M000311657

Living Water

OTHER CROSSWAY BOOKS BY MARTYN LLOYD-JONES

Alive in Christ
The Cross
The Kingdom of God
My Soul Magnifies the Lord
Out of the Depths
Revival
Seeking the Face of God
True Happiness
Truth Unchanged, Unchanging
Walking with God Day by Day
Why Does God Allow Suffering?
Why Does God Allow War?

GREAT DOCTRINES OF THE BIBLE

Great Doctrines of the Bible (3 vols. in 1)

LIFE IN CHRIST: STUDIES IN 1 JOHN

1: *Fellowship with God*
2: *Walking with God*
3: *Children of God*
4: *The Love of God*
5: *Life in God*
Life in Christ (5 vols. in 1)

STUDIES IN THE BOOK OF ACTS

1: *Authentic Christianity*
2: *Courageous Christianity*
3: *Victorious Christianity*
4: *Glorious Christianity*
5: *Triumphant Christianity*
6: *Compelling Christianity*

STUDIES IN JOHN 17

The Assurance of Our Salvation (4 vols. in 1)

Living Water

Studies in John 4

Martyn Lloyd-Jones

CROSSWAY BOOKS
WHEATON, ILLINOIS

Living Water

This edition issued by special arrangement with Kingsway Publications, Lottbridge Drove, Eastbourne, East Sussex, England BN23 6NT.

Published by Crossway Books
a publishing ministry of Good News Publishers
1300 Crescent Street
Wheaton, Illinois 60187

Cover design: Jessica Dennis

Cover photo: Veer

First printing, 2009

Printed in the United States of America

All Scripture quotations are taken from *The Holy Bible: King James Version*.

All emphases in Scripture quotations have been added by the author.

Library of Congress Cataloging-in-Publication Data

Lloyd-Jones, David Martyn.
Living water : studies in John 4 / Martyn Lloyd-Jones.
p. cm.
Includes bibliographical references.
ISBN 978-1-4335-0127-2 (hc)
1. Samaritan woman (Biblical figure)—Sermons. 2. Bible. N.T. John IV, 10-30—Sermons. 3. Sermons, English—20th century. 4. Fellowship of Independent Evangelical Churches (Great Britain)—Sermons. I. Title.
BS2520.S9L56 2008
226.5'06—dc22 2008020689

SH 19 18 17 16 15 14 13 12 11 10 09
15 14 13 12 11 10 9 8 7 6 5 4 3 2 1

Contents

1

The Possibilities of the Christian Life

Jesus answered and said unto her, Whosoever drinketh of this water shall thirst again: But whosoever drinketh of the water that I shall give him shall never thirst; but the water that I shall give him shall be in him a well of water springing up into everlasting life. (John 4:13–14)

I would like to consider with you the famous story of our Lord's meeting with the woman of Samaria, which is found in the fourth chapter of John's Gospel. It is difficult to think of any particular text from that chapter because I want to consider the story with you in general, but perhaps it is only right that we should isolate verses 13–14. I am not proposing to expound these verses now. I want merely to introduce the subject.

For some time now we have been studying John's Gospel [Editor's note: in earlier sermons), and we have been doing this in a particular manner.[1] Our concern has not been so much to go through the Gospel verse by verse as to expound and illustrate its great central theme. And I have been suggesting that the theme, in many ways, is to be found in the sixteenth verse of the first chapter where we read, "And of his fulness have all we received, and grace for grace." In other words, the theme of this Gospel is the fullness of the Lord Jesus Christ available for his people; or, to put it another way, the theme of this Gospel is eternal life.

In John 10 we read that our Lord said, "The thief cometh not, but for to steal, and to kill, and to destroy: I am come that they might have life, and that they might have it more abundantly" (v. 10), and we see that same emphasis here in John 4. So we are picking out that theme because this is, after all, what Christianity means, this is the Christian offer, the Christian possibility. Our whole trouble, surely, is that we fail to realize this: we are ever reducing the gospel, making something small out of it, something that *we* do, our practice of religion. The tragedy is that we think of our own selves and our busyness and our own activity instead of realizing that there is the wonderful possibility of receiving his fullness and more and more of it, "grace for [or upon] grace," "springing up into everlasting life." And this failure, it seems to me, is the greatest tragedy of all.

In the church today the tendency is to look at the world all the time and to see the tragedy of the world. That is perfectly right, of course; the church is to be evangelistic. But the question is, how is the church to be evangelistic? And I contend that what the New Testament itself tells us, and what the history of the church tells us, is that the church is most successful evangelistically when she herself is as she ought to be. Why are the masses of the people outside the church? I do not hesitate to say that the reason is that they fail to see in us anything that attracts them, anything that creates within them a desire to receive what we have, or anything that rebukes them and condemns them for their way of living. Not that we should necessarily put that into words, but it should be seen.

It was by the quality of its life that the church conquered the ancient world, and that is how she has always conquered during times of reformation and revival. It is revival that has been the greatest means of evangelism, and revival means Christian people, members of the Christian church, suddenly being awakened by the power and the enlightenment of the Spirit to the possibilities of the Christian life. And there is no doubt, I repeat, that the trouble at the present time is that we are living so far short of what is offered to us and of what is possible to us.

Have we received our Lord's fullness? Are we receiving it progressively? These are the all-important questions. If this well of water is not within us, we are not only robbing ourselves of the riches of his grace, but we also become unworthy representatives of the gospel, and the world outside remains in ignorance and in darkness. So the high road to revival and to evangelism is a church that realizes what she ought to be, what she can be. And when I say, "church," I mean, of course, every one of us as individuals. The church consists of a number of believers. It is not something theoretical, on paper. It is you, it is I, it is all of us. And so we face this great theme together.

Now the fullness of life available to us is, I repeat, the theme of John's Gospel. Sometimes the message is explicit and direct, as we have it here, and sometimes the Gospel puts it in terms of an anecdote, a story, an illustration—how our Lord called certain men, or how he behaved at the marriage feast in Cana of Galilee or in the Temple in Jerusalem, or how he dealt with a man called Nicodemus (the great theme of the third chapter of John). So it is direct and indirect, explicit and implicit. But it is always there. The wonderful thing about the Gospels is that they present their teaching to us in such an interesting variety of ways. Further, the teaching is most instructive with regard to the hindrances that block our receiving this fullness. The Gospels are of great value to us because humanity does not change, we are all still the same. So here, in these pictures, we see how people stumbled and what it was that held them back from this blessing, and this remains true today. So we take up this theme of the fullness of life offered by our Lord, and we take it up in terms of this great old familiar story of our Lord's dealings with the woman of Samaria.

Now it is customary to take this incident, this story, in an evangelistic sense. The woman is an unbeliever, and we are shown here how she is brought to belief. But though that is true, the message is as applicable to us as believers as it is to an unbeliever. For the astounding thing is that even when we have come into the Christian life, we tend to go on repeating the same old mistakes and carry over with us certain characteristics and habits. The apostle Paul makes this very point in dealing with the members of the church at Corinth. They had believed the gospel, they were Christian people, and he writes to them as a church, but this is what he says to them: "I have fed you with milk, and not with meat: for hitherto ye were not able to bear it, neither yet now are ye able" (1 Cor. 3:2). "And I still have to do that," he says in effect, "because of your condition. Though you are now Christians, you are reverting to the old way of thinking, and I must get you out of that. The principles of the gospel are still the same." That was the essence of the primary problem at Corinth. They were tending to introduce their old worldly wisdom even into the message concerning the cross. So Paul had to go back to first principles, and he constantly had to repeat them all the way through the epistle.

It is the simplest thing in the world for me to show you that the way in which our Lord handles this woman of Samaria is not only applicable to the handling of an unbeliever but also of believers who for some reason or another have not known much about this fullness and "grace for grace," who have known very little about this condition in which we "never thirst." So let us look at this story from this standpoint—it is put before us in a dramatic manner. For now I just want to introduce it to you because there are many general lessons here that we neglect at our peril. Indeed, some of these general lessons are, I think we will agree, among the most encouraging and moving aspects of this whole doctrine.

There are just two people to consider—the woman of Samaria and our blessed Lord and Savior Jesus Christ. Let us look at this woman for a moment. What do we learn from her as we consider her in general? The first thing, surely—and this is wonderful—is that the great and glorious blessing of the Christian gospel is offered to all types of people. This is what I have sometimes described as the romantic element in the gospel, and in these Scriptures you cannot help being struck by it. Take, for instance, the third chapter of John, which is mainly given over to that great man Nicodemus, a ruler of Israel, an erudite man, an important man in every respect. You cannot imagine a greater contrast than that between Nicodemus and the woman of Samaria; yet the same Lord deals with the two people, and he is concerned about precisely the same message.

Look at the contrast: man—woman; Jew—Samaritan. These are not just empty terms. In verse 9 of John 4 we are told in passing that Jews had no dealings with Samaritans. We will have to come to the specific meaning of that later. But there was an old feud, an old trouble, between them, so that in the ancient world Nicodemus, a Jew, and the woman, a Samaritan, presented a remarkable contrast. There was also, of course, the contrast, between men and women. Whatever else Christianity may have done, it has been the overriding power that has liberated woman and given her a standing that she had never had before. In the ancient world women were despised, and it was felt that certain things were not possible to them at all. But one of the central themes of the gospel is that in Christ Jesus, "There is neither Jew nor Greek, there is neither bond nor free, there is neither male nor female: for ye are all one in Christ Jesus" (Gal. 3:28)—which means that from the standpoint of salvation, from the standpoint of obtaining these great and glorious blessings, the distinction between male and female is gone. This is a misunderstanding that should never have come about in connection with the things of God. The difference between man and woman, however, is not abrogated, and when you come to applications and positions in the church and various other things, the essential distinction is still maintained in the teaching.

So in this story we are at once reminded that the blessings are open to all types of people: woman as well as man; Samaritan as well as Jew. But an *ignorant* woman! Not a learned man, not a teacher, not a Pharisee well versed in the Law, but a hardworking woman. But still more, a woman who is a flagrant sinner. That comes out in the course of the conversation.

"Jesus saith to her, Go, call thy husband, and come hither."

And the woman says, "I have no husband."

"Thou hast well said, I have no husband," says our Lord. "For thou hast had five husbands; and he whom thou now hast is not thy husband: in that saidst thou truly" (vv. 16–18)

That is a typical picture of life among such people—sin, open and unashamed. But it is in contrast with that remarkable man Nicodemus, who is not only a great teacher but also a good and highly moral man, a religious man. And the marvelous truth that this story teaches us here, at the very beginning, is that all that our Lord has to give, this "fulness" (John 1:16), is as open to people like the woman of Samaria as it is to the Nicodemuses of this world. Have you not often been struck by this—that the glorious statement recorded in verses 13–14 is made to this woman? That is why I say it is a very grievous mistake only to apply this story evangelistically. There is nothing higher in the whole realm of Scripture for any Christian than this:

> Whoever drinketh of this water shall thirst again: but whosoever drinketh of the water that I shall give him shall never thirst; but the water that I shall give him shall be in him a well of water springing up into everlasting life.

That is the topmost level of Christianity, and it is spoken to the woman of Samaria! This is something that we must lay hold of. Furthermore, it is to this same woman that our Lord says, "I that speak unto thee am he" (v. 26). It is to her that he says explicitly, in a way that he did not to others, that he is the Messiah.

Why are we emphasizing this point? Because if you go through the history of the church you will find there has always been a tendency to think that what may be called "the higher reaches" of the Christian life, the profound experiences of God and of the Lord Jesus Christ and of the Holy Spirit, are reserved for certain special people. You are familiar with what may be called the "Catholic" type of teaching. It starts by dividing Christian people into two groups—the religious and the laity, special Christians and ordinary Christians—and then says that only those who go in for the cultivation of the soul in this special manner can ever hope to arrive at the high and great and glorious experiences of the Christian life.

Many books trace this teaching. One of the best is the Bampton Lectures of 1928 by Kenneth Kirk, published under the title *The Vision of*

God.[2] Kirk traces this idea in the experience of God's people throughout the centuries, bringing out this well-known fact very clearly. It is at the basis of the whole concept of monasticism. The teaching is that if you want to have high and exalted spiritual experiences, then you must go out of life, as it were; they are not for you if you are in business or engaged in the ordinary affairs of life. A housewife? It is impossible—she does not have the time. This is a full-time occupation. So you segregate yourself. You go off into a cell, and there you spend your time cultivating the soul. This view, of course, is also at the very root of the whole idea of mysticism, which takes you painfully through various stages until you arrive at the ultimate stage of illumination, high knowledge that leads to such glorious experiences.

Now this is an attitude that we have tended to carry over with us into Protestantism, but it is quite wrong. It is untrue to the teaching of the Scriptures, and even if we had no other, this case of the woman of Samaria would be more than sufficient in and of itself to put us right. Nothing depends on us—nothing at all. The woman of Samaria is the absolute proof of that. We must never say, "I'm just an ordinary Christian; these realms are not for me." They *are* for you. They are all for everybody. The woman of Samaria is a great pillar, as it were, announcing this fact, calling attention to it. We must not indulge in these artificial and unscriptural divisions and distinctions. Nor must we evade the challenge of our Lord's words by saying, "Ah, well, of course, I wish . . . but I can't." That thinking is wrong.

Let me elaborate. Let us look for a moment at the unexpectedness of this event and its surprising character. It is just an ordinary day in the life of the woman of Samaria. She has her house to look after; she has food and drink to provide, we do not know for how many. But we do know it is essential that she go to this particular well to draw water. We do not know exactly how far she has to walk, but it is not difficult to see that it must be a fair distance because she regards it as an arduous task. When our Lord makes his great statement, she says, "Sir, give me this water, that I thirst not, neither come hither to draw." She has to go back and forth, often perhaps in the blazing sun. Some suggest that it is because of her character that she has gone at the sixth hour (v. 6), that is, at midday, the hottest time of the day. If she were to go at the usual times for drawing water, the other women would look at her, and she knows everybody is talking about her because of her immoral life. So a kind of shame makes her choose the hottest time of the day. So she arrives at the well on an ordinary day, expecting nothing at all to happen—the humdrum character of a life of sin. Then suddenly there is this encounter; this amazing thing happens that changes her whole life. There is this complete revolution—from nothing to fullness.

Now here again, I suggest to you, is one of the most wonderful and glorious aspects of the Christian life. There is no life as romantic as this. In every other view of life you can more or less anticipate what is going to happen. Oh, I know there are surprises now and again, but there is nothing in any way comparable to this. This is what, to me, makes a meeting in the house of God so amazing. It is the essence of the romance of preaching. I never know what is going to happen when I enter the pulpit. I do not control it. That is the wonder of it, the glory of it. A man who does control it is a poor preacher and a still poorer Christian. Oh, the unexpectedness! You go perhaps out of routine, you do things because you are called to do them and because you are expected to do them, and you may have come into a state in which you expect nothing to happen. But suddenly the Lord is there, and you are amazed at the consequences. The hymn by William Cowper sums it up so well:

Sometimes a light surprises
The Christian while he sings;
It is the Lord who rises
With healing in his wings.

Let me emphasize this point. Many Christian people today have come into a kind of humdrum state of existence—not necessarily because of anything that is wrong in them. Maybe you are one of those people. You may be a busy housewife or a busy man earning money to provide for your family. There is work to be done, there are mouths to be fed, there are clothes to be dealt with—all these tasks; and it is the simplest thing in the world to settle down, as it were, into a routine in which you expect nothing to happen. You just continue on "the daily round, the common task," the drudgery of life.

Possibly one of the most devastating things that can happen to us as Christians is that we cease to expect anything to happen. This may be one of our greatest troubles today. We come to our services, and they are orderly, they are nice—we come, we go—and sometimes they are timed almost to the minute. But that is not Christianity, my friend. Where is the Lord of glory? Where is the one sitting by the well? Are we expecting him?

Do we anticipate this? Are we open to it? Are we aware that we are ever facing this glorious possibility of having the greatest surprise of our life?

Or let me put it like this. You may feel and say, as many do, "I was converted and became a Christian. I've grown—I've grown in knowledge, I've been reading books, I've been listening to sermons—but I've arrived now at a sort of peak, and all I do is maintain that. For the rest of my life I will just go on like this."

My friend, you must get rid of that attitude; you must get rid of it once and forever. That is religion—it is not Christianity. This is Christianity: the Lord appears! Suddenly, in the midst of the drudgery and the routine and the sameness and the dullness and the drabness, unexpectedly, surprisingly, he meets with you, and he says something to you that changes the whole of your life and your outlook and lifts you to a level that you had never conceived could be possible for you. Oh, if we get nothing else from this story, I hope we will get this. Do not let the devil persuade you that you have all you are going to get, still less that you received all you were ever going to receive when you were converted. That has been a popular teaching, even among evangelicals. You get everything at your conversion, it is said, and nothing further, ever. Oh, do not believe it; it is not true. It is not true to the teaching of the Scriptures, it is not true in the experience of the saints running down the centuries. There is always this glorious possibility of meeting with him in a new and a dynamic way.

And I will emphasize that further by putting it like this: often this comes to us in the line of ordinary duty. The woman of Samaria was not in a religious service when she met our Lord. She was doing her daily work, her regular task. This is another great Protestant principle. Martin Luther rediscovered it, in a sense—at least, it was given to him to see it. And he put it in his own dramatic way. He said that you could be serving the Lord and knowing the Lord and realizing his presence just as much if you were a chambermaid brushing the floor as if you were a monk in a cell counting your beads and fasting and sweating and praying. That is the basis of the whole Protestant notion of vocation, but I am now using it in the sense that at any moment there is a great and a grand and a glorious possibility of meeting our Lord.

A minister friend was undergoing a great trial. He and his wife were passing through an unusually difficult period in their lives—sickness was involved—and as far as he was concerned, everything was calculated to crush his wife. But he told me how one evening, at the very depths of the depression and trial and tribulation that had overtaken them as a little family, his wife, having put the children to bed, went to read her daily portion of Scripture.

Now there are people, of course, who say that if you do not read the Bible and pray the first thing in the morning, it is terrible, but she did not have the time in the mornings—she had a husband and children to see to. The time does not matter. Do not become the slaves of systems, my dear friends; be open. It is not when you read the Bible that is important, it is how you read it. And the woman was right: she knew that having put the children to bed, she would have a little quiet. So she went, not expecting anything, just doing something that was routine. But suddenly she found that her Lord was there, and she had the most marvelous experience of her life, an experience that enabled her not only to have an entirely new view of what was happening to them but also to help her husband, and soon they entered into a position of release and victory.

Now this is a great principle. The experience of meeting the Lord is not confined to certain places. Of course, we must come to certain places. Do not misunderstand me. I am not foolish enough to become a devotee of this latest vogue of talking about "religionless Christianity," which says that churches are not needed. That is just nonsense, of course, even apart from being unscriptural. But what I am saying is this: do not think that such experiences only happen in a church. They can happen to you anywhere. The Lord can come anywhere. That is one of the great messages of this story—and I will be elaborating on that—"neither in this mountain, nor yet at Jerusalem," but by the side of a well—anywhere in the line of ordinary duty.

The other point I would like to stress—and to me this is an essential part of this message and is of very real significance—is that our Lord deals with this woman alone. This is not accidental. The disciples have gone into the neighboring town to buy provisions, leaving our Lord there alone, and the woman, probably for the reason I have given you, is also alone. So at the side of the well they meet alone. I think this is an important principle with regard to this whole question of truly receiving his fullness. What I mean is that in this incident there is an emphasis upon the personal element in our faith; this is an emphasis that we must not forget. Our Lord, I am going to show you, has contrived the circumstances so he can talk to this woman alone.

If we neglect the personal element in the Christian faith, we will go wrong all along the line. It is personal in the matter of our original salvation. You are not saved in crowds; you are saved individually. We come to a personal knowledge of God; we have personal dealings with God. It was a sad and sorry day in the history of the Christian church when the Emperor Constantine took the Roman Empire into the Christian church. She has never really recovered from that. You cannot be saved in families; you cannot be saved in countries; you cannot be saved in whole churches. Conversion may happen to a number of people in the same service, but it is always intensely personal and individual. So conforming to a certain moral or ethical pattern does not make you a Christian. There must be a personal encounter with Jesus Christ, personal dealing, personal knowledge.

I could illustrate this from many places in the Scripture, but one of the most tender and beautiful examples is found in the book of the prophet Hosea. The prophet is dealing with the church in the Old Testament; his book is specifically a message to the church, which is depicted as a faithless wife. But here is the message in Hosea 2:14: "Therefore"—having described her sinfulness and unfaithfulness--"behold, I will allure her, and bring her into the wilderness, and speak comfortably unto her." She will be taken out of the towns, out of the busyness of life, into a wilderness, a solitary place. There will be this isolation, this personal element. I will take her there, says God, and in the isolation and the emptiness of the wilderness I will "speak comfortably unto her."

Now this aloneness is an essential principle in connection with the whole of this particular teaching about the fullness of God. In the records of people who have been led into some deep knowledge of God you will often find that they have first of all been led into a wilderness. There has been a kind of isolation, a solitary meeting by the well-side. The principle, it seems to me, is that it is possible for us all to go on living the rest of our Christian lives as ordinary Christians: "I was saved on such-and-such a date, gave my testimony, was baptized, and am a member of a church. There I am, and I will go on being like that." There are many such people. They have never grown, and they die almost exactly as they were at their conversion.

You, too, can go on being an ordinary Christian, but you can also know something about this "well of water." And if you are to become such a person, you will find that he will "allure" you, he will separate you, he will speak to you alone. Nothing may be happening to anybody else—do not worry about that. He will draw you. Perhaps it will be to a wilderness. He may have to lead you through a period of tribulation; he may not. That is not the point at the moment. The point I am making is that this must be intensely personal.

A philosopher once wisely said about these matters, "Religion is what a man does with his own solitude." And that is true. However, I prefer it as it was put by Pascal, who was one of the great teachers on this subject. He was a man who had this meeting with the Lord by the side of the well, a man to whom this same great and glorious message was given in different words. And he put it like this: "All the miseries of mankind arise from his inability to sit still in his own room." Now if that statement applied to men and women three hundred years ago—as it certainly did—how much more so today?

One of the most difficult things in life is to be still. There is so much noise—the noises of the world, exaggerated by television, radio, and so on. Noise! But you have to be still, you must stop, you must be isolated, you must think. You cannot meet with the Lord in the midst of the noise and the bustle and the fury of life. You may be a very busy person, but stillness is still possible. You must be quiet in your own room. It is only then that you are likely to meet with him. Stillness is one of the great prerequisites.

My dear friend, I am holding before you a glorious possibility. I do not care who you are or what you are or what your work is—I am not interested in any of these things. This one case gives me authority to say this: the fullness of the Lord is open to you. So do not evade it on any grounds or bring up any arguments. This woman demolishes all your arguments. If you have not consciously received Jesus' fullness and are not rejoicing in it more and more, troubles are yours, and we shall be considering what these troubles are.

However, let us go on and take a brief glance at our blessed Lord himself. Another great lesson of this story is that this fullness is all in him, and it is all of him. As I have shown you, there is nothing in the woman of Samaria. In that sense, virtually nothing is postulated of us at all. Oh, what amazes one in this story is the glory of his person and the wonder of what he does! Have you ever looked at it like this? Look at him. What do we read here? "He must needs go through Samaria. Then cometh he to a city of Samaria . . . Jacob's well was there." Then notice this: "Jesus therefore, *being wearied with his journey*, sat thus on the well" (which means, "by the side of the well," the surroundings being included in the word "well"), "and it was about the sixth hour. There cometh a woman of Samaria to draw water: Jesus saith unto her, Give me to drink."

Now what does this tell us? It tells us that our Lord is tired and sits down to rest. He is too weary to go with his disciples to the city to buy provisions. Moreover, he is thirsty. So he asks the woman for a drink of water after she has drawn it from the well.

"What about it?" you ask.

What about it! My dear friend, that is the essence of the Christian message. Who is this sitting at this well? Who is this who is thirsty?

Who is this so weak and helpless,
Child of lowly Hebrew maid . . .

Who is he? And that is the astounding thing:

'Tis the Lord of all creation,
Who this wondrous path hath trod.

William Walsham How

Who is this who is weary? He is the Creator of the universe; it is by him that all things have been made. Who is this who asks the Samaritan woman for a drink of water? He is the one for whom the whole cosmos has been created. He is the one who, according to the first chapter of the Epistle to the Hebrews, is ". . . upholding all things by the word of his power" (v. 3).

What does this mean? Have we become so accustomed to the Christian message that we are no longer thrilled and amazed and astounded by it? This is the glory of the message of Christian salvation—the Incarnation. Our Lord has humbled himself for our sakes. He is the Lord of glory still, though he is weary and sits down and is thirsty. What has happened? It is this: in order that you and I might have this well of water in us, he has laid aside the signs of his eternal glory, he has been born in the likeness of man, he has been born, indeed, in the likeness of sinful flesh (Rom. 8:3). "And the Word was made flesh, and dwelt among us" (John 1:14). And he does not have an artificial body; it is as true a body as yours and mine. He is exhausted, and he is thirsty, and he has done all this and humbled himself in order that we might have this great gift, this great blessing of eternal life.

Now I am putting it like this because if we do not know this fullness of life, it means, in a sense, that we really have not understood the whole doctrine. What right have we to say, "I only want forgiveness from him; I only want to avoid hell" and stop at that? No, no; he came "that they might have life, and that they might have it more abundantly" (John 10:10). Let us never forget this. So if the devil tempts you and says, "This is not for you," then say, "It is! I know he has done all this for me."

So look at him. Not only did our Lord come from heaven to earth, he subjected himself to our frailties and our weaknesses. He was "made of a woman, made under the law, to redeem them that were under the law, that we might receive the adoption of sons" (Gal. 4:4–5) His was a true physical body; he was truly man. He knows something about our frailties.

But in this story he gives himself still further. Can you not see this additional outstanding aspect—that though he is tired and thirsty, he keeps that on one side, he pushes it back, because he is much more concerned about the woman's real thirst, her real need. He is not thinking about himself—he is thinking about her; and even when he asks for water, his ultimate objective is not so much that he may slake his thirst as that he may introduce the subject of salvation and this fullness. And our Lord is still like that:

In every pang that rends the heart
The Man of Sorrows had a part.

MICHAEL BRUCE

Does this not stand out about him throughout the pages of the four Gospels? Look at him there on the cross in the agony and the pain and the shame of it all; look at him crying out, "I thirst." We cannot imagine the agony that he was suffering, and yet you remember that even there he turned aside to help that dying thief who was aware of his desperate need and administered to him the word of comfort and of salvation.

So let us draw blessed encouragement and consolation from all this. He is the Lord of glory. He has all knowledge. Look at him as he talks to this woman; look at his behavior. He knows all about her. He knows all about her immoral life—and she is amazed at that. And he knows all about each of us. He knows all about our needs, our troubles and cares. "For we have not an high priest which cannot be touched with the feeling of our infirmities; but was in all points tempted like as we are, yet without sin" (Heb. 4:15). What a sympathetic High Priest! He is your High Priest if you are a Christian. Go to him; let nothing hinder you.

I must emphasize one other point, and it rises from this interesting phrase that we find in the fourth verse: "And he must needs go through Samaria." What does this mean? Most of the best commentators are quite agreed on the meaning, and it seems to me to be beyond any doubt. Some translate these words, "it behooved him to go"; others, "it was necessary for him to go." Does this mean that there was only one road between

Jerusalem and Galilee? No! It does happen to have been the shortest, but it was not the only road; he could have gone at least two other ways. So these words do not indicate a physical necessity. What then? It is a *spiritual* necessity. This is not an accident but part of the great plan. Again, here is one of the most astounding things about this whole gospel of salvation and what it offers us. The real force of these words is this: "he was aware of a compulsion sending him through Samaria." What is it? It is the meeting with the woman of Samaria.

This meeting serves many purposes, as we shall see. We have already seen that our Lord wanted to break down the division between Jews and Samaritans, between men and women. But the great thing is that it was not an accident. In this realm nothing is accidental. Is it not one of the great marks of the Christian salvation that God planned it before the foundation of the world? Not only that, he knew us individually before the foundation of the world. Our names were written in the Lamb's Book of Life before we were ever born. This is glorious! This is wonderful! The whole doctrine of the call is involved in this phrase. He knows us one by one and knows all about us, and he meets us: "he must needs . . ." He knows this compulsion. He knew it in the days of his flesh, and he singled out this woman, as he did others of whom we read at the end of the first chapter of John's Gospel.

How surprised Nathanael was when our Lord said to him, "Before that Philip called thee, when thou wast under the fig tree, I saw thee" (John 1:48). He constantly says, "Mine hour is not yet come" (for example, John 2:4). There was always "the hour." Everything is a part of God's great plan and purpose of salvation. The Son of God comes to meet us in his own appointed time and way. As we have seen, from our standpoint we never know when. We must always be expectant, always open, always, as it were, anticipating by faith. But he comes! "And he must needs go through Samaria."

These are subjects that ought to thrill us to the depth of our beings. It is what *he* does. We would not be here at all but for that. It is he who has already met you and spoken to you and called you out of darkness into his light, and he will go on doing that. This is his principle of operation. Never lose sight of his constant personal interest and concern. And it is this constraining love of his that leads him to do it. Who knows whether, in his glorious plan and eternal wisdom, the hour appointed when he will meet with you in some hitherto unknown and unexpected and unanticipated manner may not be at hand. Thank God we are his workmanship, and the work that he began is a work that he will continue. So Paul wrote, "... work out your own salvation with fear and trembling. For it is God which worketh in you both to will and to do his good pleasure" (Phil. 2:12–13).

There, then, are just some preliminary principles and lessons that we learn as we take a general glimpse at this amazing, unexpected meeting between the Lord of glory and the woman of Samaria. May God bless them and apply them to our individual souls.

2

Our Lord's Approach and Our Prejudice

Jesus answered and said unto her, Whosoever drinketh of this water shall thirst again: but whosoever drinketh of the water that I shall give him shall never thirst; but the water that I shall give him shall be in him a well of water springing up into everlasting life. (John 4:13–14)

We are looking at this great story of our Lord's encounter and dealing with the woman of Samaria from the standpoint of the light that it throws on our spiritual condition and because of the possibilities that it shows us of this spiritual, this Christian life into which we have come. The story is, of course, primarily concerned with evangelism, but the principles that govern evangelism are exactly the same as the principles that continue to govern the whole Christian life, and as I have indicated, there is here conceivably some of the richest teaching on the subject that we will ever find anywhere. The Son of God came into the world not merely to procure forgiveness of sins but also to give us the life that is life indeed, this fullness that never fails—and that is the subject matter here.

But, of course, the story does not merely consist of this statement. We are given many details about what happened between our Lord and this woman, and these show us how he dealt with the whole situation. So we have begun by taking a general view of the whole story. It is a great mistake simply to isolate certain verses of Scripture. Nothing in Scripture is unimportant. Keep your eye on everything; examine everything. There are amazing riches and most encouraging teaching to be found here if we only take the trouble to look. So we considered the woman of Samaria in general and learned certain lessons from her. And then we ended by looking at our Lord himself and at all the amazing things we are told here about him.

But there is one further important aspect of our Lord himself and his dealing with this situation that I am anxious to put before you for your consideration, for here again I think you will find that we will derive not only instruction but also great encouragement, and that is the object of all that we are attempting to do.

Look at our Lord's method—it is most important. The way in which he deals with this whole situation tells us a great deal about ourselves. The wonderful thing is that he still works in the same way with us. He is still the same in the glory. John, in the first chapter of the book of Revelation, tells us about the vision, the revelation, that he had of our Lord, and he writes, "And when I saw him, I fell at his feet as dead." But this same Lord, John says, "laid his right hand upon me, saying unto me, Fear not; I am the first and the last" (Rev. 1:17). That is what he did while he was here in the days of his flesh, and he is still doing it. He is still "the Lamb that was slain" (Rev. 5:12). He who once was dead is "alive for evermore" (Rev. 1:18). He works now, of course, chiefly through the Holy Spirit. But it is his action.

You remember how Luke starts his second book, the book of the Acts of the Apostles: "The former treatise have I made, O Theophilus, of all that Jesus began both to do and to teach" (1:1); and then Luke goes on to tell Theophilus of the continuing work of the Lord Jesus Christ that he does through the Holy Spirit. And the comfort to us through this story in John 4 is that the way our Lord handled the woman of Samaria is the way he handles us. So we meet together in church with the feeling uppermost in our minds that our being there is not accidental. "He must needs go through Samaria" in order to meet the woman of Samaria; he meets with us in the same way. Let us realize that. We may think we go there from custom or out of habit, but believe me, if you are in his hands, there is more to it than that. He arranges these things for our good and for our eternal benefit.

Let us now look at our Lord's method. We notice first that he is always in control. That is what strikes us on the very surface of this story. The meeting appears to be accidental, but it is not. Watch how he handles the whole situation from beginning to end. Thank God for this. It is our comfort, our greatest consolation. If he were not in control, not a single one of us would ever be saved and arrive in the glory. The woman with her glibness and her cleverness talks a lot and wriggles, as I am going to show you, but he is in control. Be very careful what you are doing. If you are a Christian at all, he commands your situation, and he will bring you to the desired end.

The author of the Epistle to the Hebrews puts it like this: "Whom the

Lord loveth he chasteneth, and scourgeth every son whom he receiveth" (12:6). If you are one of his people, be careful, I say again. He has taken hold of you, you are in his hands, and if you do not come willingly in response to his appeal, he will still get you there. "For whom the Lord loveth he chasteneth and scourgeth every son whom he receiveth." If you are in control of your religion, I doubt whether you are a Christian at all. If you are not conscious of being in his hands and of being dealt with, I think you had better examine your foundations again. Once he sets his heart and affection upon a person, he always takes charge, and he does not let go. So at this moment a very searching question we must each ask ourselves is, who is in charge of my life? If we know that we are in his hands, we have the greatest comfort and the greatest consolation that a human soul can ever have.

But then I immediately want to add to that our Lord's amazing gentleness. Look at his gentleness with this woman! Remember her character—she is living in adultery and has been for some time. Notice that he does not bludgeon her; he does not force the situation. He is in control, but that does not mean bullying people; it does not mean doing violence to them or dragooning them. Our Lord never did that. We are told that in him was verified the prophecy from Isaiah, "A bruised reed shall he not break, and the smoking flax shall he not quench: he shall bring forth judgment unto truth" (42:3). I say once more, thank God for this, for what are all of us but bruised reeds or smoking flax?

With smoking flax there is a good deal of smoke, but is there any fire? It is almost impossible to tell, and our tendency is to stamp it out. We say that it is only smoldering, that the fire has gone out; so we crush it. But our Lord does not do that, and I repeat, if he did, none of us would be in the church. In fact, our Lord does the exact opposite. One is amazed at his gentleness with this woman. And this is the experience of all the saints. Philip Doddridge, in his hymn "O Happy Day That Fixed My Choice," puts it like this:

He drew me, and I followed on;
Charmed to confess the voice divine.

"He drew me"! Doddridge is thinking of that word in the book of the prophet Hosea: "I drew them with cords of a man, with bands of love: and I was to them as they that take off the yoke on their jaws, and I laid meat unto them" (11:4). He draws. He never drives.

Now we are always in danger of forgetting this, are we not? We want to foist our opinions upon people and force them to accept what we say. But it cannot be done in this realm, and in any case we are unlike our Master when we attempt to do that. Oh, the gentleness! Or take it as the apostle Paul puts it in Romans 8:14: "For as many as are led by the Spirit of God, they are the sons of God." Did you notice how Paul puts it? The sons of God are those who are "led" by the Spirit—not driven, not carried, but "led." The Spirit persuades, he puts the truth to us, he enlightens us, he leads us on. This is a most remarkable aspect of this great story.

As we consider our own spiritual lives and experiences, we must always remember our Lord's gentleness. Do not forget that the Holy Spirit is said to resemble a dove. He woos; he leads; he persuades; he suggests; he works in us "both to will and to do of his good pleasure" (Phil. 2:13). He can be grieved, too, and he can be quenched. So here is a great lesson for us. We are in a realm that is very sensitive, that of the soul, the spirit. We are in a realm that is quite unlike the clash and the clamor of the world outside. We forget that at our peril and to our very great loss.

Another aspect of our Lord's approach is what I may call his indirect method. He goes to Samaria to meet this woman because he is concerned about her soul, but he does not immediately take hold of her and say, "Are you saved?" That is how some of us tend to speak, is it not? Our Lord has an indirect method. "There cometh a woman of Samaria to draw water: Jesus saith unto her, Give me to drink," and as the conversation goes on, they seem to be talking at cross-purposes. Our Lord is putting a riddle to her, as it were. The woman asks, "How is it that thou, being a Jew, askest drink of me, which am a woman of Samaria? For the Jews have no dealings with the Samaritans." Our Lord replies, "If thou knewest the gift of God, and who it is that saith to thee, Give me to drink; thou wouldest have asked of him, and he would have given thee living water." She does not know who he is, and he knows that, and he knows that he is talking about a type of water about which she does not understand or know. But this is his method, and thus, gradually and indirectly, he brings her face-to-face with the vital truth.

What is the application to us? It is that our Lord still uses this same method with us, and we often miss his purpose because we do not realize it. We have an idea that our experiences of him must happen directly, in dramatic, climactic moments. They do sometimes, but not always by any means. You never know where you are going to find the Lord. You never know what kind of question is going to bring you to him.

I am an advocate of this indirect method. I have been saying for many years that the best method of evangelism is, to me, always the indirect approach. I am saying this in passing, but what an opportunity we have for evangelism as individuals at the present time. You do not always need to start by talking to people about their souls. Talk to them about the state of the world; talk to them about the state of society. Start there, a good way off, as it were, with a general question. And then as you handle that, you will be able to lead the conversation on to their own personal condition and the state of their own soul. That is how we are able to do with others as our Lord did with this woman.

You may well find that our Lord will teach you the most wonderful spiritual lessons you have ever had in a way that you would never have imagined. Certainly that is my experience, as it has been the experience of God's people throughout the centuries. He may speak to you through a physical illness, something as far away from the spiritual context as you can imagine. It does not matter where he starts—he can use that to bring you to the center. If you will not listen to the preaching of the gospel, then perhaps you will listen when you are flat on your back in bed and cannot move and are cut off from all the things that keep you going. He does that kind of thing. The indirect method—questions that do not at first seem to be directly spiritual but lead you on until you come to the vital point. Be ready always to hear him; be ready to find him anywhere or for him to find you at any given point. You must not stereotype God's methods. You must not work them out into steps or a technique or a rule. No, no; he does not work like that. He is the Lord of creation, and he varies his methods just as much as he varies the color of the flowers. So watch his methods and especially this indirect method.

The next thing we notice is how, by means of this indirect way, our Lord arouses the interest of this woman. He is a puzzle to her. She has never met anyone like this before. What is he doing? He is leading on to a great central statement—that is what he is doing; but he does it by arousing interest and creating curiosity. And he still does this; he creates desires and longings within us. We cannot understand them, we do not know why we have them, but that is his way. He will lead you to read a book of which you had never heard. He will somehow put it before you in a most amazing manner. It seems to be accidental, but it is not. He puts things in our way, or he stops certain things, or he suggests others. And all along he is arousing our curiosity—"What is this?" We may read a biography of a saint and say, "Is this Christianity? Well, if it is, I don't have it, and if it is, then I ought to be concerned about it. I ought to be enjoying it and experiencing it." In a thousand and one different ways he creates these longings and aspirations within us.

I simply ask a question at this point: has he aroused a longing in you for this well of water? Is there a dissatisfaction, a spiritual dissatisfaction? Do you know anything about this, or are you perfectly at ease and content, feeling that you have everything and know it all? Oh, when he deals with you, he will go on arousing this curiosity, this desire, this longing for something you have never hitherto known. This dis-ease, this lack of satisfaction, perhaps at first some vague longing for something that up to now you have not known, is a sure sign that he is dealing with you.

And that brings me to my next point, which is that our Lord leads us on from step to step. This is always a great characteristic of his method. Watch it in this story. There is a kind of sequence. From the very beginning he knows what he is doing; when he starts over there, he knows he is going to end here, and he brings us step by step, stage by stage. This principle is described in the Epistle to the Hebrews: "let us go on unto perfection" (Heb. 6:1). Go on! The Christian life is a life of growth, a life of development. You do not remain as you were when you were born as a babe in Christ. "But grow in grace, and in the knowledge of our Lord and Saviour Jesus Christ" (2 Pet. 3:18). It is an increasing life, a progressing life, a well of water that goes on springing up forever and ever "into everlasting life."

The apostle Paul, at the height of his great experience as a Christian, gives an account in the third chapter of the Epistle to the Philippians of how he had been delivered from his old state and condition as a Jew. "Not having mine own righteousness, which is of the law, but that which is through the faith of Christ, the righteousness which is of God by faith."

But he is not satisfied. What does he want? What is his greatest longing and desire? It is this: "that I may know him."

But he does know him! Yes. It is because he knows him that he wants to know more and more of him and to know him better "and the power of his resurrection, and the fellowship of his sufferings, being made conformable unto his death; if by any means I might attain unto the resurrection of the dead." I believe that is final spiritual perfection. Then he adds, and this is the point, "Not as though I had already attained, either were already perfect."

He knows he is saved, he knows he is forgiven, he knows he is regenerate, but he has not fully attained yet unto perfection—"but I follow after."

"Follow after"! There is one leading him, and he is following him—"if that I may apprehend that for which also I am [I have been] apprehended of [by] Christ Jesus. Brethren, I count not myself to have apprehended."

In all its fullness, of course not; who can get a full comprehension of this? "But this one thing I do, forgetting those things which are behind, and reaching forth unto those things which are before, I press toward the mark for the prize of the high calling of God in Christ Jesus" (vv. 9–14).

Paul presses toward the mark because he is being pressed. He has already said this in the second chapter, in these words:

> Wherefore, my beloved, as ye have always obeyed, not as in my presence only, but now much more in my absence, work out your own salvation with fear and trembling. For it is God which worketh in you both to will and to do of his good pleasure. (vv. 12–13)

This, then, is always true of our Lord's method. He leads us on. Are you progressing? Do you know more about him and about these things than you did a year ago? He is never static. There are always deeper depths; there are always richer glories. Oh, to me there is nothing more pathetic than an old Christian who is always talking about his conversion and who stops there, as if nothing happened after that. It violates this great, glorious principle—growth, development, being led on by the Son of God until we reach absolute perfection.

Then notice—and thank God for this—our Lord's wonderful patience. Is he not patient with this woman? Do we not all feel rebuked as we read the story? He puts up with her interjections, her clever remarks, her glibness, her debating points—he endures it all. We might spend our whole time on that. None of us would be here were it not for the patience of God and the patience of the Lord Jesus Christ. We read in the Old Testament of God's patience and long-suffering with his ancient people: "suffered he their [evil] manners in the wilderness" (Acts 13:18). The foolish people! They insulted him, they spat upon his laws, they turned to the gods of the nations, but he did not blot them out of his book. They turned back to him when they were in trouble. Of course they did, the cowards, the cads! And we are all so like them. But his loving-kindness and his long-suffering and his patience never fail.

And we see our Lord's long-suffering with this woman—his patience with her, his tolerance. It is based upon his knowledge and upon his power. He knows the end, so he is patient with us. He knows our condition; that is why he came into the world. He knows what men and women in sin are like in a way that we will never know. We know something about it, but we do not know it in its depths. He sees what utter victims we are of the devil and his powers and his influences. And so he knows that he must be patient with us. I repeat, he does not bludgeon or dragoon us, but he is so loving and patient with us in order that he may bring us to the desired end.

But the last point I would make concerning our Lord's method, and again it stands out here so prominently, is his perseverance. He is not only patient, but because he is in charge, his patience assumes the form of perseverance and leads to it. Indeed, the patience is based upon the perseverance and his knowledge of the end. Read the story again, and watch how our Lord will not be sidetracked. The woman tries several times over, but he will not have it. He keeps on, he persists, until eventually he has brought her to face the vital question.

And it is still the same. As I said earlier, our Lord will not let us go. He does not let this woman go. She wriggles, she tries her best, but he perseveres. And this is our only hope. If it were not for his perseverance, there would be no such thing as the final perseverance of the saints. If it were left to us, we would all fail, every one of us. We have failed. How we know this! Paul says to the Ephesians, "For we are his workmanship, created in Christ Jesus" (Eph. 2:10). Some say that the original idea there is, "We are his poem." Or you can think of that verse in terms of a potter making some beautiful vase. The point in both cases is that God is the author, he is the artist, he is the maker. And he never leaves his work unfinished. We start things and then stop, leaving them in an imperfect condition. But our Lord cannot do that; he would deny himself if he did. He is God the Son; he is perfect.

He made the world perfect, and the regeneration will be perfect. We see all that in this story, in the way our Lord persists and perseveres with this woman until he brings her to the desired end.

The apostle Paul makes the same point to the Philippians. He is an old man, in prison, and there are rumors that the Emperor Nero may put him to death at any moment. But he is thinking of the little church in Philippi where there were quarrels and disputes, and you would imagine that he would be in the depth of depression. But he is not. This is what he says: "Being confident of this very thing, that he which hath begun a good work in you will perform it until the day of Jesus Christ" (Phil. 1:6). That is the rock on which we stand. As Jude says, "Now unto him that is able to keep you from falling, and to present you faultless before the presence of his glory with exceeding joy . . ." (Jude 24).

God says in his prophecy concerning this great salvation that was to come through his Son, "Yea, I have loved thee with an everlasting love" (Jer. 31:3)—not with a temporary love. As the poet so rightly states:

Mine is an unchanging love
Higher than the heights above,
Deeper than the depths beneath,
Free and faithful, strong as death.

William Cowper ("Hark, My Soul, It Is the Lord")

God's love is changeless. It is absolute. It is eternal.

Paul refers elsewhere to this perseverance that is the perseverance of God, the perseverance of Christ. "Moreover"—listen to this logic—"whom he did predestinate, them he also called: and whom he called, them he also justified: and whom he justified, them he also glorified" (Rom. 8:30).

"But," you say, "we're not yet glorified."

I know we are not in actual practice, but in the mind and the purpose and the plan of God we are already glorified, and if you are a Christian at all you will be glorified. Why? Well, the end of that chapter in Romans tells us:

> For I am persuaded [I am absolutely certain] that neither death, nor life, nor angels, nor principalities, nor powers, nor things present, nor things to come, nor height, nor depth, nor any other creature, shall be able to separate us from the love of God, which is in Christ Jesus our Lord. (vv. 38–39)

Oh, our Lord's perseverance! He will not let us go.

The work which his goodness began,
The arm of his strength will complete;
His promise is Yea and Amen,
And never was forfeited yet.
Things future, nor things that are now,
Nor all things below or above,
Can make him his purpose forgo,
Or sever my soul from his love.

Augustus Toplady ("A Debtor to Mercy Alone")

I say once more, as I said at the beginning of this study of our Lord's method, be careful, my dear friend. If he has started a good work in you, he will complete it. You may rebel, but you will suffer if you do. You may fight against him, but you are only bringing trouble upon yourself. You say, "But I want a bit of pleasure in the world. I'm young." All right, go after it, but you will pay for it. If he has started a good work in you, he will finish it. If you try to remodel this mold, you will only be inviting the chisel and the hammer, and he will go on with his work until you are faultless and blameless and spotless in his presence in the glory everlasting.

Oh, let us learn these lessons as we thus look in general at our Lord's dealing with the woman of Samaria. There is the foundation of all our hope. What hope would there be for the Christian church today if it were not the church of God? Look what men have done to her in the past centuries. Look what they are trying to do with her now. Look at what is happening. There would be no hope at all were it not that his purposes are forever sure. Whatever the position may be today, I know the ultimate is guaranteed. Though everything seems to be going the other way at the moment, that way will end in destruction. And however small a company the faithful people of God may be, it is all right—they shall shine as the sun. They will reflect the glory of God the Father, the Son, and the Holy Spirit.

The next step we come to is this one—the hindrances. Here is the goal: "Whosoever drinketh of the water that I shall give him shall never thirst; but the water that I shall give him shall be in him a well of water springing up into everlasting life." Do you have this water? Do you know about it? If not, why not? It is because of hindrances, and the hindrances are entirely of our own making. That is one of the great lessons of this story. Look at this poor woman. There is the great offer, but look at the difficulties and the obstacles that she creates and raises, spiting herself, standing in her own light, and robbing herself of this great gift. See all the hindrances—there are many here, and we must deal with them because the things that hindered this woman are still hindering God's people.

We are at a vital part of this teaching. It is no use my just saying, "Here is this well of water—do you have it?" Each of us must face the question, if I do not have it, why not? So I must deal with the hindrances as our Lord dealt with them in the case of this woman. He still does that—through preaching, through the Scripture, and in many other ways.

What are these hindrances? Well, some are immediately obvious on the surface. They are the prejudices that we hold in general. Look at this woman with her prejudice about Jews and Samaritans, about male and female, and with regard to worship, each of which I shall deal with on its own.

You may be saying, "You're wrong to deal with this chapter as you are. You should be taking it evangelistically. The moment we become Christians we are no longer troubled by those questions of Jews and Samaritans and so on."

Is that so? Are you so much of a novice in the spiritual life that you have not yet realized that many of these old prejudices follow us into the Christian life?

"But," you say, "Paul wrote, 'Therefore if any man be in Christ, he is a new creature: old things are passed away; behold, all things are become new'" (2 Cor. 5:17).

But does that mean you are therefore an entirely different person? Of course not. That idea is an abuse of Scripture. We must learn that we carry prejudices from the old life into the new life. This is not just my opinion; let me prove it to you. Look at the church at Corinth. Look at those early chapters of the First Epistle to the Corinthians. Paul there has to deal with the question of human, worldly wisdom because the members of the church at Corinth were beginning to bring that in. They had been converted, they were truly Christians, born again, but they were now beginning to look at the cross in a philosophic manner, and, Paul says, if you do that you are making it of no effect, and then he presents that great argument. But here is the material question: why were the Corinthians doing that? And there is only one answer: it was because they were Corinthians, because they were Greeks, because that was their background. Philosophy—understanding—reason! That was what they boasted of. Though they were in the Christian life, philosophy had trapped them, and Paul had great difficulty with them.

Of course, it was equally true of the Jews; you see them stumbling too. Even the apostle Peter stumbled over the question of going down to preach in the house of Cornelius. It took a vision to open his eyes. Peter! He was not only born again, he had also passed through Pentecost; yet the old Jewish prejudice was still there. And, indeed, Paul tells us in Galatians 2 how, later on at Antioch, Peter began to dissemble. You do not finish with the past; the old prejudices still tend to follow. The Epistle to the Hebrews would never have been written were it not that the people to whom it was written were Hebrews, and they, again, were tending to carry their old prejudices into the Christian life. You do not get rid of all your problems the moment you become a Christian. I know that evangelists sometimes give that impression in order to get results, but what they say is misleading, and that is why many people fall away or are disappointed. No, no; you must take the position as it is put in the Scriptures. You will find there that many prejudices tend to carry over into the Christian life and can stand between us and this great blessing.

What are they? Well, even nationality can hinder us! We must all bear this in mind. What is the place of nationality in Christianity, in the spiritual life? What a problem, what a question that is! It is very interesting to read the history of the church and the theological debates and see this influence creeping in. There is, of course, an essential difference between, say, an Englishman and a Scotsman. It is said that the Scots have theology in their bones and in their blood. Their history seems to indicate that. They are very different from the English, who are empiricists by nature and do not like definitions or too much reason. That kind of national background and prejudice is part of our makeup, and we do not finish with it when we become Christians. Then look at the Germans; their delight in words is characteristic of all German theology. The French outlook is very different, and the outlook of the Latin races is different again.

Now this, of course, can be exaggerated, and people have made too much of it. This was the whole thesis of a book I once read in which the writer said that you could explain whether people were Protestant, Reformed, Calvinistic, or Catholic in their doctrine purely in terms of climate. The further south, the nearer you go to the Equator, he said, the more likely you are to be Catholic; in the colder regions, the doctrine is harder—Calvinistic. And therefore it was not surprising that Calvinism came from John Calvin, who lived in Geneva. That author had quite forgotten that Calvin was a Frenchman! I am just showing you by illustration that these prejudices and predispositions tend to persist and to follow us. You cannot just say, "Ah, that woman was unconverted, and of course while you are unconverted you are full of prejudices." Examine yourself, my friend. We must all examine ourselves. To what extent are we allowing prejudices to influence us and to govern us—not only national prejudices but traditions and customs, the way in which we have been brought up, our background?

Have you not found in your spiritual experience that there is often a very great difference between two Christian people as a result of their backgrounds? One of them has been brought up in a church or a chapel, in a religious home, and has always been familiar with Christian teaching, but is now converted, born again, a true Christian. And here is another who comes from an entirely pagan background, with no Christian teaching at all, but is now born again. Although they are both Christians, their problems are often very different—very different indeed. The first has much more to shed than the second.

The problems of people who have always regarded themselves as Christians are often much greater than those of people who previously had nothing to do with the church. In a final sense, of course, there is no difference. All I am showing is that the devil makes use of these factors, and the prejudices will keep on creeping back—the reliance upon your works, upon your goodness, upon your attendance at the house of God, or upon saying your prayers. The tendency of these people is to fall back on works. Or there is an insistence upon worship or on a particular religious habit or custom. There is a common prejudice in this country as to what Christianity is, and it is very difficult to shake yourself free from it. These prejudices are there, they keep on seeping in, and people have to fight against them. You do not shed them completely; they do not drop off altogether the moment you come into the Christian life, and at times they constitute some of the greatest difficulties and problems faced by Christians.

People say, "Why are you talking about this 'well of water'? I've always been a Christian." Or "I've been a Christian ever since I was a child." I received a letter only this week from some people in northern England whom I do not know and have never seen, as far as I know—a husband and wife writing to me together. They'd had a bit of help from reading something that I have been privileged to write. But what was interesting in their letter was this: "At first we did not like it, we were annoyed by it." That is their term, not mine—they were "annoyed." Why were they annoyed by what I had written? Ah, because of this prejudice! They had been brought up in a certain way, the way I have been describing, and their first reaction was one of annoyance: "What is this man saying? Is he suggesting we are not Christians? But we are Christians." And so, you see, people put up a barrier. The Lord is speaking to you; he is offering you something that you do not have so you will never thirst again. But you put up an obstacle. You say, "What's this?"

Remember the Jews: it is all there in the eighth chapter of John's Gospel. Our Lord had been preaching, and we are told that as a result, "many believed on him." And he looked at them and said, "If ye continue in my word, then are ye my disciples indeed; and ye shall know the truth, and the truth shall make you free." What a wonderful promise! But do you remember the reaction? "They answered him, We be Abraham's seed, and were never in bondage to any man: how sayest thou, Ye shall be made free?" (John 8:30–33). Do you see the prejudice? There is nothing more terrible than allowing some old, general prejudice so to influence us that far from accepting this gracious, loving offer, we even resent it because it carries the implication that we are not everything that we ought to be. God, have mercy upon us!

Let us learn the lessons that we find enshrined here in the whole story of our Lord's dealing with the woman of Samaria. Thank God, he perseveres and is patient with us and is determined to bring us to the desired end.

3

Spiritual Dullness and Evasive Tactics

Jesus answered and said unto her, Whosoever drinketh of this water shall thirst again: but whosoever drinketh of the water that I shall give him shall never thirst; but the water that I shall give him shall be in him a well of water springing up into everlasting life. (John 4:13–14)

We have been seeing that the essence of Christianity, ultimately what it really means to be a Christian, is that we have within us a well of water springing up into everlasting life. And we are considering this old story, this great incident in our Lord's life and ministry, because it shows us how this can be true for us. Do we have this "well of water" that puts us into such a condition that we shall "never thirst"? "Never" is a very big word. It means everything, any conceivable condition. Need I indicate to you the importance of this great statement and the importance of our examining ourselves in the light of it? How do we stand up to life? How do we stand up to what happens to us in life? What if we should have an experience such as hundreds of people have had since Friday? What would we be like now? How would we react?[3]

This is what Christianity is about. It is not about some theoretical consideration of life; it is the most practical thing in the world. The object of this great salvation is to enable us to live in this world and to look forward to the glory that is to come. We cannot truly do that unless we are Christians. Without this life that Christ came to give, life is mere existence, and you soon discover just that when you are face-to-face with tragedy and calamity and find you have nothing at all to enable you to handle it. So this is the most important subject we can ever consider together. This is the possibility; this is what can be true of all of us; this is the great offer of the Christian gospel.

We have been taking a general look at our Lord's meeting with the woman of Samaria. We have looked at the person of our Lord himself and at the way he deals with us, and I trust this has given us great comfort and consolation. As our Lord persisted with this woman until she came to see the truth, so he persists with us. And we have now begun to consider the hindrances and obstacles that keep us from knowing much about "the well of water springing up into everlasting life." As they were true in the case of this woman, so they are, in principle, still true of all of us. We have dealt with some general prejudices that hindered this woman. She turned to our Lord in amazement when he asked her for a drink of water. She said, "How is it that thou, being a Jew, askest drink of me, which am a woman of Samaria?" We face national prejudices, class prejudices, race prejudices, gender prejudices, and so on. There is almost no end to them. What harm they have done in the life of the individual Christian, and what harm they have done in the life of the church throughout the centuries—the things we cling to so tenaciously simply because we have been born like that!

The second great hindrance is spiritual dullness or spiritual slowness. Here is an obstacle to growth that is shown very plainly by this woman of Samaria. She shows us that you can be intelligent, you can be quick and alert, you can be subtle at disputation, and yet the whole time be spiritually dull. This comes out in the way this woman materializes everything our Lord says to her. He is speaking to her in a spiritual manner, but she does not see it. Let me illustrate what I mean. Our Lord said to her, "If thou knewest the gift of God, and who it is that saith to thee, Give me to drink; thou wouldest have asked of him, and he would have given thee living water." It is a purely spiritual statement.

But in reply the woman completely misses the spiritual import of his statement. She thinks of the material well in front of her and says, "Sir, thou hast nothing to draw with, and the well is deep: from whence then hast thou that living water?" And then on she goes: "Art thou greater than our father Jacob, which gave us the well, and drank thereof himself, and his children, and his cattle?"

Then comes the great statement of our text, thoroughly spiritual, gloriously spiritual, in verses 13–14. But listen to the woman's words in verse 15: "Sir, give me this water, that I thirst not, neither come hither to draw." She is saying, "I have to keep on coming back and forth to this well to draw water. I would be very glad if you could do something to put an end to that—it would save me a lot of bother." She has no spiritual perception; she does not understand, though everything is brought down to her level.

Here again is a most important principle. It is not the first time we meet it in this great Gospel. Nicodemus, of whom we read in the early part of the third chapter, materialized our Lord's spiritual statements in exactly the same way. You see, this is not a question of learning; spiritual understanding has nothing to do with natural ability, nothing at all. Thank God for that, otherwise salvation would be the prerogative of a certain small company of people! No; when our Lord interrupted Nicodemus and said, "Except a man be born again, he cannot see the kingdom of God," Nicodemus said to him, "How can a man be born when he is old? can he enter the second time into his mother's womb, and be born?" (John 3:3–4). Poor Nicodemus! He did not see the spiritual; he could only think of the flesh, the material. And our Lord said to him, "That which is born of the flesh is flesh: and that which is born of the Spirit is spirit. Marvel not that I said unto thee, Ye must be born again" (John 3:6–7). In both Nicodemus and the woman of Samaria we are shown the kind of attitude that is a hindrance to obtaining this great fullness.

The apostle Paul says exactly the same thing about the Corinthians, and not only about them but about the "natural man" in particular. In 1 Corinthians 2 he puts forward certain propositions:

> But God hath revealed them unto us by his Spirit: for the Spirit searcheth all things, yea, the deep things of God. For what man knoweth the things of a man, save the spirit of man which is in him? even so the things of God knoweth no man, but the Spirit of God. Now we [Christians] have received, not the spirit of the world, but the spirit which is of God; that we might know the things that are freely given to us of God. Which things also we speak, not in the words which man's wisdom teacheth, but which the Holy Ghost teacheth; comparing spiritual things with spiritual. But the natural man receiveth not the things of the Spirit of God: for they are foolishness unto him: neither can he know them, because they are spiritually discerned. But he that is spiritual judgeth [understands] all things, yet he himself is judged [known] of no man. (vv. 10–15)

The cleverness, the ability, all these things that are all right in and of themselves do not help us here. Indeed, they can be a veritable hindrance.

If we constantly hold on to them, desiring this understanding that we cannot have in and of ourselves, we are raising difficulties and obstacles to receiving the fullness.

Someone may say, "But all Christians surely have the Spirit in them."

Perfectly right. "Now if any man have not the Spirit of Christ, he is none of his" (Rom. 8:9). A man or woman cannot be a Christian without having the Spirit, the Holy Spirit, in them. But then the fallacy comes in. It is assumed, therefore, that while this spiritual dullness is true of an unconverted person, like the woman of Samaria, it cannot be true of a Christian. But it can! The fact that we have become Christians, that we are born again, that the Spirit of God is in us, does not mean that we have solved all our problems; that is only a beginning. We now have to go through a great process of readjustment, and it is because so many people fail to realize that and, still more, fail to act upon it that they are constantly in trouble.

Listen to the apostle Paul putting this as an appeal to the church at Rome: "I beseech you therefore, brethren, by the mercies of God, that ye present your bodies a living sacrifice"—we must do this now; we have become Christians, but we still need to do this—"holy, acceptable unto God, which is your reasonable service. And be not conformed to this world"—Christian people have to be told that: do not go on conforming to this world—"but be ye transformed"—how?—"by the renewing of your mind"—this is what I am talking about—"that ye may prove what is that good, and acceptable, and perfect, will of God" (Rom. 12:1–2).

Now all that is addressed to Christians. Spiritual understanding is not something that happens automatically. Not at all! You must work out your own salvation in this way. You must start thinking in a new way, and apply this new thinking all along the line. Another statement of the same truth is to be found in Paul's Epistle to the Ephesians. "Do not go on living as the other Gentiles do," says Paul in effect. Then:

> Ye have not so learned Christ; if so be that ye have heard him, and have been taught by him, as the truth is in Jesus: that ye put off concerning the former conversation the old man, which is corrupt according to the deceitful lusts; and be renewed in the spirit of your mind. (4:20–23)

That is the whole problem. When men and women become Christians, they see a big truth, a broad distinction; but having seen this, they now, by renewal in the very spirit of their minds, have to go on working this out.

This principle is constantly put before us in the New Testament epistles. The apostle Paul repeats it in 1 Corinthians 3: “And I, brethren, could not speak unto you as unto spiritual, but as unto carnal, even as unto babes in Christ” (v. 1). He is saying in essence, “I cannot give you the teaching I want to give you because your thinking is still wrong. You are thinking in the old way and not in the new.”

We find the same teaching in the Epistle to the Hebrews. The writer has a great doctrine to unfold, the doctrine of our Lord as “called of God an high priest after the order of Melchisedec.” He goes on to say, “Of whom we have many things to say, and hard to be uttered, seeing ye are dull of hearing” (5:10–11). He cannot give them the comfort and consolation and the teaching he wants to give them because though they are Christians, they are still thinking in the old, unspiritual, material way.

Similarly, the apostle Peter says:

> Ye are a chosen generation, a royal priesthood, an holy nation, a peculiar people; that ye should shew forth the praises of him who hath called you out of darkness into his marvellous light: which in time past were not a people, but are now the people of God: which had not obtained mercy, but now have obtained mercy.

Then here is the appeal:

> Dearly beloved, I beseech you as strangers and pilgrims, abstain from fleshly lusts, which war against the soul; having your conversation [behavior] honest among the Gentiles. (1 Pet. 2:9–12)

Do you see the appeal? All this is addressed to Christians, and it is because we fail to realize this that we are so frequently in trouble and raise these hindrances that prevent us from receiving this well of water that springs up into everlasting life.

But why do we do this? This to me is a most important matter. It is a great tragedy that though this offer is here before us—the very thing we stand in need of, the secret of all the saints and the noblest souls that this world has ever seen—that though it is all offered to us by our Lord, as he offered it to the woman of Samaria, yet so many of us are burdened, troubled, unhappy, conscious of failure, and without consolation. What a tragedy it is that people who were meant to live as princes are living as paupers, that those who were meant to be receiving “the unsearchable riches of Christ” (Eph. 3:8) should be living in penury.

My friends, this ought not to be, and this is important not only from the standpoint of our own happiness and well-being as Christians but still more in view of the state of the world outside. People are unhappy, they do not know what to do or where to turn, and here are we claiming to be Christians. They look at us and think, *Can these people help us?* But if they see that we react as they do, that we have no comfort and consolation, that we have nothing that differentiates us and lifts us above our circumstances, they will not listen to us. They will say, "These people are all talk; there's nothing in it," and they will not be interested. So from every standpoint it is vital that we should examine ourselves in the light of this kind of hindrance, this spiritual dullness and slowness that remains on the earth on a material level and fails to realize what is being offered to us in Christ Jesus. Why, I ask again, are we like this?

Well, here are some of the answers. First of all, it is partly habit. We are all creatures of habit and custom, and I say again, the fact that you have become a Christian does not mean that all your old habits drop off; they do not. Our old habits are like autumn leaves that you see on the trees in spring. These old leaves take a long time to drop off; they have to be pushed off slowly by the new buds. You are born again. Essentially you have become a new person; yes, but you are so constituted that the body in which you live in this world—and, remember, the New Testament regards the body as a sort of tent in which people live—is a part of you. Man is body, soul, and spirit, and the body is a creature of habits and customs. And that applies to the mind as well as to the brain, distinct from the mind, the brain as an organ, the brain, if you like, as a kind of machine. It runs in grooves; it repeats things.

There is value in habit, but it can also be a great problem, for we are often unaware of it. You have a mind that has been accustomed to thinking in a given way, along a given line, and though you have changed, you will find that you have to be renewed constantly in the spirit of your mind. In order to get this mind, this faculty that I have, to change, I must train it to think in the right, the Christian, way—it will not happen automatically.

Secondly, we allow spiritual dullness because of the feeling that we have everything; we received it all at conversion, and there is nothing more to be gained. This has been a very popular teaching, and it accounts, it seems to me, for a great deal that is true of the Christian church today. Many Christian people are exactly the same now as they were fifty years ago, and they are always looking back. This is a terrible attitude, and it is an obstacle to receiving this fullness about which we are reading together.

Another cause is laziness, a failure to exercise our senses, a failure to apply ourselves to the truth and to apply the truth itself to us. This is a very serious matter, and I want to deal with it in a very serious way. Laziness, I believe, is one of the great enemies of the Christian, especially at the present time, though, of course, it is always wrong. The New Testament is always urging us to activity, and particularly to mental activity. Listen to the apostle Peter again: "Wherefore gird up the loins of your mind, be sober, and hope to the end for the grace that is brought unto you at the revelation of Jesus Christ" (1 Pet. 1:13). Now that is an appeal to Christians, but we are lazy, we do not like doing that. Or take it again as it is put by the author of Hebrews:

> For when for the time ye ought to be teachers, ye have need that one teach you again which be the first principles of the oracles of God; and are become such as have need of milk, and not of strong meat. For every one that useth milk is unskilful in the word of righteousness: for he is a babe. But strong meat belongeth to them that are of full age, even those who by reason of use have their senses exercised to discern both good and evil. (5:12–14)

If ever a text were needed by the modern Christian, it is that! What laziness there is, what failure to study, to apply the mind! We are living in an age that likes to be entertained; the element of entertainment has come increasingly into Christian activity and Christian worship—the element of singing and storytelling and talking about experiences, while there is this great truth waiting for us. We are meant to "gird up the loins of our mind," not just to sit back and say, "Wasn't it nice? Wasn't it enjoyable?" Oh, what a tragedy it is that with all of these riches people should be spending their time in sheer entertainment!

Fourthly, there is the magical view of faith taken by many people. I cannot call it anything else. These people seem to think that faith is a magic word that completely changes everything. In other words, there is the danger of putting the experiential and the subjective in too prominent a position. Now we must never forget these aspects of the Christian life—a mere theoretical Christianity is of no value, it is a contradiction in terms. But there is the opposite danger of so emphasizing the experiential and the subjective that we really know nothing about the truth as such. We have had one vital experience—thank God for it, it does make us Christians—but if we hold on to that alone we remain babes in Christ, and it is terrible to see a child who never grows up. Have you not seen this sometimes? Perhaps a person of forty or fifty years of age still with the mentality of a babe. Some of the Christians to whom the Epistle to the Hebrews was written were like that, as we have seen, and Paul suggests that the Corinthians were like that too. And that is very often because we have this magical or semi-magical view of faith.

A fifth reason is that in preaching and teaching we tend to put too much emphasis upon the will and upon surrender. This is mainly the responsibility of preachers. It has been a characteristic of evangelical Christianity since about the middle of the 1870s—a direct attack upon the will and an emphasis upon "making a decision" and upon "receiving the Lord." The great truth, the body of doctrine, has not been unfolded because people have become impatient with that; they say they do not have the time, they can no longer sit and read. Yet your great-great-great-grandparents did have the time, and they did read, though they worked much harder than you will ever work and for much lower wages. They found the time, and they went into the profundities. But this new teaching has come in that does not start with the mind and the understanding, nor even with the heart, but with the will. Surrender! Always surrender! In every type of preaching you are always being told to come forward to make some sort of a decision.

Now that is not the New Testament way. I defy you to find such teaching there. The New Testament, indeed, as I am trying to show you, does the exact opposite. So I will put my sixth point like this: all the previous suggestions that I have made to explain why Christians are being hindered in their spiritual growth are ultimately due to one basic cause, and that is a completely defective, totally inadequate view of the Christian gospel. Here is the real trouble. We reduce this "glorious gospel of the blessed God" (1 Tim. 1:11) into just one thing, and always the same thing, always this matter of deciding and receiving.

This last week I had the privilege and pleasure of talking to two ministers from another part of the world. One of them said something that I thought was most interesting because it is equally true of this country. He was talking about evangelical people, and he said, "I have a problem in my church. Ever since I have been more expository in my preaching, concentrating more on teaching them the truth, some of the people are beginning to complain that I am no longer preaching the gospel." "No longer preaching the gospel" because he was expounding the Scriptures, unfolding these great truths!

What is the matter with these people? Well, they have reduced the gospel to just one act, and that alone must be preached, so unless there is "something happening," as they put it, unless somebody is making a decision in every single service, the gospel has not been presented. Is it not astonishing that Christians can speak like that with the New Testament and the teaching of the epistles open before them? They do not know what the gospel is. That is a terrible thing to say, but it is true. At the most they just know the first beginnings of the gospel, but no more. And they think that is all. They do not want to be taught, they are intolerant, and they become critical, as that good friend was telling me.

What do I mean? Well, take that great third chapter of the Epistle to the Ephesians. My dear friends, this is the gospel! As Paul puts it, "Unto me, who am less than the least of all saints, is this grace given, that I should preach among the Gentiles." Preach what? Just "Come to Jesus and be saved"? Of course, that is the first thing. But Paul was preaching "*the unsearchable riches of Christ*. And to make all men see what is the fellowship of the mystery, which from the beginning of the world hath been hid in God, who created all things by Jesus Christ" (verses 8–9).

The great mystery about the church! The principalities and powers in the heavenly places are going to understand this, being instructed through the church, through us. And so Paul says, "For this cause I bow my knees unto the Father of our Lord Jesus Christ." What is he praying? ". . . that he would grant you, according to the riches of his glory, to be strengthened with might by his Spirit in the inner man; that Christ may dwell in your hearts by faith; that ye, being rooted and grounded in love, may be able to comprehend with all saints"—wherever they are, everywhere—"what is the breadth, and length, and depth, and height; and to know the love of Christ, which passeth knowledge, that ye might be filled with all the fullness of God" (verses 14, 16–19).

Now that is the realm into which you and I have come, but so many people are not interested. They are interested in activities. It is all right to be active and interested in evangelism, it has its place; but to give the impression that this is the first priority, the biggest thing, the central thing, the thing that is needed most of all, is to twist the Scriptures completely. That is only the beginning, and a church that remains at the beginning is infantile.

My dear friends, how much of your time do you spend in thinking about subjects such as this? Are you studying the Scriptures to find these riches, these depths and heights? Are you giving yourself to this? Do you really mean these words when you sing them:

Just as I am, of that free love,
The breadth, length, depth, and height to prove,
Here for a season, then above,
O Lamb of God, I come, I come.

Charlotte Elliott

Have you heeded the exhortation of the author of the Epistle to the Hebrews at the end of the fifth chapter? Have you, too, been chastened and reprimanded? This is what you need. The writer starts off in chapter 6 by saying, "Therefore leaving the principles [the first beginnings, the mere introduction] of the doctrine of Christ"—you must not reduce the doctrine of Christ merely to the matter of conversion; that is being done, and the church has lost her balance, she has lost the real essence of her being—"let us go on to perfection." This is what we are to pursue: "perfection." Or think of it in terms of the majestic, glorious first chapter of Paul's Epistle to the Philippians where he suddenly seems to open the front door, as it were, into the heavens and give us a glimpse of the glory of the Lord. That is what you and I are meant to enter into.

So, therefore, I would sum up this section by saying that perhaps the greatest cause of spiritual sloth is a superficial form of Bible study. We have been so concerned that people should read the Bible at all that we have fallen into the error of teaching them to read it in a superficial manner. We skim through the Scriptures, taking broad strides, chapters at a time, sometimes a book at a time, and we think we are studying the Scriptures! Then, having a general knowledge of their contents and being able to classify and tabulate them, we think we know them. But that is not the way to get at "the breadth, and length, and depth, and height," that is not the way to investigate "the unsearchable riches of Christ."

No, no; you must take time, you must go down to a deeper level, you must investigate the teaching. There are gems and nuggets here—get down to them! Not just a little portion of Scripture, with some brief words of comment, often leaving out the context. No, no! That is better than nothing, I agree, but if you stop at that, you are children and you know nothing about the unsearchable riches. The bane of our Christianity has been superficial Bible reading, superficial Bible study. It is stories as told to children, whereas we ought to be behaving as adult believers.

There, then, is a group of hindrances that I have put under the title of "spiritual slowness." Shall I put this very practically: are you with me in all this, or are you saying, "What's he talking about? What's all this about? I don't understand it. I wanted to have a nice feeling. I wanted to go out of church feeing happy, but you are making me feel unhappy"? Is that it? If it is, examine yourself, examine your very foundation. A failure to enjoy these spiritual riches, a failure to desire more and more of them, is indicative of the fact that we are but children. And we have no right to remain as children. "Gird up the loins of your mind." Pull yourself together. Give time to this. It is a painful process; it requires discipline. You must harness all your senses; you must use them. You must study in a way you have never studied before, and then you will begin to have an increasing appreciation of these "unsearchable riches of Christ."

Let me give you one other big heading, which is evasiveness. This, again, is painfully clear in the case of the woman of Samaria. Her cleverness comes out, but unfortunately it is the evasiveness that strikes us most of all—how she shifts her ground and moves from one topic to another. I have already given you examples, but let me give you one more. Our Lord now sees that he must be very personal with her and press the matter and really pin her down. So we are told in verse 16, "Jesus saith unto her, Go, call thy husband, and come hither." When the woman answers, "I have no husband," Jesus says, "Thou hast well said, I have no husband: for thou hast had five husbands; and he whom thou now hast is not thy husband: in that saidst thou truly." But, you see, instead of concentrating on that, the woman says, "Sir, I perceive that thou art a prophet"—she would have been very glad to have discussed him instead of herself. "Our father worshipped in this mountain"—he is talking to her about her adultery, her immoral life, but she wants to talk about where you worship—"and ye say, that in Jerusalem is the place where men ought to worship."

Now that is what I mean by evasiveness. We are all experts at this; we are all like this woman of Samaria. How we evade the issue, how we parry the question! It is because we do not like being searched, we do not like being examined, we do not like being disturbed. This is "the natural man," the old nature that is still with us. You do not get rid of your old nature when you become a Christian, when you are born again. The old man has gone, but the old nature has not gone; and the old nature, the natural self, does not like being searched. That element remains in us. We resent it; we do not want to be made to feel that we are wrong. We even dislike the very process that disturbs us out of our sloth: "Why, we are Christians! I was converted. There's the date, there was the test, that's how it happened." Right! But here is a man saying, "But look here, you don't have much, do you? You don't seem to know much about the real gospel and its riches." And we resent this; we thought we had it all in one packet—everything. We dislike this suggestion that there is anything wrong with us as we are. And, of course, we dislike the feeling of condemnation still more. We shuffle under it; we feel it is wrong. People in this world need condemnation, of course, but *we* . . . !

And then you see what happens. The woman evades the question by taking up other questions. And we do the same thing. We shield ourselves like she did. She is saying, "I can see that you are a prophet. Now this is interesting. I'm interested in prophets"—she knows something about the Old Testament, the five books of Moses, at any rate—"I see you are a religious teacher." Ah, then she would be very happy! She is not facing the question of her own life but wants to know about "this mountain," worship, God, and so on. And we take up these questions, we evade the issue in just the same way.

Now I have pointed out that when our Lord begins to deal with us, he does disturb us. There is no greater disturbing power in the universe than the power of the love of Christ, that "kind but searching glance"[4] of his, before which "all things are naked and opened" (Heb. 4:13). He searches us for our own good, but it is painful; so we evade it by taking up other issues. We have seen how the woman of Samaria did it, but what about us? Among the most common of all questions at the present time are questions about apartheid in South Africa. It is honorable to talk about that, is it not? You see, in denouncing somebody else, you are shielding yourself. While you are denouncing these people or friends in America or somewhere else over this racial problem, you are full of righteous indignation. That is very clever, but you are just evading the problem of your own life, the running sore of your soul.

One of the most common ways of evading the truth among those of us who are evangelical Christians is to spend the whole of our time attacking modernists and Roman Catholicism. That is all right, we must defend the truth, but if we spend all our time doing this, we are probably evading the searching glance of the Son of God. We are all experts at this, but if our purpose is to shield ourselves and to evade our Lord's words to us, we will still go on thirsting, and we will have no reserves in our lives in the hour of trial and calamity.

Along the same lines, another tendency we have is to explain away our sins and faults and deficiencies. There is a technical term for this: we are experts at *rationalizing* our sins. We can explain them. Of course, if we see the same fault in somebody else, we denounce it, but in our case, somehow or another there was a difference and extenuating circumstances. We can twist it. Oh, how clever we are! Why do we do this? Because we always want to be on good terms with ourselves. We want to be happy. Happiness must be put first, and we do not like the probing, we do not like that application to the wound that makes it smart and burn. It is for our good, it is for our healing, but we do not like it. We do not like even temporary pain, we want ease; we are like children. And so in clever ways we evade issues and explain away sin.

Finally, I will put it like this: there is no more subtle way of evading and hindering what the Son of God says to us for our good and for our happiness and for our ultimate salvation than a process of balancing, a wrong kind of balance. There is a true balance, but there is a wrong kind as well, and that is the attempt to balance failure in practice by theoretical knowledge. This woman was doing that. We all know exactly what this is. We have failed in practice; we have done something wrong. Then, against that, we say, "Ah, but we've been reading, and we've gained a lot of knowledge, and we know so much more than we knew before." We put theoretical knowledge over against the practical failure and feel we have squared the accounts. If I did not have this knowledge, of course, it would be altogether bad, but I do have it. So on balance I am really quite a good Christian, I tell myself.

We are thus balancing knowledge of theology against life and living and experience. But all the theological knowledge in the world is of no value to us unless we have a living experience of the grace of God. Do not be a fool. The final audit will take place, the ultimate Accountant will appear, and all your clever balancing will be revealed for the mere artifice, the sham, the hypocrisy that it is. God preserve us from the terrible danger of this false balance of putting one thing over against another. Christianity never does that. There is a true balance here. It is a wholeness, a completeness; it is all-inclusive.

This is what I mean. To me, the glory of the Christian gospel is that it takes in the whole person. It starts with my mind, my understanding. It is truth presented to the mind. But it does not stop with the understanding. What next? Experience. It is feeling, response, the knowledge that something is happening. And then practice. The mind, the heart, and the will are all involved. I must never put one against another. They should all be equally engaged; they should all be actively, fully involved. You do not stop on the level of activity and decision and the will. Nor do you remain always in the realm of the emotions and just be sentimental and tell stories. I have several times been in religious conferences where teaching was supposed to take place and have heard men take a text and then immediately begin to tell a story. And they will go on telling stories for an hour, with no exposition. You must not stop at experience only.

The apostle Paul expressed this truth that the whole personality is involved when he said, "But God be thanked, that ye were the servants of sin, but ye have obeyed [the will] from the heart [emotion]"—what?—"that form of [sound] doctrine [teaching] which was delivered you" (Rom. 6:17). The truth came, and the mind was given the ability to apprehend it by the Holy Spirit, but it did not remain there. It moved the heart; it melted the individual, who then put it into practice by the exercise of the will. That is Christianity, and any artificial division of these three, or, still more, any attempt to play one against two or two against one, any division, any dichotomy is wrong and is dangerous to the soul.

4

Wrong Ideas of Worship and of God

The woman saith unto him, Sir, I perceive that thou art a prophet. Our fathers worshipped in this mountain; and ye say, that in Jerusalem is the place where men ought to worship. Jesus saith unto her, Woman, believe me, the hour cometh, when ye shall neither in this mountain, nor yet at Jerusalem, worship the Father. Ye worship ye know not what: we know what we worship: for salvation is of the Jews. But the hour cometh, and now is, when the true worshippers shall worship the Father in spirit and in truth: for the Father seeketh such to worship him. God is a Spirit: and they that worship him must worship him in spirit and in truth. (John 4:19–24)

The fundamental statement with which we are dealing is to be found in John 4:13–14. But I would now like to call your attention to John 4:19–24 because we are dealing at the moment with the hindrances, the things that stand between us and the realization of what we are told in verses 13–14. It is in verses 13–14 that we are given the offer of the Christian faith, the Christian message. It is a message about life and how to live it, and here is the offer, the incomparable offer, made by the Son of God that he will give us new life that will be in us "a well of water springing up into everlasting life," and that having this we shall "never thirst." This is a promise that our Lord constantly repeats, and as I have been trying to show, it is in particular the fundamental message of this Gospel according to John. This is Christianity—nothing less than this.

The suggestion I am making is that the state of the church today, and the state of our own individual lives, is very largely to be explained by the fact that we have failed to realize that the true Christian position is this fullness—a fullness of experience of our Lord and his love and his grace. And I am calling attention to it not only that we may cease to rob ourselves of the riches of his grace, but also, still more, that we may be able to function truly as Christian people. The world, as we are aware, is in a terrible condition. It is going from bad to worse, and we know that there is nothing in it that is of any value, nothing that can avail at a time like this, except this gospel.

But people are not concerned about the gospel, they will not look at it, and I hold the view that this is because of what they see in us or, at any rate what they fail to see in us. It is because we so often give the impression that we are essentially like everybody else, but with a bit of religion added on, that people are not interested in our faith and all our claims. But when they see Christians who are filled with this fullness, Christians who have this "well of water" springing up within them, they always pay attention. That is the testimony of the great revivals in the history of the church.

To me, the most urgent need of the hour is not for evangelism but for revival of the church because it is a revived church that evangelizes in the most effective manner. That has been God's way of evangelism throughout the centuries. He has always started a work in his own people. Formal, lifeless people have suddenly been transfigured and transformed and filled with life, and the moment the world has seen that, it has come crowding into the church to hear the message. For some reason or another, we modern Christians seem to have forgotten all that. And therefore I say again, the most urgent thing for us is to make sure that we are people who correspond to this description and manifest in our daily lives what it means to be a Christian.

We have been looking at the hindrances that stand between us and the realization of this essential Christian experience. We considered first certain general prejudices and then went on to look at spiritual dullness and slowness and some of its aspects and causes. We considered also what I called evasiveness, and we saw the way in which this Samaritan woman wriggled and twisted and turned in her efforts to avoid conviction.

Let us now turn to some further hindrances. I want in particular to take the two that are suggested by verses 19–24 of this chapter—wrong ideas of worship and wrong ideas of God. These two are obviously intimately related, and in one sense you cannot separate them. Worship is worship of God. So there is a unity between the two. And yet, as I think I can show you, because we do tend to divide them, it is important that we should consider them separately.

Now this is the most crucial matter of all. What is the end and object of Christian salvation? It is to bring us to God, to reconcile us to him. Many other blessings are given—thank God for them all—but the primary object of Christianity is not to make us happy but to bring us to a knowledge of God, to enable us to worship God. We were made for that. "The chief end of man is to glorify God and to enjoy him for ever" (Westminster Shorter Catechism). Man is meant to worship God. "Thou shalt love the Lord thy God with all thy heart, and with all thy soul, and with all thy mind, and with all thy strength" (Mark 12:30). That is the ultimate object of it all. So I repeat, there is nothing more important than this—the true worship of God. And it is quite clear that failure in our worship of God is one of the great hindrances that stand in the way of receiving this blessing. It is obtained from God, and it is only as we are in a right relationship to him that we have any hope whatsoever of receiving it.

Now you notice that this story, again, gives us very clear and plain teaching with regard to the worship of God. This woman makes most of the mistakes that we all have made, and she is particularly at fault over this matter of worship. The more she talks, the more she betrays herself and reveals the inadequacy and the wrongness of her ideas. She is a religious person, remember, in spite of her sin, and she is interested in worship. She makes this point: "Our fathers worshipped in this mountain; and ye [you Jews] say that in Jerusalem is the place where men ought to worship." She is interested in this subject, and she has her point of view with regard to the God who is worshipped. But our Lord proceeds to show her the hollowness of all her talk about worship and about God, and he makes it quite plain and clear to her that all that she has is valueless and that she must think anew about these matters.

So let us try to look at these wrong ideas of worship. What is worship? What does it mean to worship God? What is prayer? I wonder how often we have stopped to ask that question. I wonder how often we have said, as the disciples said to our Lord and Savior, "Lord, teach us to pray, as John also taught his disciples" (Luke 11:1). They put that request to him as the result of observing him praying, and they must have been convicted that he was doing something that they knew nothing about, and they therefore asked for this instruction.

So I simply ask, have we ever expressed that desire? I am putting it in that way in order that I may introduce this thought: must we not all plead guilty to worship that has been completely thoughtless? We did not even stop to think of what we were doing. We did not stop to realize what we were engaged in. Surely the fundamental trouble with all of us is thoughtlessness. Is it not amazing to realize what a number of things we can do quite mechanically? Have you not often found yourself getting on your knees by the side of your bed and saying your prayers without realizing what you were doing? You were actually thinking about something else while you were uttering the words. We have all done that. It is terrible that it is possible for our worship to be quite thoughtless.

And add to thoughtlessness, ignorance. Our Lord says to this woman, "Ye worship ye know not what: we know what we worship." There is a great deal of ignorant worship. Again we must ask ourselves, do we know what we are doing? If we would know this Christian experience as it is set before us here and as we see it in the lives of the saints throughout the centuries, we must face these questions. Those men and women have always been people who have faced them, and as the result of that they have felt a profound dissatisfaction with themselves, and that is the first step, always, in the direction of this great experience.

We are all like this woman, governed by habit, custom, indeed even by tradition and, still worse, by prejudice. You see the way she puts it: "Our fathers worshipped in this mountain; and ye say, that in Jerusalem is the place where men ought to worship." Now the word translated "ought" really means "must." Our Lord used the same word in the twenty-fourth verse: "God is a Spirit: and they that worship him *must* worship him in spirit and in truth." It means "necessary." In this woman's words you see the power that tradition and prejudice exercise upon us in the matter of worship.

I think this is true of many of us. We may have been worshipping for years in a given way and manner. Why have we done that? There is only one answer: it is how we were brought up. We have never thought about it, we have never examined it, we have never asked any questions. It was the thing to do; it has always been done. We have inherited a custom; we have inherited a tradition and, indeed, a prejudice. It is amazing to read the long history of the church and see the quarrels and the fighting that have taken place over the question of worship, and that has generally been due to prejudice. People do not know why they belong to different sections of the church; they have never examined it. They were "brought up in it," and therefore they not only assume it is right, but prejudice comes in, and they will fight for their tradition with bitterness and intensity. The history of the church is unfortunately full of such battles. And the result of our thoughtlessness, our ignorance, and our prejudice is that a great deal of our worship is very hypocritical. But I am concerned to enter into the ways in which this entirely false approach to worship manifests itself in detail.

The devil, of course, is above all concerned to prevent our worshipping God. He does not mind our being happy as long as he can keep us from true worship. If the devil is likely to bring out all his reserves at one point more than another, it is when we are trying to worship God, either alone or as a company of people. And the only way to deal with him is to watch his every device, to be aware of everything that he has always done throughout the centuries and is still doing in his attempt to stand between us and the worship of God in spirit and in truth.

So what are these methods? Well, one, of course, and it is before us very obviously here, is to make us think that worship is confined only to certain places. The Samaritans said that worship could only take place in the building they had on that mountain, while the Jews tended to say that you could only worship God in the Temple, in Jerusalem. Our Lord says that they were both wrong. He says, "The hour cometh, when ye shall neither in this mountain, nor yet at Jerusalem, worship the Father . . . the hour cometh, and now is, when the true worshippers shall worship the Father in spirit and in truth."

Many people today have imagined all their lives that they are Christians, and they only worship, as they think, when they enter a church or a chapel—nowhere else. For them, worship is confined to particular buildings, and they will go into those buildings when they want to worship God, as if they cannot get into contact with God out in the open air or anywhere else. I am not talking now about a public act of worship for exposition of Scripture and for praise and so on, I mean prayer during a weekday, a lunch break—we think it must be in a particular place, as if God were confined to these places.

But not only is worship confined to certain places, still more pathetic, to me, is the way in which the worship of such people is determined and controlled by these different places. I mean something like this: when they are in a certain type of building, they adopt a certain form of worship; but in another type of building, which they regard as not consecrated, they will behave in an entirely different manner. In one building they are serious and take on what they call "a devotional air," and nothing must break into the ceremony and the form; but in a public building where there is also the reading of Scripture and prayer and so on, their behavior is different.

Now these people claim to be worshipping God in both places. But they will do things and admit things and approve of things in the public building that they would look at with horror if allowed in a building that they regard as consecrated. And that just means that their worship is entirely governed by the type of building they are in. It is not worship "in spirit"; it is not controlled by the Spirit. It is controlled by location.

Another way in which this approach to worship shows itself is that such people only pray or worship at particular times. They may express amazement at Muslims who pray at regular times, but really, in principle, they are no different. They may say their prayers morning and evening and not pray at all during the rest of the day. God is worshipped at set times. Now that is not the biblical notion of worship; that is just a habit or custom that we have developed. There are certain things we do—we get up in the morning and we wash and brush our teeth and so on, and we get on our knees and say our prayers—it is a part of the ritual, the routine of life. There it is, morning and evening, no more.

In other words, this whole conception of worship is mechanical, it is a matter of doing our duty, and indeed our very terms tend to show that. We talk about "saying our prayers." And that is what we so often do. "Saying prayers" is not necessarily praying. It can be, but generally it is not. Or people talk about "going to a building to say a prayer," while others say, "Let us have a word of prayer," and the glibness with which they say it shows that they have no conception of and have never stopped to think about what they are doing. It is impersonal; it is just something extra that they do. It is cold, it is lifeless—there is no reality at all. Is it not true to say of so many of us that our supposed worship has been quite as mechanical as that?

And then another way in which this mechanical approach shows itself is this—and this is what our Lord explains so plainly to this woman—it is an external form of worship. It is all outside us. Consider the importance some people attach to posture—you must kneel, or you must stand. Again they tend to vary the posture according to the building they are in. But is it not amazing to notice the extent to which the place we are in imposes itself upon us and determines what we do? Not that we have ever thought about it; we have just been brought up that way. Worship is therefore a matter of posture. When I am in a given posture, I am worshipping; if I am in a different posture, I am not worshipping. Is worship primarily a matter of posture?

Now these things must all be considered. Posture does come into worship, but if it comes into it at all, it must always come in, not just at certain times or places. If our posture is determined by our realization that we are in the presence of the living God and speaking to him, then that must always be the case. There must not be this variation, otherwise we are being inconsistent. But to so many of us worship is purely a matter of posture; it is nothing but form, ceremony, ritual. If you read the accounts of revivals, you will read of how two hundred years ago, and even earlier, before the Protestant Reformation, a large number of priests in this country literally could not pray. They could read prayers out of a book, but they could not offer prayer themselves. And there are many people like that still. Such worship is entirely external. It is generally conducted by somebody else, and we participate in the matter of posture but do not enter into it any more than that.

Or let me put it to you like this to show that we must be balanced: there are other people to whom worship is a purely intellectual matter. To them, worship, if you analyze it, is really just an interest in a certain type of teaching. This has been the charge that has been brought against the free churches in contrast with the liturgical, external, and elaborate. You see, it is assumed that the form and the ceremony comprise the worship, and when people say, "You don't pay much attention to worship," all they mean is that we do not read prayers and that we do not have a set form and ritual.

But there is an element of truth in this criticism, and we must face it. If we are only engaged intellectually, and if we are only concerned about ideas of salvation, and if we are only interested in doctrine in and of itself, then we are not worshipping at all. The value and the purpose of all knowledge and all doctrine and all thought is to bring us into a living communion with God, and merely to come to listen to sermons is not worship. It ought to aid worship, it ought to end in worship, it ought to promote worship, but it is not worship in and of itself. And there is no question whatsoever but that the perilous state of the Christian church today, and therefore the state of the world, is due, on the one hand, to a mechanical, lifeless worship composed of forms and externals and, on the other hand, to an intellectualization that has turned the faith into a philosophy. People speak to one another and give one another their own ideas, and God is often not worshipped at all.

So these are some of the ways in which the devil, by insinuating wrong ideas of worship into our minds, would lead us astray. Let me come to another of the devil's methods, and this is very common at the present time—it is what I would call a purely psychological notion of worship. Here, again, is something that manifests itself in myriads of ways. For years I have known men who are only interested in what they call "beautiful services." And they are experts in these matters, liturgical experts. A service can be very beautiful: everything arranged perfectly, the right kind of music at the right point, beautiful diction in the prayers.

Now the people who want this type of service are really interested in aesthetics and not in worship. For them, worship has to be beautiful, and then they come out of a service and say they feel better. But if you ask them *why* they feel better or in what way, all they can tell you is that somehow or another the atmosphere has given them a quiet or a happy feeling; they feel they have been in the presence of that which is beautiful. The Greeks worshipped goodness, beauty, and truth, and so do these people, though they use the name of God. They approach worship in the intellectual way that I have been describing, and their only test is goodness, beauty, and truth, sometimes applied quite unashamedly.

I remember once hearing a man preaching on the radio on what he called "prayer," and he had given his sermon the title, "Five Minutes a Day for Health's Sake." His point was that as you do physical exercises for five minutes a day and your body feels better, so as you give five minutes a day to prayer you will feel better in your spirit. He told us to "think beautiful thoughts," and he said that if we do, we will feel happier and will be able to go through life with a lighter step. Then he went on to say that we could even do this with regard to other people. Is somebody ill? Concentrate your thoughts upon this ill person, think kindly of him, think beautifully of him, think of him in a healing manner, and somehow or another all this will be transmitted to him and he will feel better; he may not get well, but he will feel better. That was this preacher's idea of prayer, and you can see that it is purely psychological.

Now you may be amused at that, but examine your own prayer, examine your own notion of worship! The church today is full of this kind of talk. There are people who preach what they call "positive thinking," and the idea is that you refuse negative thoughts, you cut them out. You must always be positive and always try to think beautifully as well as positively, and then you will feel better. And that is regarded as the worship of God—moral uplift.

Now these ideas are tremendously popular today, and they are regarded as truly Christian. But the great question that arises is this: are people who take them up doing anything other than giving themselves a psychological boost? Of course, psychological treatment can make you feel better, and it is foolish to say that it cannot. But the vital question is, what are you concerned about—feeling better or coming into the presence of God? Psychological treatment masquerading as worship of the living God is not worship "in spirit and in truth."

Let me sum it all up by saying that the danger confronting us all is that of taking up religion and confusing it with true worship and the praise and adoration of God. There are countries where the percentage of the population that attends a service once a Sunday is very high indeed (not so many in this country perhaps because it is not the thing to do). But the question is, what are they doing? One is often given the impression that they have simply taken up religion. But why? It may be because they feel that religion will help them. Many are led by a sheer spirit of fear and go to a place of worship purely as a bit of insurance. They are afraid—afraid of bombs, afraid of another world war, afraid of what might happen—so they take up religion exactly like the poor old pagan whom they despise, the person who worships the moon or the sun or the stars or anything else out of a spirit of fear. They do not know, but they feel that on the whole religion might help them, that it might be good for them. Yes, you can merely take up religion, but if you do, you will not be worshipping God.

And then there are others who go to church and indulge in what they call "worship" simply because they think that in this way they will acquire merit. They think God will be pleased with them and they will gain a good mark because they have done the right thing. They take up religion to placate God. They are like poor Saul, that first king of Israel. Saul was a man who fell into a terrible error. He had been given a commandment. God had told him what to do, but he did not do it. He thought he was improving on what God had said. He thought that by sacrificing the best of the animals instead of destroying them and offering them as a sacrifice to God, he would be pleasing God, but he was not. "Behold," said the prophet to him, "to obey is better than sacrifice, and to hearken than the fat of rams. For rebellion is as the sin of witchcraft" (1 Sam. 15:22–23). So often we have tried to buy merit, as it were, by externally worshipping God. We have balanced the wrong, the sin we have committed, by the good act of attendance at the house of God. We are supposed to attend the house of God, but if we regard it as merit, we might as well have stayed at home. We come to worship God.

Well, those are some of the ways in which the devil deludes us and makes us think, like this poor woman of Samaria, that we are worshipping God when we are not the "true worshippers" of whom our Lord speaks. This is what we must be concerned about. Are we true worshippers or not? So I ask you again in these terrible days in which we are living, have you ever even thought about these things? Have you examined yourself? Do you know what you are doing? Why do you go to the house of God? Do you offer true worship or something else?

Then let me just say a word about the second of the two hindrances we are now considering. We have looked at wrong ideas of worship, and now we come to wrong ideas of God, and, of course, this is the explanation of everything else. If our ideas of God are wrong, our ideas of worshipping him will be wrong. This is at the root of all the hindrances to which I have referred, all the mistakes, all the defects in our worship, and all the sin of which we are so guilty. Oh, that we might become true worshippers! You know, when we become true worshippers, the revival for which we pray and long will already have come. There is so much religion, so much form, so many services, so many meetings, but how much worship, how much contact with the living God?

What are our thoughts of God? Like the woman of Samaria, we think we know who we are worshipping, but our Lord is probably saying to us, too, "Ye worship ye know not what." Do we know? How often do we think about him? Is not this the tragedy with so many of us? We say, "I've always believed in God." And because we have always believed in him, we do not know what we believe about him.

"I was always brought up to believe; so I always have."

But have you? What is your God? Whom do you worship? What do you really know about God? The moment we examine ourselves, we discover that our ideas of him are very vague and often quite pagan. God, to so many, is nothing but some Force, some great Power. Others talk about him unhesitatingly as "the ground of being" or as "the Absolute"—some philosophical idea. And these self-same people who have such ideas of God are often ready to go through all the ceremonial and ritual and all the set forms, but there is a blank contradiction because there is no relationship. And that is why things are as they are. In our thinking about God, are we at all in advance of this woman or in advance of the poor benighted, ignorant pagan?

Then we move on a bit: some think of God as Creator only. It is this same idea of "Force." God is the great eternal Power that created everything—remote, unknown, and unknowable, not concerned about us. That was the creed of so many before the Evangelical Awakening two hundred years ago; it was called Deism. The deists believed in God, but they called him the Great Watchmaker. He had made the universe and wound it up and then put it down and ceased to have anything further to do with it. Deists cut out all God's interventions in the world, all that is miraculous and supernatural; they excluded all that is really the essence of the Christian doctrine of salvation. God, the great Creator, was cold, distant, and unconcerned. And many today have no idea of God other than just that.

Then there are others whose main feeling is one of terror. I am thinking of the people who have said their prayers regularly and perhaps have gone to public worship, but the moment anything goes wrong, either with them or their loved ones, or some kind of calamity takes place, they turn against God. They blame him and have feelings of anger and hatred with respect to him.

Their idea of the God whom they think they have been worshipping is that he is against them, that he is some awful Power that delights in playing with helpless human beings and bringing suffering upon them, some fearful Being towering over them, as it were, waiting to destroy them. Much of this has been said again this last week.[5] And many of the people who say this are church members who regard themselves as "worshipping people." But in a time of crisis we reveal our true thoughts about God. We generally go on with our habits and customs and traditions, with our forms and ceremonials or our intellectualization. It is all right as long as everything is going well. But when we are in trouble, what are our thoughts of God then? What do we feel at that moment? That is always the test.

But then I must go right to the other extreme: there are people who are guilty of sheer presumption, of an easy familiarity with God. I have often referred to the people who say, "Dear God" and talk to him easily, glibly, and familiarly and think this is the hallmark of worship and of a truly evangelical position. But it is equally wrong. Why do I say this? Because the Scripture itself tells us that we must always approach God "with reverence and godly fear," not only in certain buildings but wherever we are. Whether we are in a so-called "consecrated building" or in a public hall, God is the same, and we do not vary our approach to him according to the circumstances in which we find ourselves—"For our God is a consuming fire" (Heb. 12:28–29). Some people seem to regard God as some indulgent father who is always ready to smile upon us, and the glory, the greatness, and the majesty of God never seem to have entered into their comprehension at all.

And, finally, there are people who seem to think that God is just some kind of agency to help us. Their whole notion of God is mechanical. Are you in need? Go to the machine, offer your prayer, and take out what you want. God is really nothing but some great reservoir on which we can draw. Their whole attitude to God comes out in the way they talk and in their actions.

And so the devil in his great concern to keep us from the true and living worship of God will drive us to one or other extreme. He does not care where we are as long as we are deluding ourselves and not really worshipping God. Here is this poor woman of Samaria who can talk easily about the worship of God and yet knows nothing at all about it.

So I leave you with a great central question: when we get on our knees, what are we doing? When we come to public worship, whom have we come to meet? Have we come to meet anybody except one another? If we have come to meet with God, what are our thoughts about him? Oh, my dear friends, this is the source of all our wrong thinking in the details; it is here we go wrong. If we only started with the living God and realized that everything we do is in relationship to him, that would control everything else. We take God for granted. Indeed, he is mentioned less and less. There are those who do not even pray to him but always pray, as they put it, to "Jesus." There are those who pray only to the Holy Spirit. God over all is forgotten or ignored.

The need of the hour, the personal need of every one of us, the need of the whole church of God at this time, is to know the living God. "And this is life eternal, that they might know thee the only true God, and Jesus Christ, whom thou hast sent" (John 17:3).

5

True Worshippers

Jesus answered and said unto her, Whosoever drinketh of this water shall thirst again: but whosoever drinketh of the water that I shall give him shall never thirst; but the water that I shall give him shall be in him a well of water springing up into everlasting life. (John 4:13–14)

I start with the question that I have already put to you: what is your religion? Is it something that you do, or is it something that is happening within you? Do you have life? Do you have within you this "well of water springing up into everlasting life"? To be content with anything short of that is so wrong, so sad. It is wrong and sad from our own personal standpoint. Why should we live as paupers when we are meant to be princes? Why should we be in a state of penury when we are meant to enjoy plenty? It is tragic to see Christian people who have remained children, still concerned about the first principles of the gospel of Christ, knowing nothing about "the exceeding riches of his grace" (Eph. 2:7), "the unsearchable riches of Christ" (Eph. 3:8). It is so sad that people should have all this offered to them and still not know it, not possess it, and not enjoy it.

Why is it that so many of us fall so far short of the fullness of life offered to us in Christ Jesus? My suggestion is that in this story of our Lord's meeting with the woman of Samaria we are given in a remarkable manner an account of some of the main hindrances and obstacles to the receiving of this great gift that the Son of God came from heaven to this world to give us. We have been looking at these issues—the prejudices, the spiritual dullness, the evasiveness, and the wrong ideas about worship and about God.

But let's look at this positively. Our Lord says, "The hour cometh, and now is, when the true worshippers shall worship the Father in spirit and in truth." So here is the great question: are we "true worshippers"? What does this mean? First of all, it means *real* worshippers. We can think we are worshipping without being worshippers. How do we become genuine worshippers?

Let us start with the question, what is worship? Here, surely, is a question that needs to be asked because we tend to use this word wrongly. Indeed, we sometimes use it in such a vague way that it finally means nothing. The root meaning of the Hebrew word that is translated "worship" in the Old Testament means "to bow down," and that is the essence of true worship. It means that we bow down in the presence of God.

I could illustrate this to you at great length. Take, for instance, the second of the Ten Commandments, which, after prohibiting us from making "any graven image," goes on to say, "Thou shalt not *bow down* thyself to them, nor serve them" (Exod. 20:4–5). And then there is a particularly clear illustration in connection with the temptations of our Lord in the wilderness:

> Again, the devil taketh him up into an exceeding high mountain, and sheweth him all the kingdoms of the world, and the glory of them; and saith unto him, All these things will I give thee, if thou wilt *fall down and worship me*. Then saith Jesus unto him, Get thee hence, Satan: for it is written, Thou shalt worship the Lord thy God, and him only shalt thou serve. (Matt. 4:8–10)

There is the basic idea in connection with this word *worship*, and it is important that we should realize exactly what it means and its uniqueness.

Now the whole life of the Christian should be lived in the service of God, but the whole life of the Christian is not worship. Worship is a very special act. Our whole life should indeed be lived to the glory of God, but to say, therefore, that the whole of one's life is worship is just to confuse terms. Indeed, it is a very dangerous confusion. I am elaborating this point because there is a good deal of such teaching at the present time. There are people who say, "If you have given your life to God and if you live the whole of your life to his glory, the whole of your life is an act of worship." But that is just, I repeat, not only to confuse the meaning of the terms, it is to miss the special meaning of this word *worship*.

Some people make the same error in connection with prayer. I know of very orthodox Christian people who do not have prayer meetings in their churches. Why not? It is because they have intellectualized the whole of the Christian faith. They spend their time thinking about God and trying to work that out in practice and in detail, and they say that the whole of one's life is prayer. But it is not. Prayer, again, is a special action. It is right that one's whole life should be lived for God. The demand of God is totalitarian, and we should love him with all our heart and mind and soul and strength. Yes, that is all right—the whole of life is to be lived in the service of God—but these particular actions are special, and we are taught about them in a special way in the Bible itself. It is important, therefore, that we should realize this about prayer and thanksgiving and the various aspects of worship.

So let me put it to you negatively like this. We often call a church service "public worship," but it is not always. We can go through a whole service and, alas, there may have been no real worship at all. What we have done is all right, but we have stopped short of true worship. To read the Bible is not, in and of itself, worship. I read the Bible, and I meditate upon it, and if I do this properly and clearly it should lead me to worship God, but I can read and meditate and not worship.

This is also true even of praying. Prayer is not of necessity worship. Again, prayer should always lead to worship, but you can pray and spend your time in prayer with petitions and even with thanksgiving without worshipping. And this, I think, is where so many of us tend to go astray; we forget the most important aspect of all. It is the same with singing. Singing should always lead to worship, and if we are singing a hymn that is conducive to worship and contains the vital element of worship, it may in itself be worship, but we must not assume that all hymn singing is worship.

Similarly, listening to sermons or lectures may stop well short of worship. A sermon worthy of the name should always lead to worship, and if it does not, it is a bad sermon. If it ends with the focus on the preacher or on some particular point he has made, it has missed the mark, missed the aim. The purpose of preaching is to lead us to worship God.

What, then, does worship mean? It means bowing down before God and adoring him for himself. That is why I am drawing a distinction between prayer and worship. Prayer, if it is just petition, is not worship; if it is just thanksgiving, it is not worship. You may be grateful, you may thank God for blessings that he has given you, but you can be so interested in and concerned about the blessing that you forget the one who has blessed you. The mark of worship is that it is bowing down before God himself, being concerned about God himself, apart from what he does and all the blessings we have received from him. It is just because he is God that we fall down before him, bow before him, and adore him.

There are many examples of worship in the Bible. A perfect illustration of what I am trying to say is in the book of Exodus. When God gave a revelation of himself to Moses, Moses just fell to the ground and worshipped (Exod. 34:8). In exactly the same way, Joshua, after a revelation was given to him, "bowed down before him" and simply worshipped God.

> And it came to pass, when Joshua was by Jericho, that he lifted up his eyes and looked, and, behold, there stood a man over against him with his sword drawn in his hand: and Joshua went unto him, and said unto him, Art thou for us, or for our adversaries? And he said, Nay; but as captain of the host of the LORD am I now come. And Joshua fell on his face to the earth, and did worship. (Josh. 5:13–14)

That is worship. Joshua realized the Presence. He had not understood; he had been putting forward his question, concerned about this fight and this victory that he was desiring, as we do in so much of our praying. But when he realized the presence of God, he "fell on his face to the earth, and did worship."

I could give many other examples. There is a perfect description of worship in the fourth chapter of the book of Revelation where the twenty-four elders "fall down" before God (Rev. 4:10). That is worship. We must not forget this. Worship is very special; it is unique. It is the high watermark of the whole of our relationship with God. And our Lord is speaking about worship to the woman of Samaria. She has her mechanical notions—"in this mountain"—similar to so many today who can only worship in a given type of building with ceremony and ritual. If these aids to worship help you, use them, but all I ask is this: have they led you to worship? Do you know what it is to fall down in the presence of God and adore him because he is who and what he is?

Let me give you an example from the history of the church, just to show that genuine worship is not confined to biblical times, neither the Old Testament nor the New. Worship happens in every time of revival and reawakening, and you also find it in the individual experiences of people who have had some extraordinary manifestation of the glory of God, who have been filled with the Spirit and have been greatly used of God. Let me give you one illustration; you will find it in the journal of John Wesley for January 1, 1739. I often think this was a more important and vital experience in the life of John Wesley even than that which happened to him at Aldersgate Street on May 24, 1738. He and his brother Charles, George

Whitefield, Joseph Ingham, and some others were in the room in Fetter Lane where they used to meet. They were having what they called a "love feast" and had been together for hours. This is what Wesley writes:

> About 3 o'clock in the morning, as we were continuing instant in prayer, the power of God came mightily upon us inasmuch that many cried out for exceeding joy, and many fell to the ground. As soon as we were recovered a little from the awe and the amazement at the Presence of his majesty we broke out with one voice, "We praise thee, O God, we acknowledge thee to be the Lord."

They began to sing the *Te Deum*, which is often sung today. But do you see the difference? They did not sing it because it was announced at a given point in the service. No; they "broke out with one voice." They knew they were in the presence of God. As John Wesley put it, "as we were continuing instant in prayer, the power of God came mightily upon us."

Now there are people who not only know nothing about that, they even argue against it. They say, "As long as you are a Christian and have given your whole life to God, you do not look for anything further. You just go on serving God and do not worry about any experience." Oh, what a tragedy! This is the object of all knowledge; if your theology does not bring you to something like this, it is of very little value to you. Nor is anything else you may have; all your diligence, all your persistence in these matters, all your concern are of no value. This is what we are meant to come to; this is worship. You bow down, you are humbled, you are silent, you are filled with awe at the presence of the majesty of God, and you can do nothing but adore him. That is true worship.

Now do not misunderstand me. I am not saying, "Stop praying if you do not experience this." No, no; that would be quite wrong. We must go on praying; we must do everything else God tells us to do. All I am saying is that the real danger confronting us all is to stop with what we do, to stop at the means of grace, to stop at our own Bible reading, our own prayer, our own diligence. Oh, what a tragedy it is to stop at the means and to fail to see that God has provided them for us in order to lead us on to this act of worship, the high watermark! Go through your Bible, go through the biographies of the saints, and you will find that this is the highest point that any man or woman can ever reach. This is a foretaste of heaven. This is a glimpse of the Glory. This is a touch of the everlasting. And this is the essence of true worship.

Oh, do not merge this into something general. Do not miss this; do not lose it. The first thing we must realize is the essential character of worship, and we must be content with nothing less than this. It is right, it is our duty, to pray, but if we go through our lives just saying our prayers, without knowing anything of what it is to fall down before God—well, I am saying that is Christianity at its very lowest. We are only just in the kingdom. But here are the riches; here are the glorious possibilities. Our Lord died on the cross not merely that our sins might be forgiven, but, as Peter puts it, he died, he gave himself for us, "that he might bring us to God" (1 Pet. 3:18). Or as Hebrews 10:19 puts it, "Having therefore, brethren, boldness to enter into the holiest by the blood of Jesus." What is your thinking about "the blood of Jesus"? Do you stop at forgiveness, or do you realize that this blood brings you into the Presence, into the holiest of all? There you realize the Presence and you worship him, you bow down before him.

So, as we have seen in the case of John Wesley, we find true worship of God in individual experiences and in the great revivals, which are but wonderful records of this very thing. You read about people who have been Christians for years and are good people, but suddenly the revival comes, the Spirit of God is poured out, and they are overwhelmed, as Wesley was. If ever there was a man who was non-emotional it was John Wesley. He was hardheaded, as it were, intellectual, the scholar—as far from emotionalism as you can imagine a man to be. But remember what he had to say about himself on January 1, 1739—this is what happens in revival. There are these people praying, and suddenly the power of God, the glory of God, is manifest, and the result, as in Wesley's description, is that sometimes they literally fall to the floor, overwhelmed. They feel they are nobody; they feel they are nothing. They feel doubtful as to whether they have ever been Christians at all; they doubt whether they have ever really prayed or have ever really worshipped. They have been taking things from God. They have been using Christ just to soothe their consciences. They have been interested only in the first principles of the gospel of Christ. But now they know the fullness—and that is revival. They have a sense of the glory of God, and there is nothing to do but to fall before him and to adore him in wondering worship and praise.

There, then, is something of a definition of what is meant by worship. I am concerned to show the uniqueness of this act and to emphasize that we must be content with nothing less. Do not listen to people who say to you, "You're a Christian, you've given your life to God—just go on serving, don't worry." Oh, my dear friend, this other is what you are offered, and if you are not anxious to obtain it, if you are not thirsting for it, if you are not longing for it, then all your understanding has missed the point—you are misinterpreting the Scriptures and the great Christian tradition.

So, then, how are we to come to the point at which we worship God? Well, the second principle that I find here is this—we must submit ourselves entirely to the teaching of the Bible concerning this matter. Our Lord puts it like this: "Ye worship ye know not what: we know what we worship: for salvation is of the Jews." That is a most important statement from every standpoint. These Samaritans, as we have seen, only had the Pentateuch, that is, the five books of Moses—that is all they had of the Old Testament. They did not have the prophets and their teaching or the book of Psalms.

Now our Lord is including the Pentateuch in his statement here. But the Samaritans even narrowed the five books of Moses down to the mechanics—"this mountain" and the particular ritual that they believed in. So there was this dispute as to whether you should worship here or there. You know the interest that is so common today in postures, in whether you should stand or kneel, and in ceremony and ritual, the mere externals of religion. Oh, the tragedy of it all! No, no, says our Lord; you do not know, you do not understand: "We know what we worship: for salvation is of the Jews."

In essence, that statement by our Lord means that we do not start with our ideas of worship. That is the danger. We do not take human ideas of worship, for the history of the church shows us so plainly that as the centuries pass, people always try to add to worship and to make up a system. That is why, when you look at a church such as the Roman Catholic Church of today, and compare it with the Christian church in the New Testament, you feel you are in two entirely different realms. From where did they get all their practices? Well, they borrowed. They borrowed from Old Testament practices that, even according to the teaching of Scripture, should have been left behind, and they also borrowed from the mystery religions. And whenever the Roman Catholic Church went to a country that a Western nation had taken over, they believed it was right to incorporate into the act of Christian worship and praise various rituals from the pagan religions. So you have a kind of syncretism, and you elaborate and elaborate and elaborate, and all the attention is paid to the externals and the trappings. But the vital and real aspects are never known and are never experienced at all.

So we must turn away from that. You can have textbooks that will teach you, it is claimed, how to worship, and there are people who are "experts" in liturgies and litanies and so on. They say they can teach you, and it is all very beautiful and wonderful. Ah, but the question is, does it lead to worship? Are you being moved by the stained-glass windows? Are you being moved by the beauty of the diction or by the exact precision of the arrangement of the service? You can be moved aesthetically, and we often fool ourselves and think that is a spiritual experience. But it is not. We must, I repeat, go back and receive our instructions from the Bible itself. There and there alone do we find true worship.

Let me put it to you like this: look at the trouble God took (if I may so put it) in instructing Moses with regard to worship. I know that it was chiefly external there in the wilderness, but it was symbolic—it was all meant to convey to us the real, essential spirit of worship. That is why our Lord says, "The hour cometh, when ye shall neither in this mountain, nor yet at Jerusalem, worship the Father" (John 4:21). Not even in Jerusalem, because worship is something that is done "in spirit and in truth" (v. 24). But there in the Old Testament is this instruction, given simply to convey to us the idea that our own thoughts concerning worship are quite inadequate, and we must be instructed by God himself.

An incident in the Old Testament ought to fix this in our minds once and forever. It concerns an event that is called "the rebellion of Korah." Three men in the camp of Israel—Korah, Dathan, and Abiram—were prominent princes and were very able men. But they became jealous of Moses and Aaron. They said in essence, "Who are these two men who arrogate unto themselves the right to dictate to us as to how we should worship? We know as well as they do how God is to be worshipped." So they set themselves up and called a public meeting. Then they addressed the crowd, and the people were very ready to listen to them and to agree with them. People are always ready to listen to new ideas; they are always after some novelty. And these men persuaded the people. They said, "This is how we should worship, not the way that these others tell you." And you remember what happened: God punished Korah, Dathan, and Abiram and their households in a most terrible manner. The ground opened, and they were swallowed up and disappeared (Num. 16).

But God did not leave it at that. He called Moses and said in effect, "I want this to be fixed and established in the minds and the hearts of these people and all their descendants after them." So he told Moses to bring together the twelve princes of the twelve tribes of Israel. Each prince was to bring a rod with him, and each man was to write his name upon the rod. Aaron was to bring a rod with his name on it for the house of Levi. They handed their rods to Moses, who put them in the Tabernacle. Then God told Moses to leave the rods there overnight and look at them the following morning. God said, "The man's rod, whom I shall choose, shall blossom" (Num. 17:5)—he would be the man who was teaching the truth as God had given it.

So they did this, and when Moses went into the Tabernacle in the morning, he saw that "the rod of Aaron for the house of Levi was budded" (Num. 17:8). God told Moses to put "Aaron's rod that budded" (Heb. 9:4) in the Ark of the Covenant as a permanent token or memorial. What was it to be a token of? Well, this very question of worship. It is God who teaches us how to worship. It is he, and not men, who appoints the high priest. They may be very able and clever men such as Korah, Dathan, and Abiram, but that does not matter. It is God who is to be worshipped, and he tells us how, and we must not deviate from the teaching.

So we must not be deluded by appeals to beauty, order, and arrangement. No, no; worship is a matter of "spirit and . . . truth," and God has instructed us, and his Son has instructed us. You see him here in John 4; you see him worshipping God. Of course, his whole life was lived for God, but you find that he would rise "a great while before day" and go out to a solitary place to pray, or he would pray all night on a mountain (see, for example, Mark 1:35; Luke 6:12). He would go apart from the people in order that he might have quiet and silence and pray and adore and worship God. Our Lord constantly did this, and he teaches us to do the same. So we need the instruction that our Lord gave to the woman of Samaria at this point: "Ye worship ye know not what: we know what we worship: for salvation is of the Jews." We must look to him and listen to him and be led by him, and by him alone. The moment we deviate from that, we have already gone astray.

Those are the main matters with regard to worship that are taught here. What about the true ideas of God? You cannot separate the two; they go together. As we think of God, so we will worship. So our Lord also gives this woman instruction with regard to God. He says in effect, "You think you are worshipping God, but you are not. You are worshipping something created by your forefathers." And, oh, how terrible it is to realize how often we have been guilty of the same self-deception.

Do we know whom we worship? Who is our God? What is our God? Have you faced these questions? You can go through life dropping down on your knees, saying your prayers, without having thought about to whom you are praying. This is vital, for our ideas of God, as we have seen, can be so wrong, so false. We confine our worship to buildings. We think of God as mere Force, mere Power, "the ground of our being," and all that the modern philosophers are teaching about him, even from Christian pulpits. This is such an utter travesty of the truth. That is why the church is as she is. We must take our teaching from the Lord himself, and here it is.

The translation of the Authorized Version in verse 24 is, "God is a Spirit," but a better translation is, "God is Spirit." What a contrast this is with the localizing of God—"this mountain," "Jerusalem," particular buildings. No, no, says our Lord, get rid of that. "God is Spirit: and they that worship him must worship him in spirit and in truth." Now this is a subject that the early Christians, the apostles, and other teachers had a great fight about, even with the Jews; the Jews had gone astray on this matter. Take, for instance, the martyr Stephen. This is how he puts it in his great address to the Sanhedrin:

> But Solomon built him an house. Howbeit *the most High dwelleth not in temples made with hands*; as saith the prophet, heaven is my throne, and earth is my footstool: what house will ye build me? saith the Lord: or what is the place of my rest? Hath not my hand made all these things? (Acts 7:47–50)

And Paul has to make exactly the same point when he arrives in Athens. Here are the Athenians with their temples all over the place, and Paul says, "I perceive that in all things ye are too superstitious"—that means, "too religious," worshipping these various gods; and so the apostle puts it to them in these words—"For as I passed by, and beheld your devotions, I found an altar with this inscription, TO THE UNKNOWN GOD." Then exactly like our Lord to the woman of Samaria, Paul says, "Whom therefore ye ignorantly worship, him declare I unto you" (Acts 17:22–23). He is the apostle; he is sent. He has been given the revelation, the message, and he does not argue, he does not philosophize—he *declares*, for he has had experience of this living God through the Lord Jesus Christ. "Whom therefore ye ignorantly worship . . ."

Oh, beloved people, let us examine ourselves. Are we worshipping "ignorantly," or do we know the God whom we worship? "Him declare I unto you." And then Paul says:

> God that made the world and all things therein, seeing that he is Lord of heaven and earth, dwelleth not in temples made with hands; neither is worshipped with men's hands, as though he needed any thing, seeing he giveth to all life, and breath, and all things. (Acts 17:24–25)

There, then, is the great principle: God is Spirit. God is the living God. He is completely unlike the pagan gods, which were made out of gold and silver and wood. The people had to carry their gods and put them on pedestals before they bowed down and worshipped them. The people themselves were doing everything; their gods were dead. The psalmist ridicules this in various places. For example:

> Their idols . . . have mouths, but they speak not: eyes have they, but they see not: they have ears, but they hear not: noses have they, but they smell not: they have hands, but they handle not: feet have they, but they walk not: neither speak they through their throat. (115:4–7)

But that is not God, the living God! God is Spirit. You cannot confine God to "this mountain" or "Jerusalem." Why not? Because God is everywhere; he is omnipresent.

Listen again to the psalmist putting this in the glorious way that the psalmists do:

> Whither shall I go from thy spirit? or whither shall I flee from thy presence? If I ascend up into heaven, thou art there: if I make my bed in hell, behold, thou art there. If I take the wings of the morning, and dwell in the uttermost parts of the sea; even there shall thy hand lead me, and thy right hand shall hold me. If I say, Surely the darkness shall cover me; even the night shall be light about me. Yea, the darkness hideth not from thee; but the night shineth as the day: the darkness and the light are both alike to thee. (139:7–12)

And that is what our Lord is teaching here: God is Spirit, and he is everywhere. Nothing is hidden from his sight: "But all things are naked and opened unto the eyes of him with whom we have to do" (Heb. 4:13). Language is inadequate! Even the Bible only gives us glimpses and pictures. Oh, the glory of God, filling the universe, the universe he made. He is over all, reigning and ruling over all. "For our God is a consuming fire" (Heb. 12:29). "God is light, and in him is no darkness at all" (1 John 1:5). God is Spirit, and his might and his power are illimitable. He is the living God, the Father of all spirits. God is. And everything else has come into existence only as the result of his great and holy will and the work of his power.

But we must not stop at that. If we did, we would all be filled with terror and alarm. "God is a Spirit: and they that worship him must worship him in spirit and in truth." You cannot conceive of it, but, thank God, our Lord went on to say something further to this woman. Do not forget that he also said, "The hour cometh, and now is, when the true worshippers shall worship the Father in spirit and in truth: for *the Father seeketh such to worship him.*" And this, of course, is the special revelation that has come through our blessed Lord and Savior. In the Old Testament, we find the prophets almost grasping this truth—"Like as a father pitieth his children . . ." (Ps. 103:13)—but they do not get any further. It is the Son who shows us the tender loving care of the Father, our "*Abba*, Father" (Rom. 8:15; Gal. 4:6).

Then there is that beautiful phrase of the apostle Paul, which ought to thrill our hearts to the depths. He talks about "the God and Father of our Lord Jesus Christ" (2 Cor. 11:31). The Father and Son are like one another. So we have glimpses of Jesus, and, ah, that is the Father: "he that hath seen me hath seen the Father" (John 14:9).

What does this mean? This is wonderful truth; this is a part of this great offer of life that is life indeed—eternal life. We must ever remember that this great God, the Father of all spirits, God who is Spirit, the everlasting Creator, the God of glory, is one who, according to the counsel of his own will—and it baffles us and amazes us—has set his heart and his love upon us. Before the very foundation and creation of the world he knew you and he chose you; he has "called you out of darkness into his marvellous light" (1 Pet. 2:9). Why? So that you might "receive the adoption of sons" (Gal. 4:5).You are not merely forgiven—you are adopted into the family of heaven, you are a child of God. He is concerned about you, and he knows all about you.

A hymn ("Lord of All Being") puts it so well:

Center and soul of every sphere,
Yet to each loving heart how near.

Oliver Wendell Holmes

Do you realize that when you pray or when you worship? Before you begin to utter a sound, realize who God is. Remember the principle of recollection. You must stop; you must think about what you are doing. And then you remember who God is—"Center and soul of every sphere," and you feel, "I cannot do anything." Then you remember, "Yet to each loving heart how near." "But the very hairs of your head are all numbered" (Matt. 10:30).

We should never go into the presence of God without remembering all this rich teaching that is given to us. Let me give you one more example. It is in the sixth chapter of the Second Epistle to the Corinthians, where again this same matter is being dealt with:

> And what agreement hath the temple of God with idols? for ye are the temple of the living God; as God hath said, I will dwell in them, and walk in them; and I will be their God, and they shall be my people. Wherefore come out from among them, and be ye separate, saith the Lord . . .

It does not matter how small the number is.

> . . . and touch not the unclean thing; and I will receive you, and will be a Father unto you, and ye shall be my sons and daughters, saith the Lord Almighty. (2 Cor. 6:16–18)

And the author of the Epistle to the Hebrews crowns it all: "Wherefore God is not ashamed to be called their God" (11:16). This the Father, the one who loves you with an everlasting love, the one who is interested in you.

And Peter ends it all by saying, "Casting all your care upon him" (1 Pet. 5:7). Who? The eternal Spirit, "the Father of lights, with whom is no variableness, neither shadow of turning" (Jas. 1:17). Yes, all that is true of him. But as for you, you cannot "cast your cares." You are overwhelmed with grief or sorrow or shame or disappointment. Life has been harsh and cold; the devil has tempted you, and you are full of cares and anxiety. You are severely burdened. "Cast all your care upon him; for he careth for you." God is Spirit, yes, but God is our Father in and through our blessed Lord and Savior.

These are the preliminaries to worship, and until we are right about them, we shall know very little about "the well of water springing up into everlasting life." God grant that the particular hindrances—wrong ideas about worship, wrong ideas about God—may, in the light of the teaching we have seen, be removed and that we now may realize the presence of God and know something about that experience that Wesley and the others had in Fetter Lane: "We praise, we worship thee, O God."

6

In Spirit and in Truth

The woman saith unto him, Sir, I perceive that thou art a prophet. Our fathers worshipped in this mountain; and ye say, that in Jerusalem is the place where men ought to worship. Jesus saith unto her, Woman, believe me, the hour cometh, when ye shall neither in this mountain, nor yet at Jerusalem, worship the Father. Ye worship ye know not what: we know what we worship: for salvation is of the Jews. But the hour cometh, and now is, when the true worshippers shall worship the Father in spirit and in truth: for the Father seeketh such to worship him. God is a Spirit: and they that worship him must worship him in spirit and in truth. (John 4:19–24)

We are considering the great offer of the Christian gospel in John 4:13–14. This passage shows us the condition in which we should all be as Christian people. Our Lord's promise is that whoever drinks of the water he shall give shall never thirst—*never thirst*! *Never* is an all-inclusive word. It does not matter what the state of the world; whether we be at peace or in the midst of war, the Christian should never thirst. Christians are rendered immune to "the slings and arrows of outrageous fortune"; they are rendered immune to any trial or tribulation that may come across their paths.

But the great question is, do we know this? Do we have this well of water springing up within us? Are we in a condition in which we never thirst? And we are considering some of the hindrances to obtaining this fullness of the Lord Jesus Christ, which gives perfect, enduring satisfaction. At the moment we are dealing with the hindrance that arises from the fact that our ideas of worship and our ideas of God, the God whom we worship, tend to be so wrong.

We are looking, therefore, at verses 19–24 in this chapter, and we have seen that when we worship God, we reach the highest point that any human being can ever reach. But the great question is, do we know what it means to worship? Do we know whom we worship? How tragic it is that people should be fooling themselves by imagining they are worshipping God when they are doing something that, according to our Lord's own teaching, is quite valueless!

Now this subject is rather appropriate on this particular morning—Remembrance Sunday.[6] Various meetings are being held throughout the country, but what is their meaning? What is their value? This is an important question. If we believe that the only hope for the human race is knowledge of God and to be blessed by God, then nothing is more important than worship and prayer. Therefore we are dealing with the very essence of our modern problem and condition. Everything else is failing—there is no need to waste time in illustrating that. In spite of all the efforts of humanity throughout the centuries, the long history of what is called civilization is a record of failure, and the world is in as desperate a condition today as it has ever been, if not worse. Our only hope is in God.

And now today, Remembrance Sunday, people in large numbers are adopting the attitude and the posture of prayer and of worship. But have we not a right to ask whether they know what they are doing, whether it has any meaning for them? Is it real worship? The Samaritans thought they were worshipping God, and we ourselves know from our own experiences that we have often imagined that we have been worshipping God when we have been doing nothing of the kind according to the standpoint of this teaching in John 4. I would be wasting your time and mine if I were to address the state of the world, giving my opinion on the international problems and trying to tell statesmen how to solve them. That would be not only folly but sheer impertinence. I am in no position to do that. And when the Christian church spends a morning in that way, she is displaying her ignorance of her own truth. No, no; we are here to teach people how to worship, how to know the only "living and true God" (1 Thess. 1:9), and nothing matters but this. Rulers and monarchs, potentates and powers are all mortal and are all going to die, but the soul remains face-to-face with God.

So to look at the meaning of worship is not only the right thing to do, it is the only relevant thing to do at a time such as this. This is the instruction that the world needs above all else, and it is only obtainable from the Bible. Our Lord says, "We know what we worship: for salvation is of the Jews," and by "Jews" he means all the teaching of the Old

Testament. God had manifested himself to the Jews in a special manner. He had given his truth through them, and they were to be the teachers of the whole world. It was to them and to them alone that he had given his "lively oracles" (Acts 7:38), and there is no knowledge in connection with worship apart from that revealed to us in the Scriptures.

So we are tied entirely to this book, and we have already been seeing what worship really means. It means bowing down in the presence of God. All that we do in a church service is meant to lead to that, and to the extent that it does not, the service has failed. We started with the true idea of worship and the true idea of God. "God is Spirit," and God, blessed be his holy name, is also "the Father." Our Lord teaches this woman that she must be clear and right in her ideas as to what worship is and as to who and what God is. We must start with that.

The assumption is that we all know who God is and can go into his presence whenever we like. Some people only attempt this, or even think they are attempting it, once a year—Remembrance Sunday, and perhaps Easter Sunday in addition. But, my dear friends, that can be nothing but sheer blasphemy. If God is God, and if we know who God is and what God is, we should be constantly seeking his presence and bowing ourselves down before him. Not occasionally but constantly. "And thou shalt love the Lord thy God with all thy heart, and with all thy soul, and with all thy mind, and with all thy strength: this is the first commandment" (Mark 12:30). Everything we have and are should always be directed toward him and his eternal glory.

That is our starting point, but we do not end there. You notice that our Lord also teaches this woman what is necessary on our side, as it were. We start with a true notion of worship and a true idea of God, but still we must learn, we must all learn, how exactly we are to worship God, this only "living and true God." And our Lord's answer is that we must worship him "in spirit and in truth," and this is what I now want to direct your attention to, but I will take it in the reverse order. We must worship God in truth, and we must worship God in spirit. I take them in this order because we start with ourselves and we work up to what is ultimately most important of all.

What does our Lord mean by saying that we must worship God "in truth"? This is most important. Our Lord is contrasting true worship with the false idea of worship that characterized the life of the Samaritans. So he says worship must be "in truth." But what does this mean in practice? First of all, it means, of course, that worship must never be thoughtless.

You cannot worship God in truth if you do not stop to consider what you are doing. I need not dwell on this; we know what it means because we have all been guilty at this point. We can come to the house of God Sunday by Sunday and never realize what we are doing. We may come to meet one another, to have happy fellowship together. All right. But is that the purpose of the service? Do we stop to think? Do we ask ourselves why we are in church? Thoughtlessness is the opposite of truth. Mechanical worship is the opposite of worshipping in truth.

When I say "mechanical," I mean that we just come to church out of habit or custom or obligation. That is where you must be careful on a day like Remembrance Sunday. If your thoughts are governed by something other than God—by history, by events, by the past, by the future—if the occasion itself is more important than the act of worship, then no worship is taking place. To put anything before God is to cease to worship him; indeed, it is to insult him. But we are all subject to this; we are all prone to it. We do not stop, we do not think; it is the thing to do, everybody does it, and so, like sheep, we do too. There is national hypocrisy as well as personal hypocrisy.

All this, to me, is so important for this reason: today the masses of the people in this country, especially the so-called "working classes," are outside the Christian church. Why is this? Here is our great problem. Our great question today is, why will people not even stop to consider Christianity? And you will find, if you talk to them, that their answer, in some shape or form, is that they have reacted against hypocrisy. "It's a lot of nonsense," they say. The church, unfortunately, has given the impression that she is on the side of power and of might; and, of course, this has been the stance of the church in every country. So we see the different countries praying for their success in war, both sides praying at the same time. As a result, the average person thinks of the church as an adjunct of the state, a sort of court chaplain to whom authorities turn for prayer when they are in need or in trouble.

It is up to us to tell people that worship must be true, it must be "in truth." It must not be thoughtless; it must not be mechanical; it must not be governed by anything other than our realization of whom it is we are approaching, what he is, and why we should always approach him "with reverence and godly fear" (Heb. 12:28). This should be obvious, should it not? And yet we are all guilty. Is this not amazing? How often I have been on my knees and said my prayers but my thoughts were elsewhere. I did not stop for a second to realize what I was doing. I rushed through my prayers, as it were, so that I could go on to something else. But that is not worshipping God "in truth." My dear friends, we had better start by—and let me put it in this way in order that you may remember it—we must start by stopping. You do not start speaking at once. You stop; you think, you recollect; you realize what you are doing. You ask questions; you prepare yourself. Worship is impossible apart from that. Never must it be thoughtless; it must always be "in truth."

That leads me to the second point—and it follows from the first—worship must never be hypocritical, it must never be dishonest. Now there is always an element of thought in hypocrisy. That is why hypocrisy is actually worse than thoughtlessness. Up to a point the hypocrite does know what he is doing. There is a deliberate element, and to the extent that it is deliberate, it is dishonest. There is an idea that somehow or another we can fool God; we can use him. We imagine that he is satisfied if we turn to him now and again when we need him and then carry on without him when everything is going well.

Again, we have all been guilty of this. We imagine we can use God. Individuals have thought this; nations think it. This is an expression of the national hypocrisy to which I have been referring. But, oh, how utterly foolish such an idea is! The biggest fool in the world is the hypocrite. He is in a much worse state and condition than the person who does not think at all, because though that person is saying, "I'm going to turn to God, I'm going to worship him," for his own reasons he has not stopped to realize what he is doing.

The Bible goes out of its way to give us teaching on hypocrisy and, quite apart from anything else, on its utter folly. It gives us instruction like this: "Who shall ascend into the hill of the LORD? or who shall stand in his holy place? He that hath clean hands, and a pure heart" (Ps. 24:3–4). Or take David, who was an expert on this matter. Of course, he was a man of God, but he often played the hypocrite; his lusts, his passions, got the better of him. He had not finished with God, but he thought he was managing his sinfulness. Even in his greatest crime of all, his adultery and murder, David was happy; he thought all was well. Why? Because he had become a hypocrite. But David was brought to his senses, and he passed through an agony of repentance when God through his servant Nathan the prophet showed him the truth.

When David saw his sin, he said, "Behold, thou desirest truth in the inward parts" (Ps. 51:6). God wants inward truth. He is never satisfied with an external appearance—which is, of course, the essence of hypocrisy. Hypocrisy is putting on a mask; it is putting on an appearance. It is satisfaction in the external and the outward and covering over that which is within. "Thou desirest truth in the inward [innermost] parts," and nothing else will satisfy God. He knows all, he sees all, and nothing is or can be hidden from his holy sight.

See this again in Psalm 66, where the psalmist says, "If I regard iniquity in my heart"—if I regard it fondly; if I keep it there; if I shield it; if I go to God and my conscience accuses me, but I cover over this thing and say, "It's all right, I want this; I want God, but I want this also" and make sure it goes on, then—"the Lord will not hear me" (Ps. 66:18). I can fall on my face to the ground, but it will not help me. I can assume all the postures and the attitudes, all the appearances of worship, but it is no good: "the Lord will not hear me." So in a later psalm we find the psalmist saying, "Search me, O God, and know my heart: try me, and know my thoughts: And see if there be any wicked way in me, and lead me in the way everlasting" (Ps. 139:23–24).

That is it. Now this man is getting it right. He cannot trust himself; he cannot trust his own self-examination. He has been doing that, but he has realized that he is a hypocrite; so he stops to think and question and examine himself. But he sees that even this is not enough; we are so subtle, and sin is so subtle with us, that we manipulate things to suit our own case. So he turns to God and says, "Search me, O God"—"you do it!"

I dare not trust the sweetest frame.

EDWARD MOTE

I cannot trust myself. God must examine me. This teaching runs right through the book of Psalms, and the prophets have exactly the same message. For example, "Who among us shall dwell with the devouring fire?" (Isa. 33:14b). These are the questions that the people of God have always asked.

Exactly the same teaching is found in the New Testament. In 1 Timothy 2:8 Paul says, "I will therefore that men pray everywhere, lifting up holy hands, without wrath and doubting"—"holy hands, without wrath"! Clean hands! Without pride, without a bitter national spirit, and without wrath against an individual. And "without . . . doubting." And the author of the Epistle to the Hebrews has precisely the same teaching: "Having therefore, brethren, boldness to enter into the holiest by the blood of Jesus, by a new and living way, which he hath consecrated for us, through the veil, that is to say, his flesh; and having an high priest over the house of God; Let us draw near"—how?—"with a true heart"—that is the first thing he emphasizes—"in full assurance of faith" (10:19–22).

Notice the words, "true heart." This means "with honesty." There must not be any dishonesty in our hearts; there must be "truth in the inward parts." The heart must be honest; it must be open. And without this, whatever we may do, individually or nationally, prayer and worship are a mockery, a sham, and God will not hear us. A "true heart" is part of worshipping God in truth.

But we must go beyond that: the heart must also be a united heart—it must not be divided. The psalmist prays, "Teach me thy way, O LORD; I will walk in thy truth: unite my heart to fear thy name" (Ps. 86:11). Now, again, we all know something about a divided heart. The psalmist knew himself. He knew there were parts of him that were right, parts that were wrong, parts that desired God, parts that desired evil. The apostle Paul put it well for us when he said in effect in Romans 7, "With my mind I acknowledge the truth of God's Law and its rightness and desire to live it and to practice it, but I find another law in my members" (see vv. 22–23). Here is the division.

The great problem in life is how to have a united heart, how to be whole, how to bring the whole of our being and personality to this great place in which we realize that nothing is higher or greater or more wonderful than worshipping God and praying to him. James puts this in terms of the "double minded man" (Jas. 1:8). It is the same teaching in the sense that it shows the division again. There can be a division, an uncertainty, in the mind as well as in the desire. Is this not one of the things that curses all of us, this difficulty of uniting ourselves, bringing ourselves into oneness, into unanimity? But only then will we be in the position of truth.

There must be no lies, nothing hidden, nothing unworthy: "Unite my heart to fear thy name"—the whole being is involved. That is a part of worshipping God in truth. It is "with all thy heart, and with all thy soul, and with all thy mind, and with all thy strength." Nothing is left out. It is a total allegiance to God, a total seeking of God, a total prostration of one's self in "the presence of his Majesty," as John Wesley put it in the quotation I shared earlier. All of this is absolutely essential.

And this is what it all leads to: when we have realized something of what we are doing, and when we have realized what is true inside us, we come to a point at which we are humbled and contrite. Now look at the eloquent teaching that you find in the Bible itself—thank God for it. It is the paradox of the godly Christian life that this brokenness is what brings us immediately into the presence of God. This is directly opposite to the world's ideas. The world teaches us self-confidence, self-assurance. It gets us to take pride in ourselves, individually and nationally; in various ways it is always boosting our ego. And the more it does, of course, the farther it moves us from God. God is "the high and lofty One that inhabiteth eternity, whose name is Holy," who dwells "in the high and holy place, with him also that is of a contrite and humble spirit" (Isa. 57:15). Or take David. David was farthest from God when he was relying upon himself, upon his powers and prerogatives as a king, upon his right to get anything he wanted, even another man's wife. But he came back into the presence of God when his heart was broken, and he said, "The sacrifices of God are a broken spirit: a broken and a contrite heart, O God, thou wilt not despise" (Ps. 51:17).

We are not worshipping God unless we are humble, unless we are broken. This is an essential part of worshipping God in truth. And, surely, is not this the very element that is most lacking in us at the present time? The trouble with us as a generation of Christian people is that we are all so healthy, we are all so happy, as it were, so glib, so easy. How many "broken" Christians do you know? How many humbled Christians? There is a type of Christian today who has never repented, who does not know what that means, who has never been humbled in the presence of Almighty God. There is nothing more terrible than to go into the presence of God in a self-confident manner.

Now you need not take my word for this—it is the clear teaching of the Scriptures. This pride was the whole trouble with the Jews at the time of our Lord. It was the whole trouble, too, with the apostle Paul. This is what he says:

> For we are the circumcision, which worship God in the spirit, and rejoice in Christ Jesus, and have no confidence in the flesh. Though I might also have confidence in the flesh. If any other man thinketh that he hath whereof he might trust in the flesh, I more: circumcised the eighth day, of the stock of Israel, of the tribe of Benjamin, an Hebrew of the Hebrews; as touching the law, a Pharisee; concerning zeal, persecuting the church; touching the righteousness which is in the law, blameless. (Phil. 3:3–6)

Paul used to go to God like that, thanking God that he was such a man. But then he realized that he had never worshipped, that that was a mockery, a sham, a form of blasphemy. That was the very essence of his conversion.

Our Lord gave us exactly the same teaching in his parable about the Pharisee and the tax collector who went up to the Temple to pray. The Pharisee marched right up to the front and said, "God, I thank thee, that I am not as other men are . . . . or even as this publican. I fast twice in the week, I give tithes of all that I possess" (Luke 18:11–12). He thinks that he is worshipping, that he is pleasing God; he feels all is well. What is the matter with the man? He has never been humbled! He is congratulating himself in the presence of God; he is thanking God that he is what he is and for the contrast between him and the tax collector.

But that is the opposite of worshipping in truth. That is a lie! No one can stand like that in the presence of God. It is the other man in the story who is worshipping, the poor tax collector who just gets inside the door and who is ashamed even to lift up his face to look to heaven but beats his breast and says, "God be merciful"—be propitiated—"to me a sinner" (v. 13). That is the man who goes home justified, says our Lord. Why? Because here is a man who is humble, a man who realizes that he is nothing. To approach God with any kind of pride or self-satisfaction, whether it be personal or national, is a mockery of worship; in the sight of God, it comes near, I repeat, to blasphemy. Yet that is something of which we are all guilty. If we realize who God is, if we realize the truth about ourselves, we shall be humbled and broken.

Have you ever felt that you have no right to go to God? I do not think we have ever really been to God unless we have known that we have no right to turn to him, no right to pray. "Who am I?" says David in effect at the height of his glory. "Who am I, and who are my people that we should be building a house for your name and for your glory and for your worship? Who am I? I am unworthy, and so are my people" (see 2 Samuel 7:18). That is worshipping in truth. It is realizing your utter nothingness and your entire dependence upon the love and the grace, the mercy and the compassion of God. He is to be approached "with reverence and godly fear" (Heb. 12:28). How much "reverence and godly fear" do we see today in our bright and breezy services? My dear friends, let us come back to the Scriptures. God is to be worshipped in *truth*. You can never worship God self-confidently, though you are a Christian. Our Lord prayed like this: "Our Father, which art in heaven, hallowed be thy name" (Matt. 6:9). "Holy Father," he said when he prayed himself (John 17:11).

We come, then, confessing ours sins, acknowledging our unworthiness, admitting that we are not worthy of the very least of God's mercies. That is the way to pray! That is worshipping in truth.

But then our Lord also says that we must worship "in spirit": "They that worship him must worship him in spirit and in truth." There are those who say that this should be translated "by the spirit" and that there is really no difference between the two. This is the most important point of all. The other is preliminary; it is really dictated to us by common sense. But it is not, and we need the instruction of the Scripture. God's Word comes to us and knocks us down, and if we have not been knocked down by the Scripture, then we do not know it.

But to go on to the positive teaching, worshipping in or by the spirit is emphasized everywhere in the New Testament. You get it in the Old Testament to a degree, but really the Old Testament is prophesying this. Joel, you remember, in his great prophecy quoted by the apostle Peter on the Day of Pentecost saw this—this is what the prophets were given to see:

> And it shall come to pass in the last days, saith God, I will pour out of my Spirit upon all flesh: and your sons and your daughters shall prophesy, and your young men shall see visions, and your old men shall dream dreams: And on my servants and on my handmaidens I will pour out in those days of my Spirit; and they shall prophesy. (Acts 2:17–18)

After the coming of the Savior and the pouring out of the Spirit, the whole of worship would be revolutionized. That does not mean that the Old Testament worship was not right. It was, but it mainly involved externals—the Temple, the Tabernacle, forms, ceremonies, rituals, and so on. Now all that has come to an end. Zechariah has the same idea when he says that in those days God would shed forth "the spirit of grace and of supplications" (Zech. 12:10). The whole of the Old Testament points forward to this element of worshipping in the spirit, which is the great characteristic of the age after the coming of the Savior.

There is a great statement of this by the apostle Paul in his letter to the Romans: "I beseech you therefore, brethren, by the mercies of God, that ye present your bodies a living sacrifice, holy, acceptable unto God, which is your reasonable service" (12:1). A better translation there is, "present your bodies a living sacrifice, holy, acceptable unto God, which is your spiritual worship"—"spiritual worship"! A worship with the mind, a worship with the understanding, a worship in which the spirit is involved. It is not mechanical. Paul has a picture there. In the Old Testament the people presented the bodies of bulls and goats and lambs, but now you present your own body as a living sacrifice. You present yourself. This is spiritual worship in contrast to the external, more mechanical and localized worship of the Old Testament.

But come back again to Philippians 3:1–3. Here is a most important statement. The apostle Paul had to spend much of his time and energy in arguing against the so-called Judaizers, those Jews who were trying to add something to the gospel of Christ. Yes, they had believed the gospel, they said, but they were adding circumcision, they were trying to bring in bits of the Law. Paul was always fighting this. He says to the Philippians, "Finally, my brethren, rejoice in the Lord. To write the same things to you, to me indeed is not grievous, but for you it is safe. Beware of dogs, beware of evil workers, beware of the concision."

Then here it is—"For we are the circumcision." These people want you to be circumcised, but "we are the circumcision." Who is the circumcision? You are Gentiles, Paul says, but you are the circumcision. Why? This is the reason—"which worship God in the spirit [or by the spirit]." Do you see the contrast? It is the contrast between worshipping God in the spirit and worshipping him as the Jews wanted, in the Temple and by means of circumcision and so on. Paul continues, "and rejoice"—not in the fact that we are Jews, not in the fact that we belong to a particular nation, not because of our history and our superiority to everybody else. No, no—"in Christ Jesus." And to make it doubly certain, Paul adds, "and have no confidence in the flesh." None at all.

Paul tells us that if any man has a right to that, he has. That is how he once was, but he has been delivered from all that: "But what things were gain to me, those I counted loss for Christ" (v. 7). "No confidence in the flesh"—this is an essential part of spiritual worship.

Or take what Paul says at the end of the Epistle to the Ephesians. Having told the Christians in Ephesus to put on the different parts of the whole armor of God, he says, "Praying always with all prayer and supplication *in the Spirit*" (6:18). And nowhere is this put before us more clearly than in the little Epistle of Jude, where such wonderful things are crammed into a short space: "But ye, beloved, building up yourselves on your most holy faith, *praying in the Holy Ghost,* keep yourselves in the love of God" (v. 20). What could be clearer than that?

Or, put differently but meaning exactly the same, read Romans 8:26–27:

> Likewise the Spirit also helpeth our infirmities: for we know not what we should pray for as we ought: but the Spirit itself maketh intercession

> for us with groanings which cannot be uttered. And he that searcheth the hearts knoweth what is the mind of the Spirit, because he maketh intercession for the saints according to the will of God.

Is not that true today? "We know not what we should pray for as we ought." What can you pray for in a world like this? What does this world deserve from God? Look at the way it has behaved; look at the way it is behaving. Look at the way in which, for over a century, it has asserted its intelligence, its understanding, its philosophy, its science, and has ridiculed God. And look at the state of the world—two world wars, everything we are thinking of on this Remembrance Sunday and all that is happening at the present time. What should we pray for? Have we a right to pray for peace? Do we deserve peace? Does the world deserve peace? These are the questions we ought to be asking, and not in a spirit of self-congratulation, thanking God for this or that. No, no; we ought to be examining ourselves. Have we even a right to turn to him? "We know not what we should pray for as we ought." And when we really stop to think, we realize that we do not know. But here is this wonderful message: "The Spirit himself maketh intercession for us with groanings which cannot be uttered."

Thank God for this. This is what saves us; this is what enables us to pray at all. And you and I as Christians should be "praying in [by] the Spirit." And surely this is the greatest lack of all among us. Do we know what it means to pray in the Spirit? What is praying? I ask again, is it just saying our prayers? Is it just turning into a building and "saying a prayer," "offering a prayer"? Or as people put it, and we think sometimes that it is the hallmark of evangelicalism, is it saying, "Let's have a word of prayer"? Think of the way in which that is said, as if to say, "Let's telephone so-and-so" or "let's have a word with old so-and-so"!

Beloved people, is it not about time we began to think? Praying in the Spirit—what does it mean? Well, it means, initially, realizing our utter inability and our need of the Spirit. We cannot pray without him. It is impossible. And he has been sent and has been given to put us right on this matter. Again in his letter to the Ephesians, Paul describes praying in this way: "Through him we both have access by one Spirit unto the Father" (2:18). The three Persons in the blessed Holy Trinity are involved in this matter. The Spirit alone can get us into the right frame and condition for worship.

Would you dream of going to see the Queen at Buckingham Palace without preparing yourself? But how infinitely more important is it for us to prepare ourselves when we go to have an audience with the King of kings and the Lord of lords! You need instruction and advice from the courtiers if you are to be fit to go into the presence of the Queen. There is only one who can put us into the right frame to pray to God, and that is the Holy Spirit; and we must start by asking him to do this for us, to deal with our spirits. We need the understanding that he alone can give us so that we will "know what to pray for as we ought." We need his aid for such things as the ordering of our thoughts and the use of words. This is the beginning of praying in the Spirit—the realization that I cannot pray, that perhaps I have never prayed at all, and that it is only as the Spirit leads me, guides me, instructs me, shows me the way, and prepares me that I *can* pray at all. So I begin to worship and to pray, relying utterly and absolutely upon the power of the Holy Spirit. That is the beginning of "praying in the Spirit."

7

Praying in the Spirit

Ye worship ye know not what: we know what we worship: for salvation is of the Jews. But the hour cometh, and now is, when the true worshippers shall worship the Father in spirit and in truth: for the Father seeketh such to worship him. God is a Spirit: and they that worship him must worship him in spirit and in truth. (John 4:22-24)

The question we are dealing with at the moment is, are we true worshippers? Are we worshipping God in spirit and in truth? We have seen already that implies a true idea as to what worship is and a true idea also of God. We know nothing of God apart from the revelation in the Bible. It is in that sense that it is true to say that "salvation is of the Jews"—not of the Samaritans, nor of anybody else. Philosophers do not help us; they know no more than anyone else. We are entirely confined to this revelation that God has been pleased to give of himself, first of all through the Jews, but more fully and more gloriously in and through his Son, our blessed Lord and Savior, then through the church and through the New Testament Scriptures.

So we have been considering all that, and now we come to this very practical aspect of the matter: we must worship "in truth" and "in spirit." We have seen that to worship God "in truth" means that we must come with honest, open, true hearts and allow ourselves to be searched and examined by him. But then we moved to this second aspect of worship, which is the most important of all—we must worship him "in spirit."

We have seen that our greatest lack at the present time is our inability to pray "in the Spirit" (Eph. 6:18). There is nothing more inadequate about us all than our prayer life, both private and public, and above everything else we need the ability to "pray in [or by] the Spirit." We said in the last study that to pray in the Spirit means, first of all, a consciousness of our utter inability. We realize that by nature "we know not what we should pray for as we ought," but "the Spirit itself maketh intercession for us" (Rom. 8:26), and he will help us order our thoughts and our words. That is the beginning of praying in the Spirit. But that is not all. It also includes this: we should be sensitive to the presence and the leading and the promptings of the Spirit.

Now the Christian life is represented in many places in the Scriptures as a life in the Spirit. That is particularly the favorite contrast drawn by the apostle Paul. You find it to perfection in the eighth chapter of the Epistle to the Romans where Paul talks of the difference between being "in the flesh" and "in the Spirit": "For the law of the Spirit of life in Christ Jesus hath made me free from the law of sin and death" (v. 2). The Christian life is prompted and determined by the Spirit, and this is particularly true of our praying. There is no area in which it is more important that we should realize the influences of the Spirit than in this very matter of prayer. One of the great functions of the Holy Spirit is to lead us, to instruct us, to guide us, and, indeed, to prompt us in prayer, and it is vital that we should realize this.

Our Lord in talking to the woman of Samaria is drawing a contrast between a mechanical, formal, external type of worship and that which is "in spirit." The Spirit alone can produce this, and he does so by working upon us, working in our minds and in our desires, working in the whole of our being. Here is something that is basic to our worship. Are we aware of the working of the Spirit within us, in particular in this matter of prayer? Are we aware of the Spirit calling us to pray, indicating to us what we should pray for and how we should pray? It is very clear, surely, in the teaching of the Scriptures that the Holy Spirit does this and that this is what produces real worship and real prayer.

Let me put this in terms of the fifth chapter of the Epistle of James where James says that "the prayer of faith shall save the sick" (v. 15). I am concerned here not with the question of healing but with the character of the prayer. What exactly does James mean? People often get into trouble over this—that is why I am calling attention to it. A similar statement, which has often perplexed people and caused a good deal of misunderstanding, is found in Mark 11. We read there, "And in the morning, as they passed by, they saw the fig tree dried up from the roots." This is a barren tree that on the previous day our Lord had cursed.

> And Peter calling to remembrance saith unto him, Master, behold, the fig tree which thou cursedst is withered away. And Jesus answering saith unto them, Have faith in God. For verily I say unto you, That whosoever shall say unto this mountain, Be thou removed, and be thou cast into the sea; and shall not doubt in his heart, but shall believe that those things which he saith shall come to pass; he shall have whatsoever he saith. Therefore I say unto you, What things soever ye desire, when ye pray, believe that ye receive them, and ye shall have them. (vv. 20–24)

This is parallel to the statement made by James:

> Is any sick among you? let him call for the elders of the church; and let them pray over him, anointing him with oil in the name of the Lord: And the prayer of faith shall save the sick, and the Lord shall raise him up; and if he have committed sins, they shall be forgiven him.

And James ends by saying, "The effectual fervent prayer of a righteous man availeth much" (Jas. 5:14–16).

People have often taken those texts and have tried to work themselves up into a kind of certainty—"When you pray, believe you have already received it"—and have tried to persuade themselves that this is true. But then the prayer is not answered or at any rate not answered in the way that they asked or expected, and they are cast down and begin to doubt God and his promises. But all that is due to a misunderstanding of the meaning of this "prayer of faith." It seems to me that the only adequate explanation of these passages is that they are a typical example and illustration of praying in the Spirit. Praying in the Spirit is a prayer that is given to us by the Holy Spirit himself, created within us by him, and as he does this he gives us an absolute certainty with respect to it.

A very interesting statement throws light on this in Psalm 10: "LORD, thou hast heard the desire of the humble: thou wilt prepare their heart, thou wilt cause thine ear to hear" (v. 17). Notice the sequence here. "LORD, thou hast heard the desire of the humble." On what grounds does God hear? Here are the two steps: "Thou wilt prepare their heart" and "Thou wilt cause thine ear to hear." In other words, God prepares our hearts to pray, he gives us the petition, if you like, and then he hears the petition that he himself has placed in our hearts. But the first move is to prepare our hearts.

There are many examples in the Scriptures of God answering Spirit-led prayer, and to me they are both important and fascinating. Take, for instance, that great story to which James refers in his fifth chapter, the story of how Elijah prayed that there should be no rain, and there was none for three years and six months. Then he prayed that there should be rain, and the rain came. How did this happen?

Now there is something here that we, I am sure, tend to ignore. In 1 Kings 18 we read the dramatic story of Elijah on Mount Carmel and how he stood alone against 850 false prophets, how God answered him, and how the rain eventually came. But we tend to miss or fail to notice as we should the first verse of that great chapter: "And it came to pass after many days, that the word of the LORD came to Elijah in the third year, saying, Go, shew thyself unto Ahab; and I will send rain upon the earth" (v. 1).

By now it is, you notice, the third year of the drought. But God starts the whole movement by telling Elijah that the rain is going to come. You find a similar statement in verse 41 of that same chapter: "And Elijah said unto Ahab, Get thee up, eat and drink; for there is a sound of abundance of rain." That means that before he began to pray for the rain, Elijah had already heard the "sound of abundance of rain," even while the drought was at its highest in the surrounding countryside.

So one of the actions of the Spirit in this whole matter of prayer is to give us the prayer. He leads; he directs. This, therefore, is the prayer of faith. It is not people whistling in the dark to keep up their courage and trying to persuade themselves—"I do believe, I am believing"—while knowing the whole time that they do not believe. It is not that. There is an absolute certainty. There is calm; there is peace; there is confidence; there is great assurance. You can never work up the prayer of faith. It is impossible. It is always given.

Let me show you this from another angle. Take the book of Acts and the accounts that are given us there of the miracles that were worked by the apostles. Notice that there were no failures—the apostles were always successful. They were not making experiments; on each occasion they were given a commission. Take the first one: Peter and John were going up to the Temple at the hour of prayer—they were going there to pray. Suddenly they were confronted by a lame man sitting at the Beautiful Gate of the Temple, and he was asking for alms. He was not asking for healing but for a bit of help to eke out his miserable existence.

Then we are told, "Peter, fastening his eyes upon him with John, said, Look on us." What made them do that? There is only one explanation: they were given a commission, a command, to heal this man. All they had to do was to speak the word ("In the name of Jesus Christ of Nazareth rise up and walk"), and they knew that he would rise (Acts 3:1–11). It was not that they decided in cold blood, as it were, that they would heal this man and then worked up the appropriate faith. It was the other way around. The commission came, the Spirit guided and directed them, they spoke, and the miracle happened. And it is exactly the same with all the other examples that we are given in Acts of the wonderful works that were done by the apostles.

You and I cannot generate the prayer of faith. It is given. So one of the first things we must learn is that it is always a possibility; we are now in the realm of the Spirit and not in the flesh. The Spirit is in us, and one of his functions is to deal with us in this matter and to guide and direct us.

Let me give you an example from history. If you read the accounts of the great revivals that have taken place in the history of the church, you will generally find that long before the revival broke out, one man, or a group of people, one woman, two women—I am thinking of specific instances—suddenly felt a call to prayer. In 1858 in Northern Ireland it was just one man, a laborer, who suddenly felt a pressure on his spirit, a call to pray for the Spirit of God to come powerfully upon the churches in his area so that men and women might be converted. Now this man did not suddenly decide that he would do this. There are so many people who read these stories and read about "the prayer of faith" and then decide they are going to do something similar. This always seems to me to be pathetic. No, no; this prayer is given—people are moved and are led by the Spirit.

Again, in America in 1857, one man began praying in the city of New York; or we read about the two women who prayed for D. L. Moody. In the Welsh Revival of 1904/5 a young man named Evan Roberts began to feel a pressure to pray. People could not understand it. He had always been a good man, like many others, always religious, always zealous, but the pressure came upon him, and he could do nothing about it. It was the leading of the Spirit.

Now this precursor, this prayer before all the great revivals, is one of the most amazing factors in the whole economy of God and his dealings with men and women. Why does he work in this way? I do not know; nobody knows. But it is wonderful that he should bring us in and, as it were, give us a part. God seems to be answering the prayers of his people, and, of course, in a real sense he is doing that. But let us always remember that *he* has initiated the movement. Elijah could hear "a sound of abundance of rain" before he began to pray for the coming of the rain. So we must keep ourselves sensitive to the leadings and the promptings of the Spirit.

But we must not misunderstand this by coming to the conclusion that we just sit down until we are moved. That, of course, is the error of the Quakers. They do nothing; they might go through a whole meeting with nothing at all being said. They are waiting for the moving, the promptings, of the Spirit. That is to misunderstand the work of the Spirit because we are commanded to pray. It seems to me that we put ourselves on the direct road to being sensitive to the influences of the Spirit when we begin to pray. But we pray realizing our inability. We begin, if you like, by even asking the Spirit to move us, to guide us, and to direct us. We must start praying by asking God to help us pray, acknowledging our lifelessness and our dullness and our slowness.

We place ourselves at his disposal, telling him how unworthy we are and how dead we are and asking him to enliven us, to quicken us, and to move us. That is the best way, not to sit down passively and wait and do nothing until the moving comes. No, no; do all you can while realizing its uselessness; wait for him expectantly; ask him to come and keep on asking, yielding yourselves utterly to him. Then you will become increasingly conscious that he is moving you and leading and directing you. He will call you to pray. You will not understand it, you will not know why it is happening, but he will call you to pray for particular things, particular persons, and he will make you pray in a particular manner.

This is all important. Here is the entire contrast between true prayer and the mere formal, mechanical reading or reciting of prayers, a mere external worship. There is nothing more vital for us than that we should grasp this great contrast that our Lord is drawing here in the story of the woman of Samaria. So we must not think so much in terms of beautiful services as of spiritual services, the presence, the leading, the power, the promptings of the Spirit. We are aware that we are in the realm of the Spirit and that he is leading and directing us. Read your Scriptures bearing that in mind and you will see more and more clearly all I am trying to say.

Another part of the Spirit's work is this: he alone can make us clear as to our only way of access into the presence of God. Do we realize the difficulty of praying and of entering into God's presence? That is why the phrase "saying your prayers" is so appalling. Do we realize what it means to go into the presence of God, into the holiest of all? We are all ignorant about this. People talk glibly about prayer and say, "I don't believe in God any longer. I prayed and nothing happened." That betrays a complete ignorance of God. They do not realize who God is and what he is. They regard him as just some sort of slot machine out of which they can get what they want when they want it. No, no! When we considered what worship is, we also considered who God is, and this is an equally important question in connection with prayer. How can one pray to God at all? Apart from the instruction of the Holy Spirit, we will never know anything at all about this. How can we go into the presence of God?

Eternal Light! Eternal Light!
How pure the soul must be
When, placed within thy searching sight,
It shrinks not, but with calm delight
Can live, and look on thee.

Oh, how shall I, whose native sphere
Is dark, whose mind is dim,
Before the Ineffable appear,
And on my naked spirit bear
The uncreated beam?

Thomas Binney

Have you ever felt like that? Have you ever felt you have no right to pray? I do not think we know much about praying if we have not had some kind of consciousness of our total unworthiness and inability. "How should a man be just with God?" (Job 9:2). "Who shall ascend into the hill of the LORD? or who shall stand in his holy place?" (Ps. 24:3). These are the all-important questions. How can it be done? Of course, we all go astray by nature. We think we can go into God's presence—we have done a lot of good, we have not committed certain sins. Oh, how useless it all is!

No, no; only one can instruct us, and that is the Holy Spirit. Paul puts it like this: "Therefore being justified by faith, we have peace with God through our Lord Jesus Christ: by whom also we have access by faith into this grace wherein we stand" (Rom. 5:1–2). Nobody apart from the Spirit of God can ever show us what it means to be justified by faith. He enlightens us so that when we go on our knees and feel cold and a stranger, or when our conscience condemns us and the Law of God is thundering at us and we see our utter unworthiness so that we feel, "I cannot pray, I have no right to pray—I have forfeited every claim upon God and his love," then the Spirit will come and say, "You are justified by faith. You have peace with God. Your sins have been dealt with."

Again, in the Epistle to the Ephesians the apostle Paul reminds those people that at one time they were far from God:

> For he [the Lord Jesus Christ] is our peace, who hath made both one . . . that he might reconcile both [Jews and Gentiles] unto God in one body by the cross, having slain the enmity thereby: and came and preached peace to you which were afar off, and to them that were nigh. For through him we both have access by one Spirit unto the Father. (Eph. 2:14, 16–18)

The Spirit has enlightened us. He gives us the assurance that we can approach God, and we need this assurance every time we attempt to pray. You have to answer an accusing conscience before you can pray with any boldness and with any assurance. The author of the Epistle to the Hebrews expresses this aspect of the Spirit's work in his own striking manner: "Having therefore, brethren, boldness to enter into the holiest"—how?—"by the blood of Jesus, by a new and living way, which he hath consecrated for us, through the veil, that is to say, his flesh; and having an high priest over the house of God; let us draw near with a true heart in full assurance of faith, having our hearts sprinkled from an evil conscience, and our bodies washed with pure water" (Heb. 10:19–22).

Now only the Holy Spirit can do that for us. He answers the accusations of conscience and of the devil. He applies the truth to us. He makes it living, he makes it real, and so we are able to pray to God with this assurance. This is a very special part of the work of the Holy Spirit—he enlightens the mind. The apostle Paul draws this contrast in the First Epistle to the Corinthians: "But the natural man receiveth not the things of the Spirit of God: for they are foolishness unto him" (2:14). How, then, do we know them?

> Eye hath not seen, nor ear heard, neither have entered into the heart of man, the things which God hath prepared for them that love him. But God hath revealed them unto us by his Spirit: for the Spirit searcheth all things, yea, the deep things of God. (vv. 9–10)

Furthermore, the Holy Spirit reveals God's truth to us by creating within us what the apostle Paul calls "the Spirit of adoption": "Ye have not received the spirit of bondage again to fear; but ye have received the Spirit of adoption, whereby we cry, Abba, Father" (Rom. 8:15). Now that is real prayer. You do not bow down before "whatever gods may be";[7] you do not bow down before some God who is distant; nor do you bow down in easy familiarity with a God whom you think is much nearer than he really is. No, no; we know what we are doing because the Spirit has created within us the Spirit of adoption. He has revealed to us God the Father. This is exactly what our Lord is telling this woman of Samaria: "the true worshippers shall worship the Father in spirit and in truth."

My dear friends, when we get on our knees to pray, do we always know that God is our Father? We say, "Our Father, which art in heaven"—do we realize what this really means? Do we feel that the Spirit of adoption is in us? This is praying "in the Spirit"; it is a cry that comes up within us. Again, you cannot create this awareness—it is either there or it is not. You can utter the words, you can try hard to convince yourself, but you know perfectly well that you are failing, and the doubt remains. It is the Spirit who puts within us a Spirit of adoption that cries out, "Abba, Father."

But now let us approach this matter from the practical side. We have considered the principles governing this whole matter of praying in or by the Spirit. But someone may say, "But how can I know that I am praying in the Spirit?" That is a very good question. I would divide the answer into two main headings. First, there are certain regular ways in which we may know this. I do not use the word *ordinary* because there is nothing ordinary when the Spirit is acting in power, but I am trying to distinguish between his regular and, under the second heading, his exceptional work—the ordinary and the extraordinary—because there is a real and definite distinction. You find it in the Scriptures, you find it in the lives of the saints, and you see it also in the history of the church, in the distinction between the regular life of the church and the exceptional periods of revival and of reawakening. It is important that we should draw this broad distinction because if we set out simply to test ourselves by the exceptional or the unusual, we will depress ourselves, and that is very wrong. So we start with the regular, the usual, the customary—or, at least, what should be the customary in the lives of all people who are living in the realm of the Spirit.

How, then, can I know that I am praying in the Spirit and not just saying my prayers or taking part in a public act in which prayers are read or recited ritualistically or offering a mechanical sort of extempore prayer—you can be as unthinking in extempore prayer as you can in read prayers.

First, for me, is the realization of God's presence. If you realize God's presence, you need not have any doubt—indeed, you will not have any doubt—that you are praying in the Spirit. This is absolute. To realize the presence of God is an absolute proof that you are praying in the Spirit because it is the Spirit who gives us this blessed assurance. There is not only the assurance within us that cries out in a filial manner, "Abba, Father," but there is also the assurance that he is present and he is listening. This is possible to all of us in the realm of the Spirit.

Let me give you some examples. In the Free Church of Scotland about a hundred or so years ago there was a saintly young minister by the name of Hewitson. He actually said this: "I am better acquainted with Jesus than with any friend I have on earth." That was a sober statement, but he meant it—it was true. Or listen to another, a Methodist minister, John Brash, who lived into the present [twentieth] century. You do not always start in the way described by John Brash, and yet with the Spirit you can start in this way. Many others have been very young and yet have been able to say similar and even greater things. You will find many examples in the journals of Whitefield and others. But this is what John Brash wrote at the end of his life: "I have a singular experience in prayer; no sooner do I open my lips to God and in particular business, than a voice more distinct than I can describe says, 'Your prayer is answered.'" He wrote that it did not always happen, but it happened with increasing frequency.

Then let us go back three centuries to old Thomas Manton, one of the Puritans. On the subject of knowing that you are in the presence of God and that your prayer is heard, this is what he says: "Sometimes the Spirit witnesseth it more explicitly by expression, as if it were said when you go to prayer, 'Be of good cheer, thy sins are pardoned, God is thy God.' At other times by impressions or more secret instincts."

What he means is this—and it is so true, of course—there are degrees of this awareness of the presence of God. It can be vivid, dramatic, as it were, absolutely certain, and there are lesser degrees, but they are equally certain. Some say they are almost hearing a voice. Not that they hear an audible voice, but it is as if a voice were saying, beyond any question, "God is your God; your sins are forgiven; your prayer is already heard." Now only the Holy Spirit can do that. This is something that cannot be counterfeited. This is the particular operation of the Spirit upon us, and the moment you ever have any realization of the presence of God, you can be certain that you are praying in the Spirit.

And that, of course, leads to the second aspect of praying in the Spirit, which is this—a sense of privilege! Being in the holiest of all! Being in the presence of God! Christian friends, how much do we know about this? There are people who use strange expressions with regard to prayer. They talk glibly of having their QT. They mean "quiet time," but they refer to going into the presence of God as "I had my QT." Do we realize what we are saying? Is not this the explanation of the poverty of our lives and the poverty of the whole condition and state of the church—why she is so ineffective and why things are as they are? It is no use saying, "I pray; I've had my QT" or "I've had my DPM"—daily prayer meeting! How can these things be? What is the matter with us? Where do we get our ideas of worship and of prayer? Certainly not from the New Testament. The New Testament writers describe praying as entering into "the holiest of all" (see Hebrews 9:8).

I have often noticed the contrast between people who are punctilious about their outward behavior at garden parties and similar occasions and their behavior when they are in the presence of God. They are more careful when they meet with one another than in their meeting with God. They watch the niceties at social events but assume that you can rush into God's presence. You go in and you go out; you have done it and off you go.

My dear friends, what do we know about worship? What do we really know about prayer? You are in the holiest of all, and it is the highest; and to be admitted there, to have an audience, to have access, is the greatest privilege that can ever fall to the lot of a human being. Who are we approaching? These are the terms—"Lord of lords, and King of kings" (Rev. 17:14; 19:16). It is not surprising, therefore, that the author of the Epistle to the Hebrews tells us always to serve God "with reverence and godly fear: for our God is a consuming fire" (12:28–29).

The trouble with us is that we are all much too healthy. To say it in a different form, what is lacking among us is the fear of God. We are not humbled; we are not broken; we do not realize our unworthiness; we do not realize the greatness, the glory, the privilege of even being allowed into the presence of God, let alone to speak to him. But this realization is inevitable when the Spirit is leading us and preparing us and directing us. Prayer in the Spirit always realizes the presence of God, and there is an awe, there is a humility, there is a humbling—"reverence and godly fear."

"But," you say, "that's Old Testament."

It is not. I am quoting the New Testament to you. That is exactly where people misunderstand these distinctions. God is still the same God.

The Spirit gives me assurance of my acceptance, but that does not change my idea of God. It should deepen it, it should enhance it, and it has always done so in the case of God's true people.

Then, thirdly, any prayer in the Spirit is always a living act. We all know what it is to feel deadness in prayer, difficulty in prayer, to be tongue-tied, with nothing to say, as it were, having to force ourselves to try. Well, to the extent that is true of us, we are not praying in the Spirit. The Spirit is a Spirit of life as well as of truth, and the first thing that he always does is to make everything living and vital. And, of course, there is all the difference in the world between the life and the liveliness that is produced by the Spirit and the kind of artifact, the bright and breezy imitation, produced by people. I was once just a listener and a looker-on at a prayer meeting presided over by a lady who sat at a table with a ruler in her hand, and she was tapping the table, telling people when to stop and others when to start. She was controlling the meeting absolutely, and this was regarded as being highly spiritual!

And there are others whom I have known—God knows, we are all guilty in these matters—who have tried to work up something. I have known men in prayer meetings who, feeling there was a dryness and a hardness and a coldness—and they were right in feeling that—wanted to take charge and started singing choruses, singing hymns, trying to work it up. That is not life. The Spirit alone can give life. You and I can produce excitement. It is easy to produce excitement by speech, by singing, by many other methods, and this is constantly being done. So we have a bright and breezy prayer meeting, and we think there is great vigor and power. But it is all mechanical, it is all human and carnal. The Spirit makes it real.

In chapter 2 of his first letter to the Corinthians, Paul asks, "What man knoweth the things of a man, save the spirit of man which is in him?" (v. 11). This is a vital passage on this whole matter. How does one person communicate with another? Ah, Paul says, it is by a correspondence of spirit. You meet a man, and you take to him, and he takes to you, and you are one. There is a freedom of communion; you can speak openly; you are making contact, as it were. It is the difference between polite formality at the great receptions when you all put on an appearance of affability and friendliness but may be thinking exactly opposite thoughts and an immediate accord and unity.

That is it in the natural realm. Now apply all this to the spiritual realm: this is what the Spirit always does. He makes our relationship with

God living; he makes it vital. You know you are in the presence of God, and you are speaking to God and listening to him. You are aware of a communion, a sharing, a give-and-take, if I may use such an expression. You are not dragging yourself along; you are not forcing the situation; you are not trying to make conversation with somebody whom you do not know. No, no! The Spirit of adoption in you brings you right into the presence of God, and it is a living act of fellowship and communion, vibrant with life.

So what do we know about praying in the Spirit? Is not this the need of the hour? Look at the state of the church; look at the state of the world. We have tried everything. We have exhausted our ingenuity, our methods, our endeavors, our organizations without even touching the problem. Nothing but a great outpouring of the Spirit of God will ever touch this situation. How does that come? It comes, as I have been showing you, in answer to our prayers. Yes, but the prayer is initiated by the Spirit of God. Do we know anything about this depth of prayer, this desire for such prayer, this realization of the presence of God, this living communion, this living prayer and worship and adoration? “They that worship him must worship him in spirit and in truth.”

8

Characteristics of Praying in the Spirit

But the hour cometh, and now is, when the true worshippers shall worship the Father in spirit and in truth: for the Father seeketh such to worship him. God is a Spirit: and they that worship him must worship him in spirit and in truth. (John 4:23–24)

We have been considering the regular manifestations of worshipping or praying in the Spirit. The first is the realization of God's presence, and the second, which is invariable, is a great sense of privilege that we are admitted into the presence of God. There is nothing comparable to this. My third point is that when we are praying in the Spirit, the prayer is always a living act. The mechanical aspect has gone, and it is living, it is infused with life.

But now I want to add the next characteristic, which is always boldness and assurance. This is a most important matter. There is a kind of paradox here, and yet it is something that is taught us right through the Bible. It is that God must be approached "with reverence and godly fear" because he is "a consuming fire" (Heb. 13:28–29) and because he is who and what he is. At the same time, we are encouraged by the Scriptures to come into the presence of God with boldness and assurance.

Now this is a remarkable fact, and it is in many ways the secret of true prayer, prevailing prayer, prayer that you can be sure God will answer. Now there is a very notable example of this in the Old Testament, in the case of Elijah on Mount Carmel. We have seen how Elijah is referred to more than once in the New Testament as a great example of what it means to pray, and there is a remarkable illustration here. He was opposed by some 850 false prophets, the king and queen were against him, and he seemed to be standing almost alone. And here comes this great trial when Elijah challenged these false prophets to pray to Baal to see if he could answer them. Elijah said that the test should be this: he and they would each offer a bullock as a sacrifice. They would prepare their offerings and put them on wood on their respective altars, but without lighting a fire under the wood. Then Elijah told them to pray to their gods and ask them to send down fire from heaven, and he would do the same, "and the God that answereth by fire, let him be God" (1 Kings 18:24).

The story goes on to tell us how these false prophets did all this and prayed to their god, Baal, from morning until noon, but nothing whatsoever happened. There was a dead silence. Then Elijah called all the people to come near to him, and he repaired the altar of the Lord "that was broken down" and put everything in position for the sacrifice. Then we read:

> And it came to pass at the time of the offering of the evening sacrifice [now this is praying!] that Elijah the prophet came near, and said, LORD God of Abraham, Isaac, and of Israel, let it be known this day that thou art God in Israel, and that I am thy servant, and that I have done all these things at thy word. Hear me, O LORD, hear me, that this people may know that thou art the LORD God, and that thou hast turned their heart back again. Then the fire of the LORD fell, and consumed the burnt sacrifice, and the wood, and the stones, and the dust, and licked up the water that was in the trench. (vv. 36–38)

Now that is a great and a wonderful illustration of boldness and confidence in prayer in the presence of God. And the New Testament exhorts us to approach God with the same assurance. The author of the Epistle to the Hebrews, for instance, deals with this. He is writing to Hebrew Christians who were being persecuted and tried. They had been robbed of their possessions; they were passing through a very hard time and had become uncertain. Here were people who were thinking of going back to the Jewish Temple, reverting to the old ways and customs. You see the relevance of all this for today? We are living in an age when everybody is telling us to go back to Rome, to something that was shed four hundred years ago.

The difficulty with people who are subject to that kind of appeal is that they really do not know how to pray. To the extent that you need artificial, external aids, you are defective in your spiritual experience of worship. Anything that drives us back to priests or forms or ceremonies or rituals is indicative of the fact that we are reverting to an Old Testament rather than a New Testament view of worship. So here is the New Testament teaching as expressed by the author of Hebrews:

> Seeing then that we have a great high priest, that is passed into the heavens, Jesus the Son of God, let us hold fast our profession. For we have not an high priest which cannot be touched with the feeling of our infirmities; but was in all points tempted like as we are, yet without sin. Let us therefore [watch that "therefore"] come boldly unto the throne of grace, that we may obtain mercy, and find grace to help in time of need. (Heb. 4:14–16)

Do you see the exhortation? Be certain, be sure, come boldly in the light of this truth unto the throne of grace. The writer says it again in the tenth chapter—the repetition is necessary because we are so slow to learn these lessons!

> Having therefore, brethren, boldness to enter into the holiest by the blood of Jesus, by a new and living way, which he hath consecrated for us, through the veil, that is to say, his flesh; and having an high priest over the house of God; let us draw near with a true heart in full assurance of faith, having our hearts sprinkled from an evil conscience, and our bodies washed with pure water. (vv. 19–22)

The great thing there is the confidence in Christ and by his blood.

Now these are exhortations to boldness, to assurance, to confidence, and we must examine ourselves in the light of this teaching. Do we pray like that? Remember, this is not a contradiction of the teaching about approaching him "with reverence and godly fear," which the writer of Hebrews goes on to emphasize at the end of the twelfth chapter—no contradiction at all. A line is drawn here between a carnal confidence and a spiritual confidence. There are people who try to work up a carnal confidence and affect an easy familiarity with God. That is abominable and verges on the blasphemous. No, no; this is a spiritual confidence, and it is based upon what God has already done for us in Christ. You will find that all these exhortations to boldness in prayer are always the result of this argument. I have given you two examples from the Epistle to the Hebrews—"Having therefore" in the tenth chapter and "Let us therefore" in the fourth chapter. You do not just try to work yourself up or persuade yourself; you take the doctrine, you accept it and work it out, and then you find that it leads to this confidence.

Let me give you another example of the same argument. It is in the glorious statement in the eighth chapter of the Epistle to the Romans, where the apostle Paul is dealing with the same truth. Like the Hebrews, the Christians in Rome were passing through a time of trouble. So the apostle starts by saying, "I reckon that the sufferings of this present time are not worthy to be compared with the glory which shall be revealed in us." All right, there is the ultimate. But the problem is, how am I to live in the present time? Here is the difficulty, and we have seen that Paul has told us that part of the answer is that though "we know not what we should pray for as we ought: the Spirit itself maketh intercession for us with groanings which cannot be uttered." Then he goes on to say, "And we know that all things work together for good to them that love God" (vv. 18, 26, 28). It is this that gives us confidence.

But here is the best and most glorious statement of all: "He that spared not his own Son, but delivered him up for us all, how shall he not with him also freely give us all things?" (v. 32). Now that is the basis of confidence and assurance. It is an argument that you cannot turn back. If God has done this greatest thing of all for us in giving up his only begotten Son, even to the death and the shame and the agony of the cross, "how shall he not with him also freely give us all things?"

So put all these arguments together. Are you conscious of sin and failure? Do you have a sense of shame? You need mercy! So how do you get it? You go with boldness unto the throne of grace. If you are a Christian, you know it is a "throne of grace"; you are going "by the blood of Jesus"; there is the proof of God's grace. Or are you passing through a time of testing and trial and feel the need of strength and grace in order to keep going? Well, you will "find mercy, and obtain grace to help in time of need."

Now this boldness is always a manifestation of a true enlightenment of the Spirit. The Spirit is leading you and controlling you in all your praying. So, again, this is an infallible test of whether or not you are worshipping in the Spirit. There is no hesitation, no uncertainty, but with "full assurance of faith" you go right into the presence of God; it is purely spiritual.

But that in turn leads me to another element that is vitally important—warmth. Warmth and ardor! Is not this something on which we should concentrate? Is there warmth in our praying—warmth in our personal praying, warmth in our collective praying together? You can have a very beautiful service, but it can be as cold as an iceberg. You cannot help admiring it, but it does not move you or touch you. It has its own steel-like perfection, but that is not praying in the Spirit. Everything the Spirit does is perfect, it is full of light, it is full of knowledge, it is full of understanding. But, oh, there is something still more precious and valuable, and that is the warmth, the ardor.

When the Holy Spirit is dealing with us, he deals with the whole person. The Spirit does not merely deal with our minds, he deals with our hearts as well, and he deals with our wills. So often the tragedy in our Christian lives is that we divide ourselves up in a thoroughly wrong way. Some people are all intellect in their religion; others are all heart and no understanding, and so their spiritual lives become excess and ecstasy and false enthusiasm. Yet others are only interested in the realm of activities. But the Holy Spirit deals with the whole personality. Now, once more, this warmth is not something that you and I can work up. Many people have often tried to do that; many are still trying. There are people who even clap their hands or sing particular hymns and choruses in prayer meetings to try to work up some enthusiasm. But that is a direct assault upon the emotions, which should never be done; it is always bad. No; I am talking about something that the Holy Spirit does, and does invariably.

Let me take you back again to that incident on Mount Carmel. You remember that fire fell upon the altar. There is an element of fire in connection with Old Testament worship. The permanent fire upon the altar in the Temple is characteristic of what we are told about worship throughout the Old Testament. And this is equally true of worship in the New Testament. When the Holy Spirit came, "cloven tongues like as of fire" settled upon the heads of the people who were assembled together in that upper room (Acts 2:3). Indeed, John the Baptist said in his prophecy, "I indeed baptize you with water; but one mightier than I cometh, the latchet of whose shoes I am not worthy to unloose: he shall baptize you with the Holy Ghost and with fire" (Luke 3:16). Or take that incident in the fourth chapter of Acts when, after the release of the apostles, there was this falling of the power of the Holy Spirit and the warmth and the ecstasy (Acts 4:31).

Let me put it to you in the words of Thomas Manton, one of the Puritans: "Fire from heaven to consume the sacrifice was the solemn token of acceptance heretofore [in the Old Testament]. Fire from heaven is the token still, even a holy ardor wrought in us by the Spirit." And this is beyond dispute. You cannot read the book of Acts without being conscious of that warmth, that fire of the Spirit. The idea that the true

Christian is someone who has a cold intellectual understanding of theology is a complete denial of the whole New Testament. Nothing, in a sense, is further removed from the work of the Holy Spirit than a coldness, a lifelessness, a mechanical perfection. The Spirit always melts; he warms. He is a fire, a burning fire. You will find in the history of many branches of the Methodist Church, both Arminian and Calvinist, that *fire* was always a term they were fond of using. They would say of a certain minister, "Yes, it was at that point that he got his baptism of fire." Others talked about "a spirit of burning." These were terms that they used to describe this element of warmth that had come into their worship, this great characteristic of the operation of the Holy Spirit. An unintelligent emotionalism, however, is equally a denial of the whole New Testament. We must be careful, my friends, to observe this on both sides.

But let me give you another characteristic of the Spirit, and that is the element of freedom in prayer, the element of liberty, which again is a most thorough test. How much do we know about this? Do you know the difference between forcing yourself to pray, struggling to find words and thoughts, desires, and expressions, and, on the other hand, being carried along, as it were, on the crest of a wave while you are more or less a spectator?

Again, I could elaborate on this at great length. It is an important point. The Spirit is the Spirit of liberty and freedom as well as the Spirit of truth and love. Any man who has ever preached in a pulpit will know exactly the distinction that I am drawing. It is a most remarkable aspect of preaching. There is all the difference in the world between a preacher himself preaching and a preacher preaching in the liberty and freedom of the Spirit. Yet any man who has ever experienced this will not only know exactly what it is but he will also know that, in a sense, it is impossible to describe it; it is just one of those things that you know.

And it is precisely the same with regard to prayer. So much of our praying is halting, lacking in any warmth and inspiration. We, as it were, are having to pray, and, of course, it is right that we should. I would again issue a warning that I am not teaching a passivity. I am not saying that you do nothing until you feel moved, until you feel like it. I say, pray that you may be moved, pray until you are moved. In 1738, when they were traveling somewhere between London and Oxford, John Wesley said to Peter Boehler, "Yes, I see now this doctrine of justification by faith quite clearly. I have got it in my mind; but, you know, I don't feel it. Had I better stop preaching until I feel it?"

"No," said Peter Boehler. "Go on preaching until you do feel it."

And, of course, Wesley soon afterward did feel it, on Aldersgate Street, and that is another illustration for you about this warmth and this fire that I have been talking about. There was John Wesley, in every respect a cultured, able man, an honest man, a religious man, a man who had now come to see the meaning of justification by faith only, and yet he was cold, he was unmoved. He had not received a message; he could not preach; he was not an evangelist. But there, you remember, on Aldersgate Street, as a man was reading from the introduction to Luther's commentary on the Epistle to Romans, suddenly he felt his heart "strangely warmed," and it was the warming of his heart that turned the erudite, pedantic, scholarly John Wesley into a flaming evangelist. That is the work of the Spirit.

But the Spirit not only gave John Wesley the warmth, he also gave him freedom. He had not been able to preach without reading his sermon, and when Whitefield suggested that he should preach in the open air, he not only thought it was wrong, he felt he could not do it. But he very soon found he could—at least, he was enabled to by the Spirit. The Spirit gives liberty; he gives freedom. "Where the Spirit of the Lord is, there is liberty," says Paul (2 Cor. 3:17)—not only moral liberty but liberty in speech, liberty in prayer, liberty in every conceivable respect.

There is also a statement that Peter makes, in a slightly different connection, but he is really dealing with exactly the same experience. What is prophecy? Did the prophets give their messages as the result of their study and their observation and their thinking—is that it? No, no, says Peter, here is the truth: "Knowing this first, that no prophecy of the scripture is of any private interpretation." Now that is often misunderstood. People think that Peter means you cannot understand the prophecies unless you are inspired. But he is not talking about that; he is talking about the prophets and what they did. He means that prophecy is not a man's theory. Well, what is it? "For the prophecy came not in old time by the will of man"—a prophet could not prophesy whenever he liked; a man could not get up and say, "Now I'm going to prophesy"—"but holy men of God spake as they were moved"—carried along, borne along—"by the Holy Ghost" (2 Pet. 1:20–21).

Those holy men of God were not only given understanding, they were also given liberty, they were given freedom—freedom of expression. The words came to them. This happens in preaching, and it also happens in prayer. All I am saying is that when you do find this liberty and freedom, you can be sure that you are praying in the Spirit. Again, I add that you can pray without this, but this is the ideal, this is how we should always be praying.

An incident within my own experience demonstrates this to perfection. I remember being in a prayer meeting that I used to attend regularly every week. On this occasion it was a hot summer's evening, as I remember well, toward the end of June or the beginning of July. We started at 7:15, and I asked somebody to open the meeting by reading the Scriptures and praying. He did so, and one or two others took part in prayer. Everything was just as usual—it was always a good prayer meeting, always a benediction to one's soul. But then an older man stood up to pray, a man who was well-known to all of us as a man who normally stumbled in his praying. He was a man who knew his duty, and he took part in prayer, but—we draw these distinctions, do we not?—there was nothing very inspiring about the way he normally prayed. But this night before he had spoken two or three sentences I and everybody else present became conscious of the fact that something was happening. He was an entirely different man. His voice deepened, and he was speaking with freedom and liberty and an eloquence such as I had not only never heard from him but perhaps had never heard from anybody else in prayer. He was a transformed man, entirely transformed, and the words were pouring from his mouth in perfect order and with warmth and freedom and power and liberty.

The effect of that was that all the others felt the same power and the same freedom, and they went on praying nonstop, one after another, without anybody being called and without any intermission until about ten minutes to 10. We were all conscious that we were in the realm of the eternal and the spiritual. What was that? That was praying in the Spirit. It was the liberty and freedom of the Holy Spirit. And that is what I am referring to. It can happen in a prayer meeting, or it can happen to you individually, in private, when you are led out, as it were. The Spirit takes hold of you, and you are praying in the Spirit with glorious freedom and liberty.

Closely associated with this freedom is the element of fervency. Here, again, is something that we need to recapture—this is why I am taking time on this subject. I am one of those who holds the view that nothing is going to save the church and save the whole of civilization, as it were, but a mighty spiritual revival, and it has generally been the case, as we have seen, that God has led people to pray before revival comes. So we must learn how to pray and what it means to pray in the Spirit. Mechanical prayers, lifeless prayers, in the end avail very little, but this kind of prayer really does achieve something.

I am not saying that without reason. I am talking here about fervency, and I get my authority from statements such as these: "Epaphras, who is one of you, a servant of Christ, saluteth you, always labouring fervently for you in prayers, that ye may stand perfect and complete in all the will of God" (Col. 4:12); "The effectual fervent prayer of a righteous man availeth much" (Jas. 5:16).

What do I mean by *fervency*? It is, if you like, the element that is represented by the word "Oh" or "O," the exclamation coming out in our prayers. You find this constantly in the prayers of the psalmists, and you will find it in many of our hymns.

O for a heart to praise my God,
A heart from sin set free.

CHARLES WESLEY

O Spirit of the living God,
In all thy plenitude of grace,
Where'er the foot of man hath trod,
Descend on our apostate race.

JAMES MONTGOMERY

Such exclamation expresses the longing that leads to fervent desire in praying. This fervency always happens when the Holy Spirit is leading our prayer, and when we are truly praying "in the Spirit." Can you not see the complete contrast between this and cold, mechanical, so-called beautiful prayers? That is the great contrast that our Lord is drawing here in his conversation with this woman of Samaria, the contrast between the kind of worship that he offers and the kind of worship that is not only true of Mount Gerizim but also of so much of Temple worship with its formality and ritual. No, no, he says, the time is coming and now is when men shall worship neither here nor there, not even in the Temple.

Where then?

Well, wherever there is a soul filled with the Spirit. That is what our Lord is saying. And when the soul is filled with the Spirit, the prayer is entirely transformed; it becomes moving, and it becomes fervent.

Another great essential, and characteristic, of prayer in the Spirit is invariably the element of gratitude and thanksgiving, of praise and love. Paul puts this for us so plainly in Philippians 4: "Be careful for nothing"—whatever has happened to you, it does not matter what it is, do not be consumed with anxious care, do not let anything get you down, in nothing be anxious; but what then?—"but in every thing by prayer and supplication with thanksgiving let your requests be made known unto God. And [then] the peace of God, which passeth all understanding, shall keep your hearts and minds through Christ Jesus" (vv. 6–7).

When the Spirit is leading our worship, the element of gratitude and of praise and of thanksgiving is quite inevitable because the Spirit has been sent to glorify the Lord Jesus Christ, and the Lord Jesus Christ says that he has come to glorify the Father. And when the Spirit enlightens us and moves us, he shows us what God has done for us and all the privileges and excellencies of this Christian life.

So I would simply ask you a question: in your praying daily at home, is there thanksgiving? Is there praise, adoration, and worship? Oh, here is the characteristic of worship in the Spirit. So much of our praying is nothing but petitions and perhaps grumblings. Let me put it in a few words, and here is perhaps the best test of all by which you can tell whether or not you are worshipping the Spirit: which are you more concerned about—the glory of God or your own well-being? If your prayers are self-centered and about yourself, there is not much of the Spirit in them. Now I am not saying that you should not pray for yourself. You should; you must let your requests be made known unto God. All I am questioning is the relative proportion, the relative position, of your prayers for yourself and your praise of God. If there is no praise and thanksgiving at all, then is it really praying? If the prayer is in the Spirit, then whatever your circumstances and mine, the element of praise and of thanksgiving will predominate.

There is a classic example of this prayer of praise in the book of Acts. Paul and his companion Silas arrived at Philippi, and in a very unjust manner they were scourged—their backs lashed with whips—and then they were thrown into prison, into the innermost prison, and their feet were put fast in the stocks. It was not only painful, it was a most undignified procedure. What was their reaction? "And at midnight Paul and Silas prayed, and sang praises unto God" (16:25). Only the Holy Spirit can enable one to do that, and he always does. Whatever your circumstances, he renders you immune to them, and he gives you this knowledge of God. The saints have always testified to this, particularly in times of difficulty and trial. The Spirit has given them such understanding and such enlargement of heart that this is what they do.

Then there is that glorious example that we have already looked at in Acts 4. Here is the early church. Peter and John have only just escaped with their lives—they might very well have been put to death by the

Sanhedrin. But the council has set them free on condition that they stop teaching and preaching in the name of Jesus. So the apostles went back to the church and told them about these threats and all that has happened. And what was the result? It was this: "They lifted up their voice to God with one accord"—they began to pray.

And what did they pray about? Did they start with themselves and the fact that they were being threatened and that Peter and John have just escaped by the skin of their teeth? Did they start with their own predicament? Of course not. "Lord," they said, "thou art God, which hast made heaven, and earth, and the sea, and all that in them is" (Acts 4:24). Worship! Adoration! Praise unto God! That is praying in the Spirit. And it was because they prayed like that that the Spirit came upon them again in a great baptism of assurance and power and praise and thanksgiving, so that we read, "and great grace was upon them all." That is the characteristic of praying in the Spirit.

Now only the Holy Spirit can do that. The devil can counterfeit many things. He can make you happy; he has often made us happy, all of us, has he not? He can counterfeit happiness all right; that is how he uses the cults. And drink can make people happy; whisky can make people happy. Yes, the devil can delude us, but there is one thing he not only cannot do, he never will do, and that is to make us praise God—never! He hates God too much to do that. So whenever you find you are praising God and thanking him and adoring him and worshipping him with the whole of your being, you can be quite certain that this is no counterfeit.

The last characteristic I mention is that of persistence. "Labouring fervently," says the apostle Paul about Epaphras (Col. 4:12). This is another characteristic of the New Testament Christian. It characterized the early church even before the Day of Pentecost. They met together, and they were praying together. "These all continued with one accord in prayer and supplication, with the women, and Mary the mother of Jesus, and with his brethren" (Acts 1:14). The apostle Paul himself tells us many times how much of his life he spent in prayer: "Now I beseech you, brethren, for the Lord Jesus Christ's sake, and for the love of the Spirit, that ye strive together with me in your prayers to God for me" (Rom. 15:30). Strive! Labor! Agonize! Where has this gone in our day? You find it in the Old Testament and in the New, and if you read the history of the church and of individual saints in the church, you will read about their agonizing in prayer. But we all think that the high watermark of spirituality is a brief prayer; there it is, and it is left behind.

Take Paul again in Ephesians 3—I am just giving you illustrations:

> Wherefore I desire that ye faint not at my tribulations for you, which is your glory. For this cause I bow my knees unto the Father of our Lord Jesus Christ, of whom the whole family in heaven and earth is named, that he would grant you, according to the riches of his glory, to be strengthened with might by his Spirit in the inner man. (3:13–16)

Paul was always striving in prayer. He tells us, "Pray without ceasing" (1 Thess. 5:17)—never stop, never quit praying. Our Lord had already said it all: "Men ought always to pray, and not to faint" (Luke 18:1). The alternative to fainting is praying, and we must keep going. Paul expresses this again in Ephesians 6. Having described the elements of the whole armor of God, he ends by saying:

> Praying always with all prayer and supplication in the Spirit, and watching thereunto with all perseverance and supplication for all saints; and for me, that utterance may be given unto me, that I may open my mouth boldly, to make known the mystery of the gospel. (Eph. 6:18–19)

All I am saying to you, my dear friends, is that when the Spirit is leading us in worship and in prayer, we keep on, we persist. So it comes as a practical test. Look at the state of the church today, look at the things that are happening, look at the state of the world. We know, not only from the Scriptures but also from the past history of the Christian church, that when God intervenes in mighty revival, these things are dealt with. The church is drawn away from sleepiness or going back to Rome or whatever, and she is revived and renewed with power, and then the world outside is influenced. This can happen in no other way!

But how are we to get this revival of the church? Are we praying fervently? Are we praying persistently? Are we praying always? Are we crying out unto God to have mercy and to have pity and to come among us? We are all always called to prayer in this way—persevering thereunto, without intermission.

There, then, are some of the regular characteristics of praying and worshipping in the Spirit. The exceptional ones I can give you very briefly; then you can work them out for yourselves. The apostle John, this same man whose Gospel we are considering, says of himself:

> I John, who also am your brother, and companion in tribulation, and in the kingdom and patience of Jesus Christ, was in the isle that is called

> Patmos, for the word of God, and for the testimony of Jesus Christ. I was in the Spirit on the Lord's day. (Rev. 1:9–10)

What is John talking about? Not something ordinary, but something quite exceptional. He was taken up by the Spirit, he was lifted up out of the realm of the ordinary, the human, the natural, and he was given the vision of spiritual things.

Similarly, in 1 Corinthians 14:14–15 the apostle Paul draws a distinction between praying with the understanding and praying with the spirit. Now there is no doubt that he meant praying in tongues, but that is not essential. You can be lifted up into the realm of the Spirit, and you do not quite know what you are doing. That is praying in the Spirit in an exceptional way. And this has often been seen in times of revival; you have read about it. People are gathered together in a church, in a building, and suddenly the Spirit comes, and they begin to pray, and they go on praying for hours, perhaps into the early hours of the next morning. But nobody is conscious of boredom, nobody is conscious of time. The Spirit has come down.

The incident I talked about earlier when I was in a prayer meeting, I would describe as a touch of revival—just a touch, enough to know what it is. And anyone who has ever known that will never be satisfied with anything less—a touch of revival in which you go on for hours and hours night after night. This has happened frequently, and I would regard such experiences as exceptional instances of worshipping and praying in the Spirit.

God grants us these exceptional experiences periodically. What for? Well, just to let us know what is possible. This humdrum, mechanical worshipping of God—oh, it is all right, my friends. I am not despising the day of small things, but I am saying that we are living in such terrible times of confusion and danger to everything we hold dear and valuable that we ought to be praying without ceasing in the Spirit, fervently, warmly, ardently. Surely this is the need of the hour. But we start, of course, by realizing that this is true worship. Oh, may God give us understanding in these things; may he give us honesty as we examine ourselves. But above all may he so fill us with his Spirit that we shall be "true worshippers," worshipping the Father "in spirit and in truth."

9

Who Is He?

Jesus answered and said unto her, Whosoever drinketh of this water shall thirst again: but whosoever drinketh of the water that I shall give him shall never thirst; but that water that I shall give him shall be in him a well of water springing up into everlasting life. (John 4:13–14)

In those wonderful words in John 4:13–14 our Lord, let me remind you, gives us the essence of the Christian message. He had come into the world in order to give us this "well of water springing up into everlasting life." This is put in many different ways in this Gospel. In 1:16 the apostle John says, "And of his fulness have all we received, and grace for [upon] grace." It is the same thought. Our Lord also says later, "I am come that they might have life, and that they might have it more abundantly" (10:10).

So the question we are examining is this: have we received this fullness, this well of water, this life more abundant, this life that is life indeed? And in studying the story of this woman of Samaria, and especially our Lord's dealing with her, we have seen many of the mistakes into which we are all so liable to fall. The supreme object of our desire and of our endeavor should be to get into the position in which we shall "never thirst," and we have therefore been looking at those various hindrances to our receiving this life.

Having done that and without forgetting these very important negatives, we now turn to the positive aspect, and I ask, what is the one great essential in this whole matter of receiving this life, this fullness?

There can be no difficulty about answering that question. The one absolute essential is submission to the Lord Jesus Christ, and as I tried to show in introducing this whole subject, we have here a wonderful account of how our Lord brought this woman to that position. From her original self-confidence and glibness in her talk about worshipping here and there and so on, he led her to the place of final and complete submission. There is no hope of obtaining this fullness, this life, unless we believe in him, unless we listen to him.

But here arises the great question: who is he? Who speaks in this way? There is no hope for us until we are clear about who our Lord is. Without doubt, the main cause of trouble at the present time is ignorance with regard to the person of Jesus of Nazareth, this person of whom we read in the Gospels and who occupies the central position in the whole Bible.

Now the answer to this question is, of course, the message of this very season, this season of Advent.[8] It is his advent. It is all about him. So what better can we do during this season than consider who he is, why we should listen to him, and why we should submit ourselves to him? It is only as we discover the answers to these questions that we shall be ready to submit ourselves to him and thereby obtain this great and glorious blessing, which, after all, he came to give and which is the central and essential message of the Christian faith. And here again, in this story of the conversation between our Lord and the woman of Samaria, we are given great light and instruction on who our Lord is. This is a most comprehensive story. I say again that the great central elements of the Christian faith are all here in a most wonderful manner.

Notice how this woman seeks the truth, moving from step to step. At first she imagines she is just meeting a stranger. He is obviously a Jew, and she is rather amazed that he would have anything to do with her, a Samaritan and a woman. We have seen all that. But as our Lord leads her on, she begins to reach for the truth with respect to him. So let us look again at these verses. After our Lord has shown the woman that he knows all about the immoral state in which she is living—"Thou hast had five husbands; and he whom thou now hast is not thy husband: in that saidst thou truly"—she says to him, "Sir, I perceive that thou art a prophet." Now she is advancing; she sees he is a prophet. And then in verses 20–26 we see how our Lord leads her on from stage to stage until the final statement, "I that speak unto thee am he."

At this point we can only introduce this subject. But let me say a hurried word in passing. Is it not amazing and extraordinary that it was to this Samaritan woman, a sinful woman, that our Lord made this great revelation with respect to himself? Thank God, there is no hope for any of us but for this. He himself said such things so often—for example, "I came not to call [save] the righteous, but sinners to repentance" (Luke

5:32)—and that is the glorious hope of the gospel. It is to this woman, of all people, that he makes this tremendous disclosure.

But before we come to this final conclusion, we must consider the steps that lead to it because it is very important, if we are in any trouble about all this, that we should realize the error of the partial positions, however good they may seem to be. Now as I said, here I can only make some introductory and preliminary remarks, but let us see some of the general principles that are taught here in this whole matter of our approach to the person of our Lord Jesus Christ.

The first principle is the exclusiveness of the Christian message. Indeed, I will use a stronger term—its intolerance, its claim for an absolute uniqueness. Now that comes out in these words: "Ye worship ye know not what: we know what we worship: for salvation is of the Jews." There it is, the statement of our Lord himself—"salvation is of the Jews." This is, of course, a crucial statement and a principle that is asserted constantly in the New Testament. We find it repeatedly in this Gospel of John. Later on our Lord says, "I am the way, the truth, and the life: no man cometh unto the Father, but by me" (John 14:6). Exclusiveness! Uniqueness! He says in chapter 8 of this Gospel, "I am the light of the world"—that is an absolute statement, an absolute claim—"he that followeth me shall not walk in darkness, but shall have the light of life" (v. 12). And elsewhere he contrasts himself with other people who had offered themselves as shepherds: "All that ever came before me are thieves and robbers: but the sheep did not hear them. I am the door: by me if any man enter in, he shall be saved, and shall go in and out, and find pasture" (John 10:8–9).

And when we go on to the book of Acts and come to our Lord's first preachers, the people he had set apart and called, to whom he gave the message, we find that they make exactly the same claim. Peter, for instance, preaching in Jerusalem and addressing the Jewish authorities, the members of the great Sanhedrin, says:

> This is the stone which was set at nought of you builders, which is become the head of the corner. Neither is there salvation in any other: for there is none other name under heaven given among men, whereby we must be saved. (Acts 4:11–12)

That is an absolute statement.

There is another example in Acts 17, where the apostle Paul does not hesitate to say, "Whom therefore ye ignorantly worship, him declare I unto you" (v. 23). Again this is an absolute claim, and the apostle repeats it in his epistle to the Corinthians: "For other foundation can no man lay than that is laid, which is Jesus Christ" (1 Cor. 3:11).

Why am I giving you all these quotations? Because this is the essence of the modern difficulty. People today resent this kind of statement, and I believe that the church is as she is because of the confusion that is so obvious at this very point—the uncertainty with regard to this person and his uniqueness and to the exclusive claim of the Christian faith. We pride ourselves on living in what we like to call an age of tolerance. "Hah!" we say. "People in the past used to be so narrow-minded, so dogmatic, but we, with our enlightened ideas, have come to see that there is a little bit of good in everything. We must not say that Christianity alone is right; we must not say that the other great world religions are wrong. We must not make a claim for exclusiveness." In fact, there are some who go so far as to say that if you do, you are denying the Christian message. The whole idea of Christianity is that it is an easy tolerance, a spirit of give and take, a readiness to agree with everybody, as long as people are out for that which is good and helpful and so on.

We are living in an age that talks about a World Congress of Faiths and says we are all one, and it does not matter whether people even deny the whole of the Bible—it is still all right because there is some truth in everything. That, it is said, is the Christian spirit. And so Christianity becomes nothing but a kind of moral uplift, and the season of Christmas and of Advent is nothing but a time when we talk about goodwill and brotherliness and trying to get together and to understand one another.

But I am here to remind you that is nothing but a complete contradiction of everything we find in the New Testament, and especially from the lips of the Lord Jesus Christ himself. Now I am emphasizing this not because it gives me pleasure to do so, in one sense, but for this reason—there is no hope of salvation apart from this gospel. Our Lord here says, "salvation is of the Jews," and that is the claim that is made right through the Old Testament. This is most important, and it is why we must keep on reading the Old Testament. There we find this nation, the Jews, among a number of other nations. Who were they? This is the vital point. Their great claim, the claim of all their teachers, patriarchs, psalmists, and prophets, was always that they were the people of God, that they were not like other nations, that they were different. And their whole story, of course, demonstrates that fact. God made a nation for himself. He took a man named Abraham, called him out of paganism when he lived in

Mesopotamia, in Ur of the Chaldees, and turned him into a nation in a miraculous manner. That is the story; that is the history.

So God was making a new nation, a people for himself. And that is why he gave them the Ten Commandments. He said that they must not live like everybody else; they were his people. "Ye shall be holy: for I the LORD your God am holy" (Lev. 19:2). The other people burnt their children as offerings to their gods, they ate all sorts of food, and so on. But the people of Israel were told to live as a separate people, a people for God's particular possession, a part of his great purpose. And it was to these people alone that God was pleased to reveal himself and give the Scriptures.

Now the apostle Paul, writing to the Romans, makes use of that argument. In what way is the Jew different from everybody else? That is the question that was being put to him. He was preaching now to Jews and Gentiles alike, and so he was exposing himself to the charge, "What advantage then hath the Jew? or what profit is there of circumcision?" And he replies, "Much every way: chiefly, because that unto them were committed the oracles of God" (Rom. 3:1–2), by which Paul means the Old Testament Scriptures. The other nations did not have this revelation from God. They did not have the Ten Commandments and the Law or this great succession of prophets and psalmists and so on. This was unique to the Jews. And that is what our Lord means by saying, "Salvation is of the Jews." The Samaritans had the first five books of the Bible, the five books of Moses, but they had nothing else. Our Lord is saying in effect, "You are defective, you do not have the full truth, you do not have the real understanding, and you have misinterpreted even what you have because you lack the teaching of the prophets." "Salvation is of the Jews"; it is exclusive to them.

Now this is crucial. Either this modern thought is correct or the Bible is correct. You cannot accept both because they are in open contradiction to one another. The essence of the Christian message is this: "Neither is there salvation in any other" (Acts 4:12). "Salvation is of the Jews"—through this one who came out of the Jews, Jesus of Nazareth.

Notice how the apostle Paul puts this in Athens, of all places. Athens! The Mecca of all the philosophers, the cultural center of the then civilized world, that great city, proud of its wonderful succession of teachers. All honor to them! I am not trying to detract in any way from the greatness of Greece and especially of her great thinkers. But let us not forget this: it was to them that the apostle Paul said, "Whom therefore ye ignorantly worship, him declare I unto you" (Acts 17:23). Do you remember why he said that? He found their city crowded with temples and altars—the god of war, the god of peace, the god of love, and so on. And then there was that extraordinary altar with the inscription on it, "TO THE UNKNOWN GOD."

You see, the Greeks had gone as far as to discover that there was a God behind the gods whom they thought they knew, that there was a mysterious power at the back of them all; they were seeking after him but could not find him. They were worshipping him, as they thought, but in ignorance. Why? Because they were not Jews; they were relying upon their own thoughts, their own reason, their own understanding. So the apostle Paul did not hesitate to say to them, "Whom ye ignorantly worship, him declare I unto you."

And, of course, Paul makes exactly the same point to the Corinthians: "For after that in the wisdom of God the world by wisdom knew not God, it pleased God by the foolishness of preaching to save them that believe" (1 Cor. 1:21). That is a categorical statement: "The world by wisdom"—by philosophy, human understanding, human thought, and endeavor—"knew not God." I find it astounding that the modern world can talk as it does, and, alas, that so much of the modern church can speak as it does in the light of all this. Here are our Lord himself and his chosen apostles who founded the Christian church, standing on this one position that no one by seeking can ever find God (see Job 11:7), that the world with all its wisdom and all that it has can never arrive at a knowledge of the truth.

The world has failed to do this, and it is most important that we should realize that. This is not a matter for argument, or even for discussion: we are facing facts. The ancient world with its master philosophers failed to arrive at a knowledge of God, and all the philosophers who have lived ever since have not advanced at all upon the thinking of Plato, Socrates, Aristotle, and the rest.

And what is it we know today? What is the purpose of falling back upon human thought and ideas? Religions such as Confucianism or Buddhism or Hinduism or Islam are all man-made religions. What is the point of turning to them and saying that there is a little bit of truth in them, that they can all help us with their insights and we must all pool our ideas? That is a denial of this gospel. It was because the world in its wisdom had completely failed to find God that God manifested himself and the truth concerning himself first through the Jews, his people, and then supremely in this one who came from the Jews according to the flesh, Jesus of Nazareth, the Son of God.

I have to start with this because, I say again, it is absolutely crucial. If you do not confine yourself entirely to the Bible and its revelation, you will go astray in this question of God and of worshipping God and of obtaining this well of water springing up into everlasting life. If you are in any doubt with regard to Jesus of Nazareth, you will never get this blessing. I put it as categorically as that.

And again the history of the world substantiates this to the very hilt. Look at all the great people who have lived throughout the centuries, able, good men and women, endowed with amazing propensities, many of them, the great people of history. But read their biographies or their autobiographies, and you will find that however towering and shining their genius may have been, however wonderful and glittering their achievements, if they did not know this person, if they did not submit themselves to him, their lives were unhappy and disappointing. They went out into darkness; they had nothing to comfort them. Even at their greatest moments, they were the victims of circumstance and chance, and from the height of their achievements they could be cast down to the depths of despair and despondency.

I would almost make it compulsory for all people, especially Christian people, to read the biographies, autobiographies, and memoirs of people of this century who have mixed with some of the greatest men and women history has ever known. Read them and you will discover that no one will ever have this well of water, this peace, this satisfaction, this rest of soul and mind and spirit unless they get it from Jesus of Nazareth.

The Christian faith makes an exclusive claim, and that the church should be doubtful or hesitant about it is astonishing; that is to deny the very foundation of the whole of the faith. "Ye worship ye know not what: we know what we worship: for salvation is of the Jews." There is no hope in the world apart from the message of Scripture; there is no knowledge of God apart from the revelation that we are given there. I say we must stand on it. Not that we should be dogmatic and arrogant, but if we have any concern about the souls of men and women, if we are sorry for those who are unhappy, it is our duty to tell them not to look anywhere else; this, and this alone, holds out any hope, and it is full of hope. Oh, the exclusiveness of this message!

But I want to go on to show you why this message is exclusive and why it must be exclusive. My second principle, adduced from this teaching, is that the message we have here is a message of God acting, God doing things, and that is what explains the uniqueness. This is the essence of this great message. Peter, preaching at Jerusalem on the Day of Pentecost, made this point, and, indeed, even the people, all the strangers who were at Jerusalem on that occasion, listening to the apostles speaking in strange languages, made the same point: "Cretes and Arabians, we do hear them speak in our tongues the wonderful works of God" (Acts 2:11). That is what Christianity is about—"the wonderful works of God"!

Go back to your Old Testament—what is it about? The tragedy is that people think of the Bible as if it were a book of philosophy or a book of religion, a book just for the purpose of teaching us certain religious ideas. Of course, that is included, but before that, this is a book of the actions of God. "In the beginning God created . . ." (Gen. 1:1). That is how it starts. Read the Old Testament, and you will find God doing things! Of course, people do things too, but what they do is generally wrong, and they get themselves into misery.

Adam and Eve were perfect. God put them into Paradise, and all was well. So how has the world become as it is? It is because of their rebellion and disobedience. They brought down misery on themselves and on their world. And ever since men and women have been making a mess of things, thinking they were going to put everything right but never succeeding, buoying themselves up on a false optimism, always crashing down in the next century.

That has been the story of civilization from the very beginning, and there would be no hope for us were it not that God has acted. There are the man and woman in misery in the Garden, hiding behind the trees, and God comes down. They hear the voice of the Lord God in the cool of the evening, and he tells them what he is going to do—and here is our only hope. This is the preparation for the coming of the Son of God, this is the anticipation of the gospel—the seed of the woman shall bruise the serpent's head (Gen. 3:15). God is going to do it.

And that is what you find in the whole of the Old Testament, as I have been reminding you—God creating a nation, God giving the Law, giving his people the knowledge and the information. It is all the activity of God. And look at the story of these chosen people, these particular people whom God makes his own. Constantly they went astray; they were fools enough to envy the other nations! "Give us a king," they said. "Other nations have kings; give us a king." So God gave them a king, and kings led them into endless trouble.

The people were always lusting to live as the surrounding nations lived; they wanted the same kind of immoral life. They did not want to keep God's laws. So they always got themselves into misery and into trouble. Other nations came and conquered them, and they would soon have been finished altogether as a nation and as a people had God not delivered them time and time again. He did it when they were in Egypt; he did it when they were in Babylon. This is the whole story—God acting, God teaching them—the mighty acts of God.

And what happened at Bethlehem so long ago? The answer is this: "God so loved the world, that he gave his only begotten Son" (John 3:16). "When the fulness of the time was come, God sent forth his Son, made of a woman, made under the law" (Gal. 4:4). God acting! And that is what makes this message unique. All the so-called great world religions are the result of human efforts, as we have seen, and so are the philosophies, the art, all the thinking, every endeavor. Not one is exclusive; not one is unique. For anyone to claim uniqueness and exclusiveness and finality is sheer arrogance.

But here we are not dealing with what people have done; the whole point of this message is that God has done this. That is why it is absolutely exclusive. You do not put God into competition with human beings. So why do you want to put the Christian religion into a World Congress of Faiths? Or why do you turn to philosophy for help? You are bringing God down to a human level and putting the Son of God into competition with men. That is blasphemy! We must be intolerant about this.

Look at what the apostle Paul says to the Galatians. He had been preaching in Galatia, and churches had been established as the result of his mission there. But other teachers had come and had said, "Oh, yes, Paul was all right, but of course he doesn't understand it all. He didn't tell you that you must be circumcised. But you must, you know! It's not enough just to believe the gospel—you must be circumcised as well." The Galatians thought this teaching was an advance, and they were turning to it. But this is how Paul deals with these ideas: "Though we, or an angel from heaven, preach any other gospel unto you than that which we have preached unto you, let him be accursed" (Gal. 1:8). Now that is a very strong statement. If a man comes to preach to you, he says, I do not care if he is an angel from heaven, if he preaches a gospel that does not tally with mine, let the curse of God be upon him; he is a liar!

If you are concerned, therefore, about receiving our Lord's fullness, you must come to the position in which you accept this exclusiveness—

and you must do so because it is God acting, God offering. The gospel must be the only way because it is the action of God himself. There, then, is our second principle.

But that, in turn, of course, leads on to the third point—the historicity of this message. We must emphasize that this message is based solidly upon, and comes solely from, historical events. People sometimes put forward the question, could anyone still be a Christian if it could be proved that Jesus of Nazareth had never lived at all? Now if you are ever presented with that question and hesitate for a moment, you are denying the faith. There is no hesitation about this. This faith depends entirely, completely, solely upon the historical fact of Jesus of Nazareth and the truth concerning him.

This, again, is crucial. We are not dealing here with a teaching. "Believe me," says this Jesus of Nazareth. "I am he." The gospel is all about a person. If we do not understand that during this season of Advent, we have missed the whole point. Christianity, I say again, is not a system of ideas. It is not just a school of thought that you put by the side of other teachings or religions—call them what you like—it is not that at all. Of course, there is teaching, but it is teaching that derives from a person. Much more important than what he taught and said is the truth about the person, what that person did, what happened to him. We are not saved by ideas. To think that we are is a complete denial of all of the Christian faith.

So many people today seem to think that Christianity is just a collection of beautiful thoughts. I am not surprised that the vast majority of the people of this country are outside the church. I am not a bit surprised. They have been told by the church herself that Christianity is nothing but beautiful thoughts, that even if Jesus of Nazareth had never existed and all the facts about him were wrong, you would still have Christianity! But the man in the street has a certain native logic, and he says, "Well, I can read books and get beautiful and uplifting thoughts at home. If Christianity is just being kind and pleasant and brotherly, with vague talk about goodwill and fellowship, especially at Christmastime, then I don't need to go to church and I don't need a Bible. This is something that everyone, unless they are really beyond the pale, believes in and likes to do."

Yet that is what is passing as Christianity today. All of us are already Christians, it is said; we do not know it, but we really are, and the business of preaching is just to tell us that we are all right, that God loves us all and all is well. So you do not need this special person, Jesus of Nazareth—his birth in a stable is unnecessary. We are told that it does not matter whether it is true or not. It does not matter whether or not he died on the cross. Meeting at a Communion table is all rubbish, a bit of folklore.

But that is to deny completely the very essence of the Christian faith. This *is* all about a person. The Communion table tells us this person was nailed to a tree, his body was broken, his blood was shed. That is history; that is fact. It is as much fact as Julius Caesar conquering Britain in 55 or 54 B.C., whichever date the latest historian has decided on. Our Lord's life and death and resurrection are absolutely basic and central. If these events did not take place, then I have no message, and there is no salvation. But our Lord says, "Salvation is of the Jews" and "I am he." The Christian faith is historical and centers around this person.

I am only giving you general principles, but you must be clear about them. They control the very approach to our Lord. It is no use saying, "I'm interested in Jesus"—I want to know what your approach to Jesus is. Are you just regarding him as a great human teacher, philosopher, moral aesthete? If you are, you might as well stop being interested in him. You must take him as he is revealed in the Scriptures.

I have been emphasizing the historicity of Christianity, so I end by saying this: this person is the dividing point of history; he is the dividing point of all time. You see, Christianity is as historical as that. It not only belongs to time, it divides time. Listen to the way our Lord puts it: "Woman, believe me, the hour cometh"—what is this hour? Listen—"and now is"—it has come. What is this "hour" that he is talking about? That is one of the most wonderful things we can ever understand.

There is the past—past history. I have been reminding you of the history of the Jews and the Old Testament. We can sum it up like this: the whole of the Old Testament looked forward to the coming of a person.

This message is stated in Isaiah 40:1–5 in one of the most glorious passages in the whole Old Testament: "Comfort ye, comfort ye my people, saith your God." Why? What is the source of the comfort? It is this one who is going to come. "Prepare ye the way of the LORD"—a messenger will come; he will arrive in a wilderness and say, "Prepare ye the way of the LORD, make straight in the desert a highway for our God. Every valley shall be exalted; and every mountain and hill shall be made low." Take away the rough places; make everything smooth. It is the coming of the Lord, and all eyes shall see him. He is coming! All flesh shall see the salvation of God.

In his first letter the apostle Peter makes a statement that is germane to the whole matter we are dealing with and is wonderful in and of itself.

Peter, after reminding these people about the salvation of their souls, goes on to say:

> Of which salvation the prophets have inquired and searched diligently, who prophesied of the grace that should come unto you: searching what, or what manner of time the Spirit of Christ which was in them did signify, when it testified beforehand the sufferings of Christ, and the glory that should follow. Unto whom it was revealed, that not unto themselves, but unto us they did minister the things, which are now reported unto you by them that have preached the gospel unto you with the Holy Ghost sent down from heaven; which things the angels desire to look into. (1:10–12)

What a statement! But it is a perfect summary of the whole Old Testament. What is the meaning of the paschal lamb killed when the children of Israel left Egypt? It was a prophecy of the Lamb of God who was going to come, who would take away the sins of the whole world. And each lamb that was sacrificed morning and evening in the Tabernacle and then the Temple was also a prophecy. All the great events of the Old Testament are types and shadows—they are all pointing forward. He is to come. The seed of the woman will bruise the serpent's head (Gen. 3:15). The whole of the Old Testament is past, but it is looking forward to a new age, the coming of a new time, a glorious time when the Messiah, the Deliverer, will come.

But now he says, "Woman, believe me, the hour cometh, *and now is.*" So I ask again, what hour? It is the hour that the whole Old Testament was anticipating. Our Lord said to the Jews, "Your father Abraham rejoiced to see my day: and he saw it, and was glad" (John 8:56). What hour? The hour when God's Son, the Deliverer, is going to come. So he says, "The hour cometh, and now is." The past is ended; we are in the new age; here is a new beginning.

This is stated repeatedly in a glorious manner in the New Testament. I have already quoted from Galatians 4:4: "When the fulness of the time was come"—when all the time of the Old Testament had come to an end, had been fulfilled, when God's hour had arrived, the hour that God had in his mind from all eternity. He has an hour, a fixed point. He knows the end from the beginning—"God sent forth his Son, made of a woman, made under the law, to redeem them that were under the law" (Gal. 4:4–5). Or again, "For all the promises of God in him are yea, and in him Amen, unto the glory of God by us" (2 Cor. 1:20).

Then listen to this—what a word for a flabby, sentimental, loose-thinking age such as this: "But as God is true, our word toward you was not yea and nay" (2 Cor. 1:18). I do not make a Christian assertion at one point, then when I am given another question take it back. That is "yea and nay." You cannot at the same time say that this gospel is historical and yet be doubtful whether or not it is historical. That is "yea and nay." And the people of this country are outside the church today because the church is so anxious to please people, to try to attract them to a failing church, that she is saying "yea and nay." The people will not listen, and I do not blame them, for that is not the Christian message.

> As God is true, our word toward you was not yea and nay. For the Son of God, Jesus Christ, who was preached among you by us, even by me and Silvanus and Timotheus, was not yea and nay, but in him was yea. For all the promises of God in him are yea. (2 Cor. 1:18–20)

He is the great "Yes" of God.

He has ended an era; he has started a new one. The whole of history revolves around this blessed person who was talking to the woman of Samaria by the side of the well. He not only belongs to history, he divides history. B.C.—before Christ, preparing for him; A.D.—ANNO DOMINI—the year of our Lord. He is indeed not only Savior but the Lord of history. The hour has struck; the hour has arrived. The focal point of all history is in this one person. Who is he? That is the question. And there is only one answer—he gives it himself. "I am he"! He is the Savior of the world.

10

Our Need for Salvation

The woman saith unto him, Sir, I perceive that thou art a prophet. Our fathers worshipped in this mountain; and ye say, that in Jerusalem is the place where men ought to worship. Jesus saith unto her, Woman, believe me, the hour cometh, when ye shall neither in this mountain, nor yet at Jerusalem, worship the Father. Ye worship ye know not what: we know what we worship: for salvation is of the Jews. But the hour cometh, and now is, when the true worshippers shall worship the Father in spirit and in truth: for the Father seeketh such to worship him. God is a Spirit: and they that worship him must worship him in spirit and in truth. The woman saith unto him, I know that Messiah cometh, which is called Christ: when he is come, he will tell us all things. Jesus saith unto her, I that speak unto thee am he. (John 4:19–26)

Christians, let me remind you, are those who have received the "well of water springing up into everlasting life." They are people who, as we read in the sixteenth verse of the first chapter of John's Gospel, have received "of his fulness" and "grace for [upon] grace." This is essential Christianity; this is what we are meant to be like. We are to be a rejoicing people. When our Lord first came into this world, his coming was accompanied by a heavenly choir singing and praising, and that is the great note of the New Testament, as it must inevitably be in the light of our Lord's word here telling us what we are offered. So the great question is, do we rejoice like this? Do we rejoice in Christ Jesus?

That is what we are considering together, and having looked at the difficulties, we have come now to the positive approach. So I put to you this question: what is absolutely essential to the receiving of this great blessing that will fill us with a joy unspeakable and full of glory? And the answer is that it is an understanding and realization of the truth as it is in Christ Jesus; it is utter submission to him. He dealt with this woman in such a way that he brought her to that point, and that is the point to which we all have to come. Ultimately, the cause of our trouble is uncertainty about him, failure to realize as we should who he is, why he came, and what he has to give to us.

So we are looking at our Lord as he was pleased to manifest himself to this woman of Samaria, and to help us understand who he was, we are using her stumbling efforts because they so truly represent the position of many of us at the present time. This is, of course, the great message of Advent.[9] Why should Christian people be thrilled and rejoice as they contemplate, at this season of the year, what happened when the Son of God was born as the babe of Bethlehem? That is the question that is before us, and we are given great instruction here concerning it.

Having considered together certain general characteristics of this message, I now want to ask, in light of all that we have seen, why are people so blind to him? Why are they so slow to realize the truth of the message of Advent? Why are we all ourselves so little moved by it? Why is it that we do not rejoice in it as we should and as the first Christians so clearly did and as Christian people have always done in every great period of reformation and of revival?

I think that another answer to those questions is our failure to realize our true need, or to put it another way, our failure to realize what is to be found in him and what is possible to us and for us in him. Only the people who have realized their need truly rejoice in him. So let us see how this story of our Lord's handling of the woman of Samaria helps us realize this aspect of the truth. Earlier we considered our Lord's words to the woman of Samaria, "salvation is of the Jews," looking mainly at the words "of the Jews." Today we return to this statement, but I want now to emphasize this word "salvation."

A strictly accurate translation here would be, "We know what we worship: for *the* salvation is of the Jews." The salvation that has been talked about and for which the Jews were waiting—that is the term that our Lord uses. Then look at the terms that are used by the woman: "Sir, I perceive that thou art a prophet." A prophet! Then she goes on and says, "I know that Messias [Messiah] cometh, which is called Christ: when he is come, he will tell us all things." "Prophet," "Messias," "all things"! What does she mean by these terms? What is her connotation? And what does our Lord mean when he talks about "salvation"? This is the very essence of this matter.

Now the terms "prophet," "Messias," and "salvation" obviously refer to the Old Testament and its teaching. That is a part of the meaning of this phrase of our Lord: "salvation is of the Jews." I am not now concerned to emphasize the exclusiveness—we have done that—but do hold it in your mind; it is essential to the understanding of this teaching. Our Lord says that the salvation comes out of the Jews, and he is not only referring to the fact that he himself actually did come of the Jews according to the flesh, but he is referring also to the fact that the whole teaching, the whole concept, the whole purpose of salvation is something that God has provided and worked out through this particular nation, the Jews.

In other words, all these terms tell us that the Old Testament is the preparation for the New Testament, and there is a sense in which we simply cannot understand the New Testament truly apart from the Old Testament. We have to approach the New Testament in the light of the teaching of the Old. That is why the Holy Spirit guided the church in the early centuries to include the Old Testament with the New, and that is why it is fatal for Christian people to think they do not need the Old Testament. The two belong together, and each casts its light upon the other.

Now the main function of the Old Testament is to show us the need of the salvation that our Lord talks about; and, of course, that is the whole function of the prophets. Indeed, the term *Messiah* suggests the one who is coming to provide this deliverance, this salvation, the satisfaction of the need that exists. The Old Testament shows us this plainly and clearly, and it does so in many different ways—in particular statements, in its explicit teaching.

If you want to know the beginning of this gospel, if you want to understand the connotation of this word *salvation*, and the real meaning of the word *Messiah*, you must go back to the beginning, to Genesis 3:15, where we are told that the seed of the woman will bruise the serpent's head. That verse is the first statement, the first teaching, concerning this salvation. Man has sinned; he is in a position of hopelessness and despair. There will be enmity between him and the seed of the serpent; life has become chaotic. Is there no hope? Here is the answer: salvation will come—the seed of the woman shall bruise the serpent's head. That is the beginning of the whole message of salvation. Why does it not move us? It is because we have never realized our need of salvation as we should; we have never realized the truth about ourselves.

Then the Old Testament story continues. In promises, in covenants God keeps on repeating what he is going to do. The story of Abraham and the creation of the nation, the repetition of the promises to Abraham and the renewal of the covenant, all cast their great light upon this person who has come.

Furthermore, the Law, with its underlining and pinpointing of sins and transgressions, of disobedience, was clearly designed to show us our need, to prepare us for the great salvation that was to come. We also see it enacted in the ceremonies and rituals in connection with the Tabernacle and the Temple. What is the meaning of all the details about the furnishing of these buildings? What is the point about burnt offerings and sacrifices and meal offerings and peace offerings? Is this just some ancient history of no importance and of no interest to us? Is this just a part of the folklore of primitive people? No, no; this is God's ordinance—it is God preparing the way. These are but types and shadows pointing forward to one who was to come.

And then, of course, we find the promise of salvation in the great prophetic teaching. It is the great note of the prophets. There is a sample in chapter 40 of Isaiah's prophecy: "Comfort ye, comfort ye my people, saith your God" (v. 1), and again in Isaiah 55: "Ho, every one that thirsteth, come ye to the waters" (v. 1). These verses are all a part of the preparation for the coming of the Messiah.

The point I am establishing is that we only appreciate God's offer of salvation if we understand our need. There is no point in a promise of deliverance if we are not aware that we are captives. The Jews constantly failed at that point. There is a wonderful illustration in the eighth chapter of the Gospel of John, when our Lord says to some people one afternoon, "If ye continue in my word, then are ye my disciples indeed; and ye shall know the truth, and the truth shall make you free" (vv. 31–32). Instead of standing up and praising God and thanking him, they stand on their dignity and say, "We be Abraham's seed, and were never in bondage to any man: how sayest thou, Ye shall be made free?" (v. 33). They are saying, "We do not need your talk about freedom."

What was the matter with these Jews? They did not realize their condition of serfdom and slavery. If your heart is not moved and thrilled by the whole conception of the coming of the Son of God into this world and this great salvation, there is only one explanation—you do not know the truth about yourself, you have never seen your need, you have never learned the great lesson of the Old Testament.

So this is the background to these great statements—"Salvation is of the Jews" and "When he [the Messiah] is come, he will tell us all things"—and I repeat that we can only understand them as we realize our need. So there are two things for us to consider. The first is the need itself; the second is the salvation that our Lord came to bring.

Look, then, at this need—what is it? It is man's condition. Men and women are vaguely aware that they have a need. The most thoughtless person is aware that something is wrong. The giddiest person in London knows in his or her heart that there is some lack somewhere. The woman of Samaria, living as she is in pleasure and in sin, knows there is a need. She is interested in prophets, and she talks about the coming Messiah. Ah, yes, but the fact that the world and its individuals are aware of a need is not enough; it is of no value really. That can often lead to our just trying to forget it in another round of pleasure, or it can result in despair, cynicism, and hopelessness. The important thing for us is to discover exactly what our need is—this is a part of the preaching of the gospel. It is only those who know their exact need who will ever really rejoice in the Savior and his salvation.

We must note certain false ideas with regard to the meaning of this word *salvation*. Our Lord puts it like this deliberately: "[the] salvation is of the Jews." The Samaritans had their idea of salvation, but they had nothing but the five books of Moses; so they did not understand. Because they lacked the further prophetic teaching, their whole notion of salvation was hopelessly incomplete. Not only that, we know that the Jews themselves at the time of our Lord had an equally inadequate view of salvation and of what the Messiah would do when he came. They were so consumed by political and military notions, they thought so much in terms of the greatness of the Jews, of Israel, that they did not realize their need and therefore were blinded to the real meaning of the term *salvation*. This was the tragedy of the Pharisees, who were self-satisfied and pleased with themselves; and, indeed, we see even the disciples themselves stumbling and fumbling at this point. Even after the resurrection, they turned to our Lord and said, "Wilt thou at this time restore again the kingdom to Israel?" (Acts 1:6). That is what they were after—political, military greatness, greatness in some human sense, the nation of Israel towering over all the other nations. But that is a complete misunderstanding of the meaning of salvation. The fact that the Pharisees and Sadducees and doctors of the law were interested in salvation was not enough. They had to know the character of the salvation of which they stood in need.

And as this was the case way back at the time of our Lord's coming into this world nearly two thousand years ago, so it is equally true today, perhaps even more so. Today there is grievous misunderstanding of the meaning of this word *salvation*. It has been the curse of the last hundred years that men whose duty it has been to teach and to preach the Bible and the message of the gospel have gone on using the terms but have emptied them of their meaning. That is where the dishonesty comes in. They still talk about "the Savior," they still talk about "salvation," but when they use those terms they no longer mean by them what the New Testament means or what our Lord himself so plainly taught.

So the fact that people say they believe that Jesus is the Savior does not of necessity tell us anything at all. You have to ask them exactly what they understand by "Savior" and "salvation." And if you do, you will find that very often their idea of salvation is that we need help in order to save ourselves. That is the essence of the modern teaching and outlook. We are not basically wrong, we can save ourselves, but we do need some assistance. The whole notion of sin is no longer accepted—there is no such thing. There are inadequacies, there is a lack of development, but men and women are essentially all right and have it within them to put themselves right. There is no magic, they say; it is not done for you—you have to do it yourself.

So according to this modern view, what do people need? They need ethical and moral teaching; they need instruction on how to live. Not only that, they need especially to be taught about love. This is the popular teaching today: if only we could all grasp Jesus' teaching about love—that is how they put it—and put it into practice, all would be well. So we must listen to his teaching and we must, above all, look at him, see this love in him, see how he reacted to cruel and spiteful people, and see how he responded to persecution. Here he is—he is enacting the great principle of love. He teaches it; he lives it. He encourages us by his example, and thereby he helps us, but we must rise up and deliver ourselves.

Now I want to show you once more—and if I do not there is no point in talking about Advent and Christmas—that such teaching is all wrong. It is a denial of the whole of the teaching in the Old Testament; it is an utter contradiction of the teaching of our Lord himself and of all the apostles. What is the true view? "Salvation is of the Jews." Salvation is only understood in the light of this Jewish teaching, the Old Testament teaching, the background, the preparation.

What, then, is the teaching? At this point I am only going to give you some headings, just a broad picture of the connotation of this word *salvation*, this glorious word. Well, the first thing we are told is that men and women are spiritually dead; they are ignorant of God. "The fool hath said in his heart, There is no God" (Ps. 14:1). Our Lord in his great high-priestly prayer says, "O righteous Father, the world hath not known thee" (John 17:25). That is the trouble—it is the whole trouble with the world today. And this is still our trouble; it is our ignorance of God that explains why we are what we are. This ignorance is one of the manifestations of spiritual death.

People are not only ignorant of God, they are ignorant of the whole spiritual realm, and they are ignorant of their own true nature. They do not know the truth about themselves. Modern man, so boastful about his achievements, is insulting himself and his own true nature; he does not realize his uniqueness but glories in the fact that he has evolved from an animal! Because he is spiritually ignorant, he does not see this and does not realize the true purpose of life.

But still more serious—and this is what I want to emphasize—men and women are incapable of appreciating the truth when it is put before them. They are blinded. Because they are spiritually dead, they lack a spiritual faculty, so much so that when they are confronted by the truth, they not only do not see it, they resent it and reject it. This is the answer to the notion that people are inherently good and can save themselves if they are given a little help and instruction. They cannot.

Now this is a teaching that was laid down by our Lord himself. "How can ye believe," he said to the Jews, "which receive honour one of another, and seek not the honour that cometh from God only?" (John 5:44). And listen to the apostle Paul putting it explicitly and plainly to the Corinthians. He talks about the wonderful preparation that God made "before the world unto our glory" and then goes on to say, "which none of the princes of this world knew: for had they known it, they would not have crucified the Lord of glory" (1 Cor. 2:7–8). The Lord of glory stood before them, and they rejected him; they saw nothing in him. "Who is this fellow, this carpenter?" They dismissed him, they denounced him, they called him a blasphemer. That is blindness, spiritual blindness, spiritual death. The truth incarnate was before them, and they could not see him.

Paul goes on to put that quite explicitly: "But the natural man receiveth not the things of the Spirit of God: for they are foolishness unto him: neither can he know them, because they are spiritually discerned" (1 Cor. 2:14). That is our trouble. It is no use saying that all that people need is light and instruction. "And this is the condemnation," says John, "that light is come into the world, and men loved darkness rather than light, because their deeds were evil" (John 3:19). Men and women are confronted by the light, and they dismiss it, they joke about it, they laugh at it. They cannot see it because "the carnal mind is enmity against God: for it is not subject to the law of God, neither indeed can be" (Rom. 8:7). It is impossible. The message of the whole of the Old Testament as it prepares the way for salvation is, first, that man, when he rebelled against God, died a spiritual death.

Secondly, the Old Testament teaches that man is under the wrath and condemnation of God and his holy Law. The whole of the Old Testament deals with this. Why was the Law ever given? The Jews in their blindness misunderstood and thought that the Law was given in order that they might save themselves through it, but what a misunderstanding! The Law was never given to the Jews in order that they might put it into practice and thereby save themselves; they could not, because of their condition. No; Paul tells us, "Moreover the law entered, that the offence might abound"—that is the purpose of the Law. "But where sin abounded, grace did much more abound" (Rom. 5:20). The object of the giving of the Law was "that the offence might abound"—that it might be seen, brought out, displayed.

In Romans 7 Paul says this still more clearly: "Was then that which is good made death unto me? God forbid. But sin, that it might appear sin, working death in me by that which is good; that sin by the commandment might become exceeding sinful" (v. 13).

The object of the Law is to bring out the true nature and character of sin. In Galatians 3:24 Paul sums it up this way: "The law was our schoolmaster to bring us unto Christ." How does the Law do that? Paul writes to the Romans, "Now we know that what things soever the law saith, it saith to them who are under the law"—what for?—"that every mouth may be stopped, and all the world may become guilty before God."

That is the purpose of the Law.

> Therefore by the deeds of the law there shall no flesh be justified in his sight: for by the law is the knowledge of sin. But now the righteousness of God without [apart from] the law is manifested, being witnessed by the law and the prophets; even the righteousness of God which is by faith of Jesus Christ unto all and upon all them that believe: for there is no difference: for all have sinned, and come short of the glory of God. (Rom. 3:19–23)

That is it! That is a summary of the teaching of the whole Old Testament: man is not only dead spiritually, he is also under condemnation, he is under the wrath of God. Indeed, Paul, again, puts this perfectly when he says, "I am not ashamed of the gospel of Christ." Paul uses litotes to make his point. He means, "I am tremendously proud of it. I am thrilled by it. I boast in it. I want to tell everybody about it." Why? He goes on to say, "for it is the power of God unto salvation to every one that believeth; to the Jew first, and also to the Greek. For therein is the righteousness of God revealed from faith to faith: as it is written, The just shall live by faith. For"—here is the reason Paul glories in this great salvation, this is why he exults in it—"the wrath of God is revealed from heaven against all ungodliness and unrighteousness of men, who hold [down] the truth in unrighteousness" (Rom. 1:16–18).

That is why this salvation is so wonderful. "The wrath of God is revealed from heaven." The whole of the Old Testament reveals God's wrath; the Law does that. Man is not only dead, he is facing eternal punishment, a continuation in his state of spiritual death and torment and unhappiness forever and ever.

Not only that, man is living a life that is in the flesh and after the flesh; he is under the dominion of sin and of Satan. Our Lord once said to certain people, "Ye are of your father the devil" (John 8:44), and all men and women who are not in Christ are of the devil, as it were, and are his children. Without Christ, we are in the kingdom of darkness, the kingdom of Satan. When Paul was called on the road to Damascus, the commission that our Lord gave him was this: "I am going to send you to the people and to the Gentiles 'to open their eyes, and to turn them from darkness to light, and from the power of Satan unto God'" (Acts 26:17–18). Yes, says John, "the whole world lieth in wickedness [the evil one]" (1 John 5:19). That is the position of the world that does not believe in Christ—under the dominion of sin and Satan, slaves of evil and of the devil, and not only that, but with a nature that is polluted, with an evil heart of unbelief, loving the darkness rather than the light. Or, again, as Paul puts it, "This I say therefore, and testify in the Lord, that ye henceforth walk not as other Gentiles walk"—how?—"in the vanity of their mind, having the understanding darkened, being alienated from the life of God through the ignorance that is in them, because of the blindness of their heart: who being past feeling have given themselves over unto lasciviousness, to work all uncleanness with greediness" (Eph. 4:17–19).

That is it! The pollution of sin.

And, finally, man is under the power of death, "the last enemy" (1 Cor. 15:26), and all his lifetime he is subject to bondage because of this fear of death.

My friends, this is the need of man. It is the teaching of the Jews, the teaching of the Old Testament, the revelation of God, given before the Advent. If you do not believe that, you will see nothing in what I am going to say about the great salvation. Only those who have realized that this is the truth about themselves ever rejoice in this salvation. "Salvation is of the Jews." So listen to our Lord. What is this salvation that he is talking about?

Let me give you some further points to think about, and if they do not make you sing and rejoice, all I have said so far has meant nothing to you. You have never been convicted of sin; you just want to be religious; you just want a little bit of help. What does our Lord tell us?

He tells us, first, that he alone can give salvation; he alone can provide it. That is why he came into the world. Salvation is of the Jews, and he is one of them; he comes out from them. God brought them into being in order that his Son might come. It is a salvation that is "to the Jew first, and also to the Gentile" (Rom. 2:10); it is a salvation that is to be preached, said our Lord, first in Jerusalem, then in Samaria, then in the uttermost parts of the earth (see Acts 1:8). It is the only salvation.

Our Lord came specifically to deliver us out of the predicament that has been outlined in the Old Testament. He says, "The Son of man is come . . ." What for? To provide ethical, moral teaching? To give us an example of a life of love lived out before us? Of course, all that, but that condemns me more than anything else. I cannot face the Ten Commandments, leave alone the life of Christ. That shrivels me into hopelessness. No, no; "the Son of man is come to seek and to save that which was lost" (Luke 19:10). This is the object, this great and glorious salvation.

Secondly, our Lord gives this salvation fully, entirely, completely. It needs no supplement; it brooks no addition. You must never add anything to it, whether circumcision or Mary, the mother of Christ, or the church or a priesthood. If you add anything, you are derogating, I say again, from his glory. Read your Scriptures, my dear friends, and pray for the Holy Spirit to open your understanding before you read them, and then you will see this glory being unfolded before you. Listen to our Lord himself:

> And he came to Nazareth, where he had been brought up: and, as his custom was, he went into the synagogue on the sabbath day, and stood up for to read. And there was delivered unto him the book of the prophet Esaias. And when he had opened the book, he found the place where it was written, The Spirit of the Lord is upon me, because he hath anointed me to preach the gospel to the poor; he hath sent me to heal the brokenhearted, to preach deliverance to the captives, and recovering of sight to the blind, to set at liberty them that are bruised, to preach the acceptable year of the Lord. And he closed the book, and he gave it again to the minister, and sat down. . . . And he began to say unto them, This day is this scripture fulfilled in your ears. (Luke 4:16–21)

There it is. It is a complete, a full, a perfect salvation. He is the fulfillment of all those glorious, thrilling, moving, triumphant prophecies that are found in the Old Testament.

Not only that, here he is at the end of his life. He has finished his teaching, he is under the very shadow of the cross, and what does he say?

> These words spake Jesus, and lifted up his eyes to heaven, and said, Father, the hour is come; glorify thy Son, that thy Son also may glorify thee: as thou hast given him power over all flesh, that he should give eternal life to as many as thou hast given hm. And this is life eternal, that they might know thee the only true God, and Jesus Christ, whom thou hast sent. I have glorified thee on the earth: I have finished the work which thou gavest me to do. (John 17:1–4)

Later, from the cross he said, "It is finished" (John 19:30). Finished completely. "When he had by himself purged our sins, [he] sat down on the right hand of the Majesty on high" (Heb. 1:3). He did everything that he came to do. That is what he means by this word *salvation*—the fullness of it, the sufficiency of it. The apostle Paul, of course, is constantly trying to give expression to this. He says, do not go back to philosophies or to vague teachings about angels and hierarchies, "for in him dwelleth all the fulness of the Godhead bodily. And ye are complete in him" (Col. 2:9–10). Listen to the apostle bursting out at the very beginning of the Epistle to the Ephesians, listen to how moved he is, how thrilled: "Blessed be the God and Father of our Lord Jesus Christ, who hath blessed us with all spiritual blessings in heavenly places in Christ" (1:3). That is the meaning of the word *salvation*, nothing less.

Peter is not to be outdone. His description is not as eloquent and as moving as that of Paul, but listen to him as he puts it like this:

> Simon Peter, a servant and an apostle of Jesus Christ, to them that have obtained like precious faith with us through the righteousness of God and our Saviour Jesus Christ: Grace and peace be multiplied unto you through the knowledge of God, and of Jesus our Lord. According as his divine power hath given unto us all things [the very term used by the woman of Samaria in John 4:25] that pertain unto life and godliness, through the knowledge of him that hath called us to glory and virtue . . . (2 Pet. 1:1–3)

And Peter goes on in verse 4 to talk about "exceeding great and precious promises." Oh, this is the meaning of salvation! Take Paul again, in his letter to the Ephesians:

> . . . that I should preach among the Gentiles the unsearchable riches of Christ . . . the breadth, and length, and depth, and height; and to know the love of Christ, which passeth knowledge, that ye might be filled with all the fulness of God. (3:8, 18–19)

What is Paul describing? It is the salvation that is in our Lord himself. And to the Corinthians he says, "But of him are ye in Christ Jesus, who of God is made unto us wisdom, and righteousness, and sanctification, and redemption" (1 Cor. 1:30). When Paul talks about "wisdom," he means light, teaching. As John says, "No man hath seen God at any time; the only begotten Son, which is in the bosom of the Father, he hath declared him" (John 1:18). He has taught, he has instructed, he has manifested light and wisdom—wisdom from God. "For after that in the wisdom of God the world by wisdom knew not God, it pleased God through the foolishness of preaching to save them that believe" (1 Cor. 1:21), and that wisdom gives us understanding. That great hymn of Philip Doddridge expresses it all so perfectly:

> *He comes, from thickest films of vice*
> *To clear the mental ray,*
> *And on the eyeballs of the blind*
> *To pour celestial day.*

Do you have this life? This wisdom from God is a part of this great fullness of salvation.

Consider all righteousness. "There is none that doeth good, no, not one" (Ps. 14:3). We are all condemned; we are guilty before God; we can do nothing about it. You cannot erase your past; you can never live properly in the future. What can you do? There is only one hope for us, this salvation that he has come to give—forgiveness of sins, to be clothed with the robe of his spotless, perfect righteousness, reconciliation to God.

What else do we need? Sanctification! We need to be delivered from the power of sin, from the pollution of sin within our life and nature. Can our Lord do it? Yes, he can. It is a part of this salvation that he talks about—"Salvation is of the Jews." "I am he," says our Lord; "salvation is in me."

What is sanctification? It is a new birth, a new nature, a new life, a new beginning, adoption into the family of heaven as a child of God, a progressive work of the Holy Spirit within me getting rid of sin, undoing the work of the devil and increasingly preparing me for the glory that awaits me. Let Philip Doddridge put it again for us:

He comes, the prisoners to release,
In Satan's bondage held;
The gates of brass before him burst,
The iron fetters yield. ("Hark, the Glad Sound!")

He is the one who can cleanse us in this way and set us free "in the liberty wherewith Christ hath made us free" (Gal. 5:1). He brings us wisdom, righteousness, sanctification, and, at the end of it all, final glorification, deliverance from death. He has destroyed the last enemy and opened the gate of Paradise and of heaven. He has such power that he can change the body of my humiliation and fashion it like unto the body of his glorification. There is final, complete deliverance from sin in every shape and form.

'Tis thine to cleanse the heart,
To sanctify the soul,
To pour fresh life in every part,
And new create the whole.[10]

Everything will be perfect.

So what can we do as we contemplate this great salvation of his? We can do nothing better than remember the words of Jude:

> Now unto him that is able to keep you from falling, and to present you faultless before the presence of his glory with exceeding joy, to the only wise God our Saviour, be glory and majesty, dominion and power, both now and ever. Amen. (vv. 24–25)

Are you ready to ascribe salvation to him? Have you seen the fullness of the salvation that he came to provide? Beloved people, give yourselves no rest until you really are filled with a desire to praise him, until you rejoice in him with a joy that is "unspeakable and full of glory" (1 Pet. 1:8).

11

The Greatest Mystery of All

Jesus saith unto her, Woman, believe me, the hour cometh, when ye shall neither in this mountain, nor yet at Jerusalem worship the Father. Ye worship ye know not what: we know what we worship: for salvation is of the Jews. (John 4:21–22)

We have been looking together at our Lord's words, "Salvation is of the Jews" and have been considering the importance of realizing our need for salvation. We have looked at the biblical teaching on salvation and our Lord's teaching that full and complete salvation is found in him alone.

But that, of course, now brings us still more directly to this question: who is this person who can speak like this? Who is this one who makes such a claim? Here we come to the very heart and center of the whole Christian message. It is all about this person. It is not a philosophy; it is not just a teaching. It is not just a message about peace and goodwill, friendship, and fellowship. Christianity is Christ, the person, and unless we are perfectly clear with respect to him and the truth concerning him, we will obviously go astray with regard to the whole message.

Again, this story of the woman of Samaria gives us most valuable instruction with regard to this subject. Indeed, it is the very point of the passage we are studying. The conversation ends in that dramatic statement, "Jesus saith unto her, I that speak unto thee am he." The woman has already said, "Sir, I perceive that thou art a prophet." She is an able woman, though a terrible sinner, and this much is clear to her from what our Lord has been saying. He has been able to tell her about her own personal life and the immoral state in which she is living. He has broken through all her talk about worship here and in Jerusalem. Knowing how utterly valueless so much of our talk about religion so often is, he has cut through it all, and she recognizes that he is a prophet. Nicodemus had reached the same conclusion. John says, "[Nicodemus] came to Jesus by night, and said unto him, Rabbi, we know that thou art a teacher come from God: for no man can do these miracles that thou doest, except God be with him" (John 3:2). But this is not enough.

The New Testament often shows the failure to understand our Lord. It shows us how people were attracted and interested, could see so much, but could not really see who he was. He was a problem. "Who is he?" That was the great question when he was here on earth. As he entered Jerusalem toward the end, there was a great stir in the whole city, and everybody was asking, "Who is this?" (Matt. 21:10). On another occasion it was put in a different form. People had heard him speaking about the Son of man, and they said, "Who is this Son of man?" (John 12:34)

This was a question, indeed, that our Lord himself encouraged people to face. He himself asked it in many different forms. Once he said, "What think ye of Christ? Whose son is he?" (Matt. 22:42). On another occasion he put the question directly to his own disciples: "Whom do men say that I the Son of man am?" And they gave him various answers: "Some say that thou art John the Baptist [risen from the dead]; some, Elias [Elijah]; and others, Jeremias [Jeremiah], or one of the prophets" (Matt. 16:13–14). Even John the Baptist got into a state of confusion. There he was, lying in prison, hearing how our Lord was spending his time up in Galilee preaching to poor people instead of going down to Jerusalem to be crowned King and to gather a great army and to rid them of the tyranny of the Roman occupation. So John sent his two messengers to ask, "Art thou he that should come, or do we look for another?" (Matt. 11:3).

All these were the fumbling efforts of people to come to a conclusion with respect to this wonderful person. And it is all typified in this statement of the woman of Samaria: "Sir, I perceive that thou art a prophet." It was clear to them all that our Lord was unusual. They saw there was a problem here. He had great learning, and yet he had never been to the schools. "How knoweth this man letters [learning], having never learned?" (John 7:15). He was able to do extraordinary deeds of power, and yet he was a carpenter. Here was the enigma.

But I want to try to show that it is not surprising that they were in difficulty and that they stumbled in this way, for our Lord is a mystery, the greatest mystery of all. The apostle Paul put this once and forever in his first letter to Timothy: "Great is the mystery of godliness: God was manifest in the flesh" (3:16). And this is where we should always start—the mystery of this person who is to be found by the side of the well talking to this Samaritan woman, this sinner.

I also want to show you how, in this conversation, and especially in verses 19–26, this mystery is put before us in a very striking manner. There is a contrast here. On the one hand, our Lord turns to this woman and says, "Woman, believe me." Now that is one statement—"Believe me." And at the end he says to her, "I am he." These statements belong together: "me," "I." On the other hand, and contrasted with this, is our Lord's statement, "*We* know what we worship": "we." Let's look at these statements and the contrast between them because they hold before us the whole paradox and mystery and marvel concerning this blessed person.

First, our Lord said, "Believe me . . . I am he"—"I am the one who is going to tell you everything. I am the one who possesses all the knowledge that is necessary." He was constantly making this point. For instance, he said, "Ye have heard that it was said by them of old time . . . but I say unto you" (Matt. 5:27). Nothing is more characteristic of him than the way in which he separated himself from everybody else and put himself into a category entirely on his own. "All that ever came before me are thieves and robbers," he said. (John 10:8). The Gospel of John is full of these great statements: "I am the bread of life" (John 6:35); "I am the door" (John 10:7); "I am the light of the world" (John 8:12). And he is saying all that here when he states, "Believe me . . . I am he." He is claiming uniqueness, absolute authority as a teacher. Indeed, he is making what can only be described as a dictatorial demand for submission.

Now in our Lord's handling of people, we see many illustrations of his unique authority. For instance, we read that one day John the Baptist was standing with two of his disciples when our Lord passed by, and John said, "Behold the Lamb of God!" When they heard this, the two disciples followed Jesus, and then we read, "Then Jesus turned, and saw them following. . . . They said unto him, Rabbi . . . where dwellest thou? He saith unto them, Come and see" (John 1:36–39), and he took them with him and instructed them.

Then we read that Andrew immediately brought Simon Peter to him: "And when Jesus beheld him, he said, Thou art Simon the son of Jona: thou shalt be called Cephas, which is by interpretation, A stone" (John 1:42). He was speaking with the same authority. And the chapter continues, "The day following Jesus would go forth into Galilee, and findeth Philip, and saith unto him"—this is the typical expression—"Follow me" (John 1:43). Philip is to leave everything—"Follow me." There is the same great dictatorial claim and demand.

It is the same with Nathanael. Our Lord sees him coming and says,

"Behold an Israelite indeed, in whom is no guile!"And then he goes on to say to him, "Because I said unto thee, I saw thee under the fig tree, believest thou? thou shalt see greater things than these. And he saith unto him, Verily, verily [Amen, amen], I say unto you"—in this Gospel particularly watch this authoritative statement—"Hereafter ye shall see heaven open, and the angels of God ascending and descending upon the Son of man" (John 1:47, 50–51).

We see the same authority very clearly in the second chapter in the way he speaks to his mother. Mary has come to him at the marriage feast of Cana of Galilee and says, "They have no wine," and she suggests that he should do something about it. But he rebukes her: "Woman, what have I to do with thee? mine hour is not yet come." So he separates himself from his mother in this authoritative manner (John 2:3–4).

And then later on his authority is seen still more clearly when he goes into the Temple. John writes, "And when he had made a scourge of small cords, he drove them all out of the temple, and the sheep, and the oxen; and poured out the changers' money, and overthrew the tables." He clears them out and makes the unique claim of calling the Temple "my Father's house" (John 2:15–16).

It is the same with Nicodemus. Nicodemus comes to him as a teacher and is more or less putting himself on the same level—he regards our Lord as a teacher who just has a little bit beyond what he himself has. Our Lord interrupts him and says, "Verily, verily, I say unto thee, Except a man be born again, he cannot see the kingdom of God" (John 3:3). But more specifically, he puts it like this:

> Verily, verily, I say unto thee, We speak that we do know, and testify that we have seen; and ye receive not our witness. If I have told you earthly things, and ye believe not, how shall ye believe, if I tell you of heavenly things? And no man hath ascended up to heaven, but he that came down from heaven, even the Son of man which is in heaven. (John 3:11–13)

Now all these are but illustrations of our Lord's exclusive claim, and here he says to the woman that the water he will give will be "a well of water springing up into everlasting life." This is so characteristic of him. He puts himself into a special category: "But believe me." He had said it as a boy, twelve years of age, when he was found, you remember, by Joseph and Mary in the Temple instead of being with them on the homeward journey. They had gone back to Jerusalem, and there they found him arguing with the doctors of the law, confuting these men, and they rebuked him for not having gone with them. But he replied, "Wist ye not that I must be about my Father's business [the things of my Father]?" (Luke 2:49). Even at the age of twelve he made this unique and exceptional claim. And it is all summed up in this phrase, "Verily, verily," which means, "Believe me—listen to what I am saying."

Indeed, later on in John's Gospel we find that our Lord makes claims such as "I and my Father are one" (John 10:30) and "Before Abraham was, I am" (John 8:58). There is only one explanation of such statements. He is claiming to be God, and his enemies see that. "Who is this fellow?" they said. "This is blasphemy; he is claiming to be equal with God" (see John 5:18). Clearly, then, we are looking at one who *is* God!

But the moment we come to that conclusion, we are taken by surprise. "Woman, believe me," our Lord says, "the hour cometh, when ye shall neither in this mountain, nor yet at Jerusalem, worship the Father. Ye worship ye know not what: *we* know"—the one who has been saying "I" now says "we." The one who has been separating himself from the rest of the human race and later on says, "I ascend unto my Father, and your Father; and to my God, and your God" (John 20:17), the one who says, "Ye are from beneath; I am from above" (John 8:23), suddenly says, "we." And this is, of course, where the problem arises, where the mystery comes in, the enigma that has always puzzled humanity. The wise and the prudent came to him, and they have been looking at him ever since, but they do not know what to make of him because they are confronted by this "I" and "we," the separateness and yet the fact that he clearly belongs. He is one of the Jews; he belongs to this race of people. And that is why, at the beginning of the Gospels of Matthew and Luke, we are given those genealogies tracing his ancestry. He does belong. He is "of the seed of David"; he goes back to Abraham. Here is the line; you can see it.

And then he goes on and says, "we worship." We have seen that he is God, and yet he says he is one who worships as the Jews worship. And we read about him praying. So we can only come to the conclusion that he is a man; he is a man among men. He is saying, "I am one of the Jews, and I am speaking to you as a Jew. You are a Samaritan; I am a Jew"—"we" in contradistinction to "I."

So here, in this one incident and in just these few verses, we are led into the very heart and center of the great problem of the person of Jesus of Nazareth, and this is what baffled his contemporaries. This is something that can only be understood by those who are enlightened by the Holy Spirit. I referred you earlier to the scene at Caesarea Philippi when our

Lord puts the question to the disciples, "Whom do men say that I the Son of man am?" and they give him various answers. Then he turns to them and says, "But whom say ye that I am?" And Peter steps forward and says, "Thou art the Christ, the Son of the living God." And our Lord replies, "Blessed art thou, Simon Bar-jona: for flesh and blood hath not revealed it unto thee, but my Father which is in heaven" (Matt. 16:13, 15–17).

Now there is the only way whereby we can ever understand this problem. What is the explanation of this mystery—"Believe me" and yet "we"? What is the meaning of the Incarnation? The answer is put before us so frequently in these Scriptures. We have already seen it in this Gospel according to John:

> In the beginning was the Word, and the Word was with God, and the Word was God. The same was in the beginning with God. All things were made by him; and without him was not any thing made that was made. In him was life; and the life was the light of men. (1:1–4)

God eternal! Son of God, co-equal, co-eternal with the Father! Very God of very God! But "the Word was made flesh, and dwelt among us" (John 1:14). That is how this is put before us in the Prologue of John's Gospel, but it is stated in other places in an equally interesting manner. In introducing his great Epistle to the Romans, the apostle Paul puts it like this:

> Paul, a servant of Jesus Christ, called to be an apostle, separated unto the gospel of God, (which he had promised afore by his prophets in the holy scriptures,) concerning his Son Jesus Christ our Lord, which was made of the seed of David according to the flesh; and declared to be the Son of God with power, according to the spirit of holiness, by the resurrection from the dead. (1:1–4)

Here we have the two aspects brought together, and here the human is put first: "made of the seed of David according to the flesh." The apostle gives the same teaching in the eighth chapter: "For what the law could not do, in that it was weak through the flesh, God sending his own Son in the likeness of sinful flesh, and for sin, condemned sin in the flesh" (v. 3).

"God sending his own Son"—"me," "I," "in the likeness of sinful flesh"—"we," a Jew among Jews. But in the ninth chapter of Romans, the apostle puts it still more strikingly and specifically. He is troubled about the fact that the Jews have rejected the gospel concerning the Lord

Jesus Christ, and this is why he says he is surprised: "who are Israelites; to whom pertaineth the adoption, and the glory, and the covenants, and the giving of the law, and the service of God, and the promises; whose are the fathers, and of whom as concerning the flesh Christ came, who is over all, God blessed for ever" (vv. 4–5).

There Paul is emphasizing the words, "of whom [the Jews] as concerning the flesh Christ came, who is over all, God blessed for ever." "God blessed for ever," yes, but a Jew, an Israelite! There is the same combination. This is the great truth on which we must concentrate. There is no question about this. "Salvation," he says, "is of [us] the Jews," not of you. Samaritans are not from the Jews.

What, then, is the explanation of all this? I suppose in many ways the grandest statement of this truth that has ever been made is in the Epistle to the Philippians:

> Let this mind be in you, which was also in Christ Jesus: Who, being in the form of God, thought it not robbery to be equal with God: but made himself of no reputation, and took upon him the form of a servant, and was made in the likeness of men: and being found in fashion as a man, he humbled himself, and became obedient unto death, even the death of the cross. (2:5–8)

It is all there again—"believe me"—"we"; "being in the form of God"—along with the explanation, "he humbled himself" and "made himself of no reputation."

What does this mean? It means that he laid aside the signs and the externals, as it were, of his eternal glory and his Godhead. The translation "emptied himself" in some Bible versions is wrong because it is too all-inclusive. He did not empty himself of his Godhead; that is something that even he could not do. It is impossible for God to cease to be God. No, no; this old translation, the Authorized Version, is so much better here—he "made himself of no reputation." He still remains the one he is, he is still eternal God, but he no longer appears in the "form" of God. He now takes the "form" of a servant and is made "in the likeness of men" and is "found in fashion as a man." He is still God. This is what we must hold on to; he is still God in all the fullness. That is why he can say, "Believe me"; that is why he can say, "I am he." That is why he makes these exclusive, exceptional claims—he is God!

But—and this is the whole mystery and marvel of this message that we consider at this time of Advent[11]—he became *truly* man. He did not merely appear in a kind of phantom body. You must not misunderstand these words "fashion" and "likeness" as meaning merely some kind of pretense or some casing; that is wrong. He had a human soul—he said "we." He was truly a Jew, born of the Virgin Mary. He came, according to the flesh, from the Jews, the Israelites. He was "of the seed of David" (Rom. 1:3). He was as much of the seed of David as any other descendant of David. This substance, "the flesh," has come down from David and before that from Abraham and all the others who appear in the genealogical tables.

So here is the only answer to the problem of "I" and "we": he is still God, and yet he has become man. "The Word was made flesh, and dwelt among us" (John 1:14). He had a real human soul, and yet he was still God the eternal Son. And the explanation of this is all there, in Philippians 2:6–8, as we have just seen. What happened was that though he was still God, he came into the world and was born as a man, and though he was still God, he lived as a man.

In Galatians 4:4 Paul puts it in this way: he was "made of a woman." He was as truly born of the Virgin Mary as any one of us was born of our mother. He did not have a human father, but nevertheless his actual birth, as regards the flesh, was like every other birth. But not only that, he was "made under the law." Now this is a remarkable and amazing fact. As God he is the Lawgiver, he is above the Law. But he was "made of a woman, made under the law," and that is the ultimate proof of the fact that he was truly a Jew. That is why he says to the woman of Samaria, "We know what we worship: for salvation is of [us] the Jews."

As a Jew, he was subject to the Law. Let us not forget these facts. This is where we see the glory of the Incarnation. He was circumcised, as every Jewish male child was circumcised. He was still, remember, the eternal God, but as regards the flesh, the human part of him, he was a Jew and submitted to circumcision. Not only that, we read that he was obedient to his parents, as we see plainly in the pages of the Gospels (Luke 2:52).

Still more striking is the fact that when, at the age of thirty, he set out on his public ministry, he submitted to baptism. John the Baptist's baptism was a baptism of repentance for the remission of sins, and our Lord had never committed a sin. So John remonstrated with him. But he said, "Suffer it to be so now: for thus it becometh us to fulfil all righteousness" (Matt. 3:15). He was identifying himself with us; he was one of us.

Not only that; we read that as he was baptized by John the Baptist, there in the Jordan, the Spirit descended on him in the form of a dove.

The apostle John tells us that "God giveth not the Spirit by measure unto him" (John 3:34); and that means that God gave him the Spirit and that he needed the Spirit. Indeed, he himself said later on, "Him hath God the Father sealed" (John 6:27)—with the Spirit at Jordan and with the voice that came from heaven saying, "This is my beloved Son, in whom I am well pleased" (Matt. 3:17).

Now all these things are manifestations of his humanity, of the fact that he was truly a man. Though he was Son of God, to do his work here on earth he needed the Spirit, and the Spirit came upon him and gave him power, anointed him. So when he went back to Nazareth and entered the synagogue and was given the scroll of Isaiah, he read, "The Spirit of the Lord is upon me" (Luke 4:18; cf. Isaiah 61:1). The Spirit had come upon him there at the baptism, enabling him to speak and to preach and to do his mighty works and to engage in his ministry.

But as he says here to the woman of Samaria, he also worshipped, and we find accounts of him spending whole nights in prayer, rising up a great while before dawn in order to pray. This is what confuses people—on the one hand, this exclusive claim, and yet on the other hand we see him praying. "If he is eternal God," people say, "why did he have to pray?" But he did have to pray, and he always prayed at great length before crucial events took place in connection with his ministry.

There is only one answer, and it is, as I say, that though he was still God, he was living as a man. He was living a life of utter dependence upon God; he was living a life of obedience. He said, "I do nothing of myself" (John 8:28). The eternal God, the one by whom all things were made, and without whom nothing was made that was made (John 1:3), said, "I can of mine own self do nothing" (John 5:30). The only explanation is that though he had not lost his powers he had decided not to use them. This is the essence of the Incarnation. All the rest was still there, but he laid it aside in the sense that he was not using it. Indeed, it could not even be seen. Those who were given the insight could say, "We beheld his glory" (John 1:14)—yes, but they could not see without the Holy Spirit. Others looked at him and said, "Who is this fellow? Who is this carpenter? Away with him. Crucify him."

This leads me, of course, to the final question: Why did all this happen? Why did he do this? Why was the eternal Son of God born as a babe in the stable at Bethlehem? Why this story of the human person, Jesus of Nazareth? It took place because it was the only way whereby he could bring and give us this great salvation. "Salvation," he says, "is of the Jews," by which he is really saying, "I am the one who is bringing the salvation, and I am a Jew. I have come out of the Jews. The nation was created, in a sense, in order that it might produce me."

But why is this essential? This is the most important question that one can ever ask. Why did the Son of God have to be born as the babe of Bethlehem, born of a woman, to become a Jew among Jews—why was this necessary? And the answer is that apart from this we cannot be saved. Why not? Because "All have sinned, and come short of the glory of God" (Rom. 3:23). We have all transgressed God's holy Law; we are all under the wrath of God. So how can we be saved? We can only be saved by a representative—someone must come and represent us before God. And because we are human beings, our representative must be a human being. One hesitates to say this, and yet one must say it—even God could not have saved a single soul without the Incarnation—that is, without the life and death, burial and resurrection of the Lord Jesus Christ. God cannot just say from heaven, "I forgive you."

Why not? Because God is just, because God is holy, because God is righteous. God made a man and called him Adam; there was the representative of the whole of humanity. But Adam rebelled, he sinned, he fell. Punishment must be given, and the punishment was death, separation from God, even physical death. There is the problem. And as Adam was a man and as we are all human beings, the only one who can represent us and save us must also become a human being. The author of Hebrews puts it like this:

> For it became him, for whom are all things, and by whom are all things [this is God the Father, it "becomes" him] in bringing many sons unto glory, to make the captain [leader] of their salvation perfect through sufferings. For both he that sanctifieth and they who are sanctified are all of one [one nature]: for which cause he is not ashamed to call them brethren. . . . Forasmuch then as the children [that is to say, us] are partakers of flesh and blood, he also himself likewise took part of the same; that through death he might destroy him that had the power of death, that is, the devil; and deliver them who through fear of death were all their lifetime subject to bondage. For verily he took not on him the nature of angels; but he took on him the seed of Abraham. (2:10–16)

He does not partake of the nature of angels; he has not come to save angels. He has come to save men and women; so he must take on human nature—"the seed of Abraham."

> Wherefore in all things it behoved him to be made like unto his brethren, that he might be a merciful and faithful high priest in things pertaining to God, to make reconciliation for the sins of the people. For in that he himself hath suffered being tempted, he is able to succour them that are tempted. (Heb. 2:17–18)

That passage means we need someone to represent us. We are all sinners—what about our guilt? We cannot do anything about it, and God cannot just say, "I forgive it," as we have seen. But here is one who says in effect, "I am the one who is going to bear your sins." He has a right to do so because he is a man among men—he is not an angel. Here is a human representative, one of us—"we." "We, the Jews." "We" members of humanity. But he has to bear the punishment of our sins, and that means death. He has to deliver us from the Law of God that condemns us; he has to deliver us from death itself and from the grave. He has, at the same time, to be one who can sympathize with us and help us, for we need not only forgiveness of sins—we need help, we need strength. How can we pray? We go glibly into the presence of God and think there is no problem; but we are going into the presence of one who is "a consuming fire." He is the Judge of the universe—who can approach him? We need a representative, we need a high priest, we need a mediator—these are our needs. So he must be a man for all these reasons.

Read the Epistle to the Hebrews again, and concentrate on the Lord Jesus Christ as our High Priest.

> Seeing then that we have a great high priest, that is passed into the heavens, Jesus the Son of God, let us hold fast our profession. For we have not an high priest which cannot be touched with the feeling of our infirmities; but was in all points tempted like as we are, yet without sin. Let us therefore come boldly unto the throne of grace. (4:14–16)

And then in the next chapter, "For every high priest taken from among men is ordained for men in things pertaining to God, that he may offer both gifts and sacrifices for sins: who can have compassion on the ignorant, and on them that are out of the way" (5:1–2).

How can he have compassion on the ignorant if he is not a man? How can he bear with our frailties if he does not know something about them himself? And here he is sitting at the side of the well in Samaria, tired and weary with the journey, suffering from thirst, asking for a drink. He is a man; he must be a man. He cannot sympathize, he cannot understand, he cannot help unless he is man.

And yet he must bear the punishment of my sins; he must conquer death and the grave. No man can do it. Adam was a perfect man, sinless, and yet he failed. And if God had merely created another perfect man like Adam, he would have failed in exactly the same way. There is only one way whereby this salvation can ever come to any of us, and it is this: there must be a new humanity. And so the babe of Bethlehem was born, and the archangel in telling Mary of his coming birth said, "That holy thing . . . shall be born of thee" (Luke 1:35). "Holy thing"! The baby was not an ordinary child. "The Holy Ghost shall come upon thee, and the power of the Highest shall overshadow thee." He is the Father, as it were. There was no human father. "That holy thing . . . shall be born of thee."

In other words, he is God, and he took on to himself human nature, becoming man: "The Word was made flesh, and dwelt among us" (John 1:14). He must be both God and man. If he is not man, he cannot represent us, he cannot finally help us. But if he is only man, he cannot save us—he is not big enough, he is not great enough, he is not strong enough. So he is both God *and* man. He is God living as man and is therefore able to take upon him my sins. He has obeyed the Law on my behalf; he has borne the punishment of my sins in his own body on the tree. He has conquered death and the grave. He has conquered all our enemies, and he has risen triumphant and has taken his seat at the right hand of God in the glory everlasting. He is the only one who could not fail, he is the only one who has not failed, and therefore he is the only Savior.

There it is: "believe me"; "we know what we worship." Very God of very God and yet a man worshipping God and entirely dependent upon God. This is God's way. It was God's purpose that his only begotten, eternal Son should be born as a Jewish babe and live as a man and die as a man and rise again because the whole time he is still the eternal and everlasting God. He said he was the Son of God who had come from heaven but who was still at the same time in heaven (John 3:13). He was speaking to Nicodemus on earth, but he was still in heaven. "I"! "We"! "God"! "Man"! "The Word"! "Flesh"! And thereby, and thereby alone, are you and I saved, and in him, and in him alone, is salvation possible.

12

"I Am He"

Jesus saith unto her, I that speak unto thee am he. (John 4:26)

We are met together on this Christmas morning[12] to commemorate an event. It is always vital that we should remind ourselves of that, and that is why I, as one who is a thoroughgoing Protestant and even a Puritan, believe in the observance of Christmas Day. We are always so much in danger of forgetting that we are dealing with facts, with history. There is no greater danger than to regard the Christian faith, the Christian message, as just a philosophy, just a teaching. So it is very good that we should constantly remind ourselves that all we have and all we hope and all we hold on to is based solidly upon facts. So we meet together today to remember what is, to all Christian people, the most important and at the same time the most amazing event that has ever happened in the whole long course of human history.

Indeed, I could go beyond that and easily show you that for the whole of humanity, even for those people who do not believe this message and who do not call themselves Christians, this is nevertheless the most momentous occurrence that has ever taken place. We have already reminded ourselves that this event hanged the whole course of history. After all, why do we call this year 1966? It is because of the birth of that babe of Bethlehem—he has changed our calendars. He is the turning point of all history, and this is even recognized by secular historians.

But since Christmas Day this year happens to be on a Sunday, we are reminded in passing that he has also even changed our observance of the days of the week. Before his coming, the Jews observed the Sabbath, the seventh day, as the day that was given particularly to the worship of God. But for us Sunday is the first day of the week, and that is the day that all Christian people give to the worship of God and to the contemplation of their souls and eternal things. Why is this? Again, it is all due to this person who came into the world as the babe of Bethlehem. He has changed everything. He "towers o'er the wrecks of time." He and his cross and the great message concerning him have been the greatest factors in all human history. The question, therefore, that comes to us all is, do we realize the significance of this great, extraordinary, and momentous event that we are meeting together to commemorate and that in a sense we meet together to commemorate every Sunday?

Now it is quite clear, alas, that to many people in the world the significance of this day is not realized at all. We must all plead guilty that none of us realizes its full significance, and it does not influence the lives of any of us as it should. But it is clear that there are large masses of people in this and in other lands to whom Christmas Day really does mean nothing at all. I am not talking, obviously, about Christmas as a holiday, as it is normally regarded, but to the event that gives its name to all this—Christ's Mass, if you like—and therefore it is this that we must consider together.

Now the world remains very much as it was when this babe was born into it. Why was our Lord born in a stable? We are given the reason. It is "because there was no room for them in the inn" (Luke 2:7). Here is a woman who arrives on the verge of giving birth to her firstborn child, and yet she cannot find a room in any of the lodging-places of Bethlehem. Of course, it was an important occasion, the occasion of the taxing, and people had to go to Bethlehem from various parts of the country—they had to go wherever their household and their lineage belonged. So Mary arrived with Joseph, the man to whom she was engaged. But they found there was no room for them in the inn; nobody would vacate their room—this is sheer selfishness. We understand that this was because people did not realize what was happening. Nobody knew about the visitation of the archangel to Mary. People did not know that the baby who was to be born had been described by the archangel as "that holy thing which shall be born of thee" (Luke 1:35). To them, Mary was just a pregnant woman, and they were not concerned; they cared only about their own happiness.

And that is still a picture of the state of the world. It was a troubled world then—Palestine had been conquered by the Romans; they had to pay these taxes; there were troubles and problems and difficulties. A kind of credit squeeze obtained even then, and there was much dissatisfaction, much unhappiness. The world then, as now, was a world of war, suffering, pain, and sorrow, and it did not realize that someone was at that moment entering the world who alone could really deal with all these problems.

And the tragedy is that the world still does not realize it. A general lip service is paid to this time of the year, but the whole significance of this momentous event is not realized, is not grasped.

What I now want to consider with you is the cause of all this trouble, and I will do so in the light of this statement made here in John 4 in connection with the meeting of our Lord and the woman of Samaria. They meet by the side of a well. He is tired, so he has not gone with his disciples into the town to buy provisions. As he sits there in his weariness, this woman comes to draw water, as she regularly does, and he asks her for a drink. We have been considering their conversation and have now reached the dramatic point where our Lord tells the woman that "God is a Spirit: and they that worship him must worship him in spirit and in truth," to which she replies, "I know that Messias cometh, which is called Christ: when he is come, he will tell us all things." And our Lord says, "I that speak unto thee am he."

Now it seems to me there are great lessons here for all of us on this Christmas morning. The first is this: the inexcusableness of our failure to recognize him. What do I mean by that? Well, this woman illustrates it so well. She says that the Messiah is coming and will tell them "all things." She means, of course, that though the Samaritans only had the first five books of the Bible, the five books of Moses, and did not have the books of the Prophets and the Psalms and so on, nevertheless, even among the Samaritans there was this glimmering of a knowledge of the Deliverer, the Messiah, the Savior who was to come. So they were looking forward to him as the one who would solve all their problems. In the case of the Jews, this was, of course, still more clear because of the additional knowledge that they had from the prophets and others. The whole Jewish nation was looking forward to the coming of this great Messiah, and that is what makes their treatment of him utterly inexcusable. It is astounding that though he had been foretold, and foretold in detail right through the Old Testament—the very literature in which they gloried—when he actually came, the Pharisees and scribes, the religious leaders, the politicians, the Herodians, and others did not recognize him.

One of the most astonishing things that has ever happened in the whole course of human history is that the Jews failed to recognize their own expected Messiah. John has summed it up for us in the Prologue of his Gospel where he says, "He came unto his own, and his own received him not" (1:11). So here is the question that confronts us: why did his own people fail to recognize him in spite of the knowledge that they had and in spite of the fact that they were looking forward to the Messiah's coming? Unfortunately, the answer is not difficult to discover. The real explanation was their false understanding with respect to the Messiah. It is not enough that we should expect a deliverer; what is most important is that our ideas concerning him should be accurate.

Now the trouble with the Jews was that their notion of the Messiah was of a political or military leader. They were expecting a great king; so they were assuming that he would be born in some grand palace. They were looking for something extraordinary and unusual to announce his coming. But it had to be their idea of what was unusual, and they were expecting his actions to be primarily political and military in character. So when a baby was born in a stable, they did not understand; they had not anticipated this poverty, this lowliness. It did not fit in with their whole idea of greatness and bigness and national glory.

The Jews' trouble was that they were nationalistic in their outlook, as the nations of the world still are. This is one cause of all our troubles. They were consumed with national pride, and so they had a picture of the Messiah that was completely different from the reality. Of course, this idea of a Messiah being born in a stable and placed in a manger was monstrous; it was just rubbish and folly. So they dismissed it.

And then when this baby grew up and began to preach at the age of thirty, they were still offended. Why? Because he had not been trained as a Pharisee or as a doctor of the law. He had been working as a carpenter. He was an artisan, one who worked with his hands. They said, "Who is this fellow?" "How knoweth this man letters, having never learned?" (John 7:15). It was quite ridiculous that a peasant carpenter should stand up and claim to be an authoritative teacher. I am showing you that it is no use saying, "I know that Messias cometh" if your whole idea of what he is going to be like when he comes is completely wrong. That was the trouble then, and it is still the trouble today.

But we must take this a step further. Why did the Jews have this false idea of the Messiah? The answer to this is interesting and most important. They would have had no idea of a Messiah at all, and they would not have been expecting a Messiah, but for their Scriptures, but for their tradition. That is where the idea came from. And yet though they had the Scriptures, they were entirely wrong in their view of the Messiah. The reason was that they had not studied their Scriptures as they should have and did not believe their Scriptures. If they had only done that, they would not have gone wrong, for the astounding fact about these Old Testament Scriptures is that they not only said that a Messiah was going to come, they gave explicit details about his coming and about him. For instance, the prophecy of Micah actually says that he would be born in Bethlehem—the exact place is named. But the Jews thought that the Messiah would be born in Jerusalem, the capital city. All great things had to happen in the capital, not in a little place like Bethlehem. But if they had only read and understood their Scriptures, they would not have gone so wrong.

Then in the book of the prophet Daniel, the exact time of the Messiah's birth is prophesied. The fact that he was to be born of a virgin was prophesied by Isaiah. His poverty was prophesied as well. Jews were not aware of the facts. They took the idea of a Messiah; then they thought about it in their own terms instead of working it out and accepting it in detail as it had been expounded and unfolded in their Scriptures. Now this is a most important principle because this is still the explanation of why people do not believe in him and do not realize who he is and the significance of his coming. This in a sense is the tragedy of the whole human race. The problem is that we will not face the facts. We take ideas from the Scriptures and then we manipulate them according to our own concepts and our own philosophies. There is a lot of talk about Christianity, a lot of talk about Christian principles, but so much of it has nothing to do with what we read in the Bible. People have taken what they regard as a Christian idea and clothed it in their own language, in their own thought forms, and in the end it has no contact whatsoever with the details, the facts, that we are given in the Bible.

Many people think they know what Christianity is, but they often say, "Of course, I don't believe all that!" They do not believe in the virgin birth, they do not believe in our Lord's miraculous powers, they do not believe in his atoning death or in his literal, physical resurrection and his ascension and so on. You often hear that on television and on radio; you often read it in the newspapers. They say they like the Christian idea, the Christian teaching about love and so on. But that is to repeat the very error of the Jews and the Samaritans. He must be taken as he is, and the tragedy is that people do *not* look at him as he is. They do not read their Scriptures, the whole story about this person from his very birth right on until his death and after that his resurrection and ascension. If only the world faced these facts!

Who is this person who has even changed our calendars, changed our observance of weeks coming one after another? Who is this person who has left an impact on the whole of human history in a way that nobody else has done? How do you explain him? I suggest there is only one adequate explanation, and that is the facts as they are given to us in the Bible. That is why it is right and good for us to remember his birth in the stable and everything else that follows. If only the world faced this and accepted the whole course of the history of the Christian church! You cannot explain it away. Read the whole story of the last two thousand years. You cannot explain the church herself except in supernatural terms.

The world is always expecting to get better. Humanity still foolishly believes that it can put itself in order. It has always believed that. That is what is meant by *civilization*. And yet we see our world in utter trouble today. If only the world would pay attention to the teaching and prophecies of and about Jesus! They think he taught that war was going to be banished and that the world was going to get better and better. But he said the exact opposite. He said there would always be "wars and rumours of wars" (Matt. 24:6). He said, "As it was in the days of Noe [Noah], so shall it be also in the days of the Son of man" (Luke 17:26). He said that at the end of the world life would be very similar to life before the Flood and before Sodom and Gomorrah—"they did eat, they drank, they bought, they sold, they planted, they builded . . ." (Luke 17:28). This person, the babe of Bethlehem grown to be a man and a preacher and a teacher, prophesied that the world would not remain as it was then but would get worse, and toward the end it would be terrible, and nothing but his coming back again into it could deal with the situation, solve the problems, and restore peace and order to the entire cosmos. But the world, instead of taking him as he is, instead of believing the facts, repeats the error of the Jews and the Samaritans, taking out one idea and then manipulating it to suit its own fancy.

So the story of this woman of Samaria has a great deal to tell us today. "I know that Messias cometh." Yes, but the question is, what do you really know? Have you accepted the statements in detail concerning this Messiah who is to come?

But that leads me to another principle, and this, of course, follows directly. There must therefore be something wrong with humanity, and the Bible tells us that there is: we are all blind, spiritually blind. And so my next principle is that he can only be known as he reveals himself to us. Here is this woman of Samaria, obviously an able woman, though she lives, poor woman, such an immoral life—five husbands previously and now living with a man who is not her husband. But she is interested, and she is concerned, and our Lord speaks to her, reasons with her, leads her on, and brings her to the point when she says, "I know that Messias cometh." She says that to him! She does not recognize him. And our Lord looks at her and says, "I that speak unto thee am he." That is, "I am the very one you are talking about. You say you are expecting the Messiah and that when he comes he will teach all things. Don't you realize that I am he?" "Look at me again," he seems to say. "I am he!" He manifests himself to her.

We cannot recognize him unless he is revealed to us. The apostle Paul puts this clearly to the Corinthians:

> But we speak the wisdom of God in a mystery, even the hidden wisdom, which God ordained before the world unto our glory. Which none of the princes of this world knew: for had they known it, they would not have crucified the Lord of glory. But as it is written, Eye hath not seen, nor ear heard, neither have entered into the heart of man, the things which God hath prepared for them that love him. But God hath revealed them unto us by his Spirit: for the Spirit searcheth all things, yea, the deep things of God. (1 Cor. 2:7–10)

But our Lord himself had said this still more plainly:

> At that time Jesus answered and said, I thank thee, O Father, Lord of heaven and earth, because thou hast hid these things from the wise and prudent, and hast revealed them unto babes. Even so, Father: for so it seemed good in thy sight. All things are delivered unto me of my Father: and no man knoweth the Son, but the Father; neither knoweth any man the Father, save the Son, and he to whomsoever the Son will reveal him. (Matt. 11:25–27)

Now what could be plainer or clearer than this? In other words, the principle is that as the result of the Fall and of sin we have become such that we cannot recognize the Messiah, we cannot recognize our Savior. As the princes of this world did not know him and crucified him as an impostor and a blasphemer, so the world still does not know him, and the teaching is that the world cannot know him—he has to be revealed to us. And the wonderful thing is that he reveals himself to the woman of Samaria. She sees it at once, and she leaves her waterpot and runs back to the city to say, "Come, see a man, which told me all things that ever I did: is not this the Christ?"

As you read the story about his birth, you will find that right from the very beginning a revelation was needed. Even Mary, his own mother, did not understand. Read the first chapter of Luke's Gospel, and you will see that Mary fumbled and stumbled though an archangel was revealing the truth to her. Even after his birth she did not fully understand. The Scriptures record all this. She kept on stumbling because of the things he did and the things he would not do.

And in that wonderful second chapter of Luke's Gospel, we see how this selfsame point comes out. Look at the shepherds: why did they go to Bethlehem, and why did they become believers? The answer is that they were given a revelation. An angel had said to them, "Fear not: for, behold, I bring you good tidings of great joy, which shall be to all people. For unto you is born this day in the city of David a Saviour, which is Christ the Lord" (Luke 2:10–11). A revelation! So they said, "Let us now go even unto Bethlehem, and see this thing which is come to pass, which the Lord hath made known unto us" (Luke 2:15). And they hurried to Bethlehem where they saw everything exactly as the angel had reported it to them. The shepherds would never have recognized him but for the fact that they were given this revelation, this understanding.

The same is true of ancient Simeon, who holds the baby in his arms and says, "Lord, now lettest thou thy servant depart in peace" (Luke 2:29), and of Anna, the prophetess. Then later on, when this babe has grown up and is in his public ministry, he puts the question to the disciples at Caesarea Philippi: "Whom do men say that I the Son of man am?" They give the various answers. Then he says, "But whom say ye that I am?" Peter says, "Thou art the Christ, the Son of the living God." Then notice what our Lord says to him: "Blessed art thou, Simon Bar-jona: for flesh and blood hath not revealed this unto thee, but my Father which is in heaven" (Matt. 16:13–17). Flesh and blood! Human ability! Human intellect! Philosophies! They do not recognize him! They did not when he was here; they have never done so since. We reject him; we are blinded by sin.

God sometimes gives this revelation directly, in the way I have shown you, and as our Lord himself did here with this woman. Our Lord revealed who he was in his teaching, in the things he claimed for himself. "Ye have heard that it was said by them of old time . . . but I say unto you" (Matt. 5:27–28). "Before Abraham was, I am" (John 8:58). All this great teaching that we have been considering—"I am the light of the world"; "I am the bread of life"; "I am the way, the truth, and the life: no man cometh unto the Father but by me"—it was all revelation!

But perhaps one of the most interesting examples of all happened even after his death and resurrection. I am referring to the famous story of the two men going down from Jerusalem to Emmaus. Their leader has been killed and laid in a tomb, and they are utterly disconsolate. A stranger suddenly joins them and says, "What are you talking about?"

They say, "Haven't you heard? Jesus of Nazareth . . ."

"What about him?" he asks.

And they tell him—they do not recognize him. This is the risen Christ, the risen Lord, and he is talking to the two men. He goes on to give them instruction from the Old Testament; still they cannot recognize him. And then they get a bit tired, and they say, "Come into the house with us and have something to eat." And he goes in and takes bread, and he breaks it, and as he does, their eyes are opened. He does that deliberately. He is manifesting himself, telling them in this acted parable, "Don't you realize who I am? I am he." Their eyes are opened. Their hearts were warmed by him even when they did not know him, but now he gives this positive revelation.

And since then our Lord has been revealing himself by the Holy Spirit to all who have become Christians. If you are a Christian, do not take any credit to yourself—you have had the revelation given to you. The scales have been taken from your eyes; your eyes have been opened. Notice how Paul puts it in 1 Corinthians 2:10. The princes of this world did not know him, "but God hath revealed them [these things] unto us by his Spirit: for the Spirit searcheth all things, yea, the deep things of God." No man or woman can be a Christian unless the Spirit opens his or her eyes and gives him or her the revelation and the understanding. The Holy Spirit has been sent in order to do this. Our Lord said, "He shall glorify me" (John 16:14).

When our Lord was here in the flesh, he could say, as he said to the woman, "I am he." But he has gone, he is out of sight, but he has sent the Spirit, this "other Comforter." And the Spirit deals with us, he opens our eyes, he gives us understanding, he shows us our own need and the fullness that is in him, and we hear him whispering, "Here he is; this is he." As God during the days of his flesh spoke in a voice from heaven, saying, "This is my beloved Son, in whom I am well pleased; hear ye him" (Matt. 17:5), so the Spirit speaks within, whispers, tells us, "This Jesus is the Christ, the Savior, the Messiah you are looking for." And he can only be known as the result of this revelation. So I am not surprised that the world in general is rejecting him today. It is because of the blindness of sin. It is terrible that men and women do not recognize God's Son! He must reveal himself.

What does he reveal? Well, it is all here in this passage. He reveals the fact that he is the Messiah, the Savior. "Christ is all, and in all" (Col. 3:11). The woman has said to him, "Sir, I perceive that thou art a prophet." She now says, "We are looking for the Messiah," and he says, "I am he." So what is he?

In Old Testament history some people were prophets, some were priests, some were kings—always three different groups of people. But here is one who is himself Prophet, Priest, and King. No one person is big enough to represent him, so you have to divide up his offices. He is "all, and in all." He is everything. Why, he is even the offering that the priest offers! He is "the Lamb of God, which taketh away the sin of the world" (John 1:29). That is what he reveals. He is the fulfillment of all God's promises; he gives the satisfaction that we all need; he is everything, "the beginning and the ending," the first and the last (Rev. 1:8). He is "wisdom, and righteousness, and sanctification, and redemption" (1 Cor. 1:30). That is what he reveals.

But he also reveals something else—he reveals the love of God. Why was he in this world at all? Why was that babe ever born? There is only one answer: "God so loved the world, that he gave his only begotten Son, that whosoever believeth in him should not perish, but have everlasting life" (John 3:16). He reveals the love of God in spite of our unworthiness. He says in essence, "I am the one whom God has promised to send to deliver you."

The birth of this babe of Bethlehem is the proof of the fact that all God's promises are sure and will be honored; yes, he is the guarantee of the prophecies and the promises running through the whole of the Old Testament. "I am he." Whatever God promises, he always performs.

For his mercies ay endure;
Ever faithful, ever sure.

JOHN MILTON

Read the Bible; get ahold of the promises of God. Believe them! They are sure.

But let me end on this note: what always moves me so deeply as I read this particular story of our Lord's meeting with the woman of Samaria is his readiness to reveal himself. Look at this amazing story. Here he is, the Son of God, the Savior of the world, the long-promised Messiah. The Pharisees, the scribes, the Herodians, the philosophers do not recognize him, but he reveals himself—to whom? To this woman of Samaria, a woman living in adultery, a woman living in sin; and to the shepherds by the angels and the heavenly choir.

What is the lesson? It is this: today he again brings into this world hope for all. Not merely for intellectuals, for great and learned people. It is the exact opposite. He has not come merely for the sake of good people, religious people, moral people, Pharisees and scribes. No, no! He says himself, "I am not come to call the righteous, but sinners to repentance" (Matt. 9:13). There is hope for the woman of Samaria living in sin, in squalor, in evil—it is to her he gives this blessed word of hope! He is the opposite of Pharisaism; he is the opposite of self-righteousness: "They that be whole," he says, "need not a physician, but they that are sick" (Matt. 9:12).

The apostle Paul reminds the Corinthians:

> Ye see your calling, brethren, how that not many wise men after the flesh, not many mighty, not many noble, are called: but God hath chosen the foolish things of the world to confound the wise; and God hath chosen the weak things of the world to confound the things which are mighty; and base things of the world, and things which are despised, hath God chosen, yea, and things which are not, to bring to nought things that are. (1 Cor. 1:26–28)

What a blessed thought! What a hope he has brought into the world! There is no one too bad to be saved and redeemed; he has hope for all. Indeed, all he requires of us is what he required of the woman of Samaria. What is that? Honesty! When he challenges her about her life, she does not deny it, she admits it. Honesty! He always asks for readiness to admit the truth about ourselves, however unpleasant it may be. And then readiness to listen to him, and readiness to believe what he says.

So the one question for every one of us is this: has he revealed himself to you? Has he in some manner, some shape or form, said to you, "I am he"? "I am the one you need. I am the one you have been expecting. You have some dim, vague, uncertain notions: look at me again—I am he. I have come into the world for you, that you might be forgiven, that you might be born again, have a new nature, a new heart, start living a new life. I am the one who has come to do for you what you could not do for yourself, what the whole world could not do for you. I am the one whom God in his love has sent that you might have life, which is life indeed."

All that he demands is that we recognize our need, that we stop defending ourselves, that in honesty we admit our failure, our need, then listen to him and to all he tells us. When we believe and give ourselves to him, he will give us life, life more abundant, life that is life indeed. He came into the world that we might have life. Here, again, is the question: has he revealed himself to you? Have you heard him whispering, "I am he"?

13

The Gift of God

Jesus answered and said unto her, If thou knewest the gift of God, and who it is that saith to thee, Give me to drink; thou wouldest have asked of him, and he would have given thee living water. . . . Whosoever drinketh of this water shall thirst again: but whosoever drinketh of the water that I shall give him shall never thirst; but the water that I shall give him shall be in him a well of water springing up into everlasting life. (John 4:10, 13–14)

Here in John 4, we are confronted, let me remind you, by the great and amazing offer that the gospel makes to all people, an offer of a new life beyond everything that we could ever have thought of or even imagined. So once again I ask, do we know this new life? Have we experienced it? Indeed, I want to lead you into a further consideration of that very subject. We have been looking at many of the hindrances that stand between people and the realization of that life. And we have seen that the essential need, above everything else, is to understand who our Lord is. This is the most profound question we can ever face. "Jesus saith unto her, I that speak unto thee am he." Without the realization of who he is, there is no hope whatsoever; any uncertainty about the person of our blessed Lord and Savior makes it quite impossible for us to receive this life, this blessing that he has come to give.

But we have still not finished with the subject. These, in a sense, are but the essential preliminaries. There is so much that has to be cleared away. We think we are Christians, we think we have "religion," we think we know how to worship, we think we know about God, and we have to be put right about all these ideas. And that can happen, but we can be put right intellectually and yet still not know and experience this great salvation as it is put before us here in the words of our blessed Lord himself.

So we must come still more directly face-to-face with this great statement, and that is what I am anxious to do now.

It may be that at the beginning of a new year like this,[13] it is good and appropriate for us to consider this very subject. The new year is a time for us to take stock, to examine ourselves. We are encouraged to do that in the Scriptures. The apostle Paul says to the Corinthians, "Examine yourselves [prove yourselves], whether ye be in the faith" (2 Cor. 13:5), and there is no better way of doing that than by looking at a great statement such as the one we are now studying and again asking ourselves the question, are we possessors of this life about which our Lord speaks in the glowing words found in John 4:10–14? Do we possess this living water? If not, why not? Now here we stand directly facing this most crucial question, and all I want to do is to show you again some of the absolute essentials with respect to this whole matter.

Here is the first. We must realize our true need. I emphasize the word *true* because we are all conscious of many needs, we all have many desires. Nobody is perfectly satisfied; something is always lacking.

Since every man who lives is born to die,
And none can boast sincere felicity . . .

JOHN DRYDEN

That is it. The poet puts it quite clearly. Nobody has known "sincere felicity," by which he means unmixed joy. There is no complete satisfaction. Everybody in the world is aware of some need or other, and that, in a sense, is the greatest danger of all because these other needs often hide from us the true need, the basic need. I suppose that in many senses this is one of the great problems confronting the preaching of the gospel. Humanity is aware of many, many needs and yet the whole time is not aware of the true, the fundamental, the real need at the center. A very real danger, therefore, that confronts us all is the danger of just going on living day by day, year after year, taking life as it comes with its ups and its downs, coming to the conclusion that life always will and must be like that and that therefore we can do nothing better than just put up with it, reconcile ourselves to it, and make the best of it, extracting out of it as much happiness and joy and satisfaction as we can as we go along.

Now that is, I say, a great danger confronting every human being in this world, and it is also a danger that confronts those of us who have become Christians. So that is why it is essential that we stop and think and examine ourselves. And the kind of way in which we can prepare ourselves for this great offer, the way in which we can discover our true and basic need, is to ask questions such as this: On what are we actually living? By what are we living? On what do we really depend?

Now it is extraordinary that one has to put forward questions such as those, and yet I think you will all agree that these are the questions that really matter, because unconsciously we can be depending on quite a number of things instead of upon our Lord and Savior. Many dangers confront us; we all must examine ourselves at this point. I wonder, are we kept going by our own activities, by the various things that we have to do? This is a question that every one of us should face. I must face it as I stand in the pulpit. Am I living on my own activities? Am I living on my own preaching? I ask this question because it has been my lot in life more than once to visit men who have spent a lifetime in the ministry, preaching and teaching others, but who, because of ill health or old age, could do so no longer. I have often found such men in a state of depression, and there has been only one explanation for this. Unconsciously, they had been living on their own activities instead of living on the Lord. You can live on your preaching about the Lord instead of on the Lord himself.

Now this applies, I repeat, to all of us. The very routine of life sustains many people; they go on because they have to. Certain things must be done, and if they are not done, everything will end in chaos. So they are kept going by the demands, the needs, the necessities of life. And very often when, for various reasons such as illness or accident, they have to stop, they suddenly find that they have nothing to rest upon. Others are kept going by things that happen to them, by events and by circumstances, and so, centrally, they have nothing on which they can depend and on which they live, nothing that ultimately sustains them. So I repeat that question: What keeps you going? On what are you living? On what do you depend? What is the mainspring of your life?

Or, to put this question in a slightly different form, do you have a central rest in your life, a place of quiet, a place into which you can always retreat? Amid all the multifarious activities of life and of business, is there a place at the center where you can always go, where you know that you will have peace and quiet, where you delight to go because it gives you ultimate rest for your soul?

I suppose this is the question of questions for a busy, bustling age such as this present one, which is kept going so much by its own works and entertainment. The trouble today is that people lack tranquillity, they lack a quiet soul, a quiet heart, a peaceful, restful heart. And we, as Christians, must ask ourselves this very question because the mere fact that we are Christians does not in itself guarantee that we automatically have this place of rest within us.

Let me ask another question, therefore, that I think will help make it still more plain and clear: what is the exact difference between us as Christians and the best type of unbeliever? There are people in the world today who are not believers, they deny the Christian faith, but they are good, moral people. They are men and women of ability and understanding; they are thinkers. They realize the futility of depending upon drink and drugs and pleasure; they are people who have faced life, who have come to certain conclusions and have a working philosophy, and they keep going on that. What is the exact difference between you and such a person? Is there a vital, essential difference?

Or, to put it still more directly, what does the Lord Jesus Christ himself really mean to us? That is, ultimately, the only question that matters. We say we believe in him, that we have accepted his statement, "I that speak unto thee am he." Very well, we have correct intellectual views concerning who he is. But that still leaves the vital question that we must face: where exactly does he fit in our lives, in our whole thinking and in our whole being? We shall never know him truly, and we shall never know this experience that he himself here describes to the woman of Samaria, until we realize our deepest need, which is this ultimate rest of the soul, the final peace and quiet and confidence and assurance, the ability to stand in the midst of life with all that is happening and all that may happen and know exactly where we are because of our relationship to him.

So this is our fundamental need. Our Lord presses it upon this woman in these words: "If thou knewest the gift of God, and who it is that speaketh to thee . . ." That was her trouble. She was aware of many problems and many difficulties—that follows of necessity from the kind of life that she was leading, as we have been seeing—but she still did not know her real need. And that is the whole trouble with the world today. It does not know its central need. It says, "If only we could have this or that . . . If only this stopped, or if that did not take place." But that is not the answer. There is this ultimate, central need of the soul, and until we are aware of that, we shall never come to a true understanding of this great offer that is made by the gospel.

That, then, is the first principle, and now we move on to the second, which is this: we must realize also that this is a need that, even at its best and highest, the world can never satisfy. These are the steps through which the saints of the centuries have always passed in coming to this ultimate blessing of the Christian life, this place of peace and of quiet that nothing can disturb. Our Lord says, "Whosoever drinketh of this water shall thirst again." Now this is a specific statement, and it is very important. He is referring, of course, primarily to that actual physical well. He is speaking in parables to the woman, leading her to the spiritual truth and significance of what he is saying, and we must do the same.

Now we need to be reminded of this second principle because the devil is always tempting us, even as Christians, to find our satisfaction outside the Lord and apart from him. Our Lord himself often warns us against this very danger. It is the kind of warning that he gives to his own followers, to his own people, not to those who are outside. He says:

> And take heed to yourselves, lest at any time your hearts be overcharged with surfeiting, and drunkenness, and cares of this life, and so that day come upon you unawares. For as a snare shall it come on all them that dwell on the face of the whole earth. Watch ye therefore, and pray always, that ye may be accounted worthy to escape all these things that shall come to pass, and to stand before the Son of man. (Luke 21:34–36)

Our Lord is saying that the cares of this life, and even things that are worse, can so keep us from considering him and the state of our souls that when the crisis arrives, we suddenly find that we have nothing. The New Testament is full of warnings such as this. There is the Parable of the Ten Virgins, the five wise and the five foolish. The foolish virgins think they are all right, they think all is well, they are not aware that there is any difference between them and the other virgins, and yet when the crisis comes, they suddenly find that they have nothing at all (Matt. 25:1–13). It is this kind of negligence, this tendency to find satisfaction elsewhere, that stands between us and the receiving of this great blessing that our Lord offers.

Then we read, too, what the apostle Paul has to say about Demas. Demas was a Christian, one of the apostle Paul's helpers, but Paul wrote to Timothy, "Demas hath forsaken me, having loved this present world" (2 Tim. 4:10).

Now the danger that I am trying to indicate is that of having our Christian faith as just a compartment in our lives. Oh, yes, we believe in the Lord Jesus Christ as the Son of God, we believe that we need salvation, forgiveness, and reconciliation to God, and we are Christians. We have settled that, we say; we have become Christians. But we go on living the remainder of our lives and perhaps the bulk of our lives in terms of the things that the world has to offer us. Our faith is merely something to which we return periodically. But that is a complete misunderstanding of the Christian faith. It is not merely meant to have a place in our lives—it is meant to have the central place. Now I am not talking about evil things but about the danger of living on the world even at its best. We have this little compartment that is Christian, but the rest is taken up with philosophy, politics, art, and culture. And so often we are really living on these instead of on our Christian faith.

This is a very basic point, which our Lord makes quite plain: "Whosoever drinketh of this water shall thirst again." There is no final satisfaction there. And, of course, this applies not only to the activities and interests that I have mentioned, it applies even to our family and certain relationships in life. It is possible for you to be a Christian and yet really to be living on your family, relying on the love of your family, on the relationships in the family, the life of the family. I think this danger must be plain to all of us. It is of all these things, even at their very best, that our Lord said, "Whosoever drinketh of this water shall thirst again."

Now why does he say that? On what grounds is that true? We will never know this "well of water springing up into everlasting life" until we are perfectly clear about the insufficiency of everything else in the world even at its highest. Why is this of necessity true? Well, the answers that our Lord is obviously suggesting are these. First, all these only give us temporary relief. "Whosoever drinketh of this water shall thirst again." You take a drink of this water, and it satisfies your thirst, so you say, "This is fine, this is good! I'm satisfied." But our Lord says, "No, you are not, because this is only a temporary slaking of your thirst; it is only a temporary satisfaction."

And this is true of everything that the world has to offer. The world's pleasures give immediate satisfaction, but they are not able to do anything beyond that. They will for the time being help you, perhaps, to forget your troubles and your problems. The world knows this. It is the secret of pleasure—pleasure as a business. It succeeds because the people who run such businesses know perfectly well that we are only going to get temporary relief. While you are looking at that movie, you forget your troubles, your mind is directed away from them, and you are happy. But then the film ends, and you are left alone—and back comes your problem. All the very best that the world can give us can only bring us temporary relief.

But beyond that, the world can never give us real satisfaction for the whole of our being. It is not merely that the relief is temporary, it is that it is never fully satisfying. Many things in the world give us intellectual satisfaction. Some people find peace and quiet and rest by their study of philosophy and systems of thought. And while they are engaged in these questions, of course, they are all right. Some people turn to crossword puzzles or other word and number games—these are all escape mechanisms that take your mind off the problem, off the matter that is difficult and harassing. But they only deal with one part of you; they only deal with your mind. They do not touch your heart; they do not give you satisfaction down in the depths where your feelings are engaged and involved.

But there are other interests that deal with the heart only and have nothing to give to the mind. They can move us emotionally, sentimentally, and so on, and again they give us a temporary sense of satisfaction. Now I am not here to denounce these. All I am saying is that the mistake, the tragedy, is that men and women tend to live on these things. Music can be wonderful! "Music hath charms to soothe the savage breast," and it soothes many others as well. We should thank God for cultural pursuits and interests that are produced by human ability. There is nothing wrong in them. But if you depend upon them, if you are living on them, if these are what keep you going, you are missing the great solution itself, and that is the whole tragedy. These never give complete satisfaction. They are only partial, even at their best. They never deal with the whole problem because they never deal with the whole self.

And here is the central message. The real problem is the problem of self. A human being is not merely an intellect or a heart or an acting machine. There is a wholeness about life. It is very difficult to put this into words, and yet we all know it. "I am"—and the totality of my personality is the problem. Unless these interests and pleasures can satisfy me as a whole, then finally they are like this well of water to which our Lord pointed and said that when we drink its water we shall thirst again. We are individuals, we are entities, and inevitably we come face-to-face with our self at various points—when we have exhausted what the world can give us or when, because of our physical condition perhaps, we are no longer able to pursue these interests and to live on them. And then we are left alone.

And here is the whole problem of life; it is depicted in many pictures in the Bible itself. One of the greatest, one of the most moving of all, is the case of Jacob on that famous night when he knew he had to meet his brother Esau the next morning. He had done well; he had prospered. He had his wives and his children; he had his cattle, his herds, and his sheep. He had gone out as a fugitive, as an isolated individual, but now he was coming back to his homeland a very wealthy man. And yet the problem remained: he had to meet Esau whom he had wronged. And then we read the tremendous story of what happened to him that night. He had sent all his cattle and his sheep and his goods on ahead, and then he had sent on his wives and his children. Then there is this tremendous statement in the Scripture—"And Jacob was left alone" (Gen. 32:24).

And there was the problem. It was the greatest crisis of his life, and it led to the greatest blessing. But he had to be brought to that point. His danger was that of living on the goods, the possessions, the animals, the wives, the children, the family life. But he suddenly realized that he was alone, Jacob the individual, the entity. Though he owned all this, now he was back where he was when he had run away from the anger of his brother on that old occasion. "Jacob was left alone." And every one of us is left alone. There is that about every one of us that makes us alone, as Jacob was on that occasion, and we experience this from time to time. Then we know that all that we have and all that the world has given us, or can ever give us, can never deal with this problem of the self—I myself, my whole life, my future. Here I am; I stand alone. "Jacob was left alone." And it is because of this that these other things even at their best can never give us a true and a real satisfaction. "Whosoever drinketh of this water shall thirst again."

Now why is this the case? Well, this is the great message of the whole Bible. This is so because of the nature of man, because we are what we are. There is something tremendous about who we are, something that makes us all thank God for the fact that the world cannot satisfy us. Even if it gave us everything, if it gave us itself, it could not satisfy us. "For what shall it profit a man, if he shall gain the whole world, and lose his own soul?"(Mark 8:36). Yes, that is it. Man is bigger than the universe. He is bigger than mountains; he is bigger than seas; he is bigger than everything that creation can produce. He is made in the image and likeness of God—he is made for God; so he is too big for the world, and the world cannot satisfy him. He has a soul within him, and that soul can be satisfied by nothing less than God himself and communion with God. It is in our realization of this need that we come to a true understanding of ourselves, our nature, our true being. This is painful at first, but once you see it correctly, you will realize that it is the greatest fact about you. You are so big that all the world has to offer can never give you final satisfaction. The very nature of men and women made in the image and likeness of God makes this inevitable.

But on top of this, there is the whole fact of sin—sin in our nature, sin in our acts—and this aggravates the problem. The prophet Isaiah says, "The wicked are like the troubled sea, when it cannot rest" (Isa. 57:20), and that is why the world is restless. The world does not know the truth about itself, and it is trying to find its satisfaction where it can never find it, so it is restless, left to itself, unhappy, rushing from activity to activity to solace itself, and only ever finding temporary satisfaction. There is this motion, this constant trouble, this seeking for something it cannot find. This is the whole story of the human race.

And then, of course, there is the sense of guilt and the sense of shame and the sense of failure. There is no rest while these remain; there is no philosophy that can satisfy a troubled conscience. That is why the world at its best cannot ultimately satisfy me. My mind can be interested, my heart may be moved, but again I am left with the problem of myself. I forgot it while I was enjoying that symphony or whatever, but it has ended, and I am alone again. I lie on my bed, I am alone, and back it comes—myself. And I am aware within me of this struggle with the flesh: "For the flesh lusteth against the Spirit, and the Spirit against the flesh" (Gal. 5:17). That is why human beings are restless, and that is why it is true to say that the world, with all that it has to offer, can never satisfy our need.

"Whosoever drinketh of this water shall thirst again," and it is at this point, my dear Christian friends, that we see the real failure of humanism and the so-called "good pagan." Humanism is popular today; people are rejecting this gospel in terms of humanism. Of course, the humanist is an intellectual, and he is interested in intellectual gymnastics, in thought, but the day will come when he will be incapable of doing that, and he will be left to himself. He has to turn to other things, to stimulants, to drink and to drugs. It is just here at the center of his life that he fails most of all. You cannot live on your interests, you cannot live on your abilities, because they are all bound to come to an end, and in any case they never give you complete satisfaction, as we have seen.

So we have come to an absolute, essential principle in connection with this whole great teaching. Not only must I realize my need, I must realize that it is a need that the universe cannot satisfy. If I could possess the whole world, it would not satisfy me. There is that within me that cries out for the living God himself. That is my way of saying what Augustine said perfectly: "Thou hast made us for thyself, and our hearts are restless until they find their rest in thee." And this is true of every one of us. You all know this. If you could find rest and peace, you would have found it, but you cannot in and of yourself. Augustine has given us the reason.

Are you clear about this? Are you clear that the world in its entirety cannot satisfy you, that this need of yours is a need beyond the scope and the ability of human beings at their very highest?

And that leads me to my third and last principle. Our Lord points out that we must realize the possibilities of the Christian life. The mere fact that you are a Christian does not mean that you know these possibilities. It is because Christians do not know them that the epistles in the New Testament were all written; that is why they became necessary. If the moment people became Christians they suddenly understood and possessed all the teaching, they would not have needed these epistles with their great instruction. We need to be instructed, and our Lord instructs this woman of Samaria at this point. He puts it in these words: "If thou knewest the gift of God"—if only you knew! But she did not know, and I feel that is his word to us at the beginning of this new year. Christian people, at the present time we are in danger of limiting this gospel, in danger of reducing these glorious statements to the level of our own little experience. My dear people, we are only at the beginning of these things; we are but as children paddling at the edge of an ocean. Launch out into the deep! "If thou knewest" the depth of what is offered in the glorious gospel!

"If thou knewest the gift of God." What does our Lord mean by that? Some expositors say that he is referring to himself there. "God so loved the world, that he gave his only begotten Son" (John 3:16). I reject that explanation because he immediately goes on to refer to himself—"If thou knewest the gift of God, and who it is that saith to thee . . ." So what is the gift of God?

God's gift is everything that God has made possible for us in and through the Lord Jesus Christ. God has treasured and stored up in him all the riches of his wisdom and his grace and his knowledge. It is all the blessings that come to us through Christ, the Son of God. This is not merely a matter of being forgiven or of making a decision and becoming a Christian and a member of the church. It includes that, but that is the mere beginning, that is merely entering into the life, and the danger is that so many people stop at that. They are always looking back to something they once did, to a decision once made. They say, "I became a Christian," and from there on they have never grown, they have never developed; they know nothing about all that our Lord is referring to here. They have reduced Christian grace and the gospel to just this matter of having our sins forgiven and becoming Christians, to not doing certain things, while going on living the humdrum, inadequate kind of life that I have been describing.

That is not it. This is the biggest thing in the universe, this is the most glorious life, and our Lord says to the woman, "If thou knewest the gift of God." It is a gift from God; it is all of God; it is of God from the beginning to the end. "The wages of sin is death; but the gift of God is eternal life through Jesus Christ our Lord" (Rom. 6:23). Christianity does not just mean that you live on your own activities, even on your own goodness or your own striving. Of course, we must seek goodness, we must strive, but the essence is that God *gives* this. "If thou knewest the gift of God."

The apostle Paul puts it in this way: "the exceeding riches of his grace" (Eph. 2:7). And he says that he is privileged to "preach among the Gentiles the unsearchable riches of Christ" (Eph. 3:8). Do you know them? Do you possess them? Are you rejoicing in them? Are you thrilled by them? This is what we need to face. "If only you knew," says our Lord to this woman. So I say this to myself, and I say it to you—do you know "the unsearchable riches of Christ"? Or are you a pauper? Are you living a life of stress and strain and unhappiness? If you are, your life is not compatible with what you believe. If there is no rest, no peace or joy, it is because you do not know the gift of God; you have reduced the Christian gospel, the offer of salvation in its fullness, just to some small level that is compatible with your thinking.

"If thou knewest" the things that are possible to you, what a transformation that would produce! This, it seems to me, is what the Christian church needs to concentrate on at the present time. All right, we have been forgiven; so now let us go on to perfection. Let us know about "the breadth, and length, and depth, and height" and "the love of Christ, which passeth knowledge," that we might be "filled with all the fulness of God" (Eph. 3:18–19). That is Christianity. That is what our Lord is talking about here.

But let me close by just noting these two words that our Lord uses: "living water." This is what we must know about. What does he mean when he calls this gift "living water"? He means that it is life-giving, it is enlivening, it is stimulating, it is invigorating. Do you have this life in you? Or do you have to drag yourself to worship God? Do you have to force yourself to live the Christian life? Are you a bit ashamed of it when you meet your clever friends in the world? If so, there is something radically wrong. It is "living water." It is not some cold, detached, theoretical, intellectual understanding of a number of doctrines. Yes, it is an understanding, but if it does not give life to you, if it does not enliven you, if it does not move you, if it does not invigorate you, you do not have the "living water."

What else? Well, it is always fresh. It is not water stored in a cistern; it is not static water. It comes out of a well opened on Calvary's hill, opened in the heart of God; it is flowing, and it constantly comes with its new stream, always fresh, always living. So much Christianity seems to be stale, does it not? It is old, it is ineffective, it is dull, it is lifeless, it is insipid; you feel it needs to be purified. And the world is not interested in it because it looks at it and sees the scum on the surface and the things that should not be there. It does not see the sparkle; it does not see the light, the living quality. Oh, what a travesty all this is of the true Christian life and the true Christian message!

And, finally, this water lasts. "Whosoever drinketh of this water shall thirst again," but not those who drink the living water. Whatever may happen in the world, in the whole cosmos, nothing can stop it; it springs up into everlasting life; it goes on forever. There will never be a shortage; there will never be a drought; there will never be a lack of supply. So not merely is your thirst satisfied, but you have lasting life and power and are ready to meet the world, the flesh, and the devil and anything that may come against you in this year and in all the years that may be left to you.

I want to end by asking you a question in the form of a quotation from a hymn. I am not asking about your beliefs at the moment—I am assuming them. Here is the question—can you say something like this?

O Christ, in thee my soul hath found,
And found in thee alone,
The peace, the joy I sought so long,
The bliss till now unknown.

Now none but Christ can satisfy,
None other name for me!
There's love, and life, and lasting joy,
Lord Jesus, found in thee.

I sighed for rest and happiness,
I yearned for them, not thee.

That is what I have been trying to say: do not seek the wells of the world—seek him!

But, while I passed my Saviour by,
His love laid hold on me.

"He must needs go through Samaria." "God seeketh such to worship him."

I tried the broken cisterns, Lord,
But, ah, the waters failed;
Even as I stooped to drink they fled,
And mocked me as I wailed.

AUTHOR UNKNOWN

And that is what the world ultimately does to us. In your need, in your failure, it will mock you, it will laugh at you, it will jeer at you. It has no use for failures; it will pass you by. But, thank God, our Savior is the one who "must needs go through Samaria," meets the woman as she is, and gives her "living water."

"If thou knewest the gift of God . . ." Do you know it? Have you asked for it? Have you received it?

14

Christianity or Religion?

Jesus answered and said unto her, If thou knewest the gift of God, and who it is that saith to thee, Give me to drink; thou wouldest have asked of him, and he would have given thee living water. . . . Whosoever drinketh of this water shall thirst again: but whosoever drinketh of the water that I shall give him shall never thirst; but the water that I shall give him shall be in him a well of water springing up into everlasting life. (John 4:10, 13–14)

We have been looking at this passage for some time because it is such a crucial statement. We see here what our Lord offers to give to all who come to him, even as he offered it to the woman of Samaria. This is essential Christianity, this is what Christianity really means, and that is why we are considering these words so carefully. To me, the only hope of true revival, the only hope of the church having any influence upon the world that is outside, is that you and I should show this kind of life in our daily living. Undoubtedly, the people who are outside Christianity are in that position because they have no concept of what Christianity really is. They get their ideas from those of us who claim to be Christians, and they have come to the conclusion that we lead a miserable, poor sort of life. They feel sorry for us because they think they have gained so much by being emancipated from the shackles of religion.

So the real explanation of the present state and condition of people today is that you and I are failing to show the real meaning of the Christian life. We are apologetic; we seem to be living it with a grudge. We will allow almost anything, even the slightest excuse, to prevent our coming together to worship God. The man of the world would not dream of using such pretexts. But we do. We are halfhearted, and it is all because we ourselves do not realize as we should the nature of this life that is being offered to us.

Now is not this, I say, true of all of us in a measure at the present time? I do not hesitate to say that the greatest sin of the modern Christian is the sin of reducing Christianity to the level of our own experiences and our own understanding. We limit "the Holy One of Israel." Now this is a most serious matter. It not only robs us of the blessings of the Christian life, it makes the church weak and ineffective, and therefore, in a sense, it accounts for the condition of the world outside.

We must all be concerned about the mounting moral problem; we are aware of a declension. There were times when things were better, but why were they better? And the invariable answer is that the best periods in the life of this country, as in every other country, have always followed an evangelical revival, a true awakening produced by the Spirit of God. This does not mean that everyone has become a Christian, but when you have a powerful church, a powerful witness and testimony, it affects even those who are not Christians. The whole level of moral living is raised. Britain experienced this in the Elizabethan period, at the time of the Commonwealth, and especially after the great Evangelical Awakening of the eighteenth century, the effects of which were so clearly seen during the following century.

Now every true revival of religion is really a rediscovery of this great message that we are now considering. If you take the trouble to read the history of the church, you will find that its story can be represented in a kind of graph. It starts on the Day of Pentecost in that mighty outpouring of the Spirit, when the people were lifted up to the level described in the book of Acts and in the New Testament epistles. But after that the church went into a decline. Then there was a revival. That has been the story of the church. There has been a series of rises and falls. But there is always a fatal tendency in the church to settle down on a lower level and to be content with that. This level is characterized by an emphasis upon forms and externals, upon duties and human activities. Great emphasis is always placed upon dignity and ceremony and order, and correspondingly there is a loss of life and vigor and power. Religion tends always to become respectable, and people are content with that.

But then a number of individuals, or even one individual, become convicted about the loss of life in the church. While they are reading the Scriptures that they have read so many times before, suddenly a word is illuminated by the Spirit, and they are given to realize that their level of life is altogether too low. These people realize that they are no different from the Pharisees of old, who reduced the Law of Moses to the level of their own little rules and regulations and missed the whole spirit. They see that they have turned this great and glorious gospel into some neat little package, and they have been satisfied with that. But now they are disturbed and condemned. They begin to think that they have never been Christians at all, and they proceed to pray and to read the Scriptures, and God hears them and answers them, and they are given this "living water."

This happened before the Protestant Reformation, among little groups of people in various parts of Europe. So, for instance, we get the Waldensian Church in northern Italy and the Brethren of the Common Life.[14] These small groups of people were awakened to see that the church—the Roman Catholic Church, of course, at that time—was a travesty of New Testament Christianity and of the New Testament church. And they began to understand that Christianity is living and life-giving.

But, of course, we see this new life still more clearly in the Protestant Reformation itself. But we must be fair. The Protestant Reformation of the sixteenth century did not solve all the problems once and forever. In the seventeenth century, the early part particularly, the great truth that had been rediscovered by people such as Luther and Calvin hardened into a dead orthodoxy, a kind of scholasticism. It happened in this country [Britain] and on the continent of Europe perhaps still more strikingly. The Lutheran Church became very orthodox but dead. Theologians would argue about minutiae, and Christianity was a matter of the intellect. Then certain men arose who began to say that although all this was all right for people who had an interest in intellectual disputes, it was not the Christianity that is found in the New Testament. That was the beginning of the movement known as Pietism. In Germany certain men—Johann Arndt, Philipp Jakob Spener, and others—began to teach this message, and it led to great results on the continent of Europe.

In Britain, the Puritans, up to a point, were doing exactly the same thing. But we see this still more clearly in the eighteenth century. If you read the account of the Christian church in Britain in the early part of that century, you will see how deplorable it was, and how dead. Not only the state Anglican Church but the Nonconformist Churches also had again become intellectualized and barren, splitting hairs about doctrines; and the moral condition of the nation was, if anything, even worse than it is today.

But then there was a great revival. How did it come about? Well, this is the interesting thing: it again came through people being brought back to the kind of statement that we find in our passage. George Whitefield and the Wesley brothers were profoundly influenced by two books. The first, *The Life of God in the Soul of Man*, had been written at the end of the previous century by a Scotsman named Henry Scougal. The other was by William Law—his famous *Serious Call to a Devout and Holy Life*. But it was the book by Scougal that was especially influential. When we read the journals of Whitefield and the Wesleys, we find that all three say they read this book and saw that what they had regarded as Christianity was not Christianity at all. So they began to doubt whether they had ever been Christians; in fact, they were convinced that they had not. They did not have the "life of God" in their souls; but they were quite convinced by the argumentation of the book that that was a true representation of the New Testament teaching. And it was this realization of the truth about the Christian life that really led to the Evangelical Awakening and revival.

Now it seems to me that this message is needed today more than ever. Are we satisfied with the Christian life that we have and that we are living? Is it not our danger, too, that it all becomes hardened, that we are content with a little life, though a good life, a moral life? Up to a point, even that is now beginning to be shaken, is it not? This is always so when you lose the true life. Increasing concessions are being made by evangelical people over drink and various other issues. There is a general slackening all along the line. Christian people are also contented with a kind of decisionism. You make your decision, you take up Christianity, you attend a place of worship, and you indulge in certain activities—and there it is. You feel you have it all, and you now propose to go on living the rest of your life in this way.

But that is not New Testament Christianity. It is not the "living water" that our Lord speaks about, and that is why it is having such little effect; it is lacking at this most vital point. So that is why we must look at this statement here most carefully and prayerfully. Over and against that neat, glib, self-satisfied kind of Christian life, we must look at this description. I am once more going to show you the difference between Christianity and religion. This is a very subtle danger, this tendency to persuade ourselves that because we have taken up religion, we have become Christians. Are we aware of the distinction?

Many people decide to become religious. But the question is, are they Christians? Do we become Christians in that way? I have given you something of the testimony of history, and you will find that some of the most notable saints, people such as Whitefield and the Wesleys, had thought that because of their good works and activities, their moral efforts, their philanthropy, they were exceptionally good Christians. But they were not Christians at all. Why not? Because they knew nothing about this: "Whosoever drinketh of this water shall thirst again: but whosoever drinketh of the water that I shall give him shall never thirst; but the water that I shall give shall be in him a well of water springing up into everlasting life."

So let us look at this wonderful life that the Son of God has come to give us, and God grant that we may so see it that we shall all be ashamed of ourselves and our self-satisfaction and shall give ourselves no rest or peace until we know for certain that we have within us this "well of water springing up into everlasting life." Oh, if this but happened, the revival we long for would come, and the world and the church would soon begin to be different.

What, then, are the characteristics of this great life? Here are some that we can note. I would divide the characteristics into general and particular. And the first general characteristic is that it is experiential. It happens to us, and we know it has happened. This cannot happen without our knowing it. The water was offered to us, we received it, we drank of it. There is a vital, inescapable difference in our lives. You find this not only in these words of our Lord to the Samaritan woman and in comparable statements elsewhere in the Scriptures, but also in the biographies of the saints and in the history of the church. It is always the case.

So this is one of the ways in which we can see the difference between being religious and being Christian. You can be religious as the result of tradition—by being born and brought up in a certain country, in a certain family, by being taught to do certain things and always doing them. In this way, you are being religious, as the Jews and Muslims and members of other faiths are religious. And it is true of many people in the Christian church. These people adhere to the traditions and practices of the church. They have no idea what they are really doing or why they are doing it. All they know is that this is what they have always been taught, and they imagine that it is what makes them truly Christian. This is their idea, their notion of Christianity. But this cannot be fitted into what our Lord said to the woman of Samaria. There is nothing experiential about it. These people are not what they are because of something that has happened to them in a vital sense. We can put it in the words of the hymn by Joseph Hart: "True religion's more than notion."

These words are the title of a recently published book, *More Than Notion*.[15] Read it, and you will see the very point I am making. You will read there of a family that was considered to be a very godly and noble Christian family, but one by one the members of that family began to realize that they had never been Christians at all. They were religious, yes—very good, very moral, very active. But they had nothing within them. There was nothing vital; there was nothing living. They had not had the kind of experience of which our Lord is speaking. This, by its very nature, is experiential.

Now a further, very subtle danger comes in at this point. There are those who seem to think that experience of the power of the gospel is only possible to those who have been violent or profligate. I know something of this fallacy as I look back on my own early life and experience. You say, "Ah, yes, of course, if a man had been a drunkard or something terrible like that and then suddenly saw the truth, there would be a great change, and of course he would be well aware of it. It is something big, it is dramatic. But if we have always been good and religious and moral and have always lived a clean life, well, of course, we cannot expect anything like that."

Have you harbored that kind of argument? I remember someone once saying to me that she almost wished she had been a drunkard so that she could have had this great experience. Do you see the fallacy? It is to imagine that you can only have this great experience if you are coming from a position of violent negativity, as it were, to positivity. The answer to that way of thinking is found in Jesus' words to the woman of Samaria. There is as much, if not a greater, difference between being religious and then receiving this life as there is between violently evil conduct and good, respectable conduct. Why? Because this is life from God, and if you imagine that the difference between life from God and the good, respectable religious life is only slight, then you have misunderstood the whole case. And that is what is so wonderful about some of the experiences that I have already reminded you of. People such as Whitefield and the Wesleys were always exceptionally good, yet they were the people who had this profound experience. So you must not only think of coming up from the gutter to the level of the road. No, no; you must think of being moved from the level of the road to the skies, from man to God.

The second characteristic is that the Christian experience is received directly from the Lord Jesus Christ himself: "If thou knewest the gift of God, and who it is that saith to thee . . ." And again, in the fourteenth verse, "But whosoever drinketh of the water that I shall give him shall never thirst." Again, this is a most important point, and I must emphasize it because it is the one thing that differentiates the Christian experience from what is commonly called mysticism, which can be one of the greatest dangers to true faith. Mysticism works like this: when you begin to feel dissatisfied with the neat, glib, package kind of Christianity in which you think you have it all, and all you have to do is to go on like that for the rest of your life, the moment you see through that and begin to feel dissatisfied, you will probably start to read books, and there are many to choose from. And perhaps you will start reading about the mystics and their experience of God, their being raised to a new level of life. And you will say to yourself, "Ah, yes, that life I've always been living is all right as far as it went, but it doesn't seem to be true Christianity. I am in control of the whole thing. There is another order of life that is altogether different."

But the difficulty is that those mystics, most of them, will tell you that this life is to be attained by following certain rules or practices that they will prescribe for you. And they say that as you go on and do this, you will pass through different stages, and ultimately you will come to that stage of contemplation where you have your great experience. But the fallacy is that, generally speaking, the Lord Jesus Christ does not come into it at all. They will tell you to look into yourself; they will tell you to find God who is within you.

Quakerism, of course, has fallen into this error. Having started more or less in the right way, it went astray, and the result is that the Lord Jesus Christ has come to mean less and less. What you do is sit in silence and wait; the life is within you, and as you wait in silence, you discover this life and so develop it and foster it. Now that is the essence of the mystical notion. But the Lord Jesus Christ is not vital to it—he is not central, he is not essential. This life does not come from him directly but from the contemplation of God as the result of traveling along this mystic way. It is not the Lord Jesus Christ offering you this living water and then you drinking it. It is not directly and immediately related to him.

Our Lord's words to the woman of Samaria not only differentiate the true Christian experience from mysticism—they also, of course, show the complete difference between it and the teaching of all the cults. I am not surprised that the cults are flourishing. When Christianity is moribund, when it is merely orthodox and glib and self-satisfied and self-contained, people in trouble will turn to something else, and these other things can give some sort of an experience. It is no use denying that the cults can help you. If they did not, they would not flourish; they would have long since ceased to exist. They flourish because they can give some kind of relief, some kind of experience.

So how do you tell the difference between the cults and the fullness of life that our Lord is offering here? Well, here he is absolutely central and essential. This experience is based upon him. There must be no uncertainty about this. We see it from his words, "If thou knewest the gift of God, and who it is that saith to thee . . ." leading on to the great statement in verse 26: "Jesus saith unto her, I that speak unto thee am he." It is all based upon the fact that he is the Son of God, the one who says, "I am come that they might have life, and that they might have it more abundantly" (John 10:10). Christianity is Christ himself and his teaching.

But still more, Christianity is based upon what our Lord does, what he did when he died on the cross and rose again in the resurrection and sent the Holy Spirit upon the church on the Day of Pentecost. He says here, "The water that I shall give him . . ." and he is referring, of course, to the giving of the Holy Spirit. This is his great gift. Later in John's Gospel we find parallels to our Lord's words here. In John 7, for instance, we read, "In the last day, that great day of the feast, Jesus stood and cried, saying, If any man thirst, let him come unto me, and drink . . . out of his belly shall flow rivers of living water." And John explains, "This spake he of the Spirit, which they that believe on him should receive: for the Holy Ghost was not yet given; because that Jesus was not yet glorified" (John 7:37–39).

This is all a reference to the life of the Spirit, the Spirit whom he was going to give. And there are many other examples and illustrations of this teaching. So it is obviously an essential and central point that the Spirit is given because the Son of God has come from heaven and has become incarnate. Jesus has come that we might have life, and the life he gives us is his own life. We are made "partakers of the divine nature" (2 Pet. 1:4). I shall elaborate on these words later—all I am emphasizing now is that there are, on the very surface, those two general characteristics about this life. It is an experience, and it is a direct experience of contact with the Lord Jesus Christ, and you are aware that it comes from him and from him alone.

But now let us look at the particular characteristics of this life, and they are put quite plainly before us in this passage in John 4. "Whosoever drinketh of this water shall thirst again: but whosoever drinketh of the water that I shall give him shall never thirst"—why not? Because "the water that I shall give him shall be in him [within him]." Now the particular characteristics are vital, and none more so than this. One of the greatest differentiating points between religion and Christianity is that Christianity is always something within, whereas religion is always external.

I remember reading a book on the Victorians, entitled *Poetry and Morals*, and in it there was a most illuminating sentence that I constantly return to because it is so true. In a sense, says the author, "Religion overshadowed the Victorians, instead of penetrating them." In other words, religion never got inside them. I am often tempted to put it like this: the first thing we must do, in a sense, is to forget the Victorians—I am speaking in a religious sense primarily. The nineteenth century was a devastating century from the standpoint of true Christianity. As we have seen, there has always been a curious alternation in people's responses to God. It almost happens from century to century—a century of revival followed by a century of hardening and then a revival again. And the Victorian period was an age of respectability, an age that prided itself on its intellect and its understanding, its scientific discoveries, its discovery of unknown parts of the world. You know the whole mentality and outlook that goes under the name of Victoria.

And this outlook influenced the Christian church. It even influenced the architecture of Nonconformist chapels so that from the square places of meeting—meeting houses, buildings in which you could meet and worship God and preach the gospel, square, unadorned, but excellent for preaching because of their fine acoustics—from that they went to mock Gothic and sham and pretense, with everything big and ornate. They had lost the spirit; they had become respectable; they had turned their Christian faith into religion. Their argument was, of course, that people had now become educated, and you could no longer have the ignorant preachers of former times, Methodist or Strict Baptist or whatever you used to have. You must now have a cultured ministry. And they had it, and the more they had it, the more the Spirit went out, and the church became dead and fossilized and respectable.

That was what happened. And that was true of the so-called great Victorians—Matthew Arnold, John Ruskin, and others. They could not leave religion alone; they were always playing with it. But they knew nothing about Christianity, nothing at all. Religion was, as that author says, something that "overshadowed" them; it was there as a kind of cloud. It spoiled life for them; it made them unhappy; it made many of them morbid. But they never knew the release, the life, the power, the "living water." Tennyson, Browning, all these men, came so near, so many of them, but they never experienced it. It never penetrated into them.

But the first particular characteristic of the true Christian life and experience is that it "shall be in him"! Do you see the contrast with the well? That is outside, and the woman has to come back and forth to it. And our Lord says that religion is like that—it is always outside you. So let us examine ourselves in the light of this. Is what you regard as your Christianity something that is in you or outside you? Is it a part of you or is it apart from you?

Now there is no difficulty about answering this question. We all know this for certain one way or the other. Is what you regard as your Christianity a mere addition to your life, something that you add on to your life, or is it really central and within? This is a most terrible danger. I take it that many of us know exactly what I am talking about. Here is your life, and the only difference between you and other people is that you have an appendix to the book of your life, and in this appendix you are religious. You happen to go to a place of worship once in a while on a Sunday, whereas other people never go at all. They are as moral as you are, and their outlook on life is more or less the same as yours—you just do this odd thing that they do not do—you tack on something extra. Religion is something that you add on, just as you put on a coat and take it off again.

But by definition that is not Christianity. Or we can put it another way. Is what you regard as your Christianity something that you take up occasionally and then put down again, something that you indulge in spasmodically? Is it something that only applies to Sunday? Now that is very true of religion. Or let me put it like this: is what you regard as your Christianity something that you have to be reminded of or something, perhaps, of which you have to remind yourself—"I am a Christian, after all"—is that it? Now that again, I say, is religion.

This has been true of so many. They have assumed they are Christians, but Christianity does not mean anything to them. They have not thought about it for a long time. But then they are taken ill, and it all comes back to them. They had to be taken ill before they were reminded that they were Christians. I have seen so much of this. Any man who has been any length of time in the ministry has seen it. He has seen people who, when things are going well, fall slack and say, "Ah, there will be time for that later, but first there are interesting and wonderful things to do." Then they are taken ill, and suddenly they are most anxious to have some help, and they come back to Christianity, and they are zealous, and they are praying, and they remember their Bibles again. But that is not Christianity. That is something outside you, something that you can forget all about and have to be reminded of by illness or accident or bereavement or sorrow or something unusual.

But so much that passes as Christianity falls into that kind of category, and that is why the masses of the people are outside the church. They say, "Those people don't believe in it themselves. They can forget all about it. It's not part of them. It's something they have to be reminded of or remind themselves of when they are in trouble or at the beginning of a year or on festival days. Then they take it up, and afterward they put it down and forget all about it again."

Or, lastly, is your Christianity just some vague general influence that affects only the surface of your life, only the outward part of your life and living? These are the questions we must ask ourselves. And the extraordinary thing about this is that we all know exactly what the answer is. We can try and argue with ourselves, but we know what we are doing.

There, then, is a description of religion that is outside. But here is something entirely different. "The water that I shall give him shall be in him a well of water springing up into everlasting life." This means even more than I have been saying so far. I have said that religion is outside your life, while Christianity is a part of it, but I must go beyond that. It is not merely a part of your life—it is the center of your life. Now there is no need to argue this; it must be true, by definition. This is the Son of God speaking, remember. It is the Second Person in the blessed Holy Trinity. It is he who is giving this gift, and if you believe in him at all, you must believe that what he gives is central.

Now we know all of this, do we not, from natural analogies. We tend to evaluate the things we possess and the gifts we have in terms of the people who have given them to us. That is what puts value upon particular objects, and this is perfectly right. Very often it is not its inherent value that makes us treasure a gift so much as the person who gave it to us. Now apply all that here. He gives this gift; and if we believe that, then it is not peripheral; it is the most central thing in our lives. It is in us, and it must control the whole of our life; it becomes the spring of all our activities.

Christianity has often been called heart religion, and that is quite a good term, except that it is open to a little bit of misunderstanding. When it is called heart religion, the term *heart* is used, as it is in Scripture, to mean the center of the personality. It means that Christianity is not merely a matter of the head, not merely something intellectual, but that it really is at the very center and that it makes us what we are and controls everything we do. Now that is the essence of this whole teaching. In other words, what our Lord is saying here is the answer to certain cries that come out in the Old Testament. Let me give you one or two.

Remember David in Psalm 51? Poor David! He has been guilty of terrible sins, and he is well aware of the dreadful character of his sins; but that is not what really troubles him. What really troubles him is this: "Behold, thou desirest truth in the inward parts" (v. 6). David had gone on being religious, conforming to the externals of religion, not only before he had committed his terrible sins but even during that time and afterward, and he was not aware that anything was wrong. But when he is brought to himself and brought to the place of repentance, he sees it all: "Thou desirest truth in the inward parts." The moment we become aware of that, we begin to seek this living water, and we are open to the message that is given here by the Lord to the woman of Samaria. We are no longer content with the externals and the surface and the superficial.

"Truth in the inward parts"! That is what we need; here it is offered to us: ". . . shall be within you a well of water springing up into everlasting life." Or look at David's corresponding prayer: "Create in me a clean heart, O God; and renew a right spirit within me" (Ps. 51:10). He can see that his trouble is in his heart, and unless his heart is put right, nothing will be right. No appearances are adequate; while there is a single iniquity within, while a polluted fountain controls all my activities, all that comes out will never "create within me a clean heart" or "renew a right spirit within me." Here it is: "a well of water springing up" from the center of the personality. No longer outside or peripheral but central.

Or take the way in which it is put in the book of Ezekiel. God has promised this, you see, he is preparing his people for it. And he is always contrasting the old with the new. He says, "Then will I sprinkle clean water upon you, and ye shall be clean" (36:25). But that is not all. "A new heart also will I give you, and a new spirit will I put within you: and I will take away the stony heart out of your flesh, and I will give you an heart of flesh" (v. 26). I am simply making the general point that this living water takes out the stony heart and gives us a heart of flesh. It is experiential, as I have been saying. It is within, it is living, and it is vital.

Or take it in the way in which Jeremiah puts it as quoted in the eighth chapter of the Epistle to the Hebrews: "I will put my laws into their mind, and write them in their hearts" (8:10). Morality, laws written on tablets of stone to which you are trying to conform, are religion outside you. But here is something "within you," a spring, "a well of water springing up into everlasting life."

Do you have heart religion or only head religion or will religion? Is it inside you at the very spring and source and center of the whole of your personality? This is what our Lord gives; this is what he offers. "The water that I shall give him shall be in him [within him] a well of water springing up into everlasting life." God give us the grace to be honest with ourselves. He does require "truth in the inward parts," and he knows all about us. Let us examine ourselves honestly in the light of his word.

15

Power

Jesus answered and said unto her, If thou knewest the gift of God, and who it is that saith to thee, Give me to drink; thou wouldest have asked of him, and he would have given thee living water. . . . Whosoever drinketh of this water shall thirst again: but whosoever drinketh of the water that I shall give him shall never thirst; but the water that I shall give him shall be in him a well of water springing up into everlasting life. (John 4:10, 13–14)

We are considering this great and glorious statement of the Christian gospel as it was made by our Lord and Savior Jesus Christ himself to the woman of Samaria. This is essential Christianity, and there is nothing more important than that we should be certain that we not only know that but should have experienced something of it. We are asking why it is that we know so little about this well of water springing up into everlasting life. We have considered the many hindrances, and we are now looking at this matter positively.

I have suggested that first we must realize our need and must be aware of the quality of the life we have and how it measures up to the standard that we see here. For instance, you can look at a liquid in a glass, and it appears to be milk; but if an analyst comes to test it, he may find it is very deficient in fats and has a good deal of adulteration with water, so much so that it is not milk at all. And that is true of so much Christianity. It looks as if it is the right thing, but when you analyze it, you find that it is seriously defective. So we must really be aware of our need, and we must see that nothing else in the world can satisfy it but this living water, and we must realize that this is indeed "*living* water."

We are now considering the characteristics of this great life that our Lord has come to give us. I have suggested that they can be divided into general and particular characteristics. We have considered the two general characteristics: first, it is experiential, not theoretical; second, it is always intimately connected with the Lord Jesus Christ himself. It comes directly from him, and thereby we differentiate it from all mystical experiences and all the cults.

Then we have started on the particular characteristics of this life, and the first is, of course, that it is within us; it is a "well of water springing up into everlasting life." The next point I want to note is that this life is a power. It is a power within us, a power that acts within us—"[it] shall be in him a well of water springing up." Now if you know anything about a well, you know that is its characteristic—it is living. What a difference there is between a well and a trough or a cistern with water in it; there is no life in the latter. But here is an activity springing up, a power, dynamism, a force. And this, our Lord tells us, is one of the outstanding characteristics of this life that he has to give us.

How do we know, then, whether or not we have this life? Well, let us test ourselves by this second particular characteristic, this manifestation of power within us. It means that the Christian life is not primarily a life of *our* activity. Of course, we have things to do, but that is not the essential factor. We are bearing in our minds, I trust, the contrast between religion—any kind of religion—and true Christianity, and this is one of the chief differences. In religion, it is our activity that counts the whole time. But here we are in a different realm altogether. Here is a power that is acting within us—"a well of water springing up." Whatever we may or may not be doing, it has life and vigor and power and acts in us. And so the relationship between Christians and their activities is this—and this is where there is such a striking contrast with religion—Christians act because they are made to act; their action, their activity, is the result of this other, prior activity.

In other words, we are dealing with what may be called the dynamic of the Holy Spirit. Our Lord says that he has this to give—he gives us life; he gives us the Spirit. An old hymn says:

> *O Jesus, light of all below,*
> *Thou fount of living fire . . .*
>
> BERNARD OF CLAIRVAUX (E. CASWALL, TRANSLATOR)

You may criticize that—how can you have fire in a fountain? It does not matter. He is the fount. He is the source of life and fire. Now I want to emphasize the aspect of fire. Life, yes, but fire! There is power in a fire, and this is within us—a fountain within us—the dynamic of the Holy Spirit. The apostle Paul puts this in his own particular way in these well-known words:

> Wherefore, my beloved, as ye have always obeyed, not as in my presence only, but now much more in my absence, work out your own salvation with fear and trembling. For it is God which worketh in you both to will and to do of his good pleasure. (Phil. 2:12–13)

That is a perfect statement of this very point. We work out our own salvation "with fear and trembling," but why do we? The answer is that "it is God which worketh in you both to will and to do." We work out our salvation because he has first of all been working in us both the willing, the desiring, and everything else.

This power, this fire, is an essential characteristic of the Christian life (again, I am constrained to put it like this). But while it is very difficult to put these things into words, in the realm of experience there is no difficulty at all. It is the difference between life and a machine. The machine you have to wind up, and you wind it up and it will go for a certain length of time; but it stops, and then you have to wind it up again. But this is life, and it is life within, a power that is operating within. In other words, the impulse does not come from ourselves. I have already pointed out that when religion is external, before practicing it, you need a stimulus from outside—"Ah! Sunday morning! Yes—different from other days." So you do this and that. Or there is an illness or an accident or a death or a funeral—something pulls you up. You have to be reminded. But it is not like that here. There is an impulse within; a call, an urging, comes from within. A longing is created. At this stage it is not something you have done at all; it just happens to you. You find yourself the subject of an activity that is not your own; you are aware of a working within you.

I have often quoted or applied to this the words of Wordsworth. He meant something quite different, but we can appreciate his words:

> *And I have felt*
> *A presence that disturbs me with the joy*
> *Of elevated thoughts. . . .*
>
> LINES COMPOSED A FEW MILES ABOVE TINTERN ABBEY

That is it—a disturbing. When, perhaps, you desire to go in a given direction, you are aware of an activity within you, some impulse, some call, some urging, some longing that has not come from you. Or you may be reading something secular, your thoughts may be otherwise engaged, but suddenly you are aware that there is something, someone, within you moving you, leading you in a particular direction. "It is "God which worketh in you."

There it is; that is a very vital part of this whole Christian position. If we are not aware of the working of God in us, then I fail to see how we have any right to call ourselves Christians at all—we are merely religious. You can be religious in your use of Christian terminology; you can be religious inside a Christian church. But one of the vital aspects of Christianity is that our activities are always the result of his activity. It is the "well of water," it is the life within that stimulates. "God worketh in you both to will and to do" before you have ever done anything. Why did you desire it? Why did you will it? That is the question. We move because we are moved; we act because of the stimulus that has come apart from ourselves.

Now this, I believe, is a most important point for us at the present time. We are living in an age of activism and of activities; we are living in an age when people are so confused that they become children and like to have everything set out before them by rule and regulation, by numbers. To live according to a system, to live by rote, to live by obeying commands is a very real snare, a snare into which saints have fallen. You must "work out your own salvation with fear and trembling," yes, but it is never imposed from the outside; it works out from the inside.

Do you see the danger? The Roman Catholic type of piety is always in grave danger at this point. The life is determined by the priest or by certain books and writings, and these are imposed upon people; but that also happens to many people in Protestant circles. They make a decision in a meeting perhaps, and then they are given a list of rules they must keep because they are told to: it has become the thing to do. They exchange one pattern of behavior for another.

Now there is a danger of being misunderstood at this point—I am well aware of that. Nevertheless, this is one of the most essential points of all. I have known so many Christians, young Christians in particular, who appear to be true Christians but who later reveal that they have never become Christians at all. I have known many people who in their student days were members of Christian Unions and were carried along by the momentum of the excitement and the movement and the activity and appeared to be wonderful Christians. But then they left the university and went out into life, and once they had lost all that was round and about them as students they had nothing. They fell away completely and even scoffed at the Christian faith and ridiculed it. I have known many instances of this. It takes place in evangelistic work often, particularly among students.

Now this is just a solid fact, and I am giving you the explanation. They had a system imposed upon them; they conformed to a society to which they belonged and were carried along by something entirely outside themselves. But when a man or woman has this fountain inside them, it does not matter whether they are in a Christian society or not. The fountain is in them; they work out their own salvation with fear and trembling because it is God who works in them both to will and to do.

This is taught throughout the New Testament. We read about "the fruit of the Spirit" (Gal. 5:22) and about bringing forth "much fruit" (John 15:5)—our Lord himself uses this comparison. We are dealing with life here, not with mechanics, and if it is a question of fruit-bearing, then it is bound to come from inside outward. You do not add fruit to a tree. No, no; the life produces the fruit, and it takes time, and you get different stages—the bud, then the growth of the bud, and then full maturity. That is God's way, that is life—not the imposing of things from the outside, not doing things because you are told to, but out of a desire created within. There, then, is one manifestation of this power, one way whereby we can test whether or not this power is in us.

But let us look at another manifestation. It is similar, and yet there is a real distinction. Because this is the nature of the Christian life, it follows of necessity that it is not a life we can control; rather, we are controlled by it. Religious people are always in control of themselves and their religion. That is a further characteristic of religion—you take it up, you do it. But here we are in an entirely different realm. Because this is inside us, because it is life, because it is a power springing up, it is in control of us.

How can I put this to you? This is indeed the most wonderful thing about being a Christian, and this is what guarantees the final perseverance of the saints: we are not in control. "I live; yet not I"—that is it—". . . and the life which I now live in the flesh I live by the faith of the Son of God, who loved me, and gave himself for me" (Gal. 2:20). It sounds contradictory, and yet, again, experientially there is no difficulty about this at all. Are you in control, or are you being controlled? Are you in control of your life, or do you say with that centurion who came to our Lord, "I am a man under authority" (Matt. 8:9)? The Christian is always a man or woman under authority. There is always this power, this life, springing up and working within.

Now I want to make this point clear, so I am going to put it like this—I have found this a most valuable test, and, incidentally, an excellent ground of assurance of salvation. This life within you is a well. You have drunk the water, and it becomes within you a well of water springing up. You experience this energy, this power, this bubbling quality, this dynamic; yes, and sometimes that makes you very unhappy. By that, I mean that in a backsliding condition you may want to revert to the life of the world. Going out with your old friends may seem interesting and attractive once more, and that is what you would like to do. But this other power is there inside you, working in you, and you are annoyed; you wish you had never known anything about it. It is a nuisance. It is spoiling life, and you resent it. You struggle against it and do your utmost to silence it, to explain it away. You are glad to read in the newspaper that some critic has said this or that or some church dignitary seems to have denied the whole of Christianity. "Ah," you say, "I've been too narrow." But the more you do that, the more this other power works within you, and you cannot silence it, you cannot stop it. It goes on, and it nags at you, and it troubles you, and you are in a conflict. Now this is an absolute proof that there is this life of God within you, that there is a power working within you.

Now let me give you my authority for saying this. Listen to the apostle Paul putting it to the Galatians:

> This I say then, Walk in the Spirit, and ye shall not fulfil the lust of the flesh. For the flesh lusteth against the Spirit, and the Spirit against the flesh: and these are contrary the one to the other: so that ye cannot do the things that ye would. (5:16–17)

"But surely," you may say to me, "many an unconverted person has this kind of conflict?"

No, not this kind of conflict. Many a moral man knows the trouble he gets with his conscience and is unhappy after he has fallen into sin and experiences remorse. But that is on a very different level from this. The word used here is the word "lusteth." This is a tremendous power. It is not merely that you are aware of your conscience speaking to you—there is an intensity about it all. You are aware of a vigor, and there is a conflict within you.

James puts that even more strongly when he says, "Do ye think that the scripture saith in vain, The spirit that dwelleth in us lusteth to envy?" (Jas. 4:5). That is the translation of the King James Version, but it is generally agreed that the true idea there is that the Spirit that has been put within us as Christians—this water that we have drunk and that has become a well of water within us—and the Spirit who dwells in us is anxious about us and in a most jealous manner lusts, as it were, for our entire sanctification. What a wonderful thought it is that God has put his Spirit in us, and the Spirit now is anxious for our perfection and is even jealous! The world, the flesh, and the devil are fighting, and he knows that the flesh itself is on the side of the world and the devil, and therefore there is this lusting of the flesh.

The idea, the picture, is that of a parent looking at a child and being concerned and anxious that the child should do well—this kind of anxiety. This lusting is as strong and as powerful as that. Now this is the power of the well of water that is within us springing up into everlasting life. It is God working in us both to will and to do with a jealous envy, so great is the concern of the Spirit. And Christians, I say, are aware that they are not really in control of themselves, that they are being controlled by this Other. They can fight against him, they can quench the Spirit, they can grieve the Spirit, but the Spirit is always there.

We can go on and look at this as it is put by John in his first epistle. These verses are often misunderstood: "He that committeth sin is of the devil; for the devil sinneth from the beginning. For this purpose the Son of God was manifested, that he might destroy the works of the devil. Whosoever is born of God doth not commit sin"—why not?—"for his seed remaineth in him: and he cannot sin, because he is born of God" (3:8–9). That is a perfect statement of the point I am making. "He that committeth sin"—why does he do that? Here is a natural man, living a life of sin. Why? Because he is "of the devil." What you do is the result of what you are. You commit sin because you are *of* the devil; that is the nature that is in you.

Our Lord put this quite explicitly to the Pharisees and scribes when he said, "Ye are of your father the devil, and the lusts of your father ye will do" (John 8:44). The nature must express itself; it must come out. This is true on both sides. A life of sin is not something that is added on; it is the expression of the person. "For as he thinketh in his heart, so is he" (Prov. 23:7). Actions come from the inside. Again let me quote the words of our

Lord—people always misunderstand this—"For out of the heart proceed evil thoughts, murders, adulteries . . ." (Matt. 15:19).

The trouble with the Pharisee is always that he is concerned about the outside and that which goes in, that which he takes in. But it is the heart that is wrong; the heart is the polluted fountain (not the fountain of the Spirit but another one). "He that committeth sin is of the devil; for the devil sinneth from the beginning. For this purpose the Son of God," says John, "was manifested, that he might destroy the works of the devil." So, then, this becomes true: "Whosoever is born of God"—this is the place where you start. You do not look at a man's actions; you say, "What is the life that is in him? Is he born of God?" "Whosoever is born of God doth not commit sin" (1 John 3:8–9).

Obviously that does not mean he never commits a single act of sin. The tense of the verb used there is the continuous: he does not go on sinning. There is the contrast with the unbeliever. The unbeliever lives a life of sin; the believer does not live a life of sin. He may occasionally fall into it, but he does not go on living such a life. "Whosoever is born of God doth not commit sin"—why not?—"for his seed remaineth in him." There is a seed of new life in this man. John prefers to work with this idea of a seed of life. It is the same truth, using a different comparison. And this is one of the greatest and most profound sources of assurance and comfort and consolation. Here is a man—he is born of God, very well. But he is in this sinful world, and there are the world and the flesh and the devil, and he gets attacked, and he may fall into sin. But he cannot fall away, for "his seed remaineth in him." He will not be allowed to. He may for a while, but he cannot go back to that life that is of the devil. In chapter 5 John puts this still more explicitly: "All unrighteousness is sin: and there is a sin not unto death. We know that whosoever is born of God sinneth not; but he that is begotten of God keepeth himself, and that wicked one toucheth him not. And we know that we are of God, and the whole world lieth in wickedness" (vv. 17–19).

That is it. The man who has this life in him does not remain in wickedness—he never can. This seed, this life of God, stays in him. The evil one cannot touch us in the sense of ever getting us back into his embrace and under his control. The Christian is under the control of the Spirit of the living God. As I have said, Christians are no longer in control of themselves but are being controlled. They do not have to force themselves to live the Christian life. They are being forced to live the Christian life by the power that is within them. All you and I can do is this: we can either yield to that power or we can resist it, quench it, disobey. But if we do that, we will be miserable. When Christians go back to sin they are miserable wretches, and they continue like that; they are not allowed to enjoy it. There is this power within them. This is very wonderful. It is wonderful in pastoral experience to see a backslider restored.

All this is implicit in this idea of the well of water springing up, the power that is working within us. And this is the way in which the New Testament preaches the doctrine of sanctification. The New Testament is not always urging us to do this or that; it does not keep attacking us individually and on particular points. If you want that sort of approach, you have a religious and not a Christian outlook. All I am trying to tell you is that if you have the life of God in you and you sin, you are a fool because you are asking for misery, and you will get it, and you will go on living in hell, as it were, until you obey this power that is working in you. It will bring you back to do so, though it may knock you down, take your health from you, make you lose your money. So if you are a child of God, do not be a fool, do not resist the Spirit—you will only bring trouble on yourself.

O Love, that wilt not let me go,
I rest my weary soul in thee;
I give thee back the life I owe,
That in thine ocean depths its flow
May richer, fuller be.

George Matheson

He will follow you all your way—"The Hound of Heaven"—think of any illustration you like. This is the truth. And it all comes under the general principle that we are not in control of this life—it is in control of us.

So I make this next point, which is simple and obvious. The kind of life that is lived by the Christian is of necessity, therefore, never mechanical and never legalistic. The terms that are used in the New Testament are so wonderful—words like "living" or "lively." "If thou knewest the gift of God, and who it is that saith to thee, Give me to drink," says our Lord to this woman, "thou wouldest have asked of him and he would have given thee *living* water."

Or listen to Peter writing to people who are passing through a very difficult time:

> Blessed be the God and Father of our Lord Jesus Christ, which according to his abundant mercy hath begotten us again unto a *lively hope* [a living hope, a bubbling hope] by the resurrection of Jesus Christ from the dead, to an inheritance incorruptible, and undefiled, and that fadeth not away, reserved in heaven for you, who are kept by the power of God through faith unto salvation ready to be revealed in the last time. (1 Pet. 1:3–5)

If you read the epistles of Peter, you will find that he is very fond of emphasizing this "living," "lively," bubbling, sparkling quality, and it is right for him to do so. Again, that is one of the best ways of testing whether we are merely religious or whether we are Christians. The religious person is always mechanical, always legalistic, knows how far he can go, knows where to stop, and just lives a mechanical sort of life that keeps him just within the Law—so nice, so moral, so clean, so good! What a contrast with Christianity! This is life! This is not mechanics; this is not law; this is not legalism. Christians fulfill the Law because they are living in a realm above it; they do not just tick off whether they have done this and have not done that.

The Pharisees knew exactly what they were doing. Our Lord's parable of the Pharisee and the tax collector going up to the Temple to pray puts it perfectly. The Pharisee can get up and recite exactly what he does—fast twice in the week, give a tenth of his goods to the poor. He can tell God exactly when he prays and for how long (Luke 18:10–14). What a tragedy! What a small life that is! There is no liberty. It is not living. Religions are always dead, and that is why they are always hopeless, and that is why they never help people when they need them most of all. Religion always lets you down at the point of your greatest need. Nor can you help others if you only have religion.

Bu let me say one other thing. It follows on directly, and it is marvelous. I want to end by stressing the greatness of the power that is within us. "The water that I shall give him shall be in him a well of water springing up into everlasting life." Now this power is a variable quantity; it varies from person to person—another most important point. Christians are never identical. If you show me a church of people who are all the same, I say it is not a church, it is a religious gathering. Any teaching or system that makes everybody the same, doing the same things in the same way, is never Christianity because it is never of God. No two flowers are identical! They may appear to be, but if you examine them, you will find they are not. And no two Christians are identical; there is a wide variation in the amount of the power. The apostle Paul has put this perfectly, of course, in his great illustration of the body in 1 Corinthians 12. There are "comely parts" and less comely parts—they are all essential, they are all in the body, they all have their function, and, ultimately in the sight of God they are all one. But there is variation, and the foolish people at Corinth had not grasped this principle, so they were quarreling over gifts.

But that is not what I am interested in now. I want, rather, to establish the fact that Christian people experience variations in the degree of this power. But let me add also that there are variations in the power in the same person. Are you not aware of that? Do you know what you are going to be like when you wake up tomorrow morning? If you do, you are not a Christian. We do not control this, as I am emphasizing. What we do does affect our experience of this power, but we do not control it. If I disobey, if I rebel against the power that is in me, if I quench the Spirit or if I grieve the Spirit, that makes a difference. But it is a temporary, and not an ultimate, difference. The point I am establishing, however, is that even granting all that, you and I are not at the center of control, and we never know what that power is going to be.

I say it again, to the glory of God, the pulpit is the most romantic place in the universe as far as I am concerned because I never know what is going to happen when I get there—never. My anticipations are often falsified on both sides. This is wonderful! The temptation to a preacher is to think that if he has prepared what he regards as a good sermon, there will be a wonderful service, but it can sometimes be very bad. On the other hand, the poor man may have had a very difficult and trying week, he may have been ill, a thousand and one things may have happened to him, and he may go into the pulpit in fear and trembling, feeling that he has not done his work and has nothing. Yet that service may be one of the most glorious he has ever had the privilege of conducting. Why? Because he does not control the power; it varies.

And this is true not only in preaching but in daily life and experience. We do not control the well of water that is in us—it controls us; so the power, of necessity, varies from time to time even in the same person. Show me a person who is always the same, always on the same level—I doubt whether he is a Christian at all. Show me a preacher who is always at the same level—he is not much of a preacher. A great preacher will sometimes be a very bad preacher. It is because there is this other element, the element of the Spirit, the unknown, the unseen, the authority, the power. A man relying on his own ability can always operate on a certain level, but he is always on that level. But here there are variations; you are up, you are down, you are on top of the mountain, you are down in the depths. But, oh, the glory of the possibilities of this power, of this water bubbling up into everlasting life!

Let me just quote a few passages before I finish to show the sort of thing I am talking about. Here is the height of the power. Fairly soon after the Day of Pentecost, the apostles are on trial. When they are prohibited to preach, Peter gives the immortal answer, "We cannot but speak" (Acts 4:20). That is the power. A mere man never says a thing like that. "We cannot help speaking!" Why not? Not because they had decided they were going to preach—they were not those sorts of people. This man Peter was the one who, in order to save his life, had denied his Lord just a few weeks earlier. He had been afraid of the authorities and terrified of being arrested. He now faces the Sanhedrin and says, "For we cannot but speak the things which we have seen and heard." "It is no use telling us to stop—we cannot stop, we cannot help ourselves."

Or listen to the apostle Paul putting it in his way: "The love of Christ constraineth us" (2 Cor. 5:14)! He is like a man in a vise. It has been wound up; it is being pressed upward. "Woe is unto me, if I preach not the gospel!" (1 Cor. 9:16). You do not decide to do these things in cold blood, you do not do them mechanically, but you are aware of this tremendous pressure, power. "The love of Christ constraineth me"—a man under pressure, he cannot desist.

Or listen to the apostle Paul writing to the Colossians: "Whom [the Lord Jesus Christ] we preach, warning every man, and teaching every man in all wisdom; that we may present every man perfect in Christ Jesus"—then listen—"whereunto I also labour." Here is the secret: "I labour." Of course he does all he can—his preparation, his activities, his travelling. ". . . striving"—that is a stronger word; striving goes beyond laboring—"according to his working, which worketh in me mightily" (Col. 1:28–29). Can you not see it? He is like a volcano. There is a power, fire, within him, moving him, energizing him, carrying him along irresistibly in the performance of his great and his high calling.

Jeremiah speaks of the same power: "a . . . fire . . . in my bones." He had decided not to speak again because every time he spoke he got into trouble. "But," he said, "his word was in mine heart as a burning fire shut up in my bones" (Jer. 20:9).

My dear friends, do you know anything of this power working in you? People in times of revival know it tremendously in their personal experience. But there are variations. Do not be discouraged if it is low at the present time. Examine yourself—make sure you are not quenching or grieving the Spirit. But even when you have done all that, there is no guarantee that you will get the power. The idea that teaches, "Do this and you will get that" is not Christianity; you do not control it. There has been a foolish false teaching for eighty years or so that has told people, "Be willing to be willing and you will get it. Do this—surrender and you will have it." But you can do everything and still be lifeless. "His working, which worketh in me mightily . . . shall be within you a well of water springing up into everlasting life." *His power*! The possibilities are glorious; they are endless! Realize that. Seek this, and do not be satisfied until you know the mighty power of the life of God working in your life, lifting you above and outside yourself. And then what you do will not be mechanical works but will be the fruit of the Spirit.

16

Mind, Heart, and Will

Jesus answered and said unto her, If thou knewest the gift of God, and who it is that saith to thee, Give me to drink; thou wouldest have asked of him, and he would have given thee living water. . . . Whosoever drinketh of this water shall thirst again: but whosoever drinketh of the water that I shall give him shall never thirst; but the water that I shall give him shall be in him a well of water springing up into everlasting life. (John 4:10, 13–14)

We are considering together the main characteristics of the life that is given to us by the Son of God, this "gift of God," and we are now dealing with the particular characteristics of this life. So far we have seen that it is inward and also that it is a power within us, a power that is working within in a mighty manner, and we must never forget that.

But now I want to take this teaching a step further and point out that this power that works within us, this "well of water springing up into everlasting life," changes our lives in a radical manner. These points, you notice, follow logically one upon the other, and it is important that we should take them in that way. If this power that is working in us is the power of God—and we have seen that it is—then it is obvious that it must change us radically. It is not superficial, not on the surface. It must produce the most profound change conceivable, and this is confirmed by the terminology that is employed in the New Testament concerning this power.

One of the terms used is *regeneration*. Now there is nothing more profound than regeneration. The Christian faith is not something that merely makes us a bit better than we were; it does not just improve the surface appearance. No, no! It is *re*generation. You are generated anew and afresh. In other words, and to use a more frequent term, it is *rebirth*. Rebirth is the essence of the teaching in the third chapter to John's Gospel.

There our Lord, interrupting the speech of that great teacher Nicodemus, said, "Ye must be born again" (v. 7). Nicodemus had dropped into the customary fallacy of thinking that our Lord just had something extra to give, something that he, Nicodemus, could add on to what he already had. "No, no," said our Lord in essence, "you do not understand. You are quite wrong. You have nothing. You need to be born again. You must go back to the very beginning. The foundation needs to be changed."

The Christian life is as radical as that. But the difficulty is that people, as we have seen, fail to realize this; they will turn Christianity into a religion or into a philosophy, something that we add on to our lives. But that is quite wrong. The apostle Paul compares this new birth to a new creation. He says, "Therefore if any man be in Christ, he is a new creature [a new creation]: old things are passed away; behold, all things are become new" (2 Cor. 5:17). And in Romans 6, making the same point, he says that this life is comparable to a death followed by a resurrection—the end of one life, the beginning of another: "Likewise reckon ye also yourselves to be dead indeed unto sin, but alive unto God through Jesus Christ our Lord" (v. 11). The reference is to our Lord himself, crucified, dying upon the cross and his body buried in a grave, then the mighty resurrection in that new, glorified body.

And that, says Paul, is what happens to a Christian. We have been crucified with Christ, we have died with him, and we have also risen with him in newness of life. Now it is impossible to conceive of any stronger comparisons or analogies than this—a death, a resurrection out of death. But that is the language that is used in the Scripture in order to bring out the radical character of the change that takes place when someone becomes a Christian.

There is another way of putting this that I myself am very fond of and that Paul constantly uses in the sixth chapter of Romans, as he does in other places. "Ye were . . . ye are!" "But God be thanked, that ye were the servants of sin, but ye have . . ." (Rom. 6:17). You have, you have received, you are. And this is not confined to the apostle Paul. The apostle Peter says to Gentile people who had become Christians, "Which in time past were not a people, but are now the people of God" (1 Pet. 2:10). Here is the contrast—something that you were and something that you are, that you have become. The point is that there is a complete contrast. The New Testament uses an almost endless variety of expressions to describe this great change that takes place within us, and this makes it all the more important that we should grasp the point.

Another way in which this change is put is in terms of a contrast between living a life "after the flesh" and living a life "after the Spirit": "For they that are after the flesh do mind the things of the flesh; but they that are after the Spirit the things of the Spirit" (Rom. 8:5). And then Paul adds, "But ye are not in the flesh, but in the Spirit, if so be that the Spirit of God dwell in you" (v. 9). But perhaps it can all be summed up by putting it like this: when you become a Christian, you receive a new heart. It is nothing less than a change of heart.

Now it is very important that we should always remember that the Bible uses the term *heart* in a very special way. When we hear this word, we tend to think immediately of the affections, the emotions, the feelings; but Scripture uses the term in a much more profound sense. It includes the feelings, but it contains much more than the feelings. In Scripture, the heart stands for the center of the personality, the very core of one's being. We all have a center. We have various faculties, we have the body and its propensities and characteristics, and we have our temperaments and so on. But there is something at the center that controls all this, and that is what the Scripture means by the heart. It is the very spring of life, that which controls who the person is and what the person does.

The older theologians had a very good term to express the center of the personality—I know of no better one. They talked about one's "disposition" and said that when a man or woman becomes a Christian there is a profound and radical change in their disposition, they have received a new disposition. I have sometimes used an illustration to bring out this point, and I think it is helpful. Think of it in terms of management. Think of a man running his own business. He perhaps employs a number of others to help him, but he owns the business. He has the direction and the control; he is the ultimate authority, and he gives out the orders. Then his business is bought up or taken over by another firm. He may still continue as a manager, and the employees are there as before, but there is an essential difference. There has been a change at the center of control.

The image that our Lord uses is, "the water that I shall give him shall be in him a well of water springing up into everlasting life." There will be a new disposition, and this will govern everything else about this person. In other words, we must realize that there is a change of the whole personality.

Now I could easily show you that the failure to realize this has accounted for many of the heresies and freak religious movements of the past. The failure to realize this tends to lead us all astray. We want to be put right intellectually only or in the realm of the feelings only or in the realm of activity only, but that is not Christianity. And it is when the personality is dealt with in a piecemeal manner rather than as a whole that you have something that is spurious.

So the general statement is that this life, this well of water that is put into us, this life of God in the soul, will manifest itself in the whole of our personality. We must therefore consider what these manifestations are. But let me add this, lest someone be discouraged. It is my business, of course, to represent this new life at its maximum, at its best and highest. The New Testament itself always does that. But do not let yourself think that you are not a Christian simply because you find that you do not have 100 percent of what I have described. All I am concerned about is this: are we able to say that on the whole this is true of us? If this essential change has taken place, it is bound to manifest itself in these various ways. But, of course, there are variations in the degree to which it does so. The Scripture itself teaches us this when it says that we are born "babes in Christ" and then grow to be "children" and after that "young men," then adults, and finally "old men." There is a progression, a maturing; there is a development as one goes on in the Christian life under the instruction of Scripture and the influence of the Holy Spirit. But in the youngest babe there is this essential life, and it always shows itself.

And so we can analyze this new birth in the following way. First, there is obviously a profound change in the minds of Christian people, in their understanding. Again, here is something that is illustrated and emphasized in many places in the New Testament. It is one of the big differences between a Christian and a non-Christian. There is a different mind, a different understanding, a different outlook. Our Lord himself, for instance, puts it like this in his great high-priestly prayer when he is praying for these men whom he is going to leave behind him to carry on his work. He says, "I have manifested thy name unto the men which thou gavest me out of the world: thine they were, and thou gavest them me; and they have kept thy word."

These are men who have been given to him out of the world; they are separated people. And our Lord says that they have this characteristic: "they have kept thy word." And he continues:

> Now they have known that all things whatsoever thou hast given me are of thee. For I have given unto them the words which thou gavest me; and they have received them, and have known surely that I came

> out from thee, and they have believed that thou didst send me. I pray for them: I pray not for the world, but for them which thou hast given me; for they are thine.

He then sums it all up at the end of that same prayer when he says, "O righteous Father, the world hath not known thee: but I have known thee, and these have known that thou hast sent me" (John 17:6–9, 25).

There, you see, is the big differentiating point. Here are people who have this understanding concerning him and his purpose in the world, which the world in general does not know or recognize. This is a vital matter, and in my pastoral work as people come to me in difficulties about their spiritual or their Christian lives, I am constantly finding myself having to quote these statements. People say to me, "You know, I don't think I'm a Christian after all. I had some sort of an experience, I was forced under pressure in a meeting to say certain things, but I don't think that I have ever really been a Christian." And they are distressed about this. How can one help them?

Well, I find that one of the best ways of all is to show them that they have a new mind, a new understanding. I generally start by putting it to them like this. I say, "Why have you come to see me? Why are you troubled about this? Can't you see that you are doing something rather exceptional in this modern world? Think of your friends and associates, think of your fellow students or your friends at work—are they concerned about this? Are they questioning somebody like me because they are troubled and want to know whether or not they are Christians—is that their attitude?"

And they smile at me. "Well, no," they say.

"Of course not," I say. "They ridicule the whole thing and probably think you are a little bit mad for being troubled about such things." In this way I immediately establish that there is a difference in outlook between them and other people. Then I take them to the second chapter of the First Epistle to the Corinthians where these truths are put so plainly and clearly. The apostle is reminding the Christians in Corinth that the wisdom that he is talking about in the gospel is a mystery—"the hidden wisdom." He says:

> Which none of the princes of this world knew: for had they known it, they would not have crucified the Lord of glory. But as it is written, Eye hath not seen, nor ear heard, neither have entered into the heart of man, the things which God hath prepared for them that love him.

> But God hath revealed them unto us [to Christians] by his Spirit: for the Spirit searcheth all things, yea, the deep things of God. . . . Now we have received, not the spirit of the world, but the spirit which is of God; that we might know the things that are freely given to us of God. Which things also we speak, not in the words which man's wisdom teacheth, but which the Holy Ghost teacheth; comparing spiritual things with spiritual.

Then comes the crucial verse: "But the natural man . . ."—that is, the non-Christian. Those who are not Christians may be very able, very moral, but they do not have the Spirit in them, they do not have the well of water, they do not have the new life. A non-Christian may be a "natural man" at his very best, but here is the truth: ". . . receiveth not the things of the Spirit of God: for they are foolishness unto him: neither can he know them, because they are spiritually discerned" (1 Cor. 2:8–10, 12–14).

I say to these people, therefore, who come to me, "You are concerned about this?"

"Yes," they say.

"You are troubled and anxious about these things?"

"Yes."

"You want to know these things?"

"Certainly."

"Well, then," I say, "'the natural man receiveth not the things of the Spirit of God: for they are foolishness unto him: neither can he know them.' Are these things foolishness to you?"

"No," they say.

"Very well," I say, "you are not a natural person, and if you are not a natural person, you must be a spiritual person—there is no other possibility. You are either natural or spiritual, you are either in the flesh or in the Spirit, and the proof of your being a spiritual person is that you do not regard these things as foolishness but are anxious about them."

Then Paul goes on to say:

> But he that is spiritual judgeth [hath understanding of] all things, yet he himself is judged of no man. For who hath known the mind of the Lord, that he may instruct him? But we have the mind of Christ. (1 Cor. 2:15–16)

That is a magnificent statement and is perhaps the clearest of all the statements with respect to this matter. But let nobody think that this is just

Pauline teaching. The apostle John says exactly the same thing. As an old man writing his farewell letter to Christian people, he was worried about them because certain false teachers—antichrists—had gone abroad. There were false teachers in the church even in the first century. Let me say once more that there is nothing so fatuous and ridiculous about people who pride themselves on their modernity as their ignorance and their failure to realize that they are but the modern counterparts, and very pale imitators, of the false teachers of the first century—antichrists. But ultimately John was quite happy about the Christians to whom he was writing. He say, "They went out from us, but they were not of us; for if they had been of us, they would no doubt have continued with us: but they went out, that they might be made manifest that they were not all of us" (1 John 2:19).

Here are people who belonged to the church, but they had gone away and were now teaching heresy, and thereby, says John, they are giving proof that they did not really belong to us. But then he goes on, "But ye have an unction from the Holy One, and ye know all things. I have not written unto you because ye know not the truth, but because ye know it, and that no lie is of the truth" (vv. 20–21).

John says, "Ye have an unction." What does that mean? Well, it is not any natural ability. It is something they have been given from the Holy One, from the Holy Spirit within them. A little later John repeats this, and it is reminiscent of our Lord's words to the woman of Samaria: "The water that I shall give him shall be in him a well of water springing up into everlasting life."

> The anointing which ye have received of him abideth in you, and ye need not that any man teach you: but as the same anointing teacheth you of all things, and is truth, and is no lie, and even as it hath taught you, ye shall abide in him. (v. 27)

Now that is a perfect way of putting this very point about the change, the radical change, in the mind and understanding. This is the first profound manifestation of this new life that is within. We can enforce it still further by putting it in terms of certain great contrasts. The apostle Paul does this in the Epistle to the Ephesians: "This I say therefore, and testify in the Lord, that ye henceforth walk not as other Gentiles walk." How do they walk? How is the world living today? What is the difference between a Christian and a non-Christian? What is the effect of having within you this well of water, this life of God, this new disposition that governs everything and especially your mind? Well, here it is—"in the vanity [emptiness] of their mind, having the understanding darkened, being alienated from the life of God through the ignorance that is in them, because of the blindness of their heart" (Eph. 4:17–18). Could anything be clearer?

The trouble with people who are not Christians is that their understanding is darkened, and they are alienated from the life of God. Why? "Through the ignorance that is in them." That is the whole explanation of the state of the world. But that is no longer true of the Christian. You are not to be like those people in any respect, says Paul. Why? Because your minds have been enlightened; you have received this unction, this anointing. You have new life in you. You have "put off concerning . . . the old man" and have been "renewed in the spirit of your mind" (Eph. 4:22–23).

So how does all this show itself in actual practice? It can be put like this: a Christian is someone who knows what the truth is. Our Lord says to this woman of Samaria, "If thou knewest the gift of God, and who it is that saith to thee . . ." She did not know, but the Christian, by definition, is one who does know. Christians know the truth about the Lord Jesus Christ; they know the truth about themselves. Christians know that they are condemned sinners, under the wrath of God, who do not deserve anything but punishment and retribution. They know this, they see it quite clearly, and they see the blessed truth that God has provided the way of salvation in his only begotten Son, who saved us by dying on the cross on Calvary's hill. They know what the truth is, and they have a measure of understanding concerning it.

Now I am taking it for granted that we are all familiar with these great doctrines of the faith. But the point I want to establish at the moment is this: Christians not only know this teaching and see it, they see its inevitability. By that I mean that their old difficulties have gone, and so has their old opposition.

You know what I mean, do you not? You have known what it is to stumble at these truths and to be always arguing against them and fighting them. But the moment you became a Christian, all that came to an end. Now I am not saying that Christians understand everything. Of course they do not; they have to grow. But there has been a shift, a change in their whole position. That is what matters. So now, though they still fumble and stumble and often still do not understand and have many questions, they are on the side of truth; they are no longer against it. Before, they were always trying to find reasons to reject it, putting forth their trick questions and arguments, watching every word, trying to trip up the preacher or anybody putting forward the Christian faith. But they are now in an entirely different position. They want to know and to understand; all their sympathies are on this side, and when they come across a difficulty, they do not immediately say, "Ah, there's nothing in it after all." Rather they say, "I'm defective somewhere here; there must be an explanation."

Let me give you just one illustration. Take the great doctrine of the death of Christ, the doctrine of the atonement. It has always been a great stumbling block to the unbeliever. The apostle tells us that it was a stumbling block to Jews, and to Greeks it was foolishness. And the modern man, the intellectual, finds the whole notion quite immoral. Thereby, of course, he tells us that he is not a Christian because he does not see his own need. But the moment people become Christians, their root difficulty with regard to the atonement vanishes completely. Why? Because they are by definition men and women who have been enlightened; they have come to see that they are hopeless, condemned sinners who can do nothing at all. They have some glimmer of understanding of the righteousness and the holiness and the justice of God, but that no longer troubles them. They feel that the glory of God is that he is essentially different from us.

Then the question is, how can such a God forgive such creatures as we are? And the answer is found in the atonement. It is a mystery, it is wonderful, it is amazing. Christians do not understand it fully, but they can see now that there was no other way, that there is an inevitability about it. They are no longer against this truth. They want understanding; they want help; they do not resent it or constantly try to dismiss it. Paul sums up this change in that extraordinary statement at the end of 1 Corinthians 2: "We have the mind of Christ." What a statement! We used to have the mind of the world, but we now have "the mind of Christ."

So I put this to you as a general question: which side are you on? Let me put it still more plainly: what is your prejudice? Are you prejudiced against this truth or are you prejudiced in its favor? When men and women have this new life put into them, this well of water springing up into everlasting life, their whole disposition, their prejudice, is changed radically. They are delivered "from the power of darkness" and have been "translated . . . into the kingdom of his dear Son" (Col. 1:13). Or as Paul puts it in Romans 8:5, "They that are after the flesh do mind the things of the flesh; but they that are after the Spirit the things of the Spirit." Now this word "mind" means "are interested in," "are concerned about," "delight in." The Christian delights in the Spirit. Is this true of us? If it is not, then we are not Christians.

You can, I repeat, be a very good person; you can be doing a lot of good; you can want to make the world a better place; you may be marching and protesting about a thousand and one things. But if you do not know Jesus, I say to you that you are not a Christian. Christians "mind" these things of the soul and of the Spirit. These have the priority. This is what controls their entire outlook. And you either have this or you do not. If you do not, I say again, you are not a Christian. You can never produce this by your own efforts. All you and I can do is to drink the water that he has to give, and then it becomes in us "a well of water springing up into everlasting life."

This is the secret and the explanation of some of those amazing, dramatic stories that we read in the lives of the saints, the profound change that they underwent. It is all seen and exemplified to perfection in the apostle Paul himself, who puts it like this: "I verily thought with myself, that I ought to do many things contrary to the name of Jesus of Nazareth" (Acts 26:9). That is what he *was*. Then he becomes "the apostle of Jesus Christ" and glories in him, "determined not to know any thing . . . save Jesus Christ, and him crucified" (1 Cor. 2:2). What a profound change in the mind, the understanding, in the whole outlook and orientation!

But, secondly, there is an equally profound change in the heart. Again, you see, this is quite inevitable. If people are Christians, their feelings and their emotions are bound to be engaged. There is no such thing as a theoretical Christian; that is a contradiction in terms. That is inevitable because if you really believe the truth I have been referring to, you cannot remain unmoved; it is impossible. Of course, you can see these things intellectually and subscribe to them—I am not talking about that. I am talking about really believing them, really being governed by them.

Is not this a note that is lacking today? And it is because it is lacking that we tend so often to produce an artificial joviality and try to manufacture bright services and so on. What a travesty! If the truth is in you, the truth will move you. "God be thanked," says the apostle, "that ye were the servants of sin, but ye have obeyed from the heart that form of doctrine which was delivered you" (Rom. 6:17). Of course! Christians rejoice in the truth. They do not subscribe to it reluctantly or apologetically or halfheartedly; it is everything to them. This is the biggest thing for them. They are moved by it to the very depth of their being. That is why the apostle Paul, this giant intellect who in his epistles writes about and handles these marvelous themes with profound logic, will suddenly burst out, smash his own grammar, forget form as his heart begins to speak, and indulge in some great exclamation such as, "God forbid that I should glory, save in the cross of our Lord Jesus Christ" (Gal. 6:14). That is why Paul is always talking about glorying and rejoicing.

This, again, follows inevitably. Do you go to church to listen to the exposition of God's Word as a matter of duty? Do you go reluctantly? Do you go halfheartedly? Or do you go keenly, enthusiastically, excitedly, wanting to get more and more of it, rejoicing in it and knowing there is nothing in the world comparable to it? Nothing has done so much harm to Christianity as a formal religion that is observed as a matter of form, part of the Sunday morning service only if it is not too long. That is not Christianity at all. That is religion; that is law. We are reminded that we are not under law but under grace, and this is one of the ways in which we test that.

Is your heart, in the sense of your feelings, your emotions, engaged? The apostle John puts this perfectly. In his first epistle he has a number of tests that he applies to people so they can know whether or not they are Christians, and this is one of the best: "His commandments are not grievous" (1 John 5:3). If you find the commandments of God grievous, you had better examine yourself again. Why are they not grievous to the Christian? Because they are inevitable. Christians are men and women who have a love for God and a love for the Savior. They say, "God so loved the world [he so loved me], that he gave his only begotten Son, that whosoever believeth in him should not perish, but have everlasting life" (John 3:16); and believing that, their hearts overflow with praise and gratitude and thanksgiving. This must follow as the night follows the day.

If you believe that since "[God] spared not his own Son, but delivered him up for us all, how shall he not with him also freely give us all things?" (Rom. 8:32), then, again, your heart wells up in gratitude and in praise and in thanksgiving, and you are filled with joy. Peter defines the joy for us. "Whom having not seen," he says, referring to the Lord Jesus Christ, "ye love; in whom, though now ye see him not, yet believing, ye rejoice with joy unspeakable and full of glory" (1 Pet. 1:8). Christians find themselves bursting out and saying, "Thanks be unto God for his unspeakable gift" (2 Cor. 9:15), and with Peter, "Blessed be the God and Father of our Lord Jesus Christ, which according to his abundant mercy hath begotten us again unto a lively hope by the resurrection of Jesus Christ from the dead" (1 Pet. 1:3).

My friends, are your feelings engaged? Are you moved by the truth that you believe? There is a new emotional aspect to the life of those who are Christians, and unless you have been moved emotionally, you are not a Christian. It is contradictory to the Christian position for a man to be able to preach about these things without feeling or emotion, with a kind of detachment as if he were reading an essay, concerned about the form of his address rather than the substance. Ah, the perfection that denies the true Christianity—how terrible that is! No, no! There is a freedom here; there is a joy; there is an abandon. George Whitefield always used to say to ministers that a man should never preach unless he preaches "a felt Christ." Is it possible for a man who preaches the truth about Christ not to feel it? It is impossible. Really to see him and to know him and to believe him, you must have "a felt Christ"; the feelings are engaged as much as the intellect and the understanding.

And, thirdly, this also applies to the will. Again, note the inevitability. It is obvious. Those who believe these things are moved by them and want to do something about them. They have a desire to obey, and this desire results from the understanding and the feeling. It is not theoretical; it is not just a point of view; it is not imposed upon them. No, no! They see the whole. They reason like this: "I believe that Jesus Christ died for me on the cross. Why did he do that? He died that I might be forgiven; he died to reconcile me to God. But was that all? Has he just provided me with some kind of insurance so that now I can go on sinning as much as I like, knowing that I am covered by the blood of Christ?"

That is the very question Paul asks: "Shall we continue in sin, that grace may abound?" (Rom. 6:1). If you say that, you have not understood the gospel at all. Paul continues, "God forbid. How shall we, that are dead to sin, live any longer therein?" (v. 2). Or as he puts it to Titus, "[Christ] gave himself for us, that he might redeem us from all iniquity, and purify unto himself a peculiar people, zealous of good works" (Titus 2:14). He died that we might be forgiven, but he also died to make us good. His whole object is to destroy the works of the devil, to produce a people worthy of their Father who is in heaven.

So the moment men and women have this new life in them, this well of water springing up, they do not live the Christian life reluctantly, they do not object to the commandments. That is the whole difference between being religious or moral or ethical on the one hand and being truly Christian on the other. Moral people obey grimly. They force themselves. It is a rigid discipline, a kind of stoicism. But Christians are entirely different; their attitude is positive. They see why all these things have happened; they desire to be good; they want to please God; they want to show their gratitude.

This is the change that has taken place in the realm of the will. Christians are not fighting against the gospel; they are not moving as near as they can to the world without getting over the border and being punished. No, no! They want to be as far away from the world as they can, they want to grow in grace and in the knowledge of the Lord, and they are aware of a new ability within them. When people become Christians, this change takes place in their wills. The trouble with "the natural man" is that his will is in a state of bondage; but when men and women receive this new life, their wills are set free.

This is put so plainly by the apostle in the Epistle to the Romans. "Sin," he says, "shall not have dominion over you"—why not?—"for ye are not under the law, but under grace" (Rom. 6:14). Do you see the difference? Sin used to have dominion over you. The natural man is under the bondage and serfdom of sin and of Satan; he is in a state of bondage. But the Christian is not. Paul says in Romans 8:15, "For ye have not received the spirit of bondage again to fear; but ye have received the Spirit of adoption, whereby we cry, Abba, Father." And in Romans 8:2, "the law of the Spirit of life in Christ Jesus hath made me free from the law of sin and death." That is the argument. Paul says in Romans 7:

> When we were in the flesh, the motions of sins, which were by the law, did work in our members to bring forth fruit unto death. But now we are delivered from the law, that being dead wherein we were held; that we should serve in newness of spirit, and not in the oldness of the letter. (vv. 5–6)

And he makes exactly the same point in that great moral, ethical appeal at the beginning of Romans 12—watch the word "therefore":

> I beseech you therefore, brethren, by the mercies of God, that ye present your bodies a living sacrifice, holy, acceptable unto God, which is your reasonable service. And be not conformed to this world: but be ye transformed by the renewing of your mind, that ye may prove what is that good, and acceptable, and perfect, will of God. (vv. 1–2)

This, then, is what happens to anyone who receives this new life. The entire personality is changed; there is a new disposition. It is the disposition that governs the mind, the heart, and the will in every person, every human being. In someone who is not a Christian, the disposition is evil, and the mind and heart and will are working against God, against his or her own best interests, governed by the world, the flesh, and the devil. But those who drink of this water receive a new life and a new disposition. They are given a new mind, a new feeling, a new understanding, and it is all working in the direction of God and of the soul and of holiness and of heaven and of a joy that is unspeakable and full of glory.

Do you have this new life in you? Do you have the new disposition? Are you essentially different from the person who is not a Christian, the person you once were yourself? God give us grace to answer this profound question in the only way that matters, enabling us to say, "I was!" but now, "But by the grace of God I am what I am" (1 Cor. 15:10).

17

"The Life of God in the Soul of Man"

Jesus answered and said unto her, If thou knewest the gift of God, and who it is that saith to thee, Give me to drink; thou wouldest have asked of him, and he would have given thee living water. . . . Whosoever drinketh of the water that I shall give him shall be in him a well of water springing up into everlasting life. (John 4:10, 13–14)

We have been considering the particular characteristics of the great life offered us by our Lord. We have seen, first, that it is a heart religion, and, second, that it is a mighty power that takes up the whole person—mind, heart, and will. The whole personality is involved. It is a total change that can only be represented by referring to it as regeneration, a new birth, a new creation.

But we do not stop even there because we must again take this a step further. The text demands this, insists upon it, particularly as we consider it in the light of other and perhaps even more explicit teaching elsewhere in Scripture. In this passage our Lord is presenting a picture of this new life to the Samaritan woman. She does not understand. We have seen from the record how she stumbles and asks her questions. So our Lord puts it very generally to her. The next step, therefore, in this analysis is to see that what he is talking about is more than power. It is a power, as we have been emphasizing, that changes the whole personality; but it is more than that. It is, indeed, a *life*, and Christians are aware of a new life within them.

But the counter-distinction that I have in my mind is that our Lord is not just talking about some urge toward a new life or a new way of living. We ended our last study by saying that obviously this "well of water" that our Lord gives will lead to a new way of living—that is because it affects the will. The truth perceived moves the heart, and that in turn moves the will. So Christians do practice and live a new and a different kind of life, but what makes them do that is not merely a power that urges, it is not merely a persuasion. There is an element, of course, of moral and spiritual persuasion in it, but it is more than that. And I am trying to establish that we must realize this further truth because, after all, one of the most glorious aspects of the Christian life is that it is not merely a power in the sense of a dynamic force. There are powers, such as machines and so on, that can stimulate us; electrical vibrations can put a kind of energy into us. But this is not like that; it includes that, but it is the result of an actual life within us. We must use the terms that are found in the Scriptures themselves. It is a new life within. And, even more incredible and amazing, it is a *divine* life.

I have already referred to the book that greatly influenced Whitefield and the Wesleys two hundred years ago, a book by old Henry Scougal, a Scotsman who lived toward the end of the eighteenth century. It was called *The Life of God in the Soul of Man*. That, he said, was Christianity. And that was what awakened these great men of God to the fact that they had never been Christians. Though they had been brought up in religious homes, they realized that they had never really had this life. They had been living in a certain way, but it had been a religion based upon their activities. But now Henry Scougal convicted them. And the writings of William Law were used much to the same end, although they were not as good and as scriptural as the book by Henry Scougal. However, the truth that was brought home to them was that Christianity is nothing less than the life of God in the souls of men.

Now, of course, there are abundant statements of this truth in Scripture. We see one when our Lord was speaking to Nicodemus, when he says, "Verily, verily, I say unto thee, Except a man be born of water and of the Spirit, he cannot enter into the kingdom of God" (John 3:5). And he goes on, "That which is born of the flesh is flesh; and that which is born of the Spirit is spirit" (v. 6). Christians do not merely have a new outlook and a new disposition—they have new life in them. The new outlook is the result of the fact that they have been "born of the Spirit."

The apostle Peter, in the first chapter of his second epistle, makes the same point in different language and in very striking terms. In verse 2 he prays that "grace and peace [may] be multiplied" to these Christian believers and continues:

> . . . according as his divine power hath given unto us all things that pertain unto life and godliness, through the knowledge of him that hath called us to glory and virtue: whereby are given unto us exceeding great and precious promises: that by these ye might be partakers of the divine nature. (vv. 3–4)

That is it—"partakers of the divine nature." The apostle John in his first epistle makes the same point when he talks about the "seed" that remains in the believer, and not only the seed. He says, "These things have I written unto you that believe on the name of the Son of God; that ye may know that ye have eternal life, and that ye may believe on the name of the Son of God" (5:13). And John had just said that this life is in the Son: "He that hath the Son hath life; and he that hath not the Son of God hath not life" (v. 12).

Now these statements all bring home to us this great and staggering teaching that the power that works in us, transforming us entirely in the mighty way we have been considering, is the power of an endless life. It is the power of divine life, so that we are "partakers of the divine nature." This, of course, is a great mystery. Our Lord said that to Nicodemus: "Marvel not that I said unto thee, Ye must be born again" (John 3:7). Nicodemus was foolish enough to try to understand it, and many of us have repeated his error, but it cannot be understood. It has often been compared—and I think rightly—to our Lord's own incarnation. He was "conceived . . . of the Holy Ghost" (Matt. 1:20). He derived his human nature from Mary, his mother, but he was born of the Holy Spirit, conceived by the Holy Spirit, born as a man in that way. And, therefore, it is right to say that in a sense this is comparable to what happens to us. It is an operation of the Holy Spirit; we are "born of the Spirit." There is a new birth and a new being, and we are made "partakers of the divine nature."

Now the phrase "partakers of the divine nature" eludes our understanding. We must be careful that we do not imagine that this means that we become divine. Let me put it like this: we are told that at the very beginning of creation God created man in his own image and likeness. That is the idea that we must keep in our minds. It does not mean that when man was created, he was created a god. He was not. He was man—perfect man. The meaning of the phrase *created in the image of God* is that God gave to man certain characteristics of his own divine nature and being. This, of course, differentiates man from the animals. That is what is meant in Scripture by "the image," and it is that image that has been defaced and partly lost by the Fall. So man has lost these particular characteristics that he had originally that made him like God.

In the rebirth that is what we regain. This, again, is said by the apostle Paul in the Epistle to the Ephesians. He is reminding Gentile people who had been born again and had now become new beings that they must not go on living as they had before and as other Gentiles still were. Why not? This is how he puts it:

> Put off concerning the former conversation the old man, which is corrupt according to the deceitful lusts; and be renewed in the spirit of your mind; and . . . put on the new man, which after God is created in righteousness and true holiness. (4:22–24)

That is it! This new person is a new creation.

Now in the original creation, the man, Adam, in his perfection was righteous. God gave him an original righteousness, an original holiness; he was free from sin. And what is given to us in the rebirth—and this is the real meaning of the words "partakers of the divine nature"—is not that we become gods, nor that we become divine, but that we receive again this original righteousness, this something that is in God himself and that he puts into us, "righteousness and true holiness" or "holiness of the truth" (Eph. 4:24). And so it is right to say that we are "born of the Spirit." And, indeed, in his first epistle John goes so far as to say this about our Lord: "as he is, so are we in this world" (4:17). And, of course, implicit in all this is the notion that we become "the children of God" (1 John 3:10; Rom. 8:16).

Now that does not only mean that God takes an interest in us comparable to the interest of a father in his children—it goes beyond that. We are "the children of God" in a deeper sense, and because of that, we are "heirs of God, and joint-heirs with Christ" (Rom. 8:17). And all that is implicit in the statement that our Lord makes to the woman of Samaria. It is a power, yes, but it is the power of this life, this principle, this divine nature—"partakers of the divine nature."

How frequently we fail to realize this! Indeed, probably from day to day none of us realizes this as we should. We know that we are changed; there was no difficulty about agreeing with everything I was trying to say when we were considering the change in the mind, the outlook, the orientation in the desires and the affections and the will. But we must go beyond that. And it is, I am persuaded increasingly, because we as Christian people do not realize these profundities concerning ourselves, because we do not realize what we are as Christians, that the church is as she is and her witness is so weak and ineffective. This is the key to true Christian living and to rejoicing in Christ. It is only as we realize these truths that we shall become people whom God can use to his glory and praise.

Too often we are apologetic for our Christianity and are almost ashamed of it in our work or professions. If ever you feel at all ashamed of your Christianity, it is for one reason only—you do not realize this truth. If you were a member of the royal family, you would not try to hide it, and we are told here that we are members of the family of God. This is the great contrast that Paul is so fond of making: "ye are no more strangers and foreigners, but fellowcitizens with the saints, and of the household of God" (Eph. 2:19). We are children of God! God is our Father in a sense that he is not the Father of those who are not Christians.

This, then, is what our Lord is saying to the woman of Samaria, and we have been looking at it broadly and generally. But the Scriptures are more specific, and we come here to the fourth characteristic of this life. They actually go on to say—and this is all a part of what it means to have this well of water within us "springing up into everlasting life"—that not only are we partakers of the divine nature, but in addition God dwells within us. That is why Scougal's title to his book is so good—*The Life of God in the Soul of Man*. Now this, again, is an exposition of the great, true, mystical teaching of the Scripture. I have referred to false mysticism, but there is a true mysticism, and this is the mysticism that tells us that the Christian is joined to the life of God because of God dwelling in his or her soul.

This is divided up like this. We are told that the Holy Spirit dwells within us. This is made plain in many passages. A famous one, of course, is in this same Gospel of John where our Lord says to the religious public what he says here privately to the woman of Samaria: "In the last day, that great day of the feast, Jesus stood and cried, saying, If any man thirst, let him come unto me, and drink. He that believeth on me, as the scripture hath said, out of his belly [out of his innermost parts] shall flow rivers of living water." Then John explains, "But this spake he of the Spirit, which they that believe on him should receive: for the Holy Ghost was not yet given; because that Jesus was not yet glorified" (John 7:37–39)

Now that is a great statement of this truth. Then later our Lord, giving this final teaching to his disciples, puts it like this: "If ye love me, keep my commandments. And I will pray the Father, and he shall give you another Comforter"—our Lord was a Comforter while he was here, and now he is going to give another Comforter—"that he may abide with you for ever; even the Spirit of truth; whom the world cannot receive, because it seeth him not, neither knoweth him: but ye know him; for he dwelleth with you, and shall be in you" (John 14:15–17).

There it is put plainly and clearly that the Spirit dwells within us.

Now when we come to the exposition of that teaching in the epistles, we find the apostle Paul saying this plainly and clearly. Writing to the Romans he says, "So then they that are in the flesh"—they who are not Christians—"cannot please God. But ye are not in the flesh, but in the Spirit, if so be that the Spirit of God dwell in you" (Rom. 8:8–9). What could be plainer than that? Again in verse 11 he says, "If the Spirit of him that raised up Jesus from the dead dwell in you, he that raised up Christ from the dead shall also quicken your mortal bodies by his Spirit that dwelleth in you."

But a still more specific passage is in the First Epistle to the Corinthians. The apostle there is dealing with sins in the flesh—fornication and so on—and this is his argument:

> What? know ye not that your body is the temple of the Holy Ghost which is in you, which ye have of God, and ye are not your own? For ye are bought with a price: therefore glorify God in your body, and in your spirit, which are God's. (6:19–20)

The Holy Spirit dwells in us, in our bodies. Our bodies are temples in which he resides and in which he dwells.

So there it is beyond any doubt or question whatsoever; and James makes exactly the same point: "Do ye think that the scripture saith in vain, The spirit that dwelleth in us lusteth to envy?" (Jas. 4:5). I have already expounded the latter part of that verse, but now I am simply emphasizing the words, "Do ye think that the scripture saith in vain, the spirit that dwelleth in us . . ." He does! And, indeed, Galatians 5:17 makes the same point: "The flesh lusteth against the Spirit, and the Spirit against the flesh"—the Holy Spirit who is within us as believers.

So here is this tremendous statement that the Holy Spirit does not merely influence us. He does, but more than that, he dwells within us, he tabernacles within us in our lives. That is why we have the teaching about being careful, therefore, not to grieve him or hurt him or offend him and hinder him or quench him or resist him. "The Holy Spirit dwelleth within you." The apostle produces that as an argument for us to use in the time of temptation.

But, in exactly the same way, we are told that the Lord Jesus Christ also dwells within us. There is no higher teaching than this, but it is a part of New Testament teaching, and the danger is that in our slick and glib way of reading the Scriptures and hearing a whole chapter in a Bible lecture or something like that, we reduce all these things and regard them merely as phrases. But these are solemn facts; these are truths that are actually put before us. So listen to what our Lord himself is recorded as saying in the fourteenth chapter of this great Gospel. He says, first of all, in verse 19, "Yet a little while, and the world seeth me no more; but ye see me: because I live, ye shall live also. At that day ye shall know that I am in my Father, and ye in me, and I in you."

Then we read in 14:23, "Jesus answered and said unto him, If a man love me, he will keep my words: and my Father will love him, and we will come unto him, and make our abode with him."

There is the statement. Our Lord repeats this toward the end of the high-priestly prayer, where he is talking about the unity that should exist among Christians: "I in them, and thou in me, that they may be made perfect in one; and that the world may know that thou hast sent me, and hast loved them, as thou hast loved me" (John 17:23).

But this teaching did not end with our Lord himself; the apostles were given enlightenment and understanding. Paul writes to the Ephesians, "If ye have heard of the dispensation of the grace of God which is given me to you-ward: how that by revelation he made known unto me the mystery . . ." (Eph. 3:2–3). Christ has enlightened him; the Spirit works in him. He puts it in his characteristic way again in the eighth chapter of Romans, and it is exactly the same teaching:

> But ye are not in the flesh, but in the Spirit, if so be that the Spirit of God dwell in you. Now if any man have not the Spirit of Christ, he is none of his. And if Christ be in you, the body is dead because of sin; but the Spirit is life because of righteousness. (vv. 9–10).

Notice, "if Christ be in you." Not only the Spirit but also the Son is in us as the children of God. Again, in writing to the Corinthians, who had been falling into errors and going astray in so many ways, Paul exhorts them to examine themselves: "Examine yourselves, whether ye be in the faith; prove your own selves. Know ye not your own selves, how that Jesus Christ is in you, except ye be reprobate?" (2 Cor. 13:5). He does not say, "Do you not know that as Christians you are those who believe in the Lord Jesus Christ and know certain things about him and are trying to put his teaching into practice through the Spirit who is having an influence upon you"? No, no! Paul says, "Know ye not your own selves how that Jesus Christ is in you, except ye be reprobate?" What could be more specific than that? Nothing more specific perhaps, and certainly nothing more moving. And I suppose that in a sense nothing rises higher than Galatians 2:19–20:

> I through the law am dead to the law, that I might live unto God. I am crucified with Christ: nevertheless I live; yet not I, but Christ liveth in me: and the life which I now live in the flesh I live by the faith of the Son of God, who loved me, and gave himself for me.

Now you must not reduce that to an influence. Paul goes beyond that. He says, "I live; yet not I, *but Christ liveth in me*." And we find exactly the same truth in Ephesians 3:17, where the apostle prays, "that Christ may dwell in your hearts by faith; that ye, being rooted and grounded in love" and so on. Again, there is a staggering statement in the Epistle to the Colossians, where Paul, again talking about this great privilege that has been given to him, says, "whereof I am made a minister, according to the dispensation of God which is given to me for you, to fulfil [fill out] the word of God; even the mystery which hath been hid from ages and from generations, but now is made manifest to his saints [you and me!]: to whom God would make known"—listen!—"what is the riches of the glory of this mystery among the Gentiles." Notice the language! There is something wrong, Christian people, when we are dull and apathetic, when we are not on our feet rejoicing with our faces shining in this evil world! It is a glory, a rich glory. What is it? ". . . Christ in you, the hope of glory" (Col. 1:25–27).

Some have tried to reduce those words to mean, "Christ among you." That is included, but it cannot stop at that; it goes further. "Christ in you, the hope of glory"—the hope of glory rests upon the fact that Christ is in us, that he is dwelling in us. That is the guarantee. We have been born again; we are partakers of the divine nature. The basis of "the hope of glory" is that Christ is in us. What a glorious mystery! It is not surprising that the apostle's language seems to fail him, and he talks about "the riches of the glory of this mystery."

And, again, Paul reminds the Colossians:

> If ye then be risen with Christ, seek those things which are above, where Christ sitteth on the right hand of God. Set your affection on things above, not on things on the earth. For ye are dead, and your life is hid with Christ in God. When Christ, who is our life, shall appear . . . (Col. 3:1–4)

So it is clear that not only does the Holy Spirit dwell within us but also that our Lord and Savior, Jesus Christ, the Son of God, dwells in us. But in the twenty-third verse of the fourteenth chapter of John's Gospel that I quoted, did you notice how our Lord went even further? One almost hesitates to say such a thing, but here is what Scripture says:

> Jesus answered and said unto him, If a man love me, he will keep my words: and my Father will love him, and we will come unto him, and make our abode with him.

And remember Revelation 3:20: "Behold, I stand at the door, and knock: if any man hear my voice, and open the door, I will come in to him, and will sup with him . . ."—we can eat and have fellowship with him. Here it is—God himself, God the Father, dwelling within us. And we find the same teaching in Jesus' high-priestly prayer: "I in them, and thou in me, that they may be made perfect in one" (John 17:23). Our Lord constantly repeats this. He has given them the glory that the Father had given him (John 17:22). He is in us, and since the Father is in him, the Father is in us.

And this is what our Lord is putting in general to the woman of Samaria. He is saying in essence, "You have no idea— 'If thou knewest the gift of God . . .'" It is because people outside do not know that this is Christianity that they are not interested in it. And it is because we who are inside do not know this as we should that we are as we are and are such poor representatives of this glorious Christian gospel. The life of God in the soul!

Now do not try to understand this—it is the highest teaching. Paul constantly talks about it as a mystery, and it is. The term "mystery" in the New Testament always means something that is beyond the reach and the grasp of human understanding but that is made known. This does not mean it is a mystery to us in an ultimate sense. We have been let into the secret. It means something beyond human understanding, which God in his infinite grace has revealed. But it still is a mystery in the sense that we cannot understand it. We cannot work it out in detail, and we must not try to do so. We just know that it is true, we believe it; and as we believe it, we increasingly enter into the experience of it.

A good deal of this is expressed in our greatest hymns, especially the hymns of the eighteenth century.

A heart resigned, submissive, meek,
My great Redeemer's throne,
Where only Christ is heard to speak,
Where Jesus reigns alone;

A humble, lowly, contrite heart,
Believing, true, and clean,
Which neither life nor death can part
From him that dwells within.

CHARLES WESLEY ("O FOR A HEART TO PRAISE MY GOD")

It was this realization, first in Whitefield, then in the two Wesley brothers, that led, as I have mentioned, to the great Evangelical Awakening of the eighteenth century in Britain. The Lord Jesus Christ dwells in the heart. And so we get a prayer offered by Charles Wesley:

Love divine, all loves excelling,
Joy of heaven, to earth come down,
Fix in us thy humble dwelling,
All thy faithful mercies crown.

CHARLES WESLEY

I often listen to congregations singing that second line, and I find that they almost forget the comma. They sing it like this: "Love divine, all loves excelling joy of heaven to earth come down." No, no; it is a request, a plea: "Joy of heaven, to earth come down, fix in us thy humble dwelling." That is the meaning. And only those who know that he is already there offer that prayer. They are praying for the certainty of it, as Paul is in Ephesians 3. Christ was in the hearts of those Christians in Ephesus, and Paul is praying that they may know it, that they may be able to comprehend it more and more, "with all the saints," that they may have an active realization that Christ is "dwelling in their hearts by faith."

That is the burden of the teaching in the third chapter of Ephesians, which ends in that staggering, almost bewildering statement, "that ye might be filled with all the fulness of God." The apostle actually uses that language. That is what he is praying for these Ephesians. You find this in a negative way in that well-known hymn of poor William Cowper when he was in one of his periods of depression, with a sense of desertion. He cries out in his agony and says:

Return, O holy dove, return,
Sweet messenger of rest;
I hate the sins that made thee mourn
That drove thee from my breast.

William Cowper

This is Christian mysticism; this is the Christian life at its highest—the realization that God dwells within—God the Father, God the Son, God the Holy Spirit. And our Lord puts that in these words to the woman of Samaria: "The water that I shall give him shall be in him a well of water springing up into everlasting life."

Of course, the inevitable result of this is the point that I am putting next in order, which is my fifth particular test that we should apply to ourselves, and that is a sense of surprise, a sense of amazement and astonishment. More and more I would say this is the ultimate test. Are we surprised at ourselves? If we are not, I do not think we are Christians. If you can explain yourself, you are not a Christian. Of course, as a religious man or woman you can explain yourself. Your religion is, as I have been pointing out, something you do, something you control, something you handle. Moral people, religious people, always know exactly what they are doing, and there is no mystery in their lives at all. They are in charge; everything they have is less than themselves. But here, by definition, if the life of God is in the soul, it is something surprising, and those who know this are astounded that they should ever be in this position at all. Notice how the apostle Paul constantly says this:

> I am the least of the apostles, that am not meet [worthy] to be called an apostle, because I persecuted the church of God. But by the grace of God I am what I am: and his grace which was bestowed upon me was not in vain; but I laboured more abundantly than they all: yet not I, but the grace of God which was with me. (1 Cor. 15:9–10)

He cannot get over this; in a sense, he cannot believe this is true of him. We have already read Galatians 2:20: "I live; yet not I, but Christ liveth in me." Did you notice it again in that third chapter of Ephesians as the apostle explains why he is a preacher? "I Paul, the prisoner of Jesus Christ" (v. 1). He tells them of this great privilege that has been given him: "whereof I was made a minister" (v. 7). He has this mystic secret.

> . . . that the Gentiles should be fellowheirs, and of the same body, and partakers of his promise in Christ by the gospel: whereof I was made a minister, according to the gift of the grace of God given unto me by the effectual working of his power. Unto me, who am less than the least of all saints, is this grace given. (vv. 6–8)

Paul cannot get over this. He is astounded at it. Or, again, notice how he puts it in writing to Timothy:

> . . . according to the glorious gospel of the blessed God, which was committed to my trust. And I thank Christ Jesus our Lord, who hath enabled me, for that he counted me faithful, putting me into the ministry; who was before a blasphemer, and a persecutor, and injurious: but I obtained mercy, because I did it ignorantly in unbelief. And the grace of our Lord was exceeding abundant with faith and love which is in Christ Jesus. This is a faithful saying, and worthy of all acceptation, that Christ Jesus came into the world to save sinners; of whom I am chief. Howbeit for this cause I obtained mercy, that in me first Jesus Christ might shew forth all longsuffering, for a pattern to them which should hereafter believe on him to life everlasting. (1 Tim. 1:11–16)

Now, again, this is an expression on the part of the apostle of the fact that he is amazed that this should have happened to him. And what amazes him? It is that Christ is in him and that Christ is using him to his glory and to his praise. John says the same thing in two verses at the beginning of the third chapter of his epistle:

> Behold, what manner of love the Father hath bestowed upon us, that we should be called the sons of God: therefore the world knoweth us not, because it knew him not. Beloved, now are we the sons of God, and it doth not yet appear what we shall be: but we know that, when he shall appear, we shall be like him; for we shall see him as he is. (1 John 3:1–2)

That fact is staggering; it is amazing. Beloved, realize it, says John, even as he himself realized it and was amazed.

This is the experience of the saints throughout the centuries, and it is put perfectly in that well-known hymn of Charles Wesley:

And can it be, that I should gain
An interest in the Saviour's blood?
Died he for me, who caused his pain—
For me, who him to death pursued?
Amazing love! How can it be,
That thou, my God, shouldst die for me?

Incredible!

Finally, use this test. Men and women of whom Scougal's words are true, those who have the life of God in the soul, are aware of this difference in themselves, and they are aware that they are different from who they once were, and different from those who do not have this life of God. Now this is not Pharisaism; the Pharisee is proud that he is different because he is such a wonderful man. But that is not the feeling of the Christian. Christians know they have done nothing; the difference is because of what God has done to them. I believe this is the explanation of our Lord's teaching in the tenth chapter of Matthew's Gospel, where he says, "Think not that I am come to send peace on earth: I came not to send peace, but a sword." This is a staggering statement, and people often do not understand it.

> I am come to set a man at variance against his father, and the daughter against her mother, and the daughter in law against her mother in law. And a man's foes shall be they of his own household. (Matt. 10:34–36)

How do you explain that? The moment you receive this life of God in your soul, you are made different. Though you are still related to people in the flesh, not only do you know that you are different, they, too, know it; they sense it immediately. They do not understand you now. If you merely "take up" something, they can understand and explain it, but this they do not understand. And you cannot expect them to.

That is why when Christian people come to talk to me about the kind of difficulty that often arises when one member of a family alone becomes a Christian, I always exhort them not to be harsh, not to be impatient. These family members cannot help it; they do not understand it; it is impossible. They are like Nicodemus. So I say, be patient; bear with them, and pray for them. You have a new nature, the divine nature, and this inevitably shows itself in your life. "He that is spiritual judgeth all things, yet he himself is judged of no man" (1 Cor. 2:15).

So Peter's words are perfectly true:

> Forasmuch then as Christ hath suffered for us in the flesh, arm yourselves likewise with the same mind: for he that hath suffered in the flesh hath ceased from sin; that he no longer should live the rest of his time in the flesh to the lusts of men, but to the will of God. For the time past of our life may suffice us to have wrought the will of the Gentiles, when we walked in lasciviousness, lusts, excess of wine, revellings, banquetings, and abominable idolatries.

Then he says, "Wherein they think it strange that ye run not with them to the same excess of riot, speaking evil of you" (1 Pet. 4:1–4).

There it is. Peter says in effect, "Because you are different, your friends and relatives do not understand you. They think it strange that you are not prepared to run with them now in the way you used to, and they speak evil of you. What is happening? Oh, they are just letting you know they realize that you have the life of God in your soul; they see the difference and do not understand you."

So one of the tests that we apply to ourselves to know whether this well of water is within us springing up into everlasting life is just this: do we know that we are different? Are we amazed at it? And do other people prove it to us by telling us that we are different, perhaps even "speaking evil" of us because we can no longer live the kind of life they still live?

Here are some of the particular tests, then, that we apply to know whether we are "partakers of the divine nature."

18

"Never Thirst"

Jesus answered and said unto her, Whosoever drinketh of this water shall thirst again: but whosoever drinketh of the water that I shall give him shall never thirst; but the water that I shall give him shall be in him [become in him] a well of water springing up into everlasting life. (John 4:13–14)

We have been looking at the characteristics of the great life that is offered to us in the Christian gospel in order that we may be able to test ourselves. Christianity is not theoretical. It is not just espousing a teaching or taking up a point of view. It is a life. That is the whole point of what our Lord is saying here. If it is a "well of water" within us, the life of God in the soul, then it must express itself. And therefore if we would know for a surety whether or not we are Christians, we can test ourselves by observing the characteristics of this life that he gives us and asking ourselves whether we are aware of the manifestations of this life in our own lives.

Now having done that in general, we come to another important aspect of this statement of our Lord: "But whosoever drinketh of the water that I shall give him shall never thirst." This is a staggering statement—"shall never thirst." You see the contrast that our Lord makes: "Whosoever drinketh of this water shall thirst again." This is the element of complete satisfaction that our Lord claims for the life that he came into the world to give. There are many statements of this teaching not only in the Gospels but also, subsequently, in the New Testament Epistles. "I am come," says our Lord, "that they might have life, and that they might have it more abundantly" (John 10:10).

Here is a subject that obviously needs our close attention. It is a further test that we can apply to ourselves. Bishop Westcott says this phrase "never thirst" is a remarkable expression, and we must give it its full value. Somebody has suggested that it should be translated, "Whosoever drinketh of the water that I shall give him shall never, no, never be thirsty anymore," and even that is not quite strong enough.

This term *never* is found several times in John's Gospel. In the eighth chapter we find the words:

> Verily, verily, I say unto you, If a man keep my saying, he shall *never* see death. Then said the Jews unto him, Now we know that thou hast a devil. Abraham is dead, and the prophets; and thou sayest, If a man keep my saying, he shall *never* taste of death. (vv. 51–52)

And in the tenth chapter there is the same thought: "And I give unto them eternal life; and they shall *never* perish, neither shall any man pluck them out of my hand" (v. 28). That is, "They shall never perish, no, never, never perish." It is the same expression exactly. In chapter 11 we again find it: "Jesus said unto her, I am the resurrection, and the life: he that believeth in me, though he were dead, yet shall he live: and whosoever liveth and believeth in me shall *never* die"—never, no, never (v. 25). And once more in the thirteenth chapter: when our Lord was proposing to wash the disciples' feet, Peter said, "Thou shalt *never* wash my feet" (v. 8).

But perhaps the most interesting example of the use of this term is to be found in the First Epistle to the Corinthians. Paul has been dealing with the question of meats offered to idols. The stronger brethren had come to see that there was nothing in this at all, but the weaker brethren were still troubled when they saw fellow Christians eating this meat. So the apostle finishes by saying this: "Wherefore, if meat make my brother to offend, I will eat *no* flesh *while the world standeth*, lest I make my brother to offend" (1 Cor. 8:13).

Now it is remarkable that the translators of the Authorized Version, the very people who translated the statement "shall never thirst," when they came to translate exactly the same word in 1 Corinthians 8:13 translated it, "no . . . while the world standeth." And there is no doubt at all but that the latter is altogether better because it brings out the strength and the force of the meaning. The translation "never" is really not strong enough. Of course, if you put its full value into the word "never," I suppose it tells you everything. The language that our Lord used, and the repetition of the words, do bring out this additional emphasis. But to make clear the literal meaning, we could translate verse 14 of John 4 like this: "Whosoever drinketh of the water that I shall give him will by no means thirst unto the end of the age"; or to use the words of the translators of the Authorized Version, "Whosoever drinketh of the water that I shall give him shall not thirst while the world standeth" or "while the world is in being and in existence" or "While the world continues to be and to stand, he shall never thirst." As long as the cosmos is in existence, as long as this particular age is in existence, whoever drinks of this water shall never thirst. What could be stronger than that?

And yet, after all we have seen, this is something we should expect. It is quite inevitable and logical. We have seen already that if we drink this water, it becomes in us a well of water springing up into everlasting life and that this is God's action in us. It is the result of the miracle worked in us by the Holy Spirit. This is Christianity. It is not something we add on, not something we do, but something done to us. It is regeneration, being born again; it is being created anew; it is becoming a new creation. These are the Bible's terms, and it is all done by God himself. And supremely, as we have seen, he puts something of his own being into us; we are "partakers of the divine nature."

So in light of that, it would be a contradiction in terms to say that you can be a partaker of the divine nature and yet go on thirsting. It would mean that God's work was incomplete, that it was not perfect, that elements were still lacking. But as we know, everything that God does is perfect. We are told that when he originally created everything, the whole universe, including human beings, he looked at it all, "and, behold, it was very good" (Gen. 1:31). Of course! And the work that God does in the soul in regeneration is equally perfect. So our Lord here makes this claim for it: "Whosoever drinketh of the water that I shall give him shall never thirst."

We can, then, immediately say two things. First, the ultimate truth, the ultimate characteristic, of this life is its all-sufficiency, the complete satisfaction that it gives. And, secondly, this also becomes the ultimate test that we apply to ourselves to discover whether or not we have received this life.

Let me go on emphasizing this. I am not here to talk about these truths theoretically but because, to me, the most wonderful thing in the world that can happen to men and women is that they receive this life. And the most terrible thing I can conceive of is that people should mistake something spurious for this glorious reality. There is no greater need in the church at the present time than to have men and women who are filled in this way. We do not call for busy people or for activists; we call for people who have this life within them. These are the true evangelists, wherever they are. In all their circumstances, this life will show itself and will be obvious to all. So the question we put to ourselves, therefore, is, have we obtained this complete, final satisfaction? Do we "never thirst"?

Now it is important that we should be clear as to what the expression "never thirst" means. There is a very real danger of our so misinterpreting it that we depress ourselves, and we must not do that. There is a way of looking at this that could make us feel that we are not Christians at all, and that would obviously be wrong. What, therefore, does our Lord mean?

It seems to me that the best way of expounding this phrase is to take it together with the statement that is found in Philippians 3. The apostle is there talking in terms of what he desires. He says:

> Yea doubtless, and I count all things but loss for the excellency of the knowledge of Christ Jesus my Lord . . . that I may win Christ, and be found in him, not having mine own righteousness, which is of the law, but that which is through the faith of Christ, the righteousness which is of God by faith. (vv. 8–9)

Then in verse 10 he says, "That I may know him, and the power of his resurrection." And in verse 12 he gives us certain negatives ("Not as though I had already attained, either were already perfect: but I follow after . . .") before again repeating, in verses 13–14:

> Brethren, I count not myself to have apprehended: but this one thing I do, forgetting those things which are behind, and reaching forth unto those things which are before, I press toward the mark.

Now there is on the surface an apparent contradiction between the two statements, "Whosoever drinketh of the water that I shall give him shall never thirst" and "that [my desire is] I may know him . . . not as though I had already apprehended, either were already perfect." Are they contradictory? Of course, the answer is that they are not; they fit together perfectly. Here is the great apostle Paul at the height of his experience, in his maturity, expressing this desire, this longing, to know Christ more and more. He has not apprehended as he wishes to apprehend. He is trying, he says, to "apprehend that for which also I am apprehended of Christ Jesus" (v. 12).

How do we resolve the apparent difficulty? The answer is that it is the difference between thirsting and desiring more of this life, this water. The very expression *to thirst* implies a deep need. In thirst there are elements of profound dissatisfaction, exhaustion, and emptiness. There is an element of pain in it. *The Oxford Dictionary* describes *thirst* in these terms: "the uneasy or painful sensation caused by the need of drink." Westcott says, "Thirst is the pain of an unsatisfied want." That is a very good definition.

Our Lord is saying that the Christian will never again experience thirst. He will never have this sense of utter exhaustion, this painful sensation of need—never again. He says that Christians will never be empty or exhausted. They will never be in dire trouble or be desperate; they will never be in despair. They will never be, as it were, almost at the point of death, feeling they are going to die. Our Lord uses the word *thirst* in its full and right meaning, and this is what we must grasp.

The term "never thirst" does not mean, however, that the Christian is one who knows full satiety. Nor does it mean that Christians will not know any variations in their life and experience and will never desire more—the apostle himself says that he does, as we have just seen. Indeed, we can go so far as to say that the only people who do ever desire more of this living water are those who already have it, and that is why they desire more. This aspect of it can be put in terms of growth. If you are not alive, you cannot grow. But where there is life, there is the possibility of growth, and there should be growth. So the very fact of growth, and the desire to grow, is proof that there is life within. So we must regard this teaching mainly from the negative standpoint as meaning that once we have received this life, we will never again be empty or desperate or exhausted—never. And this can never be put too strongly.

There is, therefore, no incompatibility between these two statements, no contradiction between them. The Christian, while never empty, should always be desiring to have more and more of the fullness. Christians may at times feel they are comparatively empty, but they are never completely so. They may look at others or read the biography of a saint and say, "What do I have?" and yet they know they have something. Their very appreciation of what the other has, and their desire for it, is that which is within them crying out for more. So you must give the correct meaning to this word *thirst*.

Now I suggest that perhaps the best way of all to know the difference between thirsting, on the one hand, and desiring more, on the other, is by understanding what the apostle tells us about himself in a bit of autobiography in the Second Epistle to the Corinthians. He makes a tremendous statement: "For God, who commanded the light to shine out of darkness, hath shined in our hearts, to give the light of the knowledge of the glory of God in the face of Jesus Christ."

That is what he is glorying in—it is another way of talking about this "well of water" within. The apostle goes on, "But we have this treasure in earthen vessels, that the excellency of the power may be of God, and not of us."

Then his next words show us the difference between never thirsting and yet desiring more: "We are troubled on every side"—now watch his negatives—"yet not distressed; we are perplexed . . ." Things are happening; he does not understand them, and at times he does not know what to do. You remember the famous account of his vision at Troas (Acts 16:6–10). Paul was in great perplexity, and this happened to him on many occasions. ". . . but not in despair." You see, he does not thirst. There is great need, but he is not thirsting. ". . . persecuted, but not forsaken; cast down, but not destroyed" (2 Cor. 4:6–9).

Now there, I think, is the perfect exposition of this question of "never, no, never, thirst again." Here is the apostle surrounded by trials, troubles, tribulations, everything, as it were, going against him, but in spite of it all he brings out these positives. "Do not misunderstand me," he says in essence. "We are troubled on every side, yet *not distressed*; we are perplexed, but *not in despair*." He has drunk of this water, and he thirsts no more.

Christians, in other words, may be perplexed, they may be in trouble, they may be in difficulties, but they are never frantic. They never again search about violently for satisfaction; they never reach the point at which they wonder whether they will find satisfaction again—never. This is the vital distinction. Certain things can never happen to Christians again. Why? Because their great central need has been satisfied once and forever. That is the assertion, and that is what we must hold on to. Many things may happen to Christian people. It may be that through their neglect, their laziness, their lack of diligence, or their sinning, the water in the well, as it were, becomes muddy, filled with a lot of mire and sticks and stones, and other people may say that the well is finished. At times they themselves may be tempted by the devil to think exactly the same thing. But the point is that it will never be dry—never.

Whatever may happen to Christian people, they will never find themselves having to ask where they can find water. They will never become prospectors, or send for a prospector, and think about digging another well in order to find satisfaction. Christians at their worst, in the depth of backsliding—and Christians can backslide, and backslide so far that the world is convinced that they have never been Christians at all or that, if they ever have, they have ceased to be, having sunk to the most awful depths—will still always know that all they must do is clear out the well and get rid of the mud and the stones and the filth and all that has been clogging up the outlet of this well of water that they know is within them.

In the depths of their backsliding, Christians always know that they are children of God; that is why they are wretched and miserable. They do not have to seek for truth elsewhere; they know it is there. They know that they are responsible for their condition and that all they must do is repeat the action that Isaac the son of Abraham had to take on one occasion when he came to the valley of Gerar: "Isaac digged again the wells of water, which they had digged in the days of Abraham his father; for the Philistines had stopped them after the death of Abraham" (Gen. 26:18). Isaac did not have to dig new wells. All he had to do was get rid of the filth that the Philistines had thrown into the wells. He knew that once he got rid of the filth he would find the water in all its old pristine purity, bubbling up as in the days of Abraham. And backsliders do exactly the same thing. They have the water in them, and they know it is there, and all they must do is repent and "do works meet for repentance" (Acts 26:20).

There, then, is the way in which you interpret this word *thirst*. It does not mean you are always at the same level. The cults teach that sort of thing, and that is where they differ from this Christian teaching. Some people say that once they became Christians they never afterward had problems or troubles or doubts. That does not conform to what one reads in the Scriptures, nor in the lives of the saints. There are variations. "Never thirst again" does not mean that you are immediately put on the topmost position and remain there. That is compatible with Paul's "that I may know him." I long to know him. I feel I do not know him as much as I should.

So here is our Lord's great statement that we must consider. He says, "Whosoever drinketh of the water that I shall give him shall never thirst." Now this is true of the entire personality. We have already seen that this power within produces a *total* change, a change in the whole person. It is equally important for us to see that the satisfaction that it gives is a satisfaction that is likewise complete, and this, again, is one of the claims we make for this glorious gospel. Everything else gives us only a partial, temporary satisfaction. There is nothing else under heaven that can satisfy the complete, the total person. And it does so unfailingly and forever.

What do I mean? When we were talking about the power working within, transforming and changing us, I said it changed our mind, our outlook, our heart, our sensibilities, our affections, and our will. And this is exactly how I want to show the satisfaction that we receive.

First—now listen to this claim I am making—when we receive the life of God in our soul, we get complete intellectual satisfaction. Now that is a big claim, and yet, thank God, it is nothing but the simple truth. If you do not have final satisfaction intellectually, are you a Christian? Humanity always thirsts for intellectual satisfaction. One of the greatest characteristics of man is intellectual curiosity. Man looking at life, looking at everything that he knows of, wants understanding, wants explanation; so he begins to think and to meditate and to put forward theories. That is the meaning of philosophy: it is the love of wisdom in order to have understanding. That is why people engage in all kinds of research. The moment they begin to think at all, they find themselves up against the great mystery of the world in which they live. What is this world? Where has it come from? What is its meaning?

And then look at life—flowers, animals, human beings. What is this mysterious thing that we call life? Where has it come from? People want to know. Then, of course, there are human beings themselves. What is man? These subjects have aroused intellectual curiosity from the very beginning, and men and women have been seeking explanations.

And they have to go on, of course, if they are true thinkers. What is this thing that we call *evil*? Why is there so much failure in life? Why am I a failure? Why are you a failure? Why do we fall? Why are most people fundamentally unhappy? Why do they have to seek ways of relieving the unhappiness of which they are conscious? What is the explanation? People have been grappling with these problems, these questions, from the very beginning.

And then people are aware of the fact that they are "here today and gone tomorrow," and after they are gone there will be others, and there were people here before them. So what is this sequence? What is history? What is the meaning of history? Is there any meaning in it? What is this whole business of time? How does one understand time? And then, of course, suffering, the extraordinary suffering in the world. Pain! Humanity has grappled with these various problems all along.

And finally, of course, there is death, "the last enemy" (1 Cor. 15:26). The last mystery, too! It is the end of life in this visible world. What then? Ah, that has occupied the minds of these thinkers, and they have grappled with it. And what lies beyond death? Eternity! And behind everything, God, this being. Is he there? Who is he? What is he? You have a consciousness of him; no one has ever been born without a consciousness of God—it is universal. In the most primitive tribes there is a consciousness, an awareness, of a supreme being. Clever people try to explain it away, but it is in them; it is in everybody. There is a universal God-consciousness in the whole of humanity. These are the questions that agitate the minds of men and women.

And here is the claim that our Lord is making, and I am privileged to preach it now in his holy name. The world has no answer to these questions. It has done its utmost; it is still doing its utmost. It is no nearer to giving satisfaction than it was in the great flowering of Greek philosophy five centuries before the birth of our Lord and Savior. The world goes through phases in this quest for knowledge, for understanding. There is a sense in which this is quite amusing, were it not so vitally important and, in a sense, tragic. I am old enough to have seen the fashions in philosophy. One teaching becomes the craze, and everybody is taking it up, and it is wonderful; but it does not last, and another comes. Each one claims to be able to answer all the questions, but it never does. Indeed, we can go further—no teaching ever will. If philosophers could solve our problems, the Son of God would never have come into this world. He came to give light. "I am the light of the world," he said (John 8:12; 9:5), and he alone is the light. And here is the claim that he is making to the woman of Samaria; it is the claim that we make in his name. The only answer is the answer that is found in him, and it is, I emphasize, a complete answer.

Now I want to add a few words here as an aside. I am speaking to people who in name, I have no doubt, are evangelical people and evangelically minded. I think the greatest charge that can be brought against evangelicals in the last ninety years or so, since the 1870s, is that we have grievously failed at this point. We have tended to reduce this glorious gospel, and the life that it gives, to just a question of forgiveness, as if everything happens when a person makes a decision, as though that is the beginning and the end of the gospel. The glory, the bigness, the greatness, the complete intellectual satisfaction, has not been preached and expounded as it should have been. Indeed, evangelical people have often been charged, and I am afraid it has been a true charge, of being afraid of the intellect.

There were men forty years ago—I knew some of them and have read their books—who definitely used to advise young Christians not to read theology, saying it was dangerous. So the impression was given that to be evangelical meant to commit intellectual suicide. To be an evangelical you had to stop thinking and adopt a formula, and that put you right. That is a travesty of the gospel! The gospel of our Lord and Savior, and that alone, gives complete intellectual satisfaction. There is nothing more glorious about it than the way in which it takes up the whole person and gives a perfect understanding of all things. That is the claim.

Does this mean that every one of us, therefore, has complete understanding of everything? Of course not. All I am saying is that such an explanation is given. Many of us, like those Hebrew Christians about whom we read in the Epistle to the Hebrews, are "dull of hearing," and we are "babes," and we have not "exercised" our senses (Heb. 5:11–14). With all this wealth before us, all this amazing teaching, all this intellectual comfort, all this profound Christian philosophy, we have been content with just a first experience of conversion, and we have never grown, we have never even read, we have not thought. Shame on us! But that is entirely due to us, you see. Our Lord is saying that he is the light of the world. He is claiming that there is in this book that we call the Bible complete satisfaction intellectually, that here there is understanding of all these problems that are agitating the minds of men and women.

In other words, the Christian message is called *truth*; it is not only something you experience. It is that, as we shall see, but I never start with that; and if you start with experience, you are going against the Scriptures. This is truth, and the only experience that is of any value is experience that is based upon truth. The cults can give you experiences, but the only experience that is valid is that which our Lord gives, and it results from the truth that he himself introduces to us: "I am the way, the truth, and the life"—that is it—"no man cometh unto the Father, but by me" (John 14:6). The apostle tells Timothy to pray "for kings, and for all that are in authority" (1 Tim. 2:1–2). Why? Because, he says, "[God] will have all men to be saved, and to come unto the knowledge of the truth" (1 Tim. 2:4). Christianity is primarily "knowledge of the truth." So it comes to us in terms of this great and glorious revelation.

What do I mean by this? Take the various problems that I have mentioned. Where have they come from? What is the explanation of their origin? You are familiar with some of the theories that have been put forward. People speak of the theory of evolution as if it were an established fact, and yet increasingly scientists are admitting that it is not and that it is most inadequate. There is only one adequate explanation for the origin of the world. It is the one given at the beginning of the book of Genesis, the first book in the Bible: "In the beginning God created . . ."

I am not saying that this statement is one you can comprehend, but it is something you can understand. It is a satisfactory explanation, and it is the only one. But that leads me to ask the question, if God has created everything that is, who is God, and how can I know him? And here again the philosophers have been busy, but they have failed completely. The apostle Paul is able to say of them, "the world by wisdom knew not God" (1 Cor. 1:21). They could not get further than "the unknown God" (Acts 17:23).

There is only one who can really teach us about God: it is the blessed Lord and Savior. "No man hath seen God at any time; the only begotten Son, which is in the bosom of the Father, he hath declared him" (John 1:18). This is the only way to know God. When "the world by wisdom knew not God, it pleased God by the foolishness of preaching to save them that believe" (1 Cor. 1:21). There is no knowledge of God apart from him who says to the woman of Samaria in essence, "Take this water, and you will have complete satisfaction." Jesus says, "He that hath seen me hath seen the Father" (John 14:9). There is no other way; by knowing him, one knows God and knows God as one's Father.

And it is the same with the knowledge of man. You cannot understand man except in terms of the biblical explanation. You cannot explain man biologically; you cannot explain him materialistically, dialectically, economically, or in any other way. There is only one way to explain the greatness of man. What is it? It is that he is made in the image of God. The smallness, the despicable aspect of men—what is it? It is the doctrine of the Fall, man's disobedience and rebellion against God. You do not begin to understand the state of the world unless you accept this biblical explanation. Evolution tells you the world is getting better and better. It obviously is not. Why not? Evil! The devil! Sin! The forces of hell working against God! That is why the world is unhappy; that is why men and women are unhappy, with a sense of guilt and an accusing conscience. These are facts of experience, and yet psychology cannot explain them—the rival theories of psychology contradict one another. In the Bible is an adequate, and the only adequate, explanation.

And when you come to consider the way of deliverance from it all, oh, how much more evident is it that there is no satisfaction anywhere except in this message. Can you find peace of conscience by searching for it? Can you find rest for your soul? Can you know that your sins are forgiven? There is no other way. Here it is, and it is complete, absolute, perfect. "Whosoever drinketh of the water that I shall give him shall never thirst."

Our Lord's claim is not an idle claim. There is here in this revelation, and particularly and especially in him, the answer to all our questions. "All the promises of God in him are yea, and in him Amen, unto the glory of God by us" (2 Cor. 1:20). These words really mean just this: in him is the answer; here is the satisfaction. I do not stop thinking when I become a Christian; indeed, it is the other way around. In a sense I start thinking then, and I am now able to face all the questions, and I know there is always an answer.

19

Full Satisfaction of the Intellect

Jesus answered and said unto her, Whosoever drinketh of this water shall thirst again: but whosoever drinketh of the water that I shall give him shall never thirst; but the water that I shall give him shall be in him a well of water springing up into everlasting life. (John 4:13–14)

In our last study we saw that if Christians are ever conscious of a lack—and they often are—they always realize that it is entirely due to themselves. It is due to their own failure in some shape or form to partake of this well of water as they should, to avail themselves of it, or because of sin they have allowed the well to become almost invisible as a result of all the various things that have cluttered up its mouth. But they are always certain that it is there; they have never sought it in vain. They know there is always a sufficiency for their every need.

Indeed, as the apostle Paul puts it in a passing word, as it were, to the Philippians, "Let us therefore, as many as be perfect, be thus minded: and if in any thing ye be otherwise minded, God shall reveal even this unto you" (Phil. 3:15). He says in effect, "You were satisfied, as it were, for the time being, but there is just something else you are not quite clear about. It is all right—that will be revealed to you." Christians have this certainty, this consciousness, that there is nothing they can ever need that is not already supplied, and supplied with a great and wonderful superabundance, in our blessed Lord and Savior.

And now we are emphasizing that this is a sufficiency for the whole person—the mind, the intellect, the heart and affections, the sensibilities. Whatever the circumstances, the whole person is always fully and completely satisfied. And we are beginning to work this out in detail. We have started with the intellectual satisfaction that is given by the gospel and its teaching—teaching from our Lord himself and the life that he imparts to us. We must start here because, after all, the greatest gift that God has given to men and women is the gift of mind and the gift of understanding. It is perhaps this more than anything else that differentiates man from the animals. So we must be able to establish that the gospel, this life, gives complete intellectual satisfaction.

In a hurried word at the end of the last study, I pointed out how this life given by our Lord immediately provides satisfaction with regard to the first great problem that confronts us all, and that is our awareness of failure, our awareness of deep dissatisfaction. We do not understand the world and life and ourselves and our misery, our unhappiness; we do not know anything about God. We have a consciousness of God, but we cannot find him, and we are concerned how to be reconciled to him. These are the first fundamental human needs, and in a hurried, glancing word I reminded you of how all that is dealt with in the gospel, and only there, and dealt with perfectly, fully, and all-sufficiently. There is only one way of salvation, only one deliverance. It is not arrogance to say this—it is truthful.

But we do not stop at that, and indeed we must not. We are concerned to show the fullness, the all-sufficiency, of our Lord's words "shall never thirst." So we do not stop at entering into the Christian life and having a knowledge of sins forgiven; we must go beyond that. Let me show you in two further ways the intellectual satisfaction given by the gospel.

One is that our minds cry out for greater understanding. Questions come up, difficulties arise, and doubts may assail us, and we want to answer them. Any Christian who thinks at all, while thanking God for the knowledge of sins forgiven and a general new outlook, will still have questions and look for answers. And the devil, the adversary, hurls doubts and questions and queries at us. Not only that, there is false teaching in the church. The New Testament has a great deal to say about that. There is much false teaching at the present time, and we want to be able to deal with these issues. All this is a part of the desire for intellectual satisfaction, and our emphasis is that the gospel is able to give satisfaction by answering these questions.

The second way of showing you the greater fullness and all-sufficiency of the gospel and its way of life is just by calling your attention to the fact of the Bible. There is, perhaps, no better way of demonstrating the complete intellectual satisfaction that is given by the Christian faith than by considering the Bible itself. What is the Bible? You may think that is a foolish, almost ridiculous question, but I suggest that it is not and that oftentimes much of our trouble arises because we have never really considered this question. Or let me put it in a different way: how do you as an individual Christian use the Bible?

I have often found that many people—I am talking about Christians, those who have come into the Christian life—read the Bible because they have been told to do so; it is a duty. They have never read it before, but now they have become Christians, and one of the things a Christian does is read the Bible! So they join some scheme or other, and they begin to read it.

Other people read the Bible in what may be described as a purely devotional manner. Their attitude toward it seems to be this: they have now have what was necessary, they are converted, they are born again, they have new life, they have become Christians. So they regard the Bible as a book that is here to help them; it is an aid to their devotional life. They feel they have everything, really, and all they need to do now is just to keep this life going. As you keep your physical body going by eating and drinking day by day, so you keep on nourishing this life that you have received.

Now I want to suggest to you that while the second is legitimate and while in a sense the first is right, to read the Bible solely for those two reasons is not only inadequate, it is almost a misuse of the Bible. At least, it is a failure to realize what the Bible is and why it has been given to us.

So what is this book? Now again, there is a teaching at the present time that is very popular in the Christian church, and unfortunately it seems to be gaining a certain amount of approval among evangelical people. It is a view of the Bible that says that the Bible is the account of the experiences of various individuals in the past, and in particular of the Jewish nation. It records the experiences of the patriarchs and people such as David and the prophets and also of the children of Israel in general and shows the attempts of those people to explain and expound their experiences.

It is my business to show that this is a complete misunderstanding of the true nature of the Scripture. That view turns the Bible into a human book—people's experiences. Those who hold this view grant that the experiences were given by God, although they would tend to say that even so, they were mainly the result of human seeking and searching, but as regards these records, they are nothing but human documents written by men at various times. That is why, they say, you find errors in the Bible. These have come about in an attempt to explain the experiences. Experience is the big thing; the Bible is just the attempt to expound it.

No, no! Only one word must be used to define what the Bible is, and that is *revelation*. The Bible is not about discovering anything; it is not man attempting to do anything. The first truth about the Bible is that it is God's revelation to human beings, God making truth known to us; that is what it is. God takes the trouble to call certain people, to equip them and endow them with the necessary faculties, then to make known to them knowledge pertaining to truth, and enables them to write this revelation in an accurate, indeed, in an infallible manner. That is what the Bible claims for itself: "All scripture is given by inspiration of God" (2 Tim. 3:16). If you prefer it, you can translate that, "All scripture is God-breathed." The apostle Peter says, "Holy men of God spake as they were moved by the Holy Ghost" (2 Pet. 1:21), and "no prophecy of the scripture is of any private interpretation" (2 Pet. 1:20). There are many similar passages, and this is the claim that the writers always make for themselves.

Now this, you see, is a most important matter. Here, I say, God has been pleased to give us knowledge, to give us truth. He has taken all this trouble to deal with the people and to prepare them and then to equip them and to endow them and to give them knowledge of the truth, which they pass on to us. Why is this? Well, in order that we might have knowledge. What knowledge? Knowledge concerning God himself. That is what you find in this book. What does anyone know, really, about God apart from this?

Oh, I know you can know something about God if you look at him and his work in nature and creation. You are familiar with the arguments, so called, for the being of God—the demonstrations and proofs of the being of God. All right; grant them their full value. You can deduce—you should be able to deduce—the hand of God from nature and creation. Paul argues this in Romans 1:18–20. Modern scientists, some of them, have had the sense to say that. Sir James Jeans said that having studied science for many years, he had come to the conclusion that there must be a great mind at the back of it all and that this must be the mind of a great mathematician. All right, you deduce all that, and you can also do so from history and from providence. You can use purely philosophical reasoning to argue for the existence of God, for instance, that if there is bad and good and better, there must be a best, there must be perfection. I will grant you maximum value to all those arguments, but still I say that when you have done all that you have only, as it were, "touched the hem of his garment." You have learned a few things, but you have no real knowledge of God. And this is true, of course, of necessity. The very character of God's being, the nature of God, makes it quite impossible for finite, sinful beings ever to come to an adequate knowledge of God by their own efforts and endeavors. Of course they cannot.

But, you see, this is the glory of it—God has been pleased to make himself known to us. He has revealed himself; and not only that, he has told us what he has done. But, and this to me is most thrilling of all, in the Scriptures God not only tells us what he has done, he even takes the trouble to tell us why he has done it and why he is going to go on doing certain other things. Now we are meant to know all this; this is a part of the intellectual satisfaction, the fullness in the realm of the understanding, that is given by the gospel. "Whosoever drinketh of the water that I shall give him shall never thirst."

Now this is, of course, the sort of claim that is made in so many places in the Bible. There is perhaps no more wonderful statement of this truth than at the end of the second chapter of the First Epistle to the Corinthians, where Paul says:

> The natural man receiveth not the things of the Spirit of God: for they are foolishness unto him: neither can he know them, because they are spiritually discerned. But he that is spiritual [the Christian] judgeth [has an understanding of] all things, yet he himself is judged of no man.

Then comes the question, "For who hath known the mind of the Lord, that he may instruct him? But we have the mind of Christ" (1 Cor. 2:14–16).

Now this is a staggering claim. We have understanding, says Paul; we have the mind of Christ. He allows us to share his own understanding of these mysteries and immensities and infinities. This is the claim—complete, full, intellectual satisfaction.

Now this, of course, astonishes the non-Christian most of all. His view of Christianity is that it is based on a refusal to think. The typical modern sophisticated person thinks that those of us who are still Christians believe as we do because we are wearing blinders, burying our heads in the sand, not facing the facts, not reading the clever articles in the Sunday newspapers, and not listening to the learned discussions on television. And when we say that we have this full and complete understanding, we are regarded almost as psychopaths. And yet, you see, it is our solemn duty as Christians to make this great claim.

The person ("the natural man" as Paul calls him), who regards us as people who refuse to think, has no understanding. The reason the apostle gives for this lack of understanding is that Christianity is a mystery. In the New Testament the term *mystery* means something that is beyond human comprehension and understanding, and, of course, God is a mystery to the natural man. "Great is the mystery of godliness" in every respect (1 Tim. 3:16). It must be. It is entirely supernatural, beyond man and his highest reach.

Now, as the apostle argues, the natural man, of course, cannot possibly understand the message of the gospel and regards it as foolish. We must not be surprised at that, and it must not trouble us. I never can understand the kind of Christian who seems to be terrified and almost cast into despair when he is reminded that the great scientists and philosophers today are non-Christians. He should not be troubled. The greatest scientist, the greatest philosopher, has no advantage over Tom, Dick, and Harry in these matters; none at all. In fact, he may well be at a disadvantage because he is foolish enough to trust his own faculties in a way that the other does not. However, the point is that nobody can understand. This is beyond us; this is a mystery.

I can give a simple illustration. Many people are tone-deaf. They get nothing out of music, and to them the most glorious music is nothing but painful noise. They cannot help it; they are lacking in this faculty. Now you do not say they are unintelligent because they are not musical. You may have highly intelligent people who get nothing out of music but annoyance. And others similarly have no appreciation of art, or science means nothing to them, and so on. It is not a question of ability. You need the requisite faculty, and you either have it or you do not.

It is the same with Christianity, only infinitely more so, and so it comes to pass that very able people, great people, judged by natural human measures, know nothing about the gospel and regard it as foolishness. Not only should this not surprise us, still less depress us, it is something we should expect. But—and this is what the apostle glories in, and you and I ought to glory in—the moment you become a Christian, you are able to understand these truths. "We have received," says the apostle Paul, "not the spirit of the world, but the spirit which is of God; that we might know the things that are freely given to us of God" (1 Cor. 2:12). That is it. And the moment someone has this spirit, "he that is spiritual judgeth all things" (v. 15). That is, the spiritual person has an understanding of these truths that are foolishness to the wise and prudent. They are revealed by the Spirit, even unto babes. Therefore, we are to rejoice in this understanding. "Whosoever drinketh of the water that I shall give him shall never thirst [intellectually]." "We have the mind of Christ" (1 Cor. 2:16).

Now I am concerned to emphasize this because I have a feeling that so much of the trouble in the church today is due to the fact that this teaching has been neglected and ignored, perhaps most of all by those of us who are evangelical. We have been so afraid of higher criticism and philosophy and so on that we have tended to retreat into some corner where we say that nothing matters but experience.

Now let us be clear about this. I am concerned to show the fullness of the glorious gospel, and if it does not include the realm of the intellect, then it does not have the all-sufficiency of which I am speaking. That is why we say that Christianity is not only an experience. You notice how I put it—I say it is not *only* an experience. Thank God, it is an experience, a powerful experience, "a well of water springing up." If you do not have an experience of this living water, you are not a Christian. But I have to emphasize that Christianity is also an understanding, an understanding that is given to us and that explains what has happened to us and why it has happened and how it has happened.

Why is this so important? Because this is the way in which you always show not only the complete superiority but the complete difference between this and everything else that is offering people satisfaction and help. I am referring to teachings such as those in the cults, which offer people happiness and peace and joy, and in which you will find people testifying that they have had these experiences. That is how the cults succeed. Do you think Christian Science, for instance, would ever had succeeded as it has and become the wealthy corporation that it is, with its buildings and literature and so on, were it not that people testify that it has made all the difference in the world to them, that they have become new people? Other people, hearing this, say, "That's just what I want! I'm a worrier" or "I'm unhappy. I can't sleep" or "I'm ill—here's the answer." And they claim that they get the experience for which they are looking.

Then there are perversions or misuses of the gospel, which go by names such as "positive thinking." And there is also the misuse of Scripture by preachers who give nothing but psychological teaching dressed up in scriptural terms and terminology and bring in the name of our Lord while denying the essence of the faith. Now all these claim to give people experiences, and this is the danger—they delude people. That is why we must be careful to say that Christianity is not only an experience.

Now as I have already said, Christian people themselves have often overemphasized experience, and it has often been done in a spirit of fear. Let me give you two illustrations. In the middle of the last century, particularly after Darwin had published his famous book *The Origin of Species* in 1859, a great attack was made upon the Scripture, on the inspiration of the Scriptures, by the so-called higher-critical movement. Now a number of very good people were frightened by this. They said that science was now rising and shaking the very foundations of the faith, and they asked, how are we going to defend the faith? They had their experience, what they called the "faith experience," and they knew Christianity was true, but the question was, how were they going to defend it?

It seemed to them there was only one way. They said, "You can say that the whole of Genesis is wrong, the first chapters particularly. You can prove that Abraham was never a man, that he was a group. But let the higher critics, the scientists, say whatever they like, we have faith experience, and that is what matters." And they thought they were defending the faith by saying that. But far from defending it, they were virtually denying it because they did not demonstrate that it gives full intellectual satisfaction so that we are afraid of nothing—not science or philosophy or anything else that can raise its head against this precious truth.

I remember a man once speaking in a meeting—I had the misfortune or the difficulty at any rate of having to speak in the same meeting, but fortunately I followed him—who put the case like this. He said he had read a novel, I think it was, or had been to the movies, and the chief character was a poor old lady who spent most of her time sitting in the corner. There in the corner she sat holding a very old document. It was yellow and shriveled because of age. But as she held it and looked at it, she would smile. As I remember it, the poor old lady mistakenly believed this was a letter she had received about seventy years before from her lover. Now she had had many afflictions in life and many troubles, but as long as she could hold this letter in her hand, she was perfectly happy. Actually, said the preacher, she was wrong, but why bother to tell her it was not her lover's letter? Why should you be concerned to point out the error? Why tell her that she was unscientific and inaccurate? The document did the trick and made her happy. That is the kind of argument that has been put forward. Though critics may declare the Bible to be riddled with errors, the faith experience still remains.

I remember another occasion some thirty years ago when I was at a conference of ministers in Oxford. We were having a discussion together, I remember very well, on a Monday night, and the question came up about the veracity of the Bible and the whole foundation of the faith and our authority and basis for standing where we stood. And I remember that a number of men, who thought they were on my side, gave me the greatest difficulty in the discussion because they said to the others, "You can say what you like about your science and your criticism and so on, and I cannot answer you, but it is all right because you can never touch my experience." I say that they put me into difficulties for this reason: I felt that they were betraying the gospel. That was not the way to argue for the faith at all because they were delivering themselves over entirely to the psychologists and to these other people I have already mentioned. They were saying precisely what psychologists say about us.

Psychologists say, "We don't quarrel with you for being Christian; if it makes you happy, carry on. Anything that makes people happy—let them do it; it will help them. We're not against it. What we object to is your saying that we should be Christians, too, and your attempts to base Christianity upon what you claim is solid fact and truth."

Now, then, the answer to all that is that the Christian is not only someone who has an experience but also someone who has understanding. God has given us this book, the Bible, to give us understanding. We know what we believe; we can give explanations. We have an answer to doubts; we have an answer to criticism; we have answers for heresies. There is no need for us to be afraid; there is no need for us ever to apologize. The Bible has been given to us in order that with the understanding that comes through it we might be able to deal with all these questions that assail us.

Now, then, how does the Bible answer these questions? Well, you see, here is a great book, sixty-six different books all in one. I have never called this book "a library of books." It is not, because it is only one book. Nothing is more marvelous about it than its unity, its consistency. It has only one great message from beginning to end, and it is this message about God and his great plan and purpose. You see, the Bible tells us this. It is no use going to people and saying, "You know, if you become a Christian, you would be as happy as I am, and you would have this, that, and the other."

"All right," someone replies, "my Christian Science friend said that to me yesterday."

Then where are you? No, no, my dear friend, thank God for your experience, but oh, look at this gospel! This is God—the plan and purpose of God! In 1 Corinthians 2 Paul says:

> We speak wisdom among them that are perfect: yet not the wisdom of this world, nor of the princes of this world, that come to nought: but we speak the wisdom of God in a mystery, even the hidden wisdom, which God ordained before the world unto our glory. (vv. 6–7)

Now this is Christianity; this is what you and I are to be talking about. Christians are not people who are always talking about themselves and their experiences; they should be talking about God and what God has done. Their little experiences are only minute illustrations of this wonderful thing "which God ordained before [the foundation of the] world unto our glory," and it is revealed here. That is what the Bible is. It is the revelation of all this.

So, you see, the Bible starts with creation. Now, my dear Christian friend, do not start with your experience. Always start with God. That is what the Bible does, and you have no right to start anywhere else. You have no right to start in Matthew; you must start in Genesis because that is where God's revelation begins. Creation! The Fall! The promise of redemption! Here you stand back and look at this great plan of God for the redemption of the world.

In the Old Testament we are shown the preparation for this redemption. Having announced that he is going to bring this about, God then lets us know how he began to prepare for its actual coming. And he got men to write all this, told them the facts, gave them the information, guided them by his Spirit. So there is the account of the Flood: judgment, the saving of this one family, the family of Noah, the selection of Shem out of Noah's three boys, Shem, Ham, and Japheth. Then the great call of Abraham, beginning the nation, followed by Isaac, Jacob, the formation of the children of Israel, and the giving of the Law. What is the purpose of the Law? It is God revealing himself as a holy God and preparing a holy people for himself. And God's purpose is to redeem us from all sin and iniquity and to prepare for himself "a peculiar people, zealous of good works" (Titus 2:14).

Now I am not saying this—it is the Bible that says it, and why does the Bible say it? Why did God cause men to write this? The answer is so that you and I might *know* it. Not that we might just go about the world saying, "I've had a marvelous experience, you know, and you can have it too." All right, but you must tell them what it is, where it has come from, how it has come. Here is the answer—in the Bible. The understanding, the intellectual comprehension, is given to us by God, and it is part of the fullness of the living water.

Then we come to David, the choice of David and the promise to him that the great Messiah will come from him, from his seed. After David there are the great prophetic messages looking forward to this Coming One, pointing forward. What amazes me is that anybody can find the Bible a boring book! As you read all this, you feel the thrill that these men felt as they were given this revelation and set it forth. Of course, quite often they set it forth in historical terms—in terms of a contemporary difficulty or problem or stress. But through all that you see the purpose. Do not get distracted by the clothing; do not miss the wood because of the trees. Start with this great comprehensive picture and then see the outworking in all these detailed ways and in the variety of customs that are characteristic of the Old Testament. The author of the Epistle to the Hebrews sums it up as "at sundry times and in divers manners" (1:1)—different times, different places, different forms, but always the same message.

Then we come to the New Testament. We start with the Gospels, and we read about the birth of the babe. Who is this? The one who had been prophesied! The Messiah who had been promised! But he has come! We read about him, what he was like, how he was born, how he grew and developed, what he did, what he taught, what he promised—all this. We read about it, and, of course, having started in Genesis, we see that he is the fulfillment of all that had been promised; we see that he is the very acme of God's plan made before the foundation of the world; we see it all fitting into a great whole.

And then we go on to the Acts of the Apostles, and what do we find there? We find the fulfillment of some of the promises given by the Lord Jesus Christ. He had said to his disciples in essence, "You need not depend upon my physical presence. I am going to leave you, but do not be troubled—I will send you the Holy Spirit, and 'he will guide you into all truth'" (John 16:13). The Spirit will give you understanding; he will give you power and ability to teach and to expound these subjects.

What is the Acts of the Apostles? It is the fulfillment of that promise. The Holy Spirit came down on the Day of Pentecost, and these men who had fumbled and stumbled suddenly had understanding and spoke authoritatively and with great power, and tremendous things happened. The book of Acts is a thrilling account of that. It is all a part of this process, this sequence, "the wonderful works of God" (Acts 2:11).

And then we come to the epistles, and what are they? Well, they are but grand expositions of all this—that is why they were written. Take, for instance, the first eight chapters of the Epistle to the Romans—what are they? There is only one answer. There the apostle expounds God's great plan and shows how it is worked out. The first three chapters of the Epistle to the Ephesians do exactly the same thing, and so do the first two chapters of the Epistle to the Colossians.

Have you ever stood back and looked at these great chapters and asked yourself, what is this about, what is it for? Have you noticed the explanations, have you noticed the arguments, have you noticed the reasoning? The eleventh chapter of the Epistle to the Romans is perhaps a perfect illustration of what I am trying to say to you. The apostle takes up a question: if all that I have been saying is all right, well then, what about the Jews? They are outside the church; they are not Christians.

Here was a problem that was troubling the minds of Christian people. They had been saved, they were born again, they had their experience, but people came to them and said, "Look here, there's something wrong somewhere. You say all this, but your God has gone back on his own promises. He said the children of Israel, the Jews, were his people, but they are outside the church. Your church is mainly Gentile—how do you explain that?" And Romans 11, in fact chapters 9–10 as well, are the apostle's answer. But I want to emphasize this point: notice the way the apostle argues, the way he reasons—"If this, then that"—all the logic that is brought to bear. This is part of Scripture; this is revelation. God has taken the trouble not only to tell us what he has done but also to say why he has done it and how he has done it.

And so we come to understand why the only way of salvation is that which is in Christ. It is argued out; it is made plain and clear. The epistles show why Christ had to come, why no man could ever save us, why salvation had to be through the incarnation of the eternal Son. The apostle Paul explains why our Lord died on the cross on Calvary's hill. So many Christian people do not know why he died. If you ask them, they do not know or they are muddled. But here we are told why he died, and the Christian must know why the Son of God had to die on Calvary's hill. "There was no other good enough to pay the price of sin."[16] He is the Lamb of God slain from the foundation of the world. All that is expounded and explained here.

And then the epistles go on to explain how the perfect work of Christ in salvation is applied to us by the Holy Spirit. They even take you through the steps and the stages. Listen to this in Romans 8—what a wonderful statement it is of all this: "We know that all things work together for good to them that love God, to them who are the called according to his purpose" (v. 28). You are in trouble. Do you know that "all things work together for good to them that love God, to them who are the called according to his purpose"? How can you know that? Here is the answer:

> For whom he did foreknow, he also did predestinate to be conformed to the image of his Son, that he might be the firstborn among many brethren. Moreover whom he did predestinate, them he also called: and whom he called, them he also justified; and whom he justified, them he also glorified. What shall we then say to these things? (vv. 29–31)

Now this is part of Christianity, and if you and I do not know something about this and cannot state it, oh, what small Christians we are, what little life there is in us! We are meant to know the steps and the stages and the outworking of this grand pattern and scheme—God's foreknowledge, his election, our justification, sanctification, glorification. It is here; it is unfolded to us so that we not only know that something has happened to us, we have an understanding of what has happened and why it had to happen to us and what will happen to us.

So as you study this book, you get this great, final, and full satisfaction in every way. Are you rejoicing in this? Is this the way in which you use your Bible? Do you just read the little portion prescribed in some daily notes and then dash off, feeling you have done it? Shame upon you! Have you seen the whole? Are you working it out in its parts and portions? And above all, I ask, are you reveling in it? Here is the test. Someone who knows how to read the Bible always ends with words like these:

> O the depth of the riches both of the wisdom and knowledge of God! how unsearchable are his judgments, and his ways past finding out! For who hath known the mind of the Lord? or who hath been his counsellor? Or who hath first given to him, and it shall be recompensed unto him again? For of him, and through him, and to him, are all things: to whom be glory for ever. Amen. (Rom. 11:33–36)

20

The Authority of the Bible

Jesus answered and said unto her, Whosoever drinketh of this water shall thirst again: but whosoever drinketh of the water that I shall give him shall never thirst; but the water that I shall give him shall be in him a well of water springing up into everlasting life. (John 4:13–14)

The apostle Paul, in writing to the Ephesians, prays that ultimately they "might be filled with all the fulness of God" (Eph. 3:19). And in dealing with this and in showing how it is true that the gospel really does satisfy the whole person in every respect, we have naturally started with the intellect and with intellectual satisfaction. But though we start with the intellect, we are not going to stop there, because the gospel is equally satisfying for the heart and every other aspect of one's personality. We started with the intellect because this is God's greatest gift to men and women; it is the way in which we differ from animals. God made man in his own image and likeness; he gave him the power of reason and understanding and appreciation.

There are many reasons why it is important that we should understand something of the complete intellectual satisfaction that is given by the gospel. If we fail at this point, we may be in danger of misunderstanding the faith. In referring to Paul's epistles, the apostle Peter says, "in which are some things . . . which they that are unlearned and unstable wrest, as they do also the other scriptures, unto their own destruction" (2 Pet. 3:16). This is due to a lack of understanding. They have not used their minds as they should and so have found themselves in grievous trouble. A great warning runs right through the Bible with regard to this, especially in the New Testament.

Let us be clear therefore. The gospel, the way of salvation in Christ Jesus, is not merely meant to give us relief; it is not merely meant to give us help or experiences. Thank God, it does do that. We all need forgiveness of sins and deliverance from the power of sin; we need help, we need experiences, and the gospel gives all this. But even this is not its primary object. We tend to think this is the purpose of the Bible because we are all governed by our feelings and moods and states. We do not like to be miserable; we crave relief, peace, and joy. That is natural. But we must be careful that we never say that the whole business of the gospel is just to give us some kind of relief. It is not. That is incidental.

The primary object of the gospel is to reconcile us to God. "God was in Christ"—why? To deal with our aches and pains and little illnesses and pinpricks? Not at all. ". . . reconciling the world unto himself" (2 Cor. 5:19). That is the big, the great thing, and that is the most essential truth for us. It is our whole standing before God, our whole relationship to him, that matters primarily, and all these other benefits are, as it were, added on. As our Lord said, "Seek ye first the kingdom of God, and his righteousness; and all these things shall be added unto you" (Matt. 6:33). But the danger always is that we tend to give the whole of our attention to eating and drinking and the various reliefs that I have indicated.

If we do not sort our priorities out into the right order and proportion, we shall go astray, as the Scriptures tell us. So while we thank God for every blessing, as we shall be seeing, we must start with the intellect. In other words, the primary business of preaching and of teaching, the primary business, indeed, of the whole of Scripture, is to bring us to a knowledge of the truth. This is what we tend to forget. In his first epistle to Timothy, the apostle Paul tells Timothy to urge people that

> supplications, prayers, intercessions, and giving of thanks, be made for all men; for kings, and for all that are in authority; that we may lead a quiet and peaceable life in all godliness and honesty. For this is good and acceptable in the sight of God our Saviour; who will have all men [all kinds of people] to be saved, and to come unto *the knowledge of the truth*. (2:1–4)

The importance of knowing the truth is emphasized in the whole of Scripture. That is why preaching and teaching have such importance in the Bible; and that is why we as Protestants, evangelical Protestants in particular, are so opposed to the kind of service that puts the sacraments forward and discounts preaching and teaching. It is always a bad sign when the church gives increasing attention to forms and ceremonies and to the service as such rather than to the exposition of the Word of God. As

I am trying to show, this needs to be emphasized especially at this present time, when the whole tendency is to go back to that which, by the Spirit of God, the Protestant fathers and the Reformers were given to see was a departure from the New Testament order. We must be careful lest, unconsciously, in our subjectivity and in our concern about our own moods and feelings we also return to forms and ceremonies. There is a terrible danger today of going astray, of becoming heretics, and still more, there is a danger of confusing this gospel with the cults and their message.

The Christian gospel is not a mere matter of moral uplift and the sort of teaching put forward by proponents of positive thinking, psychology, and the cults. They are always just out to give us ease and relief in some shape or form. They have no truth. They want to help us, and that is why they appeal to people, especially people in trouble, people who are neurotic, those who are crying out for relief. There is nothing wrong in this, but it differs from the gospel in that first and foremost the gospel brings us to a knowledge of the truth and reconciles us to God. The ease and relief that people are seeking are an outcome of that, the fruit, as it were, the incidental consequence.

So that is why we start with the fullness of satisfaction that is given to the intellect, to the understanding; and as I have shown, this is brought about supremely by the Bible itself, in which God reveals himself and the truth concerning his ways. And we saw that God not only tells us what he has done and what he is going to do but also how he has done it. He gives us an understanding of it. And that should thrill us all.

You see, according to the apostle Peter, we should all be ready at all times to give a reason for the hope that is in us (1 Pet. 3:15). So it is important that we should enter into an understanding of the truth not only for our own satisfaction but also in order that we may help others. When people are shattered by things that happen to them or when they get frightened by the state of the world and are filled with forebodings, yet see that we remain calm and quiet, they say, "Why are you different? Is it merely that you have decided to adopt some psychological device and tell yourself that you need not worry about anything—there is always a silver lining to the cloud, and things will soon be all right again?" Are you just playing tricks with yourself and refusing to face facts in that way, or can you give a reason for the hope that is in you? None of us can give a reason for the hope that is in us unless we have an understanding of the truth as it is revealed in the Bible as a whole, this great revelation of God and his ways with respect to men and women and especially with respect to his dear Son, our blessed Lord and Savior. That, then, immediately gives us satisfaction.

But I am concerned that we really see the fullness of this intellectual satisfaction; so I now want to show it in a slightly different way. The gospel, and the gospel alone, satisfies our desire for authority. Now here is something that humanity has always desired. People want some certainty; they want something on which they can rest. Life is precarious, uncertain. This was true of people when they lived a nomadic life and were hunters, and it has been true ever since. Though people now build cities and have fortifications, life is still full of uncertainty. To anybody who thinks at all, life is a great mystery. There are billions and billions of viruses. You never know what is going to happen. And men and women want some assurance, some authority, but where are they to get it? So they ask their questions: How can I be sure? How can I know what is right?

Now here is a very important point, and it is a part of the glory that belongs to the gospel that it, and it alone, gives us the authority of which we stand in need. There is no authority and final satisfaction to be found in philosophy, still less in science, the god of the present time. Alas, there are those, even in the church, who are foolish enough to turn from the gospel, the only sure authority, to philosophy, "the thinkers," they say, and especially to science, scientists who seem to know and understand so much. People are ready to trust them and will hang on their every word and commit themselves to them. But I repeat that there is no authority to be found there, for a number of reasons.

First of all, before we have even listened to what they have to say, we know that all that philosophers and scientists can put before us, apart from certain well-established facts, is mere speculation. It is all theory; it is only human effort and endeavor, human attempts to solve the mystery and arrive at final assurance. We immediately know, therefore, that there is a very serious limit because of the obvious inadequacy of human ability and understanding.

And this, in the second place, is made still more evident to us when we are confronted by the rival theories. There is nothing so futile or so foolish as to think that all people who are not Christians believe the same thing. They do not, of course. There are schools among the philosophers, there are schools and rivalries among the scientists, and they contradict one another fundamentally. Two famous scientists in this country at the present time are quarreling even about the very origin of the universe! I remember reading a couple of years ago an article, I think it was by Miss

Marghanita Laski, a well-known atheist. She wrote that you must not talk about "the typical unbeliever" and said that she could not write for *the* unbeliever because there was no such person. Unbelievers differ and disagree among themselves. That is perfectly true. And so, without even looking at the details of what they say, you see at once that they can have no authority, and you cannot rest your weary soul there.

Now there is nothing wrong with science as long as it confines itself to science, as long as it examines and investigates and reports actual findings, facts that can be seen and touched and felt and weighed and handled. I am talking about science when it attempts to explain the whole of life to us and to say dogmatically, "There is no God! Miracles cannot happen!" and so on. That is no longer science; that is philosophy. While science deserves much credit, its whole trouble is that it fails most of all at the most crucial and vital points in life. It can give a lot of knowledge and information, but our problems are finally the problems of human beings themselves: What are they? What is their purpose? What is life? What is death? Scientists and philosophers can talk dogmatically, and they do, of course, but it is all theory. They do not know. They have told us nothing about death and what lies beyond.

When we come to the most fundamental problems of all, everything that opposes the Christian message and is supposed to give us scientific and solid assurance fails us and fails us completely. It was no accident that the great German philosopher Goethe cried out on his deathbed, "More light!" He had not received it; he was in the dark. He was as much in the dark as the greatest ignoramus lying on his deathbed.

And not only that, further proof that there is no authority in these realms comes from the fact that they are always changing. And they not only change, it is a part of the scientist's boast that they do. These are the people who are always talking about "the advance of knowledge," "modern thought," "the modern man," and implicit in their very statements, in their slogans, in their clichés, is a tremendous and a terrible confession. They all tell us that they are the ones who are right, they are the ones who have arrived at true knowledge; everybody in the past was wrong. Yet in the past, a hundred years ago, two thousand years ago, the same sort of people were speaking with equal dogmatism and authority.

Now it is important that we should know all this. I am referring especially to the type of uninformed, illiterate Christian who is afraid of science and of philosophy, who apologizes for the faith and is ready to accommodate it to some scientific discoveries. This is a denial of the truth, and when you do this you are robbing yourself of one of the most glorious aspects of the Christian faith.

I can easily prove this to you. Look, for instance, at the change in the attitude of scientists toward the atom. I was taught in my scientific training that the atom was indivisible, the smallest piece of matter. I was taught that with absolute authority. But we know today that is nonsense—the atom is a whole world of life and activity. There is also the change in the understanding of light, and we have the new physics, and so on. Everything has changed. How can you place yourself in the hands of such a supposed authority? There is no authority there; you are on a sliding scale. If you really accept this modern attitude, you are bound to say that however good modern theories may be, it is certain that in a few years they will have to be discarded because they have been proved to be wrong. As today that is said about the past, so in the future it will be said about the present.

Those, then, are some of the reasons why you will never find authority in science or philosophy—it is impossible. But here in the gospel we come to something absolutely different. Why? Because it is from above. It is from God. This is not human speculation, not men and women making theories; it is God teaching us, God revealing himself to us. We are in an entirely different realm here. This is the claim: "All Scripture is given by inspiration of God" (2 Tim. 3:16). It is literally "God-breathed." The biblical writers do not claim they are recording their own ideas or suppositions or insights; they say their messages were "given," they were "revealed." Study the Bible yourself, and keep your eye on that very point. It is the whole essence of the position that there is certainty in the Bible.

But we see this still more clearly when we come to our Lord himself. Take, for example, the third chapter of John's Gospel and our Lord's words to Nicodemus. Nicodemus was a great teacher, a great man, but when our Lord told him about the rebirth, Nicodemus did not understand.

> Nicodemus answered and said unto him, How can these things be? Jesus answered and said unto him, Art thou a master of Israel, and knowest not these things? Verily, verily, I say unto thee [here it is], We speak that we do know, and testify that we have seen; and ye receive not our witness. If I have told you earthly things, and ye believe not, how shall ye believe, if I tell you of heavenly things? And no man hath ascended up to heaven, but he that came down from heaven, even the Son of man which is in heaven. (John 3:9–13)

There is the authority. Here is one standing among men and saying, "I know!" Why does he say that? He says in effect, "I know for this reason—I have seen him."

The Lord Jesus Christ does not speculate about God—he declares him: "No man hath seen God at any time; the only begotten Son, which is in the bosom of the Father, he hath declared him" (John 1:18). Why? Because, he says, he has come down from heaven: "No man hath ascended up to heaven, but he that came down from heaven, even the Son of man" (John 3:13). Human beings do not know anything about God. How can they? God is in heaven; he dwells in a light that is unapproachable. Human beings cannot understand themselves and their own world, still less God. The only authority we can have on ultimate questions is the authority of one who has looked into the face of God and "came down" to tell us. That is exactly what our Lord claims: "We speak that we do know, and testify that we have seen."

So we are in an entirely different realm here. Our Lord says exactly the same thing, as we have seen, to the woman of Samaria: "Ye worship ye know not what: we know what we worship" (John 4:22). "We know"! He speaks with the authority of one who has come from heaven, from the unseen into the seen. He is just a carpenter, he has not been to the schools, and yet he speaks with authority. He says, "I am the light of the world" (John 8:12).

Here, then, is one who speaks with authority, and he proves his right to do so by his miracles, by his prophecies, by all that he did, ending supremely with the great fact of the resurrection. So the question of authority comes back to the whole question of the person of the Lord Jesus Christ himself. He is unique. This is his claim. He has dwelt with God, he was and is God, he has always been with God. He knows, and he has come down to tell us.

And then we look back at the Old Testament, and we find that this person believes it, he accepts it, he speaks of it as "God's word" and says "the scripture cannot be broken" (John 10:35). So as we face this question of authority, our real question concerns the person of the Lord Jesus Christ, and if we believe in him as the Son of God, then we know that this is God's word, this is our sole authority, and it speaks authoritatively because it has all come from God.

Now that being the case, immediately we have satisfaction, we have authority. We are not dependent upon changing human ideas and the so-called advance of knowledge. No, no; we have an absolute statement.

We have one from eternity speaking in time and revealing the mind of God.

And that tells me not only that this is true, but, further, that it always will be true—and to me this is most marvelous of all. This—I am thinking of the whole Bible—is true; it has always been true. A hundred years ago it was true, a thousand years ago it was true, two thousand years ago it was true, and because of that it always will be true. Now there is no difficulty at all in proving this, and it is one of the things in which we should glory together. There is no new truth about man or about life or about death or about God—none at all. Now this is the kind of thing, of course, that the world does not think of—and, unfortunately, many foolish Christians do not think of it either. They accept the thinking of the world—the "advance"! "We *know*." But we do not! We know nothing more about man nor about any of these great, ultimate questions than our forefathers did—nothing at all. Here it is in the Bible, and it is exactly the same truth that it has always been. There is no change, no modification whatsoever. This is very wonderful to me, and it is why I often thank God that I am preaching today and not a hundred years back.

"What?" says somebody. "Would you prefer to preach in 1967 rather than in 1867?"

Oh, yes, most definitely. This is a day of great opportunity. The poor preacher of a hundred years ago must have been in considerable difficulty—in fact, we know he was. That is why they compromised on the gospel, so many of them. The world was so steady and steadfast! Knowledge and science were growing, and man was advancing. Everything seemed to be on man's side. Most of them were bemused and deluded fools in their pride of knowledge and understanding. They were the people who talked about the world advancing and developing. The parliament of man! The federation of the world! War would be banished! The world would be made paradise by political enactments. There was nothing to stop us; everything was moving forward. Of course, we know today how utterly illusory it all was. The modern world proves that the Bible is true, that the Bible is the only authority.

A hundred years ago they read in the Bible—though they did not believe it, they said it was wrong—that man in sin will always behave in the same way, that man in sin is a fool, that man in sin is a rebel, that man in sin always brings misery down upon himself, whatever the appearances may happen to be; and the twentieth century proved that. It is more patently true today than it was a hundred years ago. Man has shown that the Bible is right, that the Bible is true. Morning newspapers proclaim the truth of the Bible; the whole world is proclaiming that truth. For all these centuries, this book has gone on saying the same things about God and man and the relationship between them, and it is as true at this moment as it has ever been. You see, here is authority, and the modern world is proving it. There is nothing more futile than trusting in man and his knowledge and his wisdom and his speculation.

But I anticipate one question here. Someone may say to me, "What about science? Are you really saying that you are putting the Bible before science?"

This is a very popular question, is it not? We obviously cannot deal with this adequately in a glancing word in a sermon; it would take a book. But there is no difficulty in principle in dealing with this. There is no contradiction whatsoever between the teaching of the Bible and science. Now notice what I am saying. I have already told you what I mean by science. Science is just the collecting of facts and putting them in order. That is the business of science.

"All right," you say, "but are you maintaining that the scientist doesn't have a right to speculate?"

I will grant him the right to speculate as long as he tells us that is what he is doing, that he is no longer dealing with facts but is putting up a theory, putting up a supposition, which he intends to test. I know that is of value—that is how you get your inventions. That is perfectly all right as long as scientists do not make dogmatic pronouncements as if they were facts. As I said, the moment they do that, they cease to be true scientists and become philosophers.

Let me make one other qualification. I draw a distinction also between the teaching of the Bible and what the Christian church has sometimes taught. It is essential to define this teaching accurately, just as it is essential to define science accurately.

Why do I say this? Because historically the church, the Roman Catholic Church in particular, has blundered by making dogmatic pronouncements in the realm of science, causing a great deal of confusion. The simple answer to that is that she had no right to do so; she was not expounding the Bible at that point. What she was doing was expounding the philosophy of Aristotle, as worked out still more fully by Thomas Aquinas and others, on which so much of her teaching has always been based. And it was when she began to do that that she went wrong, and science was able to prove that she was wrong. But science was not proving that the teaching of the Bible was wrong, merely that the speculations of certain Christian thinkers, who had become more philosophical than biblical, were wrong. So my fundamental proposition is that there is no contradiction between the teaching of the Bible and the teaching of science.

Many people are worried, of course, by the early chapters of Genesis. They say, "Surely, you can't believe that any longer? You must accept the theory of evolution."

Of course, these people do not say the "theory" of evolution; they tend to say the "fact" of evolution, and that is where they go wrong. No scientist, no teaching of science, can tell us with any authority whatsoever how things came into being. They can speculate, they can put theories forward, but they do not know—no human being was there. And they are in the difficulty of having to say that this is something that seems to have happened once and forever and why it did and so on; but they do not know. It is all speculation. Nobody knows what happened in the intervening period. They know what is happening now, and what they tend to do is to extrapolate back to what happened at the beginning. They say, "Because we observe this now, it must always have happened." But they have no right at all to say that. That is sheer supposition.

All I am trying to tell you is that science is in no position at all to disprove the teaching of the early chapters of Genesis that the world was created in six days and that man was a special creation and did not evolve through the millennia, eventually becoming man out of an animal. That is all theory and speculation, it is a contradiction of the Bible, and it does not prove anything at all. In the Epistle to the Hebrews we are given the answer to all that: "Through faith we understand that the worlds were framed by the word of God, so that things which are seen were not made of things which do appear" (11:3). And the attempt on the part of people who call themselves believers in theistic evolution is no better than non-theistic or atheistical evolution because it is still introducing the theorizing of men into the plain record of God. And the whole of our salvation, in a sense, depends upon a correct understanding of Genesis, because I am told by Paul, "As in Adam, so in Christ"—he draws a parallel.

I am trying to show you that in the Bible there is complete intellectual satisfaction, and that as this is true today and as it has always been true, we need be in no fear whatsoever with regard to any future discoveries. I make bold to assert this: scientists will never discover anything that will in any way invalidate the authority of the Scripture. They will never be able to do so because the facts of creation can never contradict the facts of revelation, and this is because it is the same God who is at the back of both.

And, indeed, I can give you some evidence to support what I am saying. I say we need not be afraid of discoveries. I would venture to prophesy that discoveries will continue, as they have done hitherto, to prove and to support the teaching of the Scriptures. Take what we read in 2 Peter 3:10 about the elements melting with fervent heat. Until comparatively recently that was regarded as nonsense by the wise and prudent, the philosophers and the scientists, but when the first atomic bomb was exploded, people began to see that there was something in this. That is exactly what happens when these atomic bombs are released—the elements melt with "fervent heat" in the great atomic explosion. I need say no more. All I am trying to show you is that the Bible gives complete and entire intellectual satisfaction and that we need never be afraid of anything that may be discovered.

I have a feeling that many Christians go to bed every night in fear, afraid they are going to read the next morning that some scientist has looked down a microscope and proved the whole of the Bible to be wrong. Oh, shame upon us Christian people! We need have no fear whatsoever. As the Bible has gone on through the ages, it will go on—it is the truth of God.

Another great argument to support the truth of the Bible is, of course, the argument of prophecy—for instance, among other prophetic examples that I could give you, God revealing the birth of Christ, with all the various details, eight centuries before it happened. Have you considered this? What a proof this is that the Bible is the Word of God and not human speculation. And then think of the whole question of the witness of the apostles. Peter writes:

> I will endeavour that ye may be able after my decease to have these things always in remembrance. For we have not followed cunningly devised fables, when we made known unto you the power and coming of our Lord Jesus Christ, but were eyewitnesses of his majesty. For he received from God the Father honour and glory, when there came such a voice to him from the excellent glory, This is my beloved Son, in whom I am well pleased. And this voice which came from heaven we heard, when we were with him in the holy mount. (2 Pet. 1:15–18)

Here is the evidence; here are the witnesses. This is not mere hearsay, this is not a novel, this is not imagination and fantasy, this is not human theorizing and speculations, not "cunningly devised fables." Rather "we heard . . . we were with him." There was witness! Here is the authority, and it is because of all this that we can say without any fear whatsoever:

O Christ, the Word of God incarnate,
O Wisdom from on high;
O Truth, unchanged, unchanging,
O Light of our dark sky!

WILLIAM WALSHAM HOW

It is the only light. It is unchanged. I am preaching the very same gospel, the same truth, the same message, that men preached a thousand years ago, the message that has always been preached, exactly the same message. What have I said that is in any sense different? Nothing at all! I have simply been showing the fallacy of modern thought. My message is not based on modern thought: it is the Bible. I am simply expounding it. A man a thousand years ago, though he would not have been able to use the same illustrations, would have preached the same message. "O Truth, unchanged, unchanging"—there is no need to modify it in any respect whatsoever. There is nothing that modern people know that requires us to qualify anything at all in the Bible. Take the Bible as it is. Differentiate between it and the speculations of able men in the church.

And that brings me to a final word—the Bible always interests us in a lasting and increasing way. This is another great desire in the human heart—we want something to interest us. By nature we get tired of things. We get tired of everything, do we not? We always want something new. We are all by nature like those Athenians who we are told "spent their time in nothing else, but either to tell, or to hear some new thing" (Acts 17:21). Everybody wants a change, on every level, including almost the animal level. People get tired of drinks—they want a new one; they change the form of leisure, sport, and entertainment. Humanity is always dissatisfied and restless.

And it is exactly the same with the most sophisticated people. It is especially typical of those who are especially intelligent and enlightened. They take up a theory, they are very intrigued, they say, and they rush after it—it is all the vogue. But it is soon dropped! Something else comes along, and that is taken up. "Have you heard of this? There's a new teacher—he has a wonderful teaching. This is quite something," and off they rush. The history of civilization is the history of changing fashions in the realm of thought and in almost every other conceivable respect.

Let me make a confession. By now I have been trying to preach this message for forty years, and I find it much easier as I go on. Do some of you think that I must be finding it difficult to have something fresh to say? Let me assure you that my difficulty is the difficulty of having enough time to say what I want to say about all that I find in the Bible! I do not mind telling you, I am already prepared for next Sunday morning and next Sunday evening—indeed, and Sundays after. This book is endless. It is an ocean, a mighty ocean, God's truth, God revealing himself.

Do you see what are we doing? In the last study I took you through the whole Bible. I was looking at the Bible through a telescope. You can do that; you should do that. But do not stop at that. Having looked at it telescopically, you then begin to look at it microscopically. I am often reminded of this: it is what I used to do in medicine, and medical people are still doing it, especially those who work in laboratories and examine specimens. This was the method that we were always taught: we were given something, and first we looked at it in general; then, having done that, we cut it into pieces and put each section under a microscope.

How did we then use the microscope? Well, this is how we were taught, and this is how medical students are still being taught. We started with a fairly low magnifying power in order to have a general view of the section that we intended to examine in detail. Having done that, we put the microscope on a higher power to get still more detail, and then higher still. And now laboratories have more advanced magnification, so that you can almost see things that are invisible.

And it is like that with the Scripture. You see the whole message of the Scripture; then you see the parts and then the portions of the parts. And it is all wonderful, it is all a miracle. It is all God in almost every detail; it is God everywhere. And so it comes to pass that it is endless, it is always enthralling, it is always exciting, it is always stimulating, it is always new, it is always amazing, it is always more and more marvelous. And it must be so, because ultimately it is all part of the knowledge of God.

Men and women will never get tired of this knowledge. It will always satisfy them as long as they live and cause their minds to expand and to develop and to reach out, and it will be the same even in eternity. That is why no one ever has been or ever will be bored in heaven. In heaven for all eternity we will know more and more about God—God the Father, God the Son, and God the Holy Spirit. It is an endless sea! It is as infinite as God himself! Oh, the fullness of the satisfaction that comes to the minds of those who drink of this water that the Lord Jesus Christ offers them! "Whosoever drinketh of the water that I shall give him shall never thirst; never, no, never."

21

The Sufficiency of the Bible

Jesus answered and said unto her, Whosoever drinketh of this water shall thirst again: but whosoever drinketh of the water that I shall give him shall never thirst; but the water that I shall give him shall be in him a well of water springing up into everlasting life. (John 4:13–14)

In our consideration of these great verses, we are now concerned with truth. The Bible is not just some sort of agency that offers us happy feelings. All our experiences, as we saw in the last study, are a result of coming to an understanding of the truth. So we must start there, and the truth, obviously, presents itself primarily to the mind. So we are looking at this glorious sufficiency that we have in the Bible for the mind and the understanding.

Here in this one book, the Bible, God has treasured up his wisdom for us. This is not an ordinary book; it starts with revelation. God has given the knowledge, the information; he has chosen men to write it and to report his message infallibly under the influence of his Holy Spirit, and so we have it here. And as we have been seeing, the Bible not only tells us about salvation but also how it works, how it has been planned.

We saw in the last study that the Bible satisfies our desire for authority, a desire that is common to the whole human race. We ended on the note that the Bible not only holds our interest but also always increases it. To me, there is nothing more pathetic and tragic than Christians who are always looking back to their first experience, always repeating that, as if nothing has happened to them since. As you go on in this Christian life, it becomes increasingly more wonderful, more enthralling, more stimulating, more exciting because it is eternal truth. There is no end to it.

That is the point at which we have arrived, but we do not stop there. The next thing I want to note is that the Bible satisfies our desire for system and for wholeness. This, again, is one of the fundamental desires of human nature. And this, of course, is what is meant by philosophy. The love of wisdom springs from the desire to have a comprehensive understanding. Man—intelligent man—has always looked at the universe and at himself and has tried to understand it. What makes man man is that he is concerned about this, and philosophy is his endeavor to reach this understanding.

We have an innate feeling that there must be some wholeness, some explanation, something that holds everything together. I put it like that in order to emphasize the difference between the Bible and certain schools of modern thinking that teach the exact opposite and tell us that life is all the result of accident and chance. Man has been searching throughout the centuries for a system—a system of truth—something comprehensive, all-inclusive, a wholeness. One school of thought is associated with the name of Field Marshal Smuts, who was a great philosopher as well as a statesman. His view, his teaching, was called Holism.

But in spite of all these endeavors, people have never been able to arrive at a comprehensive system of thought. All they have done is discover bits of knowledge, bits of information, here and there. They have tried to put them all into one piece. They have tried to complete the jigsaw puzzle, as it were, but they have never succeeded. There are always portions that they cannot fit in, that they cannot reconcile. What they discover there is contradicted by what they know here. Human knowledge is always fragmentary, even at its very best, and try as they will, people can never arrive at the wholeness, the fullness, the perfection for which they are searching. But—and this again is one of its central glories—that is precisely what the Bible gives us.

Now this is something in which we should rejoice and of which we should be increasingly aware. No greater disservice is done to the Bible than to represent it as a book that tells us about how our sins can be forgiven—that one bit of information—and after that as a book to be used mainly to stimulate our devotional life. That is a very serious misunderstanding. It is such a misuse of the Bible that it really almost contradicts its teaching.

Of course, the Bible does tell us how our sins can be forgiven. Thank God that it does. But it does not stop at that. The Bible is concerned not only about my soul in particular—thank God, I say again, that it is interested in that—but it does not stop at me and my little needs and aches and pains. The Bible is interested in the whole cosmos, the entire universe;

there is nothing that it does not take in. The apostle Paul writes, ". . . that in the dispensation of the fulness of times he might gather together in one all things in Christ, both which are in heaven, and which are on earth; even in him" (Eph. 1:10). This is the astounding thing about this book, about this revelation of God, which centers upon the blessed person who is talking to the woman of Samaria. It is all in him. He is the light of the world, and all we have is what has been given through him.

Now we must remember that while there is a great deal of particular and detailed teaching in the Bible, while there is what might be called bits and pieces, nevertheless, the great characteristic of the Bible is that in addition to the portions, there is the whole. The author of the Epistle to the Hebrews puts it like this:

> God, who at sundry times and in divers manners [in parts and portions, in bits and pieces] spake in time past unto the fathers by the prophets, hath in these last days spoken unto us by his Son, whom he hath appointed heir of all things, by whom also he made the worlds. (1:1–2)

There it is again, always starting from the particular, the bits and portions, and then coming to the whole, this Son by whom he made all things and who sustains all things. Now this satisfaction for the mind is a most wonderful aspect of our Christian life. I do not have just a bit of something here and another portion there, but these are parts of a whole, and I can look at the whole as well as at the parts.

When I am asked, as I often am, about reading the Bible, the answer that I always give is there is a sense in which you cannot understand any particular portion of the Bible until you have grasped the message of the whole Bible. Of course, you will never know the whole until you have gone through the parts, but that is the way to do it. You go through the parts, and perhaps for a while you may feel lost, but keep on—read the whole Bible. Always read the whole Bible as frequently as you can, I would say at least once a year. Then you have the whole, and the more you understand the whole, the more you will understand the parts. That is one of the thrilling things about the Bible.

Let me explain this. The Bible gives us this understanding that we crave for in two main ways. It has its plain, direct, explicit teaching—statements, propositions. We see these right through the Bible, particular statements with which we are all familiar: "God is love," "God so loved the world, that he gave his only begotten Son," and so on. But the danger is that we tend to stop there. Of course, we start with the plain statements; we are bound to. Growth in spiritual understanding and knowledge is exactly the same as the growth of a child in the natural realm. The child has to start with simple elements—letters, then words, then sentences, and so on. But the point is that you must not stop at the letters, you must not stop at the words; you must be more and more interested in the sentences, in paragraphs, in a book, and on and on it goes.

The second way in which the Bible gives us the understanding and knowledge that we innately stand in need of, and ever crave for, is by giving us knowledge that we *deduce* from the general teaching of the Scripture. Let me give you an example that I think will put it quite plainly. Take the doctrine of the blessed Holy Trinity—God the Father, God the Son, and God the Holy Spirit, three eternal Persons and yet one God. Now the doctrine of the Trinity is not stated explicitly anywhere in the Scriptures. But as we read we find God the Father, God the Son, and God the Holy Spirit. There are ample statements about these three Persons, and yet the Bible also asserts that God is one. There is only one Godhead. And by putting these together, we arrive at the doctrine of the Trinity. That is just one example, and there are others that I could give you.

As we read the Scriptures, we are meant, under the influence and inspiration of the Holy Spirit, not only to take in and to grasp and to rejoice in the direct biblical statements but also, as our minds are enlightened, to arrive at other doctrines by deduction. This is, I repeat, not only a vital but also a very thrilling matter. Let me put it like this—and this is where one begins to see the wholeness: as we read the Bible, we come across great particular truths—teaching about the nature of God, about sin, about man, about salvation, and so on. This is generally called *biblical theology*. Are you frightened of the word *theology*? Well, if you are, there is something wrong with you! Theology means "the knowledge of God," and that should be the greatest desire of every Christian. How can we arrive at a knowledge of God? Only by reading what God has been pleased to reveal about himself. It helps the mind that these great statements are given a particular form, and that is what is meant by a *doctrine*. So we have the doctrine of God, the doctrine of salvation, and so on.

The business of theology is to help us in these matters. That is why God has raised up teachers and instructors—theologians—who can teach the doctrine. They help us because the more we know about these doctrines that are revealed in Scripture, the more we shall rejoice before him and marvel and be filled with a sense of amazement.

But then we take a further step, using the mind that God has given us—it is all submitted to the Spirit. But now we find that we can take these great doctrines and see that there is a system in all this. So we arrive at *systematic theology*, which means the great doctrines of the Bible put in a logical, reasonable order. This has been done throughout the centuries. In a way the great creeds and confessions of the church have been efforts to do that very thing. And, indeed, very often in the New Testament itself we see clear evidence that the teachers of the early church, who did not have books as we have now, would produce a form of words, a kind of formula, which they taught the people to say. One great example is 1 Timothy 3:16—"Great is the mystery of godliness: God was manifest in the flesh, justified in the Spirit, seen of angels, preached unto the Gentiles, believed on in the world, received up into glory." Now that is obviously a primitive confession. That was the early church's way of making a systematic theology.

In other words, in the Scriptures there is a great chain of thought that we can work out. To me, there is nothing more satisfying, more thrilling than to have some glimpse of an insight into this. So we look, we stand back, and we start with the everlasting and eternal God. "In the beginning. . . ." That is the beginning always. Here it is in the beginning of Genesis, the beginning of the Bible. It is of necessity the beginning. We are in this mysterious universe, and we say, "I want to have understanding. Is there any plan? Is there any system, any wholeness?"

Well, here is the answer: God, and the great truths about God. One of our hymns talks about "his wise decrees," and as the apostle Paul reminds the Ephesians, these things were done "before the foundation of the world" (Eph. 1:4)—before time.

This is how we find this completeness, this wholeness, this fullness of understanding of the whole cosmos. The world is not an accident. Things have not just happened or come into being somehow. No, no! God, the three Persons, in his wisdom and understanding and purpose conceived the creation of the whole universe. As we think about this, we are working out our systematic theology, the great doctrine about God—God the Father, God the Son, God the Holy Spirit.

So we have the creation of the universe and then the creation of man. But then we come to the condition of man, humanity as it is now. What is it? And the Bible has its answer—the doctrine of the Fall. So we are taking these subjects in an intelligent, intelligible order. And there is an order in these matters. The teaching is here in the Scriptures, but it is not put in a systematic order. You get one revelation here and another there, and we are meant to take all these and to put them into this great order. Indeed, the more I read the Bible, the more I see the order coming out everywhere.

So having seen why man is as he is, we ask the question, what can be done for him? And in comes the great doctrine of salvation, again involving the person of the Son, the miracle of the Incarnation, the virgin birth—what he did—what he said. That leads to the crucial doctrine of the cross—what he was doing there, the meaning of that, the way of salvation ordained by God—the Lamb of God slain before the foundation of the world in actual practice—his death, his resurrection. And so it continues—his ascension, his return to heaven.

So the work of salvation is completed, but how am I to partake of this? Here it comes—the work of the Holy Spirit, this dispensation to which you and I belong, all mediated through the Spirit and applied through him. And even the steps and stages of that are given to us in detail—the calling and the setting apart, justification, sanctification, glorification. This is all part of this great system. And then, of course, the ultimate end of it all when this Son of God will return to this world and complete the work and establish his eternal kingdom.

That is what I mean by systematic theology, this wonderful arrangement and order. The plan, you see! People are so ignorant about these matters; some have been foolish enough to talk about the cross of Christ as if it were an afterthought, saying that something had to happen because the Jews in their folly had rejected their own Messiah. Afterthought? The Bible teaches *forethought*! Before the foundation of the world, in every single detail, there was this perfect plan. And now God in his grace has been pleased to give us the revelation of it so that we can stand back and look at it. And we end by saying, "I am a part of that!" and begin to realize what it means to be a human being and to be a Christian, and we are filled with rejoicing and praise.

To give you an illustration of what I am trying to say, let us look again at the first chapter of the Epistle to the Ephesians. What a chapter it is! The apostle is doing there the very thing that I have been trying to do in my feeble manner, and he succeeds; he gives just a glimpse of this grand sweep of it all. This is one of the most difficult chapters to read aloud in the whole Bible. Did you realize that from the beginning of the third verse to the end of the fourteenth verse there is just one sentence? We do have, unfortunately, full stops in the various versions, but in the original, from the words "Blessed be the God and Father of our Lord Jesus Christ" right until the end of the fourteenth verse, "unto the praise of his glory" there is a single sentence—but what a sentence! Into that one sentence Paul has crowded this whole great and eternal purpose. Paul begins:

> God . . . who hath blessed us with all spiritual blessings in heavenly places in Christ: according as he hath chosen us in him before the foundation of the world . . . having predestinated us unto the adoption of children by Jesus Christ to himself, according to the good pleasure of his will. . . .

Then he says, in verses 7–8:

> In whom we have redemption through his blood, the forgiveness of sins, according to the riches of his grace; wherein he hath abounded toward us in all wisdom and prudence.

Then in verse 9 we read, "Having made known unto us the mystery of his will, according to his good pleasure which he hath purposed in himself." Before the foundation of the world, he purposed it all "in himself," but it has pleased him now to make this known. All I am trying to urge upon you is the vital importance of giving yourself to this; and the more you do so, the more you will be satisfied. You will find that it really does cover everything. But what is this "good pleasure which he hath purposed in himself"? Well, there it is in the tenth verse: "that in the dispensation of the fulness of times"—by which Paul means that at an appointed time, which was known to God before he ever created the world, he will wind it all up again—"he might gather together in one all things in Christ, both which are in heaven, and which are on earth; even in him." Everything will be wound up and brought to a glorious consummation in him.

That is a great summary of this wonderful and amazing system. Now all this is not merely for the intellectual entertainment of the Ephesians, nor is what I am trying to do for your intellectual entertainment. But if you really do want intellectual entertainment, read your Bible and listen to its exposition. See how everything else is dwarfed by it and seems so trivial and piecemeal; the pompous human philosophies—how ridiculous they look. Here it is—the whole cosmos is involved.

But watch how the apostle goes on. In verses 11–12 he says, "In whom also we have obtained an inheritance." Who is he talking about? The Jews. There is the great plan. Here is humanity, and it is divided into

Jews and Gentiles. This is not our division. God has done it. God made a nation for himself—the Jews. Paul is saying that the Jews first had obtained an inheritance. He continues, "being predestinated according to the purpose of him who worketh all things after the counsel of his own will: that we should be to the praise of his glory, who first trusted in Christ."

In Romans 1:16 Paul says, "to the Jew first, and also to the Greek." We find this teaching everywhere. There are bits and portions here and there, but it is all part of this great plan of God.

Then in verse 13 of this first chapter of Ephesians, Paul says, "In whom ye also trusted." Who are the "you" here? The Gentiles. Jews first, then Gentiles. They are brought in in exactly the same way, and thus the whole of humanity is brought into God's salvation.

And in verse 14 Paul finishes by saying that we have received the "earnest" of all this by the Spirit "until the redemption of the purchased possession, unto the praise of his glory."

Very well, Paul says, there it is, that is the truth you need to understand. So he continues, in verses 15–20, "Wherefore I also, after I heard of your faith in the Lord Jesus, and love unto all the saints, cease not to give thanks for you, making mention of you in my prayers." He is praying for them. What is he praying? ". . . that the God of our Lord Jesus Christ, the Father of glory, may give unto you the spirit of wisdom and revelation in the knowledge of him: the eyes of your understanding being enlightened."

Paul is saying, "Oh, if only you saw it!" He is an apostle, of course; he has been dealt with in a special manner. He tells them that in the third chapter. He writes of how the Lord appeared to him and gave him a dispensation of the grace of God, "that I should preach among the Gentiles the unsearchable riches of Christ" (v. 8). He is not boasting. He is saying in essence, "I am an apostle. I have been given this revelation. He has appeared to me; he has taught me. He has sent me to teach you, and this is what I'm doing. I want you to see it. If only you saw these things."

> . . . that ye may know what is the hope of his calling, and what the riches of the glory of his inheritance in the saints, and what is the exceeding greatness of his power to us-ward who believe, according to the working of his mighty power, which he wrought in Christ, when he raised him from the dead [and which he is now exercising in you until he brings this church that he is forming to an absolute final completion] . . . the fulness of him that filleth all in all. (vv. 18–23)

There it is. Is it not wonderful to be able to look at something like this, especially at a time of uncertainty and confusion such as this present age? Who can find sense anywhere? It is only to be found here. A certain hymn, written by a man who was not a biblical writer, expresses it in the most glorious way that I know of:

The Lord is King! Lift up thy voice,
O earth; and all ye heavens, rejoice!
From world to world the joy shall ring,
The Lord omnipotent is King!

JOSIAH CONDER ("THE LORD IS KING")

This is the biblical way of giving us this fullness of intellectual satisfaction. We have our troubles and problems, of course, and I would like to show you how they may all be dealt with. But this is the way to begin, my dear friend: put yourself into the right setting, into the right context. If you are in trouble, do not look at yourself, look at God, and realize something of this glorious and eternal truth.

Then, having done that, you can proceed to my next point, which is that the Bible and its amazing revelation goes on to deal with our particular intellectual problems. This, again, is essential because we are in the flesh, we are in the world, we are frail creatures. Extraordinary things are happening all around us, and men and women are perplexed and bewildered and are always asking why. Why does this happen? Why is that allowed? These are certainly a part of the trouble, and if this salvation and this Savior cannot answer my questions and solve my needs in this matter of my intellectual problems and difficulties, then is he right to say, "Whosoever drinketh of the water that I shall give him shall never thirst"? And the answer is an eternal "Yes!" because he answers everything.

Now we must be clear about this, and the more we understand it, the more we will rejoice in the fullness of this great salvation. So I start with this—and again in dealing with particular problems I must emphasize the importance of order—the first thing that the Bible teaches us is that there is order in the universe. If you do not believe the revelation of the Bible, you will not believe that, and there are foolish people today who believe that all that we see is the result of blind, purposeless, mindless chance, a view that is surely monstrous and ridiculous. A famous old American preacher said recently—he at any rate had seen this clearly—that you cannot explain the universe by saying that it came about by accident or chance. As he said, you cannot explain even the works of Shakespeare in that way; these are not words that have just fallen together somehow or another.

There is only one satisfactory explanation: there is a mind behind the universe. This does not go far enough by way of explanation, but that much at any rate is plain and clear. This cosmos is not an accident. There is order; there is arrangement. We see it not only in plants and creatures and the whole order of the seasons, but especially in human beings and in the gifts they have.

Now this is always a great way of starting. If you take the position of so-called scientific humanists, atheists like Sir Julian Huxley and others, who say quite plainly and specifically that there is no order whatsoever in the universe and it all came about capriciously, by chance, and there is no discernible purpose, either in creation or history or anywhere else, then you do not know what may happen. The world may decide to move upward, or it may do the exact opposite; it may, indeed, go both up and down! And if there is no purpose, then obviously there is no explanation for anything at all.

But starting as we do with God the Creator and with an ordered universe and a purpose and a plan, we can confront the problem of pain and of suffering that agitates the minds of people. Some say they cannot believe in God when they see pain or when they see suffering, malformed children. They say, "I cannot believe that a God of love could possibly be responsible for this or even allow it." You are familiar with all these arguments that people bring forward.

I want to show you that if you take the humanist position or the position of so-called Scientism, which simply means the opinions or the philosophy of certain scientists, then you are left without any explanation at all. If it is all an accident, then accidents are to be expected, they must happen, and it is these accidents that give rise to pain. Those who take this view are foolish enough, because of their theory of evolution, to say there will be fewer and fewer accidents. But actually when we look at the world, it seems that they are increasing. So people do not understand and are completely bewildered.

But when you come to the Bible, you find an explanation. Where have pain and suffering come from? There is no difficulty here as regards the biblical teaching: they are entirely due to man's original rebellion and sin, to the fall of man. That is the simple answer. Adam and Eve were put into a place called Paradise, and there was no pain there, no problems. The man and woman were perfect, and their surroundings were perfect, and if they had continued to obey God and to share their life with him, the world would never have known all this suffering.

There is a mystery here: why did God allow evil? I shall tell you the answer later on when I deal with what may be called "residual problems," but here is an immediate and adequate explanation: man has brought all this upon himself. And it is a part of his punishment; it is not all automatic, though a lot of it is. If you put your finger in the fire, you will get pain; commit sin, and you will suffer for it. "The way of transgressors is hard" (Prov. 13:15). The poor fellow who got drunk last night is unhappy this morning and in pain. That is cause and effect.

But pain and suffering are not only the result of cause and effect; they are also partly the general punishment of sin. The biblical teaching is that all pain and suffering are the result of man's disobedience and rebellion, that God is not only a God of love but also of justice and of righteousness, that he is the moral Governor of the universe, and judgment is a part of his manifestation of himself.

Now that is a broad, general explanation that immediately satisfies people. But then, as has often happened, you may put forward certain questions. I am now referring to Christian people. It does seem at times as if godly people suffer more in this world than the ungodly, and that has often worried the saints. They see ungodly people flourishing while they themselves are in trouble. What is the answer? Well, the Bible has many, many answers. The book of Job was written to that end; it is the whole thesis of that book. And Job explains the problem perfectly. Do not forget to read that book right through; watch, as James says, "the patience of Job" (Jas. 5:11) and see how "the LORD blessed the latter end of Job more than his beginning" (Job 42:12). Job came out of all his trials and tribulations a much bigger and a much richer and a much fuller man. God used that suffering to teach his servant and to lead him on.

Psalm 73, also, is entirely given over to this problem of the success of the ungodly while the godly suffer. And what a wonderful explanation it gives! The psalmist is worried and perplexed and beginning to complain about God; he is in intellectual confusion, as we all are, until he goes into "the sanctuary of God." What does he find there? He finds the Scriptures, he finds exposition, he finds preaching, he finds understanding: "Then understood I their end" (v. 17). "It is all right," he says. "What a fool I was!" He has a perfect answer, and he goes on his way rejoicing.

Then consider Psalm 119. Here again is a man who has been in trouble, who has been ill and so on. But afterward he says, "Before I was afflicted I went astray. . . . It is good for me that I have been afflicted" (Ps. 119:67, 71).

My dear friend, one of the most marvelous things we discover in this world is that what we formerly regarded as being entirely bad is often for our good. We are such fools, we will not be taught, so God our Father chastises us. "Whom the Lord loveth he chasteneth, and scourgeth every son whom he receiveth. . . . If ye be without chastisement . . . then are ye bastards, and not sons," says the writer to the Hebrews (12:6, 8).

Can you not see that it is because of sin that all this suffering has come in? But God even uses all this to our perfection: "We have had fathers of our flesh which corrected us . . . after their own pleasure." But here is God correcting us, not for his pleasure but for our good—"but he for our profit, that we might be partakers of his holiness" (vv. 9–10). He is bringing us to glory; he wants us to have this understanding. Many people have thanked God for an illness or an accident or a loss or some suffering because it has brought them into a deeper and a greater knowledge of God. Oh, yes, says the apostle Paul, this is what he discovered: "All things"—all things!—"work together for good to them that love God, to them who are the called according to his purpose" (Rom. 8:28). Paul says "all things," and he could not have used a more inclusive word. There is literally nothing of which this is not true.

Have I told you of the illustration that an old preacher once gave of that verse? I think it is a good one. He took out his watch, and he opened it and said, "If you have a watch, open yours, and there you will see that one wheel is turning this way, and the other is turning that way. They seem to be working at cross-purposes, but they are not. That is how the pins are sent around and forward. It appears to be a mass of contradictions, but it isn't. Everything has been made by a watchmaker, and he knows that this wheel turning like this is going to move that one like that, and so each one moves the other, and the watch goes on and keeps time." "All things work together for good to them that love God." No one can say that but men or women who have this enlightenment and this instruction. They do not always understand it at the time, but they know within themselves that this is true, and as they go on living, they find it is true, and they thank God for it.

At the end of 2 Corinthians 4 we find one of the most glorious things the apostle ever wrote, and, my dear friends, this is the test of our Christianity. Can you join him in saying this? He has given the Corinthians a terrible list of his troubles and trials and tribulations, enough to crush a man and to finish him once and forever. But then he stands back and looks at it all and says, "Our light affliction, which is but for a moment, worketh for us [produces for us]"—listen!—"a far more exceeding and eternal"—some say it should be translated "an exceeding exceedingly abundant"—"weight of glory; while we look not at the things which are seen, but at the things which are not seen: for the things which are seen are temporal; but the things which are not seen are eternal" (2 Cor. 4:17–18).

The Bible teaches me that I am a stranger and a pilgrim in this world. I am only here for a while. Now people who are not Christians do not know that; to them, this is the only world, this is the only life, and if things go wrong in this world, they have lost everything. When they die, they end; their life has been in vain; they have no comfort or consolation. They are failures. But Christians say, "This, our light affliction, is only for a moment. We are only in this world for a limited time."

This time seems to be extending. It was "three score years and ten," but people are living longer, are they not? Nevertheless, there is a limit. Paul says, "for a moment," and I know that this life is but my preparatory school, this is only a stage of transition. There awaits me the everlasting and eternal glory. I expect a world like this, a world of sin and of shame, to be a difficult and cruel world. Look how it treated the Son of God. But it was only for a while. He has finished with it. He has entered again the glory that he shared with God from the foundation of the world. He has gone to prepare a place for me so that where he is I shall be also.

And, therefore, as I look at the problem of pain and of suffering—and you can throw in the problem of war—I find that the Bible, and the Bible alone, has the explanation. "From whence come wars and fightings among you? come they not hence, even of your lusts that war in your members? Ye lust, and have not" (Jas. 4:1–2). You are all against one another. War! It is caused by nothing but by lust. Why does God allow war? Because he is teaching us what fools we are and what we bring down upon ourselves because of our folly. Do not blame God for war. All these evils are the result of human folly and sin and rebellion. But the scientists, the humanists, do not understand, and they die in despair, feeling that all they have worked for is gone. The First World War and the Second World War shook many of them, and they were left speechless, hopeless. The League of Nations failed; everything fails. The Bible is not surprised at all this. It anticipates it, it prophesies it, but it also shows us that there is an ultimate that is beyond it all.

And so in these various ways with regard to these particular problems, the Bible gives us complete and entire satisfaction and understanding.

22

A Purpose for Life and Death

Jesus answered and said unto her, Whosoever drinketh of this water shall thirst again: but whosoever drinketh of the water that I shall give him shall never thirst; but the water that I shall give him shall be in him a well of water springing up into everlasting life. (John 4:13–14)

The majority of people today who are outside the church will tell you this is because of what they call "miserable Christians." They think the Christian life is a life that is almost to be despised. If we are giving them that impression, it is quite clear that we are not only missing the glory of this life ourselves, but we have not even understood it as we should. That is why it behooves us to examine a statement like this in John 4:13–14 and not just slide over it. We must see whether it is true and how it is true; we must ask whether we can substantiate it and whether we are experiencing something of it.

So we are doing that, and we have started with the complete and full intellectual satisfaction that this gospel gives. We must start there, as we have been seeing, because the truth comes to the mind, and if it fails us at that point, then it will fail us elsewhere. We do not start with feelings; we start with the mind. Feelings, the will, everything follows from that. If we do not say that, then we have no test to apply to agencies that can give experiences and affect feelings. We have seen that the gospel gives us a comprehensive view of the way of salvation and the reason for it. We have seen also that it satisfies our craving, our longing, for authority, and in our last study we saw how it satisfies our desire for system, for wholeness, for completeness and how, as the result of that, it also deals with so many of our intellectual problems. We have indicated some of them—the problem of pain, the problem of suffering, the problem of war. People are in difficulties about them, and if we cannot show that the gospel deals with these matters in a satisfactory manner, then how can it be true to say that "Whosoever drinketh of this water shall never thirst"?

But let me give you another illustration. There is the great problem of life itself. What is the meaning, the purpose, of life? Surely, at this present time this is a most urgent question. Is it not becoming increasingly evident that the tragedies that one reads of and hears of in the papers and elsewhere are so largely due to the fact that people see no point in living and do not know what to do next? There is a fundamental lack at their very center as to life itself. There is nothing new about this; when it has thought about it, humanity has always been in difficulty about this question. But it is particularly urgent, it seems to me, at the present time. It is at the very essence of the modern problem. In other words, as Christian people, when we find non-Christians who are interested in life—people who call themselves humanists and moralists and so on—we have to point out to them that since they are merely tinkering with the symptoms and manifestations, they will get nowhere. We must show them that it is the disease that matters and that this disease is the fundamental failure to know and to understand the purpose of life.

Many people regard life in the way described so eloquently by Shakespeare in *Macbeth* (Act 5, Scene 5):

To-morrow, and to-morrow, and to-morrow,
Creeps in this petty pace from day to day,
To the last syllable of recorded time;
And all our yesterdays have lighted fools
The way to dusty death. Out, out, brief candle!
Life's but a walking shadow, a poor player,
That struts and frets his hour upon the stage,
And then is heard no more: it is a tale
Told by an idiot, full of sound and fury,
Signifying nothing.

How prevalent that view is at the present time! Life is a vain show; there is nothing in it. "Let's eat, drink, and be merry, for tomorrow we die." Let us be clear about this. This is not merely true of so-called "giddy youth" but also of many others who have never read or thought at all about these matters. There is a grave danger that we will take a wrong view of today's adolescents. They are inheritors, let us not forget that, of a tradition, and much of what is true of them is the result of the failure of those who went before them.

I have often said that the people who deserve to be blamed above everybody are many of what are called "the great Victorians," the people who lived toward the latter end of the nineteenth century. We are now but reaping the end result of their concessions with regard to the Scriptures and their failure truly to understand the nature of the Christian gospel. They went on using biblical terms, but they evacuated them of their meaning, and the hopeless view of life that we see today is the result. This is found in some of the most sophisticated people, people in the very highest seats of learning. I well remember reading during the last war the autobiography of R. R. Marrett, the head of Exeter College, Oxford. I have never forgotten the words that he uttered there. He told us how he was completely shattered by the Second World War. These were his words as I remember them:

> But to me the war brought to an end the long summer of my life. Henceforth I have nothing to look forward to but chill autumn and still chillier winter; and yet I must somehow try not to despair.[17]

There it is—culture, thought at its best, philosophy with all that it has to offer, but no understanding—hopelessness, emptiness. The Victorians were fooled by appearances; everything seemed to be so secure, so firm, so solid. But this [twentieth] century has shown that there was no foundation for their optimism, that you cannot build on human greatness—financial, military, or any other sort.

And the result is that today people are bankrupt. They do not know how to live and do not know why they should go on living. The consequences are quite inevitable. People turn to pleasure in various forms. But they soon get tired of the more innocent pleasures and have to experiment with others, and so they go from drink to drugs, and it goes on and on and on. This is all but a manifestation of a central emptiness, the absence of a foundation. The whole of life is some sort of iridescent bubble that people keep going by their own breath. But as they get older and more tired they cannot do it, and it finally bursts, and there is nothing. Now this, I say again, has worried humanity from the very beginning. It is the quest of philosophers and others: What is life? What is its meaning? What is its purpose?

There is only one answer, and it is the answer that is found in the Bible. The world is in the condition that I have described because it does not believe in God, and because it does not believe in God it cannot understand itself, it cannot understand life, it cannot understand all the things that finally matter. Not believing in God, it does not know anything about his purpose, it does not understand history, and above all it does not realize that God is behind and above history, that he has his hand upon it and is controlling it, bringing all things to pass according to his own eternal will.

The Bible gives a full explanation of the state of the world. I have often said that if I had no other reason for being a Christian or for believing the Bible—and thank God I have thousands of greater reasons—this, to me, would be more than enough. I know no other book that really tells me the truth about myself and about life. But here I see it all plainly and clearly, and I see that the Bible teaches that there is a purpose in life, a purpose and an object in history. People look at the world and life around them and say that it is senseless, that there is no meaning, and this, as I have often reminded you, is granted by all the humanists, both classical and scientific.

H. A. L. Fisher, a great historian at Oxford, said that he had studied history all his life but could not see any end or purpose. Sir Julian Huxley, a scientific humanist, said exactly the same thing. That is because they are looking at segments; they do not see history as a whole. They are immersed in wars and fightings and advances and retrogressions, and they come to the conclusion that there is no true and ultimate development. But you cannot read the Bible for any length of time without discovering that there is a great central purpose predetermined by God. If you regard the origin of life as an accident, then you will inevitably have to think of the remainder of life as a series of accidents. But life is not an accident. God made this world, he had an object and a plan, and he will carry that out; nothing can stop it.

Well, then, you say, what about all the things that happen?

The Bible has an answer. It says that God's will takes two forms. There is his *directive* will, and there is his *permissive* will; both are of God. God has chosen to work in this way. He need not have, but he did, and is continuing to do so. And the moment I understand that, I am not surprised by all that happens.

God has a purpose, of course, in his permissive will. We do not see it all, but we certainly see parts of it very clearly. God permits us to do many things in order to teach us the truth about ourselves. I grew up in an agricultural district, and there is a great advantage in that. I remember very well how at times boys would come down to work for the old farmers, sometimes boys from schools in London and from other institutions. And these boys, because they had come from the town, regarded every farmer as a clodhopper, an ignoramus who knew nothing. They knew everything about farming as well as about everything else, and they were not ready to listen to instruction, they did not want any information, they knew it all. And the philosophy of the old farmers, I used to find, was always this: "He'll learn!" And these boys did learn, after many painful experiences of being thrown by horses and sticking forks into their feet instead of into the earth and so on. That was a learning process.

Now that is the way in which God permits so many things. We say, why does God allow this? And the answer is that he allows it in order that we may see what fools we are. It is his only way of bringing us to see that we do not know quite as much as we thought we did. We know too much to listen to God, we know too much to listen to his Law, we do not need his instruction, we say it is démodé, entirely of the past, and we smile in derision. Very well, says God, carry on! All that is stated perfectly in the second half of the first chapter of Paul's Epistle to the Romans. "God gave them over to a reprobate mind" (v. 28), and thereby he brings them to their senses.

These truths are taught quite plainly in the Bible. God has a positive purpose that he brings to pass in spite of us. Read your Bible from beginning to end, and you will see God's advancing purpose, all that he said being brought to pass, and then, by the side of that, this permissive aspect. As you look at it at first, you see a mass of contradictions. But it is not. It is all being directed. One of the psalmists, inspired by the Spirit, puts it like this: "Surely the wrath of man shall praise thee" (Ps. 76:10). Of course! Take this [twentieth] century with its two world wars and its tragedies. What is this? I say it is the wrath of man, and it is praising God. It is showing that what God in his Word has said about humanity is true. It has completely exploded the false optimism of the Victorians, along with every other form of false optimism and idealism. The "wrath of man" is praising God—all things do and all things finally will.

So I see the great message of the Bible: life has a purpose. And I see that by nature I had not realized this and had been fighting against it, and that is why I became disappointed and unhappy and felt that life was vain and useless. Oh, there have been some great tragedies in this respect. I remember how, over thirty years ago, a surgeon in London, one of the best surgeons, at the top of his profession, suddenly gave it all up to become just a ship's doctor on ordinary pleasure steamers. Why did he do this?

Well, he was an ambitious man, and he realized he had enemies who had thwarted his ambition to get to a certain high position in the profession; so he gave it all up in disgust.

Now that, again, is man, the natural man, in many ways at his best but lacking this fundamental understanding. He is disappointed, and he gives up. He falls into cynicism and into a kind of despair. But the moment one's eyes are opened to this Christian teaching, one sees everything in an entirely different light. The moment men and women become Christians, they not only become children of God, they also begin to see God's purpose and understand that they are a part of it, they are sharers in it. So the whole of life takes on an entirely new aspect.

This is just what the apostle Peter says in his first epistle. He says, do you realize who you are? You are "a chosen generation, a royal priesthood, an holy nation, a peculiar people"—a people for God's special possession. What are you here for?

> . . . that ye should shew forth the praises [the excellencies] of him who hath called you out of darkness into his marvellous light: which in time past were not a people, but are now the people of God: which had not obtained mercy, but now have obtained mercy. Dearly beloved, I beseech you as strangers and pilgrims, abstain from fleshly lusts, which war against the soul; having your conversation honest among the Gentiles: that, whereas they speak against you as evildoers, they may by your good works, which they shall behold, glorify God in the day of visitation. (2:9–12)

What a picture! Can you not see? Life, according to Peter, is a kind of royal march, a great crusade. You are pilgrims; you belong to God; you are God's own special people. You are his nation, as the Jews were his nation under the old dispensation. Christian people are God's nation, the holy nation, at this present time. What God said of the Jews before giving the Ten Commandments, he now, through his servant Peter, says of Christians. And our calling now is not just to live anyhow, somehow, eating, drinking, and doing what the world does, having our ambitions and being thwarted, and being cast down and made miserable, and saying, "Is there anything in it? Is there any point? Is it all just 'a tale told by an idiot, full of sound and fury, signifying nothing'?" Of course it is not! We have a great object in living; we are here to show forth the praises of God; we are here to live to the glory of God. God made the whole world to manifest his own glory, and now we become sharers in this great task. What is the chief end of man? It is "to glorify God, and to enjoy him for ever" (Westminster Catechism). We are to make these truths evident and plain.

Not only that, God has a great purpose of redemption, and we are to take part in that. The purpose of redemption is not carried out only through preachers—it is to be carried out through every one of us. As we live and mix with people, we "shew forth the praises of him who hath called [us] out of darkness into his marvellous light." Remember, then, that dignity has been bestowed upon us. We do not regard ourselves as just animals, a little more intelligent than most other animals. No, no. The image of God has been renewed in us; we have been created anew after the pattern of God's dear Son. The Son came into the world to carry out the purpose of redemption, and he continues this work in us and through us.

So the whole of life changes. We become interested in other people in a new way. We have something to tell them; we can really deal with their problems. We see them unhappy; we see tragedies. All around us we see a breakdown in marriage and in every other respect. People do not know what to do, and the world has nothing at all to offer them. Read the family histories and the personal stories of all the clever people, and you will soon see that they have nothing to offer at this point. But you and I have everything to offer. Life becomes exciting, it becomes full of interest and opportunity, it becomes thrilling. We can really help people. We do not merely pat them on the back and say a comforting word and send them away thinking what nice people we are. That does not help; it does not change anything. We have something to say to them that can change them and make them masters of their circumstances instead of victims. We really can show them this. In other words, we are participators in God's great program and sharers in this great ministry. We are guardians and custodians of the faith. And as we are doing all this, we know that we are going on steadily day by day and hour by hour to the glory that God has prepared for us and that awaits us.

This is the whole picture of the Christian life. Isaac Watts puts it in these words:

The men of grace have found
Glory begun below;
Celestial fruits on earthly ground
From faith and hope may grow.

Isaac Watts

This is the truth by which we must test ourselves. Our Lord says,

"Whosoever drinketh of the water that I shall give him shall never thirst." In other words, we will never be at a loss to know what to do with the next hour; we will never be bored; we will never say, "My time has come to retire, and now what am I going to do with myself?" They "have found glory begun below." They have the Bible, the fellowship of the saints, and all this work outside the church.

And the opportunities have never been greater. Oh, the world is in a sad condition today. Let us not speak of the world in derision—let us speak with sorrow and sympathy. Our Lord looked out upon the people and saw them "as sheep not having a shepherd" (Mark 6:34), and that is the simple truth. People are trying to find sustenance and are failing; they are hounded by dogs and marauders. And nobody can help them except the Christian—nobody at all. Nobody else has any light to give. But we have it! And this, I say again, transforms our whole view of life, our whole existence while we are still left in this world.

And then we see death in an entirely new manner—it is transfigured. "For to me to live is Christ, and to die is gain," said Paul (Phil. 1:21). Why? Because it means that we go out of this world, which, though now we are living in it as princes and are marching to Zion, is nevertheless a land of sin and woe, of trial and problems, of pain and suffering. So we look forward to the glory that awaits us. And seeing it, our whole attitude toward life in this world is transformed. We have an understanding that nobody else has, and it gives life not only meaning but also makes it great and glorious.

Shall I put it in the form of a question? Are you tired? I mean by that, are you tired of life? Are you weary? You should not be, my dear friend, if you are a Christian. The tragedy of this age is that young people are tired, they are old. They have exhausted the possibilities of life; so they are toying with things that promise to take them out of it by drugging them. Oh, how tragic that is!

But the Christian does not suffer from that. As Paul puts it in 2 Corinthians 4:16, "Though our outward man perish"—and that is bound to happen; the body will go on decaying, and death is facing us all—"yet the inward man is renewed day by day." And so I challenge you as a Christian in this way: your body is getting older, but you ought to be getting younger. Are you feeling younger than you were? Are you conscious of increasing youth because of the vigor and the power that the Spirit of God puts in you? Our "inward man is renewed day by day," and as you go nearer to the glory and see it more and more clearly, your vigor increases. That is the Christian. Christians do not tire out or fade out. Not at all.

Now this is the whole picture of the Christian as given in the Bible. This is the life that our Lord lives. Life, I say, becomes a grand march.

We're marching to Zion. . . .
The beautiful city of God.
Come, we that love the Lord,
And let our joys be known. . . .
We're marching through Immanuel's ground.

This world does not belong to the financiers or to the clever people. This world belongs to Immanuel, the Son of God.

We're marching through Immanuel's ground,
To fairer worlds on high.

Isaac Watts ("Come, We That Love the Lord")

Christian people, are you rejoicing in this? Is this your conception of your life in this world? Is this what has happened to you since you have partaken of this water? Do you have fullness of life in your understanding and in your living as you go forward on your heavenly journey?

This world is "Immanuel's ground," but we, because of the effect of sin and the Fall and shame, have become "strangers and pilgrims" in it. We do not live for this world only; we do not settle in it. We realize we are laboring here for a time but are moving on. We are away from home, as it were. "Our conversation [citizenship] is in heaven; from whence also we look for the Saviour" (Phil. 3:20). Now this is the view of life that is given to us. It is the reverse of cynicism, the reverse of mere cleverness. It is big, it is clean, it is holy, it is triumphant, it is filled with a sense of glory. And there are anticipations of it even in this world of time.

The men of grace have found
Glory begun below.

But then I go on to the next point, which is this: the Bible, having told me that this is the nature of my life in this world, then goes on to deal with the next problem that arises, which is, of course, how to live in this world while I am here. I have told you this in general, but, of course, we want to know in particular because we are confronted by different situations and choices. Is this right? Is that right? Should I or shouldn't I do this?

Problems still confront us. There is nothing automatic about the Christian life. You start with the general view, but that does not then settle every question as if it were an easy answer for all situations. You cannot just turn up the right page and find the answer. We know we cannot do that, and yet we long for teaching and guidance on how to live.

Here, of course, is another major and mounting problem. Almost every day the papers refer to a new aspect of it. Why? Because what is being queried at the present time is the very category of morality itself. Is there such a thing as morality? Is there any code of behavior? We are living in an age when the cult of self-expression is dominant, and many philosophers are telling us that our behavior is our own private business and that nobody else has a right to interfere. It is this view that accounts for the lawlessness and increasing crime at the present time. Then people go on to say that what you privately decide is governed by one thing only, and that is whether or not it gives you pleasure. So you become a hedonist.

In other words, authority is not recognized, there are no sanctions, there is no discipline, no law. This is the height of modern sophistication. Again, this is most important. It is very easy to look at some of these poor young people, who in many ways have never had a chance, and curl up your lip as you look at them and dismiss them with contempt. But let us remember that the philosophy underlying what they are doing is supplied by some of the ablest people in the country, some of the leading philosophers. This view that denies external moral sanctions or the right of anybody to tell anybody else what to do, that says that in this life it is every man for himself, that says that there is no law, no discipline, no punishment—this has been exalted into a philosophy. And we see how it is being carried out; we see the results. But these philosophers cannot see this. On the one hand, they go on asserting their great new view of liberty, as they call it, and then, on the other hand, there are these mounting problems. They cannot see the connection between them and call us philistines if we point this out to them. But it is not we who are saying these things—it is the Bible.

In other words, everything is fluid. Ideas change from generation to generation. What one generation says is derided and dismissed by the next as old-fashioned. You become out-of-date, square, or whatever they choose to call you. Everything is relative; nothing is fixed. One age condemns sexual perversions, another says they are wonderful, much better than heterosexual love, and so on. And not only that, there are different schools of thought. Philosophers are not agreed among themselves, and they are all equally dogmatic. You are familiar with all this.

But above all that, even those who still believe in morality and in a measure of discipline and control are just as useless because they simply exhort us to live up to standards to which by nature we cannot attain. There is not much idealism in the modern world; it is cynicism now. But idealism is quite useless anyway, as useless as cynicism. It is no use saying to people, "This is what you ought to do." The trouble is, they cannot. "To will is present with me; but how to perform that which is good I find not" (Rom. 7:18). This is where your idealistic systems all break down. Without Christ, the highest morality is as useless as the most profligate sin. What we need is not instruction but power. Morality fails, and the world is as it is because human beings lack power. Even someone who knows what is right cannot do it.

This is the essence of this moral problem of how to live in this world. And there is only one answer, the answer given here: "Whosoever drinketh of the water that I shall give him shall never thirst." Why? Here is the biblical scheme of things in this respect—you start with God, not with yourself. You do not start with your own likes and dislikes. You ask, where has the world come from? Where has humanity come from? What is this that one is conscious of? God!

Then we are conscious of human beings made in the image of God—their reason, their understanding, their fears, their sense of guilt. Where does all this come from? Conscience! What is the conscience? Where has that come from? You cannot say that it has developed because it is there in the most primitive people; everybody, every human being, has a sense of right and wrong. The most primitive races have this sense; they all have a fear of punishment. Not only that, the most primitive societies develop codes and rules. What makes them do it? They have not had teaching, they have not had culture, they have never read, they have never listened to a lecture, yet they have all developed these codes.

That is the question, and there is only one answer: they all have a memory of the original law that God put into the heart of human beings and subsequently in a written form only to the children of Israel. There is no other adequate explanation. So now I begin to see that there is a moral system, there are moral ideas. And then when I look at the Bible, I see that God has revealed all this. It is all here, this view of man, not as an animal but as a responsible being who was given an original righteousness, someone who was meant to correspond to God. And something in me says, "Yes, I have a feeling that there is that in me, and here I am told that God has given it to us all."

Then I see the Law, the Ten Commandments given through Moses, and I see that it is essentially right and good, that any society governed by the Ten Commandments will be a good, happy society, and I find that is true with even minor regulations. I remember as a medical student having to listen to a man lecturing on certain aspects of certain diseases, and I remember him telling us that Moses was undoubtedly the first and perhaps the greatest of all the medical officers of health that the world has ever known. Where did Moses get his knowledge from? How did he anticipate so much that has been discovered since? The answer of the Bible is that God revealed it.

And then in the Sermon on the Mount I find our Lord's exposition of the Law, and there I see life as it should be lived—a big life, a great life. Not just doing what I want to do and letting other people suffer; not just being the creature of my own lusts and passions and living like an animal. No, no, but rather consideration for others: "Love your enemies . . . do good to them that hate you" (Matt. 5:44). It is a great life, it is grand, it is uplifting, it is something that moves me.

And then I look at him who exemplified it all, the spotless, perfect Son of God. I say, "Here is man as man ought to be; that is what I ought to be. I am beginning to see a reason for living a good life." And the Bible goes on to give me motives for doing so. The Christian life is not just a series of arbitrary laws; it is not a form of legalism. The Bible does not come to us as a kind of collection of instructions and maxims and admonitions. No, no; it gives us a great view of ourselves under God, of what we are meant to be doing, and then it says, this is the way to do it.

Read the second half of all the New Testament epistles, and you will find they are all arguments, they are all reasons. They say in essence, "Realize who you are." Again Peter has said it all: "Dearly beloved, I beseech you as strangers and pilgrims, abstain from fleshly lusts, which war against the soul" (1 Pet. 2:11). In other words, Peter does not say, "Now look here, don't commit sins of lust because you will get certain diseases if you do, and you will suffer for it, and your children might suffer." That is morality. Morality just talks about the thing itself and the consequences of certain actions. Peter does not; the New Testament does not. The New Testament says, realize who you are—"a royal priesthood, an holy nation, a peculiar people" (1 Pet. 2:9). Because of that, "abstain from fleshly lusts, which war against the soul."

Why should I live a good life? Is it simply to be moral and decent and better than somebody else? No, no; that is pharisaism, the antithesis of this Christian life. Why should I live this good life? Because I am a child of God; I am a child of the heavenly Father. And we are here in this world "to shew forth the praises of him who hath called [us] out of darkness into his marvellous light" (1 Pet. 2:9).

Not only that, I have to give an account to him. I have to go home, and he will look at me as a parent looks at a child coming home from the party: How did you behave yourself? What impression did you give of the family? And then I know that if I have done anything approximating to what I should have done, there will be the great "recompence of the reward" (Heb. 11:26), a "Well done, thou good and faithful servant" (Matt. 25:21). And he does not merely ask me to do these things—he has given me a new nature, a new heart, a new desire. He has put his Spirit within me, and the power of the Spirit is in me:

He breaks the power of cancelled sin,
He sets the prisoner free.

CHARLES WESLEY ("O FOR A THOUSAND TONGUES")

"If the Son therefore shall make you free, ye shall be free indeed" (John 8:36). God even goes beyond that: he makes this good life something that I love. "His commandments are not"—are no longer—"grievous" (1 John 5:3). I see them as the pattern that God has set for the one he has made in his own image and likeness; and so I say with the psalmist, "O how love I thy law!" (Ps. 119:97). It is not against my nature but is now something I want to live, something I want to exemplify, in order that I may promote the glory of God and win my fellow men and women to him.

23

Conscience Answered

Jesus answered and said unto her, Whosoever drinketh of this water shall thirst again: but whosoever drinketh of the water that I shall give him shall never thirst; but the water that I shall give him shall be in him a well of water springing up into everlasting life. (John 4:13–14)

We are examining this great and glorious statement and have started with the intellectual aspect of the gospel. We have already seen many, many things—how the gospel gives us a general understanding with regard to our very being and existence, with regard to the universe in which we live, and with regard to the problems that arise in connection with life, such as the problems of pain, suffering, and war. We find on examination that full satisfaction is given in answer to the problems that trouble and perplex our minds.

And now we come to another aspect of the mind, and that is the conscience—the problem of its accusations. The conscience puts questions to our understanding, it raises difficulties, and one of our greatest problems is what to do with an accusing or troubled conscience. Oh, the unhappiness that this causes!

I always feel that one of the best ways of considering this question is in terms of the problem of praying and of going into the presence of God. It is then that conscience tends to be most alert and most powerful in its accusations. We can deal with other people very well—they are not the problem. The greatest difficulty we all have is to live with ourselves, and that means, partly, living with our own consciences. We can always answer the problems of other people; it is much more difficult to answer our own. The moment we go into the presence of God, or try to, conscience comes with its accusations. And behind an accusing conscience is the devil, "the accuser of our brethren" (Rev. 12:10).

So this question—whether we can go into the presence of God at all—constitutes one of our greatest needs. This is what we need to know. The question comes in many different ways, and it is put many times in the Bible in most eloquent language. Job puts it once and forever: "How should man be just with God?" (Job 9:2). Here is the question. See how it is raised in the biographies of people in the past, and we all ask it in our own lives. How can I know my sins are forgiven? How can I face God? And, ultimately, how can I die and face God at the bar of eternal judgment? These are the various ways in which this central problem of conscience tends to present itself.

Now some suggest that there is a very simple answer to all this and that, indeed, our trouble over conscience is an indication of morbidity, not to say some psychological or even psychopathic condition. They say, "You shouldn't be troubled like this."

Why not?

"Well," they say, "God is love, and is not that the final and full answer? Because God is love, there's no need to be concerned about the accusations of the conscience. God forgives everybody and everything; he would not be loving if he did not. So stop thinking! You've become morbid; you've become introspective and unhealthy. Just realize that God is love, and that is enough."

But unfortunately it is not enough for us; it certainly is not enough for anyone who has ever read the Bible. The people who talk so glibly about the love of God are generally people who are very ignorant about the Bible. They are basing what they say on their idea of God; they just think that God must of necessity be like that. It is a philosopher's idea of God. But that, of course, is of no value to us because we can always answer by saying, "How do you know that? You say that, but can you prove it? Can you demonstrate it?" There seems to be so much in the world, as we have been considering, that contradicts that idea of God that what they say does not really help us. It is especially unhelpful when we turn to the Bible, where alone we have true teaching and knowledge concerning God. Here we are told that God is love, but we are also told that he is holy, that he is righteous; we are taught about the various attributes of the being and character of God. So merely telling me that I should rest on the fact that God is love does not satisfy me.

And it is exactly the same in the case of those who tell us to rely upon the fact that occasionally we feel happy and feel that we are forgiven. But we know that feelings are so treacherous. We may be happy singing hymns in the atmosphere of a church, and we say, "Well, yes, I'm a Christian after all. I enjoy this." But then on Monday morning all the doubts and uncertainties and questionings may return along with the accusations of our conscience. So we cannot rely upon our feelings. No, we need something deeper, we need something greater. We need a satisfaction that is complete and cannot fail. We need something that will indeed conform to what our Lord says here, that will put us into a state in which we shall "never thirst" with regard to this particular question of conscience.

So, then, in order to see how it is that only the gospel and our Lord himself deal with this, we must once more state the problem. People who are not aware of problems are ignorant people. There are those who say they have never known any difficulty about prayer. I always have a feeling that such people have never prayed in their lives. Prayer is not easy. Prayer is the most difficult thing in which a person can ever engage. The saints of the centuries had to learn how to pray. You remember the disciples saying to our Lord, "Lord, teach us to pray" (Luke 11:1). Have you ever realized the difficulties in prayer? The people who tell you that prayer is quite simple tell you to relax in a comfortable chair and start listening to God. But that is not the teaching of the Bible—far from it.

Let me remind you of some of the difficulties. I have mentioned one, the most vital of all—the character, the being, of God himself. "God is light, and in him is no darkness at all" (1 John 1:5). He is righteous; he is holy; he is just. "[Thou] canst not look on iniquity," says Habakkuk (Hab. 1:13). All this is revealed in the Bible, in the Old Testament and in the New. It is here that God tells us about himself, about his holy character and the kind of life he expects from men and women whom he has created. God's character is revealed, of course, in the Law that he gave to Moses. You cannot say, "But the Law doesn't matter—only the love of God matters!" It is the God of love who gave the Law. You cannot take any one attribute in the being of God and say that is the whole.

Furthermore, if you read the Old Testament, you see some of the greatest characters humbled and trembling in the presence of God. Moses at the burning bush, we are told, "hid his face" (Exod. 3:6). Of course he did. And when the people were given the Law on Mount Sinai, the very mountain was quaking, and they were filled with terror (Exod. 19:16). The Old Testament is full of this. "Who shall ascend into the hill of the LORD? or who shall stand in his holy place?" (Ps. 24:3). "Who among us shall dwell with the devouring fire?" (Isa. 33:14). And Isaiah, one of the greatest and holiest of the men of the Old Testament, gets a vision of

God, just a glimpse, as it were, and his response is, "Woe is me! for I am undone; because I am a man of unclean lips" (Isa. 6:5). Why does he say this? It is because he has come somewhere near the presence of God, and, as the author of the Epistle to the Hebrews puts it, we must "serve God acceptably with reverence and godly fear"—why?—"for our God is a consuming fire" (Heb. 12:28–29).

Above all, we find this teaching given by our blessed Lord himself. First of all, watch him as he prays to God. This is how he prays: "Holy Father" (John 17:11), though he is the Son of God. And when he responds to the disciples' request to teach them to pray, this is how he begins: "Our Father which art in heaven, Hallowed be thy name" (Luke 11:2). That is our Lord's own teaching. So this notion that there is no difficulty about prayer, that it is quite easy and quite simple—"pray when you like"—is a contradiction of the teaching of the whole of the Bible and, above all, of the teaching of our blessed Lord and Savior himself concerning the nature and being of God. This is the first problem; this is the first difficulty about prayer. How can anyone go into such a place?

But this difficulty becomes much more acute when the accusations of conscience begin. There is the being of God; then I look at myself, and conscience reminds me of my past sins. Conscience is a very accurate recorder and has a memory that never fails. It can remember words and actions from years and years ago, and it brings them back, raises them up, and places a horrible panorama before our eyes. And we have no answer; these accusations are true—our sins, our failures. Conscience brings us to the condition of the prodigal son: "Father, I have sinned against heaven, and in thy sight, and am no more worthy to be called thy son" (Luke 15:21). Or to the position of David. Having come to a realization of his terrible sin, David writes Psalm 51 and says, "Against thee, thee only, have I sinned, and done this evil in thy sight" (v. 4). It is no use talking about the love of God, says conscience; this is what you have done. You have forfeited the love of God; you have sinned deliberately against the love of God. You cannot dispute it; you cannot deny the facts. Here is the record—there it is before you.

And then, on top of this and from this subjective standpoint, the most difficult thing of all is the sense of pollution, the sense of uncleanness, the sense of unworthiness; and nothing makes one so conscious of this as to be in the presence of God. We know this in a measure as we come into the presence of saintly, holy people; they always make us feel that we are vile, that we are unclean. A man or a woman who has never felt unclean is just not a Christian; it is impossible. You see this in the Scriptures, and you feel it. The apostle Paul expresses this in the seventh chapter of the Epistle to the Romans: "For I know that in me (that is, in my flesh,) dwelleth no good thing" (v. 18). Is that hyperbole? Is that exaggeration? Is that just a bit of rhetoric on the part of the preacher? No, no; Paul means it, he knows it—and do we not all know something about this? The hymn-writer knows it:

Eternal Light! Eternal Light!
How pure the soul must be
When, placed within thy searching sight,
It shrinks not, but with calm delight
Can live, and look on thee.

The spirits that surround thy throne
May bear the burning bliss;
But that is surely theirs alone,
Since they have never, never known
A fallen world like this.

O how shall I, whose native sphere
Is dark, whose mind is dim,
Before the Ineffable appear,
And on my naked spirit bear
The uncreated beam?

THOMAS BINNEY ("ETERNAL LIGHT")

How can I? This sense of unworthiness is not merely that one has done things that are wrong; there is something worse than that. It is the heart, the nature, that created the desire to do them. Again, Psalm 51 is a wonderful exposition of that. David is aware of the need of a clean heart: "Create in me a clean heart, O God; and renew a right spirit within me" (Ps. 51:10). And the realization of this pollution and uncleanness and unworthiness almost makes us feel that God cannot forgive us, that God, to be consistent with himself, cannot forgive the sins we have committed. He can have no fellowship, no dealings, no communion, with people of such a character and of such a nature. And so, like the wandering leper, we feel we can do nothing but spend the rest of our existence crying out in agony, "Unclean! Unclean!"

That is what conscience does to us, especially, I say, as we try to enter into the presence of God. And, of course, the whole time, as I have already indicated, the accuser of the brethren, the devil, is reminding us of these things, pressing them home—the devil as an angel of light (2 Cor. 11:14), the devil quoting Scripture, as he did to our Lord himself. Satan is an expert; he knows all the Scriptures. We begin to feel we are all right, and then he will bring up a Scripture, and it seems to cast us down again into utter condemnation, and we feel that we are completely hopeless. The devil puts us there, in this position where the Law of God is thundering against us with its terrifying accusations, and we really feel that we cannot give an answer.

There is the problem. Is there a satisfactory answer? Is there any way of receiving assurance that I am forgiven, that I can enter into the presence of God and have fellowship and communion with him?

Now here is one of the most glorious aspects of the gospel; it is the beginning, the very first step. It is one of the things our Lord has in mind as he is speaking to the woman of Samaria, this woman who at this very moment is living in adultery ("Thou hast had five husbands; and he whom thou now hast is not thy husband"), and he tells her that he can give her full satisfaction in this respect. She can not only be forgiven, she can *know* that she is forgiven. She will never thirst again; she will never be in trouble again with regard to her conscience.

But this is our message: not only can our Lord do this, but he alone can do it. It is interesting to see how at the present time many men are confessing their utter bankruptcy with regard to all this. Some of them do not recognize the category of morality, but they do admit honestly that they are miserable. They cannot find peace; there is no peace anywhere. "Peace, perfect peace, in this dark world of sin?" The world at its best, philosophy, cannot provide it. It is completely bankrupt. Here and here alone can we receive this fullness of satisfaction with regard to the forgiveness of our sins and the possibility of communion with God.

How does this happen? Well, let me remind you on this Palm Sunday morning.[18] The glory of this gospel is that it is not merely a teaching. It *is* a teaching, but it is a teaching based upon facts, upon historical events. I say that every Palm Sunday, every Good Friday, every Easter Sunday morning, every Christmas morning! My dear friends, the glory of the gospel is that it is based on facts, that it is history. That is what makes it unique.

And the facts are these: this person who is talking to the woman of Samaria is none other than the eternal Son of God. That immediately gives me a sense of relief and peace. I know that other people cannot help me. Why not? Because they have all sinned. They may say, "Ah, you know,

God is love, and everything is all right," but I reply, "You are not in a position to speak to me—you are a sinner yourself. You are saying that to cheer yourself up; you are playing a psychological trick on yourself, and you know no more than I do."

But then I am confronted by this unique person, the Son of God himself. "If thou knewest the gift of God," he says to the woman, "and who it is that saith to thee, Give me to drink; thou wouldest have asked of him. . . ." Thank God, I know who he is—he is the Son of God. Then my question is, what is he doing in this world? Why did he ever come into it? And the answer is that he is the gift of God. This is the gospel: "God so loved the world, that he gave his only begotten Son, that whosoever believeth in him should not perish, but have everlasting life" (John 3:16). "But when the fulness of the time was come, God sent forth his Son, made of a woman, made under the law" (Gal. 4:4). He was in the world because God himself sent him there.

But why did God send his Son into the world? The answer is implicit in those words that I have been quoting; but an even more specific statement is in the Epistle to the Romans: "For what the law could not do, in that it was weak through the flesh, God sending his own Son in the likeness of sinful flesh, and for sin"—which means, "on account of sin," in order to do something about sin—"condemned sin in the flesh" (8:3).

So I am beginning to feel that my problem has been dealt with, the problem of sin—in me and in the whole of humanity. People of the world cannot solve it and cannot do anything at all about it, but God sent his Son into the world especially on account of this problem. Here is one who came from the outside, from the glory, from eternity, into the world to deal with the problem of human beings in sin. I see that he is man, but I see that he is more than man. I see indications of his glory—I see his miracles, his signs. He is man; he is God. The Son of God came into the world. The Word was made flesh in order to deal with the problem of my sin.

How did he do that? Go through the Gospel stories again, reminding yourself of all that you read there, and what do you find? First, you find that he rendered a perfect obedience to his heavenly Father. He kept the Law of God perfectly. Not one of us can keep it; we have all broken it. That is the argument of the third chapter of the Epistle to the Romans: "Therefore by the deeds of the law there shall no flesh be justified in his sight: for by the law is the knowledge of sin" (v. 20). What the Law does is give me knowledge and information concerning sin and my own failure, and under the Law the whole world lies guilty before God. But here is one who never failed in any single respect. The Law of God, which we have all broken, he honored absolutely, completely, and perfectly; no one can bring a charge against him.

Now this is vital and all-important for me. I must keep the Law—God has said that. If I do not, I am under the condemnation of the Law, and the punishment it metes out is death and separation from God. And I *cannot* keep the Law. But I am beginning to see life; I am beginning to see hope. Here is one who himself honored and kept the Law of God. But still I am left with my major problem. I have sinned. My past sins I cannot remove; I cannot make atonement for them. I cannot do anything at all about them. Does he help me here? I have seen that he kept the Law. That is all right for him, as it were, but what about me?

Now we come to Palm Sunday, the triumphal entry into Jerusalem, and all that followed after it. "He stedfastly set his face to go to Jerusalem" (Luke 9:51). He knew he had to die. He could have escaped it all. He said so. He could have commanded twelve legions of angels and gone to heaven without dying. But he did not; he deliberately went to the cross. He said that he had come into the world in order to go there. This was the hour, he said, for which he had come. It was the hour of his glorification. It was all deliberate.

What does this mean? What was happening on the cross on Calvary's hill? What is the meaning of the death of the Lord Jesus Christ? And this is the most astounding thing of all. It was here that he dealt with my ultimate problem, the problem of my guilt. How did he do that? Well, this is what he says himself: he came "to give his life a ransom for many" (Matt. 20:28). The apostles, according to the light and the instruction that he himself gave them and then worked out still more clearly by the operation of the Holy Spirit within them, say, "whom God hath set forth to be a propitiation through faith in his blood" (Rom. 3:25)—and this is the most amazing thing ever said. A propitiation is a peace offering; it is something that is offered to God in order to satisfy his holy demands, the demands of his justice and righteousness. And Paul is saying that God himself provided the propitiation that he himself needed; it was God's own Son bleeding and dying upon the cross on Calvary's hill.

The apostle puts it like this in 2 Corinthians 5:21: "[God] hath made him [Jesus Christ] to be sin for us, who knew no sin." He was innocent, he was pure, he had kept the Law, but he was "made . . . sin," made a sinner. How? By our sins being laid upon him, so that "we might be made the righteousness of God in him." This is the message—God has taken your sins and mine and laid them upon him. He has *imputed* them to him; he has put them on his account. These are the terms that are used right through the Bible. It is foreshadowed in the Old Testament in all the offerings of bulls and goats and lambs. All that is just a prefiguring of this ultimate offering—"the Lamb of God, which taketh away the sin of the world" (John 1:29). Or as Isaiah puts it, "The LORD hath laid on him the iniquity of us all" (Isa. 53:6). That is what happened. God smote him: "We did esteem him stricken, smitten of God" (Isa. 53:4). The Father did this to the Son.

What was God doing? He was punishing our sins in the person of his Son. The Son came into the world in order to take our sins upon himself. God was punishing our sins through him who had not sinned. As Peter puts it, "who his own self bare our sins in his own body on the tree, that we, being dead to sins, should live unto righteousness: by whose stripes ye were healed" (1 Pet. 2:24). That is the sole explanation of the cross on Calvary's hill. He died because he was bearing the punishment meted out to our sins, and he was laid in a tomb, but he rose!

And what was the resurrection? It was God declaring to the whole world that he was satisfied with the offering of his Son. It was God pronouncing absolution of sins. It was God declaring his utter satisfaction. And then the Son ascended, and he entered into heaven, presenting himself and his own blood as an offering unto God, and there it was accepted: "[He] sat down on the right hand of the Majesty on high" (Heb. 1:3); and he is there at this moment ever living to make intercession for us (Heb. 7:25), for whom he died and bore the penalty. So this is the answer that is given in the whole of the Bible to the question raised by my conscience and by my awareness of sin.

How, then, do I receive this for myself? God applies it to me by his Holy Spirit. We are told that as God has laid my sins upon his Son, he now puts upon me the righteousness of his Son. It is all there in 2 Corinthians 5: "God was in Christ, reconciling the world unto himself, not imputing their trespasses unto them" (v. 19). This is often put in terms of clothing—he has put this great robe of righteousness of the Lord Jesus Christ upon me. God looks at me now, and he sees me clothed in the righteousness of Christ, who has obeyed the Law absolutely, without any mistake, without any shortcoming. We are "made the righteousness of God in him" (2 Cor. 5:21). And so God declares all who believe on the Lord Jesus Christ to be just. As the apostle says, "Therefore we conclude that a man is justified by faith without the deeds of the law" (Rom. 3:28).

Now that is the great declaration of the gospel. That is the message that the Son of God himself is preaching there to the woman of Samaria. That is the message of the gospel at this very moment to anyone who listens to it and is ready to receive it. But does this completely satisfy me? That is the question. Does it cover my every question? And the answer is a glorious and eternal yes! Here is the way to get assurance of faith; here is the way to know the joy of salvation. "The kingdom of God is not meat and drink; but righteousness, and peace, and joy in the Holy Ghost" (Rom. 14:17). Are you rejoicing in the knowledge of your sins forgiven? Christian people, are you happy? Do you know that you have access to God and that you are his children? This is the way to obtain that access, and we are all meant to enjoy it.

How does the gospel do this? First of all, it answers my first terrifying question about God himself. How can a God who is holy and righteous and true—a God who gave the Law and who says, "The soul that sinneth, it shall die" (Ezek. 18:4) and "The wages of sin is death" (Rom. 6:23)—how can this holy God possibly forgive me? He is the righteous God who cannot contradict himself, the God of whom the apostle Paul says to Titus, "God . . . cannot lie" (Titus 1:2). He is the just God who says in effect, "I must punish sin. I cannot pretend I have not seen it. I can have no dealings with people until sin has been punished."

As Paul puts it in Romans 3:

> Whom God hath set forth to be a propitiation through faith in his blood, to declare his righteousness for the remission of sins that are past, through the forbearance of God; to declare, I say, at this time his righteousness: that he might be just, and [at the same time] the justifier of him which believeth in Jesus. (vv. 25–26)

The death of Christ shows that God is just—my sin has received the punishment that God said he would mete out to it. As Paul puts it at the end of that third chapter of Romans, "Do we then make void the law through faith [by this gospel]?" No! "God forbid: yea, we establish the law" (v. 31). The death of Christ on the cross fulfilled the Law of God. It declared the righteousness and the justice of God. And because he has punished sin and established his eternal righteousness, he can with justice and righteousness forgive me. He can look upon me, the sinner, and justify me and smile upon me.

And so my first and greatest question is answered. The throne of God that hitherto has been to me a throne of justice has become the throne of grace. The Law of God is satisfied. God himself has satisfied his own Law in the person and death of his Son. So I can sing:

The terrors of law and of God
With me can have nothing to do;
My Saviour's obedience and blood
Hide all my transgressions from view.

AUGUSTUS TOPLADY ("A DEBTOR TO MERCY ALONE")

Because God himself has done this, I know it is true and right. The Law has been honored completely; it cannot condemn me.

And because my past sins have been forgiven, I feel I am now in a position to go into the presence of God. Ah, yes, but wait a minute—what can I do about my pollution, my unworthiness? Well, here is the answer. I have a robe of righteousness upon me. It is not mine. God does not see me; he sees me clothed with the righteousness of his dear Son. I do not go alone; I go through him. He is my High Priest. He is there to present me and my prayers. He "ever liveth to make intercession" for me (Heb. 7:25).

A debtor to mercy alone,
Of covenant mercy I sing;
Nor fear, with thy righteousness on,
My person and offering to bring.

That is it! It is his righteousness that is upon me. Or as Count Zinzendorf put it in the hymn translated by John Wesley:

Jesus, thy blood and righteousness
My beauty are, my glorious dress;
'Midst flaming worlds, in these arrayed,
With joy shall I lift up my head.

This is the glory of the gospel. I can approach the throne of grace with assurance, with boldness, because I am coming to God in the robes that he himself has put upon me. It is he who has made it possible. I am simply doing what he has told me to do.

I still have my conscience, and it continues to speak, but I can now answer it. How can my conscience condemn me if God has already absolved me? God is greater than my conscience, greater than my heart: "God is greater than our heart, and knoweth all things" (1 John 3:20). I can quote God against my own conscience, and what I say is this:

Jesus, my great High Priest,
Offered his blood, and died;
My guilty conscience seeks
No sacrifice beside:
His powerful blood did once atone,
And now it pleads before the throne.

Isaac Watts ("Join All the Glorious Names")

My conscience is satisfied. It is answered by what my great High Priest did for me when he offered his blood and died.

But there is still one enemy left—the devil, with his subtlety, his ingenuity, his power, and his malignity. He still comes, and I know that I am not strong enough to deal with him myself—he has defeated all humanity. The only one whom Satan has never defeated is this blessed Son of God who rode into Jerusalem on a donkey. And so I can turn to my Lord and say:

Be thou my shield and hiding place.
That, sheltered near thy side,
I may my fierce accuser face,
And tell him thou hast died.

John Newton ("Lord, I Approach Thy Mercy Seat")

"They overcame him by the blood of the Lamb, and by the word of their testimony" (Rev. 12:11). The devil cannot answer; he is silenced; he is dumb. As I shelter by the side of Christ, this bully, this ultimate fiendish, devilish, spiritual bully cannot any longer cause me to quake or to fear. Instead of being frightened and whimpering and running away, I can face him and cause him to flee by telling him that Christ has died for me, that the blood of Christ is on me, and that I am accepted by God.

As I take the water of life that our Lord offers me, as I drink in this message and this truth, I am put into a position in which I can answer the whole universe, and I defy the whole universe to bring me under condemnation. And I say with Paul:

> What shall we then say to these things? If God be for us, who can be against us? He that spared not his own Son, but delivered him up for us all, how shall he not with him also freely give us all things? Who shall lay any thing to the charge of God's elect? It is God that justifieth. Who is he that condemneth? It is Christ that died, yea rather, that is risen again, who is even at the right hand of God, who also maketh intercession for

> us. Who shall separate us from the love of Christ? shall tribulation, or distress, or persecution, or famine, or nakedness, or peril, or sword? . . . Nay in all these things we are more than conquerors through him that loved us. For I am persuaded, that neither death, nor life, nor angels, nor principalities, nor powers, nor things present, nor things to come, nor height, nor depth, nor any other creature [not the whole creation] shall be able to separate us from the love of God, which is in Christ Jesus our Lord. (Rom. 8:31–35, 37–39)

God himself is for us. He has proved it in the person of his Son—his birth, life, death, resurrection, ascension—his ever living to make intercession for us. He is there, he will always be there, and therefore we are eternally and everlastingly safe. "He is able also to save them to the uttermost that come unto God by him" (Heb. 7:25). Oh, the glory of the gospel that satisfies the demands of my conscience and gives complete satisfaction to my mind as I consider the greatest question of all—my relationship to God, the possibility of fellowship with him while I am left in this world, and the glorious hope of spending my eternity in his holy presence.

Oh how shall I, whose native sphere
Is dark, whose mind is dim,
Before the Ineffable appear,
And on my naked spirit bear
That uncreated beam?

There is a way for man to rise
To that sublime abode:
An offering and a sacrifice,
A Holy Spirit's energies,
An advocate with God.

These, these prepare us for the sight
Of holiness above;
The sons of ignorance and night,
May dwell in the eternal light,
Through the eternal love.

Thomas Binney

Blessed be God for such a gift. "He that drinketh of the water that I shall give him shall never"—no, never—"thirst again."

24

Death Defeated

Jesus answered and said unto her, Whosoever drinketh of this water shall thirst again: but whosoever drinketh of the water that I shall give him shall never thirst; but the water that I shall give him shall be in him a well of water springing up into everlasting life. (John 4:13–14)

We are considering the all-sufficiency of the gospel. Let me give you a better translation of our Lord's words in John 4:14: "Whosoever drinketh of the water that I shall give him shall never, no, never, thirst: never, no, never, as long as the world stands." Whoever takes of this water, takes the life that he has come to give and shall never thirst, shall never know again any final or ultimate need or emptiness. This is the great claim that we make for the Christian gospel. We have been asking, is this true? We have started with the mind and the intellect, and last time we were considering the great questions and accusations that are put to our minds by the conscience. And we saw that there is no answer except the answer that is given us in the Lord Jesus Christ and his blessed gospel.

But we must agree that the ultimate problem of all problems is that of death, the problem of the grave and of what lies beyond. The apostle Paul said, "The last enemy that shall be destroyed is death" (1 Cor. 15:26), and it is indeed the last enemy. These other problems that we have to confront come and go—scientific questions and problems, the problem of pain and suffering, political problems, the problem of war. All these may or may not be urgent, but there is one that is inevitable, inexorable, ineluctable—the problem of death. No one can evade it. And, of course, we are bound to be concerned about it. Here we are in life, full of activity and interests—then comes death. Is there any purpose in it? Does it all just end here, all the bother and all the trouble and all the agony and all the suffering—does it all finish? And what then?

So the ultimate test of the truth of this gospel that we preach, the test to apply to this statement of our Lord—"Whosoever drinketh of the water that I shall give him shall never thirst; no, never thirst"—is the question, does it help us, and does it give us satisfaction face-to-face with this last, this ultimate question of death? Easter Sunday is the answer to the question. The gospel never fails us, and it does not fail us here. It is here, indeed, that it perhaps shines out most gloriously of all.

But let us again look at this in the words the Lord used to the woman of Samaria. I put the general proposition to you in these terms: it is the gospel, and the gospel alone, that deals with the problem of death and the life beyond. I am making an exclusive claim. "Whosoever drinketh of this water shall thirst again"—there is no answer here—"but whosoever drinketh of the water that I shall give him shall never thirst."

Now the problem of death has been the problem of the ages. The literature of the world deals constantly with it. The author of the Epistle to the Hebrews expresses it in these words:

> Forasmuch then as the children are partakers of flesh and blood, he also himself likewise took part of the same; that through death he might destroy him that had the power of death, that is, the devil; and deliver them who through fear of death were all their lifetime subject to bondage. (2:14–15)

That is it. Death has been a cause of bondage for the human race from the beginning. Read the literature of ancient Greece with its mythology, and you will find that the Greeks of classical times were tremendously concerned about this question. Those great men, the Greek poets and philosophers, applied their minds to the question of death and found no answer. All they had to tell us was something vague and indefinite—the River Styx and some misty Elysium. They did not know; it was all poetic imagination and fancy. There is no satisfaction from them.

And when you come to the so-called great religions of the world, it is no better—they also just do not know. At best they offer you some sort of absorption into the absolute. Some believe you must keep coming back to this world in a series of reincarnations in order to get rid of this body, and eventually your spirit is absorbed into the ultimate, the absolute, some Nirvana. All they can offer are speculations, which are not satisfactory and which do not answer our questions. That is why all those so-called religions are profoundly pessimistic and hold their people in a thralldom of despair.

And when you come to consult the great poets, you find that they often have wonderful insights into this life, but when they face the problem of death, they fail as much as all the others. Let me quote perhaps the greatest—Shakespeare. He put it once and forever in those immortal words spoken by Hamlet:

To die—to sleep—
To sleep? perchance, to dream. Ay, there's the rub;
For in that sleep of Death what dreams may come,
When we have shuffled off this mortal coil,
Must give us pause . . .
Who would fardels [burdens] bear,
To groan and sweat under a weary life,
But that the dread of something after death,
The undiscover'd country, from whose bourne
No traveller returns, puzzles the will;
And makes us rather bear those ills we have,
Than fly to others that we know not of?
Thus conscience does make cowards of us all.

HAMLET, ACT III, SCENE 1

There is no knowledge; there is always this terrible possibility—what if? And there you have it at its best and highest in the realm of the poets—there is no answer.

And then turn to the realm of general philosophy and science—I am not thinking of the Greeks now but of the subsequent philosophers coming right up to modern times. Of course, there is a lot of talk, a lot of dogmatic talk, but they cannot prove anything. A scientist may say, "Death is the end"; but that is only his opinion, based on nothing, and, indeed, there is disagreement among the scientists themselves. We know, for example, that people such as the late Sir Oliver Lodge had a firm belief in an afterlife. In other words, there is no answer from scientists.

Let me give you one quotation from the man who is regarded as the greatest philosopher of the twentieth century. These are the words of Bertrand Russell:

> We stand on the shore of an ocean, crying to the night and to the emptiness. Sometimes a voice answers us out of the darkness, but it is the voice of one drowning, and in a moment the silence returns. The world seems to me quite dreadful.

That is it! Let us grant that Bertrand Russell is the greatest philosopher of the twentieth century, certainly a great intellect; but when he confronts this question, he just does not know. And there have been similar evidences recently of able old men who have made their contributions to literature and so on but who, faced with this question, know nothing—nothing at all.

Even when we come to the realm of spiritism, we see the same ignorance. Even if we grant that spiritism and the investigations of the Society for Psychical Research have produced certain valid evidence of an existence beyond this life, we have to conclude that what they produce is totally unsatisfactory, as has often been pointed out. Surely the most we can grant for it—and, of course, as Christians we are in no difficulty about this—is that they do establish that there is another realm, an unseen, spiritual realm.

We do not need the evidence of spiritualists, we do not need their proof; we already believe on the grounds that I am going to give you. All I am saying is that even if you give this evidence its maximum value, all it can do is give you some vague indication that death is not the end, that there is something beyond it. It does not tell you what it is. Some of us believe that all the phenomena of spiritualism can be explained very simply in terms of evil spirits, and I do not hesitate to say that is the ultimate answer. That is why the Bible tells us not to touch it—not only because it is unnecessary but because it can be dangerous.

So there is no help from any of these directions. But let me go even one step further. If you turn to the Old Testament, you will find that even the Old Testament is not clear on the subject of death, though there are some striking, glorious statements here and there. On the whole, the Old Testament is alarmed by the thought of death. It says, for example, "A living dog is better than a dead lion" (Eccl. 9:4). There was an uncertainty; there were only glimpses, adumbrations. Even the Old Testament does not get beyond that. It has faith that someone is coming who will deal even with death, but it is looking forward; it does not have a living and clear faith.

But the moment we turn to the New Testament, we find that the position is completely changed. That is why the New Testament is the most lyrical, the most exhilarating, the most cheerful book in the whole universe. Here is a book of triumph, a book of joy, a book of eternal hope. It is said, and it is true, that whenever the Christians in the early church met one another, especially on Easter Sunday morning, it was their custom to greet one another with the words, "Christ is risen!" And that is typical and representative of the Christian hope and the difference that this person who is talking to the woman of Samaria has made to this world. He is able to say, "Whosoever drinketh of the water that I shall give him shall never [no, never] thirst"—not only in life, but even in death.

Christ and his gospel give us the only satisfactory answer even with regard to this last, this ultimate question. So let us discover how our Lord does this. Of course, we do not confine this teaching to Easter Sunday, but we are particularly concerned about it then because of the historicity at the basis of all that we believe and hold.

How, then, does our Lord give us the answer to the problem of death? We start by pointing out that he does this in himself. He does it by his very presence in this world, before anything has been said by him or before anything has happened to him. His very coming into this world already answers all our ultimate questions because he is unique. All of us, from the least in the world's eyes to the greatest people the world has ever known, are born from men and women, and we understand that some have greater qualities and abilities than others; some have faculties that are more highly developed, but they are simply ourselves writ large. They belong to us, and that is why none of them can help us. But here is one who is in a category on his own—he has come into this world from the outside; he has come from the eternal realm. That babe lying in the manger in Bethlehem really answers this question about death. He is a visitor from eternity who has entered into time. "The Word was made flesh, and dwelt among us" (John 1:14). He has tabernacled for a period in this world, but he is the Word: "In the beginning was the Word, and the Word was with God, and the Word was God" (John 1:1).

Moreover, the moment we begin to listen to him, we are struck by one thing, and it struck the people at the time. We read at the end of the Sermon on the Mount that the people who had heard him looked at one another in astonishment, "For he taught them as one having authority"—authority!—"and not as the scribes" (Matt. 7:29), and that was the quality that always characterized him. He did not speculate; he did not say, "It's possible" or "Perchance it may be true." No; he spoke about God and about the eternal unseen world with ease and with a strange authority.

Now that is based on what we read in the third chapter of this Gospel of John, the words that our Lord spoke to that great man Nicodemus. Our Lord said:

> If I have told you earthly things, and ye believe not, how shall ye believe, if I tell you of heavenly things? And no man hath ascended up to heaven, but he that came down from heaven, even the Son of man which is in heaven. (John 3:12–13).

That is the explanation. Our Lord is talking about something he knows. "We speak that we do know," he said to Nicodemus, "and testify that we have seen; and ye receive not our witness" (v. 11). This is the essence of his position. He belongs solidly to history—Jesus of Nazareth. The year is dated because of this person who appeared on the stage of history. No one else has ever been able to speak as our Lord did to Nicodemus. He spoke as one who had come from the realm beyond the veil, which is hidden to us. He came out of it into our world, and he went back again into it.

This is seen in all our Lord's teaching. He kept on saying that he had come from the Father. He said to the religious leaders, "Ye are from beneath; I am from above" (John 8:23). And you cannot explain him in any other terms. He was a carpenter. He had never had the training of the Pharisees. He had never been to the schools, to the academies; he was not a Greek philosopher. And yet we are told, "The Jews marvelled, saying, How knoweth this man letters, having never learned?" (John 7:15). He was able to speak about God and heaven and man with ease and authority. And the only explanation is that what he said about himself was true: he was "from above." He was from the Father and was returning to the Father.

And when we come to this whole question of death and what lies beyond it, there are his specific teachings. I am only giving you some typical examples. Do you remember his story about Dives and Lazarus? He is not using his imagination but is talking about a realm of which he knows. He knows about "Abraham's bosom"; he knows "there is a great gulf fixed" between the abode of the blessed and the abode of the others. He knows that there is a place of torment and a place of bliss and that there is no traffic between the two. He does not speculate, he does not indicate possibilities; he speaks authoritatively, and he calls upon his listeners to accept his teaching (Luke 16:19–31).

Then on another occasion, some people came to him with their trick questions—there were people like that in the first century just as there are today! There is nothing new about the ingenious questions that are put forward by clever people on television and radio. These people are pale imitations of some of these really clever men who were alive in the days of our Lord. Listen to this: "The same day came to him the Sadducees, which say that there is no resurrection" (Matt. 22:23). You see, there is nothing new about denying the resurrection. My dear friends, if we do nothing else, let us get rid of the notion that it is modern knowledge or modern science that makes it difficult for people to believe the gospel. That has nothing to do with it. The Sadducees did not believe in the resurrection nearly two thousand years ago. This was their question:

> Master, Moses said, If a man die, having no children, his brother shall marry his wife, and raise up seed unto his brother. Now there were with us seven brethren: and the first, when he had married a wife, deceased, and, having no issue, left his wife unto his brother: likewise the second also, and the third, unto the seventh. And last of all the woman died also.

Now here is a clever question, you see; this really does knock the bottom out of all this belief in a resurrection: "Therefore in the resurrection whose wife shall she be of the seven? for they all had her."

Can you not hear the laughter and clapping of the crowd! But listen to our Lord's authoritative reply:

> Jesus answered and said unto them, Ye do err, not knowing the scriptures, nor the power of God. For in the resurrection they neither marry, nor are given in marriage, but are as the angels of God in heaven. But as touching the resurrection of the dead, have ye not read that which was spoken unto you by God, saying: I am the God of Abraham, and the God of Isaac, and the God of Jacob? God is not the God of the dead, but of the living.

And here is the footnote: "And when the multitude heard this, they were astonished at his doctrine" (Matt. 22:24–33).

Of course they were! He did not hesitate; he did not speculate. Here was one who knew what he was talking about.

And then think of that scene upon the cross—two thieves, one on each side of our Lord. One of them, in a spirit of repentance and shame, said, "Lord, remember me when thou comest into thy kingdom." And without a moment's hesitation, though he was enduring the agony of the cross, Jesus turned to this man and said, "To day shalt thou be with me in paradise" (Luke 23:42–43). Do you feel the authority? He was dying, but he knew!

Those are samples of our Lord's teaching. But beyond this, beyond the teaching, are evidences that, again, show us the reality of this other realm. Look at his miracles! What were these? He said they were manifestations of "the finger of God." He said they meant that "the kingdom of God is come upon you" (Luke 11:20). This was the power of the world to come. You cannot explain him in any other terms. The miracles were all demonstrations of the realm of God and the supernatural and the eternal.

And then you remember what happened on the Mount of Transfiguration. Our Lord took Peter and James and John with him up on top of the mountain. Suddenly they were overshadowed by a bright cloud, and when they looked at him they saw that an amazing change had taken place. He had become transfigured before them. His face shone like the sun, and his clothes were shining beyond anything that a man could ever produce. Then Moses and Elijah appeared and spoke to him, and a voice from heaven said, "This is my beloved Son, in whom I am well pleased; hear ye him" (Matt. 17:1–8). These men never forgot this transfiguration. They saw this Jesus whom they had been accompanying transformed, glorified, with a radiance of heaven shining from him and all through him, and they heard the voice of attestation from heaven.

Now I say that they never forgot this, and I have evidence to prove what I am saying. Peter, an old man, at the end of his life, writes his last letter and says:

> I think it meet, as long as I am in this tabernacle, to stir you up by putting you in remembrance; knowing that shortly I must put off this my tabernacle, even as our Lord Jesus Christ hath shewed me. Moreover I will endeavour that ye may be able after my decease to have these things always in remembrance. For we have not followed cunningly devised fables, when we made known unto you the power and coming of our Lord Jesus Christ, but were eyewitnesses of his majesty. For he received from God the Father honour and glory, when there came such a voice to him from the excellent glory, This is my beloved Son, in whom I am well pleased. And this voice which came from heaven we heard, when we were with him in the holy mount. (2 Pet. 1:13–18)

Now all this is a demonstration and proof of the reality of that life: it proves that our Lord came from it and that he spoke with knowledge and certainty concerning it. But then he was arrested, and in apparent utter weakness he was condemned to death. He was crucified on a tree, and he died. They took down his body, and they laid it in a tomb, and they put a stone in front of it, sealed it, and set soldiers to guard it.

But that is not the end of the story. We would not gather on Easter morning if it had not been for this tremendous fact of the resurrection, a literal rising from the dead. The tomb was empty. As has often been said, the resurrection of our Lord is the best-attested fact of history. Then he began to appear to chosen representatives. But there was obviously a great change in him—some of his followers did not even recognize him. Something comparable to what had happened on the Mount of Transfiguration, only still more so, had taken place. He could come into a room when all the doors were shut; yet he said he was not a ghost and demonstrated that by eating broiled fish and honey. A spirit could not have done that. This was the resurrection of the body. Here was one who had risen from the dead.

Now the preaching of the resurrection is not speculation; it is not an idea suddenly thought of by some of his followers. Indeed, after his crucifixion his own chosen followers were utterly cast down and completely disconsolate. They had lost all hope—until they saw him! This is what put them on their feet and transfigured them and transformed them—the literal fact of his rising out of the grave from the dead and appearing for forty days among the chosen witnesses who are listed in that great fifteenth chapter of 1 Corinthians. It was this that turned the unhappy, frightened apostles into bold, confident men. It was all the result of the resurrection. This is history, this is fact—not speculation.

And then he gave them his teaching, and there we find the meaning of the resurrection, its message for the early Christians, and its message for us. This is how our Lord fulfilled the promise that he gave to the woman of Samaria. Even face-to-face with death and the grave, we are never at a loss, we are never uncertain, we never thirst. This is the great message of the whole New Testament, especially the Acts of the Apostles and the epistles.

What did the first apostles preach? "Jesus, and the resurrection" (Acts 17:18). They were in trouble because of that; they were thrown into prison because of it. It is put perfectly by the apostle Paul in his second letter to Timothy. Writing of the Lord Jesus Christ, Paul says, "[He] hath abolished death, and hath brought life and immortality to light through the gospel" (1:10). What does that mean? Let me give you some headings to guide your meditation. This is the truth to live by; this is a living faith; this is the way to be triumphant in life and death.

He has "abolished death"! Now "abolish" is not perhaps the best translation. The Greek word means "made ineffective," "made powerless," "broken its power," "nullified," or perhaps, best of all, "defeated." He has defeated death! How has he done that? By actually rising from the dead. That is the final conquest of death. Death had hitherto held everybody in its grip; no one had ever risen from the dead.

"Ah," you say, "what about the case of Lazarus?"

In a sense that was not resurrection, that was resuscitation—he died again. Our Lord was the first to rise from the dead, the first to burst asunder the bands of death, the first really to conquer death—"the firstfruits of them that slept" (1 Cor. 15:20). He has literally, actually conquered death. He rose on the other side of it and appeared again in this world.

But in addition to that and because of that he has removed, for all who believe in him, the terror of death and its power over us. Read 1 Corinthians 15 where the apostle Paul puts it perfectly and wonderfully. How is it that we are able to smile in the face of death and no longer be afraid of it? The apostle gives us the explanation: "The sting of death is sin; and the strength of sin is the law. But thanks be to God, which giveth us the victory thorough our Lord Jesus Christ" (vv. 56–57).

And this is how he won the victory. The trouble about death is this sinfulness of ours. "The *sting* of death is sin"—thoughts of that unknown country, the idea of God, the idea of judgment, the idea of retribution. We know we are guilty. We try to explain our guilt away psychologically, but we cannot. The psychologists themselves are in trouble. Here it is—"and the strength of sin"—the thing that gives power to it, the thing that makes it condemnatory—"is the law [of God]."

But our Lord, by rising from the dead, gave proof positive that he had satisfied God's Law. It was God who condemned him because he had taken our sins upon him on the cross on Calvary's hill; it was the same God who raised him from the dead and thereby declared that he was satisfied: "who was delivered for our offences, and was raised again for our justification" (Rom. 4:25).

And so Christians are no longer afraid of death. They do not die; they "sleep" (1 Thess. 4:13–14). The sting has been taken out of death. In a physical sense, Christians die, but they do not taste the bitterness of death. The horror and the condemnation and the realization of their folly—they are spared all that. As our Lord put it in the account of Lazarus and Dives, "and was carried by the angels into Abraham's bosom" (Luke 16:22).

But our Lord has not only removed the terror of death and the grave from us, he has also guaranteed our rising. This is a wonderful teaching! He has risen, and all who believe in him will rise also. We are in him, in a sense; we are already risen with him.

> For we know that if our earthly house of this tabernacle were dissolved, we have a building of God, an house not made with hands, eternal in the heavens. . . . For we that are in this tabernacle do groan, being burdened: not for that we would be unclothed, but clothed upon. (2 Cor. 5:1, 4)

That is the teaching. As the apostle Paul puts it in his first chapter of the Epistle to the Philippians, Christ's rising from the dead has changed the whole aspect of death for Christians: "For to me to live is Christ, and to die is gain." Then he continues, "I am in a strait betwixt two"—to stay here is better for the Christians in Philippi, but as for Paul himself, he says, "having a desire to depart, and to be with Christ; which is far better" (Phil. 1:21, 23). Death has no terror. Death is now just a little rivulet that separates this land of sin and woe from that "land of pure delight, where saints immortal reign" (Isaac Watts).

And ultimately we await the resurrection of the body. The Spirit in us is a guarantee that our bodies will be raised. Paul again puts it in incomparable language in the eighth chapter of the Epistle to the Romans, where he says, "Ourselves also, which have the firstfruits of the Spirit, even we ourselves groan within ourselves, waiting for the adoption"—what is that?—"to wit, the redemption of our body" (Rom. 8:23). This is coming!

> If the Spirit of him that raised up Jesus from the dead dwell in you, he that raised up Christ from the dead shall also quicken your mortal bodies by his Spirit that dwelleth in you. (Rom. 8:11)

This is certain! Christ is risen! We are risen in spirit, and we will rise in the body. He guarantees this. What has happened to him will happen to us.

So Paul, in one of the most amazing things, in a sense, that he ever said, tells the Corinthians that even death has now become our servant: it is part of our possession:

> Therefore let no man glory in men. For all things are yours; Whether Paul, or Apollos, or Cephas, or the world, or life, or death, or things present, or things to come; all are yours; and ye are Christ's; and Christ is God's. (1 Cor. 3:21–23)

There, then, is the difference that his resurrection has made to all who believe in him. "He hath abolished death." He has defeated death. But beyond that, he has "brought life and immortality to light through the gospel" (2 Tim. 1:10). If you are not thrilled at the thought of this, I ask you to examine whether you are a Christian at all! "He has brought life and immortality to light." Life, not merely continuous existence, the existence that people have in this world. Full living, full being, a real life! Our Lord put it like this in some amazing words:

> Let not your heart be troubled: ye believe in God, believe also in me. In my Father's house are many mansions: if it were not so, I would have told you. I go to prepare a place for you. And if I go and prepare a place for you, I will come again, and receive you unto myself; that where I am, there ye may be also. (John 14:1–3)

That is life! Life with him, and with him forever and ever. It is a glorified life. This mortal flesh cannot inherit immortality; this corruption cannot inherit incorruption. There is going to be a change, a transformation. He was changed himself—he arose in a glorified body. And our bodies will also be glorified. No longer will we have these old bodies; the body will be the same, but it will be transfigured, transformed, glorified. There will be no disease, no weakness, no decay. There will be an eternal, a spiritual, a glorified body, and oh, the glory and the wonder of it all! There will be no sighing there, there will be no sin, there will be no sorrow, there will be no weeping, there will be no parting, there will be no death. It is an entirely new realm and an entirely new kind of life.

> *There shall we see his face*
> *And never, never sin!*
> *There, from the rivers of his grace,*
> *Drink endless pleasures in.*
>
> Isaac Watts ("O When Shall I See Jesus?")

That is what he has opened for us. He has brought this to light—real life!

Listen to this from the book of Revelation:

> After this I beheld, and, lo, a great multitude, which no man could number, of all nations, and kindreds, and people, and tongues, stood before the throne, and before the Lamb, clothed with white robes, and palms

> in their hands; and cried with a loud voice, saying, Salvation to our God which sitteth upon the throne, and unto the Lamb.

There they are praising him.

> And one of the elders answered, saying unto me, What are these which are arrayed in white robes? and whence came they? And I said unto him, Sir, thou knowest. And he said to me, These are they which came out of great tribulation, and have washed their robes, and made them white in the blood of the Lamb. Therefore are they before the throne of God, and serve him day and night in his temple: and he that sitteth on the throne shall dwell among them. They shall hunger no more, neither thirst any more; neither shall the sun light on them, nor any heat. For the Lamb which is in the midst of the throne shall feed them, and shall lead them unto living fountains of waters: and God shall wipe away all tears from their eyes. (Rev. 7:9–10, 13–17)

That is it! That is life! He has brought it to light. You and I shall be glorified. This is what Paul means when he talks in Romans 8 about "the manifestation of the sons of God":

> I reckon that the sufferings of this present time are not worthy to be compared with the glory which shall be revealed in us. For the earnest expectation of the creature waiteth for the [glorious] manifestation of the sons [children] of God. (vv. 18–19)

The whole creation is going to rejoice in it and partake of it.

But above all this, we shall see him face-to-face; we shall see him as he is. Beyond even that, we shall see God! "Blessed are the pure in heart: for they shall see God" (Matt. 5:8). That is what our Lord has opened for us. And do you know what will happen when you see God? Let the apostle Paul give you the answer. Here he is at the end of his life, writing his last letter:

> For I am now ready to be offered, and the time of my departure is at hand. I have fought a good fight, I have finished my course, I have kept the faith. Henceforth there is laid up for me a crown of righteousness, which the Lord, the righteous judge, shall give me at that day: and not to me only, but unto all them also that love his appearing. (2 Tim. 4:6–8)

Not only will we see God, but we will hear the words, "Well done, thou good and faithful servant" (Matt. 25:21), and God will put the crown of righteousness on our brows! And we shall share the bliss, the joy, the glory of eternity with God the Father, God the Son, and God the Holy Spirit. There we shall be "lost in wonder, love, and praise" (Charles Wesley).

He never fails. He gives full satisfaction—in life, in death, and forever. We shall spend our eternity singing together in great unison, "Thou art worthy . . . for thou wast slain, and hast redeemed us to God by thy blood" (Rev. 5:9).

25

Guidance

Jesus answered and said unto her, Whosoever drinketh of this water shall thirst again: but whosoever drinketh of the water that I shall give him shall never thirst; but the water that I shall give him shall be in him a well of water springing up into everlasting life. (John 14:13–14)

We have been looking together at various aspects of life as we live it, as we know it, and as we have to contend with it, and we have seen that a satisfaction is always given in the gospel that is to be found there alone.

But I move on now to a further question because it is one that often perplexes people. And again we are able to say, and must say, that our Lord's claim fails if he himself, his teaching, and all that he gives us cannot help us at this point too. I am referring to the question of guidance. Now I am not talking here so much of guidance in a moral and ethical sense as guidance from a more general aspect, guidance with respect to what we are to do in particular circumstances.

We are all very familiar with this problem. Here are certain possibilities before us—what are we to do? Perhaps no problem brings people so frequently to the minister of the gospel in his pastoral office as this question. We want to do the right thing, but the question is how to discover what that is. Our Lord says, "Whosoever drinketh of the water that I shall give him shall never thirst," which we have interpreted as meaning, "shall never be in any kind of final perplexity, shall never be beside himself, shall never be torn asunder." And that includes the whole question of guidance.

Once more, the world patently cannot help us here. The best it can offer us is worldly wisdom—"Do the best you can for yourself" and so on. But most people find that unsatisfactory. Many therefore talk about luck; they talk about chance; they consult astrologers and fortune-tellers; they dabble in spiritism. Now all this, of course, just shows that there is no satisfactory answer in this world. Yet people display a longing for some authoritative answer, for some certainty, in these matters.

Now we grant that some persons go through life fairly well, they muddle through, and things, on the whole, do not cause them much difficulty. That is very often because such people do not think; they are just content with their given lot. Their whole outlook is narrow and small. Think of the millions in this country and in every other country who live like that. They go to work because without money you cannot have a house, you cannot have food and drink, you cannot bring up a family. They fit into this little life of "nine to five," but nothing bigger is ever a consideration.

But the moment people become Christians, all sorts of other possibilities open before them. And, indeed, it is right and true to say that when one becomes a Christian, one is confronted by new problems. One can no longer go on living a mechanical life; there are new considerations, new thoughts, new possibilities, new questions. In other words—and many of you, I know, have had this experience—the first thing that happened when you became a Christian was that you asked yourself, "Is my job or the work that I am doing right for a Christian?" That is the sort of problem that we are considering.

The world, then, really cannot help us. So what is the teaching here? Can our Lord's claim be substantiated? I suggest that it can and that there are principles we can follow. This is a very difficult and large subject, and I can only lay down certain general guiding principles, but I personally find them more than adequate and have often found them to be equally helpful to others.

The first proposition we lay down is this: in the spiritual realm there is no such thing as automatic or mechanical guidance. I have to start with this because many people have gone astray at this point. They have misunderstood certain statements of Scripture, taking them to mean that the moment you become a Christian you no longer have any problems or difficulties about what to do; you are given direct and immediate guidance that is always right, and you will never go wrong again.

But we must correct that immediately. If you read the beginning of Acts 16, you will find there a final and sufficient answer to such a wrong idea. Here is the apostle Paul, of all men, with his great experiences and with his knowledge of the Lord, and this is what we are told: "Now when they had gone throughout Phrygia and the region of Galatia, and were forbidden of the Holy Ghost to preach the word in Asia . . ." The apostle Paul and his companions were anxious to preach in Asia. They clearly believed that was the right thing to do, and they were going ahead, but they "were forbidden of the Holy Ghost." Now the apostle was a great evangelist. He had been called to evangelize and preach, to found churches and establish them. The world was his parish, and he had felt that it was right to go into Asia, but he was not allowed. Then the same thing happened again: "After they were come to Mysia, they assayed to go into Bithynia: but the Spirit suffered them not" (Acts 16:6–7).

In both instances the apostle had to be restrained in some striking manner by the Holy Spirit. The only deduction that can be drawn from that is that guidance is clearly not automatic or mechanical. We must never think it is. I could give you examples from history, from the history of the church in particular, of great tragedies that have happened because very good, sincere, and honest people have gone astray in this very respect. There is always the danger of identifying our wills with the will of God.

Then, on top of that, of course, there is the teaching in the New Testament about the influence of evil spirits. The people who are most prone to the kind of danger to which I am referring are those who are most concerned about living a truly spiritual life. They are interested in the doctrine concerning the Holy Spirit and in all the activities of the Spirit. They are not cold, detached intellectuals who are merely interested in abstract truth. These are spiritual people, and they want to live life on a high spiritual level. So they put themselves, as it were, at the disposal of the Spirit, but their danger is to forget that in doing that they are partly also putting themselves at the disposal of evil spirits. So we read these exhortations in the Scriptures: "Beloved, believe not every spirit, but try the spirits whether they are of God" (1 John 4:1); "Prove all things; hold fast that which is good" (1 Thess. 5:21).

So you can see immediately that there are many great dangers just at this point of knowing God's guidance, and as this has been the experience of Christians throughout the history of the church and is still the case today, it is very important that we should consider this subject. Some of the freak religious movements that arose in the past, especially during the last century, and particularly in the USA, were characterized by this very belief in immediate, infallible guidance, and tragedies often resulted.

So we go on to a further classification of this whole matter, and I would suggest that we can divide this question of guidance into two main groups—the exceptional and the usual. We must do this because, clearly, this distinction is drawn in the Scriptures themselves, both in the Old Testament and the New. There is such a thing as exceptional guidance—it is very wrong to exclude it. We read quite a lot about dreams in the Old Testament—not so much in the New—and there are visions in both Old and New Testaments. People were directed to do things through a vision, and in that vision they were given guidance. And, similarly, guidance came to people through dreams. This is something that we must recognize.

Now it is very interesting to me to see how that one paragraph in Acts 16 deals with both the exceptional and the usual forms of guidance. Have you ever noticed this striking contrast? The apostle and his companion had been prohibited by the Holy Spirit from going to Asia and Bithynia, and as a result of that, they had to go down to Troas. They had not been able to go there, they had not been able to go here, and so they just went straight on and came to Troas, and as that happened to be a seaport, they could not go any further. Now here was the question: what were they to do? And you remember the answer that was given—a vision of "the man of Macedonia."

> A vision appeared to Paul in the night; There stood a man of Macedonia, and prayed him, saying, Come over into Macedonia, and help us. And after he had seen the vision, immediately we endeavoured to go into Macedonia, assuredly gathering that the Lord had called us for to preach the gospel unto them. (Acts 16:9–10)

Now this is quite exceptional. The apostle Paul, in the course of living his Christian life, filled with the Spirit, had thought that he ought to go to Asia and then to Bithynia, but he was wrong. Then he was given this vision in the night, and he "assuredly gathered," he was certain, that this was God's will. This is the way in which the gospel first came to Europe. It was a new departure, and God gave his servant a vision in order to show him what to do.

Peter, too, had a vision, similar in general, though not in the details. For Peter, it was with regard to his going to preach to the household of Cornelius. This was a tremendous thing for a Jew to do. Though Peter had been baptized with the Spirit on the Day of Pentecost, he was still tending to think in Jewish terms; so how could he preach this message to Gentiles? But God gave him a vision of a sheet coming down filled with all kinds of animals, clean and unclean, and then gave the command,

"Rise, Peter; kill, and eat." Peter's immediate objection was that he had never eaten anything unclean. But in that vision Peter was given guidance, understanding, and instruction (Acts 10).

Now exceptional guidance is always clear, unmistakable, and assured. There are many illustrations in the lives of the saints and in the lives of men and women of outstanding qualities whom God has raised up in connection with the life of the church. There was, for instance, the guidance given to Hudson Taylor as he was walking on a beach in southern England, in which he received the whole conception of the China Inland Mission. Now I am emphasizing that this kind of guidance is exceptional because there is a certain type of person who is always trying to live in this realm of the unusual. A man once wrote a book with the title *Ten Thousand Miles of Miracles in Great Britain*. His life was supposed to be a series of miracles. But that is a contradiction of terms—miracles are not as common as that; so what happened to him was obviously not miraculous. He was thinking in a loose kind of way. Miracles are unusual, and this kind of guidance is exceptional. But God forbid that anybody should understand me to be saying that it does not happen. It does. Thank God, it does! It has to happen at times. There are situations such as those I have described, and it may be a time such as this, when we are in need of something exceptional.

Let me give a final illustration before we move on. The kind of distinction between what I am calling the usual and the exceptional is the difference between the regular work of the Holy Spirit in the church and revival. Revival is not perpetual. By definition it is not. Revival is exceptional, and it comes in God's own time. And it is exactly the same with this immediate, unmistakable guidance that enables someone to say, "I gather assuredly that this is what God is calling me to do, and I'll go and do it," exactly as Paul went from Troas and landed in Samothracia and went through Neapolis to Philippi, bringing the gospel into Europe.

So let us turn now to the usual, to that which is more customary. This is what applies to most of us in our daily lives. The following, it seems to me, are the biblical principles with regard to this matter. First, we start with a general doctrine of vocation, a doctrine of calling. This was one of the grand discoveries made by Martin Luther. At the time of the Reformation he was given to see that God calls people who are not in the ministry or in the priesthood, that there is a calling and a vocation even with regard to such an activity as sweeping a room.

Now this is the general doctrine. It declares that God knows us individually and is concerned about us individually, that he endows us with different capacities and faculties and calls us to different tasks, to different callings. This is clearly taught in the Scriptures. For instance, in Ephesians 4 Paul says with regard to the church that "[God] gave some, apostles; and some, prophets; and some, evangelists; and some, pastors and teachers" (v. 11). All this goes under the general heading of vocation. In Romans 13:1–7 Paul says, "the powers that be are ordained of God," and people are called to these tasks. It is very important to start with that general principle, based on the fact that God is our Father, that he has numbered the very hairs of our head and knows all about us and is concerned about us. We must always keep in our minds this truth that God has a purpose for every one of us. This is a general principle, a general, overarching idea.

Then, secondly, these general biblical principles with regard to life are applied to our daily lives. We must not be absurd about this, of course. The Bible has no detailed instructions for the scientist on how he is to work in his laboratory or what he is to do next. That is not what I mean. I mean that in the Scriptures we are given certain broad principles with regard to our conduct. We are given them not only in a moral and ethical sense but also in a more general sense, and they combine with our common sense to produce what we may call the enlightened common sense that should characterize every single Christian. As we have been showing earlier, when we are born again there is not a part of us that is not affected. By nature we all have an element of judgment and of wisdom and of common sense, but when we become Christians, that is all heightened. We no longer have the world's version of common sense—rule of thumb and so on—but an enlightenment—everything in us is sharpened by the Holy Spirit, every faculty is influenced by the Spirit in this general way.

So, then, these two come together—the teaching of Scripture and enlightened common sense and understanding, so that if you have a feeling you ought not to be doing something, then, if it is something that the Bible prohibits, you need not consider it any further. You know you must not do it; you know that temptation is an attack of the devil.

Now there are people who have got into trouble over this matter; let me give you one illustration. I remember very well in the early days of the last war [World War II] reading an article by the late C. S. Lewis, who had just become a Christian. As an unbeliever he had been a lecturer, a professor in English literature in Oxford, and he wrote that when he became a Christian, he at once began to feel that he could no longer go on being a teacher of English literature. What does English literature have to do with the Christian faith, with the spiritual life? He had a feeling that he must give that up and do something more specifically Christian. Now I have no doubt that many have had this exact experience; in fact, I know that is so. Some people who have been teaching various subjects and have become Christians have said, "How can I go on teaching that any longer?" There is this feeling that we tend to get in our early days in the Christian life that we must all be doing something that is specifically Christian. But that is a fallacy.

The teaching of the Bible is that we are to do all things to the glory of God (1 Cor. 10:31), and general culture comes under that heading. It is wrong to regard anything that is not specifically Christian as therefore valueless for the Christian; there is a place for general culture. Now, of course, the Christian will always know the limits in these matters, but as C. S. Lewis came to see, his feeling had been quite wrong. So he went on with his work as a professor of English literature.

Now it is only an understanding of the biblical teaching that leads us to draw that kind of distinction. You can glorify God in art, in music, in so many realms of life. Anything that is wrong, of course, does not glorify God and so is excluded. The Scriptures show that. But if it is not wrong, it comes under the heading of all things bringing glory to God. And that is what I mean by saying that the general principles of biblical teaching plus an enlightened common sense and understanding are the basic way in which we proceed with regard to the great question of guidance.

But having put it like that very broadly and generally, I must move on to my third point, because we are not left with just the general teaching and our enlightened understanding; there is something more here—there is an inward leading. And it is at this point that so many of us have so often been in trouble. By "inward leading" I mean a pressure on one's spirit. Something comes to you; you have not sought it—it comes to you, and you try to dismiss it, but it keeps coming back. There is a kind of pressure urging you, as it were, to do something, to take up something, or to proceed to a given place and do something in a given direction.

Now this again is plainly taught in the Scriptures, and it is exemplified constantly in the lives of God's people throughout the centuries. But at this point danger again comes in. There is the danger of fanaticism or of exaggerating or misunderstanding this inward leading or of turning it into something that is isolated from the teaching of the Scripture, something that is infallible and immediate and direct. This has brought many people into trouble and into distress; so what do we do about it? We begin by recognizing this inward leading. There is nothing more valuable, nothing, in a sense, that is higher than this in the realm of experience, except that which is quite exceptional. But how do we avoid the danger of misinterpretation or of fanaticism?

Again, the Scripture provides certain tests. The first is that God's leadings always conform to certain patterns. That is what is so marvelous about the work of the Almighty. Look at the flowers, look at the seasons; God's work is always on a pattern. And if you find that you seem to be having a leading that does not fit into the general pattern found in the Scriptures and in Christian biographies, you should always be suspicious of it. The devil tries to counterfeit this, but he generally overdoes it; he makes the leading too dramatic, too wonderful. You remember how he tempted our Lord to throw himself down from the pinnacle of the Temple—that kind of exaggeration is the mark of the devil always. God's leadings are more rational; they fit into this general pattern.

Secondly, God's leadings never suggest that we should do something that is against God's own laws and ways. Let me give you two examples. I remember reading about a woman in the early centuries of the Christian church, a very godly, spiritually minded woman who believed in the leading of the Spirit. She believed the whole teaching of the Bible and was anxious to give herself and her best to God and to be doing God's will. Now this good woman reached a stage in which she believed that God was calling her to leave her husband and her children to go and live a monastic life. She really believed that she had received a direct leading of the Spirit. She was genuine and was prepared to make the sacrifice. And so that is what she did. Mark you, her heart was breaking as she was doing it, and the record even tells us that as she was going away and could hear the crying of her little children, though it was breaking her heart, she felt that it was well-pleasing to God and that the pain was the measure of her obedience.

But she was completely wrong. Why? She was wrong because she was violating one of the very principles of God's own teaching. A woman is never called upon to leave her husband and her children in order to serve God. It is plainly contradictory of God's laws with regard to marriage and the family and the home and the subjection of the wife to the husband and many other principles that I could mention. But that is the kind of tangle into which the devil in his malice can lead us; that is one of the ways in which he can lead us astray. So the principle I am laying down is that

God's inward leading never blankly contradicts his plain teaching in the Scriptures with regard to certain fundamental matters.

Let me give you another illustration. I once knew a bank manager who felt that he was called of God to give up his work in the bank and become a preacher, an evangelist, and perhaps a pastor. He had a wife and two daughters, and they were entirely opposed to this idea, but in spite of that, he went ahead, causing his family great misery. Large numbers of people regarded this man as someone who had done something very fine. They said, "This is what Christians should do." But I dissent entirely from that view. My principle, which I have often had to apply, is that when a man in such a position comes to talk to me, the first thing I always ask him is, "Is your wife in agreement?" You cannot divide yourself from your wife; you cannot leave her. The man and wife are one: "They twain shall be one flesh" (Matt. 19:5). They have been united by God, and you cannot break that. There is to be this consensus, this agreement.

This principle that the guidance of God will never lead us to break any of his own ordinances is vital and can be applied along a wide range of issues, including the order of creation, under which we put marriage, family, the home, and so on. There is consistency always in God's guidance.

The final way in which I would illustrate this principle of consistency is that God never acts in what I may call—I cannot think of a better term—a freakish manner. People who claim guidance often do behave in a very freakish way. I can deal with this by repeating a story of something that once happened to the great Charles Haddon Spurgeon. A man came to him at the end of a service and said that the Spirit had told him that he was to preach in Spurgeon's Tabernacle the following Thursday night. He was certain of this. Spurgeon's answer was not only full of common sense but also full of biblical teaching and understanding. He said, "Well, it is a very strange thing that the Spirit has not told me that," and so the man did not preach in Spurgeon's Tabernacle on the following Thursday.

Do you see the principle that is involved? If it had been the leading of the Spirit that this man should preach in Spurgeon's pulpit on that Thursday night, it is clear and obvious from God's way of acting that he would also have told Spurgeon. Spurgeon, without saying it, was applying that rule. There is a general consistency about God's way of guidance, and recognizing that is how we defeat the devil. The devil's counterfeits always overdo it; they are too clever, too wonderful; they always have this odd, freakish element and do not conform to the wholeness, the amazing pattern, that is ever the characteristic of God's dealings with us.

So, then, we have the Scriptures, we have enlightened common sense, we have an inward leading, which we can check: we must "prove all things" (1 Thess. 5:21) and "try [test] the spirits" (1 John 4:1). Do not assume that because you like the idea that comes to you, it must be from the Spirit—prove it!

And then, what else? According to the teaching of the Scripture, when we are seeking guidance, other people can be of help to us. What are pastors and teachers for? They are to give guidance; they are to give instruction and help. That is part of their function, part of why they were ordained of God. Christ has set them in the church to give answers, to give help in these matters. Therefore, we are exhorted to talk together about these questions. We do not just take a stand on our own opinion. If we do not acknowledge and respect those who are called and ordained of God to lead and guide us, we are breaking God's Law, and Christ's own law for the church. We are to respect those who are set over us in these matters of the faith. And along with them, those who are not pastors and teachers but are spiritually minded can also help us. We seek the mind of God together; we discuss the questions we have in the light of scriptural teaching, and we pray together.

Now, of course, all these ways of finding God's guidance have their risks, and one of the dangers that a pastor always has to guard himself against is that of becoming other people's conscience. Some people in perplexity make the pastor their conscience; they say, "Tell me what to do." The pastor must never do that. He can give advice, he can share his knowledge of the Scriptures and scriptural principles, he can consider the circumstances, he takes the story as it is told him into consideration, but he must never become anybody's conscience.

Indeed, I also want to emphasize our side of that statement. We must never allow anybody else to become our conscience. I have often had people come to me who are in trouble because they went to a missionary meeting where the terrible need in a certain country was put before them and pressure was brought to bear upon them. The principle that was put forward was, "The need is the call." "Here is the need," they were told; "what are you going to do about it?" And they were made to feel that they were almost criminals if they did not stand up immediately and say they were ready to give themselves in response to the missionary call.

To me that is false teaching. To start with, the need is not the call; otherwise every Christian would be in full-time service in some part of the world. Look at the need today—we would all have to go out as missionaries. To say that the need is the call contradicts the whole doctrine of vocation. But it is still worse when emotional and other forms of pressure are brought to bear upon people. God does not lead like that. It is all done with a very good motive, but it often leads to confusion and to tragedies, even on the missionary field.

That, then, is the whole principle of how other people can help but also of the need to take care lest such help be abused or we make a wrong decision through our lack of understanding. Now I come to certain final general rules that I have found to be of considerable value in my own life and in my attempts to help others.

First, never try to anticipate God's leading. That is, do not sit down and start asking yourself questions such as, is it right to be doing this? or should I be doing it? The rule is this: go on with your work, and if it is not God's will that you should be doing it, he will stop you. Do not anticipate him. Do not ask yourself theoretical questions. Do not create problems. Go on living your life; go on living the Christian life. Follow the teaching of 1 Corinthians 7:20: "Let every man abide in the same calling wherein he was called." Keep on with that; that is your business and mine.

Secondly, tell God, and tell him honestly—and this to me is perhaps the most important principle of all—that you put yourself entirely in his hands. The moment you become a Christian, you should do that. You cannot believe in Christ as simply your Savior; he is your Lord always. To say that you can take him as your Savior without taking him as your Lord is a contradiction of plain biblical teaching. You should put yourself unreservedly in God's hands, and tell him that your one desire is to know his will and to do his will. If you can say that honestly, then there is a sense in which you have done everything you can do. Say that, then leave it to him. And if you say that to God, you have no right to take it back to yourself—leave it with him. But you must be honest; you must be able to say, "I want to know your will, and I want to do your will and to live to your glory." Say that, give yourself entirely to him, then go on with your work.

Thirdly, watch for openings, and at the same time watch for closings. I am again referring to what happened to Paul in Acts 16:6–7. You keep doing your work, but you are a spiritually minded person, and while you are not creating the problem or thinking theoretically, you always have your eyes open. God approaches us and speaks to us, as we have been seeing, in many different ways. A door appears to be opening, and you will probably come to the conclusion, "Here it is," but suddenly it is shut!

Watch for that. In other words, never force a door open. If it is merely ajar, do not pull it open; never be violent. Never force it in any sense, but just be watchful.

That leads me to the next point, which is this: be prepared for delays and for testings. Oh, this is a tremendous thing! God tests us! It is his way of training us; it is his way of enabling us to grow. So nothing is more important than that we should be patient. Is that not one of our biggest problems? We are in such a hurry. God is never in a hurry, and the more Christian we become, the less we shall hurry. Foolish people have talked at different times about evangelizing the whole world in this generation or something like that. Nonsense! They were proved wrong in the past, and those who say that kind of thing today will equally prove to be wrong. Be prepared for delays, disappointments, discouragements. You say, "Here it is at last!" But then you find it is not. That is all right; be patient.

Now I come to what I have had to say more frequently than anything else in this pastoral context. Make sure to remember Philippians 4:6–7:

> Be careful for nothing [in nothing be anxious]; but in every thing by prayer and supplication with thanksgiving let your requests be made known unto God. And the peace of God, which passeth all understanding, shall keep your hearts and minds through Christ Jesus.

Never be anxious! In nothing be anxious! Never be tense, never be worried, never be troubled, never be frantic, never be divided—never.

Generally people like this come to me, and they are perplexed and troubled. Sometimes they give me the impression that I have only to say, "Do this!" and they will do it. I will not say that—I am in no position to do so. I cannot be their conscience. I do not know the will of God for people. What I say is, "You're worried about the wrong thing; you're worried about what you are supposed to be doing—is it this or is it that? But what you ought to be worried about is, do you have the peace of God that passes all understanding?"

That is a paradox, is it not? But I mean this: whether or not you are to go to Japan or to India is not the question. Though you do not know where you are to go or what you are to do or whether, perhaps, you are to continue doing what you are now doing does not matter. What is important for you is that you should *always* enjoy the peace of God that passes all understanding (Phil. 4:7). If you concentrate on that, you will find that it will solve most of your problems of guidance because that will lead you to stop analyzing and considering and weighing and measuring and always coming back to the same uncertainty. Leave it all with him, and be concerned about this relationship to him.

My final principle is this: never do anything until you are unanimous. I have talked about the unanimity of the family. I am now talking about *your* unanimity. Listen to this:

> Hast thou faith? have it to thyself before God. Happy is he that condemneth not himself in that thing which he alloweth. And he that doubteth is damned if he eat, because he eateth not of faith: for whatsoever is not of faith is sin. (Rom. 14:22–23)

These words just mean that however pure your mind may be about something, if there is doubt and hesitation, do not move—your head and your heart must be unanimous. When God guides, he guides the whole person; there is no division, no uncertainty. God persuades the mind and the heart, and they act in a great and a wonderful unison—"whatsoever is not of faith is sin." In this passage Paul is talking about eating meat that had been offered to idols, but that is only an illustration. It does not matter what it is—if there is a doubt in it or something is restraining you, do not move. Wait until the final signal drops, then move on, and you will be moving on in the direction of God's will.

You can always be certain, my dear friend, that if you have honestly fulfilled these conditions I have been laying down to you, then even if you find that you have done something that is wrong, you will never suffer for it. God is your Father, and a father does not punish a child when he knows the child is doing his best—at least not if he is a father worthy of the name. God is our Father, and if you and I have honestly sought his will and have been concerned about honoring and glorifying his great and holy name, even though we may prove to have been wrong and to have been misled, he will not punish us. Indeed, he will even be able—and he is able—to take our very mistakes and turn them into blessings; he will honor our desire and our faithfulness to him. So you need never worry, you need never be anxious; even then you will enjoy "the peace which passeth all understanding," for you will have had a vision of his heart of love such as you had never had before, and he will enfold you in his arms as his fallible child who nevertheless loves him and is anxious to promote his glory.

So you see that our Lord's claim is fully justified in this matter of guidance as in all others: "He that drinks of the water that I shall give him shall never thirst, no, never, as long as the world stands." Those who drink this water know that they are right with God and that "all things work together for good to them that love God."

26

The Secret Things of God

Jesus answered and said unto her, Whosoever drinketh of this water shall thirst again: but whosoever drinketh of the water that I shall give him shall never thirst; but the water that I shall give him shall be in him a well of water springing up into everlasting life. (John 4:13–14)

As we have been considering these words together, we have seen that the world cannot meet our needs, it cannot solve our problems, it cannot give us that for which we fundamentally long. But our Lord says that he can and will if we just drink this water that he wants to give us. So we are examining this statement, testing ourselves and our own experiences, and we have started with the mind, the intellect, and the understanding. Our Lord claims that he can give complete satisfaction to our minds—our minds with their questions.

We have examined this from various aspects and have found that it is true with regard to life in general and with regard to the way of salvation and to problems that arise, such as the problems of pain, suffering, and war. Our Lord answers the accusations of conscience, and he answers our questionings about death and the grave and what lies beyond. He has conquered even this last enemy and has "brought life and immortality to light through the gospel" (2 Tim. 1:10). In our last study, we looked at the question of guidance, a question that tends to agitate us all, and we found that there again, in his way, as revealed in the teaching of the Bible, he gives us the satisfaction of which we stand in need.

Having gone through all that, it seems to me that we have reached the point where we can consider what I would regard as the final problem. I say "final problem" in a general or generic sense because I want to consider with you some questions that we may put together under the heading of "residual problems and difficulties." I could look at these individually, but in order to save time and to advance with this great theme and show how our Lord satisfies the heart and the will as well as the mind, I am putting them all together.

What do I mean by "residual problems"? Well, I am thinking of a subject such as this: God himself! We talk about God, but the being and the nature of God and the eternity of God are a problem to the mind. Then there is the whole problem of the origin of evil. Many people are troubled and agitated about that. Where did evil come from? How is evil possible? How is it compatible with a holy God and with what we postulate with respect to him? Linked to all this is the mystery of God's ways, God's dealings with humanity in general and with men and women as individuals. This is a great problem. How are we to understand God's ways or reconcile them with other aspects of the truth concerning him? You are familiar with these questions.

To take some specific questions, there is the problem of why it is that some people are saved and become Christians and some do not. This often worries people. What determines why some are believers and some are not? Then many people are troubled about the condition of the lost—eternal punishment, hell, God's punishment of sin. How do you reconcile that with the love of God? And there is the problem of why some people die young and others live to an old age. Why is it that very often those who seem to be evil go on living a long life, while the good die young? But perhaps beyond all these there lies the question, what happens after death? What is heaven like? What happens there? Why are we told so little about it?

I could add to the list, but I am simply picking out typical problems that so often trouble the minds of men and women. Sometimes people say that these questions prevent them from being Christians, while at other times it is Christians who raise these questions because of what has happened to them or because somebody has put the question to them in an argument. Every pastor, every minister, knows what it is like to be plied with such questions.

Now all these questions have an element in common—they are all in the realm of the ultimate, they all belong to that realm that is above us. I need not waste any time in pointing out how the world quite obviously cannot help us here. The world is either not interested or when it is only adds to the difficulties and exaggerates them and aggravates the problem. The world does not understand. It is very good at asking questions, but there is nothing clever about asking questions; any fool can do that. The world never gets beyond that. It can raise the difficulties, it can show you the problems, and it does so constantly. But it cannot bring us anywhere near the beginning of understanding. It gives no satisfaction at all.

But here is the question: does our Lord satisfy us here? Can he who says, "Whosoever drinketh of the water that I shall give him shall never thirst" give satisfaction even with regard to these residual problems?

We know that he can. But can we demonstrate it? Moreover, are we ourselves able to say, "Yes, I am satisfied even here"? To help one another come to that satisfaction and to strengthen one another, let us proceed to see how our Lord does this. I would put the answer under two main headings. The first is general, and the second is detailed or particular.

I start with the general answer because it is very important that we should be clear about certain things. The first point is a negative. The Bible is the Lord's book, his word; it is here that he gives satisfaction to the mind and to the understanding. But—and I start with this as a general proposition—the Scriptures do not give us complete, detailed answers with regard to all these questions. To me, it is tremendously important that we should always be ready to say that, and we must not be afraid to say it; we must not even say it reluctantly. Christian people often get into trouble because they seem to think that they should have a detailed answer to every single question that is put to them. But that is not the case. The Bible does not pretend to put us into that position.

In other words, as I have said before, we must never regard the Bible as a sort of quick solution—here is the problem, you just turn to some verses, and there is the answer. That is never true of the Scripture. It has, as we have been seeing, its didactic teaching, its explicit statements, which are clear and unmistakable; other questions it deals with more generally, leaving us in the realm of principles. And there is a good reason for that, as we shall see.

But I hasten to another negative. Because we do not have complete and detailed answers, we must not think that we can then swing to the other extreme and be obscurantist. This is equally important. Obscurantism means that you refuse to think, you refuse to employ your understanding; you just dig in your heels, as it were, and become irritable. It means you refuse to consider any questions and even resent them, merely making dogmatic statements such as "This is what I say" or "This is what the Bible says." It is burying your head in the sand, refusing to employ the gifts that God has given you to understand the teaching of the Scripture. Obscurantism does great harm to the Christian faith. People who become obscurantist and make dogmatic statements without being able to give reasons for them have to adopt this stance because they really are in trouble and are unhappy. So they retreat and erect a barrier around themselves. They are not satisfied, and they most certainly do not help anybody else; indeed, they tend to hinder them.

We must avoid the two extremes of trying to give detailed answers to everything or of answering nothing. We cannot answer everything, but we do not retreat into a kind of castle of obscurantism and lose contact with the world that is round and about us. But what is our Lord's method? How does our Lord give satisfaction when we are faced with these residual problems?

Well, in the first instance, it seems to me, our Lord immediately takes the excitement out of these problems, and this is wonderful, as I hope to show you. I am sure that you are familiar with the way in which people come with this kind of problem and look worried: "I don't see this, I can't understand that, and I don't know how these can be reconciled." They are troubled and disturbed. And our Lord's method always is to remove completely this worry, agitation, and confusion. As far as our intellects are concerned, we are no longer like the Scripture's description of the sinner: "the wicked are like the troubled sea, when it cannot rest, whose waters cast up mire and dirt" (Isa. 57:20). There is immediately a balance and a poise that go a long way in the direction of this final satisfaction.

So there it is in general, but let us work this out together in detail. How does our Lord do this? First, he always deals with our spirit, and this is the key. The real trouble in connection with these various problems is ultimately in the realm of the spirit, our heart, if you like, in the biblical sense of that term; and our Lord gives us satisfaction by putting that right.

Now this, of course, is something that happens inevitably at conversion, and it is a proof that we are truly converted. When the Holy Spirit deals with us, he humbles us. You cannot be a Christian without being humbled. Every man and woman who has been regenerated has been humbled. The Spirit does this by convicting us of sin. Our Lord made this quite clear more than once. He said, "Except ye be converted, and become as little children, ye shall not enter into the kingdom of heaven" (Matt. 18:3). He put it similarly to Nicodemus, who asked, "How can these things be?" (John 3:9). Nicodemus wanted to understand. "How can a man be born when he is old?" (v. 4). Here it is, this agitation, this trouble, this excitement. Do you remember how our Lord treated Nicodemus? He humbled him!

> Verily, verily, I say unto thee, Except a man be born again, he cannot see the kingdom of God. . . . Except a man be born of water and of the Spirit, he cannot enter into the kingdom of God. (vv. 3, 5)

He must be humbled and become as a little child: "Marvel not that I said unto thee, Ye must be born again" (v. 7).

This is an essential part of the whole process of conversion, and remember, it happens to the whole personality. We are humbled; our spirits are put right in the sense that we are laid low.

Now you see the value of this when dealing with these residual problems. Through the Word, the Holy Spirit tells us and shows us the truth about human nature, about ourselves—not, in the first instance, about our own individual problems but about human beings in general, man as man. This is the first thing we all need. Most of the troubles in the world are due to the fact that man has a wrong idea about man. We are living in an age when man is worshipping man; man has become the god, the arbiter, of everything. It is his understanding that controls everything. So the first thing that is necessary is that we should have a true conception of man. And what we are told about him is that he is finite. Even at the beginning he was finite; even when perfect, he was still finite. He was not God; he was only a human being.

This is a tremendous fact. We must realize that man at his best is limited. There is an essential qualitative difference between God and man, and man, therefore, by definition, even when in a state of perfection, can never span the infinite, the absolute, and the eternal. And the moment you realize that, you are well on the road to dealing with these residual questions and problems at which we are looking.

But when you understand further that man is fallen and that as the result of the Fall he is not only finite but is also sinful, then your whole condition is being put right. You are reminded, in other words, that the original sin was a desire to be God. That was the temptation that the devil brought to the woman: "ye shall be as gods" (Gen. 3:5)—"you will have complete understanding." That is what man wants, and he is in trouble about the residual problems and questions because he thinks that he has it in him to understand. This great man, this great brain! Why, there is nothing he cannot do! But the moment we are dealt with by the Spirit through the Word, we see that man is a fool, that he has lost his understanding of this essential, eternal difference, and that his greatest trouble and the cause of his original fall was and has always been his presumption, this desire to know things that are beyond him. As the result of the Fall, his understanding is darkened; it is sinful. Whether he likes it or not, that is the simple truth, and his world proves it, of course.

There, then, is the condition of fallen man. He is annoyed about this. His greatest trouble is intellectual pride. You see that in so-called civilization and in the history of civilization. It is a manifestation of human pride, and especially intellectual pride. Never has this been clearer than during the twentieth century as a result of so many discoveries, inventions, and great advances. Man believes now more than ever that he has it in him to encompass all knowledge. There must be nothing that he cannot understand, and he will not believe until he does understand. This, I say again, is the original sin, and it has polluted the minds and understanding of all the progeny of the first man and woman.

But as Christian people, what we must remember in particular is that even though we are born again and are new men and women in Christ Jesus, the besetting sin for most of us is still intellectual pride; it is still the danger of presumption. It keeps on creeping back. In a sense that was the great trouble with the church at Corinth; it is, at any rate, the problem that is dealt with in the first four chapters of 1 Corinthians. Though the Christians in Corinth had believed the gospel under the teaching of Paul, other teachers had come and had brought in an additional element—philosophy, a Greek idea of wisdom—and the Corinthians were ready to take it up. They said Paul was just a simpleton—"his bodily presence is weak, and his speech contemptible" (2 Cor. 10:10); he was not eloquent, and he did not talk philosophy as Apollos did and so on. So they were being led astray by this very sin, though they were Christians.

Intellectual pride is always the danger, and so I emphasize our Lord's humbling of us and put it first because it will control everything else. Our spirits are put right when we realize how small and how finite we are, how ignorant we are, how little we really know in an ultimate sense. The teaching that he gives keeps us low, brings us down, and then we are well along on the road to dealing with these residual problems.

I put, secondly, the teaching that our Lord gives us concerning the greatness of God. You cannot consider man without this. I have already mentioned it in dealing with man, but the Scripture is full of it. This is what it says to us: God is in heaven, and you are upon earth. Be careful! Indeed, the answer to these residual problems is, in a sense, just the being of God. If we only knew more about God, we would talk much less, we would have fewer problems, we would be silenced.

It is terrible, is it not, how glibly we talk and argue about God. We have all done it. I remember years ago doing this for many, many hours, and there would be men smoking pipes and saying this and that about God and about predestination and election, lounging in chairs and getting up and laughing and joking about God! The mystery is that we are here at all, that he has not blotted us out of his sight for our arrogance. But he knows that we are ignorant; he understands our frame.

Let me put this to you as it is put in the Scriptures. The trouble with all our thinking, and especially our agitation over these particular problems, is that we are wrong at the beginning. It is our attitude that is wrong, and the moment our attitude is put right, all is well. This can be illustrated from other realms of life. We often read that in a debate in the House of Commons tempers were beginning to fray, and everybody was up in arms and shouting. Then somebody who was more of a statesman than a politician would get up and take the heat out of the discussion. That is always a great contribution to a discussion because when the heat rises you are no longer arguing about the original problem but are now dealing in personalities, and all sorts of issues have come in that have nothing to do with the primary question. And it is similar here. You must start with God and with man, and that takes the heat out.

That is what our Lord does. We see a good illustration at the end of the eleventh chapter of the Epistle to the Romans. The apostle Paul has been dealing with a great problem, an extremely difficult problem for Jews who had become Christians. The question is, how can the promises of God to Abraham be reconciled with the fact that the Jews are rejecting the gospel? And what Paul does—it is so typical of his method and of the whole method of our Lord through his servants—is to reason it out. He argues it out in detail in chapters 9, 10, and 11. But notice the conclusion at which he arrives:

> O the depth of the riches both of the wisdom and knowledge of God! how unsearchable are his judgments, and his ways past finding out! For who hath known the mind of the Lord? or who hath been his counsellor? or who hath first given to him, and it shall be recompensed unto him again? For of him, and through him, and to him, are all things: to whom be glory for ever. Amen. (Rom. 11:33–36)

Or take it as it is put in the Old Testament, in the book of the prophet Isaiah. It is the same argument exactly—it runs right through the Bible. We need to be put right, so we find this:

> For my thoughts are not your thoughts, neither are your ways my ways, saith the LORD. For as the heavens are higher than the earth, so are my ways higher than your ways, and my thoughts than your thoughts. (Isa. 55:8–9)

There it is! God is in heaven; we are on earth. "The LORD reigneth; let the people tremble . . . let the earth be moved" (Ps. 99:1). "No man hath seen God at any time; the only begotten Son, which is in the bosom of the Father, he hath declared him" (John 1:18).

This is how our Lord deals with these various questions and problems. But then he goes on; he does not leave us at that. Thank God, he gives and he gives abundantly, superabundantly, always. Take this question concerning heaven and heavenly things. People are often troubled and ask about heaven, will we know one another there? What happens? Is everyone in the same position? A thousand and one questions are raised. So how does our Lord deal with queries like this? Well, there is perfect satisfaction here. If you listen to what he tells you about these matters, you will soon stop raising your questions, for you will realize that here we are in a realm that is so transcendent and so glorious that it is entirely beyond our thoughts and, indeed, entirely beyond our imaginations.

People often say, "Here's the revelation that God has given us, but why is there so little about heaven?" They would like to know what it is like there, what we are to look forward to. Dear me, they should not be troubled; they should thank God that we are told so little. Do you know why? Heaven—the glory—is so wonderful that if our Lord had described it in our language and our categories, his words would have detracted from it. Our language is fallen; it is utterly inadequate. So the Bible gives us pictures; it gives us symbols. People often become obscurantist about these or literalize them and take a stand on them. That is not the way. These are pictures, representations. We are told that we only see now "through a glass, darkly" (1 Cor. 13:12); we see "as in a glass the glory of the Lord" (2 Cor. 3:18). We could not stand anything more. If you and I really saw heaven, we would be blinded; it might even kill us—we could not take it.

Toward the end of the third chapter of the Epistle to the Ephesians, Paul offers a prayer for the people, and it is always interesting to me to notice that the first prayer that he offers for them is this:

> That he would grant you, according to the riches of his glory, to be strengthened with might by his Spirit in the inner man; that Christ may

> dwell in your hearts by faith; that ye, being rooted and grounded in love, may be able to comprehend with all saints what is the breadth, and length, and depth, and height; and to know the love of Christ, which passeth knowledge. (Eph. 3:16–19)

It always fascinates me that in this prayer, Paul's first request is that we might be "strengthened with might by his Spirit in the inner man." Why is this? It is because if we were not, we would not be able to stand this knowledge—"the breadth, and length, and depth, and height." It would shatter us. We need to be strengthened by the Spirit in order to get just a glimmer of a knowledge of this glory.

Heaven is so amazing, it is so wonderful, it is so altogether different and utterly beyond us that we cannot understand it or have a detailed explanation. Oh, our vocabulary is inadequate, our terminology is not enough, our dictionaries are exhausted. It is an entirely different realm, and God in his grace conceals it, as it were, from us. He gives us glimpses "as through a glass, darkly"—a picture, a vision, a glimmer of understanding. That illustrates our Lord's whole approach to these questions.

As a result, we are bound to draw certain inevitable deductions, and, indeed, the Bible draws them for us. In the book of Deuteronomy, there is a specific statement that really is the answer to all our residual problems and questions. Remember it!

> The secret things belong unto the LORD our God: but those things which are revealed belong unto us and to our children for ever, that we may do all the words of this law. (Deut. 29:29)

There it is; there is the fundamental answer: "The *secret* things . . . those things which are revealed." The secret things all belong to God; the things that are revealed belong to God. Everything belongs to him, but he draws a distinction. There are things that he chooses to reveal to us, and there are things that he chooses not to reveal to us—and there is the complete answer.

"Why does he do this?" you say.

The answer is, because he is God.

Oh, how poor we are at judging our own and one another's competence. This is the great lesson that every preacher and teacher has to learn. The danger for a young preacher, of course, is to give strong meat to people who can barely take milk, while others go on giving milk to people who need strong meat. This is the whole question of the assessment of capacity. God knows what we can and cannot take, and he has drawn the ultimate division. You can come like foolish waves of the sea dashing themselves against a rock; you can ask your questions, but you will only be thrown back, and all you will have at the end is mud and mire and dirt and wreckage.

But let us work that out a little. Having started there, you can then understand, can you not, the argument of the apostle Paul in Romans 9. Paul puts forward his great argument about election, giving the example of Esau and Jacob. God had said, "Jacob have I loved, but Esau have I hated" (Rom. 9:13). Here were two children in the same womb together: "(For the children being not yet born, neither having done any good or evil, that the purpose of God according to election might stand, not of works, but of him that calleth;) it was said unto her, The elder shall serve the younger" (Rom. 9:11–12).

And Paul sums up his argument by saying, "Therefore"—in the light of all he has been quoting and saying—"hath he mercy on whom he will have mercy, and whom he will he hardeneth." And the apostle continues, "Thou wilt say then unto me . . ."—people had said this many times to the apostle. He did not need any imagination. They had been talking to him at the end of his sermons or his teaching sessions and saying, "Well, now, we don't understand this! If this is so, why that?"—"Why doth he [God] yet find fault? For who hath resisted his will?" (vv. 18–19).

How is this right? How can it be fair? That is one of the ultimate residual questions, is it not? And here is Paul's answer in verse 20: "Nay but, O man, who art thou that repliest against God?" In other words, your problem is not the problem of election, it is the problem of God!

So it is not your question that matters. What really is important at this point is that you, little pygmy, ignoramus as you are, you who do not even understand yourself, you think you can stand on your feet and say, "I want answers from God"! There is only one thing to say to you: if you persist like that, you will soon be destroyed.

> Nay but, O man, who art thou that repliest against God? Shall the thing formed say to him that formed it, Why hast thou made me thus? Hath not the potter power over the clay, of the same lump to make one vessel unto honour, and another unto dishonour? What if God, willing to shew his wrath . . . (vv. 20–22)

He is God! And that is not obscurantism; that is drawing a deduction from the being of God and the condition of man. That is the way to deal with these questions. Election is one of those "secret things" that we do not understand because obviously we are not meant to understand them. If we were meant to understand these secret things, God would have given us a revelation concerning them.

Now I want to bring this home. It is the test of the Christian, ultimately, that we not only believe there are "secret things" that belong only to God but that we accept this as inevitable. We must come as far as that. The moment we really look at all our residual problems and questions in light of the everlasting and eternal God and in the light of what we know to be so true about ourselves, we see that this truth follows of necessity. Then each of us says, "I should never have thought anything else. There are bound to be issues that I can't understand. My mind is warped; it's sinful. My ideas of loving are wrong; there's a bit of lust mixed up with them. I can't think straight. I have no idea of justice. God is God, and I am on earth! Oh, the ultimate mind and wisdom of God! I am not even going to try to understand—it would be foolish."

But we should not only recognize the inevitability of this teaching, it should be something in which we rejoice. We rejoice that God in his infinite love and kindness and compassion has been pleased even to reveal anything to us. We do not deserve anything. We have forfeited every claim upon him. To me, there is nothing more wonderful than that God as our loving Father has let us into some of his secrets. Look what he has given us; look at the revelation!

People have a problem and say, "I don't know the answer to that," but look at all *this*—have you taken all this in? Have you encompassed all he has given you, all he has revealed? The moment you look at it like that, you begin to understand poor old Job. Oh, no, he is no longer poor old Job, not at the end. You remember the story—there he is, poor fellow, suffering agonies, this terrible condition of his skin, and those foolish friends, supposed comforters, aggravating it all. But at last God deals with him. He has allowed Job to say so much, but at last God deals with him and manifests himself to him, and Job therefore ends like this:

> Then Job answered the LORD, and said, I know that thou canst do every thing, and that no thought can be withholden from thee. Who is he that hideth counsel without knowledge? therefore have I uttered that I understood not; things too wonderful for me, which I knew not. (Job 42:1–3)

Have you come to that, my friend? Job had very excellent reasons for speaking as he did in his agony. God, as it were, had handed him over for the time being to the devil to test him and to sift him. Look what he went through, but that is what he says. And he continues, "Hear, I beseech thee, and I will speak: I will demand of thee, and declare thou unto me." Then he says this:

> I have heard of thee by the hearing of the ear: but now mine eye seeth thee. Wherefore I abhor myself, and repent in dust and ashes. (Job 42:4–6)

If you have not come to that with all these residual problems and questions, you have not yet drunk as you should have of the water that he gives unto you, for the moment you drink it, this will be your experience, and thirsting will be at an end.

My dear friends, do you not realize that you are asking questions about things that even angels do not understand? Consider what Paul tells us in Ephesians 3. He is talking about God's great plan of salvation, and he says:

> . . . to make all men see what is the fellowship of the mystery, which from the beginning of the world hath been hid in God, who created all things by Jesus Christ: to the intent that now unto the principalities and powers in heavenly places might be known by [through] the church the manifold wisdom of God. (vv. 9–10)

Now the principalities and powers in heavenly places referred to there are not the evil powers, they are the good ones. These are the highest, most glorious angelic beings, who have always lived in the presence of God! But they need to be taught, they need understanding and wisdom, and God is revealing something new and fresh concerning his eternal wisdom to them through and by means of the church. And if they have not understood all this fully, who are you and I to try to understand!

Listen to Peter saying exactly the same thing:

> Of which salvation the prophets have inquired and searched diligently, who prophesied of the grace that should come unto you: searching what, or what manner of time the Spirit of Christ which was in them did signify, when it testified beforehand the sufferings of Christ, and the glory that should follow, unto whom it was revealed, that not unto themselves, but unto us they did minister the things, which are now reported unto you by them that have preached the gospel unto you with the Holy

> Ghost sent down from heaven [listen!]; which things the angels desire to look into. (1 Pet. 1:10–12)

The angels of God are looking into this great mystery of God's eternal purpose, God's everlasting wisdom, and they are amazed at it. And yet you and I are tempted arrogantly to ask, "I don't understand. If this, then why that?"

Here is your answer: "I will lay mine hand upon my mouth"; "I abhor myself, and repent in dust and ashes" (Job 40:4; 42:6). No, no; my dear friends, you must say:

My knowledge of that life is small,
The eye of faith is dim.

But here is the Christian answer:

But 'tis enough that Christ knows all,
And I shall be with him.

Richard Baxter ("Lord, It Belongs Not to My Care")

"We walk by faith, not by sight" (2 Cor. 5:7), and we are in his hand who knows all and will lead us through to the end. And so we make this kind of confession:

I cannot see the secret things
In this my dark abode;
I may not reach with earthly wings
The heights and depths of God.

So faith and patience! Wait awhile,
Not doubting, not in fear;
For soon in heaven my Father's smile
Shall render all things clear.

Then thou shalt end time's short eclipse,
Its dim uncertain night;
Bring in the grand apocalypse,
Reveal the perfect light.

"Then shall I know even as also I am [already] known" (1 Cor. 13:12)! Are you content with that? Thank God, I am content. I want no more.

Stronger his love than death or hell;
Its riches are unsearchable;
The firstborn sons of light
Desire in vain its depths to see;
They cannot reach the mystery,
The length, and breadth, and height.

CHARLES WESLEY ("O LOVE DIVINE, HOW SWEET THOU ART")

And if they cannot, who am I to seek for this knowledge that belongs to "the secret things of God"?

27

The Need for Emotional Satisfaction

Jesus answered and said unto her, Whosoever drinketh of this water shall thirst again: but whosoever drinketh of the water that I shall give him shall never thirst; but the water that I shall give him shall be in him a well of water springing up into everlasting life. (John 4:13–14)

The wonderful subject at which we are looking—and it is the great theme of the whole New Testament—is the fullness, the all-sufficiency, the never-failing character of Christian salvation, of the Christian life.

Today this is questioned. The vast majority of people regard Christianity as entirely outmoded, as ridiculous, finished, as no help at all, an anachronism in the modern world. So it is our business, for our own sake and for theirs, to show them how wrong and foolish they are, how they rob themselves of this amazing blessing that the Son of God came into the world to give us. We need to do this for our own sake because if we are not sure of it, if we are not experiencing it, we will be very poor witnesses, and after all, the gospel has always spread mainly by means of the personal witness of Christian believers. It does not matter what the preacher may be like; if his people do not commend what he is saying, his words will have very little effect.

So it is our duty not only to understand this fullness but to know and to experience it, and then others, seeing this in us, will be drawn to it. And never has the need of the world been greater than at the present time. Though in many ways we are living in discouraging days, these are also days of opportunity such as we have never seen before. As the bankruptcy of the world becomes more and more evident, so our opportunity becomes greater and greater.

But, my friends, the question is, do we realize this? Are we ready for it? Are we enabled, because of our understanding and experience, to take up this great challenge given by our Lord and Savior Jesus Christ? Now I do want to emphasize that. The trouble so often has been that Christian people come to the house of God only to receive—they just want satisfaction for themselves. That is all right, on the condition that you go beyond that. You ought to be right in order to be able to help and influence others round and about you. The world is full of trouble and problems and anxiety and pain, not only on the big scale, but also in the smaller spheres of life, and men and women do not know where to turn. Here is our opportunity. That is why it is our duty to examine this full satisfaction that our Lord gives.

So far we have shown how our Lord's claim is substantiated when you look at it from the standpoint of the intellect. We have seen that it applies to the realm of thought. I can look at it, as it were, objectively, and I can see there is a perfect system here. Moreover, it is the *only* perfect system. It is possible for intelligent men and women to see that. They can see it clearly with their minds; they can see the whole Christian position. But that does not of necessity guarantee that they are Christians. They must know that it is true for them. Inherent in each of us is the desire for Christianity to be true for me in particular.

Now this is inevitably the case because, after all, no one is mere intellect. That is the fallacy into which many fall. Some define man as a reasoning animal, and they emphasize only the intellect. It is as if man were some kind of marvelous intellectual machine, almost as if he could be made by means of computers. Now computers can do very wonderful things, but a computer can never feel, it can never register sensation or emotion. And we must realize that human beings are not mere intellects; they also have hearts. One of the greatest intellects the world has ever known, the famous Frenchman Blaise Pascal, made a wonderful statement about this. One of the most profound things he said, and he said many, is this: "The heart has its reasons which reason knows nothing of." Pascal had a gigantic intellect, but something deeper was crying out for satisfaction, a satisfaction that he could never arrive at merely with his mind, though it could soar to heights far beyond not only the average but also the greatest of people.

So because we have hearts as well as minds, because we have affections, feelings, sensibilities as well as intellectual capacity, it is not enough that our minds alone be satisfied. It is not enough for us to believe that God does forgive sin. What every one of us wants to know is, are *my* sins forgiven? Now there is a vital distinction there. We can see intellectually that God is ready to forgive sins. God is love, and we see what God has done. So we know that God does forgive sins; he is a pardoning God. But still there is that within us that cries out, "Has he forgiven my sin?"

I remember a man who was dying a very slow and agonizing death, which took many months. He was a Christian and a very able man, but he had not always responded to God as he should have. He had tended to indulge his own eccentricities and oddities. That can be quite interesting, and it can amuse people, and you can be regarded as a character, but when you come to your deathbed, when you are left alone, as it were, it can land you in trouble, and this man was unhappy. He put it in a phrase one day to a friend, who repeated it to me, and I have never forgotten it. He said, "I know the way of salvation. I know it up there." He pointed to his head. "I know it perfectly. I see it. I have preached about it." And he had, magnificently. "But what troubles me," he said, "is this." He pointed to his heart. "Has it been registered here?"

Now this is true for all of us. Take some words that I read recently about Martin Luther: "That Christianity is a matter of relationship rather than a matter of assent to truth seemed basic to Luther." This is a most important statement. This year [1967] we are celebrating the 450th anniversary of the famous occasion when Luther nailed his Ninety-five Theses to the door of the church, and it is right that we should commemorate that. But let us make use of this historic fact to remind ourselves of what really was the essence, the central point, of the Protestant Reformation. In a sense, it is all in that phrase that I have just quoted.

The Roman Catholic Church had been teaching that what makes someone a Christian is assent to the dogma of the Roman Catholic Church. But Luther had become unhappy about this; it no longer satisfied him. There was a desire within him to know that he could stand before a holy, righteous God. The word that dominated the thinking of the young Luther was the word "righteousness"—"the righteousness of God." This was what terrified him and caused him to pass through a long agony of soul. How could he stand before the righteous God? It seemed impossible.

Luther became a monk and fasted and sweated and prayed, but he was still no nearer finding an answer; indeed, he was further away. All that he did simply gave him a greater conception of God, and as this quotation puts it, he knew that what really mattered was his personal standing before God. Salvation is a matter of personal relationship, not a matter of accepting a body of truth or dogma; ultimately it comes to that. And that is what accounted for Luther's long agony, his painful struggle. He wanted this knowledge, this inner satisfaction; he wanted to know that his sins were forgiven, that he could have a righteousness that would be acceptable in the presence of God. And one day he did receive this assurance. And that is what really led to the Protestant Reformation. It came out of the experience of Martin Luther. This assurance was what set him on fire and led to all the events that followed. Luther was only one of a number of people, but his experience is one of the most striking in the whole history of the Christian church.

And in a measure all of us have this desire for certainty, this desire for safety, for peace, and for rest. We must of necessity face the fact that there is an affective side to our natures that cries out for satisfaction. So if there is not an experiential side to the Christian faith, it has failed us; and if our Lord's great statement in John 4 does not include this, it is not comprehensive and is not satisfactory. Therefore we must consider and see whether the Lord Jesus Christ himself and what he gives does satisfy the heart as well as the mind and the understanding.

Now in moving from the realm of the understanding to the realm of the heart, we are doing something that in one way is difficult, indeed very difficult. The problem is in recognizing the limits and seeing where one ends and the other begins. This is because one shades into the other, and one influences the other. The heart and the understanding are, of course, intimately interrelated. Nevertheless, it is very important that we should differentiate between them. Not that we can make absolute divisions and distinctions, but, for the sake of clarity of thought and of understanding, it is helpful and essential to draw some lines and hold them in our minds.

There is clear teaching in the Scripture that our Lord can and does deal directly with the heart, the affections, the feelings, as well as with the mind. The normal manner is to deal with the mind and through that the heart, but—and again you see this in the history of the church and some of her great people—you will find that sometimes the heart is dealt with first, and the understanding follows. That is exceptional, but it does happen.

And that leads us to this great question of the place of feeling and of emotion in our lives and especially in our Christian lives. I want to introduce this subject now because I think it is one of the greatest causes of confusion at the present time. Some people make too much of feeling and of sensation—everything that we put together under the general heading of *the heart*. Many live on their emotions and evaluate everything solely in terms of how they feel. They do not look at things objectively; they do not apply external measures of judgment. They just respond instinctually, intuitively; they are living, as it were, on a primitive level. This can have many causes. It can be due to sheer lack of intelligence. The younger we are, the more we live in the realm of feelings and instincts, of likes and dislikes, without applying much reason. This gradually changes as we get older, but if people are lacking in intelligence, they will tend to remain on this level. Experience teaches us that the less attention people give to training and developing their minds, the more they live in the realm of the emotions and feelings. That is one cause.

Another cause may be laziness. Some people live entirely on the emotional level simply because they are lazy. They do not like to use their minds; they do not like to think. This is very common, particularly in the realm of religion. This is astounding, and this is why I started with the intellect. Some people object to having to think in connection with their religion. All they want is something that gives them a nice feeling. That is the explanation of much sacramentalism and a good deal of the ceremonial and the visual that is found in many churches. There is the desire not to think but just to feel, to register sensations.

And this, I believe, is a charge that can be brought against this generation, speaking very generally. People do not like to read books as they used to; they do not like to read solid books, big books. Publishers tell me they are having increasing difficulty in selling books, though they can sell booklets and pamphlets with comparative ease. People like everything short, snappy, tabloid. This is one of the characteristics of the age in which we are living. Let me be clear about this—this is sheer laziness. It would be wrong to try to excuse it in any way whatsoever. Shame on us that we who have such opportunities are not reading as our forefathers did. Very often they could not afford to buy books; nevertheless they would save out of their meager wages in order to buy a book that would help them understand the Bible and know God.

But there is another cause that is quite common at the present time, and this is perhaps the most serious. There is a kind of modern thinking, one type of modern philosophy, that can be called anti-intellectualist. And the extraordinary thing about it, and the amusing thing in a sense, is that it is the intellectuals who teach it. Take a man such as D. H. Lawrence. He said that the whole trouble with man was that he thought too much and used his brains too much, and he must sink back to the animal level and go back to nature.

It is said that the big mistake we have made in this [twentieth] century is the attempt to think and to reason and to plan. Man is, after all, nothing but a bundle of sensations, a reaction—I must not waste your time over this, and yet it is important because it comes into the religious realm. This is true of so much modern poetry, is it not? It is no use trying to look for meaning or sense. You are not supposed to do that—it is the sound that matters, and the sound of the words is meant to do something to you. Do not ask for meaning; meaning is taboo. Do not ask for understanding. No; you react, you have a feeling, a sensation. That is said to be poetry.

So, for the reasons I have given, many, in varying degrees, make too much of feeling and exclude the intellect. But now I must consider the exact opposite attitude—making too little of feeling. In our realm this is perhaps the more important and the more common of the two. The greatest problem of all confronting evangelicals may be this particular wrong attitude toward the heart and feelings in connection with our Christian faith.

Now I am sure that part of the present reaction against the place of feeling and emotion in Christianity is due to a reaction, and though it has gone too far, I would regard it as a healthy reaction against the sheer sentimentalism, the maudlin sentimentality, of the late Victorian and the Edwardian periods. There is also a further reason for the reaction against feelings, and one that I do not think is surprising in this generation. You always tend to get this when people's feelings and sensibilities have been subjected to terrible assaults. We have lived in a century in which there have been two dreadful world wars, and there has also been the strain that we have been subjected to between these wars and after the second war.

The result of all this is that we are now in an age that more or less despises feelings, so that we have reached a point where the feelings are almost entirely excluded. Have you noticed a new word that has gained a good deal of currency in the last few years? This is interesting and revealing—it is the word *clinical*. When using that word people mean detached, objective, not involved, like a surgeon performing an operation; they mean, aseptic, perfect, mechanical. This is, incidentally, not a good use of the word *clinical*, but it is the word that is being used. This attitude is apparent in many areas—literature, novels, drama—and people are glorying in it.

Where does this come from? I have suggested that it is partly a reaction against the Victorians and also that it is a consequence of the terrible assaults that have been made upon us in this century. But it goes back even further—it is interesting to notice the elements that come into it. The man who, in a sense, started it all and made this approach to life fashionable was Thomas Arnold, the great headmaster of Rugby School, and he is still its greatest exponent. Arnold defined the perfect gentleman as a man who did not show his feelings. Primitive people show how they feel; the gentleman never reveals his feelings at all, no matter what happens. Of course, Thomas Arnold had a great illustration at hand in the Duke of Wellington, with the stories of his calm, cool indifference in battle. So this came in as a kind of philosophy.

Much more important is the view that we must define as Stoicism. It is much older, and there is much more to be said for it. Stoicism was a philosophy that was current at the time of our Lord and the apostle Paul. We read about Paul going to Athens and encountering "certain philosophers of the Epicureans, and of the Stoicks" (Acts 17:18). Stoicism was a teaching that said something like this: This is a hard, difficult, and trying world, a world that makes assaults upon us—illness, accident, disappointment, the treachery of friends, death. If you want to go through life successfully, you must face all this, but first you must put a curb on your feelings. If you allow your feelings to control you, you will be defeated because one day you will be on top of the mountain and the next day you will be down in the depth of a bog. If you do not want to suffer, if you do not want to be hurt, be balanced, be controlled and disciplined. Guard your feelings, hold them in check, keep a firm control over them with your will. Do not let things elate you too much because if you do, you will soon be disappointed; but on the other hand, do not let things get you down too much—they are never as bad as they appear to be. Hold to a middle position, a mean, a balance. That was the philosophy of the Stoics, and notice that the motive behind it was to protect yourself from being hurt.

Now it is interesting to notice that there has been a marked recrudescence of Stoicism in this century. That very able man Bertrand Russell actually says in his autobiography that when he was quite young he came to the decision that he was going to protect himself against his own feelings because otherwise he could see what would happen. He says that he did this quite deliberately; he would not allow himself to be too happy, nor would he allow himself to be too miserable. So he developed a detachment, what some would call "a scientific attitude." It is not, but that is what they call it. That is nothing but sheer Stoicism. The point is that you are protecting yourself against your feelings because you know they will be assaulted in different ways, and you will suffer and be unhappy. The only way to prevent that is by suppressing your feelings. This philosophy is inculcated by people like Thomas Arnold and others who say that if you do show your feelings you are a fool, you will be laughed at. So you hold them down, put a band of steel about them, harden yourself. Whatever happens, you will not allow yourself to feel.

Now this is all wrong, obviously, because we must not crucify parts of our being in this way. We are all meant to express all aspects of ourselves. We are all meant to live a full life, and any teaching that denies that is going against our essential nature. When we come to the realm of the Christian faith, this view becomes still more serious, and I repeat, I think it is one of our major problems. I remember a man coming to me who was delighted about a certain evangelistic campaign. "Have you been?" he asked, and when I replied, "No, not yet," he said, "It's marvelous. Crowds of people go forward. No emotion, you know. No emotion. They all just went forward." And he thought this was perfection—no emotion. People converted to God, people convicted of sin by the Holy Spirit, people regenerated, and "no emotion"!

And that is the position, I think, at which we have arrived. But when we read the accounts of the early church and the church throughout the centuries, we find a great deal about people weeping and glorying; we read about ecstasy. Why do we not see this today? Because we are living in an age when this worldly philosophy has been influencing the church. Everything has to be detached; it all has to be clinical; it all has to be kept at a distance, as it were.

Let me put it like this. How can the world help us with respect to this denial of the feelings? And the simple answer is that it cannot help us at all. "Whosoever drinketh of this water shall thirst again"—and if that is not clear to you, you must be completely blind. The most dangerous and the most obvious and evident aspect of the modern world is its failure to help people in their hearts, in their feelings, in their sensibilities. Even at its best the world has only been able to give temporary and incomplete satisfaction. It is all on the surface. I think this is alarmingly clear today.

Have you noticed the confusion in modern life, the blank contradiction in the modern outlook? On the one hand, there is the intellectualism that I have already been describing, the disdaining of the feelings, this clinical approach, and on the other hand, the pleasure mania, the constant craving for and living upon entertainment. Never has the desire for pleasure been more evident than at the present time. As I have said, people are reading less. Why? Partly because they are being entertained more. They not only crave pleasure and entertainment, they are indulging in it.

But still more than the pleasure mania, there is what can be described as sheer emotionalism. By that, I mean a kind of riot of the emotions, a working up of the emotions and a rejoicing in them. Where does this show itself? Surely, that was the main explanation of Hitlerism. Hitlerism was nothing but a riot of emotions. The shouting and the raving when Hitler appeared on the public platform was quite genuine. The people felt that. But it had been worked up in various ways. There it was in Germany, a country famous for philosophy and for the intellect and for science. These were basic contradictions. What had happened? I think those people had been repressed in the realm of their feelings. But the emotions were there, and at last they found an outlet and burst through all the barriers like a veritable flood.

Today we are far short of something extreme and political like Hitlerism, but it is still very interesting that some of the most highly sophisticated people seem to enjoy most of all the most primitive kind of music. Have you noticed this? Two types of music are popular today—clinical, intellectual, clever, mechanical music that has no melody at all but is very clever technically and, on the other hand, primitive music. People say they like both. I am not surprised. Something within them cries out for both. But what is interesting is that people are going back to the most primitive kind of music and even further back, to that which is merely elemental. This is also happening, I understand, in dancing. But perhaps the most pathetic indication and example of this at the present time is the way in which these poor, modern, young adolescents indulge in frenzies of screaming. It is their response to a certain type of music and entertainment and to certain persons.

But what is the explanation? That is what I am concerned about. I am not mentioning these things because I want to denounce them. I am sorry for people who manifest such emotions because I think the explanation is that it is all due to a lack of emotional satisfaction. There is that in human nature that cries out for emotional satisfaction, and these primitive patterns of behavior are outlets for the cry in the heart for some satisfaction that the world cannot give. And people think, "At any rate, I can express my feelings."

And have you noticed the increase in violence? People like their novels to be violent; they like violence on their television screens. It is the same craving for something that is deeper than the mind, and the world is not giving it, so they get it in this way—violence! Note too the shouting at soccer matches—the cause is the same. This is the outlet for emotions that have been held back by a false philosophy.

And it is still worse, of course, when we come to the realm of not only alcohol but also drugs. It is no use just getting irritated and annoyed and condemning these practices. If we are Christian people, we should be concerned about those who are indulging in drink and drug-taking, and we should be asking, why are they doing it? What are they after? There is only one answer: they want what they call kicks, emotional satisfaction. What is offered in the realm of intellect and of thought does not give this satisfaction, and the materialism that is so popular, the adulation of money, does not satisfy either. You have to knock out your brain so that your lower centers, as they are called, can manifest themselves. And it is all caused, I say again, by a craving for a satisfaction for the heart and for the feelings.

And on top of that some even turn to a new moral teaching that denies all morals and says, "Don't listen to all that Victorian nonsense. Let yourself go, do what you feel like doing, get satisfaction—that is the only thing that matters in a world like this." It is called the new morality, and it is sometimes even preached in the name of Christianity.

So there is a modern manifestation of this cry for satisfaction, but you can see what a subject it is, and how important it is for us all. I can sum it all up in the case of one person, who I think put this for us perfectly. I refer to the late Aldous Huxley. Here was a dazzling intellect. In the twenties he said that nothing matters but intellect. So he wrote his brilliant books in which he said that science must be the answer to everything, thought was the solution—education and knowledge. He was the high priest of this way of thinking, the most brilliant of all. But in the latter years of his life this man underwent a complete change. He began to write about mysticism, and he actually said, "The only hope of the world is mysticism," and he became a Buddhist.

But why did this happen to Huxley? It happened for the reasons I have been giving you. He saw that the intellect, however brilliant, was not enough, that there was something deeper, a heart crying out for satisfaction. He could not find it in all the intellectualism of the age in which he had been brought up, and he felt that he had found it in mysticism. Now the form of mysticism that he adopted was one that virtually tells you to stop thinking; you just abandon yourself, hoping that ultimately you will be absorbed into the Absolute. This is nothing but an interesting confession of the complete bankruptcy of the world.

"Whosoever drinketh of this water shall thirst again," and all that the modern world offers to people who are craving for some satisfaction in their hearts simply aggravates the problem. A drug will give satisfaction to you for the time being; under the influence of the drug you feel marvelous, you feel you are in paradise. But then the effect of the drug wears off, and you are in a worse position. You feel horrible; you are in hell. So you have to get more, and you increase the dose. It is the same with drink, the same with pleasure, the same with everything that the world has to give us; they make the problem worse and create fresh problems.

And this is where you and I come in. We have the answer for the world. Can we tell people in the world that there is full satisfaction without drugs, without drink, without all this anti-intellectualism, and yet without all this cutting out of the heart, without turning people into mere intellectual machines, without this dry, unmoving, clinical attitude toward life? That is the test for us. "Whosoever drinketh of the water that I shall give him shall never thirst; but the water that I shall give him shall be in him a well of water springing up into everlasting life." Oh, thank God, it is perfectly true.

Thou, O Christ, art all I want;
More than all in thee I find.

Charles Wesley

28

Moved by the Truth

Jesus answered and said unto her, Whosoever drinketh of this water shall thirst again: but whosoever drinketh of the water that I shall give him shall never thirst; but the water that I shall give him shall be in him a well of water springing up into everlasting life. (John 4:13–14)

We have seen that the gospel gives us entire intellectual satisfaction in a way that nothing else in the world can, and now we have moved on to consider the second aspect of the satisfaction that it gives, and that is the satisfaction that is offered to the heart, to the sensitivities, to the feelings. We have introduced the subject, and I felt it was essential that we should demonstrate its importance, especially for us as Christian people. The world today is perhaps less capable than ever of dealing with the feeling side of our makeup as human beings, and it is most important that we should emphasize our Lord's claim that he can give complete emotional satisfaction. One of the most wonderful and glorious aspects of this gospel is the way in which it deals with the whole personality. Everything else is partial; everything else deals with us in bits and portions.

We can put this in terms of balance. The extraordinary balance of the Scriptures is always to me both remarkable and fascinating. We are all so unbalanced. We are creatures of extremes; we swing violently from one side to another. The most obvious example of that in this [twentieth] century is the attitude of people toward Winston Churchill—vilified for so many years before the Second World War, regarded as a dangerous man and a warmonger, but after the war and up to the present time regarded almost as a superhuman being, almost a god.

We can also look at this balance in another way. By nature, people are constantly posing and taking up positions. But Christians never do that because they have a fundamental balance, a wholeness. Another way of putting it is to say that Christians never follow fashions; everybody else does, in every respect. Fashions and changes in fashion are not confined to clothing; they are quite as amusing in the realm of the intellect. As one looks back across life it is really funny to remember the crazes, the movements and emphases, the excitements that are now long since forgotten, with people under the age of thirty knowing nothing about them. This is, of course, an expression of a lack of satisfaction. We have already considered the way in which people are always looking for something that will really give them the satisfaction for which they long. There is a new craze, and they think they have found the answer. They are all out for it. "Ah, here it is," they say, and off they go. And then you find them doing perhaps the exact opposite at some later period. Civilization has been like this for many, many centuries and yet is as far away from final satisfaction as it has ever been.

But those who conform to the New Testament pattern never follow fashion; they never get excited about some new emphasis or teaching. That is always a characteristic of an unstable person. It shows there is a lack somewhere, an imbalance. It is always the mark of those who have never drawn deeply of this water that the Lord Jesus Christ offers us, this "eternal life" that he gives us and that satisfies the whole of the personality.

This is, therefore, a most important matter because we are meant to enjoy full satisfaction, and it is only as we do that we shall be able to help others. If we are the victims of crazes and fashions and changes, we shall not be able to give any help; but if people see that we are always balanced and equable, always in a position of poise, then they know they can safely talk to us and consult us and bring their problems and their questions to us. So the question to which we must address ourselves now is this: how does our Lord himself and his teaching deal with us in this matter of the emotions? What is the place of emotion in the Christian life? It is fascinating to trace this issue in the history of the church and to see how the church has always fallen into error through going to one extreme or another.

The first thing we must realize is that a mere assent to the truth or an adoption of certain principles and teachings does not make us Christians. People sometimes imagine that to agree to certain doctrines and then to show great keenness in connection with them makes them Christians. But it does not. That is, after all, one of the great differences between the cults and the Christian faith. The devotees of the cults take up their teaching, and we are aware of their keenness and their zeal. But that is, in a sense, where they betray themselves; they live on this enthusiasm. They have taken up a teaching, it is a limited one, they learn it parrot fashion and repeat it like parrots, and they keep themselves going with this artificial keenness and persuade themselves that they are happy. But if you examine them carefully, you notice that the whole time there is a fundamental lack of rest and ease and poise because it is the enthusiasm that keeps them going, and the moment they stop, they seem to have nothing. Now that is different from the Christian position.

Or let me put it to you like this. There is a grave danger of our confusing the true Christian position with what I would call believism plus sentimentality. You find people who have gone through some form of belief; they have heard a message, and they are told that if they believe this and accept it, then all will be well. So they have believed, but they have not felt anything at all. They think they should have felt something, but they have not. So what they do now is add sentimentality to this mechanical believism. This is something they produce themselves, or others produce, in order to meet the innate desire for some satisfaction in the realm of emotion. What they believed has not moved them, so something is manufactured.

There are many ways in which sentimentality can be produced. Sometimes the preacher or the evangelist does it by telling stories. They are very affecting stories, and because people find themselves weeping as they listen, they are satisfied. But the tragedy of that position is that what has made them weep is not the truth but the story. Or maybe a religious novel, so-called, or a moving account of a true incident in the life of a missionary produces a sentimental feeling. Again, as long as they can respond to this stimulus, they are satisfied.

Music is also used, and this is increasingly the tendency at the present time. The sentimentality of singing or the playing of a fiddle is added on. It is not great music, it is a sentimental type of music, and it gives a pleasurable feeling. And because it is performed in connection with a religious service or by Christians, people imagine and persuade themselves that they are feeling the truth. But they are not. This feeling has no direct connection with what they have believed.

All I am trying to show you is that this is not our Lord's method; it is not the way of the New Testament. Feeling is not something that is added on to the truth, something that has to come as a kind of supplement to the truth. Or to put it another way, we must be very careful to differentiate between emotionalism and the satisfaction that our Lord gives to the heart. Now here is another important distinction. How do you differentiate between a true emotion and emotionalism?

First of all, the essential trouble with emotionalism is always that emotion is regarded as an end in and of itself. People want the emotion; their whole attention is placed on that to the exclusion of everything else. Because they make that initial error of isolating the emotions, the feelings, the heart, and because they concentrate entirely upon this and regard it as supreme, they have to adopt various ways and methods of producing what they regard as emotion. So they deliberately work it up; they have to create it, manufacture it, and stimulate it. And they do so by making a direct assault upon the feelings.

Now I am not questioning the sincerity and honesty of such people. I am not querying their motives. I am simply putting what they do and what they believe over and against the teaching of our Lord himself and the teaching of the whole New Testament. They make a direct attack upon the feelings, and they generally do so by ignoring every other aspect of the personality for the time being. You are familiar with the many ways in which this is done.

Again, music is one of the methods most ready to hand, among the most primitive peoples and extending right along the line. Music does appeal primarily to the emotions. I am not saying there is no intellectual content in great music. There is. But there is a type of music that has no intellectual content whatsoever and is simply a direct assault upon the feelings. If you start clapping your hands or stamping your feet or moving them in a rhythmic manner, you are the whole time dealing with this realm of the emotions. And there is a great deal of that today.

Some even deliberately employ psychological methods—different colored lights, for instance—to prey upon the emotions. Perhaps the most subtle attack upon the Christian faith at the present time comes from psychologists, and I am trying to show that very often good Christian people, in their ignorance of these matters, are simply playing directly into the hands of those who attack the Christian faith in terms of psychology. This is because Christians have never understood the place of emotion in the life of the Christian and have substituted either a kind of flabby sentimentality or a more active and vigorous emotionalism.

Essentially emotionalism is emotion without any intellectual content. People deliberately abandon themselves. You will sometimes even see them leaning back and making an effort to "let themselves go," as they say, and they are encouraged to do so. A teaching today even says that the intellect is a danger and a hindrance and you must avoid it. That is a terrible thing to say, and, of course, it is an entire contradiction of the whole teaching of the New Testament. And it all rises because of this desire for feeling.

True emotion always results from truth. It is kindled by truth; it is produced by it. That is always the order in the New Testament. As our Lord puts it to the woman of Samaria, "If thou *knewest* . . ." It is because you do not know, it is because you do not understand, that you are as you are. This is the New Testament way. But with the other approach, a direct appeal is made to the emotions. And the subtlety of the devil comes in here. Because people are in a chapel or a church or a religious meeting, it is assumed that the feelings are the result of the truth. But they are not necessarily, and here, therefore, is a vital test that we must always apply: What is it that is moving me? Am I being moved by the truth, or am I just being moved by one of these agencies, such as lilting music or an affecting story?

A second and definitive test is that with emotionalism there is always an element of loss of control. Because it is divorced from the intellect and the mind and the understanding and the truth, emotionalism always has an element of excess. It is a form of intoxication similar to being under the influence of alcohol or a drug. The higher discriminating centers are eliminated, and so the more primitive and instinctual element comes to the surface. There are numerous examples in history of innocent and good Christian people who have gone into excess and brought the gospel into disrepute because they had not differentiated between a true emotion and emotionalism.

Another good test is this: emotionalism is always exhausting. It is bound to be because the mind and the will have not been affected but only the emotions. Emotionalism plays on one aspect of the personality and overdoes that. The result is that, as with artificial stimulants such as drugs and alcohol and so on, when the temporary stimulus has been removed and its influence has passed off, the person is in a state of exhaustion. Now that is a complete contrast with what we find described everywhere in the New Testament. Here you get true emotion, and true emotion, I repeat, is always the result of truth, great truth coming to the mind and coming with such clarity that the heart is moved and stimulated. And because it involves the mind and also the will, as well as the emotions of the heart, the whole person is involved. And because of that, true emotion is always invigorating, it is always stimulating.

The next test is this, therefore: emotion always leads to action. This is one of the basic distinctions between true emotion and emotionalism. Because there is no element of truth or of understanding in what they are feeling, the poor victims of emotionalism are often left not only exhausted but also with a failure in the realm of the will. So certain sins creep in, sins that always find their opportunity when the intellect is out of action and when the feelings are roused; and in this way the gospel is again brought into disrepute. But true emotion always moves and affects the will. It is deep, energizing, invigorating, and it moves the total personality. And so one desires with the whole of one's being to live to the glory of God.

Now this explanation, unfortunately, was essential. I did not want to give it, but I had to because the counterfeit is the greatest danger of all. I am simply trying to say that if I were asked to identify in a few words the greatest lack in the Christian church at the present time, I would say that it is our lack of real New Testament emotion. In contradistinction to these counterfeits that I have been describing, our Lord is talking about something that affects the whole person—the heart as well as the head. Indeed, I go as far as to say that unless our hearts as well as our heads are affected by the truth that we have believed, there is something wrong even with our belief and with our Christian position. Believism plus sentimentality does not make a Christian. Believism plus an ecstatic emotionalism does not constitute Christianity. There is no plus in Christianity. It is all one; it is all part and parcel of the same thing; you cannot make distinctions—they are artificial.

So do we agree that the heart is involved? Is it our own experience that our hearts are involved? This is a fundamental test of our whole position as Christians. The Bible is full of this. It gives great place to the heart, to the emotional side of our natures. The psalmists are very fond of expressing this. Psalm 4 puts it very well: "Thou hast put gladness in my heart, more than in the time that their corn and their wine increased" (v. 7). Of course, farmers were always very happy when they had a good harvest. When they had garnered in their corn and good crops of grapes and wine had been produced, they had a great feast. Harvest was the outstanding occasion in the life of the Jew as a farmer. Yet the psalmist says that the Lord has given him a joy and happiness that entirely exceeds all the happiness he has ever known as a farmer or as a man of the world.

We find this same rejoicing in many other psalms. One of the greatest examples, perhaps, is Psalm 107:

> O give thanks unto the LORD, for he is good: for his mercy endureth for ever. Let the redeemed of the LORD say so, whom he hath redeemed from the hand of the enemy; and gathered them out of the lands, from the east, and from the west, from the north, and from the south. . . . Oh that men would praise the LORD for his goodness, and for his wonderful works to the children of men! (vv. 1–3, 8)

Now that is typical of Psalms. The book of Psalms, remember, is a book of songs. The people sang the psalms, giving expression to the moving of their hearts, to their feelings. This is the great characteristic of the child of God, even under the Old Testament dispensation. This is yet more clear when we come to the New Testament. Why is the world as it is? Why is the church as she is today? Why does she count for so little? I have no hesitation in answering that question: it is because we are so unlike the first Christians. Look at the early church. There were only a handful of people, and unimportant people at that. They had no great learning, they had no great names, they had no wealth, they had nothing to recommend them—everything apparently was against them. And yet they shook that ancient world; they shook it to its foundations. This despised sect of the Nazarenes, these little Christians, became a dominant power in the life of the ancient world. Amid Greek philosophy and a world controlled by the power of Roman law, this power became dominating, mastering, and conquering. How did they do it? What was the secret?

Now there is no question about the answer; everybody is agreed. Even secular, anti-Christian historians agree that Christians conquered the world by their sheer joyfulness; that this was their great characteristic. They began like that. On the Day of Pentecost, after Peter had preached to the people of Jerusalem, they were deeply convicted.

> They were pricked in their heart, and said unto Peter and to the rest of the apostles, Men and brethren, what shall we do? Then Peter said unto them, Repent, and be baptized every one of you in the name of Jesus Christ for the remission of sins, and ye shall receive the gift of the Holy Ghost. . . . Then they that gladly received his word were baptized: and the same day there were added unto them about three thousand souls.

What sort of people were they? We are given a description of them. The first thing we are told is this: "And they continued stedfastly in the apostles' doctrine and fellowship, and in breaking of bread, and in prayers."

But listen to this:

> And they, continuing daily with one accord in the temple, and breaking bread from house to house, did eat their meat with gladness and singleness of heart, praising God, and having favour with all the people. (Acts 2:37–38, 41–42, 46–47)

Now that is the Christian, and that is the Christian church—gladness, singleness of heart, praising God! This is what characterized the early church and made it irresistible in that ancient world; they were a rejoicing and a praising people. I could give you endless examples. Let me give you one from the end of the fifth chapter of Acts. All the apostles had been arrested, and they were on trial, not for the first time. The members of the Sanhedrin, we are told, were cut to the heart and took counsel to slay them. The apostles would undoubtedly have been murdered there and then had it not been for a man named Gamaliel. It was a near thing; they were face to face with death. But they were told not to preach about Jesus and were released. Then this is what we read about them:

> And they departed from the presence of the council, rejoicing that they were counted worthy to suffer shame for his name. And daily in the temple, and in every house, they ceased not to teach and preach Jesus Christ. (Acts 5:41–42)

"Rejoicing"! Going on with the thing they had been prohibited from doing, something irresistible was driving them, filling them with this spirit of rejoicing. This is always the characteristic of New Testament men and women.

Another example is the eunuch whom Philip met, the eunuch from Ethiopia who had just been baptized. We read:

> And when they were come up out of the water, the Spirit of the Lord caught away Philip, that the eunuch saw him no more: and he went on his way rejoicing. (Acts 8:39)

We find it also in the Philippian jailer. This man had been on the verge of committing suicide and then he believed, and we are told:

> And he took them the same hour of the night, and washed their stripes; and was baptized, he and all his, straightway. And when he had brought

> them into his house, he set meat before them, and rejoiced, believing in God with all his house. (Acts 16:33–34)

You see, this joy is universal; it is the great characteristic.

Just before the Philippian jailer believed and was baptized, something astounding occurred. Paul and his traveling companion Silas had been arrested very wrongly, they had been scourged, their poor backs had been beaten with rods—an agonizing experience—and they had been thrown into the innermost prison with their feet put fast in the stocks. Everything was against them. But "at midnight Paul and Silas prayed, and sang praises unto God: and the prisoners heard them" (Acts 16:25). Singing in a prison! It had never been heard of before. Prisoners do not sing at midnight. And the other prisoners were there listening—what is this? What are these men? They are full of joy, praising God. They are singing, with their feet in the stocks, with agonizing backs, at midnight. "Paul and Silas prayed, and sang praises unto God."

That is Christianity, my friends, and I am suggesting to you that it is the absence of this joy that constitutes our essential problem. You see, this was not a concert that had been prepared in prison. It was spontaneous, nothing artificial, nothing manufactured, nothing organized. It was the spontaneous welling up of that which is within. The truth had captured them, moving them, so that whatever their circumstances they praised God and sang praises unto him.

Profound emotion is the whole characteristic of the New Testament. Again look at it in the case of the apostle Paul. When he met the Ephesians at Miletus, Paul reminded them of how he had conducted himself among them. He says: "Ye know, from the first day that I came into Asia, after what manner I have been with you at all seasons, serving the Lord with all humility of mind, and with many tears"—"with many tears"!—"and temptations, which befell me by the lying in wait of the Jews" (Acts 20:18–19).

Let me put it to you like this. Can you read any of Paul's epistles without feeling the tremendous emotion that is in them? Paul is interesting from every standpoint, but I am referring now to the very style of the epistles and not the content. Of course, at once you are aware of a giant mind, you are aware of a master thinker, a man who can organize his teaching, his truth; it is the sheer mastery that strikes you. But you do not stop at that; you immediately become aware of this other element, this emotion—the way that he is obviously moved and is having, as it were, to hold himself back. In addition to the reasoning and the logic, you see the emotion that comes surging through it all. The result is that in the epistles of the apostle Paul are some of the most eloquent and moving passages you will find in any literature whatsoever. Read Romans 8 again. Do you not feel the passion, the emotion, how he is thrilled with the subject about which he is writing?

And there are other examples. Take the fourth chapter of 2 Corinthians, where the apostle rises to a tremendous climax. He has been giving an account of his troubles and he says:

> We are troubled on every side, yet not distressed; we are perplexed, but not in despair; persecuted, but not forsaken; cast down, but not destroyed; always bearing about in the body the dying of the Lord Jesus [and on he goes. Then comes the climax]. . . . For our light affliction, which is but for a moment [that is not only reason. It is reason, but there is more than reason. He is ridiculing the affliction, he is standing up, he is rejoicing], worketh for us a far more exceeding and eternal weight of glory.

Language fails him there. He is moved; he is carried away; he is up in the heavens, as it were. Somebody has translated the words "far more exceeding" as "exceeding, exceeding abundant." Language is inadequate. Paul is on the crest of a mighty emotion. Not emotionalism, not something worked up by some kind of trickery or organization or preparation. No, no; it is the sheer glory of the truth.

> . . . while we look not at the things which are seen, but at the things which are not seen: for the things which are seen are temporal; but the things which are not seen are eternal. (2 Cor. 4:8–10, 17–18)

Or take Paul at the end of the third chapter of the Epistle to the Ephesians. He is praying for the Ephesians. What is he praying for? He says:

> That ye, being rooted and grounded in love, may be able to comprehend with all saints what is the breadth, and length, and depth, and height; and to know the love of Christ, which passeth knowledge, that ye might be filled with all the fulness of God. Now unto him that is able to do exceeding abundantly above all that we ask or think . . . (vv. 17–20)

This is mighty, majestic, true Christian emotion. It is the truth that moves the apostle and makes him write in this magnificent and glorious manner. And there are other examples that I could give you.

But this is not only a matter of Paul's style—he teaches it explicitly. This is something that he cannot avoid saying because it is so much a part of the truth and so much a part of his own experience. Take the first four chapters of the Epistle to the Romans—what tremendous reasoning; what a demonstration of logic! Paul is out to prove that the Jews are as guilty as the Gentiles: "For all have sinned, and come short of the glory of God" (Rom. 3:23). In chapter 4 he takes up the case of Abraham and works that out. The reasoning is subtle: where does circumcision come in? Where was the Law? And on and on he goes until he finishes at the beginning of chapter 5:

> Therefore being justified by faith, we have peace with God through our Lord Jesus Christ: by whom also we have access by faith into this grace wherein we stand, and rejoice in hope of the glory of God.

That is it! But Paul cannot stop at that; he is carried away: "And not only so, but we glory in tribulations also: knowing that tribulation worketh patience; and patience, experience; and experience, hope: and hope maketh not ashamed"—why not?—"because the love of God is shed abroad in our hearts by the Holy Ghost which is given unto us" (Rom. 5:1–5).

There it is, you see, to perfection—here is rejoicing! "The love of God . . . shed abroad in our hearts."

What is the meaning of 1 Corinthians 13? Its purpose is just the same—to show that if you do not have this love, nothing else matters.

> Though I speak with the tongues of men and of angels, and have not charity [love], I am become as sounding brass, or a tinkling cymbal. And though I have . . . all knowledge; and though I have all faith, so that I could remove mountains . . . and though I give my body to be burned . . .

It is no use. Believism plus zeal and enthusiasm and emotionalism and sentimentality, and even great sacrifices, are not the real thing. It is love that is real! Man can produce these other things, but only the Holy Spirit of God can ever shed this love abroad in our hearts, and without this love all the rest is useless: "it profiteth me nothing" (1 Cor. 13:1–3).

Now this is but a beginning of this great theme that we find running everywhere through the writings of this great apostle. Listen to him putting it again in perhaps the most lyrical of all his epistles, certainly in many ways the happiest of them all, the Epistle to the Philippians: "Finally, my brethren, rejoice in the Lord" (3:1). He thinks he is going to finish, but then he does not. He goes on to the fourth chapter! "Rejoice in the Lord always: and again I say, Rejoice" (4:4)

My dear friends, are you rejoicing? Are you like those early Christians? This is the characteristic of Christians. They have not merely made a decision and then had to do something else to give themselves a little bit of feeling. No, no! The truth has dawned upon them, captured them, captivated them, and has moved them to the depths of their beings, and they are rejoicing. "We are the circumcision," says Paul to these Philippians, "which worship God in the spirit, and rejoice in Christ Jesus"—not merely believe, but *rejoice*—"and have no confidence in the flesh" (3:3).

So here is the question: have you been moved by the truth? Does what you believe thrill you, move you to the depth of your being? Is your heart engaged? Your mind is, your will may be, but I am asking, is your heart engaged? I am not asking, is only your heart engaged, but is your mind engaged, is your heart engaged, is your will engaged? That is the Christian position—the complete personality captured, captivated by him. "Whosoever drinketh of the water that I shall give him shall never thirst; but the water that I shall give him shall be in him a well of water springing up into everlasting life."

29

Joyful Assurance

Jesus answered and said unto her, Whosoever drinketh of this water shall thirst again: but whosoever drinketh of the water that I shall give him shall never thirst; but the water that I shall give him shall be in him a well of water springing up into everlasting life. (John 4:13–14)

We have seen that the mark of the Christian is true, deep emotion. We see this in the Psalms: "Bless the LORD, O my soul: and all that is within me, bless his holy name" (103:1). We have seen that our Lord teaches this everywhere, and in the book of Acts the first Christians were "filled with joy" (13:52). We have observed, too, that the apostle Paul's great message to the Philippians is, "Rejoice in the Lord always: and again I say, Rejoice" (4:4). This, says the apostle, is how Christian people are meant to be.

It is important to realize that in the New Testament epistles, this teaching is not confined to the apostle Paul. I emphasize this because people are always ready to explain this rejoicing away in terms of temperament. So I want to call your attention just for a moment to the teaching of others. Take, for instance, what we read in the First Epistle of Peter. Peter, talking about our Lord Jesus Christ, says, "Whom having not seen, ye love"—these people were strangers scattered abroad in various parts of the world; they had never seen the Lord—"in whom, though now ye see him not, yet believing, ye *rejoice with joy unspeakable and full of glory*" (1:8).

Philip Doddridge, the hymn-writer, said that this "joy unspeakable and full of glory" is a joy that is "unspeakable" because it is already a foretaste of the joy of the everlasting glory itself—glorious beyond speech, full of joy. Christians know something about that, they have a foretaste of it, and that is what Peter says about the people to whom he is writing. He says it again in the second chapter of that first epistle. In the King James

Version, the translation is, "Unto you therefore which believe he is precious" (v. 7)—or, "Unto you therefore that believe is the precious one." It is about him. He is the foundation that God has laid, and he is precious to those who believe in him. They love him with this "joy unspeakable and full of glory."

And the apostle John has precisely the same teaching. He puts it quite plainly in his first epistle. He starts off with this great testimony:

> That which was from the beginning, which we have heard, which we have seen with our eyes, which we have looked upon, and our hands have handled, of the Word of life; (For the life was manifested, and we have seen it, and bear witness, and shew unto you that eternal life, which was with the Father, and was manifested unto us;) that which we have seen and heard declare we unto you [what for?], that ye also may have fellowship with us: and truly our fellowship is with the Father, and with his Son Jesus Christ. And these things write we unto you, that your joy may be full. (1:1–4)

Not only that your intellectual understanding may be full, but in addition that your joy may be full. This is John's whole object in writing this epistle.

This teaching on joy is the universal emphasis of the New Testament, and this is the standard by which we must measure ourselves. This was in the mind of our Lord when he said to this woman of Samaria, "Whosoever drinketh of this water that I shall give him shall never thirst." From the aspect of love and the heart and the emotions, there shall be perfect, full, and complete satisfaction.

Here, then, is the question that people tend to ask: "That's all right for New Testament times, but is it meant for all times?" People have often argued like this: "Certain things happened in the time of the apostles, but we are not to expect them now." Some people at the present time exclude the miraculous in those terms. But they have no grounds whatsoever for saying that, and it detracts from the teaching of the Scriptures. The Spirit is Lord, and he chooses to give exceptional manifestations at times. We must never say that it all ended with the apostles; otherwise we would be persuading ourselves that while the first Christians were meant to be filled with this joy, we are not, and we just have to go trudging along. What a travesty of the Scriptures it is to speak like that! It is entirely contrary to their teaching.

Furthermore, examine the testimony of history and you will find how wrong that idea is. Surely what we gather from the history of the first three or four centuries is that the joy that is taught and promised in the New Testament was exemplified constantly in the lives of the early Christians. Have you read something of the story of the martyrs and the confessors—those people who, at the very moment of being thrown to the lions in the arena, were thanking God that at last they would have the final crown, the crown of martyrdom? They rejoiced in it. "The blood of the martyrs is the seed of the church" (Tertullian). People seeing this amazing joy were apprehended and convicted and wondered what it was and began to make inquiries. This is undoubtedly the main factor in the way in which the early Christian church conquered the ancient world.

Now we must look at these issues historically, and it is the simple truth to say that unfortunately the Christian church herself began to depart from this very teaching, and as she did so, she departed increasingly from the early Christian church in her life and experience. And so you get what are sometimes described as "the dark Middle Ages"—ages of gloom. But there were certain people who kept on appearing, even in those pre-Reformation times, who, having gone back to the Scriptures and having experienced power through the Holy Spirit, knew something of this joy. Let us never forget those little groups that flourished before Luther and the Reformation—Waldensians, Brethren of the Common Life, and people like that in various parts of Europe. This irrepressible joy, this assurance, this happiness, this "joy unspeakable and full of glory," was their characteristic.

And then we come to the towering figure of Martin Luther, and whatever you may say about him, you have to grant him this—above everything else he restored the note of rejoicing. He knew what it was to fast and sweat and pray; he knew what it was to be under a system that did not believe in assurance of salvation. That was the essence of his struggle. But at last the delivering word came: "The just shall live by faith" (Rom. 1:17). The free gift of God's grace released him, and he began to sing, and he began to write his great hymns and tunes, and singing became one of the characteristics of the Protestant Reformation.

Let me give you a brief quotation. I was reading about Luther the other day, and these words put it so well:

> His basic convictions were not arrived at in the ivory tower, but in the arena of life. It was his own personal experience of forgiveness in Christ

> which initially set his movement upon its course. Because it was the Scripture which finally brought him to this experience, he emphasized its authority; because his experience had come by faith rather than works, he emphasized faith; and because the church's uncertain testimony did not lead others to the same experience, he attempted to reform it.

Now the whole point of that quotation, and it is perfectly right, is that it was this experiential element that set the whole Protestant movement going. Of course, it was worked out theologically, but it was initiated by that astounding experience that came to Luther. It came in a flash, and his whole outlook was changed. He was released, and he began to rejoice in his great salvation. This note of assurance was the great characteristic of the Protestant Reformation. It was equally true of John Calvin, temperamentally so different from Martin Luther. This is how Calvin puts it:

> Now we shall have a complete definition of faith if we say that it is a steady and certain knowledge of the divine benevolence toward us, which, being founded on the truth of the gratuitous promise in Christ, is but revealed to our minds and confirmed to our hearts by the Holy Spirit.[19]

It is a simple historical truth to say that the doctrine of the Holy Spirit was restored to the church largely by these men and their writings and their emphasis upon the assurance that is given to the heart by the operation of the Holy Spirit.

Furthermore, as we trace the whole story of the church down the centuries, we find the same note of assurance, love, and praise. Look through the hymn book, and you will find that this is the mark of all the greatest hymns. It is found in the hymns of Isaac Watts and of Charles Wesley, conceivably the two greatest masters of them all.

Thou, O Christ, art all I want;
More than all in thee I find.

Plenteous grace in thee is found,
Grace to cover all my sin.

Charles Wesley

O for a thousand tongues to sing
My great Redeemer's praise.

Charles Wesley

What is the value of one tongue? We need a thousand, and that is not enough.

Join all the glorious names
Of wisdom, love, and power,
That ever mortals knew,
That angels ever bore:
All are too mean to speak his worth,
Too mean to set my Saviour forth.

Isaac Watts

We sing these hymns, but they are not merely lines of poetry—they are the expressions of the experiences of those men, and they are meant to be our experiences.

We see this, too, in the great movements of the Spirit, the tides of the Spirit in the church, the religious awakenings or religious revivals. Take, for instance, the Evangelical or Methodist Revival of two hundred years ago. It does not matter which party believers belonged to—the Calvinists or the Arminians; common to both was the original message of assurance. This is the sole explanation of George Whitefield. Whitefield became the phenomenal preacher that he was when he received this assurance. When the Spirit sealed these certainties in his heart, he went forth as a flaming evangelist.

The same is true of John Wesley. He was an able and erudite man, very loyal and ultra-religious. But he was a very unhappy man, and though he made great sacrifices, trying, as it were, to earn his salvation, he could not get it. But then he crossed the Atlantic to go to Georgia to preach to pagans, thinking that he would add yet more to his merit. During that voyage there was a terrible storm at sea, and this proved to be a turning point in his life. Some Moravian brethren were on the same boat, and he had noticed that they seemed to be very happy people, always praying and singing hymns. When the storm came, Wesley was terrified, but these people were still singing; the storm made no difference to them. That was what really convicted him. Later, when his heart was "strangely warmed" in that little meeting in Aldersgate Street, this man's life was entirely changed, and he, too, became a great evangelist.

Now there, again, was a man who was essentially an intellectual, but he was useless until his heart was strangely warmed and he was moved, until, as he puts it, "I knew that my sins, even mine, were forgiven." There is all the difference in the world between believing that God does forgive sins and knowing that God has forgiven *my* sins, my personal sins. That is where the heart comes in. You can look on and see the truth objectively and accept it. That does not make you "rejoice with a joy unspeakable and full of glory." The truth has to be applied, to become personal.

And this is the great note of that Evangelical Awakening—not only Whitefield and Wesley but Howell Harris and Daniel Rowland as well. Whitefield and Howell Harris had heard of one another, and when they at last met—in Cardiff, if I remember rightly, in 1737—the first question that Whitefield put to Howell Harris was, "Mr. Harris, do you *know* that your sins are forgiven?" He did not ask him if he believed that but if he knew it. And Harris was able to testify gladly and joyfully that he had rejoiced in this knowledge for some two years.

Here, then, is the emphasis that comes out from all this history, and it substantiates the teaching of the Scriptures. So I move to my next point, which is that this joyful assurance is offered to us all. Now I have been giving you this evidence in order to prepare the way for this statement. The attempt is often made to deny this. People say, "But this is not meant for everyone. We all have different temperaments. There are various psychological types—some people are stolid and quiet, calm and intellectual; others are emotional. And you would expect this sort of thing with the emotional type but not with the others." That has often been brought forward as an argument, and people evade the plain teaching of the Scripture by saying, "I'm phlegmatic, not the emotional type. I don't object to it in others as long as they don't become a nuisance, but it's not for me." So they shut out the possibility for themselves.

But more than that, a kind of teaching has crept into the church that divides Christian people into two groups—the religious and the laity. This goes far back in the history of the church; the whole story of mysticism comes in at this point. The idea is that there are ordinary Christians and unusual or extraordinary Christians; and these extraordinary Christians are people who give themselves to the cultivation of the religious life. That is the genesis of monasticism. The idea is that you cannot, while living your life in this world, come to the knowledge of God that gives you the ultimate state of contemplation, which leads to joy. You only arrive at this position after you have gone through various steps and stages in your journey along the mystic way. But, of course, you do not have time to do this while you are engaged in business or in a profession; you must make it the whole of your life pursuit, which demands that you isolate yourself and become a monk or a hermit or an anchorite—the religious. Only then, at long last, do you arrive at the mystic contemplation of God.

That, I repeat, is entirely contrary to the teaching of Scripture, and it is most important that we should emphasize this. This is what Martin Luther discovered. I say "discovered," but "found to be true" is better. He did not arrive at it as the result of a process of thinking and reasoning and working it out. No, no; it flashed upon him, he saw it, and then he could work it out. And as he said, it is as possible for a girl sweeping a floor to know this joy as it is for the monk in the cell; perhaps it is even more likely.

Now this is but a repetition and an outworking of a teaching that we find so plainly in the New Testament itself. Look at Peter preaching on the Day of Pentecost. He and the others had been filled with the Holy Spirit, and it was obvious that something strange and marvelous had happened to them: they were transformed men with unusual powers and also with this joy. Then the people came together, and Peter preached, and we read that as he was preaching,

> . . . they were pricked in their heart, and said unto Peter and to the rest of the apostles, Men and brethren, what shall we do? Then Peter said unto them, Repent, and be baptized every one of you [not only some exceptional people] in the name of Jesus Christ for the remission of sins, and ye shall receive the gift of the Holy Ghost. For the promise is unto you, and to your children, and to all that are afar off, even as many as the Lord our God shall call. (Acts 2:37–39)

You must not confine this to certain temperaments, certain types. If the gospel cannot make everybody happy, it is no gospel. But not only that, surely the nature of man demands that this joy should be universal. It is wrong, it is a false anthropology and a false psychology, to say that certain people can never be happy. That is a misunderstanding. It is contrary to what is true of human nature. We all have these different aspects to our nature, and all are meant to be involved in this great salvation.

But there is also another argument. The nature of truth itself insists upon this being true of everybody. My argument is that the truth is so great, it is so glorious, so marvelous and transcendent, that it can almost move a stone. The teaching of the Scripture is that God will take away the stony heart and give a heart of flesh (Ezek. 11:19), and that is the final answer to the psychologists. It does not matter what you are by nature, what your temperament may be, you are given a new heart, and what makes this possible is the greatness and glory of the truth.

As I have been showing you, the examples of history demonstrate this beyond any doubt whatsoever. I have given you some great contrasts. You cannot imagine two more different men than Martin Luther and John Calvin—Luther, a kind of volcano, bursting forth constantly, and the systematic order and discipline of Calvin. Yet both of them testified to the same truth, and both of them experienced it. Likewise George Whitefield and John Wesley—Whitefield, the orator, the emotional personality, as the psychologists put it, and the ascetic John Wesley, the intellectual, the calm, unemotional, phlegmatic, typical Englishman. Yet here they are, both of them, with hearts moved and warmed and released and showing forth the same joy in the Lord and emphasizing it in their preaching and teaching.

So we must get rid of the notion that this deep joy is not for us, that it is only for certain people. That, of course, would be the case if we were dealing with a human teaching. People react differently to music, to films, to beauty in nature, and so on. But here we start with the doctrine of a rebirth, a new nature, a being "born of the Spirit," a "heart of flesh." Since this is common to all, the possibility of joy is open to all.

Now having said that, I must say this, lest I depress anybody—our business is to give the truth concerning these matters. So I give this as my next point: though this is for all, there are variations in its manifestation. This is an important point, but it is also very subtle and difficult. Have you ever considered the place of temperament in the Christian life? Does it come in at all? The answer is that it does. It is bound to.

"How do you reconcile that," says somebody, "with what you have just been saying about the new heart?"

There is no difficulty; we put it like this. The Christian faith, unlike the cults, never produces a uniform type. It gives a uniform, universal experience, but it does not produce a standard type of person. The cults do. Psychological movements also do that. People look the same, they repeat the same clichés, the same phrases, all in the same way. But that is not true of Christianity because here is something that deals with the whole person. Christianity does not crucify the temperament; the temperament remains. But here is the difference: whereas people who are not regenerate are governed by their temperaments, Christians can govern theirs. The unregenerate are slaves to their temperaments, but Christians never are. They become aware of the temperament and of its danger, and therefore they apply the gospel to it. They master it, they control it; and as they do so, it becomes very wonderful.

Take the obvious illustration. Look at what God does in nature. All the animals or plants within a single species have the same characteristics.

Yet no two flowers are identical. There is a variation in the intensity of the color perhaps or in the shape. There is a sameness, and yet there is a difference. And it is the same with human beings.

Take another illustration. Look at the writers of the Scriptures. All these men, we believe, were moved and led, inspired and controlled by the Holy Spirit. Peter says about the Old Testament prophecy that none of this came "of any private interpretation . . . but holy men of God spake as they were moved by the Holy Ghost" (2 Pet. 1:20–21). "All scripture is given by inspiration of God, and is profitable for doctrine, for reproof, for correction, for instruction in righteousness" (2 Tim. 3:16). But then go back and read the Old Testament prophets. Look at the different styles, for instance, of Jeremiah, Amos, and Isaiah. They are all inspired by the same Spirit. There is this common element, which is most important of all and controls everything. But that being said, notice the individual characteristics of style and emotion and reasoning.

Then come to the New Testament—it is exactly the same. Take the style of the apostle Paul, the style of Peter, and the style of John. If you are familiar with the Scriptures and somebody reads a portion to you and asks, "Who wrote that?" you ought to be able to answer without any difficulty at all. If you cannot tell the difference between a passage taken at random out of Paul or Peter or John or James, then I say you are a poor Bible student. The difference in style is obvious. In Paul's letters there is the profound reasoning, the rhythm of the argument, and then the breaks in the rules of grammar because he is suddenly caught up, as it were, and indulges in some ecstatic utterance. Then he may come back and complete his sentence or he may not. That is typical of Paul. John's style is extraordinary—instead of leading up to a conclusion, he starts with it and then explains it, and he alone does that. And then we see Peter with his more ordinary style, more like ourselves.

Here is the point: they were all controlled by the same Spirit, but the Spirit did not eliminate the temperament or personality. He used it, he controlled it, he disciplined it, he employed it in order that the one truth should be manifested to us in a variegated manner. And so the whole is a kind of spectrum manifesting the light of the glory of God in the face of Jesus Christ. Temperament, therefore, does come in, and we must not exclude it.

Now I emphasize this because it is pathetic to find a man trying to be ebullient or demonstrative when that is not his nature or temperament. There is nothing that is more ridiculous. We should be natural in this matter. Each of us in our own way shows the same truth. We must not try to conform to a type; we must not try to imitate other people. Oh, it is very sad to see people repeat glib phrases, and I know more or less where they got them! And they think this is being pious. How contradictory of the teaching of the Bible. No, no; be yourself, and under the influence of the Spirit, he will show you the joy that is in you.

Or let me put it still more clearly. There are variations even in one individual. No one is always the same all the time. And I go further—no one is meant to be. Psalm 103 reminds us that "he knoweth our frame; he remembereth that we are dust" (v. 14). While we are in the body in this life, in this world, we will experience variations and changes within ourselves. Do not be troubled by that. The body and the spirit, the mind and the heart all react upon one another. There is nothing wrong in that in and of itself, as long as we do not become victims of that. You will have moods; you will have states. Do not be a victim of them—deal with them; but do not expect always to feel the same, always to be constant. We have to know ourselves. We have to go back to the Scriptures, where our hearts will be roused and moved.

And not only that, we can go a third step and say that in the same person this joy, this happiness and love do not always show themselves in exactly the same way. I am not talking about the degree—I am talking now about the expression of these feelings. Have we not all experienced this? Let me use a familiar quotation:

> *To me the meanest [most common] flower that blows can give*
> *Thoughts that do often lie too deep for tears.*
>
> William Wordsworth ("Intimations of Immortality from Recollections of Early Childhood")

Sometimes the emotion is such that it is "too deep for tears." But you must not deduce that this man never sheds tears at other times or under other circumstances. No, no! Sometimes you are so moved that you are speechless; at other times you are so moved that you are tremendously eloquent. But they are both all right. You are not bound to be shouting, you are not bound to be singing, you are not bound to be weeping. Emotion expresses itself in a great variety of ways, and it is a great error to standardize feelings and to say that it is only when you are clapping your hands or have gone off into some ecstasy that you are really feeling a deep emotion. That is quite wrong. It is a misunderstanding of emotion.

So we must not put limits on how we experience our feelings. Be wary of putting a limit on ecstasy or upon rapture. "Quench not the Spirit," says the apostle to the members of the church at Thessalonica. We always have this danger. "Despise not prophesyings." That is said in the context of "Rejoice evermore" and "Pray without ceasing" (1 Thess. 5:19–20, 16–17). Problems had arisen in the churches. Some people were guilty of emotionalism, and others, in their dislike of that, were quenching the Spirit. Both are wrong. We must not quench the Spirit, and we must not try to work up an artificial emotion. We are to submit ourselves always to the truth as it is in Christ Jesus. It is he who gives us this "living water" that thus moves the heart.

The next question is this: how does our Lord do this? How does he give complete satisfaction to our hearts, to our emotions? How is it possible for any one of us to conform to that statement of Peter, "Whom having not seen, ye love; in whom, though now ye see him not, yet believing, ye rejoice with a joy unspeakable and full of glory"?

The secret is this: we are always told, you notice, "Rejoice *in the Lord*"—"Rejoice in the Lord always: and again I say, Rejoice" (Phil. 4:4). How do we do this? How does he give this "living water"? Here is the usual way: through the Scriptures. It is there that we find him. We search for him, we look for him, like the woman in the Song of Solomon, we find him, and our heart is moved and raptured.

30

The Coming of the Holy Spirit

Jesus answered and said unto her, Whosoever drinketh of this water shall thirst again: but whosoever drinketh of the water that I shall give him shall never thirst; but the water that I shall give him shall be in him a well of water springing up into everlasting life. (John 4:13–14)

We have seen that it is the teaching of the Bible everywhere that God's people are meant to enjoy full heart satisfaction, complete satisfaction in the realm of their emotions, and we have seen that the subsequent history of the church illustrates the truth of this teaching. It is also our fundamental postulate that unless we have known a measure of this heart satisfaction, there is something seriously wrong with our whole Christian position. So at the moment we are considering how our Lord gives this satisfaction to the heart and to the emotions. He says in essence, "Take the water that I am offering, and you will never thirst again—your heart will never be empty, you will never know that fundamental thirst."

But how does our Lord do this? Fortunately for us, he answers this question, and he does so in a very particular way in the Gospel of John, where we find the fullest teaching with regard to this whole matter. Some teaching is given in the statement from John 4 that we are considering, and we find it put still more explicitly in the seventh chapter, where we read:

> In that last day, that great day of the feast, Jesus stood and cried, saying, If any man thirst, let him come unto me, and drink. He that believeth on me, as the scripture hath said, out of his belly shall flow rivers of living water.

And the apostle John adds:

> (But this spake he of the Spirit, which they that believe on him should receive: for the Holy Ghost was not yet given; because that Jesus was not yet glorified.) (vv. 37–39)

Then in chapters 14, 15, and 16 of this great Gospel there is extensive treatment of this very theme. Our Lord has begun to tell the disciples that he is going to leave them, and they are completely downcast. So he says to them, "Let not your heart be troubled: ye believe in God, believe also in me" (14:1). And he goes on to give them comfort, and this is the real comfort:

> I will pray the Father, and he shall give you another Comforter, that he may abide with you for ever; even the Spirit of truth; whom the world cannot receive, because it seeth him not, neither knoweth him: but ye know him; for he dwelleth with you, and shall be in you. I will not leave you comfortless: I will come to you. (14:16–18)

There our Lord tells the disciples that he is going to come to them through the Holy Spirit. Indeed, he goes so far as to say to them, "It is expedient for you that I go away: for if I go not away, the Comforter will not come unto you; but if I depart, I will send him unto you" (16:7). And he tells them, "He [the Spirit] will guide you into all truth" (16:13).

He also says that he will give them his joy (John 15:11) and peace such as the world can never give (John 14:27). That is the great teaching that our Lord gives us in this Gospel. In other words, it comes to this: our Lord gives us heart satisfaction supremely through sending and giving to us the Holy Spirit and through the work of the Holy Spirit.

There is nothing more appropriate to consider on Pentecost Sunday, the day on which we remember the mighty event that took place in Jerusalem as recorded in Acts 2. Here is this notable event, the last of the great series of events recorded in the New Testament—the descent of the Holy Spirit upon the infant church and the astounding results to which it led. This is the way above all others whereby our Lord gives us this fullness of satisfaction, especially in the realm of the heart and the affections.

The coming of the Spirit had been prophesied many times in the Old Testament. That is why Peter, in preaching on that Day of Pentecost, immediately quotes Old Testament Scripture in order to explain and to expound to the people what is taking place. The crowd is aware that something strange and unusual has happened to these men, these apostles. They are but fishermen, ordinary workmen, but something outstanding has occurred. Everybody comes crowding together, and the question is, what is this? And Peter says, "This"—this event that you are seeing—"is that which was spoken by the prophet Joel" (Acts 2:16). And then he proceeds to quote that prophecy.

A similar great prophecy concerning the coming of the Holy Spirit is in Ezekiel 36, where the prophet says, "I will take away the stony heart out of your flesh, and I will give you an heart of flesh" (v. 26). There it is in very explicit and specific terms. One of the great effects of the coming of the Spirit into a human being is that the heart is changed from a heart that is stone-like and hard and unresponsive to a heart of flesh that feels, that can be profoundly disturbed with tremendous consequences.

Now this is characteristic of the prophecies in the Old Testament with regard to the coming of the Holy Spirit. Indeed, all of the prophets deal with this in some shape or form. A familiar statement by the prophet Isaiah expresses it perfectly: "Ho, every one that thirsteth, come ye to the waters, and he that hath no money; come ye, buy, and eat; yea, come, buy wine and milk without money and without price" (55:1). And again in chapter 35 of Isaiah we read, "The wilderness and the solitary place shall be glad for them; and the desert shall rejoice, and blossom as the rose. . . . And the parched ground shall become a pool, and the thirsty land springs of water" (vv. 1, 7). This is a typical prophecy of the coming of the Holy Spirit and the effect he will have upon men and women. In another and very glorious prophecy God said, "I will be as the dew unto Israel" (Hos. 14:5). Think of the dryness and the hardness of the land—but God says he will be as the dew.

Indeed, there is a sense in which the whole Old Testament is looking forward to the Holy Spirit's coming, and the point that it is establishing is that this will be the great difference between God's people under the new dispensation and his people under the Old Testament dispensation. The Jews were, after all, the people of God; they had knowledge and understanding. Yet they were being promised that something bigger, something greater, was coming. In the Old Testament the Spirit came on people occasionally. He would give ability and understanding—for instance, he would enable them to prophesy or he would give ability to make the Tabernacle (Exod. 35:31). But a promise was given that a day was coming when the Spirit would be poured out with great profusion, even upon young men and young women, "upon the servants and upon the handmaids" (Joel 2:29). It would be general and would be common to all people. In many ways the great difference between the Old Testament saints and those of the New Testament would be the coming of the Holy Spirit in this remarkable manner. The whole Old Testament looked forward to this astounding event.

Now the last of the great prophets, John the Baptist, said exactly the same thing: "I indeed baptize you with water unto repentance: but he that cometh after me is mightier than I, whose shoes I am not worthy to bear" (Matt. 3:11). Because John was unusual and a remarkable preacher, the people thought he was the Messiah. "No," said John in effect, "I am not the Messiah. He is the one who is to come after me." And the great characteristic of his coming and of his dispensation, said John, is that "he shall baptize you with the Holy Ghost, and with fire" (v. 11).

And then we come to the Day of Pentecost when the Holy Spirit, as promised, was shed forth upon the apostles and the members of the early church, the 120 who were gathered together. And what happened to them? The record makes it quite plain and clear—there was an obvious transformation in them, something astonishing, something hitherto not known. And that was the phenomenon that created that great stir of excitement in Jerusalem. You see the typical picture there in the second chapter of Acts, and you find it, in a sense, still more strikingly at the end of the chapter, not among the apostles but among the common people. This is what we read:

> Then they that gladly received his word were baptized: and the same day there were added unto them about three thousand souls. And they continued stedfastly in the apostles' doctrine and fellowship, and in breaking of bread, and in prayers. . . . And they, continuing daily with one accord in the temple, and breaking bread from house to house, did eat their meat with gladness and singleness of heart, praising God, and having favour with all the people. And the Lord added to the church daily such as should be saved. (Acts 2:41–42, 46–47)

Now that is the typical picture of the New Testament Christian; that is how we are all meant to be. Our Lord says in John 4, "Whosoever drinketh of the water that I shall give him shall never thirst; but the water that I shall give him shall be in him a well of water springing up into everlasting life." This is the message of Pentecost; this is the way in which the Lord gives this fullness of satisfaction to the heart of the one who receives the life that he has come to bring us.

So the coming of the Spirit on the Day of Pentecost should engage our most careful scrutiny. Here we see the measure of our Christianity: Do we conform to the picture and to the pattern given in Acts 2? That is what our Lord offers, and the question for us is, have we received this? Do we know this fullness of satisfaction? In order to help this examination of ourselves, let me point out to you how the apostles take up this same theme. Let us look, for instance, at the apostle Paul, who puts this in a very interesting way when writing to the Romans:

> For as many as are led by the Spirit of God, they are the sons of God. For ye have not received the spirit of bondage again to fear; but ye have received the Spirit of adoption, whereby we cry, Abba, Father. The Spirit itself beareth witness with our spirit, that we are the children of God: and if children, then heirs; heirs of God, and joint-heirs with Christ; if so be that we suffer with him, that we may be also glorified together.

Note too the mighty words that follow: "For I reckon that the sufferings of this present time are not worthy to be compared with the glory which shall be revealed in us" (8:14–18).

That is all through the Spirit. But what I am emphasizing is this: notice how the apostle defines the condition of the Christian by a negative as well as a positive. "For," he says, "ye have not received the spirit of bondage again to fear"—that is not the spirit you have received—"but ye have received the Spirit of adoption, whereby we cry, Abba, Father."

And the apostle makes exactly the same point in writing to Timothy. Timothy, by temperament and by nature, was a young man who was somewhat given to depression and to despondency. Whenever things went wrong, Timothy lost hope. He had been hearing rumors that the apostle Paul was about to be put to death by the Roman emperor. So he held up his hands in horror and said, "How can we go on? What is going to happen to the churches?" And Paul reprimands him. This is how he puts it: "Wherefore I put thee in remembrance that thou stir up the gift of God, which is in thee by the putting on of my hands."

Then listen: "For God hath not given us the spirit of fear; but of power, and of love, and of a sound mind [discipline]" (2 Tim. 1:6–7).

Here, too, the negatives are tremendously important. The apostle is saying, both to the Christians in Rome and to Timothy, something like this: You know, your condition is inconsistent with your profession of faith. You claim to have believed the gospel, but you are in a spirit of bondage, you are fearful, you are unhappy—this is wrong. Our Lord said, "Whosoever drinketh of the water that I shall give him shall never thirst," but you appear to be thirsting. What is the matter with you? You do not realize what spirit controls your life. You have no right to be despondent and heavy and lethargic.

What does this mean? Paul is saying that Christian character is produced in us by the Spirit—and this is what we should all be concerned about. Our Lord has sent the Spirit in order to give us this particular character, and we are examining it, in particular, in terms of the satisfaction that we receive in the realm of the heart and the emotions. Very well, then, let us have a look at the Christian in order to see whether or not we conform to this pattern. What are Christian people to be like? What does Christianity do to us? In the light of the Day of Pentecost, what should we be like, we who are members of the Christian church?

First of all, the negative teaching tells us that we are not merely to be religious people. There is a great difference between being religious and being truly Christian. As Christians, we are religious, but we are not only religious. In other words, our religion is not merely a matter of duty. The saints of the Old Testament were religious people. They were under the Law, and obeying the Law was a matter of duty; they went to their services and offered sacrifices in a legalistic manner because they were commanded to do so by the Law. But we are not to be merely like that.

Neither, secondly, are we to be merely good, moral people. Of course, we are to be moral, but the people were moral under the old dispensation. While that is included, we do not stop there. That is not the dominant feature of Christian people as the result of drinking this water, as the result of receiving the fullness of the Holy Spirit.

Another negative is this: Christians do not merely hope to be saved. That is not Christianity. Christians are not merely in the position of hoping that sometime before death they will know that their sins are forgiven, hoping that they *may* go into heaven. That is not the Christian; that is someone from the Old Testament. Christians, therefore, are not always struggling and striving; they are not fearful, full of problems and perplexities. They are not the sort of people who give the impression that the main effect their religion has had upon them is to create problems in their lives that they never had before. Now there are many people like that, are there not? They used to do what everybody else in the world did, but now, because they are Christians, they must stop and think about everything, and they are burdened. They would like to do the things they used to do, but they feel that they should not. Either way, they are fearful. So they are in a spirit of bondage, hesitant and doubtful, not quite knowing what to do.

My dear friends, that is not Christianity, though many people think it is. And I believe that that is why the Christian church is as she is today and why the masses of the people are outside the Christian church. We have given the impression that our Christianity is a task to be performed, a burden. Many of us have been brought up in this way and have never thought enough about it even to consider changing. Others of us, in a spirit of fear, are a bit afraid to do anything except continue as we are. We do not have absolute certainty yet, so we keep on hoping. But our Christian life remains a matter of duty, and we seem to be filled with problems and difficulties and perplexities. We are carrying this great load upon our backs, hoping that somehow, sometime or another, everything will be all right. That is the picture that has so often been given. To use the language of Milton, the Christian is often someone who "scorns delights and lives laborious days"—the miserable Christian.

And the world has reacted against this. It says it wants to be happy, it wants to live a full life, it wants freedom and enjoyment. "Ah," it says, "fancy sitting in your miserable chapels, singing your miserable hymns, afraid to do this and that. You are narrow little people; you are to be despised."

My dear friends, such Christians are nothing but a travesty of the picture given of the Christian in the New Testament, a travesty of what our Lord promises that we should be. "God hath not given us the spirit of fear"; "Ye have not received the spirit of bondage again to fear." Do you go to worship God as a matter of duty? Are you rather pleased with yourself when you go to church once a week on Sunday? Is that your conception of Christianity? You have done your duty; now you can go and do what you want to do. Is coming to church against the grain? If it is, then it is the spirit of bondage; you are in a spirit of fear; you are a legalist; you are in the Old Testament. That is not Christianity.

What, then, is the picture? Well, it is put before us plainly and clearly in the Bible. Look again at Acts 2—something has happened to these disciples and the others, and all of Jerusalem is listening to them. Some phenomenon has occurred. What is it? Some people thought these disciples were drunk! That is what they said: "These men are full of new wine" (Acts 2:13). I know they said it mockingly, but even a mocker has some reason for speaking as he does. There was something about these people that justified this remark. Indeed, the apostle Paul justifies the remark because in writing to the Ephesians he puts it like this: "And be not drunk with wine, wherein is excess; but be filled with the Spirit; speaking to yourselves in psalms and hymns and spiritual songs, singing and making melody in your heart to the Lord" (Eph. 5:18–19).

The apostle there is making a comparison similar to that which struck the members of the crowd in Jerusalem as they looked at the apostles. Here were men who had suddenly been filled with the Spirit, and it was obvious that it had produced a great transformation in them. It was not merely the speaking in other tongues, though that was remarkable enough—here were men able to speak in languages they had never learned. There is no doubt about that. But that was not the only thing. The whole aspect, the whole demeanor, of these men was astonishing and challenging. What was it? Well, they were obviously released. New wine does that; it knocks off inhibitions and restraints and sets people at liberty. And that is obviously something that is done by the Spirit of God, not the spirit of fear. There is a release, a freedom.

But there was more. There was not only an abandon and a freedom, there was happiness. There is no question but that there were smiles upon the faces of these men, that they were radiant. A joy was expressing itself outwardly in their physical appearance. Indeed, one must not hesitate to say there was obviously an ecstatic element. They were men who in many ways were beside themselves. They were so thrilled, so filled with joy and happiness that they were beyond themselves. Do you see the comparison with new wine? They manifested an entire independence of their circumstances. In the past these men had been very much afraid of the authorities. Peter had even denied his Lord because he had been so afraid. After the crucifixion they had all met in an upper room and had locked the doors because they were afraid of the Jews. But now here they were, standing in the streets of Jerusalem and in the Temple, oblivious of the presence of authorities or anybody else—unafraid, released, filled with a sense of power and of "joy unspeakable and full of glory."

And the other thing that characterized them was the way in which they kept on speaking about these "wonderful works of God" (Acts 2:11). They did not speak of anything else. A kind of amazing generosity of spirit had come upon them. They wanted everybody to hear; they wanted everybody to know; they wanted to share all that had happened. They were free men. They seemed to possess the whole universe, and they were offering it to everybody. There was abandon and generosity and happiness. Indeed, you remember how our Lord had prophesied that out of their innermost parts would flow "rivers of living water" (John 7:38). And that was the very thing that had happened to them. Out of them was now pouring forth this ecstatic joy, this abandon, this freshness, and this desire that all should participate in their great blessing and that everybody should come and share "the wonderful works of God."

That is Christianity; that is what we are meant to be like. You do not take yourself by the scruff of the neck and drag yourself to your place of worship.

> They continued stedfastly in the apostles' doctrine and fellowship, and in breaking of bread, and in prayers. . . . And they, continuing daily with one accord in the temple and breaking bread from house to house did eat their meat with gladness and singleness of heart, praising God.

This was their life; this was everything to them. "Daily"!

This, then, is the special work of the Holy Spirit; this is the great difference between the New Testament saint and the Old Testament saint. Here are men and women who are filled with rejoicing and happiness and praise of God. Their religion is no longer a task imposed upon them but is the delight of their lives, the center of their whole being, what they live for.

How does the Spirit do this? Here is a subject that is so large that I can but deal with one aspect of it now, and that very briefly. How does the Spirit produce the kind of Christian character that we have been talking about? I divide the answer into two: the first method is direct, and the second is indirect. I am looking at the direct method now because that is obviously what happened on the Day of Pentecost. It is very important for us all to realize that the Spirit does deal with us directly as well as indirectly. By indirectly, I mean the Spirit's continuous dealing with us through the teaching of the Scriptures; that is his normal, the usual method. But we must never confine the Spirit to that. The Spirit of God also operates directly upon the heart and upon the will and also upon the mind, illuminating and opening it.

I am stressing this because I know that many people in the church today are so afraid of excesses, so afraid of the ecstatic, that they go to the other extreme and "quench the Spirit." This, too, is one of the main troubles with the Christian church at the present time—with all sections of the church, evangelicals quite as much as others. We are so decent, so controlled, and everything is ordered and perfectly organized. All is under our control from beginning to end.

Now you cannot fit that into Acts 2. I repeat that we are so afraid of the excesses that have been manifested by certain people that we have undoubtedly become guilty of quenching and resisting the Spirit. We are not the only ones—the apostles had to say the same sort of thing. In their epistles they remind people who seem to have temporarily lost this happiness and peace that they are in error and have forgotten what they have received, and they must "stir up the gift of God" (2 Tim. 1:6).

The apostle Paul writes to the Thessalonians, "Rejoice evermore. Pray without ceasing. . . . Quench not the Spirit. Despise not prophesyings. Prove all things; hold fast that which is good" (1 Thess. 5:16–17, 19–21). The balance is still there, but, says Paul, in your fear of excesses, do not quench the Spirit. Of course, you must "prove all things" and "hold fast that which is good," but you must not carry that so far that you never allow the Spirit to have freedom. Do not so control your meetings that the Spirit has no opportunity at all. Do not be so mechanically, perfectly correct in your preaching and teaching and your sermon preparation that the Spirit can never come upon you and suddenly raise you up and use you in a manner that you have never understood—do not do that. Leave room for the freedom of the Spirit; leave room for revival; leave room for the unusual; leave room for the direct action of the Spirit.

This is clear New Testament teaching, and I feel that it is very badly needed at the present time. Here in this second chapter of Acts the matter is quite plain, is it not? The disciples were meeting together in the upper room. "And suddenly there came a sound from heaven as of a rushing mighty wind." They had done nothing new; they had been praying like this for ten days, and they were just going on with what they had been doing. But "suddenly" the Spirit came upon them.

And it is exactly the same in the fourth chapter of Acts. The church is praying. They are in dire straits; they do not know what is going to happen. So they pray to God to have mercy, and this is what we read:

> And when they had prayed, the place was shaken where they were assembled together; and they were all filled with the Holy Ghost, and they spake the word of God with boldness . . . and great grace was upon them all. (vv. 31, 33)

That is it. *They* do not do it. No; the Spirit comes and falls upon us.

This can happen, and should happen, to the individual. This is how Paul puts it in Romans 5: "We glory in tribulations also: knowing that tribulation worketh patience; and patience, experience; and experience, hope: And hope maketh not ashamed"—why not?—"because the love of God is shed abroad in our hearts by the Holy Ghost which is given unto us" (vv. 3–5).

Or take again Romans 8:15: "Ye have not received the spirit of bondage again to fear; but ye have received the Spirit of adoption, whereby we cry, Abba, Father."

Or take a final passage in Galatians 4:6: "And because ye are sons, God hath sent forth the Spirit of his Son into your hearts, crying, Abba, Father."

All these verses are saying the same thing. If only we had the time to analyze them, we would find that each of them says that God pours forth his Spirit and he sheds abroad in our hearts in great profusion and abundance—what?—his love! This is something that happens to us. This is not the result of our study and our preparation and our careful anticipation. We do all that, but we do not determine what happens. "Suddenly," unexpectedly, he visits us! He pours forth his Spirit; he sheds his love abroad in our hearts. And this is what moves and melts the heart and makes us realize that his love to us is overwhelming and creates a corresponding love to him in our hearts. The stony heart is taken away, and we are given hearts of flesh.

This, my dear friends, is the height of Christian experience in this world; this is what is possible to us all. And if we know nothing about this, then we are falling very short of what our Lord offered to the woman of Samaria—a heart lifted up and out of itself, a heart overflowing with "joy unspeakable and full of glory," a delight in the Lord, a rapture, an ecstasy—something beyond understanding.

Let me give you just two statements from men who experienced this. The first is old Henry Venn, a godly clergyman who lived toward the end of the eighteenth century. He lost his wife, but this is what he wrote to a friend afterward, and notice how he puts it:

> Did I not know the Lord to be mine, were I not certain his heart feels even more love for me than I am able to conceive; were not this evident to me, not by deduction and argument, but by consciousness, by his own light shining in my soul as the sun's light doth upon my bodily eyes, into what a deplorable situation should I have been now cast.

Or take Charles Simeon:

> This is a blessing which though not to be appreciated or understood by those who have not received it, is yet most assuredly enjoyed by many of God's chosen people. We scarcely know how to describe it because it consists chiefly in an impression on the mind occasioned by manifestation of God's love to the soul.

That is it. It is the direct action of the Holy Spirit upon the heart. You cannot understand it—it is beyond understanding. But he visits us, he manifests his love to us, he "sheds it abroad," and we are "lost in wonder, love and praise,"[20] our hearts fully satisfied. That is what the Holy Spirit was sent to do. That is what he did to those men on the Day of Pentecost. That is what he repeated to them the next day as recorded in Acts 4.That is what he has been doing throughout the centuries. The testimony of the saints, the testimony of our hymn-writers, the testimony of most ordinary people in revival, and even apart from revival, is that the love of God has suddenly overwhelmed them, that it has been shed abroad in their hearts, and they have been lifted up and out of themselves, unable even to express their feelings, it is so glorious, so marvelous, and so wonderful.

> *Jesus, thou joy of loving hearts,*
> *Thou Fount of life, thou Light of men,*
> *From the best bliss that earth imparts,*
> *We turn unfilled to thee again.*
>
> BERNARD OF CLAIRVAUX

My dear friends, do we know anything about this? This is what our Lord offers us. Not a correct, mechanical religion and morality; no, no! There is a fullness, there is freedom, an abandon, a joy, an ecstasy! Have you been taken out of yourself? Have you been lost in your love for him? Do you know anything about these visitations of his blessed Spirit, the Son himself coming down through the Spirit and melting and warming and moving your heart and letting you know his love to you and creating in you a love to him? That is what our Lord offered to the woman of Samaria. That is how every Christian should be. That is how the church should be. And when she is like that, the world no longer despises her, it no longer laughs at her or feels sorry for her. When this happens, the world comes looking on and listening and saying, "What is this?"

So here is the question: are you such a person that your next-door neighbors are amazed at you and find it difficult to understand you because of the joy that is yours, because of the happiness they see in you, because of the way you stand up to your trials and your tribulations, because of the way in which you are more than conqueror, because you do not have a spirit of fear "but of power, and of love, and of a sound mind"? This is what he offers to us freely. "Whosoever drinketh of the water that I shall give him shall never thirst; but the water that I shall give him shall be in him a well of water springing up into everlasting life."

31

The Fruit of the Spirit

Jesus answered and said unto her, Whosoever drinketh of this water shall thirst again: but whosoever drinketh of the water that I shall give him shall never thirst; but the water that I shall give him shall be in him a well of water springing up into everlasting life. (John 4:13–14)

We have studied the disciples on the Day of Pentecost and have seen that there was something about the quality of their lives, their joy, their abandon, their assurance, their loss of the fear of death—all of which accompanies the great experience of the work of the Holy Spirit—that astonished everybody. I am emphasizing this because it seems to me to be abundantly clear that nothing but this will have any influence upon the modern world. It is vital to see the distinction between the true joy and happiness that we read of in Acts and the kind of artificial joviality and cheeriness that at the present time is doing so much duty for the real thing.

The world can always recognize the psychological. It is not taken in by that. The world in its understanding and wisdom can see how certain effects are produced. We can read about these techniques in books on psychology and even in popular articles, and there is no difficulty at all in explaining how emotions are worked up. The world is not impressed at all. Such methods may have an influence upon certain less intelligent types, but they are of no value to the kingdom of God, and in any case this is not what our Lord is speaking about to the woman of Samaria. He is talking about another realm altogether, because as we have seen he is talking about that which is produced by the Holy Spirit, who is the special agent who has been sent to bring about true joy in the life of believers.

We have also seen that the Holy Spirit works in a number of ways. We have dealt so far with only one, which is the *direct* way. We must never forget that the Holy Spirit can come upon us directly and immediately, and we must never exclude that. If we do, we are quenching the Spirit. But now we must now go on and look at other ways in which the Holy Spirit produces this same joy and love, this same deep satisfaction to the heart and all within us that cries out to be loved and to love, to know joy and peace and so on. In addition to the immediate and direct method, he also works indirectly, and one of the ways in which he does this is by producing "the fruit of the Spirit," which is a term used by the Scriptures themselves.

As Christians, the Spirit is within us: "Now if any man have not the Spirit of Christ, he is none of his" (Rom. 8:9). It is impossible for us to be Christians without the Holy Spirit being in us. This is of vital importance. Again, the doctrine of regeneration is most important, and it is why it is possible for all of us to know this joy. We do not all have a happy type of nature, but as I have already shown, this joy is offered to us all, and whatever we are by nature and temperament, we are all meant to experience it. Look at it this way—the Christian is not merely someone who has taken up a teaching and decided to live according to it. That is not Christianity, though it often passes as such. That is religion, and as we have seen, there is no more important distinction than that between religion and Christianity.

You can take up religion; you can take up other teachings. You like a teaching, so you decide to accept it, and having adopted it, you try to put it into practice. That is the basis of all morality and ethical conduct. People face life, they see the consequences of certain actions, they read books, biographies, and direct teaching on morality, and so they solemnly decide that they will adopt a moral teaching. Similarly, people take up one of the religions—Buddhism, Hinduism, Confucianism, Islam, and so on. Some people have not been brought up in those religions, but having read about them, they decide to take one of them up, and they try to live a life in conformity with that teaching.

But Christianity is not a teaching that we take up with the mind and adopt and to which we then try to conform. There is that element in it, but that is not the main thing. Primarily Christianity happens to us. Something is done to us, something we could never do ourselves, something that God alone can do. And that is the particular work and function of the Holy Spirit; it is the third Person in the blessed Holy Trinity who does this for us. It is he who gives us a new birth.

The trouble with religious and moral men and women is that they are still essentially the same people before and after they take up a teaching.

What they are trying to do is to affect and to influence, to change and to mold their personalities. But they cannot, though they do their best. They can modify their personalities up to a point, they can restrain themselves, they can push themselves forward, but essentially they are the same. But here in the gospel everything is entirely different, and that is because of this blessed doctrine of regeneration. It is the difference of Christianity and of the very essence of our position. That we are born again is the most vital and central doctrine of all. We are not what we were; in Christ each of us has received new life, a new nature, a new heart.

The New Testament emphasizes this teaching everywhere. It is the whole point of our Lord's conversation with Nicodemus in John 3. Nicodemus comes to our Lord as a teacher, almost as an equal; he recognizes a certain element of superiority in our Lord, and he is coming to have a discussion, what is called today a dialogue. But our Lord does not have dialogues with people. He turns to Nicodemus and says, "Verily, verily, I say unto thee, except a man be born again, he cannot see the kingdom of God" (John 3:3). What is a Christian? Christians, says Peter, are "partakers of the divine nature" (2 Pet. 1:4).

The fact of regeneration is absolutely crucial to our understanding of how our Lord is able to give us complete satisfaction in the realm of the heart. Without this new birth, he could not do it. You cannot suddenly make a phlegmatic type out of a mercurial individual; you cannot take a melancholic type and suddenly persuade him to become jovial. And there is nothing more ridiculous than to see people of those various types trying to make themselves something they are not. But that is not what Christianity does. It puts this seed of new life in us. There is this new element; there is this "partak[ing] of the divine nature." Now let me show you this because it is the only way whereby it becomes possible for someone who may by nature be the most miserable creature ever born to rejoice, to be happy, and to be filled with a spirit of assurance and praise. The glory of the gospel is that nothing is impossible because of this miracle of the new birth.

What is the object of Christianity? Paul says, writing to the Romans (this is only one of many statements, but it is one of the greatest), "For whom he did foreknow, he also did predestinate to be conformed to the image of his Son" (8:29). That is what we are to be like. We are to be "conformed" to the image of the Son of God. Or take that other great statement of the apostle Paul in his letter to the Galatians: "I live; yet not I, but Christ liveth in me" (2:20). There it is perfectly—"I; yet not I."

Christians are not the people they were. There is this "new man." We must get rid once and forever of this notion that Christians are men and women who are trying to make themselves something. That is a contradiction of the very basis of the Christian position. It is God who makes a soul. It is the re-creative action of Almighty God himself. This is the point—it is this life-giving water, this well that he puts within us. So we now can say that there is a sense in which the life we are living in the flesh is not so much our living as his.

> I live; yet not I, but Christ liveth in me: and the life which I now live in the flesh I live by the faith of the Son of God, who loved me, and gave himself for me. (Gal. 2:20)

Again, in Galatians 4:19, Paul says, "My little children, of whom I travail in birth again until Christ be formed in you . . ." This is Christianity. Not that we are changing and modifying ourselves. No, no! Christ is being formed in us, until eventually he will fill us altogether.

Or, again, take the great and glorious statement at the end of Ephesians 3. The apostle tells the Ephesians that he is praying for them, and praying without ceasing, and his prayer is:

> That [God] would grant you, according to the riches of his glory, to be strengthened with might by his Spirit in the inner man [what for?]; that Christ may dwell in your hearts by faith; that ye, being rooted and grounded in love, may be able to comprehend with all saints what is the breadth, and length, and depth, and height; and to know the love of Christ, which passeth knowledge, that ye might be filled with all the fulness of God. (vv. 16–19)

Do you see how the apostle puts it? ". . . that Christ may dwell in your hearts by faith . . . that ye might be filled with all the fulness of God." It is God coming in, not the modification or adaptation of the self. That is where the difference between religion and Christianity is absolute. The greatest enemy of the Christian faith has always been religion and morality, whatever form they may take.

We see this again in Ephesians 4, where Paul, in dealing with the ethical behavior of the Ephesians, tells them they must not go on living as they used to live and as their fellow countrymen are still living. He says:

> But ye have not so learned Christ; if so be that ye have heard him, and have been taught by him, as the truth is in Jesus: that ye put off concern-

> ing the former conversation the old man, which is corrupt according to the deceitful lusts; and be renewed in the spirit of your mind; and that ye put on the new man [notice], which after God is created in righteousness and true holiness. (vv. 20–24)

A "new man" is created within us "in righteousness and true holiness." This is the action of God in us.

It is because this is true of the Christian that it is not only possible for all of us to know the heart satisfaction that our blessed Lord gives but also our duty to know it, and we are sinning if we do not. Miserable Christians should not only be ashamed of themselves, they should also realize that in many ways they are contradicting the essential teaching of the New Testament. I know the dangers of the false, but nothing is so tragic as that people should be so afraid of the false that they never realize the true.

I have said—I say it again—I am not talking about emotionalism or sentimentalism but about the joy of the Lord, about joy in the Holy Spirit. Paul says, "The kingdom of God is not meat and drink"—silly people in the church of Rome were arguing about meats and days, details and minutiae—"but righteousness, and peace, and joy in the Holy Ghost" (Rom. 14:17). That is it! And again we read in 1 Peter 1:8, "In whom, though now ye see him not, yet believing, ye rejoice with joy unspeakable and full of glory." That is what our Lord is offering. That is what he is telling this woman of Samaria.

Now the Holy Spirit, let me remind you, sometimes immediately pours his joy into our hearts, but we are now considering his indirect—his regular—way of working. He has given us the new birth; he has begun to form Christ in us; we are partakers of the divine nature. So now we are to live the kind of life that our blessed Lord himself lived, and we are to show the characteristics of the life that was so evident and so obvious in him. But how does this happen?

These are mysterious matters, and we cannot finally understand them, but we know this: a seed of divine life is put into us, Christ dwells in our hearts by faith, and the Holy Spirit is resident in us. "Know ye not that your body is the temple of the Holy Ghost which is in you . . . ?" (1 Cor. 6:19). And he gives us this heart satisfaction partly by producing in us "the fruit of the Spirit": "But the fruit of the Spirit is love, joy, peace, longsuffering, gentleness, goodness, faith, meekness, temperance" (Gal. 5:22–23).

Now that is a very wonderful way, it seems to me, of expressing this great truth that the Holy Spirit is in us and is working in us. I say again, you cannot be a Christian unless this is true. He is producing in us the characteristics of our blessed Lord himself, who was the Son of God and was filled with the Spirit. "God giveth not the Spirit by measure unto him" (John 3:34). There you see him in all the glory of his perfection. The Holy Spirit works in us, and, of course, there is much work to be done. Though we are born again, the old nature is still here. We are not rid of that. But the Spirit works, and he produces this new life in increasing abundance. So the apostle uses this comparison of "fruit."

What are the characteristics of this fruit produced by the Spirit? Paul mentions nine, which fall quite naturally into three groups of three, and it is important that we should consider them. Look at the first group of three: "the fruit of the Spirit is love, joy, peace." We can describe those three as positive fruit of the Spirit. When the Spirit is having his way in us, we are of necessity filled with love. He is the Spirit of love as well as of truth, and his action, always, is to produce love. God is love. God the Father is love. God the Son is love. God the Holy Spirit is love. There would be no salvation, there would be no gospel to preach, and there would be no church were this not true. So the Spirit works in us to produce a loving disposition.

And this is our only hope because remember what the apostle Paul—this same man who writes about this "fruit of the Spirit" and puts love in the first position—says about every one of us by nature. I do not know whether you recognize this in yourself, but this is the truth about you: "For we ourselves also were sometimes [at one time] foolish, disobedient, deceived, serving divers [diverse] lusts and pleasures, living in malice and envy, hateful, and hating one another" (Titus 3:3).

Or as he says to the Galatians, "if ye bite and devour one another . . ." (Gal. 5:15). That is what we were, every one of us, and that is the old nature still. But Paul adds:

> But after that the kindness and love of God our Saviour toward man appeared, not by works of righteousness which we have done, but according to his mercy he saved us, by the washing of regeneration, and renewing of the Holy Ghost; which he shed on us abundantly through Jesus Christ our Saviour. (Titus 3:4–6)

What the Holy Spirit does in this process of renewal is to produce this fruit, and the first is *love*. As the Spirit operates in us, we become less and less hateful, and we hate one another less and less; we are filled positively by a spirit of love. You cannot make yourself love, but the Spirit makes us love. He produces in us this love that is in God himself.

The second fruit is *joy*. You cannot argue with these facts. If the Spirit is in you, there must be love in you, and there must be joy. Now I know that some of you want to say, "Ah, but if you only knew what I do and don't do and how I fall into sin and how I am this, that, and the other." But that is true of everybody. None of us is perfect. Yet the Spirit produces joy. And as we have seen, the tragedy is that there are some people who, because of false teaching, will not allow themselves to have this joy. It is there but they try to crush it; they are afraid of it. They are afraid of animal spirits or of false joy, and they say, "Ah, but look at this . . ." But these people are putting themselves back under the Law. They are trying to say that they have no right to be joyful until they are perfect, until by their own actions and efforts they are fully satisfactory to themselves and to God. The idea is monstrous, it is ridiculous! Allow the Spirit to do his work, my dear friend. Do not resist him, do not stand in his way, do not be afraid. He will produce joy; he is bound to. It is a part of the divine character.

Love and joy—and the third fruit is *peace*. This is a heart rest, the condition of true peace, the peace the world can never give us (John 14:27), the peace that the world is ever robbing us of in so many different ways. "Peace, perfect peace, in this dark world of sin?" It is impossible apart from the Holy Spirit, but he can give us peace.

These, then, are positive productions of the Spirit. This is the outworking of the seed of life that he has implanted in us; and he tends it, he waters it, he deals with it in his own mystical manner. Let me put it to you in a very experiential and practical manner. Have you not sometimes been surprised at yourself, surprised at the fact that you are able to love the way you do? Have you not been amazed at times at this joy that is also in you? You are surprised at it, but you find it is there. The same is true of the peace. The old restlessness seems to have gone, and you have arrived at a place where at times you know "perfect peace"—you are quite sure of it. These are the firstfruits of these known aspects of the fruit of the Spirit.

But now look at the second group—it is very interesting to see how the apostle classifies them—"longsuffering, gentleness, goodness." How do these constitute a group? Well, as the first three were essentially positive and active, these are negative; but they are tremendously important. Here are Christian men and women who have this new life, and the Spirit is in them, and the Spirit is producing "love, joy, peace." But they still have to live in the world. As long as they are alone in their rooms, all is well, but the difficulty arises when they come out of their rooms and mix with other people; in a moment, but for this second group, they would lose the first three. Why? It is because people are what they are. People are so difficult, are they not? *We* are all right, but other people annoy us and irritate us; they are slow, stupid, and dull. How trying people are! You have found that, have you not? Of course you have! And they have found exactly the same about you! That is why it is so extremely difficult to maintain this love, joy, and peace. The old nature is still here, and it reacts.

But now here is *long-suffering*. It is a quality. It is not active or positive as love, joy, and peace are. Perhaps you can look at it like this: long-suffering puts the brake on so that you do not react immediately. Long-suffering takes an edge off you; it takes off a tendency toward irritability and annoyance and overreaction. This is profound psychology; this is biblical, spiritual psychology. Thank God for it, it is all so essential. God knows us perfectly, and the Spirit understands us perfectly, so he realizes that in addition to creating the positive qualities, he must do something about the old nature, and this is what he does: he puts this brake on so that we become more long-suffering. He will speak to you; he will remonstrate with you. He will point out to you how unlike our Lord this irritability is, how wrong it is in any case, how foolish it is, how it does harm, and how it has made you lose your joy. There you were—you were enjoying communion with the Lord and experiencing his love; then some triviality made you lose it all in a moment. What a tragedy!

And the Spirit agrees. So he works in us negatively and produces within us a spirit of long-suffering, which means that we can suffer long. What a difficult lesson to learn! And yet if you want to know the joy of the Lord and the joy of the Holy Spirit, you must be long-suffering; otherwise people will rob you of your joy every time. And a joy that is only experienced in God's house or when we are alone is not the real thing. This is a joy that persists wherever we are and whatever is happening, and that is the glory of it.

What else? *Gentleness*. Go back to Paul's words in Titus 3 and in many other places and you will see the fruit that we need—gentleness. How difficult it is to be gentle in a world that is full of arrogance and aggressiveness, and yet if you are not gentle, you will not be able to maintain your joy. It is so wonderful to me that the Spirit not only sheds the love of God abroad in our hearts but also safeguards it. He wants it to be perpetual, a permanent condition within us, and not spasmodic as it tends to be, and we are seeing the ways in which he does this. He creates within us long-suffering and then this spirit of gentleness.

It is wonderful, and it has been my privilege many times—I say it as a pastor to the glory of God—to watch the Spirit producing gentleness in people known to me. They were people with strong characters—we all have different battles to fight in this world; that is where these distinctions are so important—and this was one of their battles. Nobody is truly gentle by nature. Some people seem to be nicer than others, but I have found that the nicest people are often the most irritable. Have you ever thought about how the Spirit knows us all and how he alone can produce this true gentleness? He does it by reasoning with us.

The Spirit says, "Now look here, you have lost what you had, that glorious experience, and now you are cast down and unhappy. Why? Simply because you did not speak to that person in the right way. Why should you speak to another in that harsh, brusque manner?" The Spirit produces gentleness. Again, this is a way of putting on the brake, a way of mortifying and getting rid of that old nature that is in us.

The third fruit in the second group is *goodness*. And goodness here means a kind of goodness of heart, a good disposition, so that we are well disposed toward other people. The whole problem of life is, in a sense, the problem of relationships—one constantly sees this. That is why the world is on the brink of war—failure in relationships is the cause of every war. But this problem is also found in the church and in missionary societies; it is a problem everywhere. The curse of life is that man cannot get along with man. But the Spirit helps us by producing this goodness in us, this good nature that is not natural to any of us.

We now understand other people because we understand ourselves. We do not merely see what they do—we see that they are sinners, as we are, saved by grace, that the old nature is still there, that they have a fight and a problem, and we make allowances. So we develop a good disposition. Our whole attitude and outlook upon people becomes changed. And this is not only good and right in and of itself, but the point that the apostle is making is that this is the way in which you and I can preserve the love and the joy and the peace. Without these three negatives, we would very soon lose the three positives.

Then consider the last group—"faith [which really should be translated "faithfulness"], meekness, temperance." How do we classify these? I have called the first group positive, the second negative. This group is more akin to the first than to the second. And yet the apostle puts them last, and I think I begin to understand his reasons. Here is the Spirit working in us, and he positively produces "love, joy, peace." Then, in order to preserve that, he is doing this other work, which is partially negative but also has its positive element in producing a good disposition within us. Then we come to the last three, and I can simply say that these are qualities that in and of themselves promote joy.

Faithfulness means stability of character. It is not faith in the sense of saving faith, nor faith in the sense of its being a gift, as in 1 Corinthians 12. This is a quality of the Christian's whole character. A faithful person is someone who can always be relied upon, someone who has a kind of equability, a balance and steadiness. How vital this is! Oh, how the world lacks reliable people! If you are reliable, you are happy. The person who is not reliable is always changeable. Not only can you not depend upon unreliable people, they cannot depend upon themselves. And because of this, they are constantly in trouble and are always trying to get out of it, and so they lose their joy. But as you become dependable and steadfast and faithful, so the love and the joy and the peace can continue.

The second quality in this third group is, of course, absolutely essential—meekness. "Blessed are the meek," says our Lord (Matt. 5:5). One of the causes of trouble in life is an aggressive personality—someone who talks about "my rights." That is the exact opposite of meekness. Our Lord says that he himself was meek. "Come unto me," he says, "all ye that labour and are heavy laden, and I will give you rest. Take my yoke upon you, and learn of me; for I am meek and lowly in heart" (Matt. 11:28–29). Read the records in the Gospels, and you will see our Lord's meekness. Or consider Moses, the meekest of men (Num. 12:3). Then as I read the writings of the great apostle Paul, and read, too, about his gifts and his ability, there is nothing that I find more astonishing than his meekness. What a meek man he was, what a humble man!

The Spirit produces this meekness in us. The Spirit shows us that horrid "I" for what it is. He reminds us that the old self has been crucified with Christ. Thank God! But the old nature, the way in which it used to manifest itself, is still here, and the Spirit deals with this by producing this essential quality of humility. "I live; yet not I" (Gal. 2:20). We have nothing at all whereof to boast. The more we know about grace, the meeker we will be. And so this quality of meekness is developed within us.

And finally, *temperance*. This is nothing but self-control, this is discipline, this is self-restraint and orderliness, and it is absolutely essential. It is not that you become negative or repressive; that is not what is meant by temperance at all. Temperance is very wonderful. It is like a spirited, active, powerful horse under your control. He may still be galloping, and he may be jumping fences, but he knows that you are there, that you are the master and that you are holding the reins. That is temperance. Temperance is not weak; it is a very strong, a very powerful quality. It is these tremendous, active qualities and propensities harnessed, disciplined, held in the right position and the right way so that there is no dissipation of energy, no wasteful manifestation of power.

Now temperance is a great source of joy and a great guarantee of the maintenance of love and joy and peace. The apostle Paul puts this once and forever in 2 Timothy 1:7: "God hath not given us the spirit of fear"—what has he given us?—"but of power, and of love, and of a sound mind [discipline, temperance, self-control, the ability to deal, as it were, with yourself]." And so you are an equable person, you are a controlled person, and you are thrilling and vibrating with the energy of life, the life that has been put into you by the Spirit of God. But it is all under such wonderful control that you are not up and down, you are not happy and miserable, and you are not always correcting yourself. You are a complete person, a balanced person. And because of that you will go on enjoying love and joy and peace.

There, then, is another way in which the Holy Spirit works in us. We thank God for the periods of revival, but they are not his only method of operation. There is this constant work that goes on, and it all leads to the same end. There have been revivals that have not been the blessing they should have been to the church, because the church abandoned herself to the enjoyment of the unusual and the exceptional and failed to harness it all to this continuous work of the Spirit in producing his own blessed truth within us. When a revival comes, you cannot help yourself—you are filled with joy, you are carried away. But by the grace of God it is possible for us, even as things are now, to know a joy that is "unspeakable and full of glory," and this is one of the ways in which the Spirit helps us to know and to experience that.

32

The Purpose of the Scriptures

Jesus answered and said unto her, Whosoever drinketh of this water shall thirst again: but whosoever drinketh of the water that I shall give him shall never thirst; but the water that I shall give him shall be in him a well of water springing up into everlasting life. (John 4:13–14)

The point we are considering at the moment is that "joy unspeakable and full of glory" is given to us mainly as the result of the work of the Holy Spirit. That is why he in particular has been sent and given to us. He does this partly by coming upon us directly. There are visitations of the Spirit. This can happen to the individual, and it happens to numbers together in periods of what we call revival. That is what revival is: it is another descent of the Spirit, another baptism of the Spirit, an outpouring of the Spirit. It always has this same effect of filling people with joy and assurance and happiness and certainty.

But now we are considering the indirect operation of the Holy Spirit upon us. We have seen that this takes place not only in regeneration but particularly as the Spirit produces what Paul calls "the fruit of the Spirit." This is a more gradual work. The Spirit is forming Christ in us; he is reproducing in us the character, the life, of the Lord Jesus Christ himself, and that life is always characterized by what Paul calls "the fruit of the Spirit . . . love, joy, peace, longsuffering, gentleness, goodness, faith, meekness, temperance" (Gal. 5:22–23). But that does not exhaust the way in which the Spirit gives us this joy, this heart satisfaction.

The Spirit also works—and I would say that, from the practical standpoint, this is his chief method—through the Scriptures. Why do we have the Scriptures at all? There is really only one answer: it is that we may know the character of this salvation that is given to us. John, in writing his first epistle, says quite plainly, "These things have I written unto you that believe on the name of the Son of God; that ye may *know* . . ." (5:13). In other words, the object of the Scriptures is to give us assurance. That is why they were written—they came into being by the work of the Holy Spirit.

The Scriptures are not ordinary writings. They did not come about because a man sat down and decided to write certain things. The Scriptures are the result of the fact that certain men were taken hold of and were dealt with by the Spirit, who gave them, first, a revelation of the truth and, second, an understanding of it. No man can do this in and of himself, as the apostles are very careful to say. The apostle Paul keeps on saying this. For example, "A dispensation of the gospel is committed unto me" (1 Cor. 9:17). He means that the revelation has been given to him. Take, for instance, what he says about the Communion Table: "For I have received of the Lord that which also I delivered unto you, that the Lord Jesus the same night in which he was betrayed . . ." (1 Cor. 11:23). The apostle constantly repeats that this came to him "by revelation." In writing to the Galatians, he says, "I certify you, brethren"—and this is a most important statement—"that the gospel which was preached of me is not after man. For I neither received it of man, neither was I taught it, but by the revelation of Jesus Christ" (1:11–12).

Our Lord illumined the minds of these men through the Spirit; he gave them the truth, and he gave them the power to grasp it and understand it. But in addition to that he gave them the ability and the power to write it, and he controlled them in the writing of it. That is what we call *inspiration*. There is a difference between revelation and inspiration. Inspiration is the power and capacity that the Holy Spirit gave to record in an accurate manner the revelation that had been given. Now if these men had been left to themselves, though they had had the true revelation, they might somehow or another have made a mistake in the recording of it. So inspiration is as essential as revelation.

So the Holy Spirit had taken hold of certain men—these apostles but also those who were under their influence. Apostolicity is always the test of canonicity, of what is truly inspired. And the result is that you and I have the Scriptures—the work of the Spirit. Our Lord had promised this. He had said, "Howbeit when he, the Spirit of truth, is come, he will guide you into all truth" (John 16:13), and he said that the Holy Spirit would explain to them the things that he had been telling them and bring them to their remembrance.

But if the Holy Spirit had stopped at that, it would not have led to this result of joy in us. Something further is necessary, and here it is—the Bible. It is translated into our own language; it is before us all. You can buy a Bible whenever you like, and there are thousands, even millions of Bibles in this country. And yet we know that the vast majority of people do not believe the Christian message; they have not drunk of this water that Christ offers them. Why is this?

The obvious explanation is that they cannot understand the Bible. It is quite impossible for "the natural man" to understand it. People may be familiar with the words, they may give you their meaning, but it does not follow that they understand the meaning of the sentence, of the verse. They can tell you what the *letter* is, but they know nothing about the *spirit*. That is why, though people have their Bibles, that does not make them Christians. And that is why, though people are constantly writing in books and articles and journals and talking on the television and the radio about the Bible, they twist it completely. They have missed the whole point. Why? I say again that it is because they are natural men. They do not have the Spirit, and without the Spirit, no one can understand these things at all. So Paul says, "But the natural man receiveth not the things of the Spirit of God: for they are foolishness unto him: neither can he know them, because they are spiritually discerned" (1 Cor. 2:14).

People listen to the preaching of the gospel but see nothing in it. They read the Bible and see nothing in it at all. It does not matter how able they are; they may be geniuses, but it does not help them. To be able to understand English literature or philosophy or science does not help at all when you read the Scriptures. Indeed, it may be a hindrance because you are bringing your natural understanding to something that is not open to natural understanding.

There is only one way whereby any of us can ever understand the Scriptures that have been produced through men by the Holy Spirit: it is by the same Holy Spirit, who does in our minds from the standpoint of reception what he has already done in the minds of the writers from the standpoint of writing the words. Now this is marvelous, and at the present time we ought perhaps to be able to understand it more easily than our forefathers did because we are helped by the illustration of a radio broadcast. You have a transmitter, but you need to have the receiving apparatus, and you need the same electric power for the reception as for the transmission. Both are absolutely essential. Many people fail to grasp this point and seem to think that a mechanical distribution of the Scriptures is, in and of itself, going to do something. It cannot. The

Scriptures are essential, but the Scriptures alone are not sufficient, as the world proves to us.

This is how John puts it in his first epistle to these early Christians, who were a little bit confused because there were false teachers among them. There have always been false teachers. The modern heresies are not modern; they are old heresies repeated in different forms. So there were these so-called "antichrists," and John says, "They went out from us, but they were not of us; for if they had been of us, they would no doubt have continued with us: but they went out, that they might be made manifest that they were not all of us" (1 John 2:19).

How, then, were those early Christians to know who was the right teacher and who was the wrong teacher? How were they to be saved from heresy? This is part of John's answer: "But ye have an unction from the Holy One, and ye know all things" (v. 20).

John says this again later in the same chapter:

> These things have I written unto you concerning them that seduce you [with false teaching]. But the anointing which ye have received of him abideth in you, and ye need not that any man teach you: but as the same anointing teacheth you of all things, and is truth, and is no lie, and even as it hath taught you, ye shall abide in him. (vv. 26–27)

It is this "anointing" that is absolutely essential before we can derive any benefit at all from the Scriptures. The first thing we must realize, therefore, is that when we come to read the Scriptures, we are reading something that is beyond ourselves. We do not rely on human ability, human understanding, or any gift we may have. We need this "unction," this "anointing." That is why we should never read the Scriptures without praying. That is why we should never read the Bible without realizing that we are doing something exceptional and offer a prayer. We do not just pray mechanically, but we ask God to illumine and enlighten our minds and our understanding in order that we may be enabled to receive what is contained in the Scriptures.

What is contained in them? John, again, expounds this in a very wonderful way: "And these things write we unto you, that your joy may be full" (1 John 1:4). My whole contention is that one of the ways in which the Holy Spirit gives us this joy, this assurance and certainty, this extra quality that makes us more than conquerors over everything that is set against us, is by giving us the Scriptures:

> These things have I written unto you that believe on the name of the Son of God; that ye may know that ye have eternal life, and that ye may believe on the name of the Son of God. (1 John 5:13)

So here is the question: do you know that you have eternal life? Is this joy in you? Do you have in you this "well of water springing up into everlasting life"? This is full satisfaction to the heart. This is "joy unspeakable and full of glory," and you get it through the Bible. Sometimes, as I have said, God pours it into our hearts; perhaps when we are seated alone without a Bible, he suddenly does it. But not always. The regular or usual way is through the Scriptures. They have been given in order that we might have this great joy and rejoicing.

But how do the Scriptures do that? These are the truths that we take for granted, and I suppose our main trouble as Christians is that we so often miss the wood because of the trees. We are so concerned about details and minutiae that we miss the grand thing itself. The Scriptures give us this joy and assurance by unfolding to us the Lord Jesus Christ and what he has done for us. Have you noticed how the apostle Paul often puts it: "Rejoice in the Lord always: and again I say, Rejoice" (Phil. 4:4)? Yes, but "Rejoice *in the Lord*." Or again he says, "For we are the circumcision, which worship God in the spirit, and *rejoice in Christ Jesus*, and have no confidence in the flesh" (Phil. 3:3). This is the key to the whole subject.

John in his first epistle tells the Christians that he is writing to them in order that their joy may be full, and he tells them quite plainly at the very opening of the epistle how God is going to give them this fullness of joy:

> That which was from the beginning, which we have heard, which we have seen with our eyes, which we have looked upon, and our hands have handled, of the Word of life; (For the life was manifested, and we have seen it, and bear witness, and shew unto you that eternal life, which was with the Father, and was manifested unto us;) that which we have seen and heard declare we unto you, that ye also may have fellowship with us; and truly our fellowship is with the Father, and with his Son Jesus Christ. And these things write we unto you *that your joy may be full*. (1:1–4)

The emphasis is always the same. Look at John's Gospel: "In the beginning was the Word, and the Word was with God, and the Word was God" (1:1). Why did John ever write that Gospel? There is only one answer: he was writing it in order to confirm the faith of the early Christians. That is why the Gospels were written. People were Christians before the Gospels or the epistles were written. Christ was preached, and the Spirit gave the people power to believe, and they were added to the church. Why, then, were the Scriptures necessary? They were necessary to confirm Christians in the faith. The Scriptures are really for believers. Their original intent and design was to establish believers in the truth. Heresies were coming in saying that our Lord was only God and not man or that he was only man and not God; and so all the Scriptures were written. They are all about him and what he has done for us and our relationship to him; and as we grasp their teaching we should be filled with joy.

Now this is a most important matter in that it helps us to see clearly the nature of the Christian's joy. It also enables us to differentiate between this joy and all mere superficial excitements and passing emotions. Nothing is more pathetic than the church's attempts to make people happy and to produce joy. It is very sad because it is a denial of the gospel. But that is done—aesthetic and psychological methods are used, certain types of music, clapping, different colored lights, all in order to stimulate people. And then there is a psychological pep talk, as it were, all to make people bright and happy. Oh, what a contradiction of New Testament joy! No, no; we must realize that the character of the joy that the New Testament speaks about, and that our Lord speaks about, is in a category of its own. It is entirely different from all mere passing emotional excitement and titillation of the feelings. True joy and happiness are not superficial but are always profound and always have a solid foundation in the understanding. That is the great message of the New Testament.

Let me work that out in a number of propositions. First, the Christian should never seek joy as an end in itself. Never! That is a great fallacy. And if we do that, if we do seek it directly, immediately, in and of itself, then the joy will be a spurious joy. That, of course, is what the cults do. They deliberately set out to give us what we want. They know that we are unhappy, that we are troubled by the world, and that we want joy and peace. And they will give it to us; they have developed a form, a kind of ritual, a technique to give us this feeling that we want, and, of course, they do give a temporary satisfaction, like drinking water out of that well. But it does not last, it is not solid, it is not true.

Secondly, and this follows, of course, Christian joy is always a by-product of something else—our relationship with the Lord. "Rejoice in the Lord always; and again I say, Rejoice." In other words, the New Testament never comes to us and says, "Be happy! You ought to be happy;

make yourself happy. Come along, let us all be happy together." That is what the flesh says; that is exactly what the world does with its song leaders, its bands, and so on. But that is remote from the New Testament; it is really almost the exact antithesis of New Testament teaching.

Or let me put it this way: the joy that Christians have is based on the realization of what they are, and therefore, to Christians, what they are is much more important than what they may feel like, much more important than what may be happening to them. Now this again is a basic, central, foundational principle of the whole Christian position. The emphasis of all the New Testament writers, from the very beginning of the book of Acts onward—and it is particularly the theme of the epistles and is implicit in the Gospels as well—is for us to realize who and what we are. It is the failure to realize this that more commonly than anything else robs us of this joy and happiness that our Lord offers us.

Let me give you an example of how this joy is lost. Take the apostle Paul's words in Romans 8: "I reckon that the sufferings of this present time are not worthy to be compared with the glory that shall be revealed in us" (v. 18). Now he says that, and all that follows in that chapter, because these early Christian were in trouble, they were suffering and being persecuted, things were going wrong, and some of them, because of this, had lost their joy. Indeed, some were even beginning to doubt whether their faith was real and whether the gospel was true.

Why was this? It was because they obviously had a false notion, which was: believe the gospel and you will be happy ever afterward. If you believe on the Lord Jesus Christ, you will walk down the road of life with head erect and will never have any more troubles. What nonsense that is—what utter nonsense! It is putting forward the wrong emphasis. No, no; the apostle writes to get the Christians to realize that their joy must not be dependent upon what is happening to them or on how they feel but is to be based upon what they are, their relationship to the Lord Jesus Christ and where that will lead.

But how does Paul know that? He has already told us:

> The Spirit itself beareth witness with our spirit, that we are the children of God: and if children, then heirs; heirs of God, and joint-heirs with Christ; if so be that we suffer with him, that we may be also glorified together. (vv. 16–17)

Our joy is all dependent upon our relationship to him, and the way to preserve joy, therefore, is not to be controlled and governed by our feelings and moods and states, nor by what is happening to us. If we are, we will be miserable because this is an evil world and there are evil people in it and because there is illness and accident and death and sorrow. So the way of the New Testament is not seeking joy but having certainty and assurance with regard to who we are, what we are, our relationship to him, and all that is implicit in that.

And so my third proposition about the character of true joy and happiness is that the way to obtain it, therefore, is not to look into myself or to try to produce joy—never. It is always the result of "looking unto Jesus the author and finisher of our faith" (Heb. 12:2). And that is the message of the entire New Testament—look unto Jesus. He himself said, "In the world ye shall have tribulation: but be of good cheer; I have overcome the world" (John 16:33). Our Lord never promised us an easy time in this world. He never taught a kind of jovial, back-slapping Christianity. People have this foolish notion that you cannot be happy and serious at the same time. That is where the trouble comes in. But you can. The only joy worth having is a serious joy, a sober joy, a deep joy, a solid joy.

Solid joys and lasting treasure
None but Zion's children know.

John Newton

It is the element of solidity that is important, and that is always the outcome of our relationship with the Lord Jesus.

Are you a depressed Christian? Are you dejected? Do you feel that all things are against you to drive you to despair? Are you having a hard time in your Christian and your spiritual life? Do you go to church hoping for something? For what are you hoping? How do you think it is going to come to you? Is it my business to make you happy? No, no, my friend. I am not a psychologist. I am a preacher of the gospel. It is not my business to make you happy. If it were, then I would bring a supply of drugs or drink or some orchestra—I would do a thousand and one things. But that is not my calling, and the outcome would not be Christian joy.

My business is not to make you feel happy and then let you go back and face the tragedy and the problem of life exactly as you left it. That would be a cheat, a lie. It would not be true, it would not be clean, it would not be honest; above all, it would not be Christian. All I must do is tell you about him. My business is to try to do what the apostle John did.

He wrote, "These things write we unto you, that your joy may be full" (1 John 1:4), and he brought this about by telling them about him whom he had "heard," "seen," "looked upon," and "handled" (v. 1). He was bearing witness! And this is the only way in which we can have this joy and heart satisfaction about which our Lord talks. In other words, you do not look into yourself—you look out from yourself and forget yourself, and you look at him.

This is, again, a great watershed between the true Christian message and what passes in general under the name of mysticism. There is a Christian mysticism, but that is the only true mysticism. Every other type is bad because it starts by telling you, "Look for the divine spark that is in you." It says, "Do not look at the world; the world is against you. Look into yourself. You have it all there if you could only see it and let it come out."

But that, again, is the antithesis of the gospel. I say again that the only way to go through the world triumphantly and happy and joyful is to keep your eyes steadfastly upon the Son of God. But when you look at him, at what do you look? You start by realizing who he is. He says this himself to the woman of Samaria: "If thou knewest the gift of God, and who it is that saith unto thee, Give me to drink; thou wouldest have asked of him, and he would have given thee living water."

This meeting at the well is one of the greatest dramas in all literature—can you not see it? Here is a woman in desperate need, living in adultery at the moment. Oh, the poor woman! Her need is tremendous, and here is the one who can satisfy every need. But one thing is absolutely essential: he can only give this living water as she realizes who he is. If she does not realize that, she will remain as she is.

This is always the starting point. If you are in trouble, if you are unhappy, if circumstances and trials are pressing upon you, the method of the New Testament is not to deal with your problems and troubles directly—it is to ask you to look at him. He will never deal with these things directly, but only if you are in right relationship to him. The benefits of Christianity only come to those who believe the message concerning him. So you see the fallacies that come in at this point. People want the benefits of Christianity—peace, joy, healing—and they do not get them, and they say, "There's nothing in it." No, no; they have misunderstood. They think they can get the results and the benefits without the faith that is the first essential.

In other words, as I have often put it, the first thing the New Testament tells each one of us is this: the real trouble with you is what you are. It is not your circumstances, it is not your illness, it is not your accident, it is not your surroundings, it is not other people. The real trouble is yourself. The New Testament convicts us of our sin. And this is always the beginning. So it confronts us with him. It does not deal with the situation as we think it will. It has its own method, and it is a radical one—it tells us that what we are is more important than anything else. And what we are is immediately put into the relationship that is absolutely essential, namely, our relationship to him. So you start by looking at him.

You say, "This is hard. I'm in trouble."

It is because you are in trouble that I'm telling you to look at him. The woman of Samaria is in terrible trouble, and she goes on arguing and disputing until our Lord nails her down, and she has to realize who he is—then she gets the help—and not until then. And it is always like this. All our troubles arise from the fact that we are estranged from God, that we are under his wrath, and that we are not his children. So the New Testament does not try to tinker with our problems and put a patch here and a patch there. No, no; it says, "You must be born again." The whole thing must start afresh, and you do this by looking at him.

I could give you endless illustrations of what I am saying. Let me give you what is perhaps one of the most striking of all. Take the great Epistle to the Hebrews, a long epistle of thirteen chapters. Why was it ever written? That epistle was written to Hebrew Christians who were in a state of unhappiness. They were dejected. Many of them were even threatening to give up Christianity altogether and to go back to the old Jewish religion and the Temple, with the priests and the high priest and all the animal sacrifices. That was their actual position. That is why the writer had to give them such terrible warnings about turning away from the gospel.

But why were the Hebrews in that position? It was because of all that had been happening to them, as the writer reminds them:

> But call to remembrance the former days, in which, after ye were illuminated, ye endured a great fight of afflictions; partly, whilst ye were made a gazingstock both by reproaches and afflictions; and partly, whilst ye became companions of them that were so used. For ye had compassion of me in my bonds, and took joyfully the spoiling of your goods, knowing in yourselves that ye have in heaven a better and an enduring substance. Cast not away therefore your confidence, which hath great recompence of reward. (10:32–35)

He reminds them that when they first believed the gospel, they were filled with joy in spite of the fact that they were being persecuted. But all the things that were happening to them had made them unhappy. Some of them, he says, were even being robbed of their goods and were being maltreated, persecuted by their own relatives, the Jews, who hated them because they had become Christians. So these people were in a really pathetic position. But how does the writer deal with them? Here they are—keep the picture in your mind—full of unhappiness, rejection, trials, troubles, tribulations, persecutions. And this is the remedy:

> God, who at sundry times and in divers manners spake in time past unto the fathers by the prophets, hath in these last days spoken unto us by his Son, whom he hath appointed heir of all things, by whom also he made the worlds; who being the brightness of his glory, and the express image of his person, and upholding all things by the word of his power, when he had by himself purged our sins, sat down on the right hand of the Majesty on high. (Heb. 1:1–3)

That is what is supposed to make them happy. Does it make you happy? How do you view the Epistle to the Hebrews? Have you sometimes said something like, "Well, of course, those people had time to be interested in great statements like that—that's theology. I want something practical. I want something to help me. I'm in trouble; life is very hard. I don't have time to try to understand these great statements, these lofty theological propositions. I want some immediate practical help." I know you do, and that is why you are what you are.

But this is the only help, there is no other, and that is why the writer of this epistle starts with it. There is no easy comfort offered in the Epistle to the Hebrews. What he is really saying is this: "Look here, you are unhappy, and you are miserable, and you are threatening to go back. Why? Because you have failed to realize the truth about Jesus." So he starts with that. Come back, he says, and realize the truth about him, and all your troubles will leave you for the present time. They will still be there, but they will not get you down. You will be filled with joy in spite of them.

This is the only answer—"looking unto Jesus" (Heb. 12:2). The way to get joy is to contemplate the glory of this blessed person. He is "the brightness of his [God's] glory, and the express image of his person." He is God the eternal Son. He is the one about whom we are concerned. He is the one who has come into this world in order to put us right with

God. Whatever you may feel, whatever is happening to you, do not look at these things; look at him, and realize that he is able to give you all you need and infinitely more. He looks at you as you are now, in your situation, however desperate it may be, and do you know what he says to you? He says what he said to the woman of Samaria. She had said to him, "How is it that thou, being a Jew, askest drink of me, which am a woman of Samaria?" And he replied in essence, "I am not just a Jew, I am not just a man among men, I am not just a philosopher, I am not just a pacifist, I am not just a politician. Look at me! If thou knewest . . ."

And that is what he is saying to you: "If you only knew who I am and what I have to give you. Whosoever drinketh of the water that I shall give him shall never thirst; but the water that I shall give him shall be in him a well of water springing up into everlasting life." "*I*"—this is the point. "The water that *I* shall give."

Look at him again. Look into his eyes; look into his face. Realize that this is the Son of God—"the brightness of his [God's] glory, and the express image of his person." He has come to supply your every need.

33

The Ultimate Test

Jesus answered and said unto her, Whosoever drinketh of this water shall thirst again: but whosoever drinketh of the water that I shall give him shall never thirst; but the water that I shall give him shall be in him a well of water springing up into everlasting life. (John 4:13–14)

We have seen that Christians are aware of a joy in their hearts that is "unspeakable and full of glory," and we have seen that this is the work of the Spirit. We have considered together the direct influence of the Spirit and have also seen that he works indirectly by giving us new life and producing within us the fruit of the Spirit. Then in our last study we saw that the Spirit also works indirectly through the Scriptures. This is the normal way in which he works. He works in us directly, yes, but he also works in us indirectly to enable us to understand the Scriptures. He is the author of the Scriptures, and they have been given in order that we may have assurance. Above all, they point us to Christ, so that we may know what it is to rejoice in Christ Jesus.

As we read the Scriptures, we look at our Lord. That is the only way to get this full heart satisfaction. I have a message to offer you in terms of this statement of our Lord to the woman of Samaria, and it is this that can enable people to have "a joy unspeakable and full of glory." That is what matters. It is a tragedy that the Christian church should waste her time in talking about things with which she is not competent to deal. This is our message: "In the world ye shall have tribulation: but be of good cheer; I have overcome the world" (John 16:33). Here is a message that comes to us whatever the conditions in the world round and about us, and this message is always the call to look at him.

How do we get this joy as we look at him? Have you not noticed how the New Testament keeps on describing him? "In the beginning was the Word, and the Word was with God, and the Word was God" (John 1:1). ". . . who being the brightness of his glory, and the express image of his [God's] person . . ." (Heb. 1:3). ". . . who is . . . the firstborn of every creature" (Col. 1:15). "And he is before all things, and by him all things consist" (Col. 1:17).

Do you want to have Christian joy? Meditate on him; think about him. Try to think about the glory of this person, this incomparable person. The New Testament is constantly dealing with this. Our Lord told us that the Holy Spirit has been specially given in order to glorify him: "He shall not speak of himself . . . he shall glorify me" (John 16:13–14). The way to test whether or not our experiences are the work of the Spirit is always to ask what view they give us of him.

This is a most thorough test, and I want to apply that now. We need to examine ourselves. Perhaps we are living on services, on meetings; perhaps we are living on excitement or on organizations. That is not living on him. The ultimate test of our position, every one of us who claims to be a Christian, is this: do we find our joy, our peace, our contentment in him—I mean in him himself, the person of our Lord? Think of him in his own eternal glory; think of him as he is, as he is revealed to us in the Scriptures.

The only way to get real, solid, lasting joy is to know the truth about him, and it is amazing that people have lost sight of this. The modern objection to doctrine and theology is not only fatal from the standpoint of truth—it is particularly fatal in the matter of experience. It is because people have ceased to be concerned about understanding doctrine that they are having to turn to various other expedients. Have you not noticed how the element of entertainment is coming more and more into our meetings and how it is increasingly similar to the entertainment offered by the world? Christianity is having to fall back upon the world and its methods to make people happy and joyful in its meetings. This is so tragic. It is such a contradiction of what we have in the Bible. No, no; you must not borrow anything from the world to make Christian people happy. What you must do is state the doctrine concerning the person of the Lord Jesus Christ.

Do you ever sit down and contemplate him? Do you think of him—the effulgence of the everlasting and eternal God who was born as the babe of Bethlehem? Does that move you? Does it thrill you? If it does not, I must ask the question, are you a Christian? This is most important. Let me tell you what a friend from Africa once told me. He had experienced revival in Africa, and he and others had come over to this country on a visit. He had gone around telling people about the revival, and everyone had greatly enjoyed listening to him. But a year later he came back again, and he began going around to the same churches. But he had a feeling, indeed he felt certain, that it was the leading of the Holy Spirit that this time he should preach the gospel about the Lord Jesus Christ, and he began to do so. He told me that people would come to him at the end of the meeting, good, evangelical, Christian people, and say, "Thank you very much for the message, but we did hope you would tell us some more about the revival." He said, "You see, they did not want to hear about Jesus. They wanted to hear about the thrills and the excitements of revival." How devastating that is!

Does our Lord give you joy? Does he give you happiness? Does he give you peace? Let us be distrustful of any joy that we may have that is not directly related to him. Start with the glory of the person, and meditate on him. Look at him; think about him. Like the writers of the hymns, consider him: "Jesus, lover of my soul"; "Thou Son of God, and Son of Man, beloved, adored Emmanuel." That is the way to know true joy. If these things do not move us, we must examine the foundations of our faith. But then we go on from there. Our Lord was in the everlasting and eternal glory—"In the beginning was the Word"—but "the Word was made flesh, and dwelt among us" (John 1:1, 14).

Now you may say, "But I know all about that—I thought I was going to hear something that I didn't know."

It is because you think you know it that you are as you are. You are not applying it. You spend the whole of your Christian life going over these things. If you think you know all about the Gospels, you will just continue to be what you are. You are merely displaying your ignorance of spiritual things. If you think you have read the passages and know all about it, what a tragedy that is! The apostle Paul, having spent so many years in contemplating him, says to the Philippians that his deepest desire and ambition is "that I may know him" (Phil. 3:10). You get to know more and more as you contemplate him.

So I now ask this question: why was the Word made flesh? Why did the Word ever dwell among us? And then we come to one of the most amazing and glorious aspects of the gospel. You cannot ask that question without at once being driven to the only answer: it was the result of God's eternal plan and purpose. I must confess that I find it the most staggering thing that I could ever contemplate that before the world was created at all, God had planned this redemption that you and I are sharing. "We speak the wisdom of God in a mystery, even the hidden wisdom, which God ordained before the world unto our glory" (1 Cor. 2:7). "Before the world"!

Or take it as Paul puts it again in Ephesians 1:

> . . . having made known unto us the mystery of his will, according to his good pleasure which he hath purposed in himself: that in the dispensation of the fulness of times he might gather together in one all things in Christ, both which are in heaven, and which are on earth; even in him. (vv. 9–10)

This is the great plan and purpose of God, conceived and planned even before the foundation of the world. This is the source of Christian joy. Look at the world; look at all that is happening in it; look at all the failure and the misery and the shame and all that is involved. How can anyone be happy in a world like this? Is it possible? How can one have peace? "Peace, perfect peace, in this dark world of sin?" Is it possible? And there is only one answer to this—the Christian can "Rejoice in the Lord always" (Phil. 4:4).

I look at the modern scene; I see the world as it is. I will not waste your time or mine in talking about that or in telling the statesmen what to do about it. That is just a sheer waste of breath and time and energy; it is folly. I have something much more glorious to tell you: God's ultimate purpose is to restore all things in perfection and glory in Jesus Christ. All that we see in the world is the result of the Fall, of man's rebellion, and man will never be able to put it right. Anyone who still has confidence in statesmen or in Leagues of Nations or the United Nations or anything else is just a spiritual ignoramus. There is only one hope for this world—it is in this person. And I know that for one reason only, and that is that God has planned all this, and that is therefore the only real source of joy. So do not look at your circumstances and surroundings; look at God and his great plan and purpose that he has put into execution in Christ Jesus, the babe of Bethlehem.

And as you meditate on these truths, you find your joy. You "glory in tribulations" (Rom. 5:3) because you are seeing the ultimate. And the purpose itself, the very fact that God has ever planned it or even thought of it, is so glorious. We do not deserve it. We deserve hell; we deserve damnation. You should not complain about the state of the world. Man has produced it, and he deserves what he is getting; it will get worse unless he humbles himself and repents. That is the Christian message. And to blame God, to say, "If there's a God, and God is a God of love, why does he allow . . . ?" is refusing to see that the amazing thing is that God has not blotted us all out in everlasting destruction. We deserve nothing but what we are getting, and infinitely more, and worse.

The astounding fact is that "God so loved the world"—this wretched, evil world—"that he sent his only begotten Son" into it, and he planned to do it before the very foundation of the world. Does the contemplation of that not move you? Does it not thrill you that the everlasting God whom we have so insulted should be doing this for *us*? You are not thinking of your own little aches and pains now, are you, and the little pinpricks and what somebody has said or done? Look away from it all; look to him. Contemplate this, and you will know "joy unspeakable and full of glory."

Then go on—consider the way in which he came. Try to consider what it meant to him. Do you do this? This is Christianity. You do not sit passively and wait for something to make you happy or go to a meeting because you think, "Ah, they're having great happiness there!" Oh, how false that is! No; this is the method.

Let me give you another illustration of the way in which he came. Why do you think we have these accounts of our Lord's birth? Why were they ever written? They were written, of course, to establish us in the truth, but they were also written to give us comfort and consolation. The heresies had already started to come in, and John had to write his Gospel in order to show that Jesus of Nazareth is the eternal Son of God, the everlasting Word. Some people said that he was only a man, that he was only Jesus. The Gospel's emphasis is, no—he is God the eternal Son. But then John writes his first epistle with the exact opposite objective. Other people were saying that the Lord Jesus Christ was God and did not really have a true body but only a phantom body, an appearance. So then John had to write to show that he had truly come "in the flesh."

But in both cases the ultimate objective was to establish believers in the faith and in the truth as it is in Christ Jesus, in order that they might go on rejoicing in him. The false teaching had shaken them, and it had made them lose their joy. So we are given these details about his coming and what it cost him. There is no greater account of this than the one found in Philippians 2. Here again Paul is dealing with a most practical subject. If I do nothing else, I hope I am showing you the method of the Scriptures. People were quarreling with one another in the church at Philippi. So Paul says:

> Fulfil ye my joy, that ye be likeminded, having the same love, being of one accord, of one mind. Let nothing be done through strife or vainglory; but in lowliness of mind let each esteem other better than themselves. Look not every man on his own things, but every man also on the things of others.

A most practical, ordinary problem, is it not, but this is how the apostle deals with it.

"Let this mind be in you"—what mind?—"which was also in Christ Jesus: who, being in the form of God, thought it not robbery to be equal with God." He was in the form of God; he is God the eternal Son, co-equal, co-eternal with the Father. He has all the insignia and manifestations of everlasting, divine glory. But he did not regard those as prizes on which to hold. He did not say, "Whatever happens, I'm not going to let go or forgo my position and all the privileges that belong to it." That is the real meaning of "thought it not robbery to be equal with God." Far from doing that, "he made himself of no reputation." Can you feel the content of that statement? He had made men: "For by him were all things created . . . and for him" (Col. 1:16); "upholding all things by the word of his power" (Heb. 1:3). He, of whom all that is true, "made himself of no reputation, and took upon him the form of a servant, and was made in the likeness of men: and being found in fashion as a man, he humbled himself, and became obedient unto death, even the death of the cross" (vv. 2–8).

If the contemplation of that does not move us to the depth of our being, something is radically wrong with us as Christians. That is what it comes to. That is how Paul deals with a practical problem. This is the only way to know the joy of the Lord. Just look at him and consider what he did. This was planned before the foundation of the world, but the time came, the appointed time. "The fulness of the time" (Gal. 4:4) arrived, and this eternal Son of God was born as a helpless babe in the stable in Bethlehem, and his little body was put into the manger. Can you imagine what it meant for him to divest himself of his eternal glory? He laid it aside. He did not empty himself of Godhead—he could not have done that—but he laid aside all that belonged externally to the glory of heaven.

You say, "But I've always known that. I've known it since I was a child."

You say you have always known that, and yet you are miserable. How do you reconcile these two things? Can you know all that and what it really means and be miserable or selfish or wounded or slighted and all the rest of the things that get us down and make us so wretched? There is something wrong somewhere, is there not? There is all the difference in the world between being aware of a thing and really knowing it. "Let this mind be in you"! Realize what happened; realize what it meant. He who owns the universe was born into abject poverty. Mary and Joseph could not even afford a lamb to present at the Temple after his birth; they had to use two turtledoves because of their poverty. The Lord of glory, the Creator of the universe, was born in a stable—that is it. The author of life was helpless as a babe. Oh, the poverty and the lowliness of it all!

But, oh, the glory of it all! This was so tremendous that the angels were singing in heaven. That is what the shepherds heard, is it not, as they were watching their flocks. They heard the heavenly choir, a choir of angels, singing, "Glory to God in the highest, and on earth peace, good will toward men" (Luke 2:14). This was so tremendous that the angels burst forth into song, and they have been singing ever since and will go on singing to all eternity. Turn to the book of Revelation, and you hear them singing the song of "the Lamb that was slain": "Blessing, and honour, and glory, and power, be unto him that sitteth upon the throne, and unto the Lamb for ever and ever" (Rev. 5:12–13). It is all because they realize something of the glory of the way in which he came into this world.

And then look at him as he was in this world. That is why we have the four Gospels. They were not written that you and I might pass scriptural examinations; they were not written just so you and I could read daily portions. They were written to enable us to see him and to know him and to rejoice in him. How are we reading our Scriptures? We become so mechanical about it, self-righteous even! Forget your systems, and begin to read the Scriptures and to meditate upon them and to pray over them and to be filled with the Spirit as you do so. If your reading of the Scriptures does not fill you with joy, you are misreading them. You are using this book as a textbook, which it is not. Its purpose is to feed the soul and to bring us into this knowledge that leads to the joy that is beyond description. So look at him as he was in this world; look at his lowliness, "the meek and lowly Jesus"—nothing much to look at. He passed among men, and often they did not even notice him. He took upon him the form of a servant—he humbled himself to that extent.

But, oh, look at his compassion and his sympathy! This is what I want to emphasize before we leave this matter. Are you in trouble?

Art thou weary, art thou languid,
Art thou sore distressed?

JOHN MASON NEALE

Perhaps you are getting old, you are losing your health, your memory is going, you are noticing evidences of decay—you are bound to, it happens to us all. Or maybe you have lost someone who is dear to you, or someone has disappointed you, or you have had some other loss or some anxiety about your husband or about your wife or about your children, and you are in trouble and cast down, and nobody seems able to help you.

My dear friend, do you know that the four Gospels were written because you are like that? That is why we have them. We do not merely have a doctrine—we have a person. We have a picture of a person there in those four portraits of him. And what do you see as you look at them? Well, it is always his pity, his compassion. "When he saw the multitudes, he was moved with compassion on them, because they fainted, and were scattered abroad, as sheep having no shepherd" (Matt. 9:36). Do you remember what happened when he was on his way to heal the daughter of Jairus? Jairus was an important man, an official, and he had come to ask Jesus to go and heal his daughter. So our Lord went with him, and there was a great throng. But there was a poor woman there with a desperate need. Nobody knew anything about her at all, but she knew her own suffering. "The heart knoweth his own bitterness" (Prov. 14:10). And she said to herself, "If I could only touch the hem of his garment I am sure I would get something"—and she was so right. She did touch the hem of his garment, and she received healing and infinitely more (Luke 8:41–48). Why? Though Jesus was on an official errand, in a sense, he always had time for a suffering, lonely, forgotten individual. Oh, his compassion!

Our Lord was often reprimanded by his own followers because he would see and stop for a blind man or a beggar and be with tax collectors and sinners. "Ah!" they said, "this is not consistent with your position and the greatness of your teaching and the miracles that you are performing. Why do you do this sort of thing?" But he never failed.

Even on the cross, dying in shame and in agony, he had time to talk to the penitent thief, to this poor fellow who was also dying and realizing his sin and his hopelessness. Our Lord in his agony talked to him and gave him a word of consolation and help

That is the picture we see of him. Listen to his teaching, listen to what he has to say, it is always the same—love and mercy and compassion. Look at what he says to this poor woman of Samaria, the adulteress who is ostracized by the polite and respectable people who would not be seen talking to such a woman. He not only talks to her, he holds before her all the blessings that he has come into the world to give, even to her. That was his teaching, that was his practice, and he had the power to do it. He could say, "Son, be of good cheer; thy sins be forgiven thee" (Matt. 9:2). He was able to forgive; it was not merely talk—he had the power.

So there in the four Gospels, when you look at him that is what you see. And then you must apply all you see and understand. Do not stop merely at reading your daily portion of Scripture—yes, do that, but do not stop there. The whole art is application. Preaching that does not apply the message is no good, and reading the Bible without applying the message is no good either. So here is your application. You see him as he was on earth and in the depth of your need, in the agony of your condition, and you say to yourself, "He is still the same, still 'touched with the feeling of our infirmities'" (Heb. 4:15). He sees us, and he is still the same compassionate, loving person. Turn to him, and he will tell you, "I know all about you," and you will find your relief, you will find your peace, you will find your joy. That is how you do it. You do not seek peace and joy directly; you always go to him.

But then you say, "Well, what is he like? If he is now in the glory everlasting, is he still concerned?" He is. "I am he that liveth, and was dead; and, behold, I am alive for evermore" (Rev. 1:18). "Jesus Christ, the same yesterday, and to day, and for ever" (Heb. 13:8). Look at him, therefore, as you see him living his life in this contradictory, evil, sinful world, as you and I are having to do. Look at him there in the pages of the Gospels, and then go to him! You will not be miserable very long; you will not be unhappy for long. I do not care what your circumstances or your position may be, he is still the same and is ready to do for you what he did for those who were in need and suffering while he was in this world. And he will say to you, "Peace be with you," "Rise," "Walk," "See"—whatever it is—and he will send you on your way rejoicing.

34

"Looking unto Jesus"

Jesus answered and said unto her, Whosoever drinketh of this water shall thirst again: but whosoever drinketh of the water that I shall give him shall never thirst; but the water that I shall give him shall be in him a well of water springing up into everlasting life. (John 4:13–14)

The whole object of the entire New Testament is "looking unto Jesus" (Heb. 12:2), and we have been trying to do that. We have looked at him in the glory of his person—"the brightness of his [God's] glory, and the express image of his person" (Heb. 1:3)—and we have considered why he ever came into the world, the way in which he came, the humiliation that was involved, the self-abnegation, and the laying aside of the signs and the marks of his eternal glory. Finally, we have looked at him as he walked here in this world with his eye of compassion.

Now let us go on—this is the way to get happiness and peace and joy, not in some kind of psychological service that makes a direct attack upon the emotions. That is wrong. The way to have the joy of the Lord is to know the Lord. So let us continue to look at him. Here he is in the world. He is walking about the world, he sees the need, and he deals with it. But look at what he himself endured; look at what he suffered while he was here. Are you unhappy because of people or circumstances or because of something you are having to endure? Are you unhappy because you are beset by temptations or surrounded by trials and problems? These are the things that make us miserable, the things that are so constantly robbing us of our joy. But our Lord says, "Whosoever drinketh of the water that I shall give him shall never thirst." It does not matter what the circumstances may be, we are not disturbed by them; he delivers us.

And this deliverance is partly because of what our Lord endured and suffered while he was here, and that is why the Gospels were written.

There were people who said, "Ah, yes, he is eternal God and only had a kind of cloak of flesh, a kind of phantom body; he never really suffered anything at all." And the Gospels were written partly to establish the fact that such a view is heresy. He did suffer; he was truly "made flesh" (John 1:14); he really did become man. He added manhood on to his Godhead, and he lived his life in this world as a man. Now this is most important, and there is no greater comfort and consolation than to realize it.

James says to us, very rightly, "Let no man say when he is tempted, I am tempted of God: for God cannot be tempted with evil, neither tempteth he any man" (Jas. 1:13). By definition, God cannot be tempted. God also cannot lie. Certain things are impossible to God because he is God. The presence of evil in the mind of God is unthinkable: "God is light, and in him is no darkness at all" (1 John 1:5). He hates evil with the whole intensity of his eternal being; so God cannot be tempted. But we look at Jesus of Nazareth and see that he "was in all points tempted like as we are, yet without sin" (Heb. 4:15). We read the accounts of the temptations for forty days and forty nights in the wilderness, but that is only a specimen, an example. And the tempter was not some underling but the devil himself, tempting Jesus at his most sensitive points; yet our Lord did not fall into sin.

But the point for us is that our Lord has been tempted, that he has endured this. Not only that, look at the trials he suffered—what the author of the Epistle to the Hebrews calls "such contradiction of sinners against himself" (12:3). How difficult it is for us to realize what our Lord endured while he was in this world! We tend to read our Scriptures so superficially that we forget that these are facts; we tend to read the Bible as fiction. But it is all true, it actually happened—the Son of God was in this world, and look at the way he was treated. His own mother misunderstood him; he even had to rebuke her. His own brothers completely misunderstood him, even taunting him and jeering at him. We read:

> His brethren therefore said unto him, Depart hence, and go into Judaea, that thy disciples also may see the works that thou doest. For there is no man that doeth any thing in secret, and he himself seeketh to be known openly. If thou do these things, shew thyself to the world.

And John adds, "For neither did his brethren believe in him" (John 7:3–5).

Perhaps you are in trouble, you are having a hard time, people are misunderstanding you and are cruel to you, and you are losing the joy of your salvation. You are defeated, you are down, you wonder whether there is anything in Christianity after all. You are thinking of giving it up. "What is the point of it? The people in the world seem to be so happy. Are these promises true?" That is what you are feeling—that is what the devil is suggesting to you. And there is only one answer to all that: it is to look at him who endured "such contradiction of sinners against himself," in his own family and in his own home.

Yet even worse was to come. Our Lord had chosen twelve men to be specially his people, his disciples, and he had paid much attention to them, giving them considerable teaching and instruction and some very high privileges. He had let them into secrets that "the wise and prudent" knew nothing about at all (Luke 10:21). He had given them more knowledge and information than was possessed by all the Pharisees and scribes put together. They were the inner circle. But at the end of the three years, when the plans of the enemy came to fruition, we are told, "And they all forsook him, and fled" (Mark 14:50). He was left alone, forsaken, completely misunderstood, even by his own innermost circle of followers. And then, of course, there was the scoffing and the jeering and the mocking of the ignorant crowd. My dear friends, the Son experienced and endured all this.

This is how the Scriptures give us comfort and consolation. They say to us:

> Consider him that endured such contradiction of sinners against himself, lest ye be wearied and faint in your minds. Ye have not yet resisted unto blood, striving against sin. (Heb. 12:3–4)

But he did, for the end of all that betrayal and forsaking and all the rest of it was death upon the cross.

I am trying to give you a method, a picture. I am trying to show you how you are to deal with yourself when you tend to be losing your joy. This is the method:

> Looking unto Jesus the author and finisher of our faith; who for the joy that was set before him endured the cross, despising the shame, and is set down at the right hand of the throne of God. (Heb. 12:2)

When you are hard-pressed and tried, when the devil tempts you to your foundations, and when everybody else seems to be against you to drive you to despair, do you just give in? If you do, then it is entirely your own fault that you are unhappy. Our Lord says, "Whosoever drinketh of the water that I shall give him shall never thirst." How do you drink that water? Well, this is part of it—you just go straight to him, you see what he went through for you, and you realize you are not alone. Indeed, you realize that you have been given a very great and a very high privilege. Peter works that out like this when he is telling us to be obedient:

> Servants, be subject to your masters with all fear; not only to the good and gentle, but also to the froward. For this is thankworthy, if a man for conscience toward God endure grief, suffering wrongfully. For what glory is it, if, when ye be buffeted for your faults, ye shall take it patiently? but if, when ye do well, and suffer for it, ye take it patiently, this is acceptable with God. For even hereunto were ye called: because Christ also suffered for us, leaving us an example, that ye should follow his steps: who did no sin, neither was guile found in his mouth: who, when he was reviled, reviled not again; when he suffered, he threatened not: but committed himself to him that judgeth righteously. (1 Pet. 2:18–23)

And if you do the same, whatever is happening to you, you will still have "joy unspeakable and full of glory." Work that out for yourselves.

All that our Lord endured ended in death on the cross. Here, of course, is the central theme of the Christian faith. But our danger is to say, "Oh, yes, I know all about the cross. I understand exactly about the death of Christ." Is not that our tendency? But listen to what Isaac Watts tells you: "When I survey the wondrous cross . . ." You cannot take a hurried glance at the cross. It is to be contemplated, to be meditated upon for the rest of your life. You *survey* it, and you begin to see its depth and height, its breadth, its length. You see that there is no end to it, that it is the most amazing thing that has ever happened. Look at it, and the more you do, the more you will find comfort, consolation, peace, joy—everything of which you stand in need. And you will discover this: he came into the world in order to go to the cross.

Why be influenced by the thinking of the secular world that has come so much into the church? The death of Christ is not an accident; it is not pacifism. He came from heaven in order to die; he kept on saying so. "The Son of man," he said, "came not to be ministered unto, but to minister, and to give his life a ransom for many" (Matt. 20:28). The Son of man must be lifted up, he said, "as Moses lifted up the serpent in the wilderness" (John 3:14). In the Epistle to the Hebrews we read, "We see Jesus, who was made a little lower than the angels for the suffering of death, crowned with glory and honour; that he by the grace of God should taste death for every man" (2:9); and in Revelation, "the Lamb [of God] slain from the foundation of the world" (13:8). The death of the Lamb of God was in the eternal mind as the only way of salvation. What I am emphasizing is that our Lord came for this purpose. He offered himself. You will find it set out in the tenth chapter of the great Epistle to the Hebrews:

> Wherefore when he cometh into the world he saith, Sacrifice and offering thou wouldest not, but a body hast thou prepared me: in burnt offerings and sacrifices for sin thou hast had no pleasure. Then said I, Lo, I come (in the volume of the book it is written of me,) to do thy will, O God. (vv. 5–7)

He volunteered; he came deliberately. "He stedfastly set his face to go to Jerusalem" (Luke 9:51). His friends tried to dissuade him; they warned him that Herod and others were waiting for him. But he rebuked them. His object, in other words, was "to give his life a ransom for many" (Mark 10:45). The Son of God came into this world specifically to take your sins and mine upon himself, to bear our guilt, to receive our punishment, and he has done so to the full. He has paid the penalty; he has made full satisfaction for sins. "This man, after he had offered one sacrifice for sins for ever, sat down on the right hand of God" (Heb. 10:12). Here is one who was able to say, "It is finished" (John 19:30).

Are you troubled and unhappy about your sins? Tell me, you who do not have the joy of salvation, you who do not have the assurance of salvation, what is robbing you of it? You who, when you are on your knees praying to God, find yourselves uncertain and troubled, having to spend the whole of your time pleading for forgiveness, why are you like that? You are not meant to be. The Son of God came from heaven to earth and did all he did, especially the death on the cross, in order that you may never be like that again. He has once and forever borne the punishment of your sins; they are blotted out; they have already received their punishment.

> There is therefore now no condemnation to them which are in Christ Jesus [you will never get joy and assurance by just looking into yourself and examining yourself. Of course not. There is only one way to receive them] . . . for the law of the Spirit of life in Christ Jesus hath made me free from the law of sin and death. For what the law could not do, in that it

> was weak through the flesh, God sending his own Son in the likeness of sinful flesh, and for sin, condemned sin in the flesh: that the righteousness of the law might be fulfilled in us, who walk not after the flesh, but after the Spirit. (Rom. 8:1–4)

You have no right to be miserable; you have no right to be lacking in joy. If you do not have the joy of salvation—I am speaking to Christians—there is only one reason. It is because you are deliberately listening to the devil rather than to the word of God. You need to look again at the one on the cross, and you must ask questions. What is he doing there? Was it an accident or was it deliberate? If it was deliberate, why was he there? What was the object? Listen to what he says: "I came not to call the righteous, but sinners to repentance" (Mark 2:17).

You say, "But I can't be happy because I'm a sinner."

But he says he has come to call sinners to repentance. "They that are whole have no need of the physician, but they that are sick" (Mark 2:17). By your lack of joy you are denying his teaching. You think, perhaps, that it is because you are such a sensitive soul that you lack joy. It is not! It is because you are ignorant, because you do not believe the word of God, because you will not exercise your senses. You have as a Christian, I say, no right to feel under condemnation. You are detracting from the glory of God's salvation. He came not only to purchase pardon for his people but also that we might know it and might rejoice in it. "Rejoice in the Lord always: and again I say, Rejoice" (Phil. 4:4).

Now I say again that you will not get this joy by trying to work up a feeling. I often watch people in the Communion service, and I see their struggle and agony and know that they are trying to feel something. Don't do that anymore! Look at him, and consider who he is and what he has done; that is how you receive joy. Don't try to work up feelings; that is always fatal. Look unto Jesus. Look at him dying on the cross, and realize something of the depth of its meaning.

There, then, is our Lord on the cross. And he dies, and they take down the body and lay it in a tomb, and they roll the stone in front and seal it and put soldiers to guard it. But you and I would not be here now if it had stopped at that!

So then begin to look at the glory of the resurrection, which is everywhere in the New Testament. The Gospels all record it, and what was the preaching of the apostles in the book of Acts? "Jesus, and the resurrection" (Acts 17:18). They were witnesses to the resurrection. The records are so honest and so true, and they make it quite plain and clear that all these apostles would have gone home and would have given up in despair but for the glorious fact of the resurrection. Peter, we are told, was so miserable at the death of our Lord that he did not know what to do with himself. So, typically the fisherman, he said, "I go a fishing" (John 21:3)—to get a bit of relief, to do something, to get away. He had not understood it, though he had had the teaching. He was blinded by sin. But you remember what happened—the Lord appeared and kept on appearing. He spoke to the apostles and taught them.

There is something wrong with us, my dear friends, and we know what it is, do we not? It is sin remaining in us, and it is the indolence that sin leads to, and the lack of application. If you and I only lived in the light of the fact of the resurrection, we would never be downcast again. Its meaning is endless. Its first meaning is that God is fully satisfied—he has accepted the offering made by his own Son: "[He] was delivered for our offences, and was raised again for our justification" (Rom. 4:25). God raised his Son publicly, as it were, in order that we might have the joy and the comfort and assurance of knowing that our sins are forgiven.

And for us this means, as Paul puts it in writing to Timothy, "Our Saviour Jesus Christ . . . hath abolished death, and hath brought life and immortality to light through the gospel" (2 Tim. 1:10). You and I need not dabble in spiritism or with the cults and sciences, so-called, which are not sciences at all. We *know*. He has opened the gates of heaven; he has brought life and immortality to light. We have this certain, sure fact.

Not only that, but by our Lord's resurrection we know that he has conquered all our enemies—every one of them. He conquered the devil when he tempted him, and he has conquered the "last enemy": "The last enemy that shall be destroyed is death" (1 Cor. 15:26). He has taken the sting out of death; it is no longer there; for the Christian, it has gone.

So once again we see that we need to know how to study the Scriptures. Look at Timothy. He is the type of individual who is always ready to be cast down, always wondering what is going to happen—problems in the churches, people misunderstanding him. And then he hears the news that Paul is in prison and that the Emperor Nero has decided to put him to death, and poor Timothy says, "The end has come—Paul is going to die. What can we do? Look at all the problems in the churches, the old, the young—look at the opposition. How terrible!"

So Paul writes to Timothy and says, "I put thee in remembrance that thou stir up the gift of God, which is in thee by the putting on of my hands." "Pull yourself together, man," Paul says in essence. "Don't sit down and mope and whimper and cry and commiserate with yourself." Why? "For God hath not given us the spirit of fear; but of power, and of love, and of a sound mind [discipline, self-control]."

Then the apostle goes on to make this tremendous assertion, which is the essence of the Christian position: "For the which cause I also suffer these things"—because he is preaching the gospel, he is suffering and is in prison facing death—"nevertheless I am not ashamed: for I know whom I have believed, and am persuaded that he is able to keep that which I have committed unto him against that day" (2 Tim. 1:6–7, 12).

"Don't be worried about me," Paul says in effect. "Don't commiserate with me; don't offer me your sympathy—I don't need it. I'm not cast down, I'm not ashamed, I'm not frantic, and I'm not in trouble at all. 'I know whom I have believed, and am persuaded that he is able to keep that which I have committed unto him'—my soul and its eternal destiny—'against that day,'" the Day of Judgment, the day of Christ's Second Coming. Of course, Paul was always saying this. He says exactly the same thing to the Philippians when they are worrying about him:

> For I know that this shall turn to my salvation through your prayer, and the supply of the Spirit of Jesus Christ, according to my earnest expectation and my hope, that in nothing I shall be ashamed, but that with all boldness, as always, so now also Christ shall be magnified in my body, whether it be by life, or by death. For to me to live is Christ, and to die is gain. But if I live in the flesh, this is the fruit of my labour: yet what I shall choose I wot not. For I am in a strait betwixt two, having a desire to depart, and to be with Christ; which is far better: nevertheless to abide in the flesh is more needful for you. (Phil. 1:19–24)

This is the way in which one obtains this full heart satisfaction from him and will "never thirst" even in such circumstances. Paul says, "It is true. I am not ashamed—of course not; in fact, I am exulting."

We rejoice even in the midst of tribulations. And as you know full well, this rejoicing is not confined only to some outstanding persons such as the apostle Paul but was true of the most ordinary early Christians. These were the people who counted martyrdom the final crown of glory. These were the people who considered it a great honor to suffer shame for his name's sake, the people who had such joy in the Lord that nothing could rob them of it. Do you have this joy? Have you been delivered from all fear? Are you able to rejoice in the Lord always?

So look at the resurrection. Contemplate the fact; realize something of the content of its meaning. But go on. He rose from the dead, he manifested himself for forty days to chosen witnesses, and then he ascended into heaven in the presence of some of them. And where is he now? This is how you deal with these subjects, and I do not know what you feel, my friends, but the more I study these Scriptures, the more wonderful they become to me, and the less I feel I know about them.

Consider the author of the Epistle to the Hebrews. In the first three verses he tells you everything you can ever know, and then he goes on for thirteen chapters! This is the scriptural method, and it means that you have to see it all and then grasp it in portions and parts.

> God, who at sundry times and in divers manners spake in time past unto the fathers by the prophets, hath in these last days spoken unto us by his Son, whom he hath appointed heir of all things, by whom also he made the worlds; who being the brightness of his glory, and the express image of his person, and upholding all things by the word of his power, when he had by himself purged our sins, sat down on the right hand of the Majesty on high. (1:1–3)

The writer could not get over that and repeats it again in the tenth chapter:

> But this man, after he had offered one sacrifice for sins for ever, sat down on the right hand of God; from henceforth expecting till his enemies be made his footstool. (vv. 12–13)

Here is something glorious and tremendous. Here we are, a handful of people in a gainsaying world, full of wars and troubles, higher criticism, people worshipping science and other gods, and we are cast down and wondering how we can keep going. Does the church have a future? What is the matter with us? I repeat, the trouble with us is that we do not know the Scriptures because if we feel like that, a reply is given to us. Here are the last words in Matthew's Gospel:

> And Jesus [who is about to ascend to heaven] came and spake unto them, saying, All power is given unto me in heaven and in earth. Go ye therefore, and teach all nations, baptizing them in the name of the Father, and of the Son, and of the Holy Ghost: teaching them to observe all things whatsoever I have commanded you: and, lo, I am with you always, even unto the end of the world. (28:18–20)

Is that not enough for you? Do you not get up on your feet and shout and defy all your enemies? You would if you understood what that means, and you would never be cast down again. He is seated at the right hand of God, which is the position of honor, the position of power, and he says that all power has been given unto him. It has. As Paul reminds the Ephesians, God has "raised him up" because of what he has done:

> [God] raised him from the dead, and set him at his own right hand in the heavenly places, far above all principality, and power, and might, and dominion, and every name that is named [yes, Israel, Russia, the United States, Great Britain, all these powers we are hearing so much about], not only in this world, but also in that which is to come: and hath put all things under his feet, and gave him to be the head over all things to the church, which is his body, the fulness of him that filleth all in all. (Eph. 1:20–23)

He has it all, and you belong to him, and you are dear to him. What is he doing? Paul, in writing to the Romans who were also in great trouble because the sufferings of this present time had got them down, says this:

> Who shall lay any thing to the charge of God's elect? It is God that justifieth. Who is he that condemneth? It is Christ that died, yea rather, that is risen again, who is even at the right hand of God, who also maketh intercession for us. (8:33–34)

This, again, is the great theme of the author of Hebrews. In contrasting the old dispensation—the ritual of the Jewish Temple—and the Christian faith in Christ, he says:

> By so much was Jesus made a surety of a better testament. And they truly were many priests, because they were not suffered to contimue by reason of death [your priests and your high priests come and go, your popes come and go, and all your earthly priesthood]: But this man, because he continueth ever, hath an unchangeable priesthood. Wherefore he is able also to save them to the uttermost that come unto God by him, seeing he ever liveth to make intercession for them. (7:22–25)

Not only can you pray to God—the Lord Jesus Christ is praying for you, he is representing you. He is your great High Priest; he is taking your feeble cries and prayers and transmitting them and transmuting them unto God. There he is seated at the right hand of God, and he is there for you and for me.

Now these are not idle tales; these are sheer, solid facts. This is the Christian faith, the faith you think you know already. Well, if you know it, I say again, why are you miserable? Why are you defeated? Why are you filled with fears and forebodings? This is the way to have this joy and this peace and heart satisfaction. So consider what he has already done for you. He has reconciled you to God; you have forgiveness of sins; you are regenerate; you have new life within you; you have been adopted into the family of God; you are special objects of God's concern. You are "heirs of God, and joint-heirs with Christ" (Rom. 8:17). How did you go through the last week when you thought it might be the beginning of the third world war—how did you feel? How do you stand up to these possibilities? Christians see beyond all this; they know they are heirs of God and joint-heirs with Christ. They say, "The sufferings of this present time are not worthy to be compared with the glory which shall be revealed in us" (Rom. 8:18). Do you only hear the news? Do you only see literal countries in a material sense? Or do you see beyond it all to the glory? This is the question.

But you are still in this world, and you are still fighting the world, the flesh, and the devil. But remember, the Lord Jesus Christ is at the right hand of God, and he is "touched with a feeling of our infirmities" (Heb. 4:15). He has been through it all. He became man in order that he might be a merciful and faithful High Priest. He did it all in order that he might sympathize with you. He understands. Whatever has happened to you, he has been through it. Go to him, look to him; he will immediately give you peace. As he conquered it all, he will enable you to conquer it. You are not alone; he is with you. Having been tempted himself, "He is able to succour them that are tempted" (Heb. 2:18). And he tells you, "I will never leave thee, nor forsake thee" (Heb. 13:5). Never! Remember this: "Jesus Christ the same yesterday, and to day, and for ever" (Heb. 13:8). Look at him in the Gospels. See his sympathy, his understanding, his tenderness, his humility. He cannot change because of his eternal nature. All that he suffered and experienced here in this world is still there in his mind and heart, and he looks upon you and is ready and willing to help you and to succor you in all your need.

And, lastly, consider what he is yet going to do:

> [He] sat down on the right hand of God; from henceforth *expecting till his enemies be made his footstool.* (Heb. 10:12–13)

> As it is appointed unto men once to die, but after this the judgment: so Christ was once [and for all] offered to bear the sins of many; and unto them that look for him shall he appear the second time without sin [not in connection with sin, but] unto salvation. (Heb. 9:27–28)

> *Jesus shall reign where'er the sun*
> *Doth his successive journeys run;*
> *His kingdom stretch from shore to shore,*
> *Till moons shall wax and wane no more.*
>
> ISAAC WATTS

"Whosoever drinketh of the water that I shall give him shall never thirst"—never, whatever happens, whatever calamities, whatever wars, whatever pestilences. These will come; he has prophesied that. There shall be "wars and rumours of wars" (Mark 13:7) and pestilences, earthquakes, and people's hearts failing them. But it does not matter. He will come, and he will receive his own unto himself, and where he is, they shall be forever and ever.

My dear friends, "looking unto Jesus, the author and finisher of our faith," you will have the joy of the Lord, and it will become increasingly "a joy unspeakable and full of glory."

35

"Loved with Everlasting Love"

Jesus answered and said unto her, Whosoever drinketh of this water shall thirst again: but whosoever drinketh of the water that I shall give him shall never thirst; but the water that I shall give him shall be in him a well of water springing up into everlasting life. (John 4:13–14)

We have been seeing that ultimately the way to the heart satisfaction that our Lord gives and offers here so abundantly is to know him. The Spirit was sent to glorify him. The Spirit may give this joyful assurance directly—there are spiritual manifestations of the Son of God. But the normal method is through the Scriptures. The Scriptures are simply concerned to give us a portrait of him, to make us look at him. Their statements, all of them, can be summed up in the words, "looking unto Jesus" (Heb. 12:2).

We have been looking at this joy as an objective fact and have seen that we become happy by the indirect working of the Spirit as we look at our Lord in the Scriptures, as we contemplate him and meditate upon him and realize the truth concerning him. But now, having looked at this joy objectively, I think it will be most helpful to us if we also look at it subjectively. We must always take these two approaches. We must start with the objective because if we do not, we will soon be going astray. The trouble with the cults, with mere emotionalism, is that they do not start with the objective; they start with the subjective. Instead of starting with the gospel and the revelation of God in Jesus Christ, they start with man and human needs and desires. You must never do that; it is always a false approach. You start with him and contemplate the fullness that is in him, and then you see the application and the relevance of that to your particular needs.

So, having started with the objective, we come now to the subjective.

In other words, we are being very practical, and we come down to the level where we ask, what are the desires and the needs and the demands of our hearts? That is the purely subjective or experiential way of looking at it, and it is perfectly legitimate. I suggest that we can do this along two main lines. There are certain legitimate desires of the heart, and there are certain wrong or illegitimate desires, and I think we will be able to show that our Lord deals with both.

First, then, Christ satisfies the deepest *legitimate* desires of the heart. What are these? I think we will all agree that the heart cries out for rest and peace and joy and happiness. There is nothing wrong with that. It is very wrong to think that a human being should not desire rest. Man was meant to enjoy rest and peace; he was never meant to be restless. So the desire for rest and peace is good and right. It is a part of the protest that even fallen human nature makes against itself and against sin, which man as the result of his rebellion and listening to the devil has brought into the universe. So these are perfectly legitimate desires.

And likewise with joy. Just as it is wrong to think that we should always be restless or ill at ease, so it is wrong to think we should be miserable. It is right to desire to be joyful. There is no merit in being miserable. I know some people who twist and pervert themselves. You are familiar with masochism, and some people have at times foolishly thought that is the height of spirituality and that Christians are only truly functioning as Christians when they are unhappy. They think that the right thing to do is always the thing you do not want to do. What a perversion of Christianity that is! What a denial of the truth of the Fatherhood of God. No, no; the desire for rest and peace, for joy and happiness is perfectly legitimate. The point I am making, however, is that these cannot be given to us by the world. Our Lord said, "Whosoever drinketh of this water shall thirst again," and is not that the simple truth?

Now I could put this to you in many ways, but two illustrations in particular have come within my reading comparatively recently. Lord Snow—C. P. Snow—has recently written a most interesting and fascinating book called *Variety of Men*.[21] In this book, he writes of a number of great men whom he has known and of one whom he has never met. These men are some of the outstanding figures in the life of the world during the present [twentieth] century—not only statesmen and politicians but also men who were leaders in the realm of science, great men such as Einstein. But what emerges so significantly in every single case is their failure to find rest and peace and true joy and happiness. Now Lord Snow is not a Christian, and he is not concerned to bring out this point, but in being truthful and in analyzing these characters that is what he shows, and there is nothing new about this.

And then I read about the famous author of the Maigret detective stories, Georges Simenon. Here is a man who has made a fortune out of writing books—he has published 191! He has built himself a house in Switzerland above Lausanne. From the house there is a magnificent panorama stretching from the Italian Alps to Mont Blanc, including a wonderful view of the lake right down to Geneva. This is how Simenon describes his aim in building it: "I have tried to build a kind of perfection here." And, of course, it has everything that can be desired. It has wonderful windows—double glazing with gas between the two sheets of glass so that there should be no noise. He claims that "even though fifty children should be playing and shouting together outside at the same time, you would not hear a sound."

This is the way the world seeks peace and rest, happiness and joy. It is a marvelous house! We are given a list of the contents: twenty-one telephones, seven bathrooms, seven refrigerators, seven television sets, a laundry room with three washing machines, a kitchen like the galley of a liner, four or five paintings in every room, and in the main study eleven pictures by some of the masters! So there it is, but this is his confession:

> I have only one ambition left: to be completely at peace with myself; I doubt if I shall ever manage it. I do not think it is possible for anyone. It is not a question of money, for that kind of happiness must come from within yourself. I do not know any man, however successful, who is completely happy.

Now that should make us stop and think. There is a man who has everything that money can give, but he has one ambition left—"to be completely at peace with myself." Here is the great problem, the great task. How easy it is to talk cleverly. Simenon can do it; he can write brilliantly. So can the others to whom I have referred—they are possessors of great power, great money, great influence, having every conceivable thing that thought and money can provide. Yet peace and joy still elude them; they cannot find it. "Whosoever drinketh of this water shall thirst again." Read the end of the lives of the great men of the world, and that is what you always find. There is something very sad, very tragic even, about the declining years of these men. The biggest thing of all they know nothing about. To the very end it eludes them.

One of our hymn-writers puts it so well. Here is the craving, the longing, and the desire of the human heart:

I ask thee for a thoughtful love,
Through constant watching wise,
To meet the glad with joyful smiles,
And wipe the weeping eyes;
And a heart at leisure from itself,
To soothe and sympathize.

ANNA L. WARING

You cannot truly "soothe and sympathize" and help others unless you have "a heart at leisure from itself." Self is the trouble. How to find peace with oneself—here is the great quest.

All great literature really treats just this one subject. The greatest drama is always tragedy; great biographies and autobiographies all come to this. Here is the great problem of the human race, and our Lord's constant claim is that he, and he alone, can satisfy this longing and deep desire of the heart—and how abundantly does history record the truth of that claim. "Peace I leave with you," he said, "my peace I give unto you: not as the world giveth, give I unto you. Let not your heart be troubled, neither let it be afraid" (John 14:27).

And, of course, we see this promise and assurance running right through all the writings and the teachings of the epistles. For example, "Grace unto you, and peace, from God our Father and the Lord Jesus Christ" (2 Thess. 1:2). That is a very common form of salutation at the beginning of the various epistles. You also find it actually put into practice in the book of Acts. This is what stands out at once about those early Christians—they found a place of rest, a place of peace.

Of course, this is not confined only to the early Christians. This comes out so wonderfully and so gloriously in the subsequent history of the church and is celebrated in such an amazing manner in all the great hymns. Take this one, for instance, by Philip Doddridge :

Now rest, my long-divided heart;
Fixed on this blissful center, rest;
With ashes who would grudge to part,
When called on angels' bread to feast?
("O Happy Day, That Fixed My Choice")

That is it—the thing that the poor writer of literature cannot discover—

"a heart at leisure from itself," peace and rest within. Here is a man who can address his heart and say, "Now rest, my long-divided heart."

Now as we have found, there is a sense in which you cannot make too sharp a distinction between the intellectual aspect and the emotional heart aspect of the Christian life—the two go together. Doddridge is addressing his mind as well as his heart; it is true of both. The mind comes to the end of its quest, and so he can address his heart—"Rest, my long-divided heart." You remember the famous words of Augustine. This scintillating, brilliant philosopher could not find rest and peace; when at last he found it, he could only burst out and say, "Thou hast made us for thyself, and our hearts are restless until they find their rest in thee." But they do find it there.

One of the most glorious aspects of this blessed gospel is that men and women really do come to a place where they find quiet. We do not need to resort to mechanical devices; we do not need double glazing with gas in between to keep out the sounds. When Christ is in your heart, you do not hear them; you are hearing him. You have a place of rest in spite of the noise. At the very center of every hurricane there is a point of complete rest, and so does the Christian in this life, in a world like this.

And so Christians find that by our Lord they are given rest and peace—peace with God ("Therefore being justified by faith, we have peace with God through our Lord Jesus Christ," Romans 5:1); and until men and women find peace with God, they will never know true peace. They cannot. That is the cause of their restlessness. That is really what Augustine was saying. It is because they are at enmity with God and have lost the peace that they originally had with him that they are restless and unhappy and lacking in peace in every other realm of their lives. It is because they are out of right relationship with God that they are in wrong relationship even to themselves as well as to other people. This is the law of man's being.

Men and women have been made in the image and likeness of God; they are made for God. God has put such laws into human nature that they can only really function, even physically as well as mentally and spiritually, when they are obeying the laws of their nature, and obeying these laws means they are in right relationship with God. The mechanism cannot work otherwise, and without the oil of the Spirit there will be grindings, cracklings, noise, disturbance, an absence of a smooth, harmonious working. This is the message of the entire Bible. Those great men of the world who are honest all admit there is no peace to be found in the world. It is all very well to make statements, to talk cleverly and brilliantly, and to use wonderful terms that people do not understand, but the question is, are they really happy? How do they face death? How do they face their declining years? How do they face disappointment? That is the test. And all the great people of the world fail at this point. I am referring to those, of course, who are not Christians. The moment you drink of this water that Christ has come to give, the whole situation changes. You are put right at the center; you are put into the true relationship. You feel that the command has come, and everything drops into position.

Now, of course, this must be worked out, but there it is—the big change has happened. And that immediately means that you are put right with yourself, and as these men admit, self is the great problem. We find other people difficult because we find ourselves difficult. It is because we are quarreling with ourselves that we tend to quarrel with other people. I was listening to a musician talking the other afternoon about the great conductor Toscanini, who was notorious for his tantrums and bad temper. On one occasion when a certain musician was playing in the orchestra, the Maestro lost his temper and fumed and raged and walked off. The man walked out after him to apologize and said, "What were we doing wrong, Maestro? What was the matter?" Toscanini replied, "You were doing nothing wrong—it was I who was wrong."

Do you see the trouble? He could not conduct to his own satisfaction; he was ill at ease with himself; he was fighting and quarrelling with himself. So he was unpleasant to other people and quarreled with them. And this is the whole trouble in life, is it not? Man will never be at peace with himself until he is at peace with God. Why? Because until he has the right view of himself in his relationship to God, he will always see himself in the wrong way. We are ambitious, we have jealousies and rivalries, and all these take our rest and peace from us. But the moment we have peace with God, we are at peace with ourselves; we have a true view of ourselves and an object and purpose in life and in the world. We see everything in a different way. "A heart at leisure from itself"—do you have that?

My dear friend, it is not your opinions on evolution or on creation that matter; that is a lot of camouflage. The problem for you is not to understand how human beings have evolved but to know why you do not have rest and peace with yourself. Are you in the position of Georges Simenon: "I have only one ambition left: to be completely at peace with myself"? What is your answer to him? Has your self fallen into the right place, and do you know this rest? Are you able to say with the apostle Paul, who put this perfectly to the Christians in Corinth:

> But with me it is a very small thing that I should be judged of you, or of man's judgment: yea, I judge not mine own self. For I know nothing by myself; yet am I not hereby justified: but he that judgeth me is the Lord. (1 Cor. 4:3–4)

He has ceased to be concerned about himself—"a heart at leisure from itself."

It follows, obviously, that if you have peace with God and peace with yourself, you are in a position to have peace with other people. But that is the only way; it is the inevitable order. Our Lord, in giving an account of the great commandments, was very careful about the order:

> Thou shalt love the Lord thy God with all thy heart, and with all thy soul, and with all thy mind. This is the first and great commandment. And the second is like unto it, Thou shalt love thy neighbour as thyself. (Matt. 22:37–39)

The foolish world starts with the neighbor, and people come to church saying, "What is the Christian church going to do about these problems?" expecting that we can tell the statesmen what to do. That is starting with the neighbor, and it is hopeless. But if you drink of this water that our Lord is offering, you will find that it will work from above downward—God, self, others—and so you find peace, and so you find joy.

We have already considered this in dealing with the fruit of the Spirit as outlined by Paul in the fifth chapter of the Epistle to the Galatians. These things are quite inevitable. All of us by nature long for rest and peace and joy. Jesus offers it and gives it. This is the testimony of the saints through the centuries.

The next thing, I think you will agree, that the heart always cries out for is love. I need not describe this; you are familiar with it. We are so made and constituted that we all long to be loved. If you do not, you are an abnormality, a monstrosity. The feeling of being unloved is a prolific cause of the agony and the strain and the unhappiness in the world. Our Lord says, "Whosoever drinketh of the water that I shall give shall never thirst." Whatever you and I may know of human love will never fully or finally satisfy. He alone can do that, and he does.

How does our Lord satisfy this longing for love? Let me give you some of the great statements in the New Testament:

> For when we were yet without strength, in due time Christ died for the ungodly. For scarcely for a righteous man will one die: yet peradventure for a good man some would even dare to die. But God commendeth his love toward us, in that, while we were yet sinners, Christ died for us. Much more then, being now justified by his blood, we shall be saved from wrath through him. For if, when we were enemies, we were reconciled to God by the death of his Son, much more, being reconciled, we shall be saved by his life. (Rom. 5:6–10)

This is the love of God to us, and God commends it. Indeed, Paul has told us in the fifth verse, "Hope maketh not ashamed"—why?—"because the love of God is shed abroad in our hearts by the Holy Ghost which is given unto us." The Holy Spirit makes God's love real to us. We have a longing to be loved, and here we have an assurance that God himself loves us. But listen to Paul later on in the Epistle to the Romans, and you will find that he rises to some of the greatest heights, even judged by Paul's standards:

> We know that all things work together for good to them that love God, to them who are the called according to his purpose. For whom he did foreknow, he also did predestinate to be conformed to the image of his Son . . .

Some silly people ague about predestination. Predestination is not something to be argued about; it is something to be gloried in!

> . . . that he might be the firstborn among many brethren. Moreover whom he did predestinate, them he also called: and whom he called, them he also justified: and whom he justified, them he also glorified. What shall we then say to these things?

That is the inevitable question.

> If God be for us, who can be against us?

This is the great logic, is it not?

> He that spared not his own Son, but delivered him up for us all, how shall he not with him also freely give us all things? (Rom. 8:28–32)

Here is a man who knows that God loves him, that God loved him "before the foundation of the world" (Eph. 1:4) and set his affection upon him and predestined him for this glory. He knows he is loved with an everlasting love. The apostle Paul never tires of saying this, and this is just his way of telling us his experience of what Christ said to the woman of Samaria.

Before he became a Christian, Paul had been a very unhappy man, struggling, striving, sweating, trying to keep the Law. His life had been hard; it had been rigid; it had been cold. He was a genius at all times, a giant intellect, but he had known nothing about *love*. Then he met this blessed Christ, and he began to love. Why? Because he knew Christ's love to him. He says:

> For I through the law am dead to the law, that I might live unto God. I am crucified with Christ: nevertheless I live; yet not I, but Christ liveth in me: and the life which I now live in the flesh I live by the faith of the Son of God, who loved me, and gave himself for me. (Gal. 2:19–20)

"The Son of God, who loved me": this is what broke Paul's heart and enabled him to feel deeply for the first time in his life. He realized on the road to Damascus that that blessed Lord of glory whom he had dismissed as a carpenter had loved him even while he was blaspheming against him and persecuting him and trying to destroy his church. Paul knew he had been loved and was being loved and would be loved forever and ever, and he could not get over it. That was why he constantly found that he had to burst out into hymns of praise and thanksgiving. Listen to him trying to express this love in Ephesians 2. He says we were dead in trespasses and sins (v. 1).

> But God, who is rich in mercy, for his great love wherewith he loved us, even when we were dead in sins, hath quickened us together with Christ, (by grace ye are saved;) and hath raised us up together, and made us sit together in heavenly places in Christ Jesus: that in the ages to come he might shew the exceeding riches of his grace in his kindness toward us through Christ Jesus. (vv. 4–7)

Paul does not know how to express it. Later on he says in effect, "You know, I have been thanking God for you Ephesians, but you have not understood it all; but I am praying for you. What I am pleading for you is this: 'that he would grant you, according to the riches of his glory, to be strengthened with might by his Spirit in the inner man.'" What for?

> . . . that Christ may dwell in your hearts by faith; that ye, being rooted and grounded in love, may be able to comprehend with all saints what is the breadth, and length, and depth, and height; and to know the love of Christ [the love of Christ to you] which passeth knowledge. (3:16–19)

There is no end to this love. "Whosoever drinketh of the water that I shall give him shall never thirst." Peter, in his simple manner, says, in one of the most moving passages in the whole New Testament, "Humble yourselves therefore"—he is writing to people who are in trouble—"under the mighty hand of God, that he may exalt you in due time: casting all your care upon him"—why?—"*for he careth for you*" (1 Pet. 5:6–7). The whole of the heart of God is in that. God's fatherly love to you is all there—"he careth for you." He is watching over you; he is loving you with amazing love. He has numbered the hairs of your head; he knows them all. He cares for you, and nothing will ever happen to you apart from him. This is the glorious promise that our Lord is making to the woman of Samaria.

John, too, knows it—they all know it. It is what made them the men they were. "And we have known and believed the love that God hath to us." A better translation of that is, "We know the love that God hath to us, and we confide in it" (1 John 4:16). That is it! We rest in it; we are happy in it. We know it; it has been given to us.

So here it is in the New Testament, but we are always in danger, are we not, of saying, "That was all right perhaps in those days and times. But is this sort of thing still true?" Well, the hymnbook is the answer to that question, and not only the hymnbook but also the history of the church and the biographies of God's people. Listen to one of them bursting out and putting it like this:

Loved with everlasting love,
Led by grace that love to know;
Gracious Spirit from above,
Thou hast taught me it is so.
O this full and perfect peace!
O this transport all divine!
In a love which cannot cease,
I am his, and he is mine.

George Wade Robinson ("I Am His, and He Is Mine")

This is the language of love. You do not need to read novels to know about love. Read the Scriptures, read the hymnbooks, read the lives of the saints, and you begin to learn something about a love about which the world knows nothing whatsoever.

Come, thou Fount of every blessing,
Tune my heart to sing thy grace;
Streams of mercy, never ceasing,
Call for songs of loudest praise.
Teach me some melodious sonnet,
Sung by flaming tongues above.
Praise the mount! I'm fixed upon it,
Mount of thy redeeming love.

This man knows he is loved.

Here I raise my Ebenezer;
Here by thy great help I'm come;
And I hope, by thy good pleasure,
Safely to arrive at home.

Jesus sought me when a stranger,
Wandering from the fold of God;
He, to rescue me from danger,
Interposed his precious blood.

ROBERT ROBINSON ("COME, THOU FOUNT OF EVERY BLESSING")

And on they go. There is no end to this.

I've found a friend, O such a friend!
He loved me ere I knew him;
He drew me with the cords of love,
And thus he bound me to him.

I've found a friend, O such a friend!
He bled, he died to save me;
And not alone the gift of life,
But his own self he gave me.
Nought that I have my own I call,
I hold it for the giver,
My heart, my strength, my life, my all
Are his, and his forever.

I've found a friend, O such a friend!
So kind, and true, and tender,

So wise a counsellor and guide,
So mighty a defender!
From him who loves me now so well
What power my soul can sever?
Shall life, or death, or earth or hell?
No! I am his forever.

JAMES GRINDLAY SMALL ("I'VE FOUND A FRIEND")

I have often commended from this pulpit the reading of the journals of George Whitefield, and I commend them once more. Read them just for this one element, if for nothing else. Read about how he was so exhausted one day that he could scarcely speak and went to lie on a bed to have a bit of rest and leisure and to sleep. But he could not sleep. Why? Because Christ was pouring an abundance of his love into his heart. Read the early years of Howell Harris—this also happened to him. And all this is but a confirmation of our Lord's words, "Whosoever drinketh of the water that I shall give him shall never thirst." Your desire for love will be more than satisfied forever. "Loved with everlasting love"! That is it.

But let me say just one other thing. The heart not only longs to be loved, but it also wants to love; it wants an outlet for its love. And here again is a need that can only be fully satisfied in Christ, and nowhere else. "We love him, because he first loved us" (1 John 4:19). I have been quoting to you the statements of the apostle Paul about his realization of the love of God and the love of Christ to him, but he is equally eloquent in his descriptions of his love to them—he is lifted up by it. "To me to live is Christ, and to die is gain" (Phil. 1:21). This is it—"to be with Christ; which is far better" (v. 23). Read this man's epistles, and you will find that ever and again he bursts forth into some great hymn of praise and thanksgiving and worship and adoration.

What makes Paul do it? Well, he has just mentioned the word "Christ," and that thrills him, so off he goes, and his love pours forth. Once it was shut up, as it were, by legalism, pharisaism. Nothing will ever give an outlet to the heart and its love so much as this blessed and glorious gospel. And at the very height of Paul's experience you will find him saying this again in one of his most moving passages, a bit of autobiography. He has been describing what he was by nature, not boasting but saying how he once did boast:

> But what things were gain to me, those I counted loss for Christ. Yea doubtless, and I count all things but loss for the excellency of the knowl-

> edge of Christ Jesus my Lord: for whom I have suffered the loss of all things, and do count them but dung, that I may win Christ . . .

Paul will give everything to possess Christ. Nothing else is of value; this is what he wants.

> . . . and be found in him, not having mine own righteousness, which is of the law, but that which is through the faith of Christ, the righteousness which is of God by faith: that I may know him . . . (Phil. 3:7–10)

That is the language of love again. The apostle wants to know the Beloved more and more. Christians love Jesus Christ with the whole of their being; they are his bondslaves.

But again you may want to say, "Ah, that's in the New Testament, but is that normal for us?"

Of course it is. The whole of the New Testament is normal for us. The book of the Acts of the Apostles and the epistles are all normal for us; that is why we have them. And this is verified in the subsequent history of the church. If this does not move you to the depth of your being, I urge you to find out whether or not you are a Christian.

Jesus, lover of my soul,
Let me to thy bosom fly.

Do you know this?

Thou, O Christ, art all I want,
More than all in thee I find.

CHARLES WESLEY

Is that true of you?

Jesus, the very thought of thee
With sweetness fills the breast;
But sweeter far thy face to see,
And in thy presence rest.

BERNARD OF CLAIRVAUX

Object of my first desire,
Jesus crucified for me;
All to happiness aspire,
Only to be found in thee.

Thee to please, and thee to know
Constitute my bliss below;
Thee to see, and thee to love,
Constitute my bliss above.

AUGUSTUS TOPLADY

Oh, yes, says Charles Wesley:

O for a thousand tongues to sing
My great Redeemer's praise.

CHARLES WESLEY

Jesus, these eyes have never seen
That radiant form of thine;
The veil of flesh hangs dark between
Thy blessed face and mine.

I see thee not, I hear thee not,
Yet art thou oft with me;
And earth hath ne'er so dear a spot,
As where I meet with thee.

RAY PALMER ("JESUS, THESE EYES HAVE NEVER SEEN")

Yes, says Count Zinzendorf, "I have one passion; it is he and he alone." The whole of his heart was taken up.

"Whosoever drinketh of the water that I shall give him shall never thirst." You will know that you are loved, and you will love with the whole of your being.

36

The Longing of the Heart, Mind, and Will

Jesus answered and said unto her, Whosoever drinketh of this water shall thirst again: but whosoever drinketh of the water that I shall give him shall never thirst; but the water that I shall give him shall be in him a well of water springing up into everlasting life. (John 4:13–14)

We have seen that our Lord satisfies completely what I have described as the legitimate desires of the heart—rest, peace, happiness—to give us "a heart at leisure from itself" (Anna L. Waring). He alone gives that. We have also seen that our desire to be loved is fully satisfied. He lets us know that he has "loved [us] with everlasting love." And then we ended by showing how he gives us an outlet for our love. There is that within us that makes us feel the desire to love; it is a part of our very nature as God has made us. And we have seen that this, again, is primarily expressed in terms of our attitude to him.

Not only do we now love him, but also he so deals with us that we have an outlet for our desire to love others. This is equally important because the notion that a Christian is a kind of monk or anchorite, someone who chooses to be separate from the world and to live in lonely, isolated contemplation and meditation, is quite foreign to the New Testament. That is one of the fallacies of Roman Catholicism and all that type of piety, but that is not New Testament Christianity.

One of the grand discoveries made by Martin Luther was that the servant girl sweeping the floor could be as assured of God's love as the monk or the anchorite in a cell; and therefore we find that one of the great marks of New Testament Christianity is that people begin to love one another. You see the relevance of this to the age and the times in which we live. The world is torn asunder, and not merely the world in terms of nations and countries but even within nations, classes, groups, and so on. Everything is divided—"middle wall[s] of partition" (Eph. 2:14)—and there is no love.

Now our Lord satisfies that need, too. John in his first epistle puts it in a memorable phrase: "We know that we have passed from death unto life, because we love the brethren" (3:14). In other words, we have been brought into the fellowship of God's people, and we rejoice in this. We have come into a great family. We find that we are now interested in and love people in whom before we had no interest at all. Here is an extraordinary oneness—"to make in himself [Christ] . . . one new man" (Eph. 2:15)—and so the fellowship of Christian people is always a great characteristic of the Christian life. It is not surprising, therefore, that in one of the first accounts that we have of the early Christians, this element is brought out very prominently.

> Then they that gladly received his word were baptized: and the same day there were added unto them about three thousand souls. And they continued stedfastly in the apostles' doctrine and fellowship, and in breaking of bread, and in prayers. (Acts 2:41–42)

It happened immediately; they were taken out of the world and were drawn together. They wanted to spend all their time with the apostles and with the company of Christians; they wanted the teaching, the doctrine, but also the fellowship. This is always one of the first signs of rebirth. The one who is born again is anxious to be with such people; birds of a feather flock together. You are aware of this common interest, common life, common expectation, common everything.

> And fear came upon every soul: and many wonders and signs were done by the apostles. And all that believed were together, and had all things common; and sold their possessions and goods, and parted them to all men, as every man had need. And they, continuing daily with one accord in the temple, and breaking bread from house to house, did eat their meat with gladness and singleness of heart, praising God, and having favour with all the people. (Acts 2:43–47)

Now that is a lyrical picture, is it not? But that is what our Lord had promised; that is what he does. He gives an outlet to this gregarious instinct, if you like, this longing for fellowship and friendship and community, for being together. You can express it and make your contribution and give to others.

This is one of the themes of the New Testament. Our Lord, in that great statement that he made on the last day of the feast at Jerusalem, put it like this: "If any man thirst, let him come unto me, and drink. He that believeth on me, as the scripture hath said, out of his belly [out of his innermost parts] shall flow rivers of living water" (John 7:37–38). Christian men and women are a blessing and a benediction to other people; it does not matter where they are—among Christian people especially, but also everywhere. These blessings flow out, and so the land is made fruitful, as it were.

Now our Lord, and he alone, enables us to love in this way. This desire to love is in us, though it has been blunted, of course; sin has perverted and twisted everything. Humanity was never meant to be fighting as it is. We were meant to love one another and to work together and to help one another; and though sin has marred us, there is still that in us that cries out for this. Our Lord gives a full outlet to this longing to love in a way that nobody else does. And that, as I said, is the striking feature and characteristic of the life of the early church, as it has been of the church in every period of revival and reformation.

Read the history; this fellowship is one of the wonderful characteristics of the work of the Spirit. It is his special work—"the communion [the fellowship] of the Holy Ghost" (2 Cor. 13:14)—and not only fellowship with him and with the Father and the Son but fellowship with one another. The great characteristic of those little groups before the Protestant Reformation was the way they kept together and enjoyed one another's society and talked about Christian things; and it was again the mark of the early Protestants, Puritans, and early Methodists. They did not believe in isolation and only occasionally coming together. No, no! There was a blending and a unity and an outlet for the love that was within them.

Blest be the tie that binds
Our hearts in Christian love;
The fellowship of kindred minds
Is like to that above.

John Fawcett

There it is—this oneness, this unity, and it is given its full scope by this blessed life that he is ready to give us so freely.

We should think about and rejoice in that, and at the same time we should examine ourselves. Do we love the brethren? Would we sooner spend our day with Christian people than with the greatest people in the world who are not Christians? That is the sort of test we must apply. "We know that we have passed from death unto life, because we love the brethren" (1 John 3:14). We know that we belong together; we are related. We are "fellowcitizens with the saints, and of the household of God" (Eph. 2:19); we are children of the heavenly King.

But then let me go on to another aspect, which is equally important, perhaps even more so. He gives us an outlet for our desire to be *glorying*. I think you will agree again that this desire is very powerful in human nature—the desire to glory in various things. Human beings by nature like to glory in themselves; they like to glory in other people, certain outstanding people; and they like to glory in their country. I need not elaborate on this; we are all aware of it. History teaches it very plainly. Ultimately it is the cause of most wars. My country can do no wrong—this is a part of us, is it not? We are hero worshippers, and we are ever ready to glory in this or that, and we spend much of our time praising people, praising countries, praising institutions, praising different events.

You notice that I am putting this under the heading of the legitimate desires of the heart, and I want to show you why. We have perverted this desire—man in sin has perverted everything. But we must be very careful that we do not condemn something in and of itself because we have perverted it. The instinct for food must not be condemned because some people are gluttons. The desire for drink, likewise, must not be condemned because some people drink too much. You must not dismiss or condemn instincts because people abuse them and become their slaves. And I feel that this principle also applies to the whole question of glorying. Glorying is a part of human nature—badly misused, of course, and as a result productive of human tragedy. But when our Lord deals with us and when he gives us this water and we drink it, this particular desire also is given full scope and an outlet, and it becomes one of the most wonderful things of all for the Christian.

Let me show you something of what I mean. The apostle Paul particularly emphasizes this in all his writings. Read his epistles, and keep your eye on the phrase "glory in," which really should be translated "boast in." He constantly uses the word *glory*, and, of course, that is not surprising. Before his conversion, Paul was a man who knew a good deal about glorying. He was not backward in that respect. He was a man of outstanding gifts, and he was aware of them, as such men usually are. He said:

> . . . though I might also have confidence in the flesh. If any other man thinketh that he hath whereof he might trust in the flesh, I more: circumcised the eighth day, of the stock of Israel, of the tribe of Benjamin, an Hebrew of the Hebrews; as touching the law, a Pharisee; concerning zeal, persecuting the church; touching the righteousness which is in the law, blameless. (Phil. 3:4–6)

That is glorying. Paul says in effect, "If you want to start talking about boasting, I am ready to take you on. If you think you have anything to boast about, here is my record, here is my position. Look who I am; note my ancestry; note my nation; note the blood that is in me. Talk about ability, talk about morality, talk about religion—come along, I am ready to meet you." Boasting was his characteristic, not only as a Pharisee but as an exceptional man in so many respects. And there is nothing more wonderful to me about this man than the way in which all that is, as it were, taken hold of and sublimated and transformed and transfigured by the Lord Jesus Christ and made one of the most wonderful things of all.

And so it is not at all surprising that the apostle keeps on talking about glorying and referring to it in so many ways. He glories in the Lord himself. Take these words from the First Epistle to the Corinthians: "Ye see your calling, brethren, how that not many wise men after the flesh, not many mighty, not many noble, are called"—that is what the world glories in, is it not—wise men, mighty, noble—"but God hath chosen the foolish things of the world to confound the wise; and God hath chosen the weak things of the world to confound the things which are mighty; and base things of the world, and things which are despised, hath God chosen, yea, and things which are not, to bring to nought things that are"—why?—"that no flesh should glory in his presence. But of him are ye in Christ Jesus, who of God is made unto us wisdom, and righteousness, and sanctification, and redemption: that, according as it is written, He that glorieth, let him glory in the Lord" (1:26–31).

That was Paul's position. Again, he says to the Philippians in essence, "You are being troubled by certain Judaizers who are telling you that it is not enough to believe in Christ, that you must be circumcised, that you must belong to the circumcision. What are they talking about?" He says, "For we are the circumcision"—who are "we"?—"which worship God in the spirit, and rejoice in Christ Jesus, and have no confidence in the flesh" (3:3). That is it—"rejoice in Christ Jesus."

But I suppose we will all agree that one of the most moving statements that the apostle ever made in this respect is in his epistle to the Galatians. He is dealing, again, with the people who are trying to get others to become Jews, to add on this or that to their Christian faith, saying that keeping the Jewish Law was essential in addition to believing in Christ. But the apostle is impatient with it all, and this is how he puts it:

> But God forbid that I should glory, save in the cross of our Lord Jesus Christ, by whom the world is crucified unto me, and I unto the world. For in Christ Jesus neither circumcision availeth any thing, nor uncircumcision, but a new creature. And as many as walk according to this rule, peace be on them, and mercy, and upon the Israel of God. From henceforth let no man trouble me. (Gal. 6:14–17)

That is the position: "God forbid that I should glory, save in the cross of our Lord Jesus Christ." In whom are you glorying? About whom are you talking? Are you talking about men? "Let no man trouble me," says Paul (Gal. 6:17). "Do not talk to me about men." He does not want to talk about anybody except the Lord Jesus Christ. He glories in him, and in him alone.

Now this desire to glorify was always there in the apostle, but it was wrong before, it was under sin. Now it is in Christ, and all the intensity of this noble, majestic nature, this desire to praise and to glory in and to glorify, has its full outlet. Here is a theme that can never be exhausted. Here is one who is worthy to be praised. And, of course, Paul not only says this about the Lord himself, the Savior, but he glories equally in the salvation that we have in the Lord, and he is never tired of saying this. He writes to the Romans that he has been longing to come to Rome to preach the gospel to them, as he has in other places:

> I am debtor both to the Greeks, and to the Barbarians; both to the wise, and to the unwise. So, as much as in me is, I am ready to preach the gospel to you that are at Rome also. For I am not ashamed of the gospel of Christ.

Now that is a figure of speech that is called litotes. Paul puts the point he is making negatively in order to emphasize it yet more. When he says, "I am not ashamed of," he means, "I am very proud of," "I glory in," "I exult in," "I triumph in," "it is the biggest thing in my life," "I will lay aside everything else for this."

"I am not ashamed of the gospel of Christ"—he is writing to Christians in Rome, the imperial city, home of the emperors, the seat of government, a center of learning, art, literature, the center of the world of that day. "I am not ashamed of the gospel," says Paul in essence. "I am not ashamed to come to Rome. I do not care where I am. I have preached it in the villages and hamlets of Asia, and I am equally ready to come to the great imperial city because, in the last analysis, what does it have with all its pomp and show? ". . . for it is the power of God unto salvation"—greater than all your imperial powers put together and multiplied—"to every one that believeth; to the Jew first, and also to the Greek" (Rom. 1:14–16).

A universal gospel! The power of God! He is not ashamed. Of course not. He glories in it. And in the same way Paul says to the Ephesians:

> For by grace are ye saved through faith; and that not of yourselves: it is the gift of God: not of works, lest any man should boast. For we are his workmanship, created in Christ Jesus unto good works, which God hath before ordained that we should walk in them. (Eph. 2:8–10)

I could endlessly quote these magnificent statements that the apostle makes! Here is another, again one that is very moving:

> For we preach not ourselves, but Christ Jesus the Lord; and ourselves your servants for Jesus' sake. For God, who commanded the light to shine out of darkness, hath shined in our hearts, to give the light of the knowledge of the glory of God in the face of Jesus Christ. But we have this treasure [and what a treasure it is] in earthen vessels, that the excellency of the power may be of God, and not of us. (2 Cor. 4:5–7)

And then there is the grand climax of it all in the Epistle to the Romans. Paul has been working out the mighty argument concerning the gospel. He deals with every problem, even the problem of the Jews, who were not believing the gospel but rejecting it and had crucified their Messiah, and of the Gentiles, who were crowding into the kingdom. People were saying, "How do you reconcile all this? What about the promises of God to the fathers in the Old Testament? Do the promises cover all this?" And the apostle has worked out the great argument in chapters 9–10 and the bulk of chapter 11. Then, having said it all, he stops and stands back, and there is only one thing to do—break out into a great hymn of adoration and praise, a mighty parenthesis:

> O the depth of the riches both of the wisdom and knowledge of God! how unsearchable are his judgments, and his ways past finding out! For who hath known the mind of the Lord? or who hath been his counsellor? or who hath first given to him, and it shall be recompensed unto him again? For of him, and through him, and to him, are all things: to whom be glory for ever. Amen. (Rom. 11:33–36)

There it is. Paul glories in the Savior, the Lord, and he glories in his mighty salvation. Oh, yes, you can talk about "the simple gospel." It is in a sense—it can save a child. But it is not simple in an ultimate sense. It is profound—"the depth of the riches"—the treasures of God's wisdom and knowledge, all in this blessed person.

But the apostle's glorying is not confined to what he thinks and says about the Lord and about that great salvation. He goes as far as this: he is ready to die for it. This is true hero worship; he is ready to die for Christ. He has already suffered, and he is prepared to suffer endlessly for him.

But this was not confined to the great apostle; it was true of all the apostles and of other Christians. There is a wonderful statement at the end of Acts 5. The apostles had been arrested and thrown into prison, and they had escaped in a wonderful manner. Then they were arrested again and brought before the high court, the Sanhedrin, and had it not been for the pleading of a certain man, whose name was Gamaliel, they would all undoubtedly have been killed, and they knew that perfectly well. But they were sent out of court and were commanded not to speak in the name of Jesus. They were allowed to go free on condition that they stop preaching and teaching about this blessed person. "And they [the apostles and the others] departed from the presence of the council, *rejoicing that they were counted worthy to suffer shame for his name.*"

They gloried in the fact that they were suffering. Their greatest honor was to suffer dishonor for the Savior. That is the test of the true Christian. And so we read, "And daily in the temple, and in every house, they ceased not to teach and preach Jesus Christ" (Acts 5:41–42).

And, I repeat, the same is true of the apostle Paul. He gives that great list of the things in which he can boast, and then he turns on it all and says, "But what things were gain to me, those I counted loss for Christ. Yea doubtless, and I count all things but loss for the excellency of the knowledge of Christ Jesus my Lord" (Phil. 3:7–8).

Then as, an old man, probably writing his last letter, the Second Epistle to Timothy, knowing that he might be put to death at any moment, this is how he puts it:

> I am now ready to be offered, and the time of my departure is at hand. I have fought a good fight, I have finished my course, I have kept the faith: Henceforth there is laid up for me a crown of righteousness, which the Lord, the righteous judge, shall give me at that day: and not to me only, but unto all them also that love his appearing. (2 Tim. 4:6–8)

This is the characteristic of the New Testament Christians: "They loved not their lives unto the death" (Rev. 12:11). They so gloried in him that they considered it the supreme honor of their lives to be martyred. Martyrdom, to the early Christians, was the final crown of glory, the highest accolade that was given to the soldier in the army of the living God.

Now this is a part of our Lord's claim. He says, "Whosoever drinketh of the water that I shall give him shall never thirst." All this longing that is in us to give glory has its full outlet in him. And that theme will last throughout eternity. Here is a wonderful and thorough test that we can apply to ourselves. Are we glorying in him? Are we glorying in this great salvation? Are we ready, if necessary, to lay down our lives for him? Like these early Christians, would we count it the greatest honor to suffer dishonor for his name's sake? Like the apostle, can we say, "To me to live is Christ, and to die is gain"? Here is the essence of all this—glorying in him and in his cross, in his great salvation, ready to forsake the world and all it has, if needs be life itself, rather than cease to glory in him and in him alone.

Let me just mention one other matter. This theme is endless; you will never exhaust it. But let us not forget that he deals with these desires of the heart not only positively but also negatively. He does it by getting rid of and delivering us from the false and the wrong ideas that we have in our hearts. He not only gives us a positive theme to draw out all that is legitimate within us, but he also gets rid of that which is wrong and illegitimate—selfishness, ambition, lust, jealousy, envy, pride. It is these that lead to dissatisfaction, unhappiness, and restlessness. He shows us how wrong all that is.

When we look at him, how ashamed we feel when we think of selfishness! "Let this mind be in you, which was also in Christ Jesus: who, being in the form of God, thought it not robbery to be equal with God" (Phil. 2:5–6). He did not hold on to that; he laid it aside for our sake. So are we going to hold on to our rights or claims, our birth, our country, or anything else? The idea is monstrous! The meek and lowly Jesus shames us. He makes us feel that to do that is so despicable, so unworthy, so unlike him. We look at him and get to know him, and these evil desires are made so ugly and foul and vile that we long to get rid of them and be delivered from them. And he can do that.

But our Lord also gives an equal satisfaction to the conscience and to the will. If he failed at this point, again his claim would not be justified. What I am trying to say is that he deals with our failures. "Whosoever drinketh of the water that I shall give him shall never thirst." Even when I fail, even when I fall into sin, even when I do wrong? Oh, what a prolific cause of dissatisfaction and of unhappiness! How often the pastor has to deal with this! "I have fallen into sin. I have failed. I have been unworthy." The devil comes in, and I am cast down.

Now here is a tremendous need that we all know from experience. Who can give us satisfaction at this point? Of course, morality cannot, neither the old morality nor the new morality. The old morality cannot help us because it just condemns us and tells us that we should not have failed. The new morality cannot help us either because it tells us that it does not matter at all what we do, and we know that is not true because our conscience is telling us that we have done wrong. But can our Lord help us? He is the Son of God; he never sinned. Is it possible that he can help me when I fail? Surely, he who never failed at all, who was without sin and who was so pure, cannot help me here? Surely, he is the last person to whom I can turn when I fall?

But to think that is terribly wrong. This is one of the glories of the gospel. It is to him above all that we can go when we fall or when we fail. Look at him. This is what we are told about him—this was the prophecy concerning him before he ever came: "A bruised reed shall he not break, and the smoking flax shall he not quench" (Isa. 42:3). And when he came, he turned out to be like that. Who was he? He was the pure, holy Son of God. Yet what I read is, "Then drew near unto him all the publicans and sinners for to hear him" (Luke 15:1). This is one of the glories of the gospel; it is a paradox. It is the holy who attracts the publicans and sinners. They were never attracted by the Pharisees. The Pharisee in his self-righteousness kept apart; he despised and looked down on others. But here is the blessed Son of God, and publicans and sinners "drew near unto him." The poor man of Gadara with a legion of devils in him "ran" to him (Mark 5:6).

Look at his dealing with people in sin. A woman is caught in the very act of sin, and the self-righteous bring her forward, saying, "Now, what is your judgment?" He begins to write on the sand, and they all slink out. Then he says, "Where are those thine accusers? . . . Neither do I condemn thee: go, and sin no more" (John 8:10–11). His greatest characteristic was his compassion, his pity, his readiness to forgive, his encouragement to the failures.

But I suppose the supreme example is the apostle Peter, the impulsive, self-confident Peter. He says in essence, "Though all men should deny you, I will never deny you. I will walk with you through hell. There is nothing I will not do for you."

But you remember what happens. Our Lord is arrested; he is on trial. Peter, out of curiosity and also affection, slips into the courtyard. When he is recognized as a disciple of Jesus and is challenged by a maid, he denies it and says, "No, I know nothing about him." He denies his Lord with oaths and curses. And we are told one of the most tremendous things, I sometimes think, in all the accounts of our Lord: "And the Lord turned, and looked upon Peter" (Luke 22:61). Ah, there was a rebuke in that, but it was not only rebuke—it was pity, sympathy, and understanding.

And so we find in the last chapter of the Gospel of John, in that lyrical scene by the lakeside, that our Lord leads Peter to review this very failure, but he does not condemn him. He makes him realize that he must not trust in himself and in the flesh, but he also gives him his commission: "Feed my lambs . . . feed my sheep" (John 21:15–16). Peter is restored. He is not dismissed; he is not condemned. Our Lord sees that he is humble and penitent and contrite, and he forgives it all, renews the commission, and sends him on his way rejoicing. Our Lord is like that always. And this is the truth on which we rely, in which we glory, and which keeps us going. He is still the same! "I am he that liveth, and was dead; and, behold, I am alive for evermore" (Rev. 1:18).

Though now ascended up on high,
He bends on earth a brother's eye;
Partaker of the human name,
He knows the frailty of our frame.

Our fellow Sufferer yet retains
A fellow feeling of our pains:
And still remembers in the skies
His tears, his agonies, and cries.

MICHAEL BRUCE ("WHERE HIGH THE HEAVENLY TEMPLE STANDS")

He was, while he was here, "in all points tempted like as we are" (Heb. 4:15). He knows the force, the power, of the devil and of hell. So when he sees you faltering and falling, he sympathizes, and not only that, but "in that he himself hath suffered being tempted, he is able to succour them that are tempted" (Heb. 2:18)

In addition, we read in the first chapter of John's first epistle:

> If we say that we have fellowship with him, and walk in darkness, we lie, and do not the truth [we have often done that]: but if we walk in the light, as he is in the light, we have fellowship one with another, and the blood of Jesus Christ his Son cleanseth us from all sin. [Listen!] If we say that we have no sin, we deceive ourselves, and the truth is not in us. If we confess our sins, he is faithful and just to forgive us our sins, and to cleanse us from all unrighteousness. (vv. 6–9)

And that is still true.

> My little children, these things write I unto you, that ye sin not. And if any man sin [remember this; do not let the devil keep you groveling on the ground, condemning yourself and feeling you are not a Christian], we have an advocate with the Father, Jesus Christ the righteous: and he is the propitiation for our sins: and not for ours only, but also for the sins of the whole world. (1 John 2:1–2)

That is what happens when you sin. And what about your weakness? Well, it is the same: he is always there with his strength. We look at the task and at the world, the flesh, and the devil and the glory of our calling, and we say, "Who is sufficient for these things?" (2 Cor. 2:16). And there is only one answer: "Our sufficiency is of God" (2 Cor. 3:5). We look at him; it is his strength, not ours. "Come unto me," our Lord said, "all ye that labour and are heavy laden, and I will give you rest. Take my yoke upon you, and learn of me . . . my yoke is easy, and my burden is light" (Matt. 11:28–30). Be yoked with him; whatever the task, he is with you and he is bearing it with you. Look at the infinity of his power; he gives you new life, and he does not leave you to yourself.

> The law of the Spirit of life in Christ Jesus hath made me free from the law of sin and death. For what the law could not do, in that it was weak through the flesh, God sending his own Son in the likeness of sinful flesh, and for sin, condemned sin in the flesh: that the righteousness of the law might be fulfilled in us, who walk not after the flesh, but after the Spirit. (Rom. 8:2–4)

You must "mortify the deeds of the body"—how can you do that? "If ye *through the Spirit* do mortify the deeds of the body" (Rom. 8:13). Oh, yes, we are "earthen vessels": "We have this treasure in earthen vessels, that the excellency of the power may be of God, and not of us" (2 Cor. 4:7). So however weak you may feel at this moment, the word that comes to you is the word that tells you, "Put on the whole armour of God" (Eph. 6:11); "Be strong in the Lord, and in the power of his might" (Eph. 6:10). It is the only way that even Paul could keep on going and preaching. This is how he puts it:

> Whom we preach, warning every man, and teaching every man in all wisdom; that we may present every man perfect in Christ Jesus: whereunto I also labour, striving [how?] according to his working, which worketh in me mightily. (Col. 1:28–29)

And undergirding it all is this: "When I am weak, then am I strong." Why? Because "My grace is sufficient for thee" (2 Cor. 12:10, 9), and it always will be.

So, you see, he satisfies every desire, not only of the mind and of the heart but also of the conscience and the will. "Whosoever drinketh of the water that I shall give him shall never, no, *never,* thirst; but the water that I shall give him shall be in him a well of water springing up into everlasting life."

37

In Trials and Tribulations

Jesus answered and said unto her, Whosoever drinketh of this water shall thirst again: but whosoever drinketh of the water that I shall give him shall never thirst; but the water that I shall give him shall be in him a well of water springing up into everlasting life. (John 4:13–14)

We have made an extensive review of the supreme excellency of the gospel and all that our Lord has to give us. We have looked at it from all aspects and all angles. But I imagine that a question is still left in our minds and in our hearts. This is typical of unbelief, typical, particularly, of the suggestions that the devil is ever ready to insinuate into our minds. The question is this: you've displayed the gospel, you've unfolded it, and we must agree that it does seem at the moment to satisfy the various demands of our hearts and wills and minds, but will it always? Will it do so in all circumstances and under all conditions?

This question arises as the result of our experience. Many ideas have interested us and attracted us and have seemed to us to be good. We were quite well at the time, and our circumstances were very favorable, and this teaching, whatever it was, seemed eminently satisfactory. But a time came when we lost our health perhaps or had some disappointment or sorrow, or circumstances went against us, and we suddenly found that these ideas about which we had thought so much did not help us and in fact were of no value to us at all. This was a teaching, a philosophy, that was quite all right when, in a sense, we did not need any help, but just at the moment of our greatest need and trouble, it let us down.

This is a common experience. You trust teachings, you trust people, you trust things, but sooner or later you find that just when you need them most of all, they fail you completely—they are fair-weather friends that desert you in the hour of your trial. So it is not a bit surprising that this kind of questioning should arise within us, and we want to know, does the gospel *always* give satisfaction?

Our Lord's claim is that it does; so we must examine it again. We are living in a world in which trials and tribulations are inevitable. There is the whole strain of living, the contradictions of life, the contradictions within ourselves, the contradictions of people, the difficulties that seem to arise in various ways all around us. To refuse to face this is to show folly. Of course, that is the folly of the world; it does not like facing problems and difficulties. The world says, "Let's eat, drink, and be merry; let's enjoy the moment." But the Bible, while it tells us not to worry about the future, nevertheless does encourage us to think about it and to make sure that we have a view of life that covers every conceivable eventuality.

So this is the great question: does this gospel, does this life that our Lord is offering to give us so freely, really satisfy us even when all things seem against us and threaten to drive us to despair? This is obviously a most important matter. It is important from the standpoint of our experience and our happiness and joy and peace in the Christian life and from the standpoint of facing the future. It is also extremely important from the standpoint of testing us and of making sure that we really are Christians. The Bible teaches us, and we know from experience and from the history of the church in particular, that it is quite possible for people to think they are Christians when they are not Christians at all. Again we are faced with the subtlety of the devil, who can turn himself into an "angel of light" (2 Cor. 11:14), so that we imagine we are Christians and are perfectly happy until we suddenly find that we are not. We have the authority of our Lord himself for saying that we can be deceived in this way and may be just using Christian terminology without having any real life within us.

Now our Lord has put this once and for all in a clear way in the Parable of the Sower. In this parable, the sower goes out to sow and casts his seed on different kinds of ground, but only some of the seed produces grain. After telling the parable, our Lord goes on to analyze its meaning. He says:

> Hear ye therefore the parable of the sower. When any one heareth the word of the kingdom, and understandeth it not, then cometh the wicked one, and catcheth away that which was sown in his heart. This is he which received seed by the way side. But he that received the seed into stony places, the same is he that heareth the word, and anon with joy receiveth it [he thinks he has become a Christian]; yet hath he not root

> in himself, but dureth for a while: for when tribulation or persecution ariseth because of the word, by and by he is offended.

He thinks he is a Christian, he appears to be, but persecution tests him and soon shows that he is not a Christian at all; there was never any root there. There was some temporary reaction to the gospel but not a real response. Then our Lord goes on: "He also that received seed among the thorns is he that heareth the word; and the care of this world, and the deceitfulness of riches, choke the word, and he becometh unfruitful." Again, he is not a Christian, though there was an immediate, temporary response. And then comes the contrast: "But he that received seed into the good ground is he that heareth the word, and understandeth it; which also beareth fruit, and bringeth forth, some an hundredfold, some sixty, some thirty" (Matt. 13:18–23).

Now in many ways the point of that parable is that it is trials and troubles, whether persecution or the cares of life in this world, that ultimately test us. They not only show the value of the gospel but test us at the same time and reveal very clearly whether we have this well of water within us "springing up into everlasting life" or whether we have just made some temporary, superficial reaction to the gospel.

So this is a most important matter from every standpoint, and it is a very prominent teaching in the New Testament. Our Lord himself deals with this often, and it is his claim that the gospel never fails. On the question of persecution, he says:

> Blessed [happy, to be congratulated] are ye, when men shall revile you, and persecute you, and shall say all manner of evil against you falsely, for my sake. Rejoice, and be exceeding glad: for great is your reward in heaven: for so persecuted they the prophets which were before you. (Matt. 5:11–12)

Far from being offended by persecution and proving that you had no root at all, you rejoice—you are in a blessed, in a happy, position. That is our Lord's teaching. And later on he says, "In the world ye shall have tribulation: but be of good cheer; I have overcome the world" (John 16:33). He warns his followers to expect trouble: "If they have called the master of the house Beelzebub, how much more shall they call them of his household?" (Matt. 10:25). He warns that the world will be against us. The world is always against the true Christian. Christianity is not popular with the world. Our Lord says, "The world hated me before it hated you."

This teaching is not confined to our Lord himself; we find it also in the book of Acts. The apostle Paul, going around to the churches, warned the Christians that "we must through much tribulation enter into the kingdom of God" (14:22). And he is quite explicit about this in the Epistle to the Philippians: "Unto you it is given in the behalf of Christ, not only to believe on him, but also to suffer for his sake" (1:29).

We find the same teaching in James: "My brethren, count it all joy when ye fall into divers [diverse] temptations [trials]" (1:2). And Peter is equally explicit in his first epistle, where he puts it like this:

> Beloved, think it not strange concerning the fiery trial which is to try you, as though some strange thing happened unto you: but rejoice, inasmuch as ye are partakers of Christ's sufferings; that, when his glory shall be revealed, ye may be glad also with exceeding joy. If ye be reproached for the name of Christ, happy are ye; for the spirit of glory and of God resteth upon you: on their part he is evil spoken of, but on your part he is glorified . . . judgment must begin at the house of God. (4:12–14, 17)

So the teaching of Scripture is quite clear; that is one of its glories. It does not say, "Believe in the Lord Jesus Christ and you will never have another problem or trouble—all is going to be wonderful." It tells you the exact opposite. It tells you that by becoming a disciple of his, the world will be against you in a way it has never been before, and you will be tried and tested; and, of course, history proves this is what happens in practice.

I reminded you earlier of that marvelous statement at the end of Acts 5, when the apostles departed from the presence of the council, "rejoicing that they were counted worthy to suffer shame for his name" (v. 41). And we find the same theme of suffering for Christ in the wonderful story in Acts 12, where we read about the apostle Peter being arrested. James had already been arrested and put to death, and Peter was now arrested and thrown into prison. It happened to be just before Passover, and there was a rule that no man should be killed at that time (Acts 12:3–4); so Peter was allowed to languish in prison, the intention being to bring him out after Passover and put him to death. A most extraordinary thing is said in that story. Peter was there in prison, and as a Jew he knew perfectly well that he was alive only because this was the time of unleavened bread. Then we come to the very last night of the days of unleavened bread, and this is the marvelous thing we are told:

> Prayer was made without ceasing of the church unto God for him. And when Herod would have brought him forth, the same night Peter was sleeping between two soldiers, bound with two chains: and the keepers before the door kept the prison. (Acts 12:5–6)

Do you get the significance of that? Here is a man who is chained to two soldiers, one on each side, and who knows that in a few hours he is to be brought out and executed, and yet what we are told about him is that he is soundly asleep! Do you think you would be able to sleep in such circumstances? This is the gospel; here it is in operation. Our Lord says that whoever drinks the water that he will give will never thirst. Though Peter knows his life is to be taken in a few hours, he sleeps like a newborn babe.

There is another equally remarkable example in the sixteenth chapter of Acts. Paul and Silas were badly maltreated at Philippi. Their backs were scourged, they were thrust into the innermost prison, and their feet were fastened in the stocks. But "at midnight Paul and Silas prayed, and sang praises unto God" (v. 25). It is not merely that they were not grumbling and complaining—they were singing praises to God, though their backs were aching as the result of the lashing and the scourging and their poor feet were fastened in the stocks. There we see this rejoicing in practice.

So what does it all mean? It means that our Lord not only promises to enable us to bear our troubles and trials and tribulations without fainting or faltering, but he promises also—and all his apostles and teachers promise this after him—that we shall not only be able to bear them but we shall glory in them, we shall rejoice in them, we shall be more than conquerors. Not just conquerors, but *more than* conquerors (Rom. 8:37). There is a plus here.

This is one of the most marvelous and glorious aspects of the gospel, and this is where it differs from every other teaching. Our Lord is right: "Whosoever drinketh of this water shall thirst again." The world at its very best and highest knows nothing at all about this. Oh, I know the world can rise to the great heights of Stoicism, but that is the limit of its rising; it has never gone beyond that. There is something very wonderful about Stoicism, I know. Sometimes a certain statesman is regarded as "the last of the Romans." I suppose that is all right, but it is all negative, it is mere resignation. There is a kind of nobility about the person who can stand when everybody is whimpering and crying and falling or running away and disappearing. It is rather heroic to see someone just standing and refusing to give in or to give up. But such people are not singing praises, are they? They are not rejoicing, they are not smiling, they are not "more than conquerors." No, no; they just refuse to give in, they just have grit, they are sticking at it, just holding on, just standing, and no more. But here there is an entirely different atmosphere, there is a triumph, a joy: "shall never, no, never, thirst as long as the world stands." In other words, they are filled with the spirit of rejoicing and of victory and of exultation.

So here is the great question: how does the gospel do this? Or let me put it still more accurately: how does our Lord do this to us? What is this water that he gives us? How does it work? What is there about it, and how does it so operate that it brings us to this position that we are more than conquerors when everything is against us?

Many answers are given to this question in the New Testament. There is no better one than the passage from 2 Corinthians 4 where the apostle Paul deals extensively with this subject. He starts off by saying, "But we have this treasure [this gospel] in earthen vessels, that the excellency of the power may be of God, and not of us" (v. 7). He then goes on to say that this is true of him, and then he gives a list of the trials, troubles, tribulations, the bombardment of the world, the flesh, the devil, evil forces and powers, everything set against him to get him down. Yet Paul tells us that he has not been defeated, and in this passage he lets us into the secret.

And 2 Corinthians 4 is by no means the only passage. The end of the eighth chapter of the Epistle to the Romans, where the apostle gives us his great teaching concerning time and life in this world, is equally important in this respect. So let us consider what the teaching is because the end of Romans 8 is a good summary of our Lord's own teaching and of the teaching of all the other apostles. Paul says that he is more than a conqueror in spite of all that is happening to him because the gospel, this Christian view of life, this life that is in him, enables him to see everything differently. He repeats this in 2 Corinthians 5:17: "If any man be in Christ, he is a new creature [new creation]: old things are passed away; behold, all things are become new." And that is a literal fact. The Christian sees everything in a different way from the non-Christian. Do not forget the list that Paul has given in 2 Corinthians 4—it is so important. He says:

> We are troubled on every side, yet not distressed; we are perplexed, but not in despair; persecuted, but not forsaken; cast down, but not destroyed; always bearing about in the body the dying of the Lord Jesus,

> that the life also of Jesus might be made manifest in our body. For we which live are always delivered unto death for Jesus' sake, that the life also of Jesus might be made manifest in our mortal flesh. So then death worketh in us, but life in you. (2 Cor. 4:8–12)

Paul also says, "For our light affliction, which is but for a moment, worketh for us a far more exceeding and eternal weight of glory" (2 Cor. 4:17). "Our *light affliction*"—can you picture this? Consider what was happening to this man, and yet he looks at it all and says, "our light affliction"! Is this just some sort of self-hypnotism, some refusal to face the facts? Of course not. There is something profound here; any other teaching only deludes you—you are not facing the facts. But here is a man who is facing them. He gives the list, he puts it all down, and yet he says, "light affliction."

But in what way can Paul possibly say that all this is but a *light* affliction? There is only one answer. He is a man who has an entirely new view of the whole of life and of himself. Before his conversion, he used to think of himself as a man who always deserved the best. He thought he deserved happiness, joy, and peace; no problem should ever come his way. That is what the natural person always thinks and expects, and when things go against him, of course, he is annoyed, he is upset. But here is a man who has become a Christian, and he realizes now that he deserves nothing good, that if he really had his deserts, he would be in a much worse position than he is. But above all he now thinks of himself as a soul. Before he only thought of himself in his relationship to the world—success, making money, popularity, a thousand and one things. But not any longer. He knows now that the one thing that matters is that he has a soul, an eternal soul, and that he is a pilgrim of eternity.

Then add to that Paul's whole view of the meaning of life. What is life for? What is its meaning and purpose? Is it just to have enjoyment, just to get some kicks? Are we here merely to eat and drink and indulge in sex—is that the whole of life? Obviously thousands think it is, and when they are deprived of these in any shape or form, they are down; they have no resources, nothing at all to fall back on. But Christians see that the world is not their home; it is a kind of preparatory school, and their destiny is elsewhere. This is not the only world; this is not the only life. "Our light affliction," says the apostle. These things do not touch him very much. He is human; he is not unnatural. He does not, like the Christian Scientist, say there is no pain or there is no difficulty because that is not true. There is pain, there is difficulty, there is disease. But what he says is that if the world does everything that it can, if it kills him, so what? It is the soul that matters; and the soul is ultimately beyond the reach of these problems.

And then there comes in the tremendously important element of time—"our light affliction, *which is but for a moment.*" Now here is a very good way of testing whether or not you are a Christian. Here is a list of troubles and trials, and it seems that they are going on forever, that Paul has no way of escape, and yet he says that they are "but for a moment." Why does he say that? It is because he has the Christian view of time. He does not measure time in seconds and minutes and hours and days and weeks and months and years and decades and centuries. That is what the man of the world does, and that is why man is a victim of time. Time seems so long, does it not? Will there ever be an end to all this!

Let me put it like this to you. Imagine a father and a mother who lost their only son in the last war. Their immediate feeling was, "How can we possibly go on living?" They were fairly young—how could they go on facing life? It is so long. Many people commit suicide for that reason. Everything that you held dear in life is gone, and you have this awful stretch ahead—how can you bear it? But the apostle says it is only for a moment.

The Christian views everything in the light of eternity, not in the light of time. It is because we persist in judging everything from the standpoint of time that we get depressed and defeated. What is time, then? Well, time is really "but . . . a moment." You think of it in the human, ordinary, earthly manner, and you say, "Seventy years! How long it seems!" Yes, but now take that seventy years and put it into the context of eternity. What is eternity? Well, there is no end to it. Can you think of a million years? Of course not. But then think of a billion years. Of course you cannot. But think of that going on and on and on forever and ever. What is seventy years in that context? It is a moment, a flash. "What is your life?" says James. "It is even a vapour" (Jas. 4:14). Like a breath of air, it has come, and it has gone. So the apostle Paul is able to say that our "light affliction" is "but for a moment" because he has this whole new Christian view of time, and as soon as you have this, you are already more than conqueror over everything that is set against you. You say, "It doesn't matter what's happening to me now. It doesn't matter how long it's going to last in calendar terms, as far as I'm concerned—eternity is before me."

This is how Paul deals with these afflictions. But then he adds another most fascinating phrase: "Our light affliction, which is but for a moment, *worketh for us . . .*" The apostle makes the same point in the Epistle to the Romans: "And not only so, but we glory in tribulations also: knowing that tribulation worketh patience; and patience, experience; and experience, hope" (5:3–4). And James has taken hold of exactly the same idea—it is an essential part of Christian teaching. He puts it in these words: "My brethren, count it all joy when ye fall into divers temptations; knowing this, that the trying of your faith *worketh* patience" (1:2–3).

What does this mean? What is this "working"? Let the apostle Paul tell us. Here, he says, is the process:

> Therefore being justified by faith, we have peace with God through our Lord Jesus Christ: by whom also we have access by faith into this grace wherein we stand, and rejoice in hope of the glory of God. And not only so, but we glory in tribulations also: knowing that tribulation *worketh* patience. (Rom. 5:1–3)

So how does this process operate? The answer seems to me to be this: tribulation deals with the defects in us and replaces them with good qualities, virtues. Tribulation, says Paul, is a good experience for Christians because it produces something that was not there before—patience. Do you see what he means? Why are we unhappy? Why do we get defeated? It is very often because we are impatient. I say, "Why should this happen to me? I can't stand it. I can't possibly go on." The cause of much of our trouble and failure in life is our hasty spirit, our tendency to feel disappointed, our inconsistency, our reliance upon circumstances and upon conditions, and therefore our readiness always to grumble and complain. We want everything to be perfect, and if anything goes wrong, we are at once annoyed; we are full of stress and strain.

Tribulation is a very good treatment for all that. The way to get rid of that kind of spirit is to let tribulation work in you, and it does a wonderful work. It gets rid of all that impatience, it makes you think, it makes you face things instead of just reacting to them, and the result is that it produces constancy, a spirit of patient endurance, a spirit of reliability. And all this is the result of having a deeper view of ourselves, a deeper view of the Christian life, and a deeper view of our whole relationship to God. The trouble with children, always, is that they want quick results, they want things immediately, they cannot wait. But as you get older, you have to learn, do you not, that things do not come like that. You have to learn to be patient and to bear with things.

Now this is something that life does to all of us, but the gospel does it in a most amazing manner; it immediately produces patience. It makes us ask questions: Why do I always want things immediately? Why do I always want to have an unruffled kind of existence? What right do I have to ask for these things? And so it makes you more patient. And once you develop this patient endurance and reliability and steadfastness, you are already well on the road to being more than conquerors over all these things that are set against you.

And then patience, in turn, leads to "experience" (Rom. 5:4). Unfortunately "experience" is a bad translation. Patience leads to proof or approval, or as one translation puts it, "patience leads to maturity of character." This is why tribulations do good to Christian men and women—they make them mature. Peter has a wonderful way of putting this. Dealing with people who are having trials and troubles, he says that they are "kept by the power of God through faith unto salvation ready to be revealed in the last time." And he continues:

> Wherein ye greatly rejoice, though now for a season, if need be, ye are in heaviness through manifold temptations: that the trial of your faith, being much more precious than of gold that perisheth, though it be tried with fire, might be found unto praise and honour and glory at the appearing of Jesus Christ. (1 Pet. 1:5–7)

This is what trials do for us. Though we are born again and there is the pure gold of eternal life within us, there is still a lot of dross. And it is the admixture that gets us down; that is what makes us complain and feel unhappy and whimper when things go against us. But trials purge us of the dross, they purify the gold, and so they work in us, creating patience, which produces maturity of character. So we are not children, just reacting quickly, violently, superficially. There is a depth about us and a steadiness and a solidity, a maturity of character.

There is a specific treatment of this subject in chapter 12 of the great Epistle to the Hebrews. We tend to forget this, but it is most important for us to realize it. The writer says there:

> Ye have not yet resisted unto blood, striving against sin. And ye have forgotten the exhortation which speaketh unto you as unto children, My son, despise not thou the chastening of the Lord, nor faint when thou art rebuked of him: for whom the Lord loveth he chasteneth, and scourgeth every son whom he receiveth. If ye endure chastening, God dealeth with you as with sons; for what son is he whom the father chasteneth not?

> But if ye be without chastisement, whereof all are partakers, then are ye bastards, and not sons. Furthermore we have had fathers of our flesh which corrected us, and we gave them reverence: shall we not much more rather be in subjection unto the Father of spirits, and live? For they verily for a few days chastened us after their own pleasure; but he for our profit, that we might be partakers of his holiness. (12:4–10)

Tribulations enable us to see and to understand that God is at work within us purifying the gold. And that in turn leads to "hope" (Rom. 5:4). We do not feel hopeless because things are against us. No, no! We have this bigger, deeper understanding. We see the ultimate end and objective, and in the light of that we are able to continue.

That, then, is one way in which tribulations and trials work in us, and that is why we should rejoice. That first way is most important because though we are born again, much work needs to be done in us, a work of sanctification, purification, the work of purifying the gold. But in addition to that direct way of working, tribulation also does another wonderful thing. As the apostle puts it in 2 Corinthians 4:17, "For our light affliction, which is but for a moment, worketh for us *a far more exceeding and eternal weight of glory*"—it drives us to consider the glory that is awaiting us. One of our greatest lacks as Christian people and where we go wrong is that we think of salvation in terms of this world and this world alone. Thank God for all salvation does for us here, but what it does for us in this world is a mere, almost infinitesimally small fraction of what it is going to do for us.

So many people say, "I became a Christian, and I thought that now I would never have any more trouble." But then troubles come, and down these people go. What is the matter? Their real trouble, above all else, is that they have not considered what is awaiting them—"a far more exceeding and eternal weight of glory." Or listen to Paul putting it perhaps still more clearly in Romans 8:

> If [we are] children, then [we are] heirs; heirs of God, and joint-heirs with Christ; if so be that we suffer with him, that we may also be glorified together. For I reckon that the sufferings of this present time are not worthy to be compared with the glory which shall be revealed in us. For the earnest expectation of the creature waiteth for the manifestation of the sons of God. . . . Because the creature itself also shall be delivered from the bondage of corruption into the glorious liberty of the children of God. For we know that the whole creation groaneth and travaileth in pain together until now. And not only they, but ourselves also, which

> have the firstfruits of the Spirit, even we ourselves groan within ourselves, waiting for the adoption, to wit, the redemption of our body. (vv. 17–19, 21–23)

That is the glory that is coming, and that is what tribulation makes us consider. While all things are going well with us, we tend just to enjoy them. We take the Christian life more or less for granted, and we hardly ever think about what we are going to, what awaits us, what God has prepared for us, and what Christ is reserving for us. He said, "Let not your heart be troubled: ye believe in God, believe also in me. . . . I go to prepare a place for you" (John 14:1–2). How often do we think of that? And that is why we are so defeated and often so unhappy and tend to go to pieces when things are against us. "Oh," we say, "look at what's happening to me! Everything's against me. I'm losing everything." Losing everything? What about the place that he is preparing for you? You see, you have forgotten all about that.

Now the value of tribulation is—and this is how Christian men and women become more than conquerors—that it makes them think of that place. At last they realize that they have been living too much in this world, this life, the present, the seen, the temporary, and have been forgetting the other. When you have lost your health or your loved ones or your money, when everything seems to be taken from you, you are left alone, paralyzed, helpless, as it were. There is nothing that you can look forward to in this world, and that drives you to look for what God is preparing for you. What a wonderful thing tribulation is! It "worketh for us a far more exceeding and eternal weight of glory"; it makes us think of the marvel and the glory of heaven and the certainty of it. It is beyond description! That place will be life with Christ; it is a mansion that he is preparing; it will be glory everlasting. Even your very body will be glorified, with no defect whatsoever.

We have so concentrated on this life that we have forgotten the glory that is coming. What we have here, says Paul, is "the firstfruits of the Spirit" (Rom. 8:23)—only the firstfruits, the foretaste, the mere down payment. The great harvest is awaiting us, and tribulations drive us to contemplate it. So they are of value to us as they do this work within us. And the result of all this is that Christian people learn contentment. They are contented because their needs are fewer, and their needs are fewer because they live a life in the soul and in the spirit. The needs of the non-Christian are endless. They must have more and more—more money, more cigarettes, more drink, more drugs, more sex—they are never satisfied. Oh, how difficult it is, and everybody is short of money because their needs are so prolific. But when people become Christians, their needs are greatly reduced. I am not saying they have no needs or they are satisfied, but they are so satisfied by what they have that they do not need anything else.

Listen to how Paul puts it. The Philippians had sent him a gift, and he thanks them for it. Then he says:

> Not that I speak in respect of want: for I have learned, in whatsoever state I am, therewith to be content. I know both how to be abased, and I know how to abound: every where and in all things I am instructed both to be full and to be hungry, both to abound and to suffer need. (Phil. 4:11–12)

It does not matter what Paul's circumstances are—he is satisfied. Wherever he is, he has a satisfaction in Christ. He is writing to the Philippians from prison, remember, and he is an old man. He has been told that Nero has suddenly decided to put him to death. What does it matter? It does not matter at all!

On another occasion when Paul is in prison, he is brought out to speak before King Agrippa and the Roman proconsul Festus, and he says a marvelous thing to them. He is standing there with prison chains hanging heavily from both his wrists, and he is probably tied to a soldier on each side. He looks at these people in authority who have great power and everything that can be desired. They are in a bantering mood, and King Agrippa says to him, "Almost thou persuadest me to be a Christian." Then Paul replies, "I would to God, that not only thou, but also all that hear me this day, were both almost, and altogether such as I am, except these bonds" (Acts 26:28–29). He is saying in essence, "I do not wish you to become prisoners. I do not wish evil upon you. But you know, I wish you were like me."

Is this conceit? Is this just a man boasting or being egotistical? Of course not. Paul means, "You know I am a prisoner, and you have deprived me of everything. You think you have a lot, and I have nothing, but it is I who have everything and you who have nothing." That is how tribulation gives contentment and renders us immune to circumstances. It does not matter what happens—you have inner peace, inner rest; you have Christ in your heart and "the hope of glory" also. It does not matter what people may do, what circumstances may do, they cannot touch that.

And the result is that you even rejoice in your tribulations because it is tribulation that has brought you to the realization of the truth of salvation. You realize that regeneration is not little or superficial. It is profound and ends in that glory, the vision of God and the sharing of eternal bliss with God the Father, God the Son, God the Holy Spirit, and "the spirits of just men made perfect" (Heb. 12:23).

So Christians are not merely able to put up with the things that happen to them without collapsing, but they also rejoice in them. They do not rejoice in spite of them—they rejoice in them, they thank God for them. "It is good for me that I have been afflicted," says the psalmist, because "before I was afflicted I went astray" (Ps. 119:71, 67). It is afflictions that wean me from the world and drive me to consider him and the glory that he is preparing for me and the joy that is around the throne of God in the eternal bliss. "In all these things we are more than conquerors through him that loved us" (Rom. 8:37).

Do you know this, my friend? How do you react to trials and tribulations? How do you respond to adverse circumstances? Do you have patience? Do you have maturity of character as a Christian? Are you dependable, are you reliable? Are you immune to circumstances and chance? Are you able to say, "All things"—whatever they are—"work together for good"—that is my experience? Even things that are against me are good for me. Why? They drive me to him.

> For our light affliction, which is but for a moment, worketh for us a far more exceeding and eternal weight of glory; while we look not at the things which are seen, but at the things which are not seen: for the things which are seen are temporal; but the things which are not seen are eternal. (2 Cor. 4:17–18)

These are my "things" because I belong to eternity.

38

All in Christ Jesus

Jesus answered and said unto her, Whosoever drinketh of this water shall thirst again: but whosoever drinketh of the water that I shall give him shall never thirst; but the water that I shall give him shall be in him a well of water springing up into everlasting life. (John 4:13–14)

We are, let me remind you, considering this great and wonderful statement at some length because it is one of those perfect summaries of the gospel that we find scattered about here and there in the Scriptures, especially in the Gospel of John. What our Lord is offering here, and what he claims is the essential character of the Christian life, is its all-sufficiency, its fullness, its completeness, as John tells us in verse 16 of chapter 1: "And of his fulness have all we received, and grace upon grace."

This is Christianity. Christianity is not merely an intellectual belief; it is not merely moral living. It includes all that, but to stop at that is tragic. It is life and life more abundant, life in all its fullness, life that gives complete and entire satisfaction, and here our Lord is setting it forth again in an interesting pictorial manner to this woman of Samaria at the side of a well. The great question for every one of us to address at this very moment is this: is this our experience? And it is because this is not true of so many of us that the Christian church is as she is today—weak, ineffective, giving people outside the impression that the Christian faith is small, cramped, and confined, a duty to be performed, a burden that we carry, instead of this glorious life that is here indicated by our blessed Lord.

We have been examining Christianity, therefore, in the light of the full teaching of the Scriptures, particularly, of course, the New Testament, and we have seen that it really does what our Lord claims—it gives complete intellectual satisfaction, it gives complete heart satisfaction, and it deals with the will and all the problems that confront us. In the last study we saw that this is true in practice. It really does work when circumstances are against us and when we are surrounded by trials and troubles and tribulations, and we can, therefore, rejoice in tribulations—not in spite of them but in them.

In light of all this, I would say that we are entitled to make this assertion: this life that our Lord gives us enables us to face the future, whatever it may be, without any fear or foreboding. "The LORD is my shepherd; I shall not want" (Ps. 23:1). That follows of necessity. Or we can put it in the language of the apostle Paul, that man who suffered so much because he was a Christian—and let us make no mistake about this, if we are Christians, we shall suffer. "Yea," says Paul to Timothy, "and all that will live godly in Christ Jesus shall suffer persecution" (2 Tim. 3:12). And as he puts it to the Philippians, "For unto you it is given in the behalf of Christ, not only to believe on him, but also to suffer for his sake" (Phil. 1:29). If ever a man suffered, it was Paul—imprisoned, maltreated, maligned—and yet here he is writing probably his last letter, the Second Epistle to Timothy, and saying, "For the which cause I also suffer these things"—these indignities and imprisonments and so on, and then, so typical and characteristic of Paul—"nevertheless I am not ashamed"—why not?—"for I know whom I have believed, and am persuaded [certain] that he is able to keep that which I have committed unto him"—my soul and its eternal salvation and destiny—"against that day" (2 Tim. 1:12).

And that, it seems to me, sums up this great statement of our Lord concerning the gospel and its fullness. It does not matter what may come, there is no shame, there is no faltering, there is no failing. Paul is rejoicing; he is glorying.

But I would also emphasize that not only does fullness of life come immediately, it continues and increases. We worked out earlier that it really does become "a well of water springing up into everlasting life," but now I particularly want to emphasize that one of the great glories of this Christian life is that it increases and becomes more and more glorious to us and more and more wonderful; it must if we grasp our Lord's teaching here in John 4. That, again, is one of the great differentiating points between the gospel and any philosophy or cult you may happen to take up. You get as much as you are going to get out of them at once, and you do your best to hold on to that, but when you need them most of all, they will fail you most of all. They are fair-weather friends. They do not have life in them. Ultimately they all depend upon us. They are mere ideas, and you have to keep the idea going.

But the glory of the gospel is that it is life, life from God, and because it is life it grows and develops. Life does not remain stagnant but goes on growing and manifesting itself within us, and we experience it in an ever deeper and more mature manner. This is what is wonderfully true about this life. I have never understood Christians who always talk about their conversion. When I find such a person, I am saddened. I remember such people very well in my early days in the ministry, particularly in Wales. They would come to me and always tell me the same thing. It was the revival,[22] and it was "marvelous," especially their own conversion. I heard this so often from one particular individual that I once looked at him and said, "Tell me, has nothing happened to you since then? Did God finish dealing with you then? What has happened in the intervening twenty-three years or so?" This is very sad, and it is something to which evangelical people are particularly prone. My dear friends, it is all wrong.

Thank God for the beginning—without that, of course, we have nothing. But the marvelous thing is the growth and the development, the increasing understanding. Do you rejoice more in your Christian life today than a year ago? If not, there is something very wrong with you. If you do not marvel at it more than ever, if you are not moved by it more than ever, if it does not thrill you more than ever, there is something seriously wrong. This life is "a well of water" that goes on springing up into everlasting life.

We must test ourselves by this. Do you not find that as you go on in this journey, the scenery becomes more glorious, with unexpected things coming to meet you as God reveals yet further examples of what he has provided for you? This is an essential part of the description that is given here by our blessed Lord of this wonderful life that he has to give us. God grant that we all may be able to say, "The beginning? Well, it was all right, but it was just the beginning." "When I was a child," says Paul, "I spake as a child, I understood as a child, I thought as a child: but when I became a man, I put away childish things" (1 Cor. 13:11). Can you say that? Is your knowledge increasing? Is your heart being more and more warmed? Are you more and more amazed at the wonders of his ways and the increasing unfolding of his purposes with regard to you and with regard to the church and with regard to the whole world?

Now all this is implicit in the definition of this life, but what I want to leave with you as the great final thought concerning this matter is that the secret of all this, of course, is the Lord himself. "Whosoever drinketh of the water that I shall give him"—and that really means himself. That is what is meant by drinking this water; that is what is meant by possessing this well. It is "Christ in you, the hope of glory" (Col. 1:27). Paul's great prayer for the Ephesians was "that Christ may dwell in your hearts by faith" (Eph. 3:17). It is he. Life is in him. "We drink of thee, the Fountainhead."[23] "He is the head of the body, the church," and in him "all fullness" dwells (Col. 1:18–19); and it is because he is in us that this fullness is in us.

Therefore, it all comes to this: to drink of this water means getting to know him more and more and the fullness that is in him. That is what makes this life so wonderful. The moment we regard it in this way, we have a deeper understanding of it. We have been considering different aspects of this life and thinking of it as it is expounded as doctrine, but now look at it as it is in our Lord and who he is. It is because he is who he is that he is able to satisfy our every need.

The apostle Paul puts it in his own way, again in Ephesians 3, when he says he wants the Ephesians to know "what is the breadth, and length, and depth, and height; and to know the love of Christ, which passeth knowledge, that ye might be filled with all the fulness of God" (vv. 18–19). That is it.

And this is all in Christ! Paul says to the Colossians, "in whom are hid all the treasures of wisdom and knowledge" (2:3). It is all there in him, and we receive it from him, and he is everything to us. Now I think that Charles Wesley has probably excelled over everybody in expressing just this aspect in what I have increasingly come to regard as the greatest of his hymns, greater even than "Jesus, Lover of My Soul" because it goes further, though there is a wonderful beginning to that hymn and though at the end of it he goes on to say:

Thou of life the fountain art,
Freely let me take of thee;
Spring thou up within my heart,
Rise to all eternity.

But this is even better:

Thou hidden source of calm repose,
Thou all-sufficient love divine,
My help and refuge from my foes,

Secure I am if thou art mine;
And lo! from sin and grief and shame
I hide me, Jesus, in thy name.

We have worked that out. We have seen how our Lord satisfies the accusations—indeed, the demands, in a sense—of our consciences:

And lo! from sin and grief and shame,
I hide me, Jesus, in thy name.

But on he goes:

Thy mighty name salvation is,
And keeps my happy soul above;
Comfort it brings, and power and peace,
And joy and everlasting love;
To me with thy dear name are given
Pardon, and holiness, and heaven.

It is magnificent poetry, but look at the sentiment, look at what Charles Wesley is saying:

Jesus, my all in all thou art,
My rest in toil, mine ease in pain,
The healing of my broken heart;
In war my peace; in loss my gain,
My smile beneath the tyrant's frown,
In shame my glory and my crown.

In want my plentiful supply,
In weakness my almighty power,
In bonds my perfect liberty,
My light in Satan's darkest hour,
In grief my joy unspeakable,
My life in death, my heaven in hell.[24]

That is everything, is it not? Charles Wesley has covered it. In a world like this we face weakness, temptation, war, tyrants' frowns, all these many things—we are familiar with them. But as Wesley says in the second verse of that great hymn:

Thou all-sufficient love divine.

He is everything. My dear friend, you can be sure of this: nothing can ever happen to you but that he will be able to help you. Nothing—that is a simple statement of fact. It does not matter what happens to you, he is sufficient—"Thou all-sufficient love divine." And what matters is our realization of this. Have you found him to be "In want my plentiful supply"? Can you use the language of the apostle: "I have all, and abound: I am full" (Phil. 4:18)? Can you say, "I know both how to be abased, and I know how to abound" (v. 12)? The whole essence of this matter is to know him. As you know him, you find this *fullness*. He knows all; he is able to do all. There is nothing that you can ever need or desire, nothing that can ever happen to you, but that he is able to deal with it, and deal with it with this amazing fullness. He will reverse everything, and he will fill you with rejoicing in the midst of your tribulations.

Now that is one way of looking at the "well of water springing up," and in many ways it is the most important of all. You must look at him, and you must consider him. This takes time, but you must do it. You must seek his face; you must get to know him. And the more you know him, the more you will be amazed at the fullness that is in him.

But I want to add to that, and thank God for what I am going to say. It is not only what is in him that explains this fullness of life, it is also what he does, what he does to us. We go to him, but there is nothing more wonderful than the fact that he comes to us. I am referring now to what some of the saints in the past have called visitations or manifestations of the Son of God, intimations that he gives of his loving interest in us.

Now this is wonderful because there are times when perhaps because of illness, tiredness, weakness, age, or various other factors we find ourselves dull and lethargic. And it is just then that he comes and makes all the difference to us. There are wonderful examples of this in the Scriptures themselves. Look at it in connection with the apostle Paul. He was in Corinth, and he was having a particularly difficult time there. Everything had gone against him, and Paul obviously went to bed one night feeling somewhat dejected and discouraged.

> Then spake the Lord to Paul in the night by a vision, Be not afraid, but speak, and hold not thy peace: for I am with thee, and no man shall set on thee to hurt thee: for I have much people in this city. (Acts 18:9–10)

Now that is a vision. Now I am not suggesting that we should all be seeking visions! We must not do that. But what I am saying is that our

Lord, in his infinite love and mercy and compassion, chooses to visit us when we are going through times of great stress and crisis. He may visit us not in a vision, but he does visit us in our spirits. We will see nothing, we will not hear an audible voice, but we will know that he is there; there will be no uncertainty.

Or take another example. The apostle Paul was again in a very difficult situation, and he says:

> And it came to pass, that, when I was come again to Jerusalem, even while I prayed in the temple, I was in a trance [this is exceptional. You will never experience a trance perhaps. It does not matter; you can know the very experience that the apostle had]; and saw him saying unto me, Make haste, and get thee quickly out of Jerusalem: for they will not receive thy testimony concerning me. And I said, Lord, they know that I imprisoned and beat in every synagogue them that believed on thee: and when the blood of thy martyr Stephen was shed, I also was standing by, and consenting unto his death, and kept the raiment of them that slew him. And he said unto me, Depart: for I will send thee far hence unto the Gentiles. (Acts 22:17–21)

Or take a dramatic illustration, again from the book of Acts. Paul was in a ship on the way to Rome to appeal to Caesar, and a shipwreck took place. The terrible time endured by all those on board is one of the most dramatic descriptions of a storm at sea that has ever been written; but this is what interests us:

> But after long abstinence Paul stood forth in the midst of them, and said, Sirs, ye should have hearkened unto me, and not have loosed from Crete, and to have gained this harm and loss. And now I exhort you to be of good cheer: for there shall be no loss of any man's life among you, but of the ship.

How does Paul know this?

> For there stood by me this night the angel of God, whose I am, and whom I serve, saying, Fear not, Paul; thou must be brought before Caesar: and, lo, God hath given thee all them that sail with thee. (Acts 27:21–24)

Or in a less dramatic manner than that, and perhaps a little nearer to the kind of thing we are likely to experience, consider 2 Timothy 4:16–17. Paul, under arrest and awaiting trial, writes to Timothy:

> At my first answer no man stood with me, but all men forsook me: I pray God that it may not be laid to their charge. Notwithstanding the Lord stood with me, and strengthened me; that by me the preaching might be fully known, and that all the Gentiles might hear: and I was delivered out of the mouth of the lion.

"The Lord stood with me"! And this is what he promises to us all.

These are illustrations not of the apostle going to the Lord and finding this fullness but of Paul in terrible trouble and the Lord coming to him just when he needs him. This is a part of Christian experience, an essential part of the Christian life. Listen to William Cowper saying the same thing:

> *Sometimes a light surprises*
> *The Christian while he sings;*
> *It is the Lord, who rises*
> *With healing in his wings. ("Sometimes a Light Surprises")*

He comes suddenly, "To cheer the soul after rain," as Cowper goes on to say. When you are down, when you are discouraged, when the clouds are there, "sometimes a light surprises." You are amazed at it. It is he who comes; he visits you. He gives you a manifestation of his nearness, his fullness, and the glory of his presence.

Now we modern Christians have strangely neglected this teaching. Oh, how we have robbed ourselves of the riches of his grace! I am afraid some of us are so busy and have so emphasized our activity, our decision, our effort that we do not give him an opportunity to come to visit us. Let me give you a taste of this. I could give you many examples, as I have done in the past, out of the journals of George Whitefield, but now I am just going to give you something out of the diary of Augustus Toplady, the author of "Rock of Ages" and other great hymns. Here it is:

> To have a part and lot in God's salvation is the main thing; but to have the joy of it is an additional blessing which makes our way to the kingdom smooth and sweet. Here let me leave it on thankful record for my comfort and support if it please God in future times of trial and desertion, that I was never lower in the valley than last night, nor higher on the mount than today. The Lord chastened me but did not give me over unto death, and he never will. He may indeed for the small moment hide his face from me, but with everlasting kindness will he have mercy on me.
>
> From morning until now (that is to say, eleven at night) I have

> enjoyed a continual feast within. Christ has been unspeakably precious to my heart, and the blessed Spirit of God hath visited me with sweet and reviving manifestations.

Now Augustus Toplady was a great Calvinist and a great controversialist, but that is what kept this man going, that is what enabled him to write those incomparable hymns. You notice how he puts it: "manifestations." He himself did not do this. If you read his diaries and those of other people, you find they all say that it is the Lord who comes to them.

My friends, we are not worshipping a theology, we are not worshipping an orthodox belief; we are worshipping a living person, and he manifests himself, as he has promised to do. In John 14:21 we read, "[I] will manifest myself to him," and in verse 23, "My Father will love him [the one who keeps his words], and we will come unto him, and make our abode with him." As we read the biographies and autobiographies of saints throughout the centuries, we find a repetition of this. And let me make this clear—this is not confined only to outstanding Christian people, to great poets and preachers. Our Lord manifests himself to some of the most "ordinary" people, so-called. A Christian cannot be ordinary, but we use these distinctions. Some of the most ordinary Christians have testified to these inexpressible experiences. That is why Christians will never thirst. Even when they can scarcely do anything, the Lord comes to them.

Do you know these visitations of his? Does he come to you? Do you know what it is to be turned suddenly from the depth of anguish to heights of rejoicing? Do you know what it is to be overwhelmed by his love, to weep tears of joy and of rapture? He promises this. It is a personal relationship, and it is an essential part of this whole Christian teaching. And it is all in him. Thank God that our Lord comes to us even when we cannot go to him.

Another, and a most comforting and consoling thought, is our Lord's unchangeableness. Not only do we rejoice in the inexhaustible riches that are in him, but we also rejoice in the fact that they will never diminish, they will never change, they will never become small; he is "a never-ebbing sea."[25] Again the apostle Paul has given expression to this, and it gave him great comfort. Here was this man, a great man of God, a preacher, evangelist, builder of churches, contender for the faith, but, oh, the troubles he had, the persecution and the trials, people leaving him and forsaking him, rejecting the doctrine! In his second epistle to Timothy, he puts it like this when dealing with people who are denying the doctrine of the resurrection:

> Remember that Jesus Christ of the seed of David was raised from the dead according to my gospel: Wherein I suffer trouble, as an evil doer, even unto bonds; but the word of God is not bound. Therefore I endure all things for the elect's sakes, that they may also obtain the salvation which is in Christ Jesus with eternal glory.

And then:

> It is a faithful saying: For if we be dead with him, we shall also live with him: If we suffer, we shall also reign with him: if we deny him, he also will deny us . . . yet he abideth faithful: he cannot deny himself.

Is that the sheet anchor of your whole position? Is that the truth on which you are resting? Paul then says, "Nevertheless the foundation of God standeth sure, having this seal, The Lord knoweth them that are his. And, Let every one that nameth the name of Christ depart from iniquity" (2 Tim. 2:8–13, 19).

The New Testament is full of this. These people lived on it. They were having such a trying, terrible time, and death was always staring them in the face simply because they were Christians. So the writer of the Epistle to the Hebrews tells them that this is the way to deal with these tribulations:

> Seeing we also are compassed about with so great a cloud of witnesses, let us lay aside every weight, and the sin which doth so easily beset us, and let us run with patience the race that is set before us, looking unto Jesus the author and finisher of our faith; who for the joy that was set before him endured the cross, despising the shame, and is set down at the right hand of the throne of God. (12:1–3)

And then, summing it up, he says, "Jesus Christ the same yesterday, and to day, and for ever" (13:8).

And that is our only final comfort. You read of it in the four Gospels. You see who our Lord was. You see the love, the mercy, the compassion, the patience, everything that was so true of him. And you and I must realize that now, in the glory, he is still the same. In the book of Revelation, John tells us he had a great vision of our Lord, and then John says, "And when I saw him, I fell at his feet as dead." Then John adds these most wonderful words:

> And he laid his right hand upon me, saying unto me, Fear not; I am the first and the last: I am he that liveth, and was dead; and, behold, I am

alive for evermore. Amen; and have the keys of hell and of death. (Rev. 1:17–18)

That is what immediately put John right: "He laid his right hand upon me." How often had our Lord done that in the days of his flesh! And he still does that; he does not change. Read the Gospels—you will get to know him there; and as you read, remember that he is still the same.

In every pang that rends the heart,
The Man of Sorrows had a part.
Michael Bruce ("Where High the Heavenly Temple Stands")

Though he is there in the glory everlasting, he has not forgotten all that he suffered and endured while he was here. And so, in the glory, he comes, and he will put his hand on you, and you will feel the touch, and you will know that all is well. When you are agitated, when you are liable to fall, just the touch of his hand and you are well, you are strong. He comes, and he remains ever always the same.

Is not this a glorious comfort and consolation for us? We are all so changeable, and so are our circumstances. We have no idea what we will feel like tomorrow morning. We have no idea what is going to happen to us. That is the characteristic of this world in which we find ourselves, and things that bring us relief suddenly fail us. We tend to lean on things that cannot hold us; we lean on one another. But we must not. We are all here in the flesh; we are here today and gone tomorrow. We must not depend upon anybody or anything, or sooner or later we will find ourselves bereft, with nothing. But this is the glorious reality:

When all created streams are dried,
Thy fullness is the same.

When the drought has come, the spiritual drought, and things are failing us everywhere, to the right and left, he will never become dry. Droughts do not affect him. He is from everlasting to everlasting, and all the fullness of the Godhead dwells in him bodily.

May I with this be satisfied
And glory in thy name.

Of course!

He that has made my heaven secure,
Will here all good provide;
While Christ is rich, can I be poor?
What can I want beside?

John Ryland ("O Lord, I Would Delight in Thee")

That is the simple truth. He is eternally rich, and he will never change. In the glory there will never be any diminution of his power and his ability—never. He abides ever, always, everlastingly the same.

Change and decay in all around I see;
O thou who changest not, abide with me.

Henry Francis Lyte ("Abide with Me")

And he will—he has promised to. He has said, "I will never leave thee, nor forsake thee" (Heb. 13:5). Never! Whatever happens. He has given his word, and he will never break it.

And that brings us to the conclusion concerning this aspect of the matter, and that is the glory of his power, guaranteeing that nothing will ever be able to separate us from him. It is not only that he will never leave us or forsake us, but nothing will ever be allowed to come between us and him. This is the most comforting and consoling truth—not my holding on to him, but his strong grasp of me. If I felt that my eternal future depended upon me and my stability and strength and understanding, I would be lost; so would you. It is his strong grasp of us that saves us. That is the only certainty, and it is an absolute certainty. "He that spared not his own Son, but delivered him up for us all, how shall he not with him also freely give us all things?" (Rom. 8:32). "Who shall separate us from the love of Christ?" That is it. The apostle throws out this tremendous challenge at the end of that eighth chapter of Romans:

> Who shall separate us from the love of Christ? shall tribulation, or distress, or persecution, or famine, or nakedness, or peril, or sword? As it is written, For thy sake we are killed all the day long; we are accounted as sheep for the slaughter. Nay, in all these things we are more than conquerors through him that loved us.

And then comes this tremendous conclusion:

> For I am persuaded [I am absolutely certain], that neither death, nor life, nor angels, nor principalities, nor powers, nor things present, nor things

> to come, nor height, nor depth, nor any other creature [can you think of anything else? Put it in if you can, and still I say that none of them, nor all of them together], shall be able to separate us from the love of God, which is in Christ Jesus our Lord. (vv. 35–39)

We are safe!

Safe in the arms of Jesus,
Safe on his gentle breast.[26]

That is where he has put you. He has embraced you, he has enfolded you with the arms of his love, and he will never let you go. Never! And nothing will ever be able to separate you from his love and the love of God in him and through him by the Holy Spirit; it is impossible.

"Whosoever drinketh of the water that I shall give him shall never, no, never, thirst as long as the world standeth." What does he mean? He means this: "I will always be surrounding you; you will always be in the embrace of my eternal love."

Jude, in his doxology, puts it like this:

> Unto him that is able to keep you from falling, and to present you faultless before the presence of his glory with exceeding joy, to the only wise God our Saviour, be glory and majesty, dominion and power, both now and ever. Amen. (Jude 24–25)

So I leave you with a question: is this true of you? What a difference there is between being religious and being a Christian! I am not asking if you are religious. What I am asking you is this: have you found your sufficiency in him? You have known created streams going dry at times, have you not? Have you known at such times that his fullness is still the same? Have you ever gone to him in vain? Have you ever found him to disappoint you? Or let me put it in a better way: have you not always found everything in him? Oh, nothing matters but this! Nobody knows what the future is to be, internationally, nationally, in regard to family or individuals. But the point is that it does not matter. If your position, if your happiness, depends upon things that are going to happen to you, then in a sense you are of all people the most miserable. The glory of this message is that it does not matter what happens. He will be with you always—in life, in death, throughout eternity. Do you know him?

And our Lord tells you that all you need to do is to drink. "Whosoever drinketh of the water that I shall give him"—he is saying that to you, and all you must do is drink of it.

What does that mean? In its essence it means that you realize your need, your utter bankruptcy, your complete helplessness and hopelessness. You will never know this as long as you are relying on anything in yourself. It is to this poor woman of Samaria who has nothing, who does not have character or chastity, who has lost everything, that he offers everything. If you are holding on to your religion, your religiosity, your morality, your understanding, your willpower, you will not know this living water; it is a blessed gospel for paupers. This water is offered to people who are dying of thirst and who know it, those who have come to the end, who are bankrupt. That is the first and the most important thing of all. Let me put it in the words of a verse out of a hymn of Horatius Bonar:

> *I heard the voice of Jesus say,*
> *"Behold, I freely give*
> *The living water; thirsty one,*
> *Stoop down, and drink, and live."*

There is a fountain here. You are dying of thirst; you are staggering about the world. But here is everything you need. It will slake your thirst; it will put you on your feet; it will give you life. But you cannot drink from a fountain standing erect. Stoop down! Lie prostrate on the ground.

> *I came to Jesus, and I drank*
> *Of that life-giving stream;*
> *My thirst was quenched, my soul revived,*
> *And now I live in him. ("I Heard the Voice of Jesus Say")*

Come to the end of all your abilities and self-confidence and trust, all your self-defense, all your rationalizing of your imperfections and failures: "Stoop down, and drink, and live." Tell him the truth about yourself; tell him about your lack of love, your lack of joy, your lack of whatever it is. Tell him that you are like this, that you can do nothing about it, that you have tried and tried and tried and have constantly failed. Just go to him as you are; tell him all and say, "I want to have this life springing up within me. You can give it to me, and you alone." Cast yourself utterly upon him, and say, as Jacob said to him, "I will not let thee go, except thou bless me" (Gen. 32:26). And I can assure you that as certainly as you do that, he will give it you, for he has said, "Him that cometh to me I will in no wise cast out" (John 6:37).

My dear friend, go to him and drink, and you will never thirst, no, never, as long as the world stands, and you will be aware within yourself of a well of water springing up into everlasting life.

39

The Work of Christ

And upon this came his disciples, and marvelled that he talked with the woman: yet no man said, What seekest thou? or, Why talkest thou with her? The woman then left her waterpot, and went her way into the city, and saith to the men, Come, see a man, which told me all things that ever I did: is not this the Christ? Then they went out of the city, and came unto him. In the mean while his disciples prayed him, saying, Master, eat. But he said unto them, I have meat to eat that ye know not of. Therefore said the disciples one to another, Hath any man brought him ought to eat? Jesus saith unto them, My meat is to do the will of him that sent me, and to finish his work. Say not ye, There are yet four months, and then cometh harvest? behold, I say unto you, Lift up your eyes, and look on the fields; for they are white already to harvest. And he that reapeth receiveth wages, and gathereth fruit unto life eternal: that both he that soweth and he that reapeth may rejoice together. And herein is that saying true, One soweth, and another reapeth. I sent you to reap that whereon ye bestowed no labour: other man laboured, and ye are entered into their labours. (John 4:27–38)

I want now to take a general look at the teaching that stands out in the whole section that runs from verses 27 to 38 of John 4. We are picking out the great theme of this Gospel. The apostle makes that theme perfectly clear in the first chapter. It is that the Lord Jesus Christ, the Son of God, has come into this world to give us the right and the authority to become the children of God and to be filled with his fullness: "And of his fulness have all we received, and grace for [upon] grace" (John 1:16).[27]

Our Lord constantly repeats this promise. He says, "I am come that they might have life, and that they might have it more abundantly" (John

10:10). And, as we have been seeing at great length, "Whosoever drinketh of the water that I shall give him shall never thirst; but the water that I shall give him shall be in him a well of water springing up into everlasting life" (John 4:14). This fullness, this abundant life, is the great theme of this Gospel, and we are concerned to find out how it is to be obtained. In the various incidents that are recorded in John's Gospel, we are given an account of the difficulties, the obstacles, to receiving this fullness. Can we all say, "Of his fullness have I received, and grace upon grace"? Can I say of a surety that I have this "well of water" in me and that it is "springing up into everlasting life" so that I do not thirst? This is the great question.

Now in dealing with this passage in John 4 from verse 4 up to the end of verse 26, we have seen many of these difficulties, and we are aware of them in our own lives. But we have also seen how our Lord enables us to overcome them, how he deals with us, and we have looked at this wonderful, positive teaching. And now we come to the stage at which we see the result in this woman's life. It is very important that we should consider this because in a sense it is always the same for everyone, and as we have tested ourselves in terms of the difficulties and the obstacles, so we can also test ourselves in terms of the result. This is a most practical matter, and that is why we deal with it.

But before we even do that, we must remind ourselves again of who makes all this possible. A great danger confronting us all at the present time is to keep on talking about Christianity instead of talking about the Lord Jesus Christ. We start with ourselves, we start with our problems and difficulties, we start with the world as it is, and we end with that, and people are merely interested in the application of Christianity to this, that, and the other problem. The whole emphasis today is upon the practical application. Now that is all right, that must be done, but the constant danger is that in the process we forget about him. And the devil, of course, seeks to make this happen.

Others seem to have lost the Lord in the doctrines concerning him. They approach the doctrines in a theoretical and purely intellectual manner. Again, of course, it is right to study the doctrines, but if we stop at that, if we forget him, we shall soon be in trouble. And in any case we are missing and failing to enjoy what is, after all, the greatest lesson of all, and that is our personal relationship to him. So we must concentrate on our Lord himself.

Why do we have the Gospels? Why were they ever written? Well, they have two main functions. One is, of course, to establish the facts concerning our Lord and to remind us constantly of who he is and what he is. But they have an additional function, and that is to remind us that he is still the same, that as he was on earth, so he is now. Though high and exalted, at the right hand of God in the glory everlasting, he still remembers all that he suffered in this world. He is still the same one who spoke to the woman of Samaria by the side of the well. All that characterized him then characterizes him now.

Do we know him? Are we able to go to him? Are we able to speak to him as this woman spoke to him, as the disciples spoke to him? This, after all, is what matters. If our faith, if our Christianity that we talk about, is not of value to us in the ordinary circumstances and details of life, there is something tragically wrong with us. The very heart and nerve of this message is to tell us that it is possible for us to know him and to go immediately and directly to him. So we must look at him again. He dominates the situation, always. In the sequel to this incident, he is still the most important person.

So what do we find here? Let me just present some of these truths for your consideration, for they are wonderful and most comforting and encouraging. The trouble is that the church, with its ceremonies and rituals and by putting others between us and him, has so often hidden him from us. He is put at some distance, and people do not derive the great benefits of the Christian life that are waiting for them. But they are open before us in the New Testament. Let us, then, above all else realize the truth concerning our Lord.

I have taken this one paragraph—verses 27–38—and have put all that we are told here under two main headings. There are certain general things that we learn about our Lord, and then there are certain things that are more particular and that he himself brings out in his teaching. The first comment I would make concerns the opening of verse 27. It reads like this: "And upon this came his disciples, and marvelled that he talked with the woman." The expression "upon this" is not the best translation. A better way of translating these words is, "just then," or better still, "at that moment." What moment? Well, obviously the reference is to what has just gone before. Our Lord is instructing this woman, and she says to him, "I know that Messiah cometh, which is called Christ: when he is come, he will tell us all things." And Jesus replies, "I that speak unto thee am he." At that moment the disciples came. Just as he says that, the disciples arrive.

What is the significance of this? This is to me one of those glorious things that we find so constantly in the Scriptures. A few years back, a man wrote a book called *Golden Nuggets in the New Testament*,[28] and he is quite right—there are "golden nuggets" here. But you must seek them. If you take the trouble to look for them, you will find how wonderful they are. Now you must not suppose that the disciples interrupt the conversation. That is what we are tempted to think. You remember that they have gone to buy provisions; they are all very tired, and they have not eaten. We are told that our Lord, "being wearied with his journey, sat thus on the well," and then we think that just as he is talking with the woman, back they come. But to think that is to miss the glory of this particular teaching. It is not that the disciples return and interrupt the conversation, but that our Lord has finished saying to this woman what he intended to say. He has reached the climax—"I that speak unto thee am he." He has delivered his message, and immediately afterward, or just as he is finishing, they come back.

This is one of these golden nuggets that should give us such comfort and consolation. He is always in charge of the situation. He knows everything; nothing is accidental. All his conversation with the Samaritan woman is so arranged that he finishes his statement and makes his declaration before the disciples come back. Nothing can interrupt his work. We tend to think that his work can be interrupted, but that idea is a fallacy; it is our self-importance that makes us think that. What he has purposed he will always do. He can control time; he can control persons; there is nothing that he does not do for them. He knows everything. We have already seen how he knows all about this woman. He knows about her immoral life; he knows that she has had five husbands. She does not understand this and is astonished, but this is simply the truth about him. Therefore, in chapter 2 we read:

> Now when he was in Jerusalem at the passover, in the feast day, many believed in his name, when they saw the miracles which he did. But Jesus did not commit himself unto them, because he knew all men, and needed not that any should testify of man: for he knew what was in man. (vv. 23–25)

And John 3 similarly tells us that he knew the exact position of Nicodemus, and so could cut through his conversation.

Now here, it seems to me, is one of these great principles that we should always bear in mind. There is nothing about our circumstances that our Lord does not know; he is the Lord of all circumstances. There can be no interruption; his plan is perfect, and he will certainly carry it through. We are so self-important and put such emphasis upon our decisions, as if we can keep the Lord waiting. My dear friend, get rid of that notion. He is always in charge; he knows what he is doing.

> *He knows the way he taketh,*
> *And I will walk with him.*
>
> Anna L. Waring ("In Heavenly Love Abiding")

Just at that moment! Not before, not after, but just at the right moment the disciples come back. Do you realize that you are in the hands of this Lord, this blessed person, this one who is in charge and in control of the entire universe? He has said, "All power is given unto me in heaven and in earth" (Matt. 28:18).

The next thing we notice is that he does surprising things. "And upon this came his disciples, and marvelled that he talked with the woman." They do not understand. Of course not; they are Jews and are creatures of tradition. It was the teaching of the rabbis—and this had been made into an absolute law—that a man was not to speak to a woman in a public place. A husband should not even speak to his wife in public if they happened to meet accidentally on the street. So this is part of the disciples' difficulty. The further reason, as we have seen, is that she is a Samaritan, and still more, there is her particular character.

We all have our preconceived notions, and we often get into trouble, both before and after we have come into the Christian life, because we are bound and fettered by our prejudices. But our Lord breaks through them all. This is one of the first things we must realize about him. He acts in ways that are utterly unexpected. He sometimes does the exact opposite of what we think he should be doing. But this just opens out to us the utter folly of trying to dictate to him, of trying to tell him what he should do. We need to cultivate the attitude and the spirit of these disciples who, because they do not understand, behave in the right way. We are told, "[They] marvelled that he talked with this woman: yet no man said, What seekest thou? or, Why talkest thou with her?" They have enough sense to say nothing, and this is one of the lessons we learn in passing.

> For my thoughts are not your thoughts, neither are your ways my ways, saith the Lord. For as the heavens are higher than the earth, so are my ways higher than your ways, and my thoughts than your thoughts. (Isa. 55:8–9)

So the lesson we must learn is that we are dealing with this great and glorious person, and we must shed our prejudices, our preconceived notions and ideas. We must not turn our Christianity into something little that is just set and formal and polite and respectable and so ordered. No, no; we must abandon ourselves, watch what he does, and be open to his leadings. We never know which way he is going to take us; we never know what he is going to do. He does things that, to us, are unusual and strange and seem at times to be wrong.

This was the whole tragedy of the Pharisees and the scribes when our Lord was in this world. Here were these people—remember that they were godly, religious people—who were always being stumbled by him. He seemed to them to be a law-breaker. They were so narrow and rigid in their ideas that when they saw him healing a man on the Sabbath, they said, "He is breaking the Law." They did not realize that "The sabbath was made for man, and not man for the sabbath" (Mark 2:27). These are the sorts of legalism and prejudices that we tend to carry with us into the Christian life, and therefore at times we will be shocked and amazed at his treatment of us or at his handling of some situation. We marvel, and we also tend to grumble and complain. So let us learn the lesson from these disciples and not say anything. If we do not understand, we must remember that he knows what he is doing. We must have faith in him and keep silent. We must let him lead us. Our business is to follow him.

And that leads to the next general point, which is the fact that he is one who always commands respect. He is always to be approached with reverence and awe. Though the disciples do not understand him, though they "marvel," they keep silent. Why? Well, there is something about him, and you find this running right through the Gospels. How important it is for us, periodically at any rate, to stand back and just look at him again, to see him as he was here on earth, and to remember that he is the same one, but infinitely glorified, there above the heavens at the right hand of God! So we are delivered from the temptation to approach him with an easy familiarity.

Now there is a paradox here. I am going to tell you about his condescension and about how the woman of Samaria and the disciples can speak to him and put forward their questions; but at the same time there is something about him that holds them back—"Yet no man said, What seekest thou? or Why talkest thou with her?" Read the story concerning him in the Gospels, and you will see how he could silence his enemies. When the very soldiers who came to arrest him saw him, they fell back.

He was just a carpenter, he appeared to be an ordinary man, and yet there was something about him that created a sense of awe, a sense of respect, a sense of "someone other." As you read about the miracles and his teaching, you will find that people were amazed. "And they were astonished at his doctrine: for he taught them as one that had authority, and not as the scribes" (Mark 1:22). They were filled with wonder; they praised and worshipped God. They said, "We have seen strange things to day" (Luke 5:26). So let us remember that we are in the realm of the miraculous, the supernatural, the divine. Let us remember that we are dealing with the everlasting and eternal God in three Persons—Father, Son, and Holy Spirit.

But, come, let us listen to his own teaching as we find it in this paragraph. You notice his self-revelation. He puts it in terms, as he so generally did, of "I" and "you." "My meat," he says, in contradistinction to the food of the disciples: "His disciples prayed him, saying, Master, eat. But he said unto them, I have meat to eat that ye know not of. . . . My meat is to do the will of him that sent me, and to finish his work" (John 4:31–32, 34).

Here, again, is something that should be fundamental in all our thinking. It is a tragedy that I even have to mention such a point as this, but we are living in an age when people who call themselves Christians do not seem to believe any longer in our Lord's unique deity. They not only believe that he was merely a man, but they are capable of believing that he was a pervert. If there is any suggestion of such thinking in your approach to him, do not be surprised if you do not know these great blessings and have not received of his fullness and grace upon grace (John 1:16).

This is the very beginning of it all. He is a man, but he is not only a man. He stands among us as a man among men, but he says "I"—"you." We must get rid of any notion that he is one of us in that sense. The devil is so subtle. I am not querying the motives of people who teach these blasphemous heresies, but they go wrong because they do not approach these issues in the right way. They say, "If he is to help modern people, then he must be like them." So they reduce him to our level and argue that he can help perverts by being something of a pervert himself and so on. The whole tragedy is that is the wrong way round. You start with *him*! The only hope of our salvation is that he is not one of us, that he can say "I." He is the great "I am that I am" (Exod. 3:14). He is the Lord Jehovah appearing in the flesh as the Son: "I' and "you."

Now I repeat that if there is any question in our minds with regard to his blessed person, there is no hope of any blessing. We immediately reduce him to the level of an earthly human teacher, making him just one in a series with the great men of the ages. But that is a lie; it is wrong. This is what these disciples have grasped. They are still unlearned and are lacking in their understanding of him and of his way, but they have already felt something that keeps them quiet.

But then our Lord puts the truth of who he is plainly and clearly to the disciples, as he had put it to the woman when he said, "I that speak unto thee am he" (v. 26). He says, "My meat is to do the will of him that sent me" (v. 34). By nature he does not belong to this world. He has come *into* the world; he has been sent *into* the world. This, of course, is just another way of summing up the whole of what we read in the prologue of John's Gospel. This is just another way of saying, "In the beginning was the Word, and the Word was with God, and the Word was God" (1:1), and "And the Word was made flesh, and dwelt among us" (1:14).

Now, again, this is a basic Christian truth. Unfortunately, I have to say these things because of this foolish age in which we live, which talks about "tolerance" and says that though you may not believe the truth about the person of Christ, you can still be a Christian if you do good and so on. But there is no Christianity if that is true. This is one of the subjects about which there can be no discussion. There is no "well of water springing up into everlasting life" if Jesus of Nazareth was only a man. These infidels have their own consistency. They say that he did not even have this fullness of life himself—that he was a fallible, ignorant man and a failure. So there is no hope for us, and there was failure in him.

But, oh, how wrong this is! Our whole salvation depends upon the fact that God sent into the world his only begotten Son: "The Word was made flesh." Man, yes, but also God the eternal Son taking upon himself human nature: "I"—"you." "I am the sent one—I have come into the world." That was what he kept on saying. He did not say, "I was born," but "I am come." He was a visitor. "[God] hath visited and redeemed his people" (Luke 1:68). If we are not clear about all this, it is not surprising that we do not know about the fullnesss. Let us realize, then, that what we have here is just another way of saying, "When the fulness of the time was come, God sent forth his Son, made of a woman, made under the law, to redeem them that were under the law" (Gal. 4:4–5). "I am come." He is the sent one.

But let us go on: our Lord takes it upon himself to do this work. He says, "My meat [my whole purpose] is to do the will of him that sent me, and to finish his work." Do you see the content of that? There is the whole of Christianity in a nutshell. Why has this person come into this world? Why is this blessed Son of God speaking to the woman of Samaria? What is he doing here? And he tells us he has come to do the will of God, "the will of him that sent me." What does that mean? It refers to Christian salvation. He came to carry out God's plan of salvation. That is what he was doing in this world. He was not merely here to teach us, though that is a part of it; the plan of God is for the redemption of the world! This is the great plan conceived in the mind of God before the very foundation of the world, that "hidden wisdom" about which the apostle Paul so delights to write:

> Howbeit we speak wisdom among them that are perfect: yet not the wisdom of this world, nor of the princes of this world, that come to nought: But we speak the wisdom of God in a mystery, even the hidden wisdom, which God ordained before the world unto our glory. (1 Cor. 2:6–7)

Or as Paul puts it in writing to the Ephesians, God's purpose is "that in the dispensation of the fulness of times he might gather together in one all things in Christ, both which are in heaven, and which are on earth; even in him" (Eph. 1:10).

We must not think of salvation only in subjective terms—what it means to us. We must do that and thank God for it; we are to enjoy this personally. But let us see, I say, the whole grand, glorious purpose—"the will of him that sent me." Our Lord was a messenger, an envoy, one who had been given an allotted task, and the way to be delivered from so many of the difficulties and miseries of the Christian life, which we should never be in at all, is just to look up and to look at him and to see this grand and glorious unfolding purpose.

And our Lord adds to that, to open it out still further, "to finish his work." What does this mean? Well, this is a summary of all that he came to do. He means that he came into this world to finish the work that God had sent him to do. And what is that work? It is your salvation, it is my salvation, but it is also the salvation of the world. This is an antidote to every form of spiritual depression. He did not merely come to experiment, he did not merely come to try to do something—he came to finish it. Certain things had to be done before you and I could be saved. My dear friend, how can you ever get this glorious Christian experience that the saints of centuries have always enjoyed? You can never get it until you are clear about the way of salvation.

Many people do not realize that our Lord came to finish the work of salvation, and that is why they spend their whole lives seeking it. This is the basic error of what is called mysticism. There is a true and there is a false mysticism. The true mysticism is the mysticism of a personal relationship to the Lord Jesus Christ in the way that is indicated in the New Testament. The false mysticism bypasses the work he came to do, that work that he has finished. That mystic starts by saying, "God is in you, and what you must do now is to seek the God that is in you." So you go through a long process of meditation and contemplation—"the dark night of the soul"—and at last you may get some sort of an experience. What it is one does not know. It can be purely psychological. It can make people happy at times, for the few who succeed in getting through the process. But that it is not Christianity at all.

There is only one way to this blessed fullness of which our Lord speaks, and that is to realize that it is only possible as the result of his finished work. So many people go to God in trouble. They pray, and they are surprised that they are not answered; indeed, many Christians go to God and do not get satisfaction. Again, it is because they are forgetting the essential fact that there is a finished work. I am only mentioning this in passing because we are looking at our Lord as he is and as he enunciates these basic questions. You should always read what he says here in the light of his High-Priestly prayer in John 17.

> Father, the hour is come; glorify thy Son, that thy Son also may glorify thee: as thou hast given him power over all flesh, that he should give eternal life to as many as thou hast given him. And this is life eternal, that they might know thee the only true God, and Jesus Christ, whom thou hast sent. I have glorified thee on the earth: I have finished the work which thou gavest me to do. (vv. 1–4)

There our Lord sums up his work.

He gave himself to the death of the cross "to finish his work." What is this work? It is all that he gave in his teaching, it is all that he manifested in his person and power, but supremely it is what he went on to talk about in that seventeenth chapter of John: "I sanctify myself" (v. 19). This work is to redeem us, to reconcile us to God. There is no hope for us until we are reconciled to him. It is no use seeking blessings from God until you are reconciled to him, until you realize, in other words, that you have sinned against him, that you are guilty before him, that his wrath is upon you, and that he will not bless a sinner. God may grant you certain temporal or general blessings, but he will never give you this intimate and greatest blessing of all, which is the knowledge of God and of his Son. That knowledge is eternal life, and it is only given to those who are covered by the finished work of Christ, which means that the only way whereby we can be reconciled to God is by realizing that God has laid our sins upon his own Son. This is the finishing of the work. It is his going as a lamb to the slaughter, yielding himself passively, allowing the Father to lay our sins upon him, becoming the Lamb of God, and, without grumbling and complaining, being smitten by God. And there he finishes the work of this grand redemption and cries out, "It is finished" (John 19:30).

And then he rose again to justify us, and he "ever liveth to make intercession for [us]" (Heb. 7:25). That is what our Lord is saying here in John 4. This is what he has come to do. He has come to do the will of him who sent him and to finish the work. And he finished it; nothing could stop him. All the powers of hell arrayed against him could not stop him.

Have you realized this? When you go to him or when you seek him in prayer, do you always realize that the only way into the presence of God is "by the blood of Jesus" (Heb. 10:19)? Without the finished work there is no access. You will spend the rest of your life seeking, but you will never find the living water. This is the possession only of those who realize the truth concerning this finished work, God's plan in redemption, which is Jesus Christ, and him crucified. Without this atoning death, no blessing is offered to us, and we have no right to expect it.

And then to complete this picture, notice our Lord's zeal in this work that he has been sent to do, this commission that has been given to him. Oh, what comforting words these are! "My meat is to do the will of him that sent me." The disciples do not understand this. "I have meat to eat," he says, "that ye know not of." They are pressing him to eat, but he does not. Why not? He says in effect, "For one thing, though I am a man, and though I need food, and though I know what it is to be weary, these do not control me. I have hidden resources that you do not understand. I have sources of satisfaction beyond anything that you have ever imagined."

He is saying, "Yes, I stayed here, and I let you go to buy the provisions because I was feeling tired, but now I do not need the food—I am absolutely refreshed." Why? "Because I have been doing the very work I was sent to do. I have been engaged in spiritual activity. I have been handling a soul. I have brought a woman to the place of understanding and of joy. I can live on this; this is my meat, and this is my drink. These are the resources; these are the things by which I live."

What a tremendous consolation it is for us that the Son of God not only came but came with delight, with pleasure, that he enjoyed doing this work for you and for me. And you can be certain that in exactly the same way he enjoys working for us now—"he ever liveth to make intercession" for us, he is ever ready to listen to us. It is his meat and drink. This is what ravishes his soul. This is what fills him with delight and glory.

But another truth is hidden in this same statement, and that is our Lord's utter forgetfulness of himself, his readiness to sacrifice himself. He needs the food, in a sense, but when it becomes a question of handling this soul and the possibilities of life for the Samaritans through this woman, he forgets food and drink; he is not interested in them for the time being. He gives himself. The disciples press him. We read here that they "prayed him" (v. 31). The Greek word is very strong. It means they try to persuade him, they bring pressure to bear upon him to make him eat. They say, "You know, you're tired and you need food. You must eat. It will all be too much for you, and you'll break down under the strain." Our Lord's mother and brothers did the same thing on a different occasion. They said, "He is beside himself" (Mark 3:21)—he cannot go on like this, he will break down. Here our Lord forgets everything; he sacrifices himself completely for the sake of this woman's soul and the souls of the others.

And our Lord is still the same, my dear friends; this is the very essence of the gospel; this is what we are told everywhere in the New Testament. It is stated supremely in that well-known passage in the second chapter of the Epistle to the Philippians:

> Let this mind be in you, which was also in Christ Jesus: who, being in the form of God, thought it not robbery to be equal with God. . . .

In other words, he did not hold on to that; he did not say, "Well, yes, I am prepared to help those people, but I cannot give up the signs of my eternal glory." He did not regard this as a prize that he was to hold on to at all costs. No, no; he laid it aside, he laid aside the "signs."

> But [he] made himself of no reputation, and took upon him the form of a servant, and was made in the likeness of men: and being found in fashion as a man, he humbled himself, and became obedient unto death, even the death of the cross. (Phil. 2:5–8)

This is it—self-forgetfulness, self-abnegation, self-abasement. The insignia of the everlasting glory do not stand in the way. He puts them aside, as he puts the food and the drink aside here in order to help these people. For you and for me he put it all aside and humbled himself and became a man and was tempted and suffered—yes, "even the death of the cross" and the shame accompanying it—and was laid in a tomb. This is his meat and drink. This is his concern for you and for me. And the whole object of recording this is that you and I should remember it. As you go to him in your need, remember all this about him. Though there in that excellent and eternal glory, he still looks at you with a brother's sympathizing eye. He is aware of your need, and he is with you. This is the whole point of this teaching. So remember the zeal that he displayed.

And then there is the joy of which our Lord talks, the joy of sowing and the joy of reaping—it gladdens his heart. Whenever a soul is saved, it gives him joy. There is also joy among the angels of heaven, and you and I are to be participators, he says, in this joy.

And, finally, remember his glorious and amazing condescension. This one who does not hesitate to say "I" in contradistinction to "you" is not only ready to talk to a woman but is ready to talk to this "fallen" woman, this woman who is living in sin, and he allows her to speak to him and to put forward her fumbling questions and her clever arguments. Oh, the infinite condescension of the Son of God! And he is still the same; he is the same blessed person. Do not let your weakness keep you from him; do not let your sin keep you from him. His heart is the most tender in the whole universe. Though high and exalted and pure and apart from sin, he will never refuse you; he will never reject you if you go to him penitent and repentant, humble and contrite, if you really seek his face.

Here he is—infinite in his glory, infinite in his condescension, infinite in his pity, his sympathy, his tenderness, and his readiness to deal with us. He stands before the woman of Samaria and the disciples and later the Samaritans, but, thank God, also before us now. That is who he is!

40

Conviction of Sin

The woman then left her waterpot, and went her way into the city, and saith to the men, Come, see a man, which told me all things that ever I did: is not this the Christ? (John 4:28–29)

I want in particular to deal with the words spoken by the woman of Samaria when she hurries back to the town in which she lives and invites the men there to come out and see this strange and wonderful person whom she has just met herself, the Lord Jesus Christ, the Son of God. We have been seeing together that our great endeavor should be to know and to be certain that we have received, and are receiving, of his fullness and grace upon grace.

Last time we saw that we must always start with the Lord Jesus Christ himself. If we do not do that, we are inevitably doomed to go wrong because everything is in him. The apostle Paul likes to compare the Christian church to a body, of which we individually are members. Christ is the head, and we all receive from that head. The fullness is in him: "[The church] is his body, the fulness of him that filleth all and in all" (Eph. 1:23). Or, again, as Paul puts it in a pregnant statement in the Epistle to the Colossians—this, in a sense, is the great theme of all the Epistles—"I would that ye knew what great conflict I have for you, and for them at Laodicea, and for as many as have not seen my face in the flesh. . . ." What is the apostle concerned about? He continues:

> . . . that their hearts might be comforted, being knit together in love, and unto all riches of the full assurance of understanding, to the acknowledgement of the mystery of God, and of the Father, and of Christ; in whom are hid all the treasures of wisdom and knowledge.

That is it. "For in him dwelleth all the fulness of the Godhead bodily. And ye are complete in him" (Col. 2:1–3, 9–10). So we must start with him.

The great question, therefore, is, I repeat, have we received of this fullness? If not, what is the obstacle? What is the hindrance? Everything that was possessed by the greatest saints that the church has ever known was all derived from the Lord Jesus Christ. The saints were not what they were because of some natural powers and faculties. That does come in, in ministry and so on, but the experiences that they had came from nothing in them. If you read about them before their conversion, before they were born again, you see that they were failures like everybody else, in spite of their shining gifts. The whole secret was that they were in communion and fellowship with him; they were receiving this fullness from him. So what was possible to them is possible to us, and therefore we must discover the obstacles that are preventing our experiencing this fullness.

We will find that we are given further instruction as we examine the case of this woman of Samaria. We have already seen many principles, but here is a fresh one, and we find it in the statement that she makes to the people of her city. "Come," she says, "see a man, which told me all things that ever I did." That is the first thing that she says about him. And I want to direct your attention to just that very point and to ask a question: why does she say that? Why is that the particular way in which she issues her invitation to come and see the Lord Jesus Christ? Why does she not talk about his personality or describe his physical appearance? Why not tell them some of these wonderful truths that he has taught her about worship?

What is this? It is what we call conviction of sin, and I want to show you the primacy of this, for if we are not clear about this, it is not surprising that we know nothing else. Certain rules in the spiritual life must be observed. There are no shortcuts in the spiritual realm. There are certain absolutes, and unless we conform to them, we shall never know much about this fullness that is in him. And the first is conviction of sin—"a man, which told me all things that ever I did." This is what is uppermost in her mind.

On the surface there appears to be an element of exaggeration in this woman's words. She says that our Lord has told her "all things" that she has ever done. That is not a lie; it is hyperbole. What our Lord actually told her, of course, was that he knew all about the immoral life she was living and the fact that she had had five husbands and that the man she was now living with was not her husband. That is all he said about her life. When she refers to "all things that ever I did," she means that as our Lord revealed to her his knowledge of her present life and of what she was actually guilty, both at that moment and in the recent past, he made her feel that he knew everything. And though our Lord did not put it into words, he produced it, he resurrected it as it were, and she saw on a screen flashing past her eyes the whole of her life and all her misdeeds and sins.

This is frequently found in the testimonies that saints of God have left behind them. Some people have testified to this kind of experience when their conversion has been due to some crisis or to some accident. I remember one man in particular who was converted as the result of a terrible accident, an explosion in a mine. He suddenly heard the noise and saw the flash, and he realized that his end might be at hand. He testified that immediately there passed before him the whole of his life, as it were, and his individual misdeeds.

Now it is difficult to understand or to accept this, is it not? And yet we know that even in the natural realm this whole problem of time is very strange; there can be a foreshortening that we do not understand. This kind of thing happens. We think so much in terms of clocks and watches, of seconds and minutes and hours, but there is this extraordinary capacity to see the whole, as it were, in a flash. This is, of course, still easier to comprehend in the spiritual dimension, and there is no doubt at all but that this is precisely what happened in the case of this woman. Our Lord only mentions one thing, but that brings her face-to-face with herself and her life and her misdeeds. So she says and says quite truly therefore, "Come, see a man, which told me all things that ever I did." It is clear that this woman was more conscious of a conviction of sin than of anything else, and it is in terms of this that she invites her fellow townspeople to come and see our Lord.

This is most important. If I were asked to say what, in my opinion, is most lacking in the life of the Christian church at the present time, without any hesitation I would answer that it is just this—a conviction of sin, a sense of our unworthiness, and a sense of the glory of God. We are too healthy; we are too satisfied; we are too pleased with ourselves. When we contrast the state of the church today with what we read of in past ages, what strikes us immediately is that there is an absence of humility, an absence of repentance. This, of course, is vital, and if we are to know individual or general revival, we must start here.

Let me give you one example of how this works out. It is Harvest Thanksgiving. Is the world interested in such times? Why doesn't the world thank God? Why do we not always realize our indebtedness to him? The answer of the New Testament is that this is all due to the fact that we have never realized the truth about ourselves and the truth about God. This is the great argument of the apostle Paul in the second half of Romans 1. He says:

> For the wrath of God is revealed from heaven against all ungodliness and unrighteousness of men, who hold [down] the truth in unrighteousness; because that which may be known of God is manifest in them; for God hath shewed it unto them. For the invisible things of him from the creation of the world are clearly seen, being understood by the things that are made, even his eternal power and Godhead; so that they are without excuse: because that, when they knew God, they glorified him not as God, neither were thankful; but became vain in their imaginations, and their foolish heart was darkened. Professing themselves to be wise, they became fools, and changed the glory of the uncorruptible God into an image made like to corruptible man, and to birds, and four-footed beasts, and creeping things. (vv. 18–23)

Now all that just means that the world does not realize the truth about creation, about daily life and living and the very means whereby we go on living. This is because of its "ungodliness and unrighteousness." In other words, you will never persuade men and women to realize the truth until they are in right relationship to God, until they are godly and righteous. They need to be convicted of their sin; they need to repent; they need to turn to God. It is then, and only then, that they will be able to see things truly.

Now this is a most important point because there are those who think that you can persuade men and women about these things by sheer argumentation. You cannot. They cannot even see the universe and creation truly unless they have new life in them. The "natural man" (1 Cor. 2:14) is incapable of this and sees the creature rather than the Creator.

> *A primrose by a river's brim*
> *A yellow primrose was to him,*
> *And it was nothing more.*
>
> William Wordsworth, "Peter Bell"

But a man or woman with a new nature and a mind illuminated by the Holy Spirit sees God in the flower. You can only truly see creation and all things as you have this mind, this eye of Christ. So these things all hang together. And it is exactly the same with receiving his fullness and grace upon grace. The last people to receive it are always the people who think they are already full. You do not seek for fullness if you think you have it; that would be foolish. It is the people who have never gone down who never go up. It is the people who have never realized their emptiness and their woe who never know very much about "the exceeding riches of his grace" (Eph. 2:7). And I want to show you that it is our failure to put conviction of sin in the first position that accounts for so many of our troubles and certainly accounts for the poverty of our Christian lives.

Why must conviction of sin be put first? Here are some answers. First, the great difference, in the last analysis, between the cults and the Christian faith is just this very point. Has that ever occurred to you? It is no use denying that the cults can help people. They do; they would not succeed but for that. Look at Christian Science and similar movements. Look at their buildings; look at their wealth. That is because of the numbers of their adherents. And listen to their testimonies. Yes, the cults can do many things for many people, but there is one thing that cults never do—they never produce in anybody a sense of guilt. And, of course, that is a part of their popularity. The cults always come to you and more or less tell you that you are all right as you are, that it is circumstances or other people that are the problem, and all you need is a bit of help. They are most ingratiating and pleasant. They never disturb you; they never make you feel uneasy. You never come under any sense of conviction; they never make you feel that you do not deserve any blessing. No, no; they tell you that you deserve everything and can get everything.

And that is where cults differ so essentially from this Christian message; that is what makes Christianity unique. The trouble is that so many people approach the Christian faith as if it were but one in a series with the cults, and they come expecting that kind of teaching. But they do not get it. They say, "I came for comfort and for help, but you make me feel uncomfortable, and I don't like it." Exactly! But you will never know this blessing until you have been made to feel uncomfortable.

And, of course, this is equally true of the difference between all psychological treatments and movements and Christianity. This again must be emphasized because there are people who turn the Christian faith into a psychological method of treatment. You are familiar with this. There are men well known in what are called Christian pulpits who do nothing but treat people psychologically. There are people flourishing at the present time who talk about the power of "positive thinking," as if that were the Christian message. That is pure psychology, nothing else—psychology using Christian terminology.

How do you tell the difference? What right do I have to say that is not Christianity, that it is not even pseudo-Christianity but a travesty of Christianity? I say it solely on the strength of this one point: all that psychological misuse of the Scriptures never produces a conviction of sin. Indeed, you will find that the purveyors of those false teachings generally denounce the biblical doctrine of sin. They are the very people who talk about "that God sitting on the top of Mount Sinai" in whom they do not believe. "Ah," they say, "we don't believe in the God of the Old Testament, the God of law, the God of wrath." They dislike that. They say, "That's a travesty—don't accept it." They believe in the God of Jesus, who is nothing but love, in their view.

That is their way of putting their whole case, and they go on to say that nothing has done so much harm to people as the preaching of the doctrine of conviction of sin. They say, "You've given people complexes; you've made them lose confidence in themselves; you've kept them down. That's wrong; it's a perversion. The first thing you must do is get rid of the whole notion of sin, which has so depressed people and stood between them and all there is to enjoy." But thereby they betray themselves completely. Nobody who has gone to them can come back and say, "Come, see a man, which told me all things that ever I did." Never! Because they never produce that effect. They never make us feel worse than we were; they never make us feel hopeless.

Do you see the vital importance of all this? If the Christian message has never made you feel worse than you were before you first heard it, you have never really heard it. If it has never made you feel hopeless, you do not know it. This is the very essence of the Christian faith, as one can illustrate so easily and in so many different ways. When old Simeon held our blessed Lord in his arms, he said, "This child is set for the fall and rising again of many in Israel" (Luke 2:34). Did you notice the order? The "fall"! There is no "rising" without going down; there is no salvation without preliminary condemnation. People come to me as if they were coming to the cults—they want this, that, and the other; and at first they are shocked and amazed—at least, they should be. If they are truly hearing the gospel, they always will be. They say, "I know I have my problems, but now I'm made to feel that I'm wrong, that I'm a worm," and they dislike it. But this is always what our Lord does.

And we find all this in the case of the woman of Samaria. We see how this woman with her glib argumentation is very ready to talk about this world and about worship—"this mountain," "Jerusalem." Oh, how easy that is! But then our Lord becomes personal. He puts his finger on the running sore of her life. He reveals her utter sinfulness, and that is essential before she can ever be led to this great and glorious salvation.

Then, secondly, conviction of sin is also the crucial point of difference between taking up religion and becoming truly Christian. Here, again, is a most important distinction. It is possible for us to take up religion, it is possible for us to take up what we regard as Christianity, and there are many who do that. But there is a vital, essential difference between that and truly becoming a Christian.

What am I talking about? It is possible for men and women—"the natural man"—to be interested in Christ. Many are. After all, he is a remarkable phenomenon of history. When you have always thought in terms of evolution and gradual development and progress, it is startling suddenly to find, very nearly two thousand years ago, this towering figure. And when people who are merely interested in history and in the processes of thought and in philosophy confront him, they have been fascinated by him.

And then there is an interest in our Lord's teaching. People who are concerned about the state of the world and have made many attempts to find solutions say, "You know, what's really needed is the application of the Sermon on the Mount." There are still many who say this—there used to be many more in the early years of this present [twentieth] century. It used to be the prevailing teaching—"the social gospel," it was called. It was really believed that the Sermon on the Mount could be turned into acts of Parliament and that the world could thereby be put right.

Not only that, there are many who desire to live a good, a better life. Not every sinner is as bad as he can possibly be. There are great differences among sinners. Some poor sinners wallow in the mire and the filth and the gutters of life; but others are very concerned about living a good life, though they are equally sinners and are no more Christian than the man in the gutter. There is idealism, and there are idealists. Large numbers of people really want to be good. They are troubled, they have consciences—every man and woman has a conscience, and some are more sensitive than others. Some people have taken the trouble to read and are concerned about the whole problem of life in this world. They have studied ethical, moral systems; they have read not only the Greek philosophers but also the maxims of Marcus Aurelius and other idealistic writings about life, and their whole desire is to be able to live that sort of life.

And there are others who desire to do good. The world has large numbers of such people. We must never, as Christians, say that nobody but the Christian wants to do any good in the world. It is not so. These people are anxious to improve the world, to uplift the human race, to put an end to war. Our Lord is, to them, the great pacifist, and the Sermon on the Mount, they say, teaches that war is wrong. So they take up what they regard as Christianity and set about trying to do good.

And then at the top of the list, perhaps, we have the people whose great ambition in life is to imitate Christ. It is fascinating to trace the history of this idea in the long story of the Christian church; it has been one of the greatest snares for many an honest soul who has been seeking salvation. "The imitation of Christ"—it sounds so good, does it not? These people are obviously anxious to be good, they are anxious to do good, and they go on to say, "Here is one who has lived a perfect life in this world. He is the person I must emulate. I must follow him." So they find books and manuals to encourage them in the imitation of Christ, and they are ready to make sacrifices; and this is regarded as the height of Christianity and the Christian profession.

Again, we must be very careful how we speak. There are people in the world today who quite genuinely and honestly have set out to imitate Christ. They have given up good positions and prospects in the world; they have made great financial and other sacrifices to follow him. We do not hear as much of this as we used to because the two wars [World Wars I and II] have shattered people's belief in the ability to imitate Christ, but this teaching still often appears in different guises. I remember very well—I mention this simply as a typical illustration of what I am saying—attending a young people's rally over forty years ago. Three speakers had been given the same subject—"The appeal of Christ to the enthusiasm and heroism of young people." Do you get the idea? He was to be depicted as a young man, full of heroism, full of enthusiasm, full of idealism—"here is the one for you to follow." Now this, it is said, is the way to win young people, this is the way to get ahold of them. Young people always admire heroism; they are enthusiastic; they have it in them to do good. They want to follow Christ, so here he is; let us hold him before them, and he will appeal to them.

But do you see how this all betrays itself? All that teaching, all this interest in the person of our Lord, in his teaching, in the desire to be good, to improve the world and to imitate him, is based on one assumption—that we have it in us to be like him. So all we need to do is to be enthused, to rise up and follow him in this great crusade. This teaching has never made us feel uncomfortable, has it? Indeed, it has done the very opposite; it has made us feel we are rather wonderful, that we can do this. Indeed, we feel there is something good in us or we would not be responding in this way. The person who has come under this kind of influence does not rush back and say, "Come, see a man, which told me all things that ever I did." No, no! It is, "Come, see a man who has told me that I have it in me to live as he lived, that I can put the world right, that all we need to do is band together and march down this highway and the world will become paradise." This teaching says, believe in yourselves—follow him—he is what you can be.

That is religion; you can take up that kind of teaching, and many have done so. And, alas, is it not one of the great problems of the church that it regards this as Christianity? It is just calling upon people to take it up, to go into some great crusade. The world can be invited, of course. So the biblical doctrine of sin is denounced, and people are appealed to in terms of the idealism of Christ and the wonderful teaching and the possibilities he holds out. But he does not do that. What he does is expose you to yourself and make you see yourself as you really are, and you feel you are unworthy to do anything. Here, therefore, is something about which we must obviously be very clear. It is not surprising that people say they have tried Christianity and have found it wanting. Such people have started with the wrong conceptions. This is a message that first and foremost convicts us of sin.

Let me put it like this, and this is the third reason why conviction of sin must be put first. The New Testament teaching itself makes it perfectly plain and clear that it is impossible for us to be truly Christian without conviction of sin. How does it show this? The first way is by giving this teaching priority.

Let us assume for a moment that we do not believe this message at all but that we are approaching the Bible as literary critics who are going to make an analysis of the New Testament. We are given this question: what is the first teaching in the New Testament? I think you will have to agree that we will discover that it is always a message of repentance.

Who is the first preacher in the New Testament? The answer is, John the Baptist. We are told about his wonderful birth and then about how he set out on his ministry. This is the introduction; this is the prologue. What did John preach about? There is no difficulty about this—he preached "the baptism of repentance for the remission of sins" (Mark 1:4). Now there had been four hundred years of silence, as it were, after the time of the prophet Malachi—not a word of prophecy Then suddenly came a phenomenon—a strange man preaching in the wilderness, clothed with camel's hair and with a leather belt about his loins, eating locusts and wild honey. A strange man with an extraordinary message—"the baptism of repentance for the remission of sins." And the people came crowding out to listen to him, the Pharisees included, and look at the reception he gave them. He did not say, "I'm glad to see you. Are you ready to go forward in this great crusade I'm starting in order to put the world right?" No, he looked at them and said:

> O generation of vipers, who hath warned you to flee from the wrath to come? . . . And think not to say within yourselves, We have Abraham to our father: for I say unto you, that God is able of these stones to raise up children unto Abraham.

Do not make any mistake about this, says John the Baptist.

> The axe is laid unto the root of the trees; therefore every tree which bringeth not forth good fruit is hewn down, and cast into the fire. (Matt. 3:7, 9–10)

"The baptism of repentance for the remission of sins"—that was the first message of the first preacher. "I indeed baptize you with water" (Matt. 3:11). There it is; nobody can dispute that.

The second great preacher, of course, was none other than our Lord himself. What did he preach about? The message is exactly the same:

> Now after that John was put in prison, Jesus came into Galilee, preaching the gospel of the kingdom of God, and saying, The time is fulfilled, and the kingdom of God is at hand: repent ye, and believe the gospel. (Mark 1:14–15)

Then in John 3 we see Nicodemus, a ruler of the Jews, a teacher, a good man, a religious man, a moral man, who wanted to be arguing with our Lord on equal terms, as it were, and was ready to receive a little further information. But this is what our Lord said to him: "Verily, verily, I say unto thee, Except a man be born of water and of the Spirit, he cannot enter into the kingdom of God" (John 3:5). "Born of water"—that is repentance again; that is baptism again; that is acknowledgment and confession of utter sinfulness. To a man such as Nicodemus, who wanted to start from where he was and go on, our Lord said in essence, "No, no!

Start again. You must be born again; you must go through the water; you must be baptized."

Repentance! Our Lord was constantly making this point, especially to the Pharisees. In one of the parables that he addressed to them, he said:

> But what think ye? A certain man had two sons; and he came to the first, and said, Son, go work to day in my vineyard. He answered and said, I will not: but afterward he repented, and went. And he came to the second, and said likewise. And he answered and said, I go, sir: and went not. Whether of them twain did the will of his father? They say unto him, The first. Jesus saith unto them, Verily I say unto you, That the publicans and the harlots go into the kingdom of God before you. For John came unto you in the way of righteousness, and ye believed him not: but the publicans and the harlots believed him: and ye, when ye had seen it, repented not afterward, that ye might believe him. (Matt. 21:28–32)

This is what determines our entry into the kingdom of God. You cannot enter the kingdom of God without repentance. It does not matter who you are or how good you are—the tax collectors and harlots will go in before you. Why? Because they repented! It is the very essence of his teaching.

We find exactly the same teaching in the famous parable about the tax collector and the Pharisee who went up into the Temple to pray. What could be plainer and clearer?

> Two men went up into the temple to pray; the one a Pharisee, and the other a publican. The Pharisee stood and prayed thus with himself, God, I thank thee that I am not as other men are, extortioners, unjust, adulterers, or even as this publican. I fast twice in the week, I give tithes of all that I possess.

"Here is a typical follower of Christ," people think. "Here is a man who has taken up Christ." But it is all wrong.

> And the publican, standing afar off, would not lift up so much as his eyes unto heaven, but smote upon his breast, saying, God be merciful to me a sinner. I tell you, this man went down to his house justified rather than the other: for every one that exalteth himself shall be abased; and he that humbleth himself shall be exalted. (Luke 18:10–14)

And this need for repentance is implicit in the whole of our Lord's teaching. Look again at the Sermon on the Mount, which the kind of person we are dealing with always admires and is ready to take up and to put into practice in order to follow Christ and imitate his example. Such a person says, "This is what the world needs." But what a complete misunderstanding of the Sermon on the Mount and its purpose! The Sermon on the Mount is nothing but an exposition of the Law. Our Lord did not preach it because he thought that men and women as they were could keep it; it was the exact opposite. He gave the Sermon on the Mount to convict those who felt they could keep the Law of God and to show them that they could never do so. In effect he said, "The moment you really understand the Law, you will see how impossible that is." As an example, consider a man who says he has never committed murder. But, says our Lord, have you understood that? You say that because you have never murdered a man you have kept the Law in this respect, but have you? Have you ever said of your brother, "You fool!"? Have you ever murdered him in your heart and in your mind? If you have, you are guilty of murder.

Now does that mean that the Sermon on the Mount is possible? No; it means it is impossible. Is the Law possible? No; it is impossible. The Law is concerned with my motives, my desires, my hidden imaginations, and therefore the moment I see it, I am undone. The Sermon on the Mount was given to convict people of their utter helplessness and to show that our Lord had come to save them out of their helpless and hopeless position.

And it is the same with the whole of our Lord's teaching. All along he shows men and women that they cannot save themselves. "The things which are impossible with men," he says, "are possible with God" (Luke 18:27). That is his reply to the question, "Who then can be saved?" As Simeon prophesied of him, he casts down, he condemns. That is why the Pharisees hated him. And here, with this woman of Samaria, we see how he cuts across all the talk and the pleasant argument and immediately comes down to the question of sin and guilt—conviction of sin.

And as this is true of the teaching of our Lord, so it is equally true of the teaching of the apostles. Turn to the book of Acts and you will find this theme at the very beginning and running right through. Here is Peter filled with the Spirit on the Day of Pentecost, and he is expounding the Old Testament Scriptures. He declares that God has raised Jesus from the dead and shows that this is what was prophesied of the Messiah because the body of David is in the sepulchre and remains there. And on Peter goes, expounding these Scriptures; he declares that God has at last sent the Deliverer and that the coming of the Holy Spirit upon them is the absolute proof of this. Then Peter says, "Therefore let all the house of Israel know assuredly, that God hath made that same Jesus, whom ye have crucified, both Lord and Christ."

We are told that when all the people heard this, "They were pricked in their heart, and said unto Peter and to the rest of the apostles, Men and brethren, what shall we do?" Here is the announcement of the gospel, the proclamation of the kingdom of God, and the first effect it has is that people say, "Men and brethren, what shall we do?"

And Peter says, "Repent." Repent! Acknowledge and confess your sin. You have felt a pricking in your hearts; you are aware of your guilt. It has been exposed to you for the first time. Now acknowledge it, give up your defense, cast yourself at his feet, 'and be baptized every one of you in the name of Jesus Christ for the remission of sins'" (Acts 2:29–38). That is Peter, the first preacher among the apostles.

Then look at the apostle Paul with his mighty ministry. What did he preach? In Athens, what does he preach in that cultured, sophisticated society, to that gathering of Stoics and Epicureans? This is the message:

> Whom therefore ye ignorantly worship, him declare I unto you. God that made the world and all things therein, seeing that he is Lord of heaven and earth, dwelleth not in temples made with hands; neither is worshipped with men's hands, as though he needed any thing, seeing he giveth to all life, and breath, and all things; and hath made of one blood all nations of men for to dwell on all the face of the earth, and hath determined the times before appointed, and the bounds of their habitation; that they should seek the Lord, if haply they might feel after him, and find him, though he be not far from every one of us: for in him we live, and move, and have our being; as certain also of your own poets have said, For we are also his offspring. Forasmuch then as we are the offspring of God, we ought not to think that the Godhead is like unto gold, or silver, or stone, graven by art and man's device. And the times of this ignorance God winked at; but now commandeth all men every where to repent. (Acts 17:23–30)

Philosophers, idealists, repent! This is the universal message. And, finally, when Paul takes his farewell of the elders of the church at Ephesus, he says:

> Ye know, from the first day that I came into Asia, after what manner I have been with you at all seasons, serving the Lord with all humility of mind, and with many tears, and temptations, which befell me by the

> lying in wait of the Jews: and how I kept back nothing that was profitable unto you, but have shewed you, and have taught you publickly, and from house to house, testifying both to the Jews, and also to the Greeks, repentance toward God, and faith toward our Lord Jesus Christ. (Acts 20:18–21)

If you merely take the New Testament teaching chronologically, in the order of priorities, there is no question but that the need for repentance is the first message. The gospel starts with this: "'Come, see a man, which has told me all things that ever I did'—a man who has made me see myself as I am, my guilt, my emptiness, my woe, my helplessness, my hopelessness." That is always the first effect that he has.

Has he had this effect upon you? There is no hope of receiving his fullness and grace upon grace until you have known conviction of sin and have realized your appalling need and your precarious position. Have you known this? Start with this because without it he has nothing to give you; but having had this, he has everything to give you. Make certain that you start at the beginning.

41

The Essential First Step

The woman then left her waterpot, and went her way into the city, and saith to the men, Come, see a man, which told me all things that ever I did: is not this the Christ? (John 4:28–29)

We are dealing, let me remind you, with the woman of Samaria's response to our Lord and to what he has been saying to her. We are looking at this whole incident because we are anxious to see what it is that hinders so many from knowing this final satisfaction, this sufficiency that our Lord has to give. We have seen that she is convicted of sin, and we are trying to show that this conviction of sin is always essential for a true receiving of the well of water that springs up into everlasting life.

Now I have already given you some reasons for emphasizing this need and for putting it first. I suggested, first, that it shows us the difference between the teaching of psychologists and the cults, on the one hand, and the true Christian faith on the other; and, secondly, I pointed out that it is the difference between taking up religion and becoming truly Christian. Then, thirdly, I suggested that we must put this first because it always comes first in the New Testament itself.

But there are further reasons for putting conviction of sin first, and I want to consider them with you. Have you ever looked at it from this standpoint: if you read these four Gospels, at once you will be impressed by the opposition that our Lord received. It is extraordinary that he, the Son of God, who had come to bless humanity, should have had such opposition. Much space is given in the Gospels to the wranglings of the Pharisees, the Sadducees, the doctors of the Law, and all these other people. Why did they oppose him? To what did they object? I think you will agree that the answer is quite simple. They always hated the fact that he convicted them of their sin. This was the great trouble, especially with the Pharisees. It cut right across all their ideas. They had divided people into Pharisees and sinners. The tax collectors were among the sinners, of course, while they, the Pharisees, were the godly, the self-righteous. We see this to perfection in our Lord's parable of the Pharisee and the tax collector who both went up to the Temple to pray (Luke 18:10–14).

The religious leaders finally crucified him simply because he made them feel that they were sinners. Indeed, he not only made them feel it by the general tenor of his teaching, he put it specifically to them: "I am not come to call the righteous, but sinners to repentance" (Matt. 9:13). He was saying, "You reject my gospel. You say it is not for you. 'They that be whole need not a physician, but they that are sick'" (Matt. 9:12). In those words, he was simply telling them plainly and directly that they were putting themselves outside the salvation that he had come to give. But perhaps one of our Lord's clearest statements is at the end of John 9:

> And Jesus said, For judgment I am come into this world, that they which see not might see; and that they which see might be made blind. And some of the Pharisees which were with him heard these words, and said unto him, Are we blind also?

That is it! "Are you saying that we are blind?"

> Jesus said unto them, If ye were blind, ye should have no sin; but now ye say, We see; therefore your sin remaineth. (John 9:39–41)

This was the explanation of the constant argumentation and wrangling of these Pharisees and scribes against our Lord. So it was obviously the aspect that stood out prominently in his teaching. The Pharisees saw it negatively, and they reacted against it, but thereby they were giving proof that the first thing that he always did was convict of sin. The woman of Samaria saw it. The Pharisees felt it but hated it. So I repeat that we must put this in the first position.

Or note the way in which the apostle Paul puts it at the beginning of Romans 7. Saul of Tarsus had been a man who was very satisfied with himself. As a Pharisee, he had resented this particular teaching. He puts it like this: "I was alive without the law once" (v. 9). He had thought he was all right, he had been perfectly satisfied, but then he had suddenly realized the meaning of the Law. You can know the letter of the Law. You can be an expert at keeping it, from a purely external point of view, and you will say, "Touching the righteousness which is in the law, [I am] blameless" (Phil. 3:6), and that had been Paul's position. In that third chapter of his letter to the Philippians and especially in verses 4–6, you find that he gives a list of all his reasons for being pleased with himself as a religious, moral man and an expert in the Law.

But then suddenly the Spirit came upon him, and he saw it all: "I was alive without the law once: but when the commandment came"—by that he means, "when the Spirit came upon it and came upon me, then it really did get me, it came to me"—"sin revived, and I died" (v. 9). He saw then that he was the chief of sinners, and that is what he says about himself: "This is a faithful saying, and worthy of all acceptation, that Christ Jesus came into the world to save sinners; of whom I am chief" (1 Tim. 1:15). That is the difference between someone who is religious and a Christian. Religious people are not aware that they are sinners at all. The determining factor that shows whether we are just religious or whether we are truly Christians is that the commandment comes to Christians with the enlightenment of the Spirit, and we are convicted and undone.

Then Paul goes on in Romans 7:

> Was then that which is good made death unto me? God forbid. But sin, that it might appear sin, working death in me by that which is good; that sin by the commandment might become exceeding sinful. For we know that the law is spiritual: but I am carnal, sold under sin. (vv. 13–14)

That is it! As a Pharisee, it was the last thing the apostle would ever have said, but the moment conviction came, this is what he found, and he was ready to admit it. And so he goes on with this analysis, ending with the final cry, "O wretched man that I am! who shall deliver me from the body of this death?" (v. 24).

So it is obvious that it is conviction of sin that always comes out first and most prominently in the whole of our Lord's ministry. The reactions of the self-righteous Pharisee and the religious person are proof of the fact that without conviction of sin there is no such thing as becoming a Christian.

But even apart from our Lord's teaching, is it not interesting to observe how his very presence, his person, and all that he was so often produced this same effect upon people, even at times without his saying a single word? This is found through the whole Bible. We are concerned about our relationship to God, and the Bible emphasizes that this is not intellectual but is personal. Some people say, "I've always believed in God. I was brought up to believe in him." But thereby these people betray themselves. They argue about God and what God should and should not do and so on, but that is not the atmosphere of the Bible at all.

Let me give you just one or two examples of what I mean. It is one thing to believe intellectually, but people who only believe intellectually know very little about the "well of water springing up into everlasting life." They know nothing practically about this fullness that is in him. The moment you are in that realm there is a change in your whole demeanor, your whole attitude. There is a perfect example of this in the case of Jacob. Jacob had been brought up to believe in God; he was a religious man. But then he had an experience that changed his whole life, and he never forgot it. It happened when he was running away from the wrath of his brother Esau after he had supplanted Esau and received Esau's blessing from their father. His mother had suggested to him that he had better go if he wanted to save his life; so off he went.

But here he is, troubled. He has been running, and he is weary. So he puts himself down to sleep with a stone under his head as a pillow, and there he has an extraordinary dream. Then he wakes up, and this is what we read:

> He said, Surely the Lord is in this place; and I knew it not. And he was afraid, and said, How dreadful is this place! this is none other but the house of God, and this is the gate of heaven. (Gen. 28:16–17)

That is it! You see, he is a man who believes in God; and he goes to sleep, but something happens, and he has a direct, immediate experience of God.

We find many other examples. When Moses had finished erecting the Tabernacle in the wilderness for the people and had furnished it perfectly and everything was in position, suddenly the glory of the Lord descended upon it all, and Moses, we are told, "was not able to enter into the tent of the congregation, because the cloud abode thereon, and the glory of the Lord filled the tabernacle" (Exod. 40:35).

This personal experience of God's glorious presence is emphasized right through the Bible. The same thing happened to Isaiah. It was a part of the very call of this man, a part of his commissioning:

> In the year that king Uzziah died I saw also the Lord sitting upon a throne, high and lifted up, and his train filled the temple. Above it stood the seraphims: each one had six wings; with twain he covered his face, and with twain he covered his feet, and with twain he did fly. And one

> cried unto another, and said, Holy, holy, holy, is the LORD of hosts: the whole earth is full of his glory. And the posts of the door moved at the voice of him that cried, and the house was filled with smoke.

This was a wonderful vision given to Isaiah. What was its effect?

> Then said I, Woe is me! for I am undone; because I am a man of unclean lips, and I dwell in the midst of a people of unclean lips: for mine eyes have seen the King, the LORD of hosts. (Isa. 6:1–5)

Do you see the effect of having a vision of God! Do you see the result of coming anywhere near the presence of God? Isaiah had not seen God, "For there shall no man see me, and live," God had said to Moses (Exod. 33:20). But he had had a vision, he had had a glimpse, and the immediate, invariable effect was, "Woe is me! for I am undone; because I am a man of unclean lips." No condemnation had come from the throne of God to Isaiah, the Law had not thundered at him, he had not been condemned in detail—there was no need. He had come into the presence of God. There was no self-defense. He saw the truth about himself, and he was "undone."

All I am suggesting to you is this: we are not mere believers in God with our minds and intellects. We claim to know him, we say we are his people, but that is impossible without our knowing something of what Isaiah felt on that occasion. I agree that is an exceptional experience; but it is only exceptional to indicate what is the norm. This is where we are supposed to be.

Let us go on and consider the New Testament teaching, and here, as one reads the Gospels, one is struck constantly by the way in which our Lord himself had this effect upon people, especially at moments when he had worked a miracle or had done something unusual and remarkable. Every time you read the accounts of the miracles, watch the effect upon the disciples and upon the people—the sense of marvel and amazement or their worship of God for this strange power that he had given.

One of the most interesting occasions is in the case of Peter. The disciples had been out fishing all night long and had caught nothing. In the morning our Lord appeared and got into Peter's boat to preach from it. He later told Peter to go farther out and throw the net into the sea, and they caught so many fish that the net broke. Those in the boat called James and John to help, and both boats were so full of fish that they began to sink. It is interesting to read the effect that had upon Peter. When he saw this tremendous haul of fish after a night of failure, he said, "Depart from me; for I am a sinful man, O Lord" (Luke 5:8).

Why did Peter feel that? Our Lord had not rebuked him; he had not said that Peter was a sinner or read out a list of his particular sins. No, no! Our Lord had just given the word, "Let down your nets for a catch," and they had. But the effect upon Peter was to make him feel that he was a sinner, that he could not stand it. What was this? He had just had a glimpse of the glory of the Son of God and the power of the infinite and the eternal, and whenever one has that, it always has this effect. "Come, see a man, which told me all things that ever I did: is not this the Christ?"

Here, I repeat, is something that is at the very heart and center of the whole of the teaching of the Bible concerning our relationship to God. How can we say that we know God if we know nothing of this? And yet at the present time we are subjective, we are self-centered, we want blessings, we do this and that—and God himself is forgotten. The sense of awe and of reverence, the sense of sinfulness and of unworthiness and of vileness that should come first do not seem to be there at all.

Take another instance. In John 18 we read the account of our Lord's arrest, and we are told:

> And Judas also, which betrayed him, knew the place. . . . Judas then, having received a band of men and officers from the chief priests and Pharisees, cometh thither with lanterns and torches and weapons. Jesus therefore, knowing all things that should come upon him, went forth, and said unto them, Whom seek ye? They answered him, Jesus of Nazareth. Jesus saith unto them, I am he. And Judas also, which betrayed him, stood with them. As soon then as he had said unto them, I am he, they went backward, and fell to the ground. (John 18:2–6)

They did not rush forward to arrest him; they "went backward, and fell to the ground." And all he had said was, "I am he," the words he had spoken to the woman of Samaria. Why did they fall to the ground? They suddenly realized something of the truth of this statement that he was indeed not only Jesus of Nazareth but the everlasting Son of God. They were in the presence of his majesty, and they were humbled and alarmed, and they fell down.

We find this also after our Lord's resurrection and ascension. John tells us in the first chapter of the book of Revelation how he was given a vision of this blessed risen Lord:

> . . . in the midst of the seven candlesticks one like unto the Son of man, clothed with a garment down to the foot, and girt about the paps with a golden girdle. His head and his hairs were white like wool, as white as snow; and his eyes were as a flame of fire; and his feet like unto fine brass, as if they burned in a furnace; and his voice as the sound of many waters. and he had in his right hand seven stars: and out of his mouth went a sharp twoedged sword: and his countenance was as the sun shineth in his strength. And when I saw him, I fell at his feet as dead. (Rev. 1:13–17)

My friends, this is the glory of God. And Paul says this is the truth about the Christian: "For God, who commanded the light to shine out of darkness, hath shined in our hearts, to give the light of the knowledge of the glory of God in the face of Jesus Christ." That is what makes me a Christian, says Paul. "But we have [received] this treasure in earthen vessels" (2 Cor. 4:6–7).

What we have received is "the glory of God in the face of Jesus Christ," and the effect of that, invariably, is to humble, to subdue, to silence, to convict, to reveal to us our true state and condition, our emptiness and woe, our sinfulness, our unworthiness. You cannot be healthy in his presence; you cannot be self-satisfied and glib and slick. It is impossible.

You and I are not people who merely believe a number of propositions with our intellects. We do that, but what makes us truly Christian is that we know something of him. There is this personal fellowship and communion, and the moment this comes in, the effect is, "I fell down as one dead." "Come, see a man, which told me all things that ever I did: is not this the Christ?" Quite apart from his explicit teaching, his very person, his very presence, does this.

This conviction of sin is always also, is it not, the primary work of the Holy Spirit. Our Lord has returned to heaven and is seated at the right hand of God in the glory everlasting, but he had said to his followers, "Let not your heart be troubled"—do not be distressed. Why? "I will send you another Comforter. I am not going to leave you orphans, I will send you another Teacher, one who will stand by your side. He will be with you, he will lead you, he will guide you into all truth, he will instruct you. You will be in a better position after I have gone than you are in now. 'It is expedient for you that I go away: for if I go not away, the Comforter will not come unto you; but if I depart, I will send him unto you'" (John 16:7). And he did.

So what is the work of this Comforter, the Holy Spirit? This is especially clear in this Gospel according to John. This is how our Lord himself teaches his disciples about it:

> And when he is come [what will he do? what is the first work of the Holy Spirit?], he will reprove the world of sin, and of righteousness, and of judgment: of sin, because they believe not on me; of righteousness, because I go to my Father, and ye see me no more; of judgment, because the prince of this world is judged. (John 16:8–11)

This, according to our Lord, is to be the first and essential work of the Spirit—the Spirit who is now in the church, the Spirit who is now the teacher, the one through whom the risen Lord himself is working and active among his people and through them to those who are outside. This, he says, is to be the primary work, this will characterize his ministry—conviction of sin. And as our Lord prophesied, so it turned out to be.

In the second chapter of the book of Acts, we have the great account of the coming of the Holy Spirit upon the church in Jerusalem in a mighty baptism of power on the Day of Pentecost. Filled with this tremendous power of the Spirit to preach, the apostle Peter stands up and expounds the Scriptures, preaching the first sermon, in a sense, under the auspices of the Christian church as we now know her. What effect does this have? It is no longer Peter—it is Peter filled with the Spirit, it is Peter being clothed with the Spirit, Peter as the vehicle of the Spirit and his power. What does the Spirit do through Peter? You remember what happened: "When they heard this, they were pricked in their heart, and said unto Peter and to the rest of the apostles, Men and brethren, what shall we do?" (Acts 2:37).

What is this? It is conviction. These people listening to Peter are in trouble. They are unhappy; they are ill at ease; they are made to feel desperate. The Law has come, it has found them, and they cry out in their agony, "Men and brethren, what shall we do?"

And Peter answers, "Repent"! In a sense he says, "Let this work happen in you. Do not defend yourselves. Give in to what you are feeling. You see how wrong you have been and how unworthy you are. Do not resist the Spirit. 'Repent, and be baptized every one of you in the name of Jesus Christ for the remission of sins, and ye shall receive the gift of the Holy Ghost'" (Acts 2:38). There it is, the very first instance of the operation of the power of the Spirit in the church. The Spirit does the very thing that our Lord had prophesied that he would do.

And as we work our way through the book of Acts, we find this same conviction everywhere. Take the ninth chapter, where we see Saul of Tarsus on the road to Damascus. The powerful, defiant Pharisee who hates Christ and is going down to exterminate his church in Damascus suddenly sees the Lord, and he falls to the ground and in his helplessness says, "Lord, what wilt thou have me to do?" (Acts 9:6). He is finished; he sees his vileness and emptiness, his woe, his utter wrongness.

Then take the famous case of the Philippian jailer in Acts 16. Here is a man who has carried out his instructions and has thrust Paul and Silas into the innermost part of the prison and put their feet fast in the stocks, having already scourged them. And Paul and Silas are praying and singing praises unto God at midnight when suddenly there is a tremendous earthquake, and this man, the keeper, wakes up thinking all the prisoners have fled. But we read, "But Paul cried with a loud voice, saying, Do thyself no harm"—the jailer is on the point of committing suicide—"for we are all here."

What effect does that have upon the Philippian jailer? These records are so wonderful in their detail; it is all here, perfectly simple and plain before us. "He called for a light, and sprang in, and came trembling, and fell down before Paul and Silas." He falls down before the men whom he has just been scourging, the men whom he has put into the innermost prison, whose feet he has fastened in the stocks! He falls down before them—what is the matter with this man? And he says, "Sirs, what must I do to be saved?" But they have not preached to him; they have not condemned him; they have not tried to convict him of anything. What is happening?

This man has sensed the presence of God, and he is convicted of sin. He does not mean, "What must I do to retain my job?" but "What must I do to get saved? What must I do to be like you are? Where can I get this joy that you have, that makes you sing when you are in the innermost prison with your feet in the stocks? You are happier than I am as the keeper—what is this?" He feels his sinfulness; he is convicted. That is the effect—trembling, falling down, even before the servants of the Lord. Everything about them and this tremendous action in the earthquake has convinced and convicted this man of sin, and, as in the case of the woman of Samaria, suddenly all that he is flashes before him on a screen, as it were, and he is horrified. So he says, "What must I do?" (Acts 16:23–30).

We cannot be Christians without something of this; it is impossible. This is everywhere in the Scriptures. I say again that conviction of sin is one of the essential preliminaries to receiving his fullness and grace upon grace, to having this "well of water springing up into everlasting life."

"But," you say, "this all belongs to New Testament times." That is the argument today, is it not? All that was all right in the time of the apostles, but not any longer. You mustn't judge yourself by the New Testament, we are told—that was an exceptional period.

What a terrible lie that is! How dreadful to narrow the word of God down to the measure of our little understanding! That view is not even true historically. Read the history of the church, read the biographies of the saints, the stories of these outstanding men and women, and you will invariably find what you have found in the Scriptures. Start, if you like, with St. Augustine of Hippo—read the story of his conversion. There was an increasing conviction of sin before he found peace and joy and release and happiness. There was desperation, unhappiness, struggling, knowing he was wrong, being convicted but resisting, and then at last abandon. It is invariable.

Or consider Martin Luther. We commemorate that great day when he nailed the Ninety-five Theses to the door of the church at Wittenberg. What is the story of Luther? The essential story was conviction of sin. You do not understand the Protestant Reformation apart from this. We are living in an age of conferences and of clergymen. They meet in a conference and decide this and that. You never get a Reformation like that! No, no; it happened in the soul of a man who was convicted of sin, who was in agony.

Perhaps one of the greatest classics in these matters is John Bunyan's *Grace Abounding* or, if you like, *The Pilgrim's Progress*. It does not matter. Read both books and you will find exactly the same depiction of conviction of sin. That mighty man, John Bunyan, tinker as he was, with his great soul, for eighteen months passed through an agony of repentance, sensing the vileness of his own heart, seeing his utter helplessness and hopelessness.

Then go on to the next century and read about the conversion of George Whitefield and the two Wesleys, John and Charles. These men felt such a conviction of sin that they became physically ill; at some points they almost felt they were losing their reason. Why was this? It was due to an agony of soul in these mighty men of God. This is the invariable rule; it is the work of the Holy Spirit. When the Holy Spirit deals with people, he invariably must produce conviction of sin. "See a man, which told me all things that ever I did." You see yourself for the first time in your life. The man of the world has never seen himself, and that is why he goes on as he is.

But then read as well the stories of the great revivals in the long history of the church, and you will find, without a single exception, that in the early stages of every revival the first effect was a terrifying conviction of sin. Now this happened to people who had been brought up in the church, who had been church members, perhaps for many years, and were highly respected and regarded as religious people. Suddenly the Spirit would come down, and these very people would begin to feel they had never been Christians at all. This conviction could sometimes be so powerful that they would fall to the ground in a great spiritual agony and crisis.

Now I am not the one saying this—this is history, and I am just commending you to read history. All I am trying to show you is that the Spirit always does what our Lord prophesied he would do—he starts by convicting us of sin. You do not start where you are, feeling nothing, and then suddenly accept Christ into your heart. No, no! "See a man, which told me all things that ever I did, is not this the Christ?" Conviction of sin is invariable in all the great movements of the Spirit, whether in individuals or in masses of people at the same time.

Let me conclude with this argument: surely there is no meaning in the word *salvation* apart from conviction of sin. Is Christ your Savior? What do you mean by that? What is a savior? What is salvation? Surely, by definition a savior is one who saves us from something, from a predicament, from trouble. The Savior! Salvation! What is it? There is only one answer to all this in the whole Bible. Think of the angel who appeared to Joseph, the husband of Mary, the mother of our Lord. The angel made this quite plain to Joseph at the very beginning, putting it in explicit terms so that there should never be any misunderstanding.

> But while he thought on these things, behold, the angel of the Lord appeared unto him in a dream, saying, Joseph, thou son of David, fear not to take unto thee Mary thy wife: for that which is conceived in her is of the Holy Ghost. And she shall bring forth a son, and thou shalt call his name JESUS: for he shall save his people from their sins. (Matt. 1:20–21)

That is why he is to be called Jesus; that is why he is called the Christ, the Messiah, the Savior. There is no sense, no meaning to the word *salvation* apart from this. He saves us from what? From the condemnation of the Law.

It is all there in Paul's epistles, expressed in different ways. Paul, writing to the Galatians, says, "Wherefore the law was our schoolmaster to bring us unto Christ" (3:24). What brings us to Christ? The schoolmaster, the pedagogue. How does he do it? He convicts us of our sin; he shows us our need. That is the whole business of the Law. All of the Old Testament is preparation for the New. The Law brings us to Christ by revealing to us our need, our emptiness, and our woe. And, indeed, this is what we are told of our Lord himself: "When the fulness of the time was come, God sent forth his Son, made of a woman, made under the law"—what for?—"to redeem them that were under the law" (Gal. 4:4–5). That was why he came.

So when our Lord came, he said, "The Son of man is come to seek and to save that which was lost" (Luke 19:10) and "The Son of man came not to be ministered unto, but to minister, and to give his life a ransom for many" (Matt. 20:28). Why do they need a ransom? Why do they need to be saved? What is it all about? There is only one answer—it is to save us from sin, to save us from the condemnation of the Law. "God was in Christ, reconciling the world unto himself, not imputing their trespasses unto them" (2 Cor. 5:19). That is it! "He hath made him to be sin for us, who knew no sin; that we might be made the righteousness of God in him" (2 Cor. 5:21). We are under the Law: "the whole world lieth in wickedness" (1 John 5:19).

There is no sense in the words *Savior* and *salvation* unless we realize our guilt, our condemnation. And so the triumphant cry of the redeemed is, "There is therefore now no condemnation to them which are in Christ Jesus" (Rom. 8:1). And if you do not say that first of all, the question must be, are you saved? Do you know what *salvation* means? The first thing is that we are saved from the guilt and the condemnation of sin.

And so, you see, the very terms that we use carry this essential principle. The first thing that any kind of contact with our Lord does, whether in his teaching or in some experience of him, is make us feel, as the woman of Samaria felt, that we are vile in his presence, that we are unworthy, that we are foul. Have you felt that? I am not asking you about the degree or the intensity of your feelings. I am simply asking, as you think of him, whether the first thing that comes into your mind is that he has saved you from the guilt of your sin, from the condemnation of the Law, that he has revealed to you what you are and your utter hopelessness and vileness and has delivered you from it. "Come, see a man, which told me all things which ever I did: is not this the Christ?" That is the order, and it is the only order.

42

What Is Meant by Conviction of Sin?

The woman then left her waterpot, and went her way into the city, and saith to the men, Come, see a man, which told me all things that ever I did: is not this the Christ? (John 4:28–29)

We are still dealing in particular with the words of this woman of Samaria as, leaving her waterpot and our Lord, she rushes to the city and says to the people there, "Come, see a man, which told me all things that ever I did: is not this the Christ?" The first words she speaks reveal conviction of sin. I have been giving a number of reasons to show why this must always come first. First, this is the way in which we differentiate between the cults and Christianity, and, second, it differentiates between religion and Christianity. Third, conviction of sin always comes first in the teaching of the New Testament. Fourth, as we saw in the previous study, we cannot come into God's presence without feeling our sinfulness, our utter unworthiness.

This is so vital that we cannot afford to be uncertain about it. Let us, therefore, make sure that we are clear as to the meaning of the term *conviction of sin*. I am emphasizing this not only because it is a tragedy that anybody should claim to be Christian and yet not enjoy this great fullness offered by our Lord, but also because I am convinced that the great cause of trouble in the Christian church today, including the evangelical section, is the absence of conviction of sin, the absence of humility, the absence of the godliness that runs right through the whole Bible. We are too healthy, we are too glib, we are too self-assured, too confident in ourselves and what we do. "The fear of the LORD is the beginning of wisdom" (Ps. 111:10). How much of "the fear of the LORD" is there among us and in the church in general at the present time? We must be clear about this.

So what is meant by conviction of sin? Let me put it negatively first. It is not enough to recognize that some things are wrong. Some people think conviction of sin means recognizing that there is right and wrong and that certain things in particular are especially wrong. Now that, obviously, is not conviction of sin because most people in the world are aware of this distinction. We all have a conscience within us that makes us aware of right and wrong. Pharisees always had that awareness; they were experts on this subject. Moralists are always perfectly clear on this. Indeed, it is the one thing they are clear about, and they never talk about anything else because it is generally the only thing that they do see. But conviction of sin is something quite different.

Neither is it enough to know that we sometimes do wrong. This, again, often passes for conviction of sin, for true repentance. People feel that as long as they occasionally realize that they have done something wrong and should not have done it, they have experienced conviction of sin. But again, for the same reasons, this cannot be accepted as a definition because "natural" men and woman (1 Cor. 2:14), especially those who are moral and religious, are aware of that. Their whole idea of Christianity is that you do not do certain things and you do others. So if they do the prohibited things, they feel they are wrong. But that is not of necessity conviction of sin.

I will go further. Somebody may say, "Well, all right, I agree with all this, but surely if people are really annoyed with themselves when they do wrong, that must be conviction of sin?"

No, it is not. This again falls short of conviction of sin. We know something about this, do we not? We do something wrong, and we feel we have let ourselves down and are annoyed with ourselves. But the natural person does that; religious people, especially, know that. It is a part of conviction, but in and of itself it is not sufficient. It is remorse, but remorse is not conviction of sin.

What is the difference between remorse and conviction of sin? Well, the person who is only conscious of remorse is one who has a temporary feeling of unhappiness and a temporary desire to be delivered from this sin that gets them down. Remorse is concerned primarily with the consequences of sin. Men and women do something that is wrong and are unhappy afterward. They feel they have been fools and have let themselves down. They should not have done it and are miserable. They dislike that feeling and say, "Oh, I wish I could get rid of it." All that is just remorse.

In 2 Corinthians 7 the apostle Paul draws a distinction between "the sorrow of the world" and "godly sorrow" (v. 10). The world, I say again, knows what it is to be sorry because of having done wrong things. Many people suffer remorse because they drank too much or took drugs or have done something else that is wrong. Now they are miserable, suffering the physical consequences perhaps and consequences in their spirits. But that is not repentance, that is not conviction of sin; that again is only remorse. These people regret the wrong because it caused these particular consequences, which they now want to get rid of. That does not come near to being conviction of sin.

What, then, is conviction of sin? Here is the vital question, and the answer is quite clear. The essence of conviction of sin is the realization that our very natures are sinful. It is the difference between particular actions and our condition. Those who are truly convicted of sin realize that their very nature is wrong and perverted and polluted. That is why this woman of Samaria's way of putting it is so interesting. Though our Lord only mentions certain particulars in her life, she says, "all things that ever I did." She realizes her nature; for the first time she sees herself for what she is. She knows that people, pharisaical types in particular, point at her and say, "Look at her!" But she could always retort, "I do these things, but they think them, miserable hypocrites that they are!" She has always been able to defend herself—people living in gross sin can always put up a marvelous defense. But now she realizes that her trouble is not so much that she does particular things that are wrong as that her heart is wrong, her desires are wrong.

Now this is a profound understanding. Read Psalm 51, where David sees this so clearly. He had committed terrible sin, adultery and murder, but he was still perfectly happy until the prophet Nathan was sent by God to convict him, and then he saw it all. But what troubled David was not even the adultery and the murder, it was that he had ever desired to do these things. He saw his nature; he saw that there was something there that produced these desires. So he cried out in his agony, "Create in me a clean heart, O God; and renew a right spirit within me" (Ps. 51:10). He had gone beyond the realm of actions to his condition, to his state, to his whole life; he realized that his very heart was foul and ugly and vile; his whole spirit was wrong.

This is of the very essence of conviction of sin, and this is where it is differentiated from the sorrow of this world that is merely remorse. In the seventh chapter of the Epistle to the Romans, the apostle Paul puts it in a similarly graphic way: "For we know that the law is spiritual: but I am carnal, sold under sin" (v. 14). That is the point. He is not talking about actions but about his whole state. He says, "I see another law in my members, warring against the law of my mind, and bringing me into captivity to the law of sin which is in my members. O wretched man that I am!" (vv. 23–24). People who experience remorse never know that. They feel that as long as they can put certain actions right, all will be well. They have not realized that it is their *nature* that matters. But Paul had. "For I was alive without the law once," he says, "but when the commandment came, sin revived, and I died" (v. 9).

So here is the first point: you are convicted of sin when you are troubled not so much about the things you do as about what you are—your whole hopeless condition. "False and full of sin I am," says Charles Wesley.

But let us go on. The second aspect, obviously—I am putting these as we experience them and as we feel them—that we must emphasize about true conviction of sin is that it always creates within us a realization that we have sinned against God. What a tremendous point this is. People of the world, even those who are moral or religious, are only concerned with themselves. They have let themselves down; they have done something they should not have done. What will people say? What will the consequences be? God does not come into it. But the moment they are convicted of sin by the Holy Spirit, their concern is that they have sinned against God and have broken his holy laws.

Note again how David brings this out in Psalm 51:

> Have mercy upon me, O God, according to thy lovingkindness: according unto the multitude of thy tender mercies blot out my transgressions. . . . For I acknowledge my transgressions: and my sin is ever before me. Against thee, thee only, have I sinned, and done this evil in thy sight: that thou mightest be justified when thou speakest, and be clear when thou judgest. (Ps. 51:1, 3–4)

This is what now troubles David. He sees the enormity of his sin. By that I mean he is no longer concerned primarily about the wrong things he has done, but that he has done them against God, the God who gave him the honor and the dignity of being a human being, created in the image and likeness of God himself, who made man for his own pleasure, that he might have a companion.

God made man the lord of creation and set him in authority over everything in creation. That is the dignity that God has given us; and God looked upon it all, and he saw that it was good. But we have let God down, the God who has made us like this, the God who has been so kind, the God who has been so loving toward us. We have deliberately flouted his laws. We have wounded him; we have hurt him. We have violated what he intended us to be. We see now that sin is not merely a matter of wrong actions but is lawlessness. It is arrogance; it is pitting ourselves against God, rebelling against him. Having some realization of the character and the being of God, we see the enormity of it all and are appalled that we should thus offend a holy and a loving and a righteous God. "Against thee, thee only, have I sinned, and done this evil in thy sight."

This is the response of the prodigal son after he has come to himself. He has been a fool, he has squandered his money, he has allowed his fair-weather friends to take his money from him for entertainment and so on, and now he has lost everything and even finds himself in the field with the swine and the husks. Oh, the degradation and the shame of it all. That is what would have worried him if he had only felt remorse, but now that he has truly come to himself, what does he realize? He sees that he has sinned against his father, sinned against the one who showered his love upon him and did so much for him; this is what seems to him to be unforgivable. "I have sinned against heaven, and in thy sight, and am no more worthy to be called thy son" (Luke 15:18–19, 21). He now sees his actions in the true way.

It is the question of this personal relationship to God that is the very essence of the conviction of sin. Whatever we may feel about our actions, however acute the remorse may be, however violent our reaction, it is not conviction of sin, it is not repentance until we have seen it in terms of our rebellion against God, our violation not only of his laws but of his fatherly relationship to us.

I must now emphasize a third element, which is feeling. This, again, is most important. True conviction of sin never stops at mere intellectual apprehension. That comes in, of course, but conviction does not stop at that; and as I have said, it does not even stop at annoyance. An essential part of conviction of sin and repentance is a feeling of true sorrow, what the apostle calls "*godly* sorrow" (2 Cor. 7:10). Godly sorrow is very difficult to define, and yet once one has ever known it, there is no difficulty at all. It is unique to the Christian. It is not irritation, it is not that you are annoyed with yourself; no, it is much deeper. You are troubled; you are grieved. It is a deep sorrow in the heart, in the center of your being, that you are what you are, that you should ever have been guilty of such behavior against God.

Further, godly sorrow is not transient. It is always very deep. It cannot easily be healed. This, too, is widely expounded in the Old Testament. The charge that God always brought against the false prophets of Israel was that "they have healed the hurt of the daughter of my people slightly, saying, Peace, peace; when there is no peace" (Jer. 8:11). That is always the characteristic of the false prophet and false teaching. Ah, yes, you have a bit of sorrow, but you are quickly over it and have soon forgotten it. But you cannot do that when you are truly convicted of sin; you do not get over it so quickly. This sorrow is deeper than a surface emotion or some temporary feeling.

And that, in turn, leads, of course, to this: people who have been convicted of sin always have a realization that their first need is the need of mercy, the need of forgiveness. Now I emphasize that for this reason: you are well aware that this element is missing in so much of today's evangelism. Salvation is represented as something that can help us conquer particular sins or give us peace, happiness, and joy. The need for mercy and forgiveness is often not even mentioned, and that is why true conviction of sin is so largely absent at the present time. But once we are convicted of sin, then more than anything else whatsoever, we are aware of our need of the compassion of God. This awareness is either there or it is not there. It is not enough that you feel, "I wish I didn't do these things. I wish I could be free of this thing that gets me down." That is all right, that comes into the Christian life, but if that is first and if you have never known the need of forgiveness, if you have never realized that you do not deserve forgiveness, then you have never known true conviction of sin.

Let our Lord say it himself. In his picture of the Pharisee and the tax collector who go up to the Temple to pray, he tells us about the poor tax collector who is at the back and cannot even lift up his head. He is beating his chest, and all he can say is, "God be merciful to me a sinner"—"be propitiated toward me." He is so aware of his sin that his greatest needs are for forgiveness, mercy, pity, compassion. "Can God forgive me? Is it possible that such a wretch as I am, such a vile creature, can be forgiven even by God?" (Luke 18:10–14). That is what he needs above everything else. That is inevitable when there is a true conviction of sin. But you can be highly religious and never know that at all, and that is one of the differences between being religious and being a Christian.

Or let me put it like this: another feeling experienced by those truly convicted of sin—and we put these true feelings over against the false—is that the desire to be holy is altogether greater than the desire to be happy. Of course, by nature we all want to be happy. The real explanation of remorse is that we do not like to be unhappy. If only we could sin without suffering, if only the consequences did not follow, we would have a wonderful time, we think. And that is the problem with people who feel remorse. They are miserable and will promise anything for the time being in order to get rid of the unhappiness. But that is not the effect of conviction of sin. Someone who is convicted of sin has a great desire to be free from sin. "Create in me a clean heart, O God; and renew a right spirit within me" (Ps. 51:10).

O for a heart to praise my God,
A heart from sin set free.

CHARLES WESLEY ("O FOR A HEART TO PRAISE MY GOD")

Once we see the true nature of sin, we realize that it is a pollution of our very nature. It is not merely a matter of doing wrong things or a problem of the will—that is the fatal teaching that came in with Finney above all others and has been so popular—but is a matter of the nature. So this is a way whereby we can test ourselves as to whether we know true conviction of sin. "Though he slay me," says Job, "yet will I trust him" (Job 13:15). Anyone who is truly Christian says, "I don't care what I may have to suffer, I don't care what tribulations I may have to go through, as long as I am clean, as long as I am holy, as long as I am worthy of him, as long as he is well-pleased with me." Holiness comes before happiness. We desire not merely to be delivered from things but to be like God, to be worthy of him. We have heard his command, "Be ye holy; for I am holy" (1 Pet. 1:16). Our supreme desire is to be holy because God is holy and because it is the will of God—"For this is the will of God, even your sanctification" (1 Thess. 4:3).

These are vital matters, are they not? Have you been convicted of sin? Have you, like this woman of Samaria, felt that your heart is opened, and have you been astounded at what you have seen? Have you gone beyond the realm of being interested only in conduct to concern about the state, the plague, of your own heart, the pollution of your own spirit? Have you ever seen that?

Do not misunderstand me—I do not hold the view that the test of Christian people is that they are always miserable about themselves. It is not. All I am saying is that they should have passed through that stage some time or another. The Christian knows about this "well of water." But this sorrow is not glib. It is not superficial or intellectual; it is much deeper. There is a kind of paradox in the Christian. One of the great statements made by Martin Luther is that the Christian is at one and the same time a great sinner and a great saint; he is extremely miserable, and he is extremely happy.

But now let me come to a question. I am sure that many are saying to themselves, "Are you saying that all should feel this conviction of sin? Are you laying this down as a universal rule?" Some people maintain that what I am saying here is quite wrong. Some go as far as to say that repentance was only for the Jews at the time of our Lord. This is the teaching of the ultra-dispensationalists. "Oh, yes," they say, "of course John the Baptist and our Lord preached repentance, but they only preached it to the Jews." These people have divided God's plan of salvation into "dispensations"—periods of time—and say repentance was only for the Jews, and nobody needed to repent after that. But, to start with, they are utterly unscriptural, denying what we are plainly told in the book of Acts and the epistles where we see that the apostle Paul preached repentance to the Gentiles. They evade the need to repent by saying that all you need to do is accept Jesus and take him into your heart. This is being taught today. More than once I have had friends consulting me in my vestry because this is the prevailing teaching in the church to which they belong.

Others feel that surely teaching about conviction of sin and the need to repent is only for people who are guilty of some gross sin—a drunkard or a drug addict or a prostitute. Someone who holds this view will say, "You've quoted David, and of course he committed adultery and murder. If I'd been guilty of sins like that, then I'd see the need of conviction of sin, but I've not done any of those things."

Thirdly, some say, "That may be all right for people who've been brought up in godless homes and were never taken to a place of worship, people who really did not know any better. But we've been brought up in Christian homes and have always gone to a place of worship and Sunday school. You surely are not saying that *we* ought to experience this kind of thing? Surely," they say, "what you are talking about—this conviction of sin—was necessary for the woman of Samaria who had five husbands and the man with whom she was living was not her husband—we can understand all that. But what does that have to do with us?"

This is how the devil comes in. What is the answer? It is very plain—the facts are entirely opposed to that argument. There is no such distinction; nothing in Scripture says that repentance is to be confined to the Jews only or to certain other people only. The fact of the matter is that in the history of the church, the people who have known most intensely what I have defined to you as conviction of sin have been people who have been brought up in a most godly manner. I refer again to Martin Luther. If ever a man knew conviction of sin, it was Martin Luther. But what a godly young man he was, brought up in an entirely religious home. He had never committed what we call gross sins; yet look at the conviction of sin that he experienced. It was while he was a monk that he endured an agony of repentance.

I could keep you for hours telling you about such people. Look at the two Wesleys. If ever two men were brought up in a Christian home, it was John and Charles Wesley. Yet these two men knew such intense conviction of sin that they became desperately ill, both of them. The same was true of George Whitefield. Is it not amazing how we can do things without thinking? We all like Charles Wesley's great hymn "Jesus, Lover of My Soul," do we not? But remember, Charles Wesley, this man brought up in a rectory, with an exceptionally godly father and mother, who had given his life to godliness, said, "False and full of sin I am." And this is not a poet's rhetoric; this is not hyperbole created by a poetic imagination. The man meant it. He had been through agony and felt that he was beyond forgiveness.

And, indeed, I go further and say, in the second place, there can be no question at all but that such people have felt conviction of sin and grief and godly sorrow more than anybody else. You simply have to read the biographies to see what I mean. These people have experienced it much more intensely than your ex-drunkards, ex-adulterers, ex-murderers, or anyone else.

And, thirdly, you will generally find—and this is a part of the paradox I am referring to—that as saints go on in the Christian life, their awareness of the rottenness of their natural self becomes greater and greater. Again, do not misunderstand me. The saints are not people who are therefore always moaning and groaning. No, no; they have the well of water in them, but at the same time, they know the truth about the old nature that is still in them, and it is this that troubles them. I was reading again the other day about Daniel Rowland, the great Methodist father in Wales two hundred years ago. He was dying and knew he was dying. Some of his brethren went to see him and asked him how he felt. He said, "I am an old sinner saved by the grace of God." That is the way. Oh, yes, he was rejoicing in his salvation, but on his deathbed he knew that he was an old sinner still. He went through triumphantly and gloriously, but the other consciousness was still there.

I can prove all this in another way. When a revival breaks out, the first effect of the falling of the Spirit of God upon a people, a congregation, a group of churches, or a nation is invariably conviction of utter sinfulness. It always happens; it has always happened. People who have been members of a church perhaps for fifty years begin very seriously to doubt whether they have ever been Christians at all, and they are in real trouble. The revival is in the church, not outside. We are all so clear about the outsider, but these are the people inside. They feel they are nothing. So you see how utterly wrong it is to argue that conviction of sin is only for certain people, for notorious sinners, or for Jews only.

But let me wind this point up by putting it like this: why is it so wrong to argue that we respectable people, as it were, do not need to feel conviction of sin, that it is only for the flagrant sinner? Here is the final reason. That argument is based on an entirely wrong position. What matters is not the number of sins we have committed, nor their character or quality. What matters, and what matters alone, is our relationship to God. Of course, if it is a matter of the number of sins or the quality of the sins, then it is perfectly all right to say, "Look at that man! He has a full page of sins while I've only a few at the top of the page. Look at the quality of his sins—they're vile, they're foul! Mine aren't! I've done wrong things, but thank God I've not done *those* things!" It is the devil who teaches us to keep ledgers and account books. God does not; Christ does not. I say again that it is not the number of your sins, it is not the character of your sins, it is your relationship to God that counts.

When you come into God's presence, you realize the truth about yourself. And it does not matter who comes into his presence—there is no difference when you are face-to-face with him. You have your comparisons, your contrasts; then you come to him, the burning light. "God is light, and in him is no darkness at all" (1 John 1:5). "There is none righteous, no, not one" (Rom. 3:10). "The whole world lieth in wickedness" (1 John 5:19). The greatest sin of all is the failure to see your need of salvation; that is much worse than murder. To feel that you can stand in the presence of God because you are who you are and what you are and what you have not done is the greatest of all sins because it means that you do not need the death of the Son of God on the cross on Calvary's hill. And that is the greatest insult you can ever offer to God. The nearer you get to him, the more you are aware of your guilt, your unworthiness, and your foulness. Conviction of sin is positive, not negative.

What makes a good young man like Charles Wesley say, "False and full of sin I am"? Read the hymn again, and you will see how it works. This is always the argument and the only true argument.

Just and holy is thy Name.

You do not start with yourself. If you start with yourself, you will never know conviction of sin because you will always see that you are better than somebody else, and you will always be able to square the books. Charles Wesley does not start with himself.

Just and holy is thy Name.

And in the light of that, and that only, he says:

I am all unrighteousness;
False and full of sin I am;
Thou art full of truth and grace.

This is the only way whereby you will ever be convicted of sin. So people who talk about "big sins" and "being brought up respectably and religiously" and so on have missed the whole point. To speak like that is a denial of the doctrine. Are you interested in actions and in their number and character? You must not be.

Just and holy is thy Name.

It is only when you are in his presence that you see this; and if you have not seen it, it means you have never been in his presence. It comes to that.

So if you have never felt your vileness or if you object to preaching that tells you that you ought to feel vile, you are entirely on the human level. Numbers and categories are irrelevant. They are madness; they are folly. They are from the devil.

Thou art full of grace and truth.

As I look at him, there is only one thing that I can say about myself at my best:

I am all unrighteousness;
False and full of sin I am.

But blessed be his name who said, "They that be whole need not a physician, but they that are sick. . . . I am not come to call the righteous, but sinners to repentance" (Matt. 9:12–13). And the men and women who go to the greatest heights in their knowledge of the Christian life and in the receiving of his fullness are those who have been deepest in the depths under conviction of sin and a realization of their utter hopelessness. Before I ask you whether you have been raised to the heights, I ask, have you been down in the depths of your own vileness?

43

Salvation and Sanctification

The woman then left her waterpot, and went her way into the city, and saith to the men, Come, see a man, which told me all things that ever I did: is not this the Christ? (John 4:28–29)

I have been demonstrating to you from the Scriptures the centrality of the teaching that forgiveness of sins follows a sense of guilt and unworthiness. The first message is a call to repentance. Repentance is the key that leads to all the treasures and riches of the gospel. And I have shown you also the central and vital place of this teaching in the experience of Christian people throughout the centuries. Indeed, beyond any question at all, it can be laid down as a law that the greater the saint, the greater his understanding of his sinfulness and guilt.

I once stayed with a man who was an expert in growing sweet peas and had won prizes many times at the Royal Horticultural Society shows. I noticed the extraordinary length of the stalks and asked him the secret. He said, "There's only one secret to having a long stalk like this and a wonderful bloom. You must dig as far down as you desire the plant to be high. Many people," he said, "do not seem to realize this, but if you want great height, you must dig a deep trench." It is exactly the same in the spiritual life, and I am suggesting that many fail to realize the importance of the fact that it is only as we truly see our need that we shall ever receive fullness and satisfaction from the Lord. This applies to all people, whatever their background.

I am anxious to make it clear, however, that I am not suggesting that we should all experience conviction of guilt in exactly the same way and to the same degree. Nor am I saying that it is bound to come at exactly the same point in the experience of each Christian. What I am asserting is that it is an invariable rule that at some time or another there has to be a consciousness of guilt and of unworthiness. Furthermore, I postulate that the closer we draw to God, the more likely we are to be convicted of our guilt. Let me illustrate this.

George Muller exercised an astounding ministry in the nineteenth century, particularly in connection with orphanages in Bristol. He was a man who was given a very unusual gift of faith, a man whose faith was unshakable. In his autobiography he writes that as a young man he lived a dissolute, unworthy, and immoral life. Yet he says:

> In the midst of all this I had a desire to renounce this wretched life, for I had no enjoyment of it and had sense enough to see that the end one day or another would be miserable, for I should never be able to get a living. But I had no sorrow of heart on account of offending God.

In other words, Muller felt remorse, as I have defined it. He was miserable; he was living a life of sin, but he was not really enjoying it, and he could see the consequences. But notice his emphasis: "I had no sorrow of heart on account of offending God." Then in 1825 he was taken by a friend to a small gathering of Christian people who met together to pray, read the Scriptures, and read sermons (the law of Prussia, where he grew up, did not allow anybody unordained to preach, so they would read sermons aloud). He writes that in that little meeting he began to enjoy great peace and happiness, which continued when he went home. Then he adds:

> . . . if I had been asked how I was happy, I could not clearly have explained it. This shows that the Lord may begin his work in different ways, for I have not the least doubt that on that evening he began a work of grace in me, though I obtained joy without any sorrow of heart and with scarcely any knowledge.

God does this work and brings us to this experience in different ways. We must not stereotype the work of salvation. I remember a man who was very worried about his son. He had no need to be, but he was a man with a rigid mind. He kept on shaking his head and saying, "My son has never had the Damascus Road experience." But as Muller shows here, we must not postulate that God can only work in one way. Though Muller had little understanding and no deep sorrow of heart with respect to sin, he was confident that God had started a work in him.

That was in 1825. In 1829, four years later, Muller was very ill, and this is what he says:

> The weaker I got in body, the happier I was in spirit. Never in my whole life had I seen myself so vile, so guilty, so altogether what I ought not to have been as at this time. It was as if every sin of which I had been guilty was brought to my remembrance. . . .

"A man, which told me all things that ever I did"—it is the same.

> . . . but at the same time I could realize that all my sins were completely forgiven. The result of this was great peace; I longed exceedingly to depart and be with Christ.

He was still a young man; but what is important is that this was four years after the event that he himself regards as his conversion. He certainly had been living an entirely different life from 1825 onward, and I have no doubt, as he says, that he was truly a Christian. But you would never have heard of George Muller if it had not been for this experience in 1829. It was from there on that he became the exceptional, unusual man of God who enjoyed such peace and tranquillity, such joy in the Lord, and was given such outstanding faith, which enabled him to do mighty things to the glory of God.

But the essential part of this experience was, "Never in my whole life had I seen myself so vile, so guilty, so altogether what I ought not to have been as at this time." It was as if every sin he had ever committed flashed in front of him as some terrible panorama, and he saw his utter emptiness and woe. And as the result of that he truly saw the fullness that is in Christ and saw it to such an extent that, as he says, he did not want to live. And he says that when later he was told by his doctor that he was beginning to get better, he was truly disappointed. He had already come to the state in which he could say with the apostle Paul, "For to me to live is Christ, and to die is gain" (Phil. 1:21). Not that he wanted to get out of this world, but he wanted to be "with Christ" whom he had now come to know in this manner and whose love was filling his heart.

Now there is a perfect illustration, and it really is, I repeat, a universal law—I do not know a single exception. People such as Muller who have had exceptional experiences of the love of God and who have consequently been used in an exceptional manner invariably have had the deepest view of their sinfulness, their guilt, their emptiness, their woe. And this, I say again, is not confined to these outstanding people. We happen to have their biographies and autobiographies, but it is equally true of others of whom we read in connection with the lives of great people but whose names one does not remember.

So, then, the great question for us is, do we know anything about this conviction? To me, this is one of the most urgent questions facing the church today—every section of the church. It is obvious that the church is not counting as she should, but are we as individuals exemplifying the New Testament picture of people with this well of water within them springing up into everlasting life? And if we are conscious of not knowing much about this fullness, we must face this question: why is this sense of guilt so absent today? Different periods in the history of the church have different characteristics, and there is no doubt at all but that this present age to which we belong, with all its activities, is an age that is lacking in this depth of the realization of guilt and of sin. Correspondingly, it knows very little about the profundities and the heights of the Christian life. Why is this? I think there are certain answers to that question.

The first answer, surely, is that somehow or another we must have a wrong view of salvation. What is our conception of salvation? I think we will find that many of us have been concerned only about particular blessings. We were after happiness; we were miserable for various reasons. Perhaps, like George Muller, we were living a wrong life, which brought us into a miserable state of remorse. The one thing we wanted was to be delivered from all this, and then we were told that the Christian faith would give us happiness. So we turned our attention to Christianity, and our sole purpose was to obtain this happiness. It may be that in our unhappiness we were in a Christian meeting or we met someone who had been like us and we heard of an experience that had been given to that person as a result of believing this message. And we wanted that experience.

So often people seem to make a decision, as they put it, "for Christ" with no thought of God at all—all they have done is think about themselves. They want what somebody else has. Then they adopt a formula and seem to have what they sought, but the idea of offending God has never been present. That was what Muller, in writing his autobiography and looking back across his life, was able to see so clearly. So he said, "I had no sorrow of heart on account of offending God." You simply cannot accept that as a true view of salvation if you are guided by the Scriptures as to what salvation really means. Everywhere in Scripture salvation is described in terms of being "reconciled to God." Reconciliation to God is the beginning and the end of salvation.

Why did our Lord Jesus Christ come? Why did he die? According to Peter, he did all this "to bring us to God" (1 Pet. 3:18). Or as Paul puts it, "God was in Christ, reconciling the world unto himself, not imputing their trespasses unto them" (2 Cor. 5:19). This is salvation. The Old Testament comes before the New; the Law precedes the gospel. It is wrong, it gives us a false view of salvation, to ignore the Old Testament, to ignore the Law, to start just where we are and to "come to Christ," as it is expressed. Salvation means being reconciled to God, and if we have no awareness of having offended God, if we are in no sense concerned about the fact that we have rebelled against him and offended him and wounded him and transgressed his laws, and done so deliberately, indeed, if we are not aware of the fact that the most terrible sin of all is to be so self-centered that we are not concerned about God and our relationship to him, then we do not know what salvation means.

This is a most solemn matter. Of course, it shows itself in many ways. For instance, many Christian people always pray to the Lord Jesus Christ, and to him alone, and never talk about anybody else—and thereby they betray themselves. This just shows that they have never understood what salvation means. The Lord Jesus Christ is the mediator—he brings us to God. We do not stop with him. He was sent by God and was sent to reconcile us to God. It is through him that we enjoy access to God.

Now it is most extraordinary, but I think you will agree that if you examine yourselves and examine many whom you know, you will find that probably the greatest danger of all is to be purely subjective and to fail to realize that the first principle of salvation is our relationship to God. How can we be truly godly? How can we, indeed, be truly Christian in any deep sense without being aware that we have offended God and are guilty before him?

But, further, it seems to me that there is also in this matter very clear evidence of a lack of a true belief in the Holy Spirit and his work, a lack of faith in him. I was able to show you earlier that our Lord himself, in telling his disciples about the coming of the Spirit, said, "He will reprove [convince, AV margin; convict] the world of sin, and of righteousness, and of judgment" (John 16:8). And when he came on the Day of Pentecost that is precisely what he did. The Holy Spirit has been sent primarily to apply the finished salvation that has been obtained for us by the Lord Jesus Christ in all his work on our behalf, in his death and burial and resurrection and ascension. It is the Holy Spirit who mediates that to us; that is his particular work. There is the completed salvation, but how does it come to me? Primarily by the Holy Spirit's work of conviction.

But must we not agree that far too often in connection with evangelism there is no ultimate reliance upon the Spirit? This shows itself in many ways, and I think it accounts for the absence in so many today of the sense of guilt that is so characteristic of the saints. The very atmosphere of evangelistic meetings is often quite contrary to everything we read of in the Scriptures and would expect when the Holy Spirit is operating. It is not part of my business to say that Christian preachers should be solemn—they should not be mournful. But there are also certain other things that they should not be: they should never be light, they should never be flippant, they should never indulge in what the Scriptures refer to as "foolish talking" and "jesting" (Eph. 5:4). In other words, if we really have met together to consider the eternal God and our relationship to him, it is he who should dominate the meetings. When we realize that we are in the presence of God, then what happens to us is what happened to Jacob who, when he was at Bethel, was filled with fear as he said, "Surely the LORD is in this place; and I knew it not" (Gen. 28:16).

Now I am not concerned about motives—I know that the motive is to attract people and to give the impression that Christianity is bright and happy and so on. But, my dear friends, need we do that? Is it not the work of the Holy Spirit to attract people? We are talking about immortal souls and their eternal destiny; we are talking about people who may go to hell and eternal misery. This is the most solemn thing in the whole universe. We are very serious, are we not, if somebody is dangerously ill? Life-threatening illness immediately sobers everybody. If there is a danger of a person dying, there is no levity, no jocularity then. But apparently when we are dealing with the danger to a soul of eternal death, we must become like the world. Do you not see that this is a quenching of the Spirit? The motive may be excellent, but surely the method is desperately and dangerously wrong and militates against the operation of the Spirit. He is a dove; he is gentle. He can be grieved; he can be quenched.

Is it not extraordinary that we are starting with people instead of starting with God? And then because we are starting with people, we are anxious to ingratiate ourselves, we are anxious to make the gospel palatable and nice and acceptable. But that is not our business. All we are told to do is to "preach the word" (2 Tim. 4:2), to declare the gospel of salvation. We are "ambassadors for Christ" (2 Cor. 5:20) and speak and act in his name. As we are so often reminded these days, ambassadors, foreign secretaries, and others have the reputation of the country in their hands, and their conduct must correspond to those whom they are representing.

Very well, there it is in general. But that leads to our Lord himself being presented in the wrong way. He is offered as someone who will make us happy, someone who will take all our problems from us. Now, of course, he does do all this, but I am concerned about the way in which he is presented, which is as a friend or as a companion, someone who will put everything right, someone who will bring blessing if we but come to him. But that is not the way in which he is presented in the New Testament. Surely the great emphasis there is always the same: he is the only one who can save us from the wrath of God and eternal destruction. That is who he is. He died—he had to die; his body was broken, his blood shed. It was as tremendous as that. He is the Savior, "the Lamb of God, which taketh away the sin of the world" (John 1:29). If this is not central in the whole of our thinking, we are already wrong.

What is he to you, my friend? This is the question. You say you have believed in him, but why did you believe? How did you believe in him? What did you believe concerning him? We must examine ourselves in the light of the prominence of the teaching about this need for a sense of guilt and of sin—"a man, which told me all things that ever I did."

Furthermore, often an appeal is made to us "to take Christ" or we are urged to "decide for Christ" or "follow Christ" or "give ourselves to Christ" or "give our hearts to Christ." But, again, I think we must examine this. Is this scriptural? Does the Scripture put it in that way? Surely the Scripture does not ask, "Will you take Christ?" but "Will Christ take you?" Is it possible for him to take me in view of my sinfulness, my vileness, my guilt, my hopelessness? This idea that I can take Christ or not or that I should be pleaded with or cajoled, that pressure should be brought to bear upon me to "take Christ" or "follow him" is wrong—it is "I" all along. But I am a miserable worm, a wretch!

Here is the most terrifying question: can he possibly look upon me? That is what the poor tax collector felt in our Lord's parable of the tax collector and the Pharisee going up to the Temple to pray (Luke 18:10–14). Look at this man striking his chest as he pleads for mercy. There is nothing else to plead for. He does not say, "Well, I think I'll decide for Christ; I'll follow him." Dear me, no! He is desperate. The New Testament does not exhort us to "take Christ" but to believe on him. Then when we see our guilt, our unworthiness, our emptiness, and our woe, when we see that we are perishing, it says in summary, "Though that is true of you, he has died for you. Believe that! Believe on him and what he has done for you, and you will be rescued." That is how the gospel is presented everywhere.

And so it is in our hymns:

Foul, I to the fountain fly:
Wash me, Saviour, or I die.

This idea that we can weigh up the gospel and balance out the arguments and decide and, yes, make a decision is remote from everything we read in the Bible and in all our great hymns and in all the biographies, as I am showing you.

Nothing in my hand I bring,
Simply to thy cross I cling;
Naked, come to thee for dress;
Helpless, look to thee for grace.

That is it! And it is that always.

Rock of Ages, cleft for me,
Let me hide myself in thee.

Augustus Toplady ("Rock of Ages")

Can we truly come to Christ unless we are desperate, unless we see our utter hopelessness and helplessness? Our whole conception of salvation has gone astray. It is subjective; it is always seen in human terms. Salvation is never understood in terms of our ultimate relationship to God, this holy God who has manifested himself in his Law, and to Christ as the only way, at such a cost.

The last observation I would make under this heading is that the moment you look at salvation in this biblical way, you see that any pressure for a quick decision is of necessity a form of "quenching the Spirit." There are terrible phrases that people use that have always alarmed and frightened me. They talk about "getting people through," and the impression they give is that they push them through. My dear friends, you can push people to make a decision, but you can never push them to true conversion. That is the work and the prerogative of the Holy Spirit. I know the motive is excellent; I am not querying motives. But this overanxiety, resulting from a false way of understanding, leads to trouble.

Of course, we are anxious that people should be saved, but let the Spirit work in his own way, let him convict. We are very anxious for people to be happy, but there is something more important than that, and it is that they should be truly regenerate, that they should be truly reconciled to God. The Spirit does not need your help, and we must certainly not try to go ahead of him or hurry the work, as so many do. The result of trying to take over the Holy Spirit's work is that not only are there reactions, with only a very small percentage of decisions being accepted as true conversions, but even among those there are often tragedies. The Holy Spirit alone can convict, he alone can apply the Law, he alone can bring us to see our utter emptiness and vileness, and he alone can reveal the Lord Jesus Christ to us in the plenitude of his work as divine Savior. Let the Spirit do his law-work.

Again, I could give you endless examples of people such as Muller who were familiar with the statements of the gospel and had attended gospel services but who nevertheless had to pass through a process of conviction. I am not standardizing this. It is possible for men and women to be converted the first time they hear the gospel, but it does not always happen like that. The Spirit has his different methods and knows us one by one. We must leave the work to him. We state the truth, we pray for people, we do everything we can, but no decision must ever be produced by human pressure. It is not surprising that today many people know nothing about a sense of guilt and sin and correspondingly know practically nothing about the higher reaches of the Christian life. These all belong indissolubly together. If the birth has been wrong or faulty, it will tend to show itself throughout that person's life. This is a most serious and solemn matter. Have we known much about a sense of guilt? If not, why not?

But not only is there a lack of faith in the power of the Holy Spirit in the matter of evangelism, the same lack of faith is also evident in the whole question of sanctification. I do advise you to read the history of the church, especially the great revivals of history, the great tides and movements of the Spirit. If you do, you will find that during the last hundred years or so something new has come in, something different from what had always obtained previously. Before then, we read of men and women undergoing terrible periods of conviction—groaning in agony, doubting whether they can ever be saved, almost desperate. But that seems to be gone; now everything is so slick and easy and can be done quickly. And there is a corresponding absence of godliness and sobriety and of all that is depicted of Christians in the New Testament itself.

Why is this? Well, I am suggesting that it is partly due to the type of evangelism that is found today, but it is equally because of the teaching with regard to sanctification. For some reason or another, the idea has come in that sanctification is mainly negative. People are taught that it just means getting rid of certain sins. Conventions are held that are described as casualty clearing stations. People are told, "You're a Christian, but you keep falling into sin. Now you want to get rid of that, don't you? Come along, we'll be able to deal with this—we can help you." And then it is put in terms of victory. "We'll give you victory. We'll teach you how to live the victorious life." This has been the popular approach for the last hundred years. The emphasis is on getting rid of particular sins. Again, this type of holiness and teaching always starts with *the individual*. Are you happy? Are you victorious? If you're not, this is how you can be put right.

Then the steps that need to be taken are spelled out, and they are consistent with the essential fallacy. These teachings are always consistent with themselves. Having found out that I am unhappy because of my failures and because of certain things that get me down—and these are specified—they go into details: Have you answered that letter that you should have answered? Have you made this apology? There will be a whole list of things that you are guilty of not having done, and you are told, "Now you must get rid of all this."

How do you get rid of it?

You must come to a crisis decision in which you surrender all these things and yourself too. And if you do that, you have had this great experience that is now going to release you and will lead to victory and to the rest of your life being spent "abiding in Christ." A man who was a great exponent of this teaching used to describe his experience in a very graphic manner. He had been a Christian and truly converted, and he was enjoying much assurance of salvation and much usefulness in the Christian life as a preacher, but still something was lacking. Then he went to a certain gathering, and there he was convicted because in one pocket he had a pipe and in the opposite pocket a pouch. In that meeting he went through agony over the pipe and the tobacco pouch. And at last he felt he must go and get this right; so he climbed up the side of a hill near the place where the meeting was held, and there this tremendous struggle took place. But at last out came the pipe and the pouch, and from there on all was different.

Now do not misunderstand me. I am not here to say that particulars do not matter—they do; details do count. But that is not New Testament holiness and sanctification. From the standpoint of sanctification, a man can be in as bad a state after he has thrown the pipe and the pouch away as he was before; indeed, he may even be worse because he is tending to rest upon this action. This whole view is negative; it involves getting rid of particular things. And then formulas come in, techniques to enable you to do this. You see the parallel with the cults, do you not? The cults can do all that, and they do. They can make people throw away pipes and pouches and give money and make sacrifices. They are doing it, hence their success. But my point is that this is not New Testament holiness; this is not New Testament sanctification.

What is New Testament holiness? What is sanctification? It is "to be conformed to the image of his [God's] Son" (Rom. 8:29). And it is because we forget this and concentrate on details that we can become such spiritual monstrosities. I have known people following the kind of negative teaching that I have described who have been very loud in their denunciation of Christians who still continue with certain practices such as smoking, which to them is horrible and terrible; but I have known the same people to be flagrantly guilty of wasting money.

I remember, it must be twenty-five or thirty years ago, a businessman who was attending services at our church. He had come under conviction and was aware that he had a soul and that he was a sinner. He asked me if I would tell him when I was going away to preach within fifty or sixty miles of his home. He said he wanted to know because he would like to come with me in order to "keep under the sound of the gospel." An occasion came when I had to preach elsewhere in the afternoon and evening; so I told him, and he kindly took me in his car. I was invited to tea there, and as my companion, he was invited with me.

I knew the people of the house well, but there was a visitor there, the sister of the lady of the house, whom I did not know. She had come up for these services, and we were having tea together. We had just finished tea when this poor fellow with me, who was under conviction of sin, quite automatically pulled out his cigarette case and lit a cigarette. The moment he did so, this sister of my hostess attacked him viciously for smoking. Now these were very good Christian people, and yet she was attacking him. She did not know the truth about him, of course, and should not have interfered; she should have assumed that he was in my care. She was now undoing all that had been done over the weeks through the preaching under the power of the Spirit. But quite apart from this, she was concentrating on this one thing. The poor man was uncomfortable and unhappy and did not know what to do with himself, obviously feeling that he had let me down.

I had to decide what to do very quickly—I believe the decision was left up to me. The lady was waxing eloquent on the waste of money that was involved, saying that all this money that he was spending on cigarettes could be given to missionary funds and so on; you are familiar with the argument. When she had finished, I said, "I do not want to be rude, but I would like to ask you one question: how much did you pay for that dress you are wearing?" And she blushed crimson. Of course she did. I said, "Did you have to buy as expensive a dress as that? Could you not have bought a cheaper dress that would look as nice and neat and becoming in every respect? Then you would have been able to give probably half of what you paid for this dress to the missionary fund." That had never occurred to her. But that is the sort of thing that happens if you start with yourself and with your actions and with particular sins. You throw away your pipe and pouch and think you have done everything. You do not smoke cigarettes, but you are not aware of what you are doing in some other respect.

How do you deal with all this? Is there no way whereby we can cover all these possibilities and defects? There is, the way shown in the New Testament. You do not start with yourself, you do not start with particular actions, but you start with Jesus Christ, and you say, "I as a Christian am meant to be conformed to the image of God's Son." If you have that in the center of your thinking, the details will soon look after themselves. He will make certain things impossible, and they will not be only the ones that you happen to be very keen on avoiding and somebody else does not think about at all, but he will deal with everything. This is the only way. Holiness and sanctification are positive. It is not that I get rid of certain things and then am a paragon of perfection. I am more likely to be a miserable, self-righteous Pharisee, criticizing others and setting myself up as a judge. Thank God, that is not New Testament holiness and sanctification.

New Testament holiness is positive. I see that God's Son, having given himself, having died for me, his body broken, his blood shed, has purchased me. I am not my own; I am bought with a price (see 1 Corinthians 6:19–20). What matters is what he thinks of me, my relationship to him, and when I am in this relationship with him, I will soon find what I am to do and what I am not to do. So you do not have to have these lists and techniques and categories—get rid of this or that and you are all right. No, no! "Take time to be holy." It cannot be done once and forever on the side of a hill. "Grow in grace, and in the knowledge of our Lord and Saviour Jesus Christ" (2 Pet. 3:18). "Work out your own salvation with fear and trembling. For it is God which worketh in you both to will and to do of his good pleasure" (Phil. 2:12–13).

My dear friends, these are the reasons why people know so little about conviction of sin and a sense of guilt. We are so self-centered, subjective, and introspective; we start and end with ourselves, and the Holy Spirit becomes just some sort of agency to help us. No, no; sanctification is getting to know him. This woman of Samaria has met him; she has looked into his eyes; she has heard him. "Come, see a man, which told me all things that ever I did." George Muller said, "Every sin that I had ever committed seemed to come back." That is what our Lord does—let him do it. He will through the Spirit. Do not quench the Spirit. Leave your overanxieties with your methods and techniques and systems, and let the Holy Spirit do his own work.

44

A Message for Remembrance Sunday

The woman then left her waterpot, and went her way into the city, and saith to the men, Come, see a man which told me all things that ever I did: is not this the Christ? (John 4:28–29)

We turn again to the first words that were uttered by the woman of Samaria to her fellow-townsmen when, having met the Lord Jesus Christ and having come to some understanding of who he is, she rushed to tell them the news. It is the story of a great transformation that takes place in this woman's life, a woman who has been living in sin for years and is undoubtedly notorious for her sinfulness in the city in which she lives. She has to go backward and forward several times a day to draw water from the well, and our Lord makes use of this to give her a great spiritual lesson. He says, "Whosoever drinketh of this water [the water in the well] shall thirst again"—that is the world. The world cannot satisfy; it gives temporary relief, but it can never do more than that. "But whosoever drinketh of the water that I shall give him shall never thirst; but the water that I shall give him shall be in him a well of water springing up into everlasting life."

Now that is the message of the Christian faith, and that is what it offers to give us, that is what it offers to do for us. This message offers us a life that can give us complete satisfaction—"shall never thirst"—whatever may happen. We are considering this great message because this is the most important question that can ever face any human being. I remember reading a book that started with these words: "It is not life that matters, but the courage that you bring to it." Well, the thesis of that book was wrong; not everybody has courage, and some have more than others. That book leaves it up to us to cope. But there is a sense in which there is something right in that statement. It is not life that matters. What really matters is whether or not we have the secret of the way of living that enables us to go through life triumphantly.

So I want to consider this great message given here by our blessed Lord to the woman of Samaria in the context of this particular day that is observed [in Britain] as Remembrance Sunday.[29] This passage shows us what the gospel does and what it really has to give, and it also shows us how false ideas with regard to Christianity are generally the greatest hindrance to men and women receiving this great and wonderful blessing. We have considered many such hindrances as we have gone through this story. This woman, like all of us, stumbles; she thinks she knows much more than she does. Our Lord has to deal with her, and eventually he brings her to see the central truth, and that is what we are concerned about.

What does Remembrance Sunday mean to us? What have we ever derived from the observance of this day? What is the world deriving from it? Many thousands of people probably go to religious services only this one day a year. What do they get out of it? What does it represent? Is that Christianity?

Now we know perfectly well that to many this Remembrance Day service is a formal, mechanical act, a kind of parade. There are those in the armed forces and in various movements and organizations who only go because it is the thing to do, and attendance may mean they can avoid other duties. That has nothing whatsoever to do with true Christian living—nothing at all.

Then for large numbers of people in this country and many other countries, this service is purely national in its connotation. These people are concerned with their patriotic thoughts. This is an occasion for national pride and self-satisfaction. Clearly, again this has nothing to do with the Christian faith.

To others this occasion is purely sentimental. It makes them think of death and suffering; it makes them think of loved ones who perhaps lost their lives in war. I am not saying there is anything inherently wrong in this, but does it go beyond that? To many this day is wholly depressing because of thoughts of war and loss and bereavement and sorrow. A certain type of music is always put on; there is an air of solemnity. I myself can clearly recall a time in my own experience when this day and similar days brought nothing but sheer depression, a sense of mystery, something pagan, thoughts of death and the fear of death. But is that Christianity? Is it not, rather, paganism?

A great characteristic of paganism, and of many of the religions that belong to the realm of paganism, is that they are all mournful and sad. Let us say this for them—they, at any rate, have sufficient understanding to see that you cannot dance your way through life. They see very clearly that life is real, life is earnest, full of problems and difficulties. But they have no relief, and everything is finally completely hopeless. And a great deal that passes for Christianity is precisely that.

People often observe Remembrance Sunday because, in a sense, they are afraid not to or they may think it is the right thing to do. But what is the effect that it has upon them? How does it leave them? Do they seek relief the moment the service has ended? Do they have to turn to alcohol to get over it? It is depressing, and you try to forget it as soon as you can. Is that Christianity? No; Christianity is the exact opposite! People are hindered from really enjoying the blessings of the Christian faith because they imagine that something is the true faith when it is not.

And then, to finish this miserable list, there are those for whom Remembrance Sunday is merely an occasion to indulge in political talk. They use this day only to protest against war and against governments. It is an opportunity to talk vaguely of general uplift and to try to get people to unite together to put an end to war. People think that Christianity is just some teaching about stopping conflicts in the world. And many have said that if that is Christianity, they are not interested in it; they can see through all that. So they have turned their backs upon God and upon the Christian faith. But I hope to make it perfectly clear that this, again, is not Christianity at all.

Then there are others—and I am much more concerned about them—who have been bitterly disappointed. They are searching for comfort. Life has dealt blows to them; they have lost loved ones, their hearts are broken, and they want help. So they come to the Christian church. And there is something soothing about it. While they are there they feel eased and calmed by the solemnity and the ritual. But then they go out, and where are they? Have they received anything that they did not have when they went in? Have they been given anything permanent? Are they able to look at life differently? And they find they are not. They just have to depend upon this Remembrance Day ritual as it comes around year by year, and they are sad and disappointed and begin to wonder what this Christian faith is all about.

I want to show you, in the light of what we find here in John 4, how far removed all that is from the glorious, blessed truth of the gospel. Here is the Christian message to the world, to this country, on a morning such as this. Let us look again at this woman of Samaria. If we would have this "well of water springing up into everlasting life" within us, if we would be in the position in which we shall never thirst again, if we would receive of this fullness and grace upon grace, we must learn from our Lord's words to her. There are certain vital lessons here that are utter, absolute necessities, and if we do not accept them, if we quarrel with them, our entire lives will be spent in shallows and in miseries.

What are these lessons? Well, the first great lesson is that we must submit ourselves entirely to God and to his handling of our life. In many ways, this is the most difficult lesson of all. The trouble with all of us is that we tend to come with our own ideas and demands. We want certain things; so we approach Christ, we approach the Christian church, which represents him and which has his message. What do we want? Well, we bring to him an almost endless variety of questions and problems and demands. Some are purely personal and subjective—we want comfort perhaps; we want consolation; we want some healing substance that can deal with the bruises of life. Or it may be that we want peace in the world and war to be banished; we are concerned about the state of the world and want to put things right. So we approach him and insist, as it were, on an answer to whatever problem has brought us to him.

And I do not hesitate to assert that as long as we are doing that, we will never get this well of water—never. That approach is entirely wrong and is the supreme hindrance to receiving the fullness of Christ. As long as we are coming with our demands and desires, almost insisting upon them and virtually telling God that if he does not give us what we want we are not interested in him and will turn our backs upon Christianity or denounce him, we will continue as we are. That is the very reason why we are in trouble and in pain, in sorrow and in misunderstanding, knowing nothing about this blessed life that the Son of God came into the world to give.

Why is this? Well, one of the great fundamental principles of this faith is that the blessings of the Christian life are always only obtained as the result of something else. They can never be obtained directly. What a vital principle this is! We come, as I say, with particular desires, particular demands, and we believe we can get them directly. I have often used this illustration: we regard our Lord, we regard God, as some kind of slot machine. We come with our desires and make a request—we put our coin in the slot—"this is what I want and I expect to get it." We are all doing that in some shape or form. But I do not get what I want, and so I say, "Well, Christianity doesn't do what it promised to do. I've done my best, I've prayed, I've asked, but I'm still unhappy. I don't have the consolation I was looking for. I see the world in trouble still." And the answer is, I repeat, that all the blessings of the Christian life are by-products. They cannot be obtained directly.

Now this is a teaching that comes out constantly in the New Testament. In the Gospel of John it is particularly evident. This was the mistake that was made by Mary, the mother of our Lord, in the incident at the marriage feast in Cana of Galilee: "And both Jesus was called, and his disciples, to the marriage. And when they wanted wine, the mother of Jesus saith unto him, They have no wine."

What was she doing? She was telling him in effect, "Look here, the wine is finished—do something about it." Do you remember his reply? "Jesus saith unto her, Woman, what have I to do with thee? mine hour is not yet come" (John 2:2–4).

Now that is a rebuke. He did deal with the situation, but not at Mary's request, not in her time. He did it in his own way and in his own time. Even his own mother had to be rebuked because of this very attitude.

And then in the same chapter we read, "Then answered the Jews and said unto him, What sign shewest thou unto us, seeing that thou doest these things?"

They were saying, "You're making a great claim for yourself, and we're ready to listen to you—just give us a sign and we'll believe in you." And then we read, "Jesus answered and said unto them, Destroy this temple, and in three days I will raise it up" (vv. 18–19).

He answered them in a parable, and they did not understand it. But that is the only way he does answer such people. At the very end of that chapter we read, "Now when he was in Jerusalem at the passover, in the feast day, many believed in his name, when they saw the miracles which he did."

Exactly! People come to him wanting miracles, they want healing, or they want comfort or peace. "But Jesus did not commit himself unto them, because he knew all men, and needed not that any should testify of man: for he knew what was in man" (vv. 23–25).

You see how fatal this is! You come with your demands and insist upon something, but you will not get it. Now this is clearly one of the fundamental facts that operates at the very beginning; our whole approach to God is involved here.

We find exactly the same misapprehension in the third chapter with regard to Nicodemus. He, again, thought he was in a position to say, "I've been watching you, and I admire you. You're wonderful and must be a teacher sent from God, otherwise you couldn't do these things. Now then . . ." But our Lord stopped him: "Verily, verily, I say unto thee, Except a man be born again, he cannot see the kingdom of God" (v. 3). Stop! You must not come like this. The approach is wrong, and it inhibits the activity that leads to this great blessing.

Now in the case of the woman of Samaria, our Lord does exactly the same thing. He has to be almost brutal with her as he cuts across all her talk and says, "Go, call thy husband, and come hither," revealing to her that he knows all about the fact that she has had five husbands and that the man she is living with now is not her husband at all, that she is living in adultery and in sin. This is essential; he takes charge. Fullness of life has to come in his way.

Consider one other example because it is so striking. In the sixth chapter we find that after our Lord performed the miracle of feeding the five thousand, the people got very excited. We read in the fifteenth verse, "When Jesus therefore perceived that they would come and take him by force, to make him a king, he departed again into a mountain himself alone." They were actually going to lay hands on him. They had seen something of his tremendous power and said in essence, "This is the Deliverer; this is the one who is going to give us a great victory over our Roman conquerors. He will set himself up as king in Jerusalem, and we Jews will be elevated to our old position. This is marvelous!"

They were going to take him by force, and, oh, how many are doing that today! They are trying to take him by force to make him a politician or a pacifist or a socialist or a conservative; they are all trying to use him for their own ends. And he will not have it. If you try to lay your hands upon him, he will depart from you; you will not get his blessing.

So you see, my dear friends, how vitally important this principle is. He has his own method, and blessings are only obtained as we submit ourselves utterly to him. I say once more that this Christian faith has no comfort, no consolation whatsoever, to offer to those who are not Christians. Now that sounds hard, does it not? But it is true, as every pastor, every minister, knows from his own unhappy experiences. There is nothing more difficult for a Christian pastor than to be confronted by a non-Christian who is desperately ill and may be dying or to visit a non-Christian family that has lost a dear one—what comfort can he give? To talk sentimentally is not Christian comfort. These blessings can only be given to those who have an understanding of the gospel. There must be something for you to build on.

For the Christian, there is glorious comfort and consolation. There is nothing like it; it makes us more than conquerors. But most Christian comfort is the result of a logical argument. It is a deduction, it is a by-product, and if certain fundamental postulates are not there, there is no comfort to give. Unless people are in a relationship with him, they cannot follow the argument. So the Christian church has no comfort whatsoever to give to people who are not Christians. You cannot obtain the comforts and the blessings of the Christian life unless you first of all become a Christian.

Now all the confusion today in the church and in the world arises directly from the failure to understand this truth, which is so elementary, so primary, so fundamental in the whole of the teaching of the New Testament; and the church, of course, is mainly responsible. She has allowed herself to be put into the position of being just some great institution that gives people vague comfort and consolation. She is called in on certain occasions—a birth or a marriage or a death—to do something vague and general. People think that is Christianity, but it is the very thing that is robbing them of the real blessings of the Christian faith. There are even people who are seeking sanctification before they have justification, but it cannot be done. We cannot live holy lives until we are *made* holy, until we are regenerate, until there is in us the seed of the divine nature, until, indeed, we become, as Peter puts it, "partakers of the divine nature" (2 Pet. 1:4).

So I put this in the form of a general proposition: the first thing we must do is realize that we must put aside our demands and requests and just submit to him. We come as we are, and we allow him to deal with us and to handle us.

And then what will he do? This is again one of the primary, fundamental truths of Christianity. Do you know the first step the Lord Jesus Christ leads us to take? It is to ask the right questions. He makes us face the real problems, and these are very different from everything we have ever thought. The gospel is a complete contrast to all that we know by nature. That is why those who would represent Christianity as just one of the world philosophies or a movement for political change are the greatest deniers of the gospel. Our Lord never does what we expect him to do; he does the exact opposite. Even his own disciples, remember, were amazed that he was talking to this woman—any woman would have been bad enough, but talking to a Samaritan woman, and especially to a woman of this character was astounding. But that is the sort of thing he does, and thank God for that! Thank God, he shocks us. If he has not shocked you, there is only one thing I can say to you, and that is that you have never met him, you do not know him. You get the biggest shock of your life when you meet Christ. He gets us to face the real, instead of the wrong, questions.

What do I mean? Well, as with this woman, he always starts by making us face ourselves. "Come, see a man which told me all things that ever I did: is not this the Christ?" She has not been made to face herself before; none of us have. We come with our questions, and our questions may be, why does God allow war? Or, if God is a God of love, why does he allow the carnage to go on? Why does God allow handicapped children to be born?

You know the questions. We say, "These are the questions to which I want answers. Why is the world as it is? Why does the world deal with me as it does? Why have I known sorrow and bereavement? Why have I had trouble and unhappiness that other people haven't?" We come with all these problems—the problem of suffering, the problem of pain, the problem of war, the problem of misunderstanding—and we say these are the great issues.

But, my dear friend, they are not. The first great question for every one of us is ourselves. It is astounding how blind we are to this; nobody thinks of it. I have been reading an article by an outstanding man who did brilliantly in Oxford and became a professor and a minister in a Christian church. But unfortunately, poor fellow, he gave way to drink and as a result lost his professorship and his position in the church. In the article he refers to another man, also a minister in the church, who, like him, had been defrocked because of drunkenness. This second man was a poet and believed that a poet had license to do more or less what he liked. The writer of the article says that he cannot understand why life has dealt so harshly with both of them. But notice, it is *life* that has done it. There is not a suspicion or a shadow of a suspicion in his article that he has done anything wrong at all. "Some of us," he says, "do get dealt with very harshly by life in this world." Self-pity!

And here in John 4 is a woman living in adultery. She probably feels that she is having a very hard time, that her great problem is not her adultery but the way people look at her when she walks down the street and when they nod to one another or wink at one another. That is her problem, she thinks, this society in which she is living. Perhaps she, like many today in this permissive society, says, "Am I doing anything wrong at all? I'm as good as they are! What if their thoughts were revealed—who are they?" And she justifies herself. It does not matter how low people may fall, they can still justify themselves. It is innate—the world is at fault or other people or something. But our Lord, when he takes charge, immediately puts an end to all that. He makes us realize that the first question to be answered concerns ourselves, just as we are.

Our Lord so deals with us that we stop asking: Why does God allow war? Why do I suffer? Why am I sad? Why am I in pain? Instead we ask, what do I really deserve? This is a very different question, is it not? Who am I? What have I a right to expect in this life, seeing I am what I am? These are the questions that he makes me face. I stop thinking of what the world does to me, what other people do to me, and just look at myself and say, what am I?

Then our Lord makes me think of my relationship to God. He makes me answer these questions. You ask why God allows war, but how often do you actually think about God? What are your ideas about him? Where did you get them from? On what are they based? What right do you even have to ask that question? What right do you have to sit in judgment on God? He makes us turn right in upon ourselves and face ourselves in this way. It is no longer something outside us—it is ourselves.

And then I come with my question—war and the horror of war and young men being killed in the very bloom and blossom of life—oh, what a terrible thing it is! And our Lord says, "Yes, it is terrible, but you know, the question for you is, are you ready to die yourself? You are protesting, you are making your great statements, and it is all outside you. But are you yourself ready to die? You do not know when that will be. This is your first problem. And not only that, what happens, do you think, after you die? What lies beyond?"

Is it not tragic that the world does not look at the really big issues? There will be all this talk today and preaching and so on about the horror of war because it leads to death. Yet people refuse to face the fact that whether or not there is a war, they have to die. It is not bombs that matter. It is not the way in which you die; it is the fact that you must die. There is no difference between being blown to bits by a bomb and dying peacefully and quietly on a bed at home or in a hospital—essentially no difference at all. What is of the utmost importance is the fact of death, this great, startling thing, and whether we are ready to meet it.

All our questions are external, outside ourselves. Our Lord questions us personally, individually, directly, leading us to ask: Where am I involved in all this? What right do I have to ask my questions? What do I deserve in life? What right do I have to expect blessings from God? What has been my relationship to him? Do I live to his glory? Do I keep his commandments? Do I worship him? Do I adore him? Who am I to ask for blessings? Who am I even to seek forgiveness?

These are the problems that our Lord makes us face. We do not like this, do we? The world does not like it either. Our world is always living outside itself, and when we live in this way we manage pretty well with ourselves. But our Lord will not have this. If we are to know this well of water, he must first clear out all that is inside us and make room for it. If you want the blessings, submit to him.

In contradistinction to our idea, based on the assumption that we are all right as we are and that the problems are outside us and that all we need is a better world in which to live, our Lord tells us in essence, "Not so. It was in Paradise that your first parents fell, and if you did banish war, life would still be what it is. It would still be a problem; it would still be pain and suffering and selfishness. All these horrible things are in the world because they are in us all. So you do not put yourself right by changing your circumstances. You are asking the wrong questions."

In other words, as we have seen, it is basic to the whole of the biblical teaching that the people who have received the greatest blessings of the Lord and have known this well of water springing up within them have always been those who have had the greatest realization of their sinfulness and their unworthiness. It is an absolute rule, an absolute law, that if you want to know what it is never to thirst but to have within you a well of water springing up into everlasting life, you must submit entirely to him and allow him to show you the truth about yourself. "Come, see a man, which told me all things that ever I did."

That is the first step, but there is a second, which is vital. Having made us face ourselves, our Lord makes us face him. "Is not this the Christ?" That is what he did with this woman. Having shown her the truth about herself, he reveals himself to her. He makes us face himself as he is, and not merely his teaching. That is the travesty that takes place every year on Remembrance Sunday—the emphasis is on the teaching of Christ, but it is a misinterpretation. Some people think the Sermon on the Mount is nothing but a treatise on pacifism, and others have different interpretations, but all say that to solve its problems, all the world needs to do is apply the teaching of Christ. But that is wrong! If you take the teaching of Christ and turn it into a philosophy or an ideology or a political system, it will not work. He said so himself. It cannot work because we are left to put it into practice, and as we are we cannot.

What our Lord does is to bring us into a relationship with himself; he brings us to know him. That is what happened to this woman. She says, "Is not this the Christ?" It is a rhetorical question—she is expecting the answer, "It is!" She is not in any doubt at all. She is saying, "Come and see him—this is the Christ." It is the person of Christ himself and not his teaching that gives us hope and consolation.

So the great question we ask is not, am I familiar with his teaching in a theoretical manner? but, do I know him? This is because all blessings are in him. "For it pleased the Father," says Paul, "that in him should all fulness dwell" (Col. 1:19). Or listen to Paul again: "In whom are hid all the treasures of wisdom and knowledge" (Col. 2:3). In Christ are "unsearchable riches" (Eph. 3:8). All God's blessings for us are in him, and in him alone. And we only obtain them as we get into contact with him, as we realize the truth about him. So we stop thinking preeminently about war and about bombs, and we think of Christ. The tragedy is that people are talking about everything but Christ, the Messiah, the Savior, the Deliverer.

And what does he make us see? He makes us see who he is: "Is not this the Christ?" My dear friends, the only hope for every one of us is that "God so loved the world, that he gave his only begotten Son, that whosoever believeth in him should not perish, but have everlasting life" (John 3:16). This is the Son of God! I am not here to say you should not read history. Read it; history is important. Read about births, marriages, deaths, wars, campaigns, victories, empires, but in the name of God, do not stop at that. All that becomes nothing when put by the side of the fact that "when the fulness of the time was come, God sent forth his Son, made of a woman, made under the law, to redeem them that were under the law" (Gal. 4:4–5). The birth of the babe of Bethlehem is the most staggering, amazing event that has ever taken place in history. Start with him. He has come into the world; he has taken our nature upon him. "And the Word was made flesh, and dwelt among us" (John 1:14). "I am he," says he to this woman.

And then we consider what he has done: "Is not this the Christ?" What does that mean? Well, *Christ* is the Greek term for the Hebrew word *Messiah*, the promised Deliverer. The Samaritans were waiting for the

Messiah; so were all the Jews. What was he coming to do? He was coming to "save his people" (Matt. 1:21). He was coming to rescue us from "this present evil world" (Gal. 1:4). He was coming so we would be "reconciled to God" (2 Cor. 5:20). He was coming to make us "the children of God" (Gal. 3:26). And he has come! He wants us to realize that he has made it possible for us to have access into the presence of God. So we no longer talk about God and ask God pompous questions like "Why do you allow this?" or "If you are a God of love. . ."

We stop all that and get to know God. We learn the way into the presence of God. We learn how our lives can be linked to God. Messiah! Christ! The one who can save us from this horrible thing that we have become as the result of sin and can make us new people even while we are still in this world. "Is not this the Christ?"

He does that for us, and then he goes on to let us know what he can do for us after making us the children of God. What does he do? I shall only give you a few headings. First, he will give you an entirely new understanding of life and of death and of eternity. "This is the victory that overcometh the world, even our faith" (1 John 5:4). The moment you have faith in him, the moment he gives you this new life, you have new understanding, and do you know the first thing that will do for you? It will enable you to see through the world, through all its illusions. I mean by that, you can see it for what it is. The pomp and the power and the glitter are nothing, nothing at all; it is all child's play. He will enable you to see through all the sham and hollowness and vanity of the world and to see all that leads to—the misery and the shame and all the problems.

At its best this is a land of sin and shame. So you will not pin your hopes to this world; you will realize that this is a temporary life only and that you are just passing through. You belong to another realm now; your citizenship is in heaven. And so he will render you immune to all "the slings and arrows of outrageous fortune." You will come into the position of the apostle Paul: "Not that I speak in respect of want: for I have learned, in whatsoever state I am, therewith to be content." Is that true of you? This is true of anybody who has this well of water. "I know both how to be abased, and I know how to abound"—I am not miserable when I have nothing; I do not lose my head when I have a lot—"every where and in all things I am instructed both to be full and to be hungry, both to abound and to suffer need. I can do all things through Christ which strengtheneth me [while I am left in this world]" (Phil. 4:11–13).

Then he will enable you to see death in a different way, and you will even see through that and beyond it.

There is a land of pure delight,
Where saints immortal reign.

Isaac Watts ("There Is a Land of Pure Delight")

Death is just a narrow sea that divides me from that "land of pure delight." You know the story, do you not, behind that hymn of Isaac Watts? He was born and brought up in Southampton, and it is said that he got the whole idea for the words of this hymn from looking across that narrow strip of sea to the Isle of Wight. That, he said, is death, nothing more. Look at it; look at the green fields; look at what is beyond the river, beyond the sea. Jesus Christ will enable you to see right into eternity, beyond time altogether. Christians have the "blessed hope" (Titus 2:13); they see the glory that is awaiting them. So they do not shiver on the brink! No, no; they see beyond it. They "set [their] affection on things above, not on things on the earth" (Col. 3:2), and even death loses its terrors and its horrors.

And while they are still left in this world of time, this blessed person, this Christ, is still with them. "I can do all things through Christ which strengtheneth me" (Phil. 4:13). So whatever may come to meet me, I shall not be moved. "Whosoever drinketh of the water that I shall give him shall never thirst"—never, whatever happens—"but the water that I shall give him shall be in him a well of water springing up into everlasting life."

All the way my Savior leads me;
What have I to ask beside?
Can I doubt his tender mercy,
Who through life has been my Guide?

Frances J. Crosby ("All the Way My Savior Leads Me")

No, no! This is the Christ, the Savior of the world, my Savior, my Lord.

He knows the way he taketh,
And I will walk with him.

Anna L. Waring ("In Heavenly Love Abiding")

45

Captivated by Him

The woman left her waterpot, and went her way into the city, and saith to the men, Come, see a man, which told me all things that ever I did: is not this the Christ? (John 4:28–29)

The Christian faith offers us a life in which we shall "never thirst." Christians never thirst because they have life, abundant life, within them. As I have been emphasizing, it is most important for us to be certain that we have this life, and if we do not, to find out why not and to discover how we can obtain it. It is for this reason that the Scriptures have been given to us. We are told by Paul in Ephesians 4, "When he [Jesus] ascended up on high . . . [he] gave gifts unto men. . . . And he gave some, apostles; and some, prophets; and some, evangelists; and some, pastors and teachers" (vv. 8, 11). He gave these gifts so that we might know the teaching given in the Scriptures. Though we are born again, we are not perfect; the world, the flesh, and the devil are round and about us and are ever trying to rob us of the abundant life that our Lord gives. God has made this wonderful provision for us so that we might examine ourselves in its light. We then discover what it is that stands between us and entering into this great possession.

We have been looking at the response of the woman of Samaria to our Lord and have seen that the first essential to receiving this fullness of life is conviction of sin. The woman was humbled and really saw herself for the first time. As a result, she submitted herself to him. And we have seen that if we resist him in any way, if we come with our demands, we will not get anything. We must come to him realizing that we do not know what to ask for and therefore leave ourselves in his hand, letting him speak to us and deal with us. He will do this—he has promised to. What he did for this woman, he will do for us. Thank God he will if we only allow him to.

But I would now like to call your attention to a further obstacle to receiving this fullness of life—namely, our whole notion of the Christian life is defective. We may see our guilt clearly, and we may see the folly of ever trying to justify ourselves by our works or our understanding. We may see clearly the need of justification by faith only and of regeneration. We may see all this and yet still have very inadequate views of the true nature of the Christian life.

I suppose that one of the main causes of our trouble is the instinct for safety and preservation. This instinct makes us realize acutely the need for forgiveness, but then we tend to stop at that; we are safe, and so we stay there. Notice how frequently in these New Testament epistles the various writers—not only the apostle Paul but the others as well—reprimand the people to whom they were writing because they were remaining mere "babes" in Christ. They were not progressing; they were not going on to perfection; they did not "have their senses exercised" (Heb. 5:14). So the writers had to keep on dealing with the first principles of the gospel of Christ while reminding their readers of the danger of staying there and of not realizing the tremendous and the glorious possibilities of this life into which he has brought us.

Here again we are helped by the woman of Samaria. We are told, "The woman left her waterpot, and went her way into the city." It is very important that we should understand exactly what she does and why she does it. One tends instinctively to imagine that she has been having a conversation with our Lord and he has just spoken to her about himself when the disciples suddenly appear, and seeing them, the woman gets excited and rushes back to the city, forgetting her waterpot.

But I think that is a complete misunderstanding. This is not a case of excitement or forgetfulness, as I think I can prove. She rushes to the men in the city and says, "Come, see a man, which told me all things that ever I did: is not this the Christ?" Now she does not say, "Go"; she says, "Come." In other words, she has not forgotten her waterpot. She has not just been carried away, as it were, and, not realizing what she is doing, suddenly rushed back to the city. No, no; she quite deliberately leaves the waterpot at the well and goes to the city in order to invite these people and take them back with her. This is her whole intention.

So what does this teach us? Well, here we are led to two principles that I am anxious to enunciate. The first is that this woman has undergone a radical change. All her values have changed; she has become a different person. Hitherto her life was a life of sin and drudgery, of daily household chores, especially the tiring work of going back and forth to fetch water from the well. As we have seen, she goes to the well at midday, when the sun is directly overhead. She does not like to go when other people are about because she knows what they think of her and what they are saying about her. But now everything is changed. There is a revolution, and this comes out, it seems to me, in the fact that she deliberately leaves her waterpot and hurries back to the town to get the people.

This is a tremendous change, and it leads us to see a number of facts that are always true about this Christian life of ours. It is important to examine ourselves in the light of all that we learn here. Let me begin with some negative points. The Christian life is not merely a slight modification, a slight change, in our existing lives but is a complete change. The New Testament is full of this teaching. Our Lord has already put it to Nicodemus: "Ye must be born again" (John 3:7). That is the essential truth about this Christian faith. Our Lord's conversation with the woman of Samaria demonstrates clearly that this is indeed a *life*—that is what he tells her: it is "a well of water springing up into everlasting life." Or let us put it like this—and this is where we are challenged and searched by this message—the life of the Christian is not like the life of everybody else with just the one difference that Christians have an extra interest added on. People should not look at Christians and come to the conclusion, "Well, they're human beings like everybody else, with the same interests, the same pursuits as the rest of us. For six days of the week there is no difference, but they do this odd thing on the seventh day."

Yet is this indictment not true of so many of us in this Christian life? You look at someone and are rather surprised that he or she is a Christian. I remember a story told to me by a man who had recently become a Christian. Shortly after his conversion, he fell ill and for the sake of his health was advised to take a Mediterranean cruise. On their way down to breakfast on the first Sunday, he and his wife looked at the notice board and were delighted to see that at 11 o'clock the captain would be holding a service in the lounge. They went to their table where there were a number of people whom they were getting to know and immediately said how glad they were to notice that there was to be a service at 11. To their utter astonishment, a lady sitting at the table also expressed her great delight and said how much she looked forward to it. Why were they shocked? It had never occurred to them that she was a fellow Christian. Her conversation, her appearance, her demeanor had given exactly the opposite impression.

That is an extreme example perhaps, but is it not so often true that our Christian faith does not seem to be an essential, central part of our lives but an addition? Or let me put it like this: far too often we give the impression that our Christianity is nothing but some sort of a brake upon our lives—I mean that mainly in a moral sense. There we are, doing what everybody else does, and then, suddenly we will not do something and people are amazed. "Why won't you do this?" they ask. They had never thought we were different, and this holding back strikes them as an oddity. They are perplexed, but perplexed not so much that we do not do this particular thing as that this contradicts their estimate of our lives. Because there is not a wholeness about our lives and demeanor, we give people the impression that to be a Christian is to be an odd person.

Another way in which we can put this same point is this: far too often our Christianity seems to be something about which we have to remind ourselves. We have to pull ourselves up and remember that we are Christians. Or we may be in such a state that other things have to pull us up. I have often been told by people, and I am sure this is true in the experience of all of us, that an illness or some disaster once pulled them up sharply, and they were reminded of how they had been assuming their Christianity while, in a sense, forgetting it. If they had been questioned or examined, they would have been fundamentally all right and would have given the right answers, but in their daily living their faith had more or less not been there, and their life might have been the life of any non-Christian. But suddenly the illness reminded them.

Oh, how often this happens! The New Testament tells us that God himself has to chastise us at times because we are his children. "For whom the Lord loveth he chasteneth" (Heb. 12:6), and if we will not give positive obedience, he will employ other methods to remind us of who we are and of our relationship to him. He reminds us that the whole glory of his gospel is in our hands, as it were, and that it is being tarnished. This is another way, therefore, in which we fail to demonstrate clearly the essential character of the Christian life.

Another way in which I can put this first principle is this: is our Christianity something that we take up as a duty? It is a duty that we have, perhaps, to force ourselves to carry out. So often it is as if it is a sort of burden, a kind of weight that we are carrying. In other words, we have turned Christianity into a law, and we give the impression, very often, that it is against the grain, and we just have to make ourselves obey God's instructions; and then we give ourselves credit because we have done our duty.

But this is a kind of mechanical religion; we take it up, and we put it down, and we force ourselves to take it up again, and we feel we really have done very well because we have carried out certain duties—attendance at the house of God and so on. This is the opposite of what is illustrated in the story of the woman of Samaria and of the teaching throughout the New Testament.

Finally under this negative heading let me put it like this: is our Christianity merely a vague, general influence, something about which we are not clear and that we do not quite understand?

In other words, I am asking this one big question: what is the place and position of your Christian faith in your life? I have subdivided this first principle in order to make it more obvious, but it really all comes to this: where exactly does the Christian faith come in my life? Is it only the appendix, or is it right through the whole book? And this is what I see so clearly in the case of this woman. She is an illustration of our Lord's teaching about the rebirth, about being born again. Here is a woman who has been changed entirely.

Of course—and this is the second principle—we must go on to point out that this change is entirely due to the fact that the woman's life is now dominated by our Lord. Until this point she herself has been in control of her life—I mean, in the sense of what she did. She had to do her work; she thought about it and carried it out. She had gone from home with the intention of filling that waterpot again and taking it back and going on with the work in the house. Then she had her pleasure and her unworthy lifestyle. She had her program, and she lived according to it.

But suddenly that program is upset. She leaves her waterpot and does something else. Why? A revolution has taken place; her outlook upon waterpots and everything else has changed completely. What has caused the change? The Lord Jesus Christ himself. This is the great central theme of the New Testament. When we really are in this position to which he would have us come, he determines our lives, he controls them and dominates them in every respect. And this, once more, is the difference between religion and Christianity.

Now in the days of his flesh, our Lord was always making this kind of demand. He would constantly look at a man and say to him, "Follow me." And by that he meant the man had to leave what he was doing. He said, "Follow me" to Peter and Andrew and James and John, fishermen. James and John were with their father, Zebedee, mending their nets, and Simon and Andrew were fishing when suddenly our Lord came and said,

"Follow me." They left Zebedee and the boats and the nets and everything else and went after him (Mark 1:16–20). Matthew was "sitting at the receipt of custom"—that was his job, he was earning his living—when again our Lord said, "Follow me." And Matthew got up and left it all (Matt. 9:9).

Now this was our Lord's demand, and it was always a totalitarian demand. The point I am emphasizing is that following him is not merely a question of taking up his teaching and trying to implement it. He goes beyond that. You and I can take up teachings, and the grave danger is that we may take up the Christian faith in that way, taking it up and then putting it down again, living lives that are exactly the same as everybody else's. That is not what he wants; that is not what he will have. "If any man will come after me, let him deny himself, and take up his cross daily, and follow me" (Luke 9:23). He is the leader, he is the director, he is "the author and finisher of our faith" (Heb. 12:2), and we follow him. He controls our life; he dominates our life. It is obvious that the Samaritan woman's life has now been changed entirely. It is now, "Come, see this man." There will be time for the waterpot; it will find its own place.

There are many illustrations of this principle. We see it perfectly in two other women and the contrast between them—Martha and Mary (Luke 10:38–42). There is Martha, busy with many tasks—coming and going, making food. And there is Mary, sitting at the feet of the Master. Of course, it is important to be hospitable and to prepare food and to be kind and so on, but when he has arrived, there is something more important—you sit at his feet instead of fussing and bothering. "One thing is needful: and Mary hath chosen that good part."

We find the same teaching in the epistles of the great apostle Paul. Look at how he puts it in writing to the Galatians:

> I am crucified with Christ: nevertheless I live; yet not I, but Christ liveth in me: and the life which I now live in the flesh I live by the faith of the Son of God, who loved me, and gave himself for me. (2:20)

And, again, we read the great statement in the first chapter of the Epistle to the Philippians: "To me to live is Christ" (1:21). Paul said in essence, "This is life; this is the essence of life. Christ is not somebody I remember now and again; he is not somebody whose teaching I am trying painfully to put into practice. He is my life; he dominates my life."

Someone once said that Paul was a Christ-intoxicated man. That is a good expression. But the apostle himself has a better way of putting it. He likes to call himself "the bondslave of Jesus Christ" (Rom. 1:1)—the Authorized Version has "a servant," but the Greek word means not only "slave" but "bondslave." "I am not my own," Paul says; he belongs to his Master. In other words, though Paul was a genius, and though as a natural man he was very self-willed, as he makes plain in that bit of autobiography that we read in Philippians 3, the astounding thing that happened to him was that this determined, self-righteous, brilliant man became as a little child, and his whole life was dominated by the Lord Jesus Christ.

Ask yourself for a moment, what governs my life? What is it that determines how I will live this next week? As we answer those questions, we will soon discover, I think, that we have become the victims, the slaves, of habits and customs and duties. Now do not misunderstand this. The woman of Samaria did not leave her waterpot by the well permanently. No, no; life has to go on, and we must live; we have our duties to carry out. All I am saying is that the relative position changes. The waterpot no longer dominates; it does not determine her life.

I am trying to show that the central control of life changes—that Christianity is not something added on, it is not a cloak we put on, it is not a bag that we take up or something that comes and goes spasmodically, but it is "a well of water [within you] springing up into everlasting life" and fructifying everything, making a difference to everything that it controls.

How, then, does this change of control within us show itself? The first way is this: there is a change in our mind and in our outlook and in our thinking. In 1 Corinthians 2:16 the apostle Paul says one of the most amazing things he ever said: "We have the mind of Christ." These words are a climax to the chapter. In verse 15 Paul says, "He that is spiritual judgeth [understands] all things, yet he himself is judged of no man." He has become a problem and an enigma. He is a changed person, and he has an understanding of spiritual things. The natural man does not—Paul has just been saying that (v. 14)—but the spiritual man does: "Who hath known the mind of the Lord, that he may instruct him? But we have the mind of Christ." Now Paul means that the Lord Jesus Christ dominates our thinking, and we no longer think as we used to think or as others do.

First and foremost, of course, this applies to our way of looking at things. You remember how in the Epistle to the Romans the apostle Paul contrasts "they that are after the flesh" and "they that are after the Spirit." This is the fundamental difference. By nature we are all of the flesh, and we think according to the flesh. Let Paul say it:

> They that are after the flesh do mind [think of] the things of the flesh; but they that are after the Spirit the things of the Spirit. For to be carnally minded is death; but to be spiritually minded is life and peace. Because the carnal mind is enmity against God: for it is not subject to the law of God, neither indeed can be. (Rom. 8:5–7)

One of the first things that happens when you become a Christian is a complete change of mind. Paul says we are "renewed in the spirit of your mind" (Eph. 4:23). Now this is a tremendous fact, and it is because of this that the whole life is changed. So we ask ourselves this simple question: do we see everything in a different way from the people in the world? If we are Christians, we should. Again, we see this in the change that took place in the apostle Paul: "But what things were gain to me, those I counted loss for Christ" (Phil. 3:7).

Now you cannot argue with this; it is something that happens. You do not have to force yourself; you do not suddenly put down one set of spectacles, as it were, and put on another. No, no; it is there within you, and it comes out. By nature we are all out for the world, and the world appeals to us. What the world has is so wonderful, it is so marvelous—look at the way people get excited about it all. But Christians find that they are no longer interested. They see the world in a different way. As the apostle James puts it, they see that "whosoever therefore will be a friend of the world is the enemy of God" (Jas. 4:4). And as John in his first epistle says, they know that "all that is in the world, the lust of the flesh, and the lust of the eyes, and the pride of life, is not of the Father, but is of the world" (2:16). And they are amazed to find themselves looking at everything in this new way.

But I am anxious to put it in this form also: this change is not merely a different way of looking at things but is also a considering of all things in terms of the Lord Jesus Christ. Now we sometimes use the word *Christian* in a very loose way, with people talking about Christendom, Christian culture, and so on. I know that in a sense they are right, and there is a kind of Christian philosophy, but using these terms can be a great danger because what you find in the New Testament is not a Christian philosophy but a mind and an outlook dominated by the Lord himself. And that, in turn, means that we view all things in light of the fact of the Lord's coming and of what he has done and where he is and what he is yet going to do; this dominates the whole of our lives and all our thinking. In the life of the woman of Samaria, this shows itself in a big detail—the waterpot and the place of the waterpot in her life, as we have seen—but this is only one illustration.

So we examine ourselves. Do we view all things in the light of the facts that we believe concerning our blessed Lord? How do we react to things that happen? This is a very good test. Christians "set [their] affections on things above, not on things on the earth" (Col. 3:2). And because of that, they develop a relative immunity to the things that happen around them. "His heart is fixed, trusting in the LORD" (Ps. 112:7). They do not become panicky; there is a stability about them. The Lord has opened their eyes. They see through the world; they see it for what it is; they see beyond it. They do not expect too much in this world, and therefore they are not disappointed.

It is only in Christ that we know the truth about this world and all its attendant circumstances. The apostles are constantly pressing this point. In all their writings, they begin by laying down the great doctrine, and then they apply it. We see this in Romans 12:1–2, where Paul says: "I beseech you, therefore, brethren, by the mercies of God, that ye present your bodies a living sacrifice, holy, acceptable unto God, which is your reasonable service. And be not conformed to this world"—that is first, remember, in your thinking—"but be ye transformed by the renewing of your mind, that ye may prove what is that good, and acceptable, and perfect, will of God."

That is it—transformation. The Christian is no longer "conformed to this world."

Now when Paul says, "present your *bodies* a living sacrifice," he does not only refer to the body and what we put on it and what we put in it and what we do with it. Paul's words do include those details but also refer to the whole of our thinking. We are not to be conformed to the world in our political thinking, for instance. We do not get excited about politics if we are Christians. Now I am not denouncing politics. Politics is essential; government is essential. Whether we live in a monarchy or a republic, under a democracy or under some other form of government, does not matter. "The powers that be are ordained of God" (Rom. 13:1). What I am saying is this: Christians do not pin their faith to it, and they are not disappointed when things go wrong. They know that this is a world of sin. They understand the problems of their country as nobody else does. It is not a question of a quarrel between the one party and another. Both parties have the same problem, which is that nobody believes in work, and everybody is out for pleasure, whether employer or employee. They have other interests, and money is just a means for them to get their pleasure. Nobody wants to work, but each, of course, blames the other for not working.

Christians see through both sides of the argument, and they know that all our fundamental problems are due to the fact that men and women are selfish in sin, they are lawless, they are disobedient. Ah, yes, you can get excited, perhaps, if you hold a certain set of views about the lawlessness of the trade unions, but what about the lawlessness of the whole of humanity before God? It is the same type of sin but to an infinitely worse degree; that is the only difference. How easily we condemn others! Christians see life in its totality; they see everything in the light of this blessed Lord who has come into the world. And he came because the world was in such a rotten condition, such a desperate plight, that nothing else and no one else could possibly save it. He came "to seek and to save that which was lost" (Luke 19:10).

Christians see all that; they are not "conformed" to the world in any sense whatsoever. As Paul puts it in Ephesians 4, "Ye henceforth walk not as other Gentiles walk, in the vanity of their mind, having the understanding darkened" (vv. 17–18). They used to be like that, but they are no longer: "Ye have not so learned Christ; if so be that ye have heard him" (vv. 20–21). He says in effect, "I am beginning to be doubtful about you—the way you think, the way you speak, the way you live. Have you really heard and begun to follow Christ? Have you really learned from him?" This is a complete change in the mind.

But I want to show you there is also a complete change in our interests. This is very clear in the case of this woman, is it not? What a change! Waterpot, family, all that she had to do, the drudgery of domestic duties had dominated her life and her sinful manner of living, but now she leaves her waterpot, goes to the city, and brings the men back with her. Why? Her interest now is in Jesus; he is what matters. The rest can wait. A modern phrase puts it so well: What are your priorities? Is Jesus always first? Does he dominate everything else? To the Christian he is the main interest in life!

This shows itself in many ways. Look at what we are told about the very first converts in Jerusalem on the Day of Pentecost. Here are people who have known many a previous Day of Pentecost, and here comes another—of course, an important festival. But they have no idea what is going to happen to them. They are a part of the mob, the crowd that had cried a few weeks before concerning our blessed Lord, "Away with him!

Crucify him!" But now they suddenly hear a great commotion. Something has happened to the men who used to follow Jesus. They are standing up, and one of them is preaching. The people begin to listen, and as they listen they are convicted, for the speaker tells them that they have crucified the Son of God, that they, by wicked hands and through wicked men, have crucified the Lord of glory, and that they and their rulers are guilty of the most terrible crime, the greatest enormity ever committed by humanity. And suddenly they are convicted of this, and they see it, and they cry out, "Men and brethren, what shall we do?" They are given the answer, and they are entirely changed. Three thousand of them!

And what do they do? Immediately they do the very thing that this woman did: they give evidence that their whole life has been changed. There is a new evaluation of everything; there is a new orientation; there is a difference in the center.

> They continued stedfastly in the apostles' doctrine and fellowship, and in breaking of bread, and in prayers. . . . And they, *continuing daily*, with one accord in the temple and breaking bread from house to house, did eat their meat with gladness and singleness of heart. (Acts 2:42, 46)

This was the big thing in their lives. They did not think they had done wonderfully if they went to church once every Sunday or perhaps once a month; they did not have to be driven and cajoled. Nothing could keep them away, it was the one dominating interest, and it governed everything. This is Christianity.

Look at the great apostle Paul—what a revolution! The old things had become "dung" (Phil. 3:8), and what was his desire? "That I may know him, and the power of his resurrection, and the fellowship of his sufferings" (Phil. 3:10). Paul was a very busy man, remember—traveling, preaching, organizing churches, working with his own hands as a tentmaker—never did a man work harder. But his was the dominating desire: "that I may know him." This is the Christian's saving interest. Or to put it negatively, the Christian is unlike Demas, who "loved this present world" more than the Lord and all who belonged to him and his kingdom (2 Tim. 4:10).

And then in exactly the same way, there is also a change in the realm of the will. The will is dominated by our Lord. Your relationship with him is such that the will is won over. You do not have to force yourself to live the Christian life; it is what you desire to do and enjoy doing. Again look at the apostle Paul in his very conversion on the road to Damascus. One of the first things he says is, "Lord, what wilt thou have me to do?" (Acts 9:6). Until then he had made the decisions. "I verily thought with myself, that I ought to do many things contrary to the name of Jesus of Nazareth" (Acts 26:9). It was he who decided to go down from Jerusalem to Damascus. He was in control; he ruled his own will. But then, "Lord, what wilt thou have me to do?" He was almost afraid to do anything. He had made such tragic mistakes; he wanted to know his Lord's will.

Thy way, not mine, O Lord,
However dark it be!

Horatius Bonar

And, finally, there is a complete revolution also in the realm of the heart and of the feelings. Do you not see it in the case of this woman? See her rushing off to the city. That is not performing a duty, is it? That is not mechanically saying that you are a Christian. No, no; quite the opposite. Can you not picture her? Can you not see the animation in her face? Can you not hear the excitement in her voice? I do not see how anyone can be a Christian without being thrilled. There is a passion; there is feeling. You cannot really believe in the Lord Jesus Christ without any movement of your heart.

If our hearts are not moved, my dear friends, are we Christians at all? This idea that our Christianity is a duty, this being rather pleased with ourselves when we have not done some things and when we have done others, is almost a contradiction of Christianity. If you are not moved and thrilled, if knowing him and belonging to him is not to you the most wonderful thing on earth and the most wonderful thing in heaven, you had better examine yourself again. I have often quoted that statement of Count Zinzendorf: "I have one passion! It is he and he alone!"

May God give us such a knowledge of him that we shall be able to say the same thing honestly. The mind, the interest, the understanding and will, the heart, the passion are all captivated by him.

O Jesus Christ, grow thou in me,
And all things else recede!

Johann C. Lavater; trans. Elizabeth L. Smith
("O Jesus Christ, Grow Thou in Me")

46

A Living Communion

The woman then left her waterpot, and went her way into the city, and saith to the men, Come, see a man, which told me all things that ever I did: is not this the Christ? (John 4:28–29)

The true Christian, we have seen, is "the bondslave of Jesus Christ." We have looked at this in general and have shown that he dominates us in mind and heart and will. But now we must take this a step further because over and above this general influence that he exerts is the fact of our Lord himself, the realization of his presence and of his nearness and of his companionship. In other words, I am anxious to show that the relationship between Christian believers and their Lord is not confined to a general influence but goes beyond that. There is, indeed, a personal relationship, and the life of the Christian is a life that is lived in his presence, a life of companionship and of fellowship with him.

This is very obvious in the case of the woman of Samaria. Christians are not merely those who believe a number of correct things about this person who lived two thousand years ago and now belongs to history. Christians do not merely believe in the truths that are derived from the account of what that person said and did. They do, of course, believe in the historical person of Jesus of Nazareth, whom they believe to be the Son of God. He belongs to history. But Christians do not merely believe in him as someone who once acted in this world but who has ceased to do so except that there is some kind of continuing general influence through the activity of the Spirit.

Far too often people's idea of Christianity is that you take this body of truth, these propositions, concerning the Lord Jesus Christ and accept them and now do your utmost to live according to them, praying to God for strength and help. But I want to show you that this is a quite inadequate idea of the Christian life. Indeed, it can even be false because the very essence of the Christian position is that it is a life that is lived with him, in the consciousness of his presence.

Let us approach this whole matter by asking, is what I have just said really possible at the present time? In other words, is it in your mind to say something like this: "Of course, I can understand the case of the woman of Samaria. At that time our Lord was actually in the world, and she was in direct, personal contact with him. She could look into his face; she could hear his actual words. But that is no longer possible—he is no longer in this world." Have you ever thought that? Have you not sometimes had this kind of feeling and wished you had been alive at that time? You have said to yourself, "If only I could see him, if only I could literally meet him, then, of course, all my problems would disappear immediately—there would be no difficulties left. If only! But we don't see him—he's no longer here." And therefore one has a feeling that then was the glorious time, and somehow we are now at a disadvantage.

This is a very common attitude, and it is a most serious cause of trouble in the Christian church at the present time; and when I say *Christian* church I am referring particularly to those who do still believe the truth. There are those who do not believe in the deity of Christ—I am not concerned about them, they are not Christians. They call themselves Christians, many of them, and they may be members of a church, but that does not make them Christians. I am talking about people who really do believe the correct truths concerning the Son of God. I am talking about those who believe the Bible as the Word of God and who are orthodox in every possible respect. Often the most serious cause of trouble for such people is this very tendency to say that the experiences people had of our Lord in the New Testament were only for the people who lived then. Or they may go further and include the period of the apostles, but since that time is now over and since we have the written Word of God, the position is now quite different.

Here is obviously a very serious matter. You are familiar, I am sure, with this very common position. That is what I would call turning Christianity into religion; it is something that excludes the subjective element, something that, in a way, excludes the heart and the feelings and the emotion. I was recently reading an article by a well-known evangelical writer who quite deliberately said that assurance of salvation has nothing to do with feelings. Assurance of salvation, he said, consists entirely of "believing the statements of the Scriptures." It is not a matter of emotion, not a matter of the sensibilities; it is simply believing the Scriptures.

Today this is the commonly held view of assurance of salvation. If you go to people who hold this view and say, "I'm not quite happy about my salvation," they will say, "Well, it's quite simple; listen . . ." Then they will take you to a chapter such as the third chapter of the Gospel according to John, and read, "God so loved the world, that he gave his only begotten Son, that whosoever believeth in him should not perish, but have everlasting life. For God sent not his Son into the world to condemn the world; but that the world through him might be saved. He that believeth on him is not condemned: but he that believeth not is condemned already" (John 3:16–18).

Then they say, "Do you believe in him?"

You reply, "Yes, I do believe."

"Very well," they say, "don't worry about your feelings—just believe in him. We're told here that 'he that believeth on him is not condemned.' What more do you want?"

And that, they say, is the totality of assurance. I agree, of course, that accepting the statement of the Scripture is the beginning of assurance, but I am here to suggest as strongly as I can, by the aid of the Spirit and under the power of the Spirit, that this is the lowest level of assurance and that there is a higher form, which includes the sensibilities and the feelings and which is direct and immediate.

I use that simply as an illustration of the whole modern tendency. The position I am depicting is the commonly held view that there is no consciousness of the Lord himself, that there are no direct dealings with him, that he does not deal with us intimately and directly as he did with the woman of Samaria and others in the Scriptures. Since he is no longer in the world, all that has finished.

Now I say again that this is obviously a very serious matter, and to me it involves, in many ways, the very essence of the Christian faith. I am certain that the main trouble with the Christian church today is that it tends to be dominated by that kind of thinking, and that is why we do not experience revival, that is why the church counts for so little in the modern world, and that is why the position today is such a contrast to the New Testament itself and to what has invariably been the case in all periods of reformation and of revival. We really must examine this, therefore, because if we are bypassing what the Scriptures teach on this subject, we obviously will continue exactly as we are, and we shall never know much about this "well of water springing up into everlasting life."

But why do I say that this kind of attitude is entirely wrong? There are a number of reasons. First of all, I would suggest that it involves a misunderstanding of salvation itself. What is salvation? My answer would be that salvation is not merely accepting a number of propositions, however right and true they may be. Salvation does not consist in accepting teaching. I realize that everything I am saying is liable to misunderstanding. Obviously, salvation includes believing these propositions, but what I am asserting is, that is not salvation. The essence of salvation is a relationship to God through our Lord Jesus Christ and coming to know him as our Father. Man was originally made, as you know, in the image and likeness of God, and he had companionship with God, he had fellowship with him. But sin broke that fellowship. Salvation, therefore, obviously, by definition, restores the fellowship.

Now fellowship does not just mean believing that God is and that certain other things are true about him. Fellowship means communion, it means communication, it means entering into a personal relationship. So the terrible possibility is that you can subscribe to a number of perfectly orthodox propositions and yet, because you have not entered into this fellowship, not be a true Christian.

Often evangelism itself causes this misunderstanding, does it not? You are presented with a number of propositions: Do you believe this? Do you accept that?

You say, "Yes!"

All right!

But is it all right? That is the great question. It seems to me that at this point we are tending to forget the whole doctrine of regeneration and the new birth. You have to believe the truth, you have to believe the propositions, but I say again that is not salvation.

Or let me put it like this: what is the real purpose of the Scriptures? I think this will bring us to the heart of the matter. The answer is that the Scriptures in and of themselves are not salvation. What saves us is not so much that we believe the Scriptures as that we believe what the Scriptures say concerning Jesus Christ. Do you see the distinction? It is possible for us to be interested in the Scriptures, it is possible for us even to defend them, it is possible for us to defend the particular propositions of the Scriptures, while remaining purely intellectual. We can study the Scriptures exactly as we take up any other subject—geometry, science, or whatever. We can take hold of the biblical principles and believe them and accept them, but if we stop at that, it is not true Christianity, and indeed we are misusing the Scriptures. We must not stop with the Scriptures. They are the means of bringing us to him.

Now let me prove this to you. I can do so quite simply. Take this modern teaching that we have just considered that tells us we must not consider our feelings when looking for assurance but must simply accept what we find in the Word of God. Well, then, all I ask is this: how did the early Christians have assurance of salvation since they did not have the Scriptures? Jews had the Old Testament, but Gentiles did not even have that. There were no Gospels, no book of Acts, none of the epistles. How did the first believers have assurance of salvation if assurance of salvation is simply taking the Word and accepting what it says without feeling anything at all? That was not possible, and yet they had a great and glorious assurance. So you see the contradiction in the position.

Someone may think that I am now setting the Scriptures aside. They may say, "You are maintaining that the first Christians did not have the Scriptures but had these marvelous experiences. Are you not suggesting, therefore, that we do not need the Scriptures at all but should try to recapture what the early Christians had?" That, of course, is a very serious error. It is the error into which the Quakers fell and into which many of the mystics have fallen. But I am not saying that. The Scriptures have a very definite and a very real function and purpose.

There are two extremes here—those who are bound only to the Scriptures and who simply accept scriptural statements without their feelings being involved and those who say we do not need the Scriptures at all. Both are wrong. The true position is to say, the Word is essential—that is why it has been given. The Scriptures are essential because their purpose, finally, is to strengthen our faith. In the early church, there were false teachers who were querying and questioning many aspects of the truth, such as the truth about our Lord's deity and the truth of the Incarnation. So one of the reasons for the Gospels was—as John tells us in this very Gospel—to let us know "that Jesus is the Christ, the Son of God" (20:31). Strengthening faith—that is one of the functions of the Scriptures. Another function, of course, is to instruct us and to lead us on. The apostles did that while they were alive and wrote their teaching down under divine inspiration in order to give us greater knowledge. Not only that, the Scriptures are given to us in order that we may check our experiences, in order that we may be safeguarded against heresy and against various forms of false teaching that can lead us into grievous error and trouble.

Now those are the main functions of the Scriptures. They have been given to establish us, to teach us, to lead us on, to safeguard us, to give us checks, helps, and aids, and so to make us perfect and complete. But salvation is possible without the Scriptures, as we see in the case of the first Christians. So we must not say that it is all in the Scriptures exclusively and entirely. We must not exalt the Scriptures into the supreme position. We must never say that the truth about Christian people is that they believe the Scriptures. You do not stop at that. They believe the Scriptures only in the sense that they help them to come to a belief in the Lord of the Scriptures, in the Lord Jesus Christ himself. The Scriptures per se do not save us, but they tell us of the one who does save us.

Another argument, therefore, that I can adduce, is that if the Scriptures are really only describing the Christian life as it could be lived in the first century, then they are very misleading. If they are all I have, and I am told, "Ah, you must not expect that now—that was only true while he was here or while the apostles were still alive," then I ask, what is the value of the New Testament to me as a whole? What is the value of an incident such as our Lord's meeting with the woman of Samaria? What is the value of the history of the book of the Acts of the Apostles? What is the value of the teaching of the epistles? If I am to be told that I must not expect it all to be true for me now, that means that the New Testament is always exhorting us to a level of life unto which we cannot attain, and that surely would discourage us and be utterly unfair to us.

Or, finally, if this attitude toward salvation and toward the Scriptures is true, then it seems to me that we must say that the people in the Old Testament dispensation were in a superior position to us, because in the Old Testament God dealt directly with men and women and spoke to them, as we see in the experiences of the psalmists and David and others. And, of course, many Christians are honest enough to admit that. Many are ready to confess they are on a lower level than the psalmists. They have not had the experience of those men, who could say, "When my father and my mother forsake me, then the LORD will take me up" (Ps. 27:10). They have to confess that they do not know much about that.

Now that is quite inevitable according to this teaching that I am criticizing, but it is hopelessly and entirely wrong. The Christian is in a superior position to all the saints of the Old Testament. Our Lord himself said concerning John the Baptist, the last of those great prophetic figures of the Old Testament dispensation, that while it was true to say that "Among them that are born of women there hath not risen a greater than John the Baptist: notwithstanding he that is least in the kingdom of heaven is greater than he" (Matt. 11:11). Any teaching that makes you feel that the Old Testament saints were in a superior position to you or had an advantage over you is of necessity a false teaching.

There, then, are some general considerations to show you the fallacy of this modern teaching that tends to represent the Christian as someone who simply accepts New Testament statements and propositions without of necessity feeling anything at all. But I want to go further—it is a blank contradiction of our Lord's own teaching, and this is what we are particularly concerned about as we study John 4. Let us never forget that our Lord said that he had come to give us life. Life! He did not merely come to give us a teaching that would satisfy us in certain respects, but he came that we might have life, and that we might have it "more abundantly" (John 10:10).

Now life, as we have been seeing, includes every part of us. Life does not merely satisfy the intellect and make us live solely in terms of our understanding. No, no; it takes up the entire person, the totality of our being. This is of necessity true, by definition. But take some of the specific statements that are found in John 14. "Let not your heart be troubled" (v. 1). Why did our Lord say that? He said it because he had just told the disciples that he was about to leave them:

> Now is the Son of man glorified, and God is glorified in him. . . . Little children, yet a little while I am with you. Ye shall seek me: and as I said unto the Jews, Whither I go, ye cannot come; so now I say to you . . . (John 13:31, 33)

Peter as usual acted as spokesman:

> Simon Peter said unto him, Lord, whither goest thou? Jesus answered him, Whither I go, thou canst not follow me now; but thou shalt follow me afterwards. (John 13:36)

That was why they were utterly cast down—their Lord was telling them that he was on the verge of leaving them. But this was his response: "Let not your heart be troubled: ye believe in God, believe also in me. In my Father's house are many mansions. . . ."

The whole of chapter 14 is devoted to this theme. This is what our Lord keeps saying. "I will not leave you comfortless: I will come to you." Here is one who has just said that he is going to leave them: "Yet a little while, and the world seeth me no more; but ye see me: because I live, ye shall live also" (vv. 18–19).

These words of our Lord do not only refer to the resurrection; that is included, but they go beyond that. Later in this chapter, our Lord puts it quite plainly:

> He that hath my commandments, and keepeth them, he it is that loveth me: and he that loveth me shall be loved of my Father, and I will love him, and will manifest myself to him. (v. 21)

This does not simply refer to the forty days of our Lord's resurrection appearances. This is permanent. This is the Christian life as it is going to be lived; and the great emphasis is, "I will not leave you comfortless: I will come to you." Our Lord is going to manifest himself, of course, in a different way, but the point that he constantly emphasizes is that they have nothing about which to be downcast. This is not the end of that marvelous period when he was with them. But that is the tendency of this teaching that is so popular. "If only we had been alive then!" No, no; our Lord says. "Do not be comfortless."

And in the sixteenth chapter he goes even further:

> But these things have I told you, that when the time shall come, ye may remember that I told you of them. And these things I said not unto you at the beginning, because I was with you. But now I go my way to him that sent me; and none of you asketh me, Whither goest thou? But because I have said these things unto you, sorrow hath filled your heart. Nevertheless I tell you the truth; It is expedient for you that I go away [could anything be clearer? It is a good thing for you; it is to your advantage; it is "expedient" for you that I go away]: for if I go not away, the Comforter will not come unto you; but if I depart, I will send him unto you. (John 16:4–7)

And, indeed, our Lord goes further and tells his disciples that far from weeping, they ought to be rejoicing in this:

> Ye have heard how I said unto you, I go away, and come again unto you. If ye loved me, ye would rejoice, because I said, I go unto the Father: for my Father is greater than I. (John 14:28)

Now all this teaching fits in together, and what it really means is this: our Lord is saying to these men in effect, "I have been with you for three years, and during this time I have shown you what is possible for you. But you are going to experience much greater and bigger things." This is astounding! He looks forward to the future after he has departed and after he has sent the Holy Spirit. That is what he is dealing with in John 14, 15, and 16. He is saying in effect, "Do not be mournful. You ought to rejoice because it means I am going to my Father, and he will give me the gift of the Spirit, and I will send him upon you. What has been happening now while I am here is nothing in comparison with what will happen then." He even says that they ought to believe him because of his very works:

> Believe me that I am in the Father, and the Father in me: or else believe me for the very works' sake. Verily, verily, I say unto you, He that believeth on me, the works that I do shall he do also; and greater works than these shall he do; because I go unto my Father. (John 14:11–12)

In other words, in the Gospels we are just given illustrations in a very human, practical form of something much greater that will happen after Christ has returned to the glory. So what he is able to give to the woman of Samaria in the days of his flesh, he is able to give us, but in a greater manner. Let me give you another statement of his on this same theme of the Holy Spirit:

> In the last day, that great day of the feast, Jesus stood and cried, saying, If any man thirst, let him come unto me, and drink. He that believeth on me, as the scripture hath said, out of his belly shall flow rivers of living water.

And then John explains: "(But this spake he of the Spirit, which they that believe on him should receive: for the Holy Ghost was not yet given; because that Jesus was not yet glorified)" (John 7:37–38).

The teaching is exactly the same both here and in the fourteenth, fifteenth, and sixteenth chapters of John's Gospel. Our Lord says, "It is expedient for you that I go away." It is better for Christians that he should not be here in the flesh, but that he should be dealing with us as he now deals with us. Not only is our position not inferior to those who were alive in the days of his flesh, it is superior.

And then go on to the seventeenth chapter of John: "This is life eternal, that they might know thee the only true God, and Jesus Christ, whom thou hast sent" (v. 3). What a statement! But to "know the only true God, and Jesus Christ" does not mean "accept the propositions concerning him." He does not say that eternal life consists in knowing *about* God. Many people know about God but are not Christians. The Jews know about God. You can know about God as Creator; you can know the teaching of the Scriptures about God. You can accept all the theology, all the propositions, but that is not what our Lord is talking about. Adam knew him, but Adam sinned and lost that knowledge, and man has lost the knowledge ever since. The restoration that salvation brings is not a mere knowledge about God—"The devils also believe, and tremble," as James tells us (Jas. 2:19)—but it is to know God. The knowledge we have lost is thus restored, and it is a knowledge of communion and of fellowship. There is an intimacy, there is a personal quality; we must never detract from this.

And then, to clinch the whole thing as it were, we have those famous words that our Lord uttered to doubting Thomas, Thomas who could not believe the testimony of his fellow apostles that the Lord really had risen. Our Lord had appeared to them when they were gathered together, but Thomas had not been there. And Thomas had said very stubbornly, "Except I shall see in his hands the print of the nails, and put my finger into the print of the nails, and thrust my hand into his side, I will not believe." This is how John's Gospel continues:

> And after eight days again his disciples were within, and Thomas with them: then came Jesus, the doors being shut, and stood in the midst, and said, Peace be unto you. Then saith he to Thomas, Reach hither thy finger, and behold my hands; and reach hither thy hand, and thrust it into my side: and be not faithless, but believing. And Thomas answered and said unto him, My Lord and my God. Jesus saith unto him, Thomas, because thou hast seen me, thou hast believed: blessed are they that have not seen, and yet have believed." (John 20:25–29)

That is a rebuke, and I feel it is a rebuke that comes to many of us who tend to say the same sort of thing, but we put it like this: "If only I had been alive then. If only I could have seen him." As if the manifestations of the Son of God were confined solely to his days on earth.

So there it is in the plain teaching of our Lord himself. To say that the Christian simply lives on believing and accepting intellectually the statements and the propositions of the Scriptures is a denial of our Lord's own teaching. To exclude the feelings, the emotions, the whole person, the sense of personal relationship is to deny his own teaching.

And it also denies the teaching of the book of the Acts of the Apostles.

Do you not see, as you read through that book, that those people were living a life in conscious communion with the Lord? They were not living on memories; they were not living simply on what he had taught them. In the fourth chapter, we read that they are in trouble, and we find them praying. They pray to God directly, and God answers them directly: "When they had prayed, the place was shaken." These people were not holding on to propositions only. Many were doing that, of course, but they wanted more than that, they wanted some demonstration, and they asked for it and got it:

> And when they had prayed, the place was shaken where they were assembled together; and they were all filled with the Holy Ghost, and they spake the word of God with boldness. . . . And with great power gave the apostles witness of the resurrection of the Lord Jesus: and great grace was upon them all. (Acts 4:31, 33)

The apostles, you see, did not merely make an intellectual statement, putting forward the propositions concerning Jesus Christ and what they had heard him say and how they had seen him crucified and how he had been buried and how they had seen him risen. They did that, but what is emphasized is the power, the authority, the might of the Spirit upon them. The certainty, the absoluteness—this is what is stressed. And this, of course, is what we find running right through the whole book of Acts. Take, for instance, the story of that man Stephen, who became the first martyr. This is the description we are given when he was brought before the court: "And all that sat in the council, looking stedfastly on him, saw his face as it had been the face of an angel" (6:15).

This had happened to Moses after he had spent forty days with God on Mount Sinai. He had been in a living, vital communion with God, and his face was shining when he came down. Stephen, too, was in the realm of the Spirit, and his face was shining like that of an angel. But do you remember the end of the story? At the end of Acts 7, where we read about the martyrdom of Stephen, we are told:

> But he, being full of the Holy Ghost, looked up stedfastly into heaven, and saw the glory of God, and Jesus standing on the right hand of God, and said, Behold, I see the heavens opened, and the Son of man standing on the right hand of God. (vv. 55–56)

Now Stephen was not merely bearing witness to a number of propositions that he had believed. He was seeing the risen Lord in some manner or other. This happened after our Lord had gone back to heaven. It was real, it was living, and it was vital. So he was able to die "calling upon God, and saying, Lord Jesus, receive my spirit" (v. 59).

Now I am simply quoting these passages to you to show you that these people expected that kind of thing. I shall deal with this later, God willing, lest anyone misunderstand what I am saying. For now I am simply giving you the evidence, I am simply breaking down this notion that all we can do today is live by faith in propositions, that we are left to that and cannot expect a living communion such as the woman of Samaria had. I am simply breaking down that erroneous, crippling teaching by giving you scriptural evidence.

These people did not live on propositions—there was a living communion. Listen to the beginning of the thirteenth chapter of Acts: "As they ministered to the Lord, and fasted, the Holy Ghost said, Separate me Barnabas and Saul for the work whereunto I have called them" (v. 2). How did he say that? They did not have these Scriptures. He spoke directly. The Holy Spirit does speak directly. He deals with us. Christians are not merely trying to live on and implement the propositions they have believed concerning the Lord Jesus Christ. I say again, there is a living communion with the Holy Spirit—"the communion of the Holy Ghost" (2 Cor. 13:14) and the communion with the Son and the communion with the Father.

We see this again in Acts 15. The council of Christians at Jerusalem sent a letter to the churches, and this is how they put it: "It seemed good to the Holy Ghost, and to us" (v. 28). They knew that it seemed good to the Holy Ghost because he had told them so. This is a living relationship. In Acts 16, too, it is the same:

> Now when they had gone throughout Phrygia and the region of Galatia, and were forbidden of the Holy Ghost to preach the word in Asia, after they were come to Mysia, they assayed to go into Bithynia: but the Spirit suffered them not. (vv. 6–7)

This is the direct, immediate guidance of the Spirit, and if you are denying this, you are robbing yourself of a living fellowship with the blessed Persons in the Holy Trinity. You are robbing yourself of this "well of water springing up into everlasting life." Listen to this again in Acts 18. Paul is in trouble at Corinth and has great opposition, but we read in the ninth verse, "Then spake the Lord to Paul in the night by a vision, Be not afraid, but speak, and hold not thy peace."

My friends, this is direct dealing with human beings by the living, risen Lord. He has not ceased to do this. Another example—to complete this evidence for you—is in Acts 22. Paul is giving his defense and he says, "And it came to pass, that, when I was come again to Jerusalem, even while I prayed in the temple, I was in a trance; and saw him saying unto me"—Paul saw this blessed Lord saying to him—"Make haste, and get thee quickly out of Jerusalem: for they will not receive thy testimony concerning me" (vv. 17–18).

And again in Acts 23:

> The night following the Lord stood by him, and said, Be of good cheer, Paul: for as thou hast testified of me in Jerusalem, so must thou bear witness also at Rome. (vv. 11)

Our Lord ministered to the woman of Samaria in the days of his flesh, and he does so still, and we must not rob ourselves of the glorious benefits and blessing and privilege of his ministrations. "A well of water springing up into everlasting life"—it is through that life that we have fellowship and communion with him.

47

Joy beyond Words

The woman then left her waterpot, and went her way into the city, and saith to the men, Come, see a man, which told me all things that ever I did: is not this the Christ? (John 4:28–29)

The Christian, as we have seen, is not only someone who believes in the Lord Jesus Christ as a man who lived nearly two thousand years ago, who gave incomparable teaching, who died and rose again, and who outlined a way of life for us. Christians believe that, but they do not stop there. They believe their salvation is the result of the death of the Lord Jesus Christ, and over and above that, they believe they are meant to enjoy fellowship, communion, with him—they believe they meet with him.

We have been dealing with this tremendously important matter. Many people shut out a living, real experience of our Lord and try to argue that obviously this cannot happen now but belongs only to the days of his flesh. Many are afraid of enthusiasm, they are afraid of ecstasy, they are afraid of excesses; and they are so afraid of these things that they have reduced the Christian faith and the Christian experience merely to an intellectual acceptance of a number of propositions. We have seen that this view is utterly wrong and contradicts the plain teaching of the Scripture itself. I have adduced words from our Lord's own lips to prove this and have quoted from the book of the Acts of the Apostles to show how, after our Lord's death and resurrection and ascension, he still continued to manifest himself to people, as he had said he would.

It is tremendously important that we realize what the Scriptures really do teach us. So I would now like to show you further evidence from the epistles. We have many examples of this teaching—I am simply picking out one or two that show it very clearly. Take, for instance, the apostle Paul's words about himself in 2 Corinthians 12:

> It is not expedient for me doubtless to glory. I will come to visions and revelations of the Lord. I knew a man in Christ above fourteen years ago, (whether in the body, I cannot tell; or whether out of the body, I cannot tell: God knoweth;) such an one caught up to the third heaven. And I knew such a man, (whether in the body, or out of the body, I cannot tell: God knoweth;) How that he was caught up into paradise, and heard unspeakable words, which it is not lawful for a man to utter. Of such an one will I glory: yet of myself I will not glory, but in mine infirmities. (vv. 1–5)

The apostle is there relating an experience that had happened to him fourteen years earlier. He confesses he does not quite understand it, "whether in the body, or out of the body," but what he does know is the reality of the experience. It was a manifestation of the Son of God. He calls it "revelations of the Lord," and he was lifted up into the third heaven. That was an experience given to the apostle long after the ascension of our blessed Lord and Savior, and it is in line with his experiences that are recorded in the book of Acts. He puts this in a more didactic form in the Epistle to the Philippians, where he describes his supreme ambition: ". . . that I may know him, and the power of his resurrection, and the fellowship of his sufferings, being made conformable unto his death" (3:10).

Now the important expression there is, "that I may know him," and that clearly does not mean to know *about* him because the apostle already had that knowledge in great fullness and was a teacher and an apostle. All the authorities are agreed that it cannot be reduced to anything less than personal knowledge, intimate knowledge, direct communion. The apostle is there expressing his desire that over and above all the direct and immediate knowledge that he had, he might have yet more. That was his greatest desire, the greatest longing of his heart. He had had these experiences, and because of that he desired to have more. And so you find him saying in his very last letter, the Second Epistle to Timothy, where he is giving an account of what had happened to him in his trial, "At my first answer no man stood with me, but all men forsook me: I pray God that it may not be laid to their charge. Notwithstanding the Lord stood with me, and strengthened me" (4:16–17).

Paul is conscious of the Lord's presence. He is not making a general statement that he was given strength and power but goes beyond that: "The Lord stood with me." At this trial no men had stood with him; as far as his accusers were concerned, Paul was standing alone. But he was aware in the dock that the Lord was standing by him. This was real to him; it was living. There are other examples as well. I am only selecting a few out of the writings of the apostle Paul.

And it is the same with all the other apostles. The apostle Peter has exactly the same teaching. I have often quoted the next verse because I have always regarded it as the greatest challenge to all Christian people. This is Christianity. Peter is writing to a number of people whom he has never seen and does not know. He can only address them as "strangers scattered throughout Pontus, Galatia, Cappadocia, Asia, and Bithynia" (1 Pet. 1:1). But what he does know is that they are passing through a great trial. He says:

> Wherein ye greatly rejoice, though now for a season, if need be, ye are in heaviness through manifold temptations: that the trial of your faith, being much more precious than of gold that perisheth, though it be tried with fire, might be found unto praise and honour and glory at the appearing of Jesus Christ: whom having not seen, ye love; in whom, though now ye see him not, yet believing, ye rejoice with joy unspeakable and full of glory. (1 Pet. 1:6–8)

Now Peter is not writing, let me remind you, to apostles but to people we may term ordinary Christians. You know what I mean by that—no Christian is ordinary, but there are differences between Christians. These people are not officers, they are not apostles or leaders in the church, and he says that they rejoice in Christ with a joy that is "unspeakable," and even more, this joy of theirs has something of the glory of heaven itself—"full of glory."

That is Christianity. It is not merely that you deduce from the Scriptures that you are saved—"Whosoever believeth is not condemned"—I believe and therefore I am not condemned, an intellectual acknowledgment and that is it. No, no! It is that you know a joy that is beyond words; it cannot be expressed. The apostle Paul said the same of the words he heard in his vision (2 Cor. 12:4). Though the Christians to whom Peter is writing are passing through "manifold temptations" or trials, they have a joy that is "unspeakable and full of glory." This same joy is meant for us and is possible for us. That is the teaching. And you and I have no business to be content with anything less. This is another way of putting the statements in John about never thirsting again and the "well of water springing up into everlasting life."

Or take it as the apostle John expresses it: "These things write we unto you, that your joy may be full" (1 John 1:4). What are "these things"? They are "that which we have seen and heard." John says that these "declare we unto you"—what for?—"that ye also may have fellowship with us: and truly our fellowship is with the Father, and with his Son Jesus Christ" (v. 3). Now the words that are really important there are, "that ye also may *have fellowship* with us." Have you ever realized what that means? Some grammarians, those people who are interested in the Scripture from the standpoint of words and exact meanings, say this is an extremely strong expression and denotes enjoyment and the realization of fellowship as compared with the mere fact of fellowship. In other words, John is not merely concerned to let his readers know that because they are believers, they have fellowship with the apostles and in turn, therefore, with the Father and the Son. No; he says in essence, "I am writing in order that you may have the enjoyment and the realization of this fellowship that is with the Father and with his Son Jesus Christ."

Now there again is something that I must emphasize. John does not say, "and truly our fellowship is with the Father and Jesus Christ his Son." He goes out of his way to say, "our fellowship is with the Father, and with his Son Jesus Christ." They have fellowship with the Father, they have fellowship with the Son, they have fellowship with the Holy Spirit—distinct and separate. This is not merely something of which you say, "Oh, of course, this must be true of us because we are Christians." I am emphasizing this because I know how glib we are in our thinking and in our speaking. We slide over these momentous, profound statements and miss the glory and the experience of them. John would not have written this letter merely to tell his readers that because they are Christians, they have fellowship with the Father and with the Son. He is saying, "I am writing that you may have the enjoyment and the realization of this." Not the fact, but beyond it. So he adds, "These things write we unto you, that your joy may be full" (v. 4). This is the plain teaching, you see, of the First Epistle of John, and the whole object of that entire epistle is really just to bring out that teaching.

Then we turn to the last book of the Bible, the book of Revelation, and we know its message from its very title, do we not? It is a book of revelations—not mere teaching but beyond teaching, revelations given to John. Read that book again for yourselves, and be especially careful about reading the introduction where John is quite plain and clear about what has happened to him: "The Revelation of Jesus Christ, which God gave unto him, to shew unto his servants things which must shortly come to pass," and so on. And then John goes on to say how this revelation, this manifestation of the Son of God, came to him:

> I John, who also am your brother, and companion in tribulation, and in the kingdom and patience of Jesus Christ, was in the isle that is called Patmos, for the word of God, and for the testimony of Jesus Christ. I was in the Spirit on the Lord's day, and heard behind me a great voice, as of a trumpet, saying, I am Alpha and Omega, the first and the last: and, What thou seest, write in a book. . . . And I turned to see the voice that spake with me. (Rev. 1:9–12)

John goes on to give an account of the vision. But I want to emphasize in particular verse 20 of chapter 3 of Revelation: "Behold, I stand at the door and knock: if any man hear my voice, and open the door, I will come in to him, and will sup with him, and he with me." Do not forget that this was written to church members, to Christian believers, and our Lord is saying that over and above the fact that they are Christians, he is prepared to enter in, to sup with them and have this intimate fellowship and communion.

There, then, is the evidence of the Scriptures. But people say in reply, "Yes, that's quite true. But all that came to an end with the death of the apostles. That is how God dealt with his people until the Scriptures were written, but after the Scriptures had been given, that sort of thing was not needed any longer. As Christians, we are to live on the Scriptures." This means that all the passages that I have been referring to are not for us, and we should not expect the experiences they describe—indeed, it is wrong for us to expect them. We are facing the great danger of becoming enthusiasts if we look for these experiences, we are told.

Now this is a very serious tendency in the Christian church at the present time. But it seems to me to be a tragic misuse of the Scriptures. What is the object of the Scriptures? When I read of the early Christians rejoicing with a "joy unspeakable and full of glory," do I say, "Well, of course, that is not meant for me—I am not near enough to the Lord. The apostles are not still alive, and therefore I cannot expect to rejoice with that joy. That was only for the first century"? If so, why are the Scriptures preserved? Why was the church guided in the arrangement of the canon? What is the value of the Scriptures at all if that is what I think about them? Yet that is the common argument in evangelical circles at this present time, and it seems to me that it accounts for the poverty of the life of the church and her ineffectiveness and therefore the condition of the world.

The Bible tells us that God reveals and manifests himself. Let me put it to you like this: if this modern attitude is right and we as Christians must never expect anything beyond reading and understanding the Scriptures, at times feeling a sense of joy and of happiness as we do so but nothing beyond that, then I stress again that in that case the Christian today is in an inferior position to the Old Testament saints. God made himself known to the boy Samuel, did he not? He spoke to him. Samuel did not understand it; nor did Eli at first. But subsequently the boy did. Look at all those instances in the Old Testament. I am not thinking only of the theophanies, the appearances of God in human form, for example, to Abraham on more than one occasion. I am thinking also of occasions such as the call of Gideon in the time of the judges. Gideon had one of these manifestations, one of these revelations, quite unexpectedly; he was called in that way to perform his great task (Judg. 6).

The Old Testament saints had direct dealings with God, and are we not to have direct dealings also? The author of the Epistle to the Hebrews put this in a very striking way, which denies all this modern teaching completely. In the eleventh chapter he gives a great list of Old Testament heroes of the faith, and then, having told us of some of the astounding experiences that they had, he says, "And these all, having obtained a good report through faith, received not the promise: God having provided some better thing for us, that they without us should not be made perfect" (vv. 39–40). This teaches that not only do we have something more than they had, which is the teaching of the New Testament everywhere—indeed, of the Old as well because the Old is always pointing forward to the New—but also that still greater things are coming. The great prophetic message is that the Spirit will be poured forth in great profusion in that future time, not occasionally as in the Old Testament dispensation. But this modern teaching denies that completely.

That is why, as I have said, it so often comes to pass that many modern Christians reading the Psalms feel that they do not know God as well as the psalmists did, and that is a terrible thing to say. You and I are in a better position than the psalmists—even, as we have seen, in a better position than John the Baptist. Why did our Lord come into this world? Peter tells us he came "that he might bring us to God" (1 Pet. 3:18). Not theoretically but in a living, experiential, vital manner, so that we might *know* God. This is what we are meant to enjoy. This is the glory about which the New Testament constantly speaks. Therefore to deny that this is possible for us is to deny the Scriptures themselves and, indeed, to make them very misleading. They have no function at all if I am to explain away all their greatest statements as belonging only to the first century.

But I have a stronger argument still to put to you. It is that the subsequent experience of God's people throughout the centuries shows how utterly false the notion is that it is not possible today to have direct and immediate experiences of God. Long after the end of the time of the apostles of the first century, long after the canon of Scripture had been fixed, people continued to have living and direct communion with the Lord. We read of great revivals in the church. What is a revival? A revival is nothing but a repetition of the book of Acts. The whole story of revivals is of God manifesting himself in an unmistakable manner. In a revival, a large number of people at the same time are aware of God. I was reading again a manuscript on the history of the last revival in Wales in 1904/1905, and that is what stands out so directly and amazingly.

I remember the story of one man in a meeting. For years he had been going to Christian meetings, he was a good Christian man, but when he was in this meeting, he said, "God is in this place." And God *was* in that place and was making himself known. His power was there. They were conscious of his very presence. This happens in revivals, and what I am trying to emphasize is that it should happen to every Christian, and every Christian should be seeking this experience of God.

Now, I repeat, this does not apply only to exceptional people. This is another favorite way of getting out of all this, is it not? People say, "Ah, yes, you've been quoting Paul, you've been quoting John—apostles; you've been quoting Samuel—a mighty prophet; you've been quoting Gideon—a great judge. Of course," they say, "we expect these exceptional people to have such experiences." The answer to that is found in Peter's words in 1 Peter 1, and they are enough: "strangers scattered throughout." The Bible never says that this is limited only to the exceptional: "For the promise is unto you, and to your children, and to all that are afar off" (Acts 2:39). It is all-inclusive! To deny that is to be guilty of introducing distinctions that are never found in the Scriptures or, as I have said, in the subsequent history of the church.

In order to establish this point, I want to read to you some experiences of Christian people so that you may know the kind of thing about which I am speaking. Let me tell you about A. B. Earl, a man who was greatly used in America in the last [nineteenth] century. He was born in 1812 and began preaching in 1830 after his conversion at the age of eighteen. He was a good preacher and for the next thirty-three years had a successful ministry. But in 1863 he began to feel that there was something lacking, that he was just an advocate instead of being a witness—and what a difference there is between the two! The advocate talks about what has been happening to others; he has his brief, but he is outside it. The witness, on the other hand, tells what has happened to him; he is giving his testimony. This is what A. B. Earl says:

> I felt that I must have in my heart something that I did not then possess. Before I could be filled with the fullness of Christ's love I must be emptied of self. Oh, the longing of my heart for what I then believed, and now believe, to be sweet and constant rest in Jesus. I believed I should receive and thought it was near.

He was right, of course, for Jesus had said to the woman of Samaria, "Whosoever drinketh of the water that I shall give him shall never thirst." Do you see it?—"sweet and constant rest"; "never thirst." Then Earl says:

> I soon found it was easier to resist temptation. I began to trust Christ and his promise more fully. With this mingling of faith, desire, and expectation I commenced meeting on Cape Cod. After rededicating myself, in company with others, anew to God, I was in my room alone pleading for the fullness of Christ's love, when all at once a sweet, heavenly peace filled all the vacuum in my soul, leaving no longing, no unrest, no dissatisfied feeling in my bosom. I felt I knew that I was accepted fully in Jesus. A calm, simple, childlike trust took possession of my whole being; then for the first time in my life [he was fifty-one then, remember] I had the rest which is more than peace. I had felt peace before but feared I should not retain it. Now I had peace without fear and which really became rest. This change occurred about five o'clock on the evening of the second day of November 1863, and although I never felt so weak and small, yet Jesus has been my all since then. There has not been an hour of conscious doubt or darkness since that time. A heaven of peace and rest fills my soul. Day and night the Savior stands by me. My success in leading souls to Jesus has been much greater than before. Temptation is presented, but the power of it is broken. I seem to have a present Savior in every kind of need, so that for several years I have done the trusting and Jesus the keeping.

Now that is Christianity, and that is a man in the nineteenth century.

"Ah," you say, "but there again is a preacher, an evangelist, a man whom God was using in a special manner."

Well, consider the experience of a woman who became a minister's wife, a very able woman who had been born into a wealthy family and was brought under conviction and converted, as a result of which she suffered a lot, even at the hands of her own mother. But though she was a true Christian, she was still not satisfied. She describes how she was listening to a sermon on Trinity Sunday in June 1776 and tells how the preacher had been preaching about the Holy Spirit:

> He spoke also much of the near union and communion with God that believers might enjoy, especially those perfected in love. My soul was led into depths unspeakable and saw such a fullness of God ready for me to plunge into that what I now felt seemed only as a drop compared with the ocean. As I came into the chapel yard I felt peculiar communion with the adorable Jesus in all his offices of redeeming love, and that verse of a hymn was so powerfully sweet as I had never felt it before:
>
> *The opening heavens around me shine*
> *With beams of sacred bliss,*
> *If Jesus shows his mercy mine,*
> *And whispers, I am his.*
>
> I was deeply penetrated with his presence and stood as if unable to move and was insensible to all around me. While thus lost in communion with my Savior, he spake these words to my heart: "All that I have is thine. I am Jesus in whom dwells all the fullness of the Godhead bodily. I am thine. My Spirit is thine, my Father is thine, and they love thee as I love thee; the whole Deity is thine. All God is and all he has is thine; he even now overshadows thee; he now covers thee with a cloud of his presence." All this was so realized to my soul in a manner I cannot explain that I sank down motionless, being unable to sustain the weight of his glorious presence and fullness of love.
>
> At the altar this was renewed to me but not in so large a measure. I believe indeed if this had continued as I felt it before but for one hour, mortality must have been dissolved and the soul dislodged from its tenement of clay. . . .
>
> I grew through boundless mercy and free grace in increasing intercourse and communion with my God every day. I live and move in him alone. Wherever I go, whatever I do, I feel the presence of the great Three in One. Yea, he dwelleth with me and shall be in me. This is his promise to my soul. I feel I am under his loving eye and the continual guidance of his Spirit. I do indeed dwell in God, and God in me. O love unsearchable to such a worm! I loathe myself when God I see, and into nothing I fall.

Here is a final quotation from that life. She describes how her husband was suddenly stricken by illness. He had fallen down as suddenly as if he had been shot and was still unwell.

> Yet in secret prayer the Lord assured me that he should not die at this time but live. Oh, what should I do at a time like this if I had not a constant intercourse with God. But blessed be his dear name, I have access to him. He is indeed my refuge and strength, a very present help in trouble, and fills my soul with strong consolation.

These are but two illustrations out of a large number, a great host, that I could have given you. I have quoted elsewhere the experience of some of the Puritans. John Flavel said that in one moment of this realization of the manifestation of the Son of God, he had learned more than he had learned from all his books and all his own preaching and teaching over fifty years. The same is true of John Howe. How often have I quoted from Whitefield's journals! How often have I reminded you of what happened to D. L. Moody and Charles Haddon Spurgeon. Now these are men and women of different types, of great abilities and ordinary abilities. In revival, as I say, some of the most ordinary people have had some of the most amazing experiences of the direct and immediate presence of the Lord.

You say, "Is this enthusiasm [emotional excess]?"

All I can say is that if it is, God grant that we all may become enthusiasts. These are sane, balanced people—people of intellect, people of knowledge, people of understanding, many of them people with great training, people who have been benefactors to the church, to their own families, and to the community at large. These are nothing but people who through the running centuries are verifying in their experience precisely what we are told in the New Testament is possible to every Christian. These examples I have just given are but examples and illustrations of people in the eighteenth and nineteenth centuries rejoicing in the Savior "with a joy unspeakable and full of glory," so conscious of him, and of his nearness and of his presence, his love and his glory and his power, that it was almost more than their physical frames could stand.

God in his infinite kindness and grace has seen to it that the story of the meeting of the woman of Samaria with the Lord Jesus Christ was recorded and is available to us in order that you and I might know that as she met him by the well, so you and I can meet with him. Remember the words I quoted earlier—our Lord said to his disciples, "It is expedient for you that I go away" (John 16:7). "You will be in a better position," he said in essence, "when I go away."

So you need not say, and you must never say again, "Oh, that I were there with the woman of Samaria! Oh, that I were one of those Samaritans whom she called out to see him! Oh, I can imagine what I would have felt!" If you say that, you are denying the teaching of the Scriptures, you are denying his own words. This incident at the well is only an illustration to show us that we can enjoy that same fellowship, the same communion even in a much greater manner than the woman of Samaria did at that particular time in the history of the world.

He manifests himself, and unless we know something about this, we are robbing ourselves and at the same time putting a limit upon the greatness and the glory of the salvation that he came into the world to give us. May God open our eyes and deliver us from reducing the Scriptures to the level of our own poor experiences; may he open our eyes to the full message of the Son of God and his so great salvation.

48

Experiences of the Lord's Presence

The woman then left her waterpot, and went her way into the city, and saith to the men, Come, see a man, which told me all things that ever I did: is not this the Christ? (John 4:28–29)

We have been seeing that according to the Scriptures, it is as possible for us to realize the presence of our Lord today as it was for the woman of Samaria. Having established that, we must now go on to consider a question that people are always, and very rightly, ready to ask: how does our Lord manifest himself now to Christian people? He has promised to do so. He has said, "I will love him, and will manifest myself to him" (John 14:21). But how does he do this?

This question has perplexed many people, and in many ways it is a subject that is surrounded by certain dangers. Everything in this Christian life or teaching is surrounded by danger. That is because of the devil and because of the effect of sin and the Fall upon us—every one of us. People sometimes go off on a tangent and seek visions and confuse the psychological with the spiritual. But that does not mean we are to avoid the subject altogether: quite the reverse. That should urge us to examine it scripturally, carefully, in the light of the help that we are given by the saints throughout the centuries.

Because of certain possible dangers, there is a fatal tendency at the present time to have nothing to do with the subject. Some people are so afraid of excesses that there has really never been much evidence of life in them. As I have often pointed out, it is not difficult to keep order in a cemetery, but when you have a houseful of children, you have a problem, and I prefer the problem of a houseful of children to the dead, legalistic orderliness of people who are afraid of excesses and of enthusiasm and of ecstasy. Do not be troubled by that. But I say this because it is important that we should have some clear idea in our minds as to what we can legitimately expect and, indeed, what we can legitimately seek.

So how does our Lord manifest himself? The answer is, of course, that it is a spiritual manifestation. The woman of Samaria was in our Lord's physical presence. We do not seek that. We seek *spiritual* manifestations. And what are they like? Let me quote the saintly John Fletcher of Madeley who knew so much about this: "The tongues of men and angels want proper words to express the sweetness and the glory with which the Son of God visits the soul that cannot rest without him." It is to the people who cannot rest without him that our Lord manifests himself. But what Fletcher is emphasizing here is that the manifestations are such that words are inadequate. So he goes on to say, "It is not to be described but to be enjoyed." This is something, of course, that transcends all human ability to describe. It is comparable to what we saw when we were looking at the experience that Paul described in 2 Corinthians 12.

We must expect this. It is fatal to try to confine what is possible to us in the Christian life to our understanding and our terminology. Let me use an illustration to show what I am mean. People often ask questions about heaven. They want to know what it is like and what will happen there and so on. I suppose that such questions are among those I am most frequently asked. Many people are a bit troubled by the fact that we are not told very much about heaven in the Scriptures. But you should not be surprised by that; the explanation is perfectly simple. The glory of heaven is such that our highest and best language is inadequate to describe it and is inevitably bound to detract from it.

There is a similar difficulty with the word *love*. However noble your conception of love, it falls almost infinitely short of what love really is, for God is love. You and I cannot use the word *love* without, of necessity, its carrying certain human, carnal, even sinful implications. And I believe that this failure of language is why, in the kindness and the goodness of God, we are not told more than we are about heaven. We are told enough to make us realize that it is infinite in its glory, perfection, and joy. We are told that, but we cannot be given detailed descriptions. The nearest the Scriptures come to it is to say that "the street of the city was pure gold" (Rev. 21:21). Now that is imagery. It is not a literal description. The book of Revelation is a book of imagery and symbols, and this is just an attempt at a description by using human categories. Gold is regarded as wonderful. Yet to say that the streets are paved with gold is totally inadequate; it simply gives us some vague notion.

And that is precisely what John Fletcher of Madeley is saying in those words that he uses. It follows from this that you find certain symbolic terms and metaphors employed in the Scriptures. Take, for example, the expression used in the letter to the church in Pergamum: "I will give to eat of the hidden manna" (Rev. 2:17). That term indicates the kind of experience that this is. Manna was given to the children of Israel. It was miraculous food from heaven, something nobody could explain, but it satisfied the people in the wilderness when they had no food to eat. But this is "*hidden* manna," which means that there is an element of mystery about it. It is something strange and unusual. Our Lord, as we have seen in connection with the woman of Samaria, tells the disciples, "I have meat to eat that ye know not of." This is the hidden manna. Another expression with a similar connotation is found in the letter to the church in Philadelphia: "I will write upon him my new name" (Rev. 3:12). It is a name that nobody knows about.

These terms suggest that there is an element of mystery, in the New Testament sense, and that the experience of our Lord's presence so transcends our ordinary experience and even our thinking and all our categories that symbolism has to be used in order to give some impression of it. What we are talking about is, by definition, something that is completely meaningless to people in the world. They cannot begin to understand it. They do not understand the gospel in its most open and explicit form; they do not understand the way of salvation—it is rubbish to them. So if they do not understand that, how can they understand this? And that is why the world has always tended to regard Christians who know something about these experiences as being almost insane. This, of course, is a very good test of those of us who are members of the Christian church. People in the church who have known this experience have generally been regarded as oddities by the majority of church members. They even ask, are they Christians at all? The manna is "hidden manna," and only those who have tasted it know about it. And this "new name" is a secret between the Lord and the believer.

The love of Jesus, what it is,
None but his loved ones know.

BERNARD OF CLAIRVAUX ("JESUS, THE VERY THOUGHT OF THEE")

It is not to the world that our Lord says he will manifest himself (John 14:19, 22). And he says of the Holy Spirit, "whom the world cannot receive, because it seeth him not, neither knoweth him: but ye know him" (John 14:17).

All this is one of the most remarkable and glorious aspects of the Christian life. That is why Paul says about the Christian, "He that is spiritual judgeth all things, yet he himself is judged of no man" (1 Cor. 2:15)—which simply means, "he that is spiritual" has an insight into these things and a knowledge of them, and the non-Christian does not understand him at all and thinks there is something peculiar about him. He can see that the Christian is being ravished by something that is real to him, but he himself knows nothing at all about it. This is something that is difficult to describe because it belongs to a realm and to an order that is so essentially different from everything to which we are accustomed.

It also follows that the experience is not only very wonderful but also sacred. That is why you will find that the people who have known most about it have generally been reluctant to say very much. For instance, even D. L. Moody, who was by nature an extrovert, very rarely spoke of that great experience that he had in New York City, that experience that changed his whole life. And the reason is that it is wonderful, it is spiritual, it is mysterious, and it has an element of intimacy with the Lord. There are certain things in natural, ordinary life that you do not broadcast. You do not share your most wonderful experiences with many people, and you do not make known to the public the most intimate parts of your life story.

This is a very good way of testing a spiritual experience and the ways you are helped when you are concerned to avoid the psychological or even the emotional. People who have had some psychological experience are always ready to talk about it. Those who are always getting visions are always talking about them. That is how they betray themselves. But the very characteristic of this experience of which we are talking is that there is, I repeat, something sacred about it, and therefore one is afraid, as it were, of betraying a confidence. There is a secret between you and the Lover of your soul, and you do not broadcast that. In order to help others, you may mention it. You want them to know something about it, and thank God that people have done so, but almost without exception there is a reluctance or hesitation. There is a fear lest you detract from it or boast of it in the flesh. But you cannot boast in this realm. It is too sacred; it is too pure; it is too wonderful. So it follows that all who know something about this are careful and hesitant and do not parade it. The whole trouble with the church in Corinth was that it was parading the gifts. Bear that in mind. It is one of the best and most delicate tests when you are sifting between the true spiritual experience and the psychological or emotional.

A further general remark is that there is also a great variation in spiritual manifestations. Sometimes such an experience will come instantaneously, without people seeking it, without their having known much about it. For other people, it may be very gradual. Some have sought this and sought it diligently and long and have almost come to the point of despair before entering into it. You cannot stereotype these things. Again, this is a useful and a valuable discriminating test. Any experience that you can produce at will—I do not care what it is, speaking in tongues or anything else—is by definition not a spiritual experience. If a man tells me he can speak in tongues whenever he likes, I am doubtful as to the character and the nature of his speaking in tongues. We do not control these things. There are no absolute rules we can apply to bring them about; there is no legalistic element, as it were.

These spiritual manifestations lie entirely in our Lord's sovereign power—that is the reason for their great variety. You cannot find him whenever you like. You can seek him, but you cannot guarantee that you will find him. We ought to be able to see this quite clearly from human analogies. If delicate human relationships and associations cannot be commanded, how much less can these spiritual manifestations of the Son of God.

Not only the timing but the type of experience also varies greatly from person to person. It is very difficult to know why. The only explanation that I would have is that, again, in a sense, you would expect this because, using once more the human analogy, you do not treat all the people you know in exactly the same way. This applies even to people who, as far as you can tell, you like and love to the same extent. This is because if you are a person with any sensitivity at all, you are so concerned to help others and to be pleasing to them that unconsciously your conduct changes as they call out different things in you. Not only that, you consciously change as you feel they need different things from you. And so, looked at in general, though you may take the same view of persons, there is always a subtle difference in your treatment of them.

You do not deal with two or three or four or five children in a family in exactly the same way. If you are a good parent, you do not have favorites, and fundamentally you treat them all in the same manner. Yet you are aware that there are differences in these children, and you deal with them according to your knowledge of these differences. One child, for instance, is born demonstrative, while another is almost offended by displays of feeling. Though you love both equally, you do not show your love to them in exactly the same way. I believe that is true in the spiritual realm, and I thank God for it. We are not machines; we are persons. We are human beings, and God our Father and the Lord Jesus Christ know us; and they know us so intimately that one person gets this kind of manifestation, while the other gets that.

Now I say this because there is always a tendency for people to stereotype these things. This is where the influence of the cults and psychological methods tend to come in. The same thing is always done in the same way. That to me is abhorrent. Forgive the expression, but there is a kind of sausage-machine mentality in which people are treated almost as if they are all identical. Now that approach is mechanical—it is not spiritual. With the Holy Spirit there is always a wonderful variation, showing the marvelous fatherly love of God to us.

But we can go even beyond that and assert that there are variations in the same person, and this, too, is most important. How often have the saints got into trouble over this! How often have we got into trouble ourselves because having had one experience, we set that up as a norm and a standard and are so intent upon getting a repetition of that, we do not recognize other manifestations. Do you see the danger? God our Father gives us other things, but we are not looking for them. We are looking *there*, and we do not realize what is happening *here*.

It is so sad that we so often rob ourselves because we do not realize that God varies the experience even from person to person. Some people have an extraordinary experience at the beginning of their Christian life that they can never get again, but they receive many others and should not be sad. With others it is the other way around; they seem to spend many years in shallows and miseries. They spend a long time under clouds, but suddenly the clouds break, and the sun shines upon them, some even on their deathbed. It is of great importance that we should understand these factors as they help us sift the true from the spurious.

Another general point that I must make is that generally these experiences come to us through the medium of the Scriptures—generally, I say. But I must be careful to point out that they are not confined to that, that though they are normally mediated to us through the Scriptures, they may come directly. Again, thank God for this. And this is where we must be so careful: we must watch that we do not exclude certain elements of our Lord's dealing with us. Again, it is the spirit of fear that makes people do this. They are so afraid of anything that happens to us apart from reading the Scriptures that they shut it all out and thereby rob themselves in a most grievous manner, because as we have been seeing, the fact is that our Lord comes to us not only in the mediate but in the immediate, not only in the indirect but in the direct. It is for him to decide. He cannot be limited. As he appeared to men and women in the Old Testament and in the New, so he can still. But normally—and you would expect this—he comes to us as we are reading the Scriptures or by bringing into our minds a verse of Scripture; but I repeat that we must not lay down rigid rules.

And then my last general point is that most frequently our Lord comes to us through our internal senses; but once more we must not make this absolute. He may, and sometimes he does, appear to the external senses also. What do I mean by that distinction? When I refer to the external senses I mean seeing with the literal, physical eye, hearing with the external ear, feeling, and touching. John in his first epistle puts it in terms of the external senses: "That which was from the beginning, which we have heard, which we have seen with our eyes, which we have looked upon, and our hands have handled, of the Word of life" (1:1).

But in addition to our external senses, we have internal senses. The apostle Paul, for instance, in writing to the Ephesians says in his prayer for them, "the eyes of your understanding being enlightened . . ." (Eph. 1:18). He does not mean the physical eyes. There is a spiritual eye, a spiritual way of perceiving. Similarly, there are spiritual ears. You can hear without hearing an audible voice; you are hearing by the internal senses. And it is the same with all the other senses. And generally speaking the intimations and manifestations that come to us from God are given to the internal senses.

Let me give you some illustrations of what I mean when I talk of the spiritual eye being opened. The practical outworking of what Paul was praying for those Ephesians may be experienced in this way: you are reading Scriptures, which you may have read many, many times before, Scriptures concerning him, the Son of God, and suddenly they are illuminated, and you are conscious that you are meeting with him, that he is there. You do not see him, but you see him in the Scripture. He becomes alive to you. You see the person of our Lord, his person is made real to you, and you realize you are not merely reading about some historical figure. You not only see the truth about him but you realize the glory of his person in a way that you never have before.

And in addition to that, you realize the truth concerning him as it is revealed in the Scripture. You realize in a new and living and more vital way the great truth concerning what he has done for us and for our salvation. Now you knew this before, you knew it with your brain, you knew it with your intellect, you knew it with your understanding in the way that anyone can perceive certain truths. But there is all the difference in the world between seeing that with your mind and suddenly seeing it in a living, internal, spiritual manner. You knew it, you were aware of the statements, you were aware of the facts, you could have given the correct answers, but suddenly it all becomes alive to you.

I am using terms that we tend to use, do we not, even in a natural and secular sense. You may, for example, be listening to a piece of music that you have always enjoyed when suddenly it becomes alive to you. This can happen with a poem also or with something you are studying. You struggle along, and you are taking in the facts, and you know them, but suddenly they all fuse together, and you experience it in a way you had not before. I am only using illustrations, but the spiritual experience I am describing is comparable to that. So it is possible for us to see and know something of the glory of his person and the glory of what he has done for us and, indeed, of the glory that he is preparing for us even while we are here in this world of time.

The men of grace have found,
Glory begun below.
Celestial fruits on earthly ground
From faith and hope may grow.

ISAAC WATTS ("MARCHING TO ZION")

Your spiritual eyes are open, and he manifests himself to you.

Similarly, we may hear him with the spiritual ear, and this is a marvelous aspect of this spiritual experience. We find it in the testimonies I quoted to you earlier. There is a hearing that is not physical; it is a realm of mystery. Take what we are told about the conversion of Saul of Tarsus on the road to Damascus. He had a number of people with him, and when he was suddenly addressed by the voice from heaven, these other people, we are told, heard a sound but could not make out what it was (Acts 9:7).

Can you explain that sort of thing? I cannot. I remember a man once trying to explain it; he said it is a matter of new electronics, wavelengths and so on. If your natural, material explanations help you go a certain way along this line, all well and good. All I can say is that if it is true in that realm, how infinitely more true it is in the other realm. There are spiritual wavelengths that enable you to hear without hearing an audible voice; and this internal hearing is much more wonderful than the external hearing. Our Lord can tell you in an unmistakable manner certain things that will give you a clear and a full assurance. He can say to you, "Thou art mine, and I am thine." He can say, "Thy sins are forgiven." That is what happened to John Wesley at that meeting in Aldersgate Street about which he wrote in his journal. He said he knew that "my sins, even mine" were taken away. The Son of God may say to you, "I died for thee." He may speak through the Scriptures. He may say, "What you are reading is true of you," or he may speak directly when you are not reading the Scriptures.

This is what I mean when I refer to this hearing with the spiritual, the internal, ear. No voice is heard, but it is not only as definite, it is more definite than hearing a voice; there is absolute certainty. This is why many of the saints, especially the hymn-writers desire this. They are asking for something that they know can happen:

Speak, I pray thee, gentle Jesus!
Oh, how passing sweet thy words. . . .
Tell me thou art mine, O Savior,
Grant me an assurance clear.

William Williams ("Speak, I Pray Thee, Gentle Jesus")

Or he may communicate directly to the feelings and to the emotions. You may have been under a spirit of heaviness or dullness or bondage for months. You may have been doing everything you can to be free of this—reading your Scriptures, praying, attending public worship—but still there is a sort of heaviness that you cannot get rid of. Then suddenly you find it has gone. The cloud breaks, the sun shines, and a beam darts upon your soul. You cannot explain it, you cannot understand it, but you have a sense of peace and joy. Again, the hymn-writer expresses this:

Sometimes a light surprises
The Christian while he sings;
It is the Lord who rises,
With healing in his wings.

William Cowper ("Sometimes a Light Surprises")

It is surprising, but the Lord does it, and you cannot explain it. Suddenly your whole mood, as it were, has been changed. You are transformed, the heaviness has gone, and you are free, and you cannot believe that you had ever known a spirit of heaviness.

In the same way, you can have a sense of his presence and of his glory. You do not see him with your physical, external eye, but you know he is there. There is nothing more wonderful than just to feel that the Lord is with you in the room—the glory of God, the glory of the Son. Without your doing anything, in his love and in his mercy and in his compassion he suddenly gives you this manifestation. Once a man or woman has known something about that, they will never be the same again, and they will never be really satisfied until they know this more and more. Take the words of another hymn:

Oh that I could forever sit
With Mary at the Master's feet;
Be this my happy choice;
My only care, delight, and bliss,
My joy, my heaven on earth, be this,
To hear the Bridegroom's voice.

CHARLES WESLEY ("O LOVE DIVINE, HOW SWEET THOU ART")

That is the prayer and the longing of anyone who knows anything about these manifestations of the Son of God to the internal senses.

Then, finally, sometimes he manifests himself to the external senses. This is, of course, most mysterious, but you find it in both the Old Testament and the New. In the Old Testament there are what are called theophanies, when suddenly the Angel of the Covenant appears in a human form. The authorities are agreed, and it seems to me to be beyond any doubt, that these were always appearances of the Lord Jesus Christ himself. The people saw him, and then he would suddenly disappear.

It is the same in the New Testament and in the history of the church. Now this is the point at which, of course, we have to be most careful, and I will give you just one example and illustration. There is a book with the title *Remarkable Passages in the Life of Colonel Gardiner*. This was written by the famous Philip Doddridge, the hymn-writer, a preacher of two hundred years ago, a man who ministered at Northampton and kept an academy there to train young preachers. I am saying all this to tell you that by nature Philip Doddridge was one of the most careful and judicious of men—not a hothead, not an excitable person, but a calm and cool and highly rational person. He wrote this account of his friend Colonel Gardiner, and Colonel Gardiner, again, was a man who was famous for and characterized by his judicious spirit, not only in his military career but in every respect.

With some reluctance, Colonel Gardiner told this story, emphasizing that he told it only for the glory of God. He was a man who had done well in his profession, but he was living an utterly godless life, until one night when a great experience came to him. He had spent the evening drinking and talking, not to excess, but amusing and entertaining himself. Then he had gone back to his room to wait until midnight when he planned to meet with another man's wife. Not knowing quite what to do while he waited, he casually picked up a book, a religious book, which his good mother or aunt had slipped into his suitcase without his knowledge. The title of the book was *The Christian Soldier or Heaven Taken by Storm*, and it was written by Thomas Watson. As Colonel Gardiner was holding this book and glancing through it, an impression was made upon his mind that drew after it a train of the most important and happy consequences.

What happened? Well, this is what he describes. He repeated it more than once to Philip Doddridge, and he also repeated it to another spiritual leader. Philip Doddridge writes:

> He thought he saw an unusual blaze of light fall on the book while he was reading, which at first he imagined might happen by some accident in the candle. But lifting up his eyes he apprehended to his extreme amazement that there was before him, as it were, suspended in the air, a visible representation of the Lord Jesus Christ upon the cross, surrounded on all sides with a glory, and was impressed as if a voice or something equivalent to a voice had come to him to this effect (for he was not confident as to the very words), but the voice said, "O sinner, did I suffer this for thee, and are these the return?" But whether this were an audible voice, or only a strong impression on his mind, equally striking, he did not seem very confident, though to the best of my remembrance he rather judged it to be the former.
>
> Struck with so amazing a phenomenon as this, there remained hardly any life in him, so that he sank down in the armchair in which he sat and continued he knew not how long insensible. But however that were, he quickly after opened his eyes and saw nothing more than usual. But, of course, from that point on he was a new man, a complete change in his life, he became a great saint.

Like Philip Doddridge, I quote this to you for one reason only, and that is to warn you not to put limits upon what the everlasting God may do. We must not deny these things; we must not dismiss them as belonging to the realm of fancy, a disordered brain, enthusiasm, or dangerous ecstasy. We do not seek them; we seek the spiritual manifestation. But we must not deny that in his own time and according to his own sovereign will, God may choose to do to some what he did to Colonel Gardiner on that amazing occasion.

My dear friends, heaven is round and about us. The supernatural is ever with us. There are myriads of angels. Do you believe in angels? The spiritual realm is all around us if we but realized it. And as I say, these are some of the ways in which the Son of God may manifest himself to his children. You realize, therefore, how careful all those who know anything about this kind of experience have always been and how reluctantly they have spoken about it, and yet, my dear friends, we must speak because this is the salvation that is offered to us. Not a mere intellectual belief about which you are always having to persuade yourself. No, no; our Lord died to bring us to God, to restore to the fallen race of Adam the knowledge of God that he lost.

Talk with us, Lord, thyself reveal,
While here o'er earth we rove;
Speak to our hearts, and let us feel
The kindling of thy love.

Charles Wesley ("Talk with Us, Lord")

49

Finding the Lord's Presence

The woman then left her waterpot, and went her way into the city, and saith to the men, Come, see a man, which told me all things that ever I did: is not this the Christ? (John 4:28–29)

We have realized that the whole purpose of our Lord's meeting with the woman of Samaria is to bring us to that place where we shall see that it is possible for us to have communion and fellowship with the Lord, even as these people did in the days of his flesh, and we have been dealing with the ways in which this becomes possible. We have seen that we must not put limits upon what God does but rather recognize that there is a great variety in the ways in which our Lord manifests himself to his people in a spiritual sense. While we normally know our Lord's presence by means of our internal senses, he does sometimes manifest himself even to our external senses.

This, then, is the point at which we have arrived. Our position as Christians is not simply that we believe certain things about someone who once lived, and now we live on the teaching that we have concerning him in the Bible. Over and above that, the Scriptures clearly teach that we can have a spiritual fellowship with him, a communion with him, the kind of experience that the apostle Paul has in mind when he says in Philippians 3:10, "That I may know him, and the power of his resurrection, and the fellowship of his sufferings." And when Paul goes on to say, "Not as though I had already attained," he does not mean that he is uncertain about his salvation—he is absolutely certain about that—but that what he longs to have is more and more of this personal, intimate, immediate knowledge of the Lord himself. That is what Paul is striving after, the mark he is pressing toward (Phil. 3:14). He knows that this personal communion and knowledge will only be perfect, of course, at that great day when the Son of God will come again from heaven and manifest himself in all his glory. That is the day when we shall be changed and see him as he is. But in the meantime Paul's greatest desire is to know Christ.

So the question therefore that remains for us is this: if this knowledge of our Lord is possible for us all, how do we attain it? This is a very practical matter, and unless we can deal with it, we will fall far short of our Lord's purpose for us. But, thank God, there is sufficient instruction given to us in various parts of the Scriptures to enable us to answer this question.

The first essential is that we believe in its possibility. Undoubtedly the greatest difficulty is that people do not believe in the very possibility of this personal communion. We have become so accustomed to something purely objective that we tend to forget the subjective. It is interesting to notice that throughout the history of the church there has been a kind of oscillation from one to the other. We also find these different emphases in different types of people. Some are purely objective, some are purely subjective—and both extremes are wrong. The glory of the gospel is that it takes up the whole person. It is not merely for the intellect; it is also for the sensibilities and for the feelings. Some people are afraid of excesses, and others are afraid they are entering into the realm of the mystical. But we find a constant warning in the New Testament not to "quench the Spirit" (1 Thess. 5:19), not to put our carnal, human limits upon what is made possible for us by this great and wonderful gospel in which we partake together. So we must get rid of all negative ideas.

And then we must get rid of the notion that this experience is only for very outstanding people. That is a very common ruse of the devil. He says that it is all right for apostles, that it is all right for saints. Under Roman Catholicism there is a very wrong and unscriptural division not only between the clergy and the laity, which in itself is not a New Testament distinction, but also even beyond that into extraordinary and ordinary Christians, saints and those who are not saints. But the New Testament says that we are all "called to be saints" (Rom. 1:7), and therefore all these experiences are possible to all of us. There is no need to become a monk or a nun and to go out of everyday life in order to cultivate this religious life and then receive great and marvelous experiences. That is one of the most erroneous teachings that has ever been introduced into the church; yet the tendency to think in this way has percolated into even Reformed and Protestant circles, so that we say, "Ah, yes, that's all right for people who don't have to go to work every day or who aren't engaged in business or aren't housewives with a lot of work. If only I had nothing to do but cultivate my soul, then I could expect this kind of experience."

And the simple answer to that, I repeat, is that people of all types have known this experience. If you are not clear about its possibility, then you cannot proceed any further. If in some way or another you are saying, "This isn't for me," if you begin to bring in psychological terms and say there are certain people who by nature seem to be given to this kind of mystical experience, then again you are making the whole thing impossible as far as you are concerned. There are no such distinctions in the New Testament, none whatsoever. "For the promise is unto you, and to your children, and to all that are afar off" (Acts 2:39). We must be clear about that.

Then, secondly, we must seek this diligently. Now I put my emphasis upon the word *diligently*, but I must also stress the seeking. There is great variation in how this kind of experience comes to people, as we have seen. Sometimes it is given without any seeking at all. But that is not the common rule. The usual experience is that men and women, having realized the possibility of this communion with our Lord, have started to seek. How do you do this? Well, the first way is to seek him in the Scriptures.

Let me give you an example. It is shown perfectly in Luke 24, in the famous story of the two men on the road to Emmaus after the resurrection. Here are two men, cast down and dejected. When the Lord joins them, they do not know him. What does he do with them? He takes them through the Scriptures. That is his antidote to their depression. He says, "O fools, and slow of heart to believe all that the prophets have spoken: ought not Christ to have suffered these things, and to enter into his glory?" And so, we are told, "Beginning at Moses and all the prophets, he expounded unto them in all the scriptures the things concerning himself" (vv. 25–27). That is the perfect example.

And later on in the same final chapter of Luke's Gospel, we find the same method. Our Lord says:

> These are the words which I spake unto you, while I was yet with you, that all things must be fulfilled, which were written in the law of Moses, and in the prophets, and in the psalms, concerning me. Then opened he their understanding, that they might understand the scriptures. (Luke 24:44–45)

If you want to find him, therefore, the first place to look for him is in the Scriptures. So you must read the Scriptures, not in a mechanical, thoughtless manner, not simply that you may read your portion of

Scripture. No; deliberately read your Scriptures to look for him, and suddenly you will find him. You will find him in unexpected places in the Old Testament, in the prophecies, in the Psalms, and even in the five books of Moses, as he said himself. And he will come to you and speak to you through the Scriptures. He says in essence, "All that is about me."

Then you come to the New Testament, and you do not just read the four Gospels as ancient history. They are that, but you say to yourself, "As he appeared to these people when he was here in the days of his flesh, so he still appears to his people. Here I read of somebody meeting him—I can meet him! Here's a woman who met him by the side of a well—he's still the same person. I don't see him with the naked eye, but he's exactly the same person and is as real as he was when he met with that woman. I, too, can meet with him." And as you read in this living way, you will often find that you meet with him, and he becomes real and manifests himself to you.

Then you go on; you read the book of Acts and find how he appears to people. You read the epistles, you read the book of Revelation, and all along what you are being told is that he is present, he is everywhere, and he is always ready and willing to meet with his people. That is the most common way of all, and that is the way that God has most blessed his people throughout the running centuries. You deliberately seek him in the Scriptures. As you do that, he will come to you.

And you do exactly the same thing in the sacraments. That is one of the objects of the sacraments—not so much what they do to us as what they tell us about him. So often people have met with him in obedience to his command when they have partaken of the sacraments, the Lord's Supper in particular, which is just, in the first instance, a reminder of the Last Supper. Our Lord said to his disciples, "This do ye, as oft as ye drink it, in remembrance of me" (1 Cor. 11:25), and one of the objects of meeting together at the Lord's Table is to remind ourselves of him. He said that he would meet with his people in that special way.

Now, again, the devil has obviously been very busy at this point, and that is where the whole notion of transubstantiation has come in. Transubstantiation, which is the idea that the bread changes into our Lord's very body, is an attempt to make his presence real, "the real presence," as it is called. But it is not a real presence at all; it is a mere figment. But the idea behind that was right, in a sense, and that was that people should realize that they were not only eating bread, they were not doing something in a mechanical manner in connection with someone who now belonged to the past. The idea was to realize his presence. But the way we understand that is to say that he is present spiritually. This has been the great Reformation declaration on the Lord's Supper—the spiritual presence of the Son of God.

You say, "But is he in the bread?"

No, he is not, and he is not with the bread, as Luther taught. He himself has said in effect, "As you do this in remembrance of me, in accordance with my command to you, I will be with you. I will manifest myself to you."

And thus, as you read the long history of the church, you will find that there have been glorious manifestations of the Son of God at various Communion seasons. I have often referred to that famous occasion at Cambuslang, now part of Glasgow, in the eighteenth century, that famous Communion season when George Whitefield was present and was preaching. That is perhaps one of the most astounding manifestations of the Son of God among his people ever recorded in history. It was a great revival, a great outpouring of the Spirit of God, and came about through the medium of the Communion service. As the Lord's death was declared and remembered, suddenly he appeared among his people. So that is one of the reasons for partaking of this sacrament.

And then, of course, another way of finding the Lord is prayer—prayer that concentrates on this very thing. You are not merely praying in general; you are not only worshipping God; you are not only making known your petitions and desires. You are going beyond that and are deliberately seeking, deliberately making this effort and asking him to manifest himself to you. You start with the desire—"Oh, that I knew where I might find him!"—and then you go after him, as it were, and you plead with him to manifest himself to you. This is something that the saints have done. The words of one of our hymns are a perfect illustration of this cry that you make to him:

Speak, I pray thee, gentle Jesus!
Oh, how passing sweet thy words,
Breathing o'er my troubled spirit
Peace which never earth affords.

William Williams ("Speak, I Pray Thee, Gentle Jesus!")

This is something that we have to do deliberately, volitionally, realizing that there is a possibility. You go out, as it were, in prayer, and you try to lay hold upon him, and you cry unto him to be pleased to look upon you and to manifest himself to you.

The third very practical step is the one I have already been illustrating to you—read the lives of the saints. Deliberately study the biographies and the histories of men and women who have had great and notable experiences of this very experience to which I am referring.

Let me give you one further example to stimulate you yet more, a practical example of what I mean. I shall read something written by a most remarkable man, a man by the name of John Lilburne. He is a man of interest, quite apart from his Christian experience. He was the real founder of the people who became known as the Levellers, and in many ways he is the father of democracy in this country [Britain]. Here is a man who, three hundred years ago, agitated for certain things that have only come to pass in this present [twentieth] century. But he was first and foremost a highly spiritual man, and he had amazing experiences. Listen to this:

> I assuredly know that all the power in earth, yea and the gates of hell itself shall never be able to move me or prevail against me, for the Lord, who is the worker of all my works in me and for me, hath founded and built me upon that sure and unmovable foundation, the Lord Jesus Christ . . . for which with courage and rejoicing I now bear witness to and am a prisoner in bonds [he was in prison when he was writing this], lying day and night in fetters of iron, both hands and legs. If even worse things should be inflicted upon me, I should sing, rejoice, and triumph in them all, for my God makes me glory in my tribulation, and my soul is filled so full of that sweetness and joy that it finds in my God alone that my tongue and pen are never able to the full to express and utter it. . . .
>
> He hath crucified the world and all things here below unto me and hath enabled me to account and esteem all things beside himself as dung and dirt, not being worth of casting any affectionate eye upon them. I am as merry, yea, more cheerful than ever I was in any condition in my life and can sleep as soundly in my boots and irons as Peter did between the two soldiers when he was in prison.

There is a man enduring in the Fleet Prison in London the most cruel imprisonment, yet who is able to say that he is having the full experience of the apostles. He does not hesitate to claim that he has as much joy and peace and happiness as Peter when he was asleep that night before he was due to die, lying between two soldiers and bound with chains (Acts 12). Here is a man, a man like ourselves, a man of ability and understanding, not this strange, ascetic kind of person that the psychologists would speak of, but a man who was intensely practical in his outlook. Here he is, having such experiences that he is able to say, "If even worse things should be afflicted upon me, I should sing, rejoice, and triumph." He has reached a place in which he is so certain of God the Father, God the Son, and God the Holy Spirit that he is quite immune to anything that man in his malice might do to him.

So this is the way to seek this experience; you read an account like that, and you say to yourself, "If that was possible to John Lilburne, why is it not possible to me?" And he is only one of many, many, in that century in particular. Read the stories of some of the early Quakers—it is just the same.

I know something about the danger of reading the Scripture in a mechanical manner. You can, as I say, read your daily portion and perhaps a little commentary on it, and you think you have done well. But the question is, have you really grasped the message of the Scriptures? Do you have a living message? Do you just stop at having done your duty, as it were, or does this urge you to seek the fullness that is in Christ Jesus? I am a great advocate of reading about the actual lives of men and women like ourselves, people living in this world, people who are suffering—not monks, not anchorites, not hermits, but people in the midst of life, with all its difficulties and trials and problems. This is how they were able to find the Lord in their need and to rejoice in him "with joy unspeakable and full of glory." So, my dear friends, use the biographies of the saints as commentaries upon your commentaries; use them as commentaries on the Scriptures. Here are people who have applied the Scriptures, and if they were able to do it, you and I should be able to do it also.

Then, fourthly, I come to another very practical matter—we must always be obedient to him. We must never lose sight of the fact that we are dealing with a personal relationship and with an experience of a person. I am not talking merely about feelings and sensations; I am referring to what the apostle Paul talks of in Philippians 3:10—"that I may know him." We are seeking knowledge of a person; we are seeking experiences of communion and fellowship with this blessed person. So there is nothing more important than that we should be obedient to him. In what way? We must learn to be responsive to his drawings. That expression *his drawings* was used by the Puritans and has always been used by the great Christian mystics. This is a scriptural term: "I drew them with cords of a man, with bands of love" (Hos. 11:4). Or as Philip Doddridge puts it:

He drew me, and I followed on;
Charmed to confess [and to follow] the voice divine.
("O Happy Day, That Fixed My Choice")

Here is something that is most wonderful in the Christian life and experience. It is, of course, indicated clearly in the Scriptures. The greatest possible encouragement we can have is that God approaches us through the Spirit. He does not leave it entirely to us. He gives us encouragements, and there is nothing more important in the Christian life than to be sensitive to his approaches, to the times when he draws near and gives us a kind of manifestation of himself. You know the sort of thing to which I am referring. It is generally a surprise to you, sometimes coming when you least expect it. It is expressed in that hymn to which I referred earlier:

Sometimes a light surprises
The Christian while he sings.
William Cowper ("Sometimes a Light Surprises")

You are aware of a kind of softening of experience, a tenderness in your spirit. That is undoubtedly one of his drawings. So Isaiah, in a prophetic manner, says, "Seek ye the Lord while he may be found"—that is it—"call ye upon him while he is near" (Isa. 55:6). Is this not something you know in experience? There is this variation; sometimes he is near, sometimes he seems to be far-off, distant, remote. And the essence of wisdom in this matter is that if you ever have the feeling that he is near, that he is drawing you, that he is speaking to you, respond immediately.

I could show you this in many different ways. I will put it in the negative, which is perhaps the most helpful of all—we must be the exact opposite of the spouse, the bride, who is depicted in the Song of Solomon:

> I am come into my garden, my sister, my spouse: I have gathered my myrrh with my spice; I have eaten my honeycomb with my honey; I have drunk my wine with my milk: eat, O friends; drink, yea, drink abundantly, O beloved.

She continues:

> I sleep, but my heart waketh: it is the voice of my beloved that knocketh, saying, Open to me, my sister, my love, my dove, my undefiled: for my head is filled with dew, and my locks with the drops of the night.

But then she replies:

> I have put off my coat; how shall I put it on? I have washed my feet; how shall I defile them? My beloved put in his hand by the hole of the door, and my bowels were moved for him. I rose up to open to my beloved; and my hands dropped with myrrh, and my fingers with sweet smelling myrrh, upon the handles of the lock. I opened to my beloved; but my beloved had withdrawn himself, and was gone: my soul failed when he spake: I sought him, but I could not find him; I called him, but he gave me no answer. (Song 5:1–6)

He approaches her; he draws nigh. This is one of the drawings. He asks her to open the door and so admit him into fellowship, but she cannot be bothered, she cannot put on her cloak again, she cannot defile her feet—they would need washing again—and so she resists him. Then he gives a further manifestation, and now her heart is ravished, and she rushes to open the door, but he has departed. Why? She did not respond to the first approach! And this is so true in this spiritual life. Apart from anything else, there is nothing so foolish as to put him to one side because we are too busy.

If I may give a word from my own experience, there is nothing that I have had to learn more—and I thank God that I have at last learned the lesson, but it took me time to learn it. It does not matter what you are doing—if he draws near to you, put everything else down. Even if what you are doing is reading your Bible, stop for the time being and talk to him directly. Whatever your occupation, clutch at every approach, take advantage of every drawing. Give him this implicit obedience; leave yourself in his hands.

But we must not only obey our Lord in his drawings—it is equally important that we obey him in his rebuking, because he *will* rebuke us. He is concerned about our sanctification. He came into the world, he died, he rose again, and he is at the right hand of God in order that we might come to a final, full redemption and glorification. But he knows us in a way that we do not know ourselves. That is the meaning of those great words in Hebrews 12:6: "For whom the Lord loveth he chasteneth, and scourgeth every son whom he receiveth," whom he is calling unto righteousness. In other words, in order to bring us into this intimate fellowship and communion with himself, he will point out to us the hindrances, the obstacles. The effect of sin upon us and the effect of the devil is to make us think, "Yes, I would like this wonderful experience," but we rather want to have that and to have something else at the same time. But the two are incompatible, and he will tell us so in various ways. He says, "I cannot come to you while that is true of you."

Go back to the letter that the Lord wrote to the church of the Laodiceans. Before he says, "Behold, I stand at the door, and knock," he tells them exactly what they must give up and what they must take on (Rev. 3:14–20). There are certain rooms into which he will not come; there are certain things that must be put out before he will enter. He will point this out to us, and he will chide us and rebuke us. He speaks within us in the Spirit, and this often happens when we are not even thinking about these things. Something will be put before us, and we will try to explain it away. But if we go on trying to explain it away, we need not expect to have any knowledge of these spiritual manifestations of the Son of God. He will rebuke, he will chastise, and he will make it quite clear to us that they must be got rid of, and then—and only then—will he manifest himself to us. So we must be entirely obedient to him. I add to that, we must resign ourselves to him completely and entirely. The lesson here is just this—he is not at our command; we are to be entirely at his command.

Shall I give you a simple illustration that will put it quite plainly? Take the condition or the relationship of a British citizen to a royal personage. You do not make demands of the Queen, but you respond to what she says, what she does. You do not bombard such a person; because of the dignity of the person and the office, because of all that is so true of such a person, your attitude is one of resignation. You do not send a request demanding an appointment; you do not lay down the terms and conditions. You do not say, "I'm very busy all day, but at 6 o'clock it is possible for me to see you." Multiply that by infinity, and there is your relationship and mine to our blessed Lord. It is he who determines the time, not us. We have a tendency to say, "When I have done other things, then . . ." That is no good, my friend. We must be at his disposal.

And our Lord not only determines the time, he determines the manner in which he will manifest himself to us or grant us an audience or admit us into his presence. It is entirely his royal prerogative, and he will never surrender it. You find this not only in the Scriptures but everywhere in the subsequent testimony of God's people. They have been most careful and punctilious to stipulate that they do not demand, they do not insist, they do not become impatient and show their annoyance; they leave themselves entirely in his hands. The time, the way, the manner, the particular form are all left to him.

So you do not go on demanding an experience exactly like that of somebody you have read about or somebody you know. You say, "All I am anxious for is to know him and to love him and to serve him. I don't care how he manifests himself as long as he does. What I want is to know him. As the apostle Paul says, 'That I may know him, and the power of his resurrection, and the fellowship of his sufferings, being made conformable unto his death'" (Phil. 3:10). But, remember, to say that is to say a very big thing. One of our hymns puts this in an extreme form;

Nearer, my God, to thee,
Nearer to thee!
E'en though it be a cross
That raiseth me.

SARAH F. ADAMS ("NEARER, MY GOD, TO THEE")

Here are people at the topmost height of their experience, and they know that nothing matters as far as they are concerned except that they have this experience. They do not care what it is as long as it brings them "nearer . . . to thee." And remember, what we feel should always be a footnote to that. You do not offer the prayer in that hymn only when the *Titanic* has struck the iceberg and you are sinking. You always offer that prayer; you are always in that condition; it is a desperate cry. You do not get the answer very often, and you are not entitled to expect one. This is the prayer of someone who realizes what is possible and says, "I don't care how as long as I know you." "Though he slay me," says Job, "yet will I trust in him" (Job 13:15). That is the final resignation that is so essential in these matters.

That brings me to my last point, which is obvious—the element of persistence. "Take time to be holy," says a hymn, and how true that is. This is the whole trouble with the modern world, is it not? We all say we are so busy. But that, of course, is ridiculous. Why should we find the problem of time so difficult? We have more leisure than people have ever had. Our whole outlook upon life is wrong if we, as Christians, say, "I don't have the time." You have to take time; you have to make time; you have to get your priorities right.

You must draw up a program; you must realize that you have to fight for these things. The world does not want you to; "the world is too much with us";[30] that is our whole trouble. The world determines our programs, and we are manipulated by other forces and factors. You must take charge of yourself and say, "I don't care what happens—this is the most important thing of all." Persistence! Not fits and starts. Not a great spasm and cooling off and forgetting and then returning. But that is our story, is it not?

This demands great discipline. The saints have always been characterized by stern self-discipline, and it is absolutely essential. We fritter away our days, and then we excuse ourselves with the words, "Of course, I'm not an apostle. I'm not a saint. I'm not living in the first century. These experiences are not meant for us now. Other people don't read the Bible at all, so if I read a few verses, I'm very spiritual." Spiritual? You are a little babe, the merest infant. This is a way of persistence, a way of discipline. We must take the steps that our Lord has indicated—"ask . . . seek . . . knock" (Matt. 7:7). This is a rising gradation. You ask, but you do not seem to get an answer; then you begin to seek, like the bride n the Song of Solomon, and you look for him everywhere, and you ask people, "Where is he?" Like Job, you say, "Oh that I knew where I might find him!" (Job 23:3). You have gone beyond asking, you are seeking, and now you have become desperate, and you are knocking. "Ask . . . seek . . . knock." Those are our Lord's own words.

Or let me put it to you in the words of Jacob: "I will not let thee go, except thou bless me" (Gen. 32:26). Our Lord likes that kind of holy boldness. Let there be an urgency; let there be this spirit of seeking; let us know something of the holy ambition of the apostle Paul: "I press toward the mark" (Phil. 3:14). He is saying, "I am always seeking him. I have known so much of him that I want more of him." "For to me to live is Christ, and to die is gain" (Phil. 1:21). So we seek him in these various ways. Consider those words that were so vital to Hudson Taylor and others:

Lord Jesus, make thyself to me
A living, bright reality;
More present to faith's vision keen
Than any outward object seen;
More dear, more intimately nigh
Than e'en the sweetest earthly tie.

CHARLOTTE ELLIOTT ("O JESUS, MAKE THYSELF TO ME")

That was Hudson Taylor's prayer. It has been the prayer of every saint in some shape or form. It should be our prayer. There you have the possibility and the persistence. Refuse to be discouraged; do not give in; go on. "Watch and pray" (Matt. 26:41). Seek him! Be sensitive to him. He will lead you on. There are some things about which we are not certain, but of this we can be certain—it is his desire that we should know him. He is standing at the door and knocking. Have you heard him? Take time to listen to him. Always be ready. Whatever you are doing, have your ears open. Whatever you are concentrating on, always be sure that you can hear him. He will knock at the door, and the moment you hear that knock, put everything down, open the door, and he will enter in and have fellowship with you, and he will sup with you, and your heart will be ravished.

Now it is an extraordinary fact, and it is a terrible condemnation of us as human beings, but it does seem to me to be the case as I judge from my reading in these matters, that the people who have had the most experience of what we are talking about have tended to be people who have been enduring some cruel persecution. I have read to you from John Lilburne. John Lilburne had his greatest experiences when he was in the prison, and so did John Bunyan. What a terrible condemnation of us that it takes a prison or something like that to cut us off from the things that stand between us and him. But we should learn a lesson from that. Let us put ourselves into a kind of prison by cutting off these things in order that we may have time for him.

There can also be no doubt of the fact that our Lord has often given manifestations of his presence to people before they have had prison experiences, to prepare them for it. You will often find that revivals come to countries that have some great trial to pass through. It happened in the Congo, in Korea, and in many other countries. So this experience may happen before a trial, or you may be put through the trial in order that you may meet with God. But both come down to the same thing, and that is that we have to concentrate on him. It is when we are cut off from everything else that so many of us begin to seek him and to seek this intimate knowledge. Many people have even waited until their deathbed, but thank God he has not refused them even there. Even there he has granted them the manifestation of his presence, and looking back on their life, they say, "What a fool I've been! I might have enjoyed this throughout the years, but I was so busy here and there, coming and going . . . Oh, what a fool!" They have left a dying testimony and statement.

So let us learn from them, and let us realize that our Lord is as ready to speak to us today as he was to that woman by the side of the well. He is ready to give us assurances of his love and to make himself known to us.

50

"Is Not This the Christ?"

The woman then left her waterpot and went her way into the city, and saith to the men, Come, see a man, which told me all things that ever I did: is not this the Christ? (John 4:28–29)

I now want to consider with you this great question that was put forward by the woman of Samaria after her encounter with our Lord and Savior at the well, the question that she put to her fellow townsmen: "Is not this the Christ?"

She puts this question in a form that makes it quite clear that she is in no doubt whatsoever with regard to the answer. It is not a question asking for information; it is an assertion. She does not ask, "Is this the Christ?" but "Is not this the Christ?" by which she means, obviously, that he is, he must be. It is important that we should realize that as she presents the question she expects a positive answer.

So here we are face-to-face with the most important question that can ever be asked. Many serious questions face the countries of the world at the present time, but as Christians we say that this is the greatest of all. Who is he, this babe who was born in Bethlehem nearly two thousand years ago?[31] Is he or is he not the Christ?

Let me start by putting a question to you: have you ever asked this question and have you been so certain of the answer that you have put the question to others as this woman of Samaria did? She is now on an evangelistic errand; it is because she is so certain that he is the Christ that she wants these people to come to meet him and to hear from his own lips the kind of thing that she has already been hearing. This is what makes us Christians, and this is what proves that we are Christians—we have come to see that Jesus of Nazareth is the Christ, the Messiah, the Deliverer, the Savior of the world, and we are anxious for others, too, to know this.

But that immediately raises in our minds this question: on what grounds are we satisfied that he is the Christ? The word *Christ* is the Greek form of the Hebrew term *Messiah*, the Deliverer who was to come. Here is a woman who is quite sure of it and gives us her main reason: "Come, see a man, which told me all things that ever I did." We have been seeing that this statement is a vital part of the evidence, but it is not the only evidence. If we are satisfied that he is the Christ, on what grounds are we satisfied? It seems to me that the only object and purpose of our observing the Christmas season is that we may put questions like this to ourselves. Some sections of the Christian church do not believe in observing Christmas. I think they are wrong. I understand their point of view, I know that it is a reaction against the errors and the paganism that has been introduced, mainly by the Roman Catholic Church, into this season, but, nevertheless, I think it is an error because it is good for us from time to time to face the facts and to look at our whole position, lest we assume certain things without being clear in our minds about them.

On what grounds do we believe that Jesus of Nazareth is the Christ? Fortunately this claim can be tested objectively, and the point that I want to establish this morning is that our faith is not based on some subjective experience. There is a subjective experience in the Christian life, otherwise we are not Christians at all; but our position is not based upon anything we may feel. So our approach as Christians to this season is not the sentimental one with which the world approaches it; rather, we approach it historically, and we do so because the very glory of our position as Christians is that our faith is based upon a very solid foundation, upon facts. We are not worshipping a beautiful theory; we do not just have an idea.

Many today are trying to persuade us to think not so much of the Lord Jesus Christ as of love as a principle. The great message of Christmas, they say, is the message of love. I think that is quite wrong. The great message of Christmas is not the message of love—though it is incidentally and indirectly a message of love—but of these great historical events that have taken place. So we do not consider love primarily—we consider the person, the Lord Jesus Christ, as this woman does. She does not go to the city to tell men to consider some teaching. She says, "Come, see a man . . . is not this the Christ?"—this Deliverer.

So we can ask ourselves this question: are we satisfied that Jesus is the Christ? If so, why are we? What are our criteria? It is not enough just to say, "I believe this is the Christ." Somebody may say to us, "What are your reasons?" There are all sorts of myths and stories in literature and in history. How do we substantiate our claim that this baby is the Christ? What tests do we apply?

I suggest that the following tests must be applied, and as we do this, they should strengthen our faith and give us a great certainty and assurance concerning our whole position. How do I know that he is the Christ? What do I insist upon before I come to this conclusion? Well, the first answer is this: he must fulfill the prophecies of the Old Testament. I put that as my first test because that is what is done in the New Testament itself. In practically every book of the New Testament this point is made strongly. The apostle Paul, for instance, in a very typical manner, puts it like this in the Second Epistle to the Corinthians: "For all the promises of God in him are yea, and in him Amen, unto the glory of God by us" (1:20).

Peter makes the same point. "We have not followed cunningly devised fables," he says and goes on to give the evidence of what happened on the Mount of Transfiguration, but then he hastens to say, "We have also a more sure word of prophecy; whereunto ye do well that ye take heed, as unto a light that shineth in a dark place, until the day dawn, and the day star arise in your hearts" (2 Pet. 1:16, 19). The fulfillment of prophecy is the first great proof, therefore.

So, then, let us apply this test to Christ. What have the prophecies of the Old Testament told us concerning the Messiah who was to come? They are there in great profusion. First, there are certain general statements. The first of these is found way back in the third chapter of Genesis: "Her [the woman's] seed shall bruise thy [the serpent's] head" (v. 15). Those are the words of God himself immediately after the Fall. The enemy has conquered, the serpent has prevailed, and mankind has fallen and is in a state of sin and bondage; and God goes on to say that there will be a great enmity between the seed of the woman and the seed of the serpent. But here is the great promise—the first great promise—of the coming of the Messiah, the Christ.

Now that expression "the seed of the woman" is very significant. No father is mentioned; the suggestion is immediately conveyed that the Deliverer will arrive in this world from a woman, and from a woman only. So it is not surprising to find the prophetic statement in the book of the prophet Isaiah: "Behold, a virgin shall conceive, and bear a son" (7:14). Do not be misled by popular talk on this subject. The best scholarship still says that this word means "virgin," as it has always been taken to mean throughout the centuries. So there we have Old Testament prophecies with the strong suggestion that the Christ, the Messiah, when he comes will come of a woman and specifically of a virgin.

So when we come to the New Testament, it is not surprising to find an emphasis upon this very prophecy. Matthew's Gospel states explicitly that our Lord had no human father, that he was born of a virgin. You find exactly the same statement in the announcement to Mary, his mother, by the angel Gabriel: "The Holy Ghost shall come upon thee . . . therefore also that holy thing which shall be born of thee shall be called the Son of God" (Luke 1:35). And the apostle Paul, looking back, describes him as having been "made of a woman, made under the law" (Gal. 4:4). So here is our first test, and it is more than fully satisfied. It had been said in the Old Testament that when the Messiah did come, he would come in this way, in a strange, miraculous, marvelous manner, without a human father—the miracle of the virgin birth. This is one of our greatest proofs. It is not something that you can sacrifice lightly; it is one of the most striking fulfillments of prophecy that we have.

I am trying to give you a list of points to strengthen your faith. What else are we told about him? Well, according to the prophecies, he must also be of the seed of Abraham. When God called Abraham out of Ur of the Chaldees, he told him immediately that in him all the nations of the world would be blessed (Gen. 12:1–3), and he promised him a seed (Gen. 13:16). This is the great line that runs right through the Old Testament from that twelfth chapter of Genesis onward, and all along there is an emphasis upon the fact that the Christ, the Messiah, would be of the seed of Abraham. This promise was repeated both to Isaac and to Jacob.

Then comes a most interesting and important point. Jacob had twelve sons, and one of these sons, Levi, was the one from whom the priesthood came. One would have naturally expected that the Deliverer would belong to this particular tribe. But the promise was not given with respect to Levi; it was given to the tribe of Judah. You will find that in the forty-ninth chapter of Genesis. The promise is being narrowed down. It is now specifically this child out of the tribe of Judah. Of course, Judah had many children, and they had children, and they had children and so on, but the promise is narrowed down further by the prophecies to a particular descendant of Judah, and his name was David—King David. The Deliverer would be of the seed of David (2 Sam. 7:16; Psalm 8:3–4). You cannot read the Old Testament without being impressed by the fact that this promise has been narrowing down like this, so that the Messiah when he comes must be of the seed of Abraham, the seed of Jacob, the tribe of Judah, and in particular "of the house and lineage of David" (Luke 2:4). This is one of those prophecies, therefore, that must be satisfied and fulfilled.

So when we come to the New Testament, we see how punctilious the writers are to give absolute proof of the fact that our Lord has indeed come from this particular line. Take, for instance, the way Matthew opens his Gospel: "The book of the generation of Jesus Christ, the son of David, the son of Abraham." There it is in summary form. Paul, years afterward, wrote to Timothy, "Remember that Jesus Christ of the seed of David was raised from the dead according to my gospel" (2 Tim. 2:8). Remember, too, the blind men shouting out to our Lord, "Thou Son of David, have mercy on us" (Matt. 9:27). So, again, this criterion is more than fully satisfied.

In addition, something else is said that is of great importance. The Old Testament is very careful to point out to us that while the Messiah will obviously be a man, "born of a woman," of a specified line and lineage, there will also be a mystery about him, something strange, something inexplicable, something that suggests that he is more than a man. Take Psalm 110, where David writes, "The LORD said unto my Lord, Sit thou at my right hand, until I make thine enemies thy footstool" (v. 1). Here is a suggestion of someone greater. Our Lord himself made use of that argument later on. When he was being questioned and cross-examined by the Pharisees and others, he asked them to explain David's words in Psalm 110. These words cannot refer to David's son because David says, "The LORD said unto my Lord . . ." There is someone above and beyond David (see Matt. 22:41–45).

And as we read a great passage like Isaiah 40, we get the same impression of a great person who is going to come. He is such a mighty personage that a great highway must be prepared for him: "Every valley shall be exalted, and every mountain and hill shall be made low" (v. 4). So these two elements are here for us in the prophecies of the Old Testament. And when we come to the New Testament, we see both so clearly every time we look at him.

Something else that is stated in the prophecies is the particular time of his coming, and this is most astounding. There are many suggestions about the timing, but in the ninth chapter of the book of the prophet Daniel the very period is narrowed down in a most explicit manner. It was not that he might come some time or other in some vague distant future. No, no; it is narrowed down, and when the experts came to look up the records, they were able to verify this. So he even fulfills this particular test of the time when he would appear in this world. But, of course, the Jews had become neglectful of this teaching, and so when the Messiah did come, they were not expecting him. That was due to their lack of diligence and to their failure to understand the character of their own prophecies.

Even the place of Christ's birth is prophesied—by the prophet Micah, who said that the Messiah would be born in Bethlehem (Mic. 5:2; Matt. 2:5–6). Here, again, is something that is astonishing. It is unexpected, yet it is true. Reading the Old Testament prophecies, I see that when the Christ comes he must be born in Bethlehem—and he *was* born in Bethlehem. Not only that, I find according to these prophecies that he must have lived for some time in a place called Nazareth. And so when Matthew comes to write his Gospel, he says in the last verse of the second chapter that Joseph and Mary took the child and "came and dwelt in a city called Nazareth: that it might be fulfilled which was spoken by the prophets, He shall be called a Nazarene" (Matt. 2:23). And he *was* called a Nazarene—he was known as Jesus of Nazareth, as foretold in the Old Testament prophecies.

The final fact that I adduce under this general heading is that it was even prophesied that he should be taken down to Egypt. In that second chapter of Matthew's Gospel, we are told that because of the malice of King Herod, who was trying to put Jesus to death, Joseph took Mary and the child down into Egypt "and was there until the death of Herod: that it might be fulfilled which was spoken of the Lord by the prophet, saying, Out of Egypt have I called my son" (v. 15; Hos. 11:1).

Now here is most striking evidence. "Is not this the Christ?" Certain essential evidences are put forward by the Old Testament prophets, and whatever effect Jesus has upon me, he is not truly the Christ unless he satisfies these criteria. But he does satisfy them—he satisfies every one—and this is a part of the basis on which our faith rests.

But let us go on and consider, in the second place, his character. The prophecies emphasize the Messiah's greatness, his majesty, his dignity. I have quoted to you from the fortieth chapter of Isaiah—everything there suggests that he will be someone quite unusual. In verse 5 Isaiah writes, "And the glory of the LORD shall be revealed, and all flesh shall see it together." There would be a glory about the Messiah, and the moment we come to the New Testament we find that prominence is given to this glory—look, for example, at the announcement to the shepherds. This is not an ordinary birth; this is something unusual. The angelic hosts are singing, an announcement is made to the shepherds, and they go and see. Ancient Simeon, too, is filled with a sense of marvel, Anna the prophetess also, and the wise men from the east. Why? Because this child, this babe, is a great King, the King of kings, the Lord of lords. There is a majesty and a glory about him. All this is foreshadowed and prophesied in the Old Testament Scriptures.

Yet here we come to something remarkable, because alongside these prophecies of glory, the Old Testament makes it quite clear that the Messiah will be exceptionally meek and peaceable. Isaiah, for instance, compares him to a lamb led to the slaughter (53:7). This is the paradox of the person. One very striking prophecy is quoted in Matthew's Gospel. In chapter 12 we read:

> Then the Pharisees went out, and held a council against him, how they might destroy him. But when Jesus knew it, he withdrew himself from thence: and great multitudes followed him, and he healed them all; and charged them that they should not make him known.

Why did he do this?

> That it might be fulfilled which was spoken by Esaias the prophet, saying, Behold my servant, whom I have chosen; my beloved, in whom my soul is well pleased: I will put my spirit upon him, and he shall shew judgment to the Gentiles. He shall not strive, nor cry; neither shall any man hear his voice in the streets. A bruised reed shall he not break, and smoking flax shall he not quench, till he send forth judgment unto victory. And in his name shall the Gentiles trust. (Matt. 12:14–21; Isa. 42:1–4)

And when we look at him, that is what we find—this mighty King, this King of kings and Lord of lords, yet how humble, how gentle. Tax collectors and sinners draw nigh unto him, the poor draw nigh unto him, and the people who were condemned as outcasts by the Pharisees he was prepared to touch and to help. This is the great characteristic that we find in him. And so, again, as we look at his character, we see that he fulfills the two elements that are most emphasized about him in the Old Testament Scriptures.

And then we come to our Lord's works—his miracles. In many places in the Old Testament there are prophecies that the Messiah will work miracles. In many places it is forecast that the blind will see, the deaf hear, the lame man leap as the hart, and the dumb sing (for example, Isaiah 35:5–6). It is to be expected, of course, that there will be something unusual about him because if the Son of God is going to come into the world, he will attest his person, he will give evidence of being someone entirely above ordinary humanity. And when our Lord came, this is precisely what he did. He himself made use of this very argument on a very interesting and important occasion connected with John the Baptist.

John was the forerunner; he had the great privilege of "preparing the way" for the Lord (Isa. 40:3), and yet John was arrested and thrown into prison. There in prison, he is obviously ill. Doubts begin to assail him, so much so that when he hears about the works of Christ, he sends two of his disciples with the question, "Art thou he that should come, or do we look for another?" (Matt. 11:3). Do you see the difference between John's question and the question of the woman of Samaria? The woman of Samaria rushes to the men and says, "Is not this the Christ? Come!" John the Baptist asks whether they should look for another. Having thought that our Lord was the Christ, he is now beginning to doubt whether he is the Christ. Why is this?

It is because John is surprised that our Lord has not gone up to Jerusalem and set himself up as a King and gathered an army together. John, a typical Jew, has, in a measure, a false notion concerning the Messiah. Poor John, there he is languishing in prison. He is the one who foretold the coming of the Messiah; surely, if our Lord is the Messiah, he will set John free. But he is not doing that. "Is this the Christ?" This is our Lord's reply to John's disciples: "Go and shew John again those things which ye do hear and see." What are they? "The blind receive their sight, and the lame walk, the lepers are cleansed, and the deaf hear, the dead are raised up, and the poor have the gospel preached to them" (Matt. 11:4–5).

What is our Lord doing when he replies like that? In effect he is saying, "Go back and tell John to read his prophecies again. Tell him to read the prophets, and there he will find they have said that the sign of the Messiah when he comes will be just what you have seen and heard. Go and tell him." It was predicted that the Messiah would work miracles, and if he had not done so, he would not have been the Christ. But he *did* work miracles, and therefore we say with the woman of Samaria, "Is not this the Christ?"

Or take another example. Here he is working some of his mighty miracles, and Matthew reports it like this:

> When the even was come, they brought unto him many that were possessed with devils; and he cast out the spirits with his word, and healed all that were sick: that it might be fulfilled which was spoken by Esaias the prophet, saying, Himself took our infirmities, and bare our sicknesses. (Matt. 8:16–17)

The miracles are a fulfilment of the prophecies. Our Lord himself again makes use of the same argument when he turns to those doubting disciples of his and says in essence, "If you do not believe me when I speak to you, 'Believe me for the very works' sake' [John 14:11]. The works that I do prove to you that I am indeed the Christ, the Son of God, the Savior of the world."

Further proof that he is the Christ is seen in our Lord's death and his resurrection because these, again, were prophesied and predicted in the Old Testament. This is a most valuable part of our proof and a substantiating of our belief. Even our Lord's disciples were too blind to see this. They had become so ignorant of their Scriptures and so misled by the wrong teaching of the Pharisees that when he was put to death, they were dumbfounded and cast down and came to the conclusion that the one whom they had thought was the Christ was actually not the Christ at all. You find this typified perfectly in the story of the two dejected men on the road to Emmaus on the evening of the day our Lord rose from the dead. Our Lord joins them, and at last, when they give him a chance, he speaks to them, and this is what he says:

> O fools, and slow of heart to believe all that the prophets have spoken: Ought not the Christ to have suffered these things, and to enter into his glory? And beginning at Moses and all the prophets, he expounded unto them in all the Scriptures the things concerning himself. (Luke 24:25–27)

Now this is a most vital bit of proof for us. Some people today are troubled by our Lord's death and resurrection—they do not understand them. They do not understand them in terms of the biblical teaching and depict him dying as a pacifist. They do not believe in the resurrection of the body, and thereby, of course, they show their utter disbelief. I put it as strongly as this: if our Lord had not been crucified, if he had not risen again in the body out of the tomb, I would say, "He is not the Christ." But because he was crucified and fulfilled Psalm 22 as he was hanging there on the tree and because he literally came in the body out of the grave, I say,

"Is not this the Christ?" He is! He has fulfilled the prophecies concerning his death on the cross and his resurrection in the body.

What else? The next bit of fulfilled prophecy is in the sending of the Holy Spirit on the Day of Pentecost. Go back to the Old Testament, and you will find prophecies that will tell you that this Messiah, when he comes, will send the Holy Spirit in mighty profusion upon his people. You find it in Ezekiel 36 and in many other places. And so the Holy Spirit is called "the promise of the Father" (Acts 1:4). You remember the prophecies of Joel in Joel 2:28–32: "It shall come to pass afterward, that I will pour out my spirit upon all flesh"—this great outpouring of the Spirit of God. And so as I look at him I ask myself, "Is this the Christ?" I say, "Has he shed forth the Holy Spirit?" And I go to Acts 2, and I find that he has, and I say with the woman of Samaria, "Is not this the Christ?" If he had not shed forth the Holy Spirit on the Day of Pentecost in Jerusalem, he would not be the Christ. But this was prophesied, and he has carried it out.

The last bit of evidence concerning the prophets is that though he himself is a Jew, he will have a message for the Gentiles. Search the Old Testament, and you will find this prophesied; come to the New Testament, and you will see that this is the very thing that happened. He prophesied himself that his message should go out not only to Jerusalem but to the whole of Judea, to Samaria, and to the uttermost part of the earth (Acts 1:8) and that "this gospel of the kingdom shall be preached in all the world for a witness unto all nations; and then shall the end come" (Matt. 24:14). So you see this abundant and amazing and astonishing evidence that we have concerning this person.

"Is this not the Christ?"

"Of course he is!" He fulfils all these prophecies. "For all the promises of God in him are yea, and in him Amen, unto the glory of God by us" (2 Cor. 1:20).

But I have still other tests that I must apply. We have already referred to the prophecy in Genesis 3:15 that the seed of the woman shall bruise the serpent's head. The Messiah, the Christ, when he comes, must be one who can conquer the devil and destroy all his works. Here is a promise, plain and clear. This is what the Christ is going to do. As the result of listening to the devil, man has become the bondslave of the devil and needs to be set at liberty. So the Christ must deliver us from the devil and all his power and all his might. Let us apply this test to him. What do we see? In his life our Lord conquered the devil completely; he repulsed his every attack. For forty days and forty nights the devil tempted him in the wilderness and was routed. In his life our Lord cast out devils; no devil could withstand him. He is Master over the realm of evil and all its forces.

But still more strikingly, he finally routed the devil in his death on the cross. He said so himself just before he died: "Now shall the prince of this world be cast out" (John 12:31). As Paul puts it to the Colossians, in the cross he defeated all the principalities and powers and "made a shew of them openly, triumphing over them in it" (Col. 2:15).

And this defeat is seen even more clearly in the resurrection: "The last enemy that shall be destroyed is death" (1 Cor. 15:26). By the resurrection our Lord has conquered the devil, who is the one who has "the power of death" (Heb. 2:14). He has destroyed the devil himself, all his emissaries and powers and works, and our Lord has set free all those who believe in him.

Having, then, looked at the objective criteria for believing that our Lord is the Christ, let me in a few words also suggest a few subjective criteria. You notice the order in which I have put them before you. Always start with the objective. Here you have evidence that is irrefutable; it can never be turned back. You have the Old Testament prophecies written before he ever came, you have the fulfillment in the New, and they fit perfectly. That is the evidence; there is the basis.

But we are all in the flesh, and we are subjective, and we have our subjective tests. There are certain things that I, as a human being, ask of the Messiah, of the Christ. There are certain things that I need. What are they? First, I need wisdom, I need knowledge. How little we know, how dark our understandings. We do not understand life; we do not understand ourselves; we do not know God. We know nothing about death; we know nothing about what lies beyond it. We are ignorant. We need light, and we need instruction. I am faced with these ultimate questions, and no man can give me the information I need.

Here is the only one who can help me. God gives "the light of the knowledge of the glory of God in the face of Jesus Christ" (2 Cor. 4:6). I do not want human speculation about God. I can speculate as well as anybody else, but it is only speculation. I want someone who can speak with authority, and here is the one who does. "We speak," he says, "that we do know, and testify that we have seen" (John 3:11). "No man hath seen God at any time; the only begotten Son, which is in the bosom of the Father, he hath declared him" (John 1:18).

Here is the only knowledge of God. He gives me knowledge of myself;

he shows me my sin. I say with the woman of Samaria, "Come, see a man, which told me all things that ever I did." It is in him that I see my sin, my lost condition. He condemns me utterly. He alone reveals to me the condemnation of the Law. He does it in his teaching, in his perfect life, as he dies upon the cross.

What else do I need? I need righteousness. I know that I am guilty before God. I need to be forgiven; I need to be reconciled with God. I want to get rid of the fear of God that is in me instinctively. I want to feel that I can approach God. Who can help me? The Christ when he comes must do this. And as I look at this babe of Bethlehem, I find the only one who does: "who his own self bare our sins in his own body on the tree, that we, being dead to sins, should live unto righteousness" (1 Pet. 2:24). "God was in Christ, reconciling the world unto himself" (2 Cor. 5:19). My sins are forgiven. I am reconciled to God by this person and by him alone. He satisfies that need.

But I want more. I want a nature that corresponds with the nature of God. I want to commune with God; I want to have fellowship with him, but "what communion hath light with darkness?" (2 Cor. 6:14). I want eventually to stand in the presence of God and to spend eternity with him. So I must be like God, but how can I be? I cannot change myself; no man or woman can change me. I need a new nature, and that is precisely what he gives me. He said, "Verily, verily, I say unto thee, Except a man be born again, he cannot see the kingdom of God. . . . Marvel not that I said unto thee, Ye must be born again" (John 3:3, 7). I can be born again. I am born again. He has given me new life, and it is his own life, a holy life. He has put his Spirit within me, and the Spirit does his progressive work of delivering me from the pollution as well as the power of sin in order that eventually I might stand before God—and that is the ultimate thing that I need.

I have told you that he has already conquered my last enemy, which is death, but what of the realm that lies beyond? And there he still satisfies me. ". . . Christ Jesus, who of God is made unto us wisdom, and righteousness, and sanctification, and redemption" (1 Cor. 1:30). "Redemption" there means glorification—my very body delivered, free from infirmities, free from sin, free from all weakness, free from disease, free from everything that gets me down. He guarantees my eternal future. "Beloved, now are we the sons of God, and it doth not yet appear what we shall be: but we know that, when he shall appear, we shall be like him; for we shall see him as he is" (1 John 3:2).

So there he is, the babe of Bethlehem. Watch him growing as a boy, on into manhood; see him setting out at the age of thirty to preach, to teach, to work miracles; see him dying on the cross; see him laid in a tomb; see his rising; see him ascended; watch him sending the Holy Spirit; think of him seated at the right hand of God. "Is this not the Christ?" We have examined him in the light of the evidence that God himself has given us in all the teaching of the prophecies of the Old Testament. There is the picture of what he will be like. Look at him in the days of his flesh—what do you see? A fulfillment in every detail, in every jot and tittle. He satisfies every prophecy, and he satisfies my every need.

There is only one thing that we can say, having looked at him together again, and this is what we must say to everybody whom we know and everybody in the world as we are given opportunity to do so. We must rush to them and say, "Come, see a man, which told me all things that ever I did: Is not this the Christ?" Come and see him, test him, and see with us that this is indeed the Christ of God, the Savior of the world.

51

Facing a New Year

The woman then left her waterpot, and went her way into the city, and saith to the men, Come, see a man, which told me all things that ever I did: is not this the Christ? (John 4:28–29)

We are interested in this extraordinary act on the part of this woman of Samaria because by doing what she did and saying what she said, she gave what we must regard as the typical response to the Lord Jesus Christ of all who believe in him.

Here we are on the first Sunday morning of a new year. As Christians, we have a new view of time. Time, for us, is divided up entirely in terms of the Lord Jesus Christ. We think of time as time before he came, when he came, after he came, and when he will come again. But as the world to which we belong does recognize distinctions and divisions, and since this is the first time we are meeting together on a Sunday morning in 1968, it is good that we should examine ourselves and our whole relationship to time and to life in this world.

How do we examine ourselves? Well, the one thing that matters above everything else is that we should do so in terms of our relationship to the person of the Lord Jesus Christ. Here is a woman who, having met him and heard him, realizes that he matters above everything else and that her relationship to him is the most important thing in the world. That is why she rushes back to the city to invite her fellow townsmen to come out to see him. So let us examine ourselves in the light of what we are told here about this woman.

There are many reasons why this process of self-examination is very necessary. One is that Scripture itself frequently commands and exhorts it. Perhaps one of the most striking examples is in the Second Epistle to the Corinthians: "Examine yourselves, whether ye be in the faith; prove your own selves. Know ye not your own selves, how that Jesus Christ is in you, except ye be reprobates?" (13:5). The apostle says this because of certain things that were happening in the church at Corinth. This church, though it was a Christian church, was in a very unsatisfactory condition, both in general and in the lives of many individual members. In the light of this, Paul tells them that he can do nothing but exhort them to examine themselves. Are they truly Christians? Are they in the faith? Is Christ Jesus in them? The New Testament, with its characteristic honesty, makes it quite clear to us that it is possible for us to be members of the church without being Christians.

John reminds us that some had joined the church and yet, he says in effect, "They have gone out from us because, though they were among us, they never really belonged to us" (see 1 John 2:19). I have written elsewhere about Simon Magus in the city of Samaria who had been accepted into the church and had been baptized but clearly was never a Christian at all (Acts 8:9–24).[32] The Scriptures exhort us to examine ourselves lest we assume that we are Christians when we are not. We are all open to this delusion; we are all liable to it. Many of us have been brought up in Christian homes and taken to a Christian church and have assumed, therefore, that we are Christians. But that does not make us Christians.

But even if we have had a definite Christian experience, it is necessary—indeed, it is essential—that we should periodically examine ourselves and make sure that we are in the faith because, again, the New Testament shows us the danger of drifting. "Therefore we ought to give the more earnest heed to the things which we have heard," says the author of the Epistle to the Hebrews, "lest at any time we should let them slip" (2:1). There is a danger of drifting away from the foundations, drifting away from the moorings, drifting away from everything that should hold us to the truth.

The experience of the church throughout the centuries confirms this danger. The graph of the history of the church is never a steady one; certainly there is not a perpetual ascent. It is a history of ups and down, great periods of revival followed by periods of lethargy, of deadness and failure, and of formality. That, again, should urge us to examine ourselves. You can be a Christian, and yet you can become slack; you can become indolent; you can drop to a lower level and fail to maintain an experience you once had.

But how do we examine ourselves? It seems to me there is only one big question to ask, and it is the very question suggested by this story of the woman of Samaria. In the end it all comes down to this: what does our Lord himself mean to us? That is the great question. "Come, see a man, which told me all things that ever I did: is not this the Christ?" This woman is now dominated by this person. He is everything to her.

But even here we need help and instruction. I ask what our Lord means to us, but how do we decide that? Do we find out in a purely subjective manner? No! We must have certain objective standards and tests in order to make sure that our subjective reactions and responses are really true. What is the true response that is required of us? There is abundant material in the Scriptures to help us. To find out what he means to us, we must go back to the Gospels and see how men and women responded to him in the days of his flesh. The Gospels were written partly in order to bring this out and to help us. We see people amazed at him, astonished at him, loving him, falling at his feet. And when we look at those who were given the great privilege of seeing him after his return to heaven, we see that what always impressed them was that he was the same person. Though glorified, he is still "the Lamb that was slain" (Rev. 5:12).

But then we go on to the Acts of the Apostles. Our Lord has gone back to heaven, and his people are left in the world with persecutions and trials and troubles and tribulations. What was their relationship to him? What did they think of him? What part did he play in their lives? And I would remind you again that the book of Acts is meant to be a norm. Of course, in Acts there is an unusual intensity, but we must not isolate this book and segregate it, as it were, and say that it has nothing to teach us. We see there how Christian people are meant to live; so there we have another test.

Then we go on to the teaching of the epistles, and constantly, as I have shown you, the apostles are asking their questions. They remind the readers of their true relationship with Christ: "ye have not so learned Christ" (Eph. 4:20). And they put forward questions: is he that to you? "Examine yourselves, whether ye be in the faith; prove your own selves" (2 Cor. 13:5) and so on. And we end with the book of Revelation, where he again dominates the whole scene and where the concluding cry is, "Even so, come, Lord Jesus." His followers are still in this intimate communion with him. So there we have abundant evidence whereby we can test our relationship to the Lord.

But we can supplement even that, and it is most important that we should. I have already emphasized that a great danger in the Christian church at the present time is the danger of putting a wedge, as it were, between the New Testament and ourselves and saying that all we read there only belongs to that time and is impossible now, so we should not even seek it. There is a fatal assumption that the whole of the New Testament describes some ideal position that never is to be repeated. To me, this is the greatest fallacy of all; nothing is so responsible for the quenching of the Spirit as that attitude.

The best way to correct that wrong view is to turn to the whole history of the church subsequent to the first century. We can do that in many ways. We can read church history itself and see the great tides, the great movements, of the Spirit of God when the church and her people were lifted back up again to the position of the book of Acts. Then we can take the biographies of individuals. Sometimes, even in a time of drought and aridity, some saints were given experiences that were exactly like those that we read of in the New Testament, thus refuting the false teaching that would discourage us from seeking the New Testament kind of experience. And then we can always turn to our hymnbooks, and especially the great hymns of certain centuries. Go back to these hymns, and you will find accounts in verse of experiences of the relationship between these people and our blessed Lord and Savior. So let us make use of all this, and as we do so, we get a clear picture—it is the picture we are given here of this woman of Samaria. He means everything to her: "Come, see a man . . ." The picture is always the same.

In the light of all this, let us examine ourselves on this first Sunday morning of a new year. I again put my question to you—it is the one thing that matters—what does he mean to you? Let us consider this question in two main ways—first, by looking back at the past. Here we are, changing from one year to another, and as we start a new year, it is good to look back. The Bible is always doing this. Take the psalmists—they are constantly reviewing their own personal histories and the history of the nation of Israel. They look back at the history; they start from the beginning and see the various vicissitudes that occurred. It is excellent to do this. Let us do the same.

As we look back, I think these are the questions we should face. First, can we say quite honestly that our coming to know him is the greatest thing that has ever happened to us? That was true of this woman. She had her past history, but here she is affirming that meeting this person is the biggest event of her life; at last she has discovered reality. As we look back across our lives, can we say that without any question that is also true of us? Many things have happened that have given us much pleasure—we have had successes, joys—but here is the question: are we perfectly clear that greater than all else is our relationship to him?

Many things have controlled our lives; many factors have been bearing upon us—family, home, upbringing, associations, university, perhaps business. Whatever it is, it does not matter. Many things and many people have influenced us. But here is the second major question: what has been the biggest influence in our lives? What has been the dominating influence? It is no use saying, "Yes, I'm a Christian, and I'm applying certain Christian principles in my living." All right, that is important, but it is not quite enough. Here is the question of questions: is Jesus the biggest factor in your life? Has he been controlling your life? Can you say as you look back, "I've made many mistakes, I've fallen into sin, yet I know that the controlling influence in my life has been the Lord Jesus Christ"?

Or, thirdly, let me put it like this: are we more proud of our association with him than of anything else? We are proud of many things in our lives, proud of many associations—there is nothing wrong in that. The Bible does not condemn them as long as they do not become "inordinate" (Col. 3:5). We must not love the world, but it is right and legitimate to take pride in certain things that have happened to us in this world and of certain associations that we have. But this third question is always the test of tests. If called upon to do so, would we always have been ready to sacrifice every other association for his sake?

These first Christians were called upon to make such a decision. This was the great problem for every Christian in the Roman Empire: were they prepared to go on saying, "Jesus is Lord" or would they say, "Caesar is Lord"? They were pressed to make this decision, and they were told that unless they said, "Caesar is Lord," they would be put to death. And this was the test that they passed so gloriously. They would not deny Jesus Christ for the sake of Caesar, for the sake of saving their lives. They preferred to be martyred, crucified, torn limb from limb by the lions in the arena. "Jesus is the Lord!" Their boast was in him.

Has our boast been of him, or have we denied him for the sake of popularity or applause from human beings? Have we denied him in order to gain something for ourselves? This is the question. This woman, because of her evil life, because she knows exactly what everybody thinks about her, avoided people, as we have seen. But all that has gone now. She does not care what they think of her; what matters is what they think of him. And so we can test ourselves in that way.

Fourthly, a very good way of examining ourselves is to ask, what has he done for me? You have rejoiced, you have known happiness, but is the great source of your joy and rejoicing your knowledge of what he has done for you? This woman says, "Come, see a man, which told me all things that ever I did." He has done that for her. She knows he has done other things for her, too—she is aware of a change within herself. And that is the question I am asking: do you know that your sins are forgiven? These are the questions by which we examine ourselves and decide whether or not we are Christians. We are paying heed to the apostle's exhortation, "Examine yourselves, whether ye be in the faith; prove your own selves."

Are you still troubled about your past sins? Are you still doubting whether you are forgiven? If you are, my friend, I take leave to ask you to be sure again that you are a Christian at all, for Christians are people who know that their sins have been forgiven. They know that among the other sins that God the Father laid upon our Lord were their sins; they know that their sins have received their punishment, that Christ has borne them and they have been blotted out of God's book. And as the result of that, they have peace with God. "Being justified by faith, we have peace with God through our Lord Jesus Christ" (Rom. 5:1). Are your heart and conscience at peace? Peace in your mind, peace in your conscience, peace between you and God.

Oh, let us examine ourselves! Are you still trying to make yourself a Christian? Are you still trying to find a way of delivery and of salvation? Are you waiting for some book to appear that will give you some new insight? Are you dependent upon the researches of modern scientists—is that your position? Are you still in uncertainty and looking and searching and hoping to arrive at some truth? Or do you know that he is "the way, the truth, and the life" (John 14:6) and that you have come to the Father by him? Is your mind at rest? Has the weary searching and straining and travailing of looking come to an end, and do you know him who is the light of the world, and can you say with the apostle Paul, "God, who commanded the light to shine out of darkness, hath shined in our hearts, to give the light of the knowledge of the glory of God in the face of Jesus Christ" (2 Cor. 4:6)? Do you know that all is well with your soul, and well between you and him?

Or let me put it like this to you: do you have peace with God through Jesus Christ? Is this what matters to you above everything else? If it is, you are a Christian, however unworthy you are, however much you fail. If it is not, I take leave to suggest that you are not a Christian. And do you have, in addition to that, a sense of sonship, a sense of belonging to God as his child? Paul says, "For as many as are led by the Spirit of God, they are the sons of God" (Rom. 8:14). He continues, "For ye have not received the spirit of bondage again to fear." Are you living in fear, the fear of God, the fear of judgement, the fear of death, the fear of hell? Are you still in a spirit of heaviness and bondage? That is not the spirit of the child of God. No, no! ". . . but ye have received the Spirit of adoption, whereby we cry, Abba, Father" (v. 15). Tell me, has that cry arisen from your heart as you look back? I say again, however unworthy and failing, you can still say with Peter, "thou knowest that I love thee" (John 21:17).

And are we aware, as we look back, that we have had a sense of his nearness and of his help? This is real; it is not theoretical. "He hath said, I will never leave thee, nor forsake thee" (Heb. 13:5). Have you found him "a very present help in trouble" (Ps. 46:1)? Has he made all the difference to you at certain points of crisis? This is the test. It is comparatively easy for a man like me to preach and for you to come and listen and worship God, but the real tests of life and of our faith and of our relationship to him come when we are in trouble. What are we like in temptation and trial? Look back across your life—has he made all the difference to you? He always does when you really know him. You see, it is not enough to say, "Yes, I believe. I have subscribed to the truth." You can do that intellectually. Here is a profound test: in the moment of agony has he suddenly appeared, and then has everything been different? I must quote that hymn again:

Sometimes a light surprises
The Christian while he sings;
It is the Lord, who rises
With healing in his wings.

William Cowper

Have you known that? It has been the universal experience of the saints throughout the centuries.

Lastly, as you look back, have you been conscious of his working in you? Have you been conscious of the fact that he will not leave you alone? Oh, that is a wonderful test! It can be a very painful one, but it is a very determined test. He will not allow you to go away. "O love that wilt not let me go"—have you known that? Have you known that the pressure of his hand is upon you, that he is dealing with you, manipulating your life? For he does. This is the whole teaching of the Scripture. Again this is the universal testimony of his saints at all times. As you look back, are you staggered as you see the way that he has led you and brought you, anticipated you, manipulated circumstances—how all along he has been there? Are you conscious that he has been working in you "both to will and to do of his good pleasure" (Phil. 2:13)? These are infallible signs of our being in true and right relationship to him.

I want to supplement all this with yet another question before I leave the past: has your knowledge of him increased during the last year? It should have. The notion that you get your really big experience when you make your decision for Christ and for the rest of your life you try to maintain that and probably fail rather than succeed is an utter travesty of the New Testament teaching. Jesus Christ is a person, and he is endless. The apostle Paul, in praying for the Ephesians, asks that they "may be able to comprehend with all saints what is the breadth, and length, and depth, and height; and to know the love of Christ, which passeth knowledge" (Eph. 3:18–19).

Do you know him better than you did twelve months ago? Is he more real to you, more vital? Are these assurances that come from him more and more precious to you? Tell me, my dear friends, are you more amazed at him than you have ever been? Are you amazed at the Scriptures? Are you enjoying them more than you did? Are you ravished by them? Are you thrilled by them? Does this knowledge seem to you more and more precious? Your personal knowledge of him, your awareness of his presence, your confidence in him, your understanding of the way of salvation—has all this been increasing? These are the ways whereby we discover our true relationship to him. These are what ultimately count.

We have been looking at the past; now let us turn and look at the future. That is what you inevitably do at the beginning of a year, is it not? And it is important that we should do this. We are starting a new year—how do we contemplate it? Again I would say that the vital test is this: are all of us facing the future in terms of our relationship to him? I do not mean that we do not consider anything else; all I am asking is, is he the dominating factor here? We look to this unknown future, we think of possibilities, but here is the question—is he central to all our hopes and plans?

The apostle Paul in the Epistle to the Romans shows us the right perspective. This, he says, is how a Christian looks at the future:

> . . . knowing the time . . . now it is high time to awake out of sleep: for now is our salvation nearer than when we believed. The night is far

spent, the day is at hand: let us therefore cast off the works of darkness, and let us put on the armour of light. Let us walk honestly, as in the day; not in rioting and drunkenness, not in chambering and wantonness, not in strife and envying. But put ye on the Lord Jesus Christ, and make not provision for the flesh, to fulfil the lusts thereof. (13:11–14)

So, then, as you look at the future, is it essentially in terms of him?

Let me put that to you in a number of subsidiary questions. What is your greatest desire as you face the future? We all have desires, we all have wishes, there are certain things we would all like to happen, and we think as we look at the future, what does it have in store for me? All right, I ask, what do you want? What is your greatest desire? This is a vital test, and the Christian response to that test is this: it is the desire to know him better. "Come, see a man, which told me all things that ever I did." Come and listen to him; come and look at him. The woman of Samaria wants to know more and more of him, and she forgets the waterpot, puts it aside, and goes back and fetches the people!

Consider Mary of Bethany sitting at his feet:

O that I could forever sit
With Mary at the Master's feet;
Be this my happy choice;
My only care, delight, and bliss,
My joy, my heaven on earth, be this,
To hear the Bridegroom's voice.

CHARLES WESLEY ("O LOVE DIVINE, HOW SWEET THOU ART")

Tell me, can you honestly say as you face this new year that your greatest desire is to know him better because of what you have already known of him? Like the apostle Paul, can you say that the greatest desire of all in your life is "that I may know him, and the power of his resurrection, and the fellowship of his sufferings, being made conformable unto his death; if by any means I might attain unto the resurrection of the dead" (Phil. 3:10–11)?

Tell me, my dear friend, is that your supreme desire more than everything else? Is it your desire to serve him truly and to please him in all your ways?

Tell me another thing—above everything else in this coming year, do you desire to see the success of his kingdom? We look at our world, we look at our country, and it is right and good that we should wish for economic improvement and prosperity. We seek health, strength, happiness, wealth—I am not criticizing any of these desires, but I am asking this: above and beyond all this, do we long for revival, reformation, for his truth to be manifested with power, sin rebuked, men and women converted, falling at his feet, leaving evil? Do we wish to see this country renewed spiritually for his glory's sake? Are we grieved at the blasphemy of this age, and do we long, even beyond the prosperity of the country, to see the prosperity of the kingdom of our God and of our Christ? This is inevitably the response of all who are in this true and living relationship to him.

And then I want to ask another question—it is an obvious one, is it not? How do we face the unseen possibilities? What does this year hold for us? Who knows? But the question is, are you afraid of the future? Are you afraid to face it? Are you apprehensive? Does the future hold terror from which you shrink so that you try just to enjoy yourself for the moment? This is a vital matter.

At this point we must draw a crucial distinction. There are two ways of looking at the future. There is a wrong way, a morbid way, which our Lord himself condemned in the Sermon on the Mount:

> Therefore I say unto you, Take no thought for your life, what ye shall eat or what ye shall drink; nor yet for your body, what ye shall put on. Is not the life more than meat, and the body than raiment? . . . Wherefore, if God so clothe the grass of the field, which to day is, and to morrow is cast into the oven, shall he not much more clothe you, O ye of little faith? Therefore take no thought, saying, What shall we eat? or, What shall we drink? or, Wherewithal shall we be clothed? (For after all these things do the Gentiles seek:) for your heavenly Father knoweth that ye have need of all these things. But seek ye first the kingdom of God, and his righteousness; and all these things shall be added unto you. Take therefore no thought for the morrow: for the morrow shall take thought for the things of itself. Sufficient unto the day is the evil thereof. (Matt. 6:25, 30–34)

Now people sometimes misinterpret that by saying that Christianity tells us, "Never look to the future at all—do not consider the possibilities—just live for today." But that is a misunderstanding of this teaching. Our Lord is saying that we should not be the victims of a morbid care and anxiety; we should not worry about the future. But that does not mean that we should not consider it at all. What, then, is the right way to face the future? It is the way of the apostle Paul. He looks at the future and says:

> For I am persuaded, that neither death, nor life, nor angels, nor principalities, nor powers, nor things present, nor things to come, nor height, nor depth, nor any other creature, shall be able to separate us from the love of God, which is in Christ Jesus our Lord. (Rom. 8:38–39)

That is the right way, and it is very important that we do that. The Christian is not afraid to look to the future. The Christian does look at it and envisages all the worst possibilities but then triumphs over them all in Christ Jesus.[33] That is the Christian's response.

So we are unlike the world in every respect. We do face the future, and we face it honestly. It is right that we should do so. We will be a year older if we are still alive in a year's time. So face it—remind yourself that ill health, failure of your faculties, and so on are all bound to come, and eventually death itself.

It is, therefore, the essence of Christianity that we face these things. We do not just say, "Don't think of them—they will come soon enough." That is the world's way! Christian men and women look at them all, but they are able to face them and to be more than conquerors through him who loved them. This is the way. So apply that in detail. Look at the immediate future—we do not know what may come. We may have a year of great happiness and joy; we may have disappointment and sorrow. We may have abounding health; we may lose it. We may have loss; we may have success. Accidents may come, or sorrow and bereavement. My dear friends, we are in the midst of life, and in the midst of life we are in death. "Change and decay in all around I see."[34]

But here is the question: having looked at these possibilities, these certainties, how do we react to them? And this is where our Lord comes in. Do you rely on him? Do you know that his promises are sure? Do you know that he will always be sufficient, that he will never fail you? That is the question. That is how the apostle faced the future; that is how the first Christians faced it; that is how Christians throughout the centuries have faced it. The Christian is the greatest realist in the world. Christians can afford to face their fears and problems, and they believe in facing them. It is the world that tries to forget its problems by entertainment or drink or drugs, by playing and escaping.

Christians are able to face the future because they know him; they have met this man. "Come, see this man, which told me all things that ever I did: is not this the Christ?" Christians have met him, and they say, "This one can do everything for me. It matters not what may come to meet me. I am ready for all things because he is the ruler of the universe, the Lord of history, the controller of my destiny. Though I am led as a lamb to the slaughter, whatever may happen to me, I know that nothing shall be able to separate me from the love of God, which is in Christ Jesus our Lord." This is the test of the Christian. Charles Wesley looks at the Lord, and this is what he says:

Thou hidden source of calm repose,
Thou all-sufficient love divine,
My help and refuge from my foes,
Secure I am if thou art mine;
And lo! from sin and grief and shame
I hide me, Jesus, in thy name.

Thy mighty Name salvation is,
And keeps my happy soul above;
Comfort it brings, and power and peace,
And joy and everlasting love;
To me with thy dear name are given
Pardon and holiness and heaven.

Jesus, my all in all thou art,
My rest in toil, mine ease in pain,
The healing of my broken heart . . .

Does he mean this to you? Has he been that to you? And as you look to the unknown future, do you know he is going to be medicine for your broken heart?

In war my peace; in loss my gain,
My smile beneath the tyrant's frown,
In shame my glory and my crown.

In want my plentiful supply,
In weakness my almighty power,
In bonds my perfect liberty,
My light in Satan's darkest hour. . . .

Has he been all this to you? Do you know he will be?

My help and stay whene'er I call,
My life in death, my heaven, my all.
(Charles Wesley, "Thou Hidden Source of Calm Repose")

Has he been that to you? Is he that to you now? Do you know that he will ever be that to you, so that whatever may come all is well with your soul? And ultimately as you look into the haggard face of death, can you smile and say, "O death, where is thy sting? O grave, where is thy victory?" (1 Cor. 15:55). Well, there it is, my friends: what is he to you? Can you say quite honestly:

Thou, O Christ, art all I want,
More than all in thee I find.[35]

I have found, I find, I know that I ever shall find this so, for Jesus Christ is "the same yesterday, today, and for ever."

52

The Witness

The woman then left her waterpot, and went her way into the city, and saith to the men, Come, see a man, which told me all things that ever I did: is not this the Christ? Then they went out of the city, and came unto him. (John 4:28–30)

We have been considering together the reaction of the woman of Samaria to our Lord's conversation with her. We have seen that one of the first things that happens to her is a profound conviction of sin, and then that this overwhelming person becomes the dominating factor in her life—that is why she leaves her waterpot. We have seen what this means as it is expounded to us in the pages of the New Testament, as it was confirmed in the lives of the saints in the church throughout the running centuries, and as we know it ourselves.

So now we come to the next step, and these steps follow, I think you will agree, in a kind of logical necessity. They are true psychologically and are true according to the teaching of the Word. The next step is that this woman invites her fellow townspeople to come at once and see this person who has made such a difference to her and listen to him. This, again, is something against which we must obviously test ourselves. There is a kind of wholeness about the Christian life or, if you like, about the response of the Christian to the Lord Jesus Christ. One step always leads to another; they are indissolubly bound and linked together. So we examine ourselves by each of the particulars, and we also examine ourselves to see if we are manifesting something of the whole. Both are very necessary; otherwise we may very well go astray. If we fix on one aspect only, we lack balance, we develop a lopsided Christianity, and we can indeed fall into grievous error.

Let us, then, look at this together. Here is this woman—she has had the experience of meeting this blessed person, and her immediate response is to rush to the city to say to the people there, "Come, see a man, which told me all things that ever I did: is not this the Christ?" Now the first point that we must notice about her action is that it arose spontaneously. This is most important, and that is why I am starting with it. The way in which this arises is important in and of itself and particularly, I feel, at the present time. You will often hear Christian people like ourselves criticized on the grounds that in this matter we contrast unfavorably with the adherents of the cults. We are told how these people give themselves enthusiastically to their work: young men give up an afternoon to knock on doors and sell their literature. This is a great characteristic of the cults, and it is said of Christians that as long as they can go and enjoy their acts of worship they think they are all right. Then they do these other things when they have time and when nothing more important is calling for their attention. So they spend most of their lives failing to show the concern about other people and the zeal that are so characteristic of the members of the cults.

Now it is not up to me or to any preacher to excuse the failure of Christian people, and it is not my purpose to do so now. My comments are not primarily meant for the comfort of the Christian but are intended to bring out certain characteristics of the cults. I want to try to show you that, speaking generally, in this very difference between the behavior of the adherents of the cults and of Christian people we see a vital distinction between the two, a distinction that is clearly seen here in the spontaneity of the woman of Samaria.

To describe in general the characteristics of any of the cults, we simply have to use one word—carnality. By that, I mean that they are of the flesh, of the natural man; they are carnal in contradistinction to that which is spiritual, which is ever the characteristic of the true Christian. Let me analyze that a little to show you what I mean. Here is the picture I trust you have in your mind: here is the woman of Samaria rushing back to the city; she typifies Christian people. Then think of what you know to be so true of the followers of the cults at the present time. What is happening today is not new; there have always been cults, but under different names. There were mystery religions in the time of the New Testament and other false, specious teachings that at first seemed to be very Christian but were not Christian at all.

One of the characteristics of the cults is their method of approaching people. First of all, their members have to be urged to go out and do this. The moment they join, they are told that the right thing to do is to get others also. Then a definite scheme or system is always imposed upon them—they all say the same things in the same way. It could really be done almost as well by a record or tape player, and indeed sometimes is. This, of course, leads to the third point, which is that they have to be trained and taught how to go out and speak to people. They are given the formula. It is drummed into them; they are drilled, in order that they may be effective and efficient. I think you will agree that always marks the way in which the cults operate.

In other words, their method is mechanical. The machine-like element is always very prominent. If you start listening to such people but then interrupt them and put questions to them, you will find that they are nonplussed because what they have to say is a sort of circle that goes round and round. They are generally taught a certain number of Scriptures, and they can always produce them, but give them one they have never heard of or have never been taught to repeat or to expound and they are lost and fumble, not knowing quite what to say. There is no freedom about their words, but they are learned and repeated parrot-fashion.

The other characteristic of cults is a zeal for proselytizing and for gaining adherents; that seems to be their great motive. Now there are fine distinctions here. Obviously, the Christian is anxious that others should become Christians, as I am going to show you, but there is all the difference in the world between being moved by a desire to get adherents to your particular cult or teaching and the true desire that people should get the blessings of the Lord Jesus Christ. These people are anxious for us to get "it." There is always some "it," some particular thing. And they are very zealous—there is no question about that. The New Testament tells us that the Pharisees would "compass sea and land" to make one proselyte (Matt. 23:15). They were great proselytizers, and the false teachers, the New Testament tells us in many places, have always been characterized by a similar zeal. They know that people have "itching ears" (2 Tim. 4:3), and they show an enthusiasm and an energy that is quite astonishing until you begin to examine it. But the moment you examine it, you see that it belongs to the flesh rather than to the spirit; it is an imposed system that is carried out in a mechanical manner.

Of course, these days this approach is by no means confined to followers of cults and false religions; we see it also in the realm of business. If you listen to the patter of people who want to sell you a vacuum cleaner or anything else, you can see that they have been trained and that they are repeating parrot-fashion something that they have been told to say.

But in contrast to all that, we see this woman of Samaria, and what hits us at once as we read this story is the spontaneity of her action. Nobody told her to rush to the city and invite the people to come and see the Lord Jesus Christ. Nobody told her, nobody taught her, nobody urged her. The glorious and remarkable aspect of this story is that she just found herself doing it. She did not even have to think about it; she just did it. And this spontaneity is characteristic of the Christian. Now you see the essential difference. That is why I say that this principle is so important. False proselytizing zeal is the characteristic of the spurious rather that of the true.

Linked with this is the fact that it is obviously the Lord himself who is at the center of the woman's concern. She is not primarily out to get adherents to the cause to which she is now going to belong, she is not concerned above all else that others should have her experience, though that comes in, but she is motivated by the desire that everybody should come to meet him. This is what is overwhelming her. She wants everybody to listen to him as she has been doing. He is the center of everything, and this is the most valuable test of all. Even in our Christian work we can quite unconsciously have wrong motives. A minister may be anxious to have more church members or an increase in the collections so that he can boast about it. A congregation, likewise, can be moved by the same desire to show off "our church," "our cause." But all this is so remote from what we have here. Look at the delightful, glorious simplicity and spontaneity of someone captivated and captured by the Lord. The woman acts as one inevitably acts in such circumstances.

Let me give you further demonstrations of this. My whole purpose is to show that the Christian response is spontaneous and not imposed. Christians witness to others because of something that is working in them. There is one notable example at the end of the first chapter of the Gospel of John. One afternoon John the Baptist is with two of his disciples when our Lord passes by, and John says, "Behold, the Lamb of God." So these two disciples go after him, and he speaks to them. Then we are told, "[They] abode with him that day: for it was about the tenth hour. One of the two which heard John speak, and followed him, was Andrew, Simon Peter's brother."

What does Andrew do, having met the Lord and having listened to him? "He first findeth his own brother Simon, and saith unto him, We have found the Messias, which is, being interpreted, the Christ. And he brought him to Jesus." What then? "The day following Jesus would go forth into Galilee, and findeth Philip, and saith unto him, Follow me."

What is Philip's response? "Philip findeth Nathanael, and saith unto him, We have found him, of whom Moses in the law, and the prophets, did write, Jesus of Nazareth, the son of Joseph" (John 1:35–45).

My argument is that this is inevitable. You cannot meet with this person without responding. If it has been suggested to you that this is a duty for which you have to be trained and drilled, there is something wrong and you belong to another realm; it is not the Christian response. We must examine ourselves in the light of this.

Or, again, consider fully what we read in Acts 4—this is the Christian response:

> Peter and John answered and said unto them, Whether it be right in the sight of God to hearken unto you more than unto God, judge ye. For we cannot but speak the things which we have seen and heard. (vv. 19–20)

We cannot help it; we cannot stop it; we are bound to do this. "We cannot but speak."

Or take another still more striking example. You may say, "That is still about apostles—what about ordinary Christians?" Look at Acts 8. We read at the beginning of the chapter:

> And at that time there was a great persecution against the church which was at Jerusalem; and they were all scattered abroad throughout the regions of Judaea and Samaria, except the apostles.

What did these people who were scattered abroad do? The fourth verse tells us, "Therefore they that were scattered abroad went every where preaching the word." Then verse 5 goes on to say, "Then Philip went down to the city of Samaria, and preached Christ unto them."

In verses 4–5 the same English word—"preaching/preached"—is used to translate two different Greek words. This is a pity because there is an important difference in the meaning of the two Greek words. The difference is this: in verse 5 Philip, who was an evangelist, "proclaimed" or "heralded" Christ to the people. The suggestion here is of a man addressing a congregation; that is the meaning of the word actually used by Luke. By contrast, it has been very rightly suggested by someone that a very good translation of the word in verse 4, referring to ordinary people, is this: "Therefore they that were scattered abroad went everywhere gossiping the word." They did not stand up in pulpits. The word "preaching" now carries that connotation for us, and so when we read about the first Christians "preaching the word," we picture them standing up and addressing congregations. But these people did not do that; they just talked about the gospel. They were "scattered abroad" because of the persecution, and some kind people in Judea and Samaria received them into their homes, and the believers they just talked to them—it was gospel conversation.

This is the instinctive, characteristic Christian response—Christians cannot help talking about the Lord. These first Christians not only told the people why they were being persecuted and why they had to escape from Jerusalem, they wanted to tell them about this person and this experience that they had received through him. It was not confined to apostles or to some exceptional people. Here were ordinary members of the church—I use the word *ordinary* because of the limitation of language. There is no such person as an ordinary Christian, but there are distinctions in offices in the church, and these are the people who did not hold any office—they went everywhere speaking, gossiping, telling people this blessed word of salvation in Christ Jesus.

Now this is so vital that I cannot leave it; let me give you another example. Listen to the apostle Paul writing to the church at Rome and telling the people there about his desire to be with them. This is how he puts it:

> For I long to see you [what for?], that I may impart unto you some spiritual gift, to the end ye may be established; that is, that I may be comforted together with you by the mutual faith of both you and me. Now I would not have you ignorant, brethren, that oftentimes I purposed to come unto you, (but was let [hindered] hitherto,) that I might have some fruit among you also, even as among other Gentiles. I am debtor both to the Greeks, and to the Barbarians; both to the wise, and to the unwise. So, as much as in me is, I am ready to preach the gospel to you that are at Rome also. (Rom. 1:11–15)

Do you see the idea? "I am debtor." What does the apostle mean by that? He means that he owes it to them. In the word "debtor" there is the whole idea of compulsion, is there not? The very word conjures up a court and a man with legal pressure being brought to bear upon him to pay a debt. So Paul is saying, "I am similar to that man. A kind of pressure is on me. I am a debtor. I owe this. I have the good news, and I want to give it, and I feel I must give it."

This is a concept that Paul returns to in many other places. For instance, he says to the Corinthians, "Though I preach the gospel, I have nothing to glory of: for *necessity is laid upon me*; yea, woe is unto me, if I preach not the gospel!" (1 Cor. 9:16). "Necessity"! "Woe unto me if I do not!" "You ask me why I preach like this," says Paul in effect, "and why I go on in spite of obstacles and persecutions and so on. I have no choice. I don't deliberately decide to go out and preach; there is a necessity." The same necessity sent the woman of Samaria rushing to the city: "Come, see this man . . ." Spontaneity! You are in a different realm from drilling and ordering and the mechanics of it all.

Again, in writing to the Corinthians, Paul says, "Wherefore we labour, that, whether present or absent, we may be accepted of him. For we must all appear before the judgment seat of Christ." And then he ends with this tremendous statement—the fact is, he says, "the love of Christ constraineth us" (2 Cor. 5:9–10, 14). "Constraineth" is a great word. Apparently the original word, in its root meaning, is this: you put something into a vise, and you turn it, and it gets tighter and tighter, and the pressure from the two sides becomes greater and greater. That is the idea—"the love of Christ"—this constraint, this pressure. Paul is like a man in a vise: I do not decide; I do not get trained. I must do this; I am bound to.

That comes out everywhere in all these examples and illustrations in the New Testament, and the big principle, therefore, is this: the difference between the cults and the Christian is the difference between something that is put on from the outside and something that comes from the inside. Adherents of the cults are people who belong to the flesh and behave accordingly. They think after the flesh; they act after the flesh. Not so the Christian. There is in the Christian something compelling, something driving, something urgent, a kind of dynamo. Our words *dynamo* and *dynamic* derive from the Greek word for power. There is a dynamism within Christians, something that is operating inside. And this Samaritan woman shows it all to perfection. What is driving her? Oh, it is this inward constraint, this dynamic element; it is this force and this power of the truth that has become hers.

And as we read the history of the Christian church in general throughout the running centuries, and as we read it in particular in the lives of individuals, we always find this same element—ordinary, simple people talking about the gospel. We are told that Communism spread in a similar way. Communism was not spread by public meetings; it was spread in a more subtle and thorough manner by conversation. A man on a bench talked to his colleagues on the right and on the left, and so it spread. It was called "cellular infiltration."

As Christianity spread mainly like that at the beginning, so it has spread many, many times since then in periods of revival. Even when the church has been persecuted, people have been born again, and they have just talked to one another. And so the gospel has spread from one to the other. I say again that the whole idea of training people to witness is quite foreign to the New Testament, as it is to the whole history of the Christian church. That belongs to the realm of the cults, the false, the spurious, the human. Of course, human beings by nature have to operate in this way; it is their only way. They always multiply their organizations and institutions; they are bound to. But it is foreign to the church's method; she has something infinitely greater. So the whole idea of training people to witness, giving them the formulas and the phrases, telling them steps and numbers, and especially making them pass an examination afterward and then giving them a certificate and commissioning them, is ridiculous and laughable from the standpoint of the New Testament and the history of the Christian church.

But even worse, even more serious, is the fact that this approach shows a failure to rely upon the power of the Holy Spirit. There is something ludicrous about this age in which we live. It is astonishing that modern people never ask the most obvious question with regard to all these matters: how did Christianity spread in the past? How did Christian people behave in former ages? If only they asked that question, they would save themselves a lot of trouble and avoid many serious pitfalls. Instead, we are told we all must become psychologists and must be trained psychologically to talk about Christianity.

The salesman has to pass a training course, it is said. He cannot be a salesman if he has not had the appropriate psychological training. Well, how do you think the people of the last century, and many centuries before, built up their businesses? According to the modern idea, they could never have built up a business, they could never have succeeded. How could they sell goods? They had never been trained in salesmanship; they had never been drilled; they had never been told that if such and such a question comes, this is the reply. And the answer is perfectly clear—and if it is clear in the realm of business and of secular affairs, how much more so is it in the realm of these spiritual matters with which we are dealing?

"Are you saying," says someone, "that the Christian does not need any training?"

No, no! But I am saying that he does not need any teaching or training in techniques and methods. The woman of Samaria did not get it; the early Christians did not have it. They were very successful and effective, and their results were more lasting than the modern methods that get you an immediate result that does not last. The early Christians had something more important.

What, then, do we need to be taught? We need to be taught about Christ Jesus; we need to get to know him; we need to be taught the truth as it is in him. That is where the training and the teaching come in. This, again, is the testimony of the New Testament and of history. The best workers in the Christian church, those who have been greatly used in winning others for Christ, have always been those who have been best, not in techniques, not in carnal zeal, but in their knowledge and understanding of the truth; they have been those with the most profound experience.

Experience is of the very essence in this matter. It is the man or woman who has experience who can help others. They can understand, they can sympathize, they can be patient. The life in them enables them. The best workers, eventually, are those who are living the best kind of life. The world soon sees through false Christians, who are skillful with their words perhaps but whose lives do not bear witness to the words. At first people are taken in—what is offered seems glamorous and wonderful; that is why the cults are successful. But when they apply the test of time, people begin to see through the talk.

Do you know what is the supreme necessity in order to be a witness for Christ and to bring others to him? It is to be filled with the Holy Spirit. That is the secret of the early Christians, as it has been the secret of Christians who have been most used in this respect through the centuries. It is at times of revival that people always do so magnificently what the woman of Samaria did. The secret, the key, is the Spirit within us, enlightening the mind and moving the heart, giving wisdom and understanding, leading and directing. The New Testament is full of this. For instance, take the case of the evangelist Philip. We read that after he had done his work in Samaria, "The angel of the Lord spake unto Philip, saying, Arise, and go toward the south." Then after Philip had arrived on the road, he saw the Ethiopian eunuch, and "the Spirit said unto Philip, Go near, and join thyself to this chariot" (Acts 8:26, 29). The Spirit is the teacher; the Spirit is the guide and director. Any drilling that is done is done by the Holy Spirit; it is his constraint. It is always the Holy Spirit.

You see, my friends, if our object were just to get adherents to a cause or a cult or a teaching, then mechanical training is all right; but we are not dealing with that, we are in the realm of life. This eventually includes being born again, and formulas cannot give new birth to anybody. Someone can persuade you to join a movement; logic can get you to buy a commodity on your doorstep or join a political party or a cult. You listen to the arguments. "Ah, yes," you say, "I've never thought of that before," and you take it up. But that is not Christianity! You do not take this up—you are taken up by it. This involves being born again, born of the Spirit. It is the mighty activity of the Holy Spirit of God himself.

So I deduce from all that this great principle: anything that attributes results to particular methods is of necessity wrong. That is a very serious statement to make, but it needs to be made in the light of certain modern tendencies. Anything that attributes success to the methods employed is not truly Christian because everything that happens in this realm must be attributed solely to the operation of the Holy Spirit of God. To rely on methods is therefore wrong. Of course, we must have flexibility, we must use all our faculties rightly, we must do all we can, but we must never rely on these things.

Do you see how important this is for you and for me? Do you have the power of the Holy Spirit in you? It is no use our shielding ourselves behind this teaching and saying, "Of course, these people who belong to the cults are all wrong. I can see that." That is all right, but the question then is, what about us? Is anything moving us? I would prefer, in a sense, the person who witnesses mechanically than the person who does nothing and who is not aware of any compulsion and has none of this spontaneity that sent the woman hurrying back to the city. Here is the vital and the positive question: do I know this inward constraint, this "love of Christ constraining me," that makes me say, "Woe is unto me, if I preach not the gospel" (1 Cor. 9:16), necessity is laid upon me, I must, I am bound to?

There, then, is the first great principle—it is a spontaneous action. But that compels us to ask a further question: why does this action arise spontaneously in this woman? She has lived in that city, leading this wretched kind of life, and everybody knows the sort of woman she is. So why does she now rush back and give this invitation? Why does she act in this manner? There are a number of answers. I will just mention one or two.

The first is this: it is because of what she has found. She is a new woman; she has been changed. We have considered that. But now I want to emphasize that it is because of what she has found. The Christian is not a mere seeker and searcher after the truth. That is the modern idea.

You can hear this whenever you like on television. It is very clever. People discuss theories and ideas, they debate philosophies, they drag in the Russian novelists, of the last [nineteenth] century particularly, and it is all so wonderful—we are seeking, searching after the truth. Nonsense! The Christian is not a seeker; the Christian is one who has found. "Come, see a man . . ." Or as Andrew and Philip put it, "We have *found*"—that is the invitation—"the Messias, which is, being interpreted, the Christ" (John 1:41). Philip says the same thing: "We have *found* him, of whom Moses in the law, and the prophets, did write, Jesus of Nazareth, the son of Joseph" (John 1:45). Oh, my dear friends, here is the great thing—once you have "found," you want others to know.

I would like to ask this question: have you found him? If you have not, of course you have nothing to say. "Can the blind lead the blind?" asks our Lord on a famous occasion. "Shall they not both fall into the ditch?" (Luke 6:39). The blind cannot lead the blind. Christians are men and women who have found; they have something to give; they are not merely seeking. How can you help others if you do not have anything yourself? What is the use of going to somebody else and saying, "Well, I see that you're interested in the truth and you're seeking and searching after it; so am I. We must keep on, you know. There's a great book coming out next week, and I'm hoping to get something out of that." What is the value of that to somebody who is in need and in trouble?

By definition Christians have something; they have something to say. The woman of Samaria would not have left her waterpot and rushed into the city and addressed the people unless she had something to say to them, and what she says is, "Come, see this man: this is the Christ—you are bound to agree with me that he is." She has found, she has arrived, and this is always the first element. It acts in a dynamic manner in every true Christian. It is inconceivable that anybody who has found in this sense can remain silent. But this does account, does it not, for so much failure in many Christians or in those who regard themselves as Christians.

So the great question we must all ask ourselves is this: do we have something to give to people who are in need? I like to think of it like this. Imagine that tonight when you are in your home, somebody knocks at your door or rings the bell. You go to the door, and there you find a messenger. What is the message? Well, it is a request, an appeal, from a man whom you have known for years; perhaps you have known him since you were children together. Unfortunately, poor fellow, he has gone wrong in life, he has lived a godless life, and yet you somehow liked him. Whenever you met him, you were glad to see him, and you always spoke to him, and you often tried to urge him to come with you to listen to the gospel. But he would not come; he laughed it off, as such people often do.

Now here is the message—this afternoon that poor fellow had a sudden heart attack, and he is desperately ill; in fact, he is dying. The doctor can do no more for him. He has told the family, and this man realizes the truth—he can see it in their faces. And suddenly he has come to himself. He sees that his life is finished, and he is going to the unknown and to darkness. He has nothing—nothing to lean on in his past life, nothing to lean on in the present. Nobody can help him. He is absolutely alone, as we all shall be sooner or later, as our soul passes from time to eternity and into the presence of God. He does not know what to do or where to turn; he is in agony of soul. But suddenly he has thought of you because he thinks of you as a Christian and as a member of a church because you have invited him to go with you to church. So he has sent for you—that is the message. Of course, you have no choice; you must go. And when you arrive in the room, there is your friend lying on his back in bed.

This is the test as to whether or not we are Christians. Do you have something you can give him that will make all the difference in the world to him? What is the point of telling this man that you are also a seeker and a searcher after the truth—he will be dead before midnight? What is the point of saying to him, "I hope that my sins are going to be forgiven sometime, I'm doing my best, I'm living a good life"? Does that help him? That puts him into hell while he is still alive. Or how does it help him if you turn to him and say, "Well, at last you see it. How many times have I told you that the life you were living was wrong? If only you had lived as I live!" What is the value of that? That is sheer cruelty. That, again, is putting him in hell while he is still alive. It is of no value at all.

No, no; that is not the Christian way. Christians are not seeking truth or seeking forgiveness. They are not trying to make themselves Christians by living good lives; they are not merely church members. What are they? Well, in the end it just comes to this: they are men and women who, like the woman of Samaria, have met Christ, the Son of God. They are able to tell this poor fellow that it is not too late, that it is not hopeless, that no one is justified by their works or by their lives, that we are all sinners, and that there is no ultimate difference between us at all, but that this is the message: "God so loved the world, that he gave his only begotten Son, that whosoever [even he] believeth in him should not perish, but have everlasting life" (John 3:16).

Christians can tell this man not about their own experience but about Jesus Christ. There is no time to give experiences; there is no time to go through your drill and mechanically quote this or that. All they can say is, "Jesus Christ—look to him!" They just tell the dying man about him, who he is, what he has done. And that is the only way this man can be helped, the only way he can find peace and rest for his soul.

Christians have this knowledge, they have this information, and as Paul puts it to the Romans, they are able to "impart" it. "I long to see you," he says, "that I may impart unto you . . ." (Rom. 1:11)—pass it on, hand it over, tell others about it, gossip it. So often we are not concerned about others simply because we have nothing to say to them. But if we know this, how can we possibly refrain from telling others about it?

53

Rejoicing in Christ

The woman then left her waterpot, and went her way into the city, and saith to the men, Come, see a man, which told me all things that ever I did: is not this the Christ? Then they went out of the city, and came unto him. (John 4:28–30)

We have been considering together the fact that the woman of Samaria does not have to be trained to give her witness or trained to do personal work; she witnesses automatically, almost instinctively. I am very concerned to stress this principle. This activity of the Christian should always come from within. It should not be imposed upon us as a duty. We should not have to be drilled and then almost dragooned into doing it. If that is our condition, there is something seriously wrong with us. The whole glory of this activity, as we find in the Scriptures, and still more perhaps in the subsequent history of the church, is the spontaneity. This is a great principle.

Having dealt with that, we began in our last study to consider a second question, which is this: why does the Samaritan woman behave in this spontaneous, instinctive manner? I have given one answer, and that is that she clearly has something to give. That is the first great reason. But let us continue with this question. What else do you think has moved this woman? Why has she left her waterpot, a deliberate action, to go to the city and say, "Come, see a man . . ."? The very way in which she puts it, of course, gives us our second explanation—it is her realization of the uniqueness and the glory of this person. Here again is a most important point. All these points help us understand what is so wrong with the Christian church at the present time—it is that all our emphases have gone wrong. But here they can be corrected for us.

The woman of Samaria is motivated by the greatness and the glory and the uniqueness of this person she has just met. This is something we can illustrate from the natural level. If ever you are in contact with some great person, you are not only impressed, you also want everybody to know about your meeting. If you ever have an audience with the Queen, you will not have had to be trained how to tell people. Nobody will have to urge you to tell others. The difficulty, in a sense, is to control your telling, and you may become a bore because you keep on repeating the details. That is natural; it is instinctive. Multiply that by infinity, and you begin to understand the reaction of the woman of Samaria.

So many of our troubles arise because we forget the objectivity of our faith; we are too subjective. We dwell in the realm of experience; we emphasize experience. But the order of these matters is what is important, and we must always keep in the forefront the objectivity, the person. This emphasis is characteristic of the great eighteenth-century hymns:

O happy bond, that seals my vows
To him who merits all my love!

PHILIP DODDRIDGE ("O HAPPY DAY, THAT FIXED MY CHOICE")

It is typical, too, of the New Testament. Take, for instance, the apostle Paul's constant exhortation to people to "rejoice." But notice how he always puts it—"Rejoice in the Lord always: and again I say, Rejoice" (Phil. 4:4). Paul is not exhorting the Philippian Christians to try to create within themselves some feeling of happiness; quite the opposite. But many people do that; in meetings they try to work up the congregation with preliminary singing, making a direct assault upon the feelings. That is not the Christian method—"Rejoice *in the Lord.*"

In other words, you can rejoice at all times, whatever your feelings or mood; whatever your circumstances, you can be a rejoicing Christian. How? By rejoicing "in the Lord." You do not look into yourself—you look at him. And if you look at him and realize who he is and what he has done, you will be filled, if you are a Christian, with a spirit of rejoicing.

And that is what has happened in the case of this woman. It is the person and her realization of who he is and what he is and the glory of his being that has moved her and created within her the desire that the people in her town should also have the privilege of seeing him and listening to him. I have to stress this because in many ways the most important thing of all is the realization that he is who and what he is and that he is there outside us, beyond us, in the glory. Of course, he is in us, as Christians, as well, but we start with the grand and glorious objective truth. The

Christian, ultimately, is a person who realizes that the most important event that has ever happened in this world is the coming of the Son of God into it.

By nature, we human beings are all interested in history, but our history books have tended to be nothing but an account of kings and great generals and captains and so on. There is a sense in which all this is all right. I still maintain that is true history and that "modern history" is not true history at all. The great things in this world have been done by great people, and our troubles today are due to the fact that we no longer have such people. So let us try to understand our history anew and afresh, and let us accept that as a true way of looking at history and that it is right that these great people should stand out. But Christian men and women are people who, while they subscribe to all that, say that the event of events was the birth of the babe at Bethlehem. If you are interested in people, says the Christian, great and glorious people, here is one who stands alone.

Now the uniqueness and glory of our Lord, surely, ought to be self-evident to us. It is everywhere in the New Testament. As is often pointed out, the book of the Acts of the Apostles is merely the book of the acts of the Lord Jesus Christ. "The former treatise have I made, O Theophilus," says Luke, "of all that Jesus began both to do and to teach" (Acts 1:1), and now Luke is going on to tell Theophilus what Jesus continued to do and to teach. Our Lord dominated the life of the apostles. He dominated the thinking of the apostle Paul—"that I may know him" (Phil. 3:10).

While Christians, therefore, are interested in all secular history and in all that man has done and can do and has produced, they say that what matters is that our Lord came out of the glory: "But when the fulness of the time was come, God sent forth his Son, made of a woman, made under the law, to redeem them that were under the law" (Gal. 4:4–5). This was the climactic, crucial event in the history of the world, and consequently Christian people now see everything in terms of Jesus Christ. Christians look back at history, but they also look at the present, and they look to the future, and they see everything in the light of Christ. Christ has divided history for them, as he has divided everything else. He determines and controls the whole of life.

Now here is another point against which we must test ourselves and one another. As we talk with people about present circumstances, as we look upon life in the past and as we look to the future, is our Lord prominent in our thinking, and do we tell others that here is the sole explanation of our world, here is the guarantee of the future? The Son of God has been in this world. "[God] hath visited and redeemed his people" (Luke 1:68) in the person of his own Son. Nothing else comes anywhere near this momentous event.

The question we must therefore ask ourselves is this: is the whole of our thinking dominated by the Lord Jesus Christ? Over and above all we have known and experienced, is our chief glory the fact that Jesus is the Son of God? Are we taken out of ourselves in this respect, and are we amazed and filled with a sense of wonder and glory at the person of Christ?

Work this out for yourselves. As we have seen, we cannot read the New Testament without being aware that everything is constantly pointing to him. This is where Christianity is essentially different from the cults. They are always turning you in on yourself: "Are you happy? Are you sleeping? Do you have good health?" It is always *you*. But with Christianity we start by looking at him, and if we are not doing that, then we must be careful that we are not using the Christian message in a kind of cultic manner. We start with the blessed person, this one whom we have met face-to-face, this one who has entered into history and into our lives, this one who has made everything different and new. "Come, see a man who has done this amazing thing."

There, then, is the second great explanation of this woman's actions. But having said that, I come to a more personal, experiential level. We must always keep a balance. Some people seem to be almost entirely subjective, others entirely objective in their thinking, and they are both wrong. The Christian truth is both; that is the glory of it. It starts with great objective facts and truths and events—a person. But it is not only that; it is not merely theoretical and academic and intellectual. No, no. Christianity is experiential, it is practical, it is living, it is vital, and if we do not combine these two aspects, then at the very best we have a poor kind of imbalanced, lopsided Christianity. This must be corrected. We must test ourselves at all these points.

So what has our Lord done for the woman of Samaria? You can manifest our Lord's work in your life and exemplify it without fully understanding it, but as you go on in the Christian life, you are able to analyze. You do so in the light of the scriptural teaching, and you very soon see what has really been happening. What has this woman found? Well, first, she has found authority. This is something for which everybody is looking. We are in a world that is full of troubles, full of difficulties and perplexities. We are surrounded by a veritable babble of voices, all of them telling us they know the answer—we have only to listen to them and to follow them and all will be well with us. But we try them one after the other and never get satisfaction. And we come to realize that we are listening to human voices, and none of them speaks with authority. They have an assumed and spurious authority, which we begin to see through because we realize that they have not found the answer themselves. They are failures in their own lives and do not know it.

Now I need not elaborate too much on this, but the question of authority is a most urgent problem in the world at the present time. Some of the greatest dangers in the world today and some of the greatest disasters in the past, including in the immediate past, have all arisen out of the desire for authority. When there are troubles, people always look for an authoritative statement, an authoritative leader. That is why perhaps the greatest danger at a time like this is the danger of dictatorship. Certainly that was the sole explanation of Hitlerism. Hitler came into power in Germany because of the troubles and the difficulties facing his country. The politicians had been trying; they were honest men, and they had done their best, but they could not solve the country's problems. Suddenly a man stood up and said, "I know! Listen to me. Follow me." And instinctively they followed him. They wanted authority; they wanted a voice.

Now this need for authority has also largely been the explanation of the success of Roman Catholicism and of the cults. The world is longing for some authoritative statement, someone to listen to, someone to follow who seems to have knowledge. There is nothing wrong in this; it is inevitable because of our condition as the result of the Fall. This need is in all of us, and when we meet this authoritative word that we are looking for, at once we listen and are ready to follow.

Now this undoubtedly happened to this poor woman. We have seen the state of her life; it is familiar to you. She has been living a miserable existence, and nobody has been able to help her. But at last she meets somebody who seems to understand, who speaks with authority. She is interested in the question of worship and of religion. "Our father," she says, "worshipped in this mountain; and ye say, that in Jerusalem . . ." and she goes on talking and arguing. But a point comes when she is silent; here is one who knows, and he says so. "Ye worship ye know not what," he says; "we know what we worship: for salvation is of the Jews" (John 4:22). She has met authority, someone whom she feels she can follow.

And as we read the pages of the four Gospels, we find that this note of authority stands out constantly. Have you not been amazed at this? Take the call of the disciples. There are Peter and Andrew fishing, and James and John with their father in their boat mending the nets, doing their work as usual. Suddenly this person appears and says, "Follow me," and they just leave everything and go after him (Mark 1:16–20). And we read, "As Jesus passed forth from thence, he saw a man, named Matthew, sitting at the receipt of custom" (Matt. 9:9)—a tax collector just doing his job. Suddenly this person comes along and says, "Follow me," and Matthew gets up and follows him. What is this? This is authority, this quality that men and women are instinctively drawn to in their lost condition, the authority for which they have been looking.

And, of course, the people recognized our Lord's authority. At the end of the Sermon on the Mount, when our Lord had finished speaking, we are told, "And it came to pass, when Jesus had ended these sayings, the people were astonished at his doctrine: for he taught them as one having authority, and not as the scribes" (Matt. 7:28–29). This was the inevitable comment. We see there a very interesting contrast. How did the scribes teach? Well, they were always quoting authorities, but here *is* authority. What a difference there is between quoting authorities and speaking authoritatively. One of the troubles in the church today is that people are quoting authorities: What does Tillich say? What does Barth say? And Bultmann? But there is no authority. Humanity longs for this word, this authoritative word, this assured word, and the only person who can give it to us is this blessed person who has met the woman of Samaria. So she now invites her fellow townspeople to come and meet with him and to hear what he has to say.

And, thank God, our Lord has given his Holy Spirit, and in great profusion and power. When he does that, he can cause even a human being to be steeped with authority. This is what he has done in the people whom he has raised up throughout the centuries in reformation and revival. The world recognized the power of the Holy Spirit in the people, the church recognized it in a measure, and others recognized it too. A note of authority came from Martin Luther. You can only explain him in that one way. It was the authority that the Lord gave to him through the Holy Spirit.

But here is the next question: why do we need this authority? What is it in us, in detail, that looks for it and cries out for it? The answers to this question are almost endless. I shall only throw out some suggestions and some hints for you to work out for yourselves. What do we need from authority? First, we need rest of mind, do we not? The mind is restless and curious; the mind seeks satisfaction. That is the whole meaning of philosophy; it is men and women trying to arrive at an understanding of everything, "arriving at truth," as they put it. Confronted by themselves and the whole problem of life and of the world, of existence and of history, people say, "Is there any sense in it? Is there any meaning, any explanation? What is it all about? To what will it all lead?" The mind is looking and searching, but it cannot find any answers and is restless. But here at last is one who can give rest to the mind and bring the questings to an end. Of course, our Lord was always claiming this. He says, "I am the light of the world: he that followeth me shall not walk in darkness, but shall have the light of life" (John 8:12). "I am the way, the truth, and the life: no man cometh unto the Father, but by me" (John 14:6).

What do we want to know? We want to know God. The whole world has been seeking after him. There is not a race of people that did not have this vague sense of some Supreme Being. As Paul put it to the Athenians, "If haply they might feel after him, and find him" (Acts 17:27)—this search for "the unknown God" (v. 23). Humanity instinctively feels there is someone beyond it all, but we cannot find him. "Canst thou by searching find out God?" asks Job (Job 11:7). No, we cannot. But here is one who can bring us to that very knowledge. We find it in the prologue of this very Gospel: "No man hath seen God at any time"—so is there no hope? Yes, there is—"the only begotten Son, which is in the bosom of the Father, he hath declared him" (1:18). This is the answer. He alone can do it. We have had speculation, but speculation does not satisfy us because we know it is speculation. And though people may speculate with arrogance and human self-confidence, we know there is nothing in it; it is only their opinion, and it will change soon, as all these opinions constantly do. There is only one who has authority, and John's prologue tells us who he is.

But then our Lord put it still more plainly, you remember, to Nicodemus. "Jesus answered and said unto him, Art thou a master of Israel, and knowest not these things?" Nicodemus was one of the authorities, a great teacher and a great man, but he did not know. There were limits, as there always are. So our Lord addressed him as "a master of Israel" but then went on:

> Verily, verily, I say unto thee, We speak that we do know, and testify that we have seen; and ye receive not our witness. If I have told you earthly things, and ye believe not, how shall ye believe, if I tell you of heavenly

> things? And no man hath ascended up to heaven, but he that came down from heaven, even the Son of man which is in heaven. (John 3:10–13)

Here is authority. Here is an answer about God. Here is one who has looked eternally into the face of God and has come down to tell us about him and to lead us into the blessed knowledge of him. And so our Lord gives this immediate rest of mind, and this is one of the most wonderful things that one can ever receive. You are no longer bewildered about life and about yourself and about your destiny. You have answers to these great questions—he has given them. So you say with the writer of the hymn:

> *O Christ, in thee my soul hath found,*
> *And found in thee alone,*
> *The peace, the joy I sought so long,*
> *The bliss till now unknown.*
>
> AUTHOR UNKNOWN

This is the answer. Or remember how Charles Wesley put it when, at the time of his own conversion, he cried:

> *O! when shall all my strivings cease?*

But they did. He found this intellectual peace, this rest of mind, and the fact is—and this is what we claim—all knowledge is in him, and it is all here in this Book. This does not mean that we understand it all, but it is all here. There is a complete philosophy of life here; there is nothing left without explanation. It is all here; it is the mind of God. Again, the apostle Paul is able to make that astounding claim, "We have the mind of Christ" (1 Cor. 2:16), and we are entering more and more into the full and complete understanding that he gives.

But, thank God, our Lord does not stop at giving us rest of mind and peace in the intellect; we find exactly the same peace in our conscience. The conscience is in even greater trouble, is it not? The more we know about God, the more our conscience troubles us because God knows all things. "If our heart condemn us," says John, "God is greater than our heart" (1 John 3:20). The writer of the Epistle to the Hebrews says, "All things are naked and opened unto the eyes of him with whom we have to do" (Heb. 4:13), and every one of us knows this. However ignorant we may be of God, there is a conscience in every one of us. We cannot get rid of it, and it goes on troubling us more and more so that we long for peace of conscience, rest of conscience.

The human race has been seeking and striving after peace of conscience. We have a sense of guilt, a sense of unworthiness, a sense of shame, and the great question is, how can this be satisfied? How can this be answered? Much human activity is explained solely in terms of the quest for this peace. The world, of course, has its glib and easy answers, but they do not satisfy us. People try to forget their consciences. They rush into pleasure or take drugs or turn to the teaching of the cults. In these ways they find temporary satisfaction, but always the great ultimate question arises, and there they are alone, facing the eternal Judge, and they do not know what they can do about it.

This is the essence of Christianity, is it not? Christian men and women know that they find peace of conscience in one place only, and that is in this one person only, this same blessed person who was speaking to the woman of Samaria. Here is the only one who can say, "Come unto me, *all ye that labour and are heavy laden*, and I will give you rest" (Matt. 11:28). What are you laboring at? Laboring to make yourself righteous; laboring to atone for your past sins; laboring to make yourself fit to stand in the presence of God? You are "labouring" and "heavy laden" because of the load of your sins. And you are striving and sweating and fasting and praying. You are doing all you can, and the more you do, the more you see his holiness and your own unworthiness. You are at the end of your tether; your conscience is thundering at you, and nothing you do can silence it.

But then you meet this blessed Savior, this blessed person. You hear this sweet invitation, and you feel he is speaking with authority; he knows what he is saying. He says, "The Son of man came not to be ministered unto, but to minister, and to give his life a ransom for many" (Matt. 20:28). He speaks a parable such as the Parable of the Prodigal Son, and there is authority again. He knows; he speaks and acts with assurance and certainty. And the end of it is that in believing him and his message, you find that you have peace with God. "Therefore being justified by faith, we have peace with God" (Rom. 5:1). This is the outstanding thing—you know it, you feel it instinctively now, your conscience is cleared, you enjoy peace.

Let me quote another verse from Romans: "There is therefore now no condemnation to them which are in Christ Jesus" (Rom. 8:1). "No condemnation"! Why? Because we have an explanation, a satisfactory explanation. It is not that God is merely saying, "I have forgiven you," but that he has done something. He has made a way of forgiveness. And the Bible tells us how we can be sure. The Scriptures expound to us the whole blessed doctrine of the atonement. This is argued out by Paul in the third chapter of Romans. God is just, says Paul, "and the justifier of him which believeth in Jesus" (Rom. 3:26). God does not set aside the Law—he honors the Law, he fulfills it. God's own Son "bare our sins in his own body on the tree" (1 Pet. 2:24). God "has made him to be sin for us, who knew no sin; that we might be made the righteousness of God in him" (2 Cor. 5:21). So we know that our sins are forgiven, and knowing that, we have peace and rest in our consciences. This is the most blessed knowledge that we can ever have. And it is only the Christian who knows it. This woman of Samaria has felt it. She does not fully understand it, but our Lord has not only revealed to her every sin "that ever I did," but she knows he is also able to deal with her sins. Though he condemns, he heals.

And then we go on to the next point, which is this: beyond any question, this woman is aware of new life within herself. Forgiveness alone is not enough; we need new life. Look at her; look at the kind of life she has been living, that has produced the misery, the social ostracism. But having met this person, she not only knows she is forgiven, she is aware of a new kind of life. You cannot be a Christian without this new life. A Christian is someone who is born again—born of the Spirit, born from above. This woman is aware that she has new desires within her, a desire for a new type of life, not that old life she has been living. She did not know any better then, and she did not have the desire for anything better. But now she has looked into the face of purity, everlasting purity, the holiness of God in the face of Jesus Christ, and she has a desire within her for purity and cleanliness, chastity, a holiness that she has never known of before. And, still more important, she is aware of the fact that this is possible for her.

It is very difficult for us, is it not, to realize the fullness of this woman's feelings at this point, but this is Christian testimony, this is the experience of the saints throughout the centuries. The miracle is that a woman who has lived this kind of life, who has had five husbands and is now living with someone who is not her husband, as she confessed to our Lord, not only wants to be out of all that and to live a new life but knows it can be done. It does not need much imagination to know that she has often become so miserable in that old life that she has longed to get out of it. She has tried, she has made resolutions, she has made efforts, but she has always gone back. Try to extricate yourself from any one of the things that grip you, and you cannot do it.

Now the amazing truth is that the effect of meeting Jesus Christ is that he not only creates within you the desire to be different, but he also gives you the feeling that you can be. He transmits something of his own purity and his own strength and his own power to you so that you have the blessed feeling that it can be done. And so you feel you can trust him; you can trust in his protection and his guardian care. He puts into you, somehow, unconsciously, this feeling of a new strength, a new understanding, and a new power that will enable you to live this new and glorious life to which he has opened your eyes.

But our Lord goes beyond that—he gives you a new view of life itself and of your own future. You see opening before you a new kind of existence. You are no longer dependent upon the world, its excitements, its pleasures, its opinions, and its comings and goings. You are aware that though you are still in this world, you do not belong to it; you see through it and beyond it. You find you are living as a stranger; your citizenship is in heaven. You feel at once that you belong to a new realm, that God has delivered you "from the power of darkness, and hath translated [you] into the kingdom of his dear Son" (Col. 1:13); you know this.

Now you do not fully understand all this, but you will grow in your understanding. He has cleansed your past, you have certainty in the present, and now you look to the future without terror, without alarm. And, remember, this includes death and the grave, the last enemy. Christians already have their conquest; they are no longer terrified of illness or of death or of the grave. They can look at it and say:

> O death, where is thy sting? O grave, where is thy victory? The sting of death is sin; and the strength of sin is the law. But thanks be to God, which giveth us the victory through our Lord Jesus Christ. (1 Cor. 15:55–57)

Read for yourselves the fifteenth chapter of the Gospel according to Luke because three times over our Lord makes this very point. You see there, in a sense, the difference between the Christian and the Pharisee. Both the Christian and the religious person can be measured entirely by this note of joy. You may be religious, but if you are, it will be self-contained, there will not be much joy about it. Like the Pharisees, you have to spend the whole of your time being religious, trying to please God, hemming yourself in. You have no contact with other people; you have nothing to tell them. You are so busy putting yourself right and safeguarding what you have that you have nothing to give, and so you do not give. You are not happy yourself, and you do not want to make other people happy. That is very different from the woman of Samaria and from the true Christian, always.

In Luke 15, by contrast, we read how the woman lost her coin and then found it. "Come," she says, inviting her neighbors. "Rejoice with me." The shepherd who loses his sheep searches for it and finds it. Back he goes and says, "Come. Rejoice with me." And the father who has found his son again—or whose son has come back to him—says, "Put the best robe on him, kill the fatted calf, invite the neighbors, let's have a feast. Come." Of course, the elder brother, the religious man, does not approve of this. He has no joy, and he sees no occasion for rejoicing. But the moment one really understands these things, there is this dynamic element. Those who are truly Christians must rejoice, and they want everybody to rejoice with them. That is what happens to this woman.

And so the final test we apply to ourselves in this connection is just that: has the Lord Jesus Christ made you rejoice? Has he filled you with a spirit of praise? You can be a great theologian but have no joy. You can be very religious but without joy. You can be very moral, but is there joy? Joy is the particular mark of the Christian. "Rejoice in the Lord always: and again I say, Rejoice" (Phil. 4:4). There is no better test of our knowledge of our Lord and of what we claim he has done for us than the extent of our joy and our rejoicing in him and in what he has done for our souls.

54

The Need and the Cure

The woman then left her waterpot, and went her way into the city, and saith to the men, Come, see a man, which told me all things that ever I did: is not this the Christ? Then they went out of the city, and came unto him. (John 4:28–30)

In these verses we have seen how the woman of Samaria was moved spontaneously to fetch her fellow townspeople to come and see the Lord. We have shown that it was the person of our Lord himself and her joy in her encounter with him that made her do this. But that is not all—there are still further reasons, further motives, that impel her to behave in this way, and we must examine ourselves in their light.

But first I want once more to put forward my general question: do you find yourself like this woman? That is the point. We are not just looking at her in some kind of detached manner, interested in psychology, in phenomena. No, no; the whole point of this incident is that it examines us and searches us. Are we behaving as this woman behaved? Is the response that she made to the Lord also our response? Do we know something of her spontaneity? Are we moved by her motives?

So I come to the next characteristic of the woman of Samaria, which is that she obviously has a great concern for the people of her town. Her first reaction, once she is aware of all this within herself, is immediately to think of them. Once more, we all agree, this is always true in the natural realm. When we derive some great benefit, this is the way we tend to behave—we do not even think about it. We saw this kind of response in the three parables in Luke 15. We want people to rejoice with us, but it goes beyond that, and we have a concern for others. Our natural concern for one another is greatly heightened when we become Christians because, as I shall show you, one of the first things that happens to us is that we cease to be entirely self-centered. We are more or less self-centered until we become Christians. The great trouble in the world is selfishness, self-centeredness—*I*. You do not care about anybody or anything else, you do not care about your country, as long as you are all right. But the Christian is not like that.

There are two elements, I think, to the concern that the woman of Samaria feels and that any Christian must feel about those who are not Christians. But before I come to this double analysis, let me ask a question: are you concerned about other people, about those who are not Christians? I am not asking if you denounce them or condemn them. The world can condemn, and it does. I am not asking if you are irritated by them or horrified by the immorality and the vice and the slackness and all that is portrayed to us in the newspapers and on television. I am asking, are you concerned about it? Does it trouble you? Are you concerned about the people who are in that condition?

Now this concern divides itself into two elements. The first is that this woman has undoubtedly become concerned about the utter superficiality and the final futility of the lives of non-Christians. We know the kind of life she has been living, a life of immorality. The world thinks that is wonderful. That is what it is boasting of today, is it not? This is the thing to do. You are old-fashioned if you do not do these things. The world says this is life. And I am not only talking about the life of the world when it lives as this poor woman has been living. I am thinking of the world at its very best, its highest. The Christian immediately sees the superficiality and the emptiness of it all in a final sense.

Now this is established and emphasized in many places in the teaching of the Scriptures. One of the first signs that one has become a Christian is that one sees through the world. Having been born into the world, we had been dominated by it, by its mind and outlook. Paul says in Ephesians 2:2, "Wherein in time past ye walked according to the course of this world"—the worldly view, the "thing to do," all that the world regards as thrilling, the reason why people brought up in the English countryside long to get to London—"the life of London." Marvelous! If as a Christian you do not see through all this, you had better examine your foundations again. You cannot be a Christian and go on regarding the world and its life as people of the world do; it is impossible. The Bible tells us:

> Love not the world, neither the things that are in the world. If any man love the world, the love of the Father is not in him. For all that is in the world, the lust of the flesh, and the lust of the eyes, and the pride of life,

> is not of the Father, but is of the world. And the world passeth away, and the lust thereof: but he that doeth the will of God abideth for ever. Little children, it is the last time. (1 John 2:15–18)

Read those verses, study them, and examine yourselves in their light. The Christian has seen through it all—the vanity, the emptiness. John was very concerned about this, so later in his epistle he says it again: "For whatsoever is born of God overcometh the world: and this is the victory that overcometh the world, even our faith" (5:4). Do you see the contrast? The life of the Christian and the life of the world are opposites. The world organizes itself to be inimical to us and to our best interests. If you have not discovered that, you are not a Christian at all. The world does not even believe in the soul, it does not believe in God, it does not believe in an afterlife. Its sole concern is the present life and people and what they do—their thrilling wonderful activities, which the world judges by its own standards.

I am anxious to make this clear, so I repeat that I am not only thinking of life as lived by this poor woman of Samaria but am also thinking of it in its most cultivated and cultured aspects, all that the world regards as glittering. The kind of people who call themselves intellectual feel sorry for us as we meet on a Sunday morning. We ought to be reading the Sunday newspaper supplements, the book and music reviews. But Christian men and women see through the artificiality of all that. They see that even at its best there is no depth in it, no satisfaction; there is nothing for the soul.

Oh, you can have intellectual interests, you can be moved emotionally and in other respects, but it is all rather like an iridescent bubble. It looks very beautiful, but you have to keep it going, and it demands energy. You are fascinated by it, but at any moment it can burst and you have nothing left. The world is all very largely a pose, an affectation. What is so pathetic is its superficiality. You see people affecting an interest in things that they do not really care about at all, putting on interest like a cloak or a mask in order to be able to have a wonderful conversation. That is what I mean by the superficiality of it all. It does not answer the profundities that are in human nature, for human beings, after all, have souls and cry out for something bigger, something deeper.

But you really see through the world when you come to a time of need or a crisis, and all that the world has does not help you at all. The sophistication will never give you comfort or ease; it will never give you rest; it always abandons you. The world always does that to us if we belong to it—remember what it did to poor Judas Iscariot. He was a traitor to our Lord, and he plotted with our Lord's enemies, and they were very kind and ingratiating. Then Judas, when he had betrayed our Lord, suddenly realized what he had done. He was sorry and went to them to tell them about it. But they said, "What does that have to do with us? That's your business." They abandoned him, left him to himself, and he committed suicide (Matt. 27:3–5). That is the world always. The world never gives you anything when you really need it.

That is what the poor prodigal son found, was it not? While he had his pockets full of money in that strange "far country," he had any number of friends. As long as you pay, the world will fawn upon you and praise you. But the famine came, his money was all spent, and he "began to be in need." You remember the pregnant phrase, "and no man gave unto him" (Luke 15:16). Of course not! They were all out for themselves, those supposed friends, those well-wishers. And the world always does that. When you need it most, it has nothing to give you, it abandons you.

Now the Christian realizes this at once. The apostle Paul talks about "the unfruitful works of darkness" (Eph. 5:11)—and what a wonderful phrase that is. That kind of life is unprofitable; it never produces fruit. It has its immediate results, but as with drink and all these things, the effects wear off. The writer of the Epistle to the Hebrews talks about "dead works" (Heb. 6:1), and again what a marvelous phrase. Dead works—there is no life in them. It is all mechanical, it all has to be kept going, so you need money and organization.

But the Christian sees through that immediately. Our Lord says, "For what shall it profit a man, if he shall gain the whole world, and lose his own soul? Or what shall a man give in exchange for his soul?" (Mark 8:36–37). That is the very essence of the Christian outlook. Christians look at the world as it is, at its best and highest as well as in the gutters where this poor woman lived. They look at it all, and that is their question: "What shall it profit a man, if he shall gain the whole world"—the wealth and the knowledge, the sophistication and the applause, everything the world prizes—"and lose his own soul?"—this imperishable thing, this thing that belongs to God and is bigger than the whole universe, this thing that nothing but God can finally satisfy.

Our Lord puts this in another way that shows us still more clearly the kind of feeling that this woman felt instinctively. We are told:

> But when he saw the multitudes, he was moved with compassion on them, because they fainted, and were scattered abroad, as sheep having no shepherd. Then saith he unto his disciples, The harvest truly is plenteous, but the labourers are few; pray ye therefore the Lord of the harvest, that he will send forth labourers into his harvest. (Matt. 9:36–38)

You see the picture. That was our Lord's view of humanity apart from him—fainting and sheep without a shepherd. Now that description of sheep means the two things I have been mentioning. It means, first, that the people were not getting proper sustenance. One of the main functions of the shepherd is to lead the sheep into the green pastures. He knows where there is food, where there is pasture; so he leads them there, and they follow him. But these people were fainting because they were not having proper food, like sheep without a shepherd. And that is the truth about the world today. All that it has to offer and of which it is so proud does not feed the soul; it leaves us fainting.

The second point is that a shepherd protected his sheep. There were dogs, marauding dogs, that came and attacked and harassed the sheep and would even kill them at times. Having no shepherd, the sheep had no protection. In the same way, when life begins to attack you—illness or disease or old age—you are left on the scrap heap, you are left to yourself: "No man gave unto him."

So Christians see this. They see that this supposed marvelous life is the emptiest thing, it is just a bubble. "For what is your life? It is even a vapour" (Jas. 4:14). That is the same idea exactly. This is what this woman sees in a flash, as it were. She sees through the futility, the vanity of the life she used to live and others are still living, and she wants them to see through it, too. We find this expressed constantly in our hymns:

> *Fading is the worldling's pleasure,*
> *All his boasted pomp and show;*
> *Solid joys and lasting treasure*
> *None but Zion's children know.*
>
> John Newton ("Glorious Things of Thee Are Spoken")

My dear friends, before we go any further, let me ask, have you seen through the world? Have you really seen through what it offers and glories in? Have you seen its emptiness, its shallowness, its final futility? For the Christian, this is inevitable. Everywhere in the Bible there is the great contrast between the world and the people of God. That is the whole secret of the Old Testament saints, those mighty giants. That is the great argument, is it not, of Hebrews 11. Why did those people live as they did? The answer is that they saw through the world and were looking for "a city which hath foundations, whose builder and maker is God" (Heb. 11:10). That is why they forsook the world. That is why they became pilgrims and strangers and travelers and sojourners. That is what made Abraham obey the call of God in Ur of the Chaldees. That is what made Moses renounce it all at that critical point when, having been adopted by Pharaoh's daughter, he might have become the greatest man in Egypt. Instead, he joined himself to these slave people, the Hebrews, to whom he belonged. "He had respect unto the recompence of the reward . . . as seeing him who is invisible" (Heb. 11:26–27). He saw through all that the world had to offer because he saw it in the light of that which belongs to God.

There, then, is the first element in this woman's concern about these other people. But there is another factor that in a way is still more important—she not only sees through the emptiness and the futility of their lives, she sees the danger of their position, and this is where the element of urgency always comes in. You cannot become a Christian without realizing at once that the non-Christian is in a very dangerous position. Again, this applies on a natural level. As soon as you realize that somebody is unknowingly in danger, you warn them. You give them the necessary information. You say, "Look here, perhaps I shouldn't be doing this, but I must tell you, I'm concerned about you. I'm warning you—be careful." And you tell them that this and that is happening or is going to take place. That is quite natural, is it not?

How much greater should be our concern about the precariousness, indeed, the extreme danger, of people's situation in the spiritual realm! Read the sixteenth chapter of Luke in order to see this put to us in a plain and alarming manner. Dives was a rich man who lived the life of the world. Dressed in gorgeous robes, he "fared sumptuously every day," and his whole family was living in the same way. But he died, and now here he is in hell. His chief desire is that he may escape from there and go to be in Abraham's bosom with the poor beggar, Lazarus, whom he ignored while he was still alive. But that cannot be granted. Then he asks, "I pray thee therefore, father, that thou wouldest send him [Lazarus] to my father's house: for I have five brethren; that he may testify unto them, lest they also come into this place of torment" (vv. 27–28). Dives has realized it now. He has not only seen through the vanity of the world, he sees that he is where he is because he had lived a worldly life and did not know, did not realize, what he was doing. So he says in effect, "Send word to my five brothers. They are still in the ignorance that I was in. Send Lazarus to warn them so that they may not arrive in this same place and suffer this same horrible fate that has overcome me."

This is the very thing that the woman of Samaria has realized. "Come, see a man, which told me all things that ever I did." We have emphasized this—her sense of sin, her conviction, the guilt of sin, realizing something of what sin is in the sight of God. This is the very center of her experience. Christians are first of all convicted of the fact that they are sinners in the sight of God, that they are in a dangerous position. Having realized this, the woman of Samaria rushes to tell the people in her town because they have no idea. Not only the people who have lived as she has, but even the best people in the city are quite unaware of their position. This is the whole tragedy with men and women as they are by nature, unenlightened by the Scriptures and the Holy Spirit. They think that this world is everything; they are proud of it and never consider their death and the judgment beyond it. They regard such thoughts as morbid and try to explain them away—you are familiar with all this. So this woman, realizing that other people are in this appalling ignorance, inevitably wants to tell them or at any rate wants to bring them to the one who can make it all plain and clear to them.

Now we have come to a very important point, a point that I think is the key to many of our troubles in the Christian church at the present time, perhaps especially among those of us who are evangelical. I ask once more: are or are we not like this woman? If we are not, if we do not feel this concern for others, and if we are not doing anything about them, the question is, why not? I suggest that probably the main explanation is our failure to realize the danger that people are in when they are outside Christ.

Why do we fail here? I feel it is largely because we have a defective sense of sin in ourselves. That is why I started with conviction of sin and emphasized it in earlier sermons. The danger of the soul outside of Christ has not been emphasized in this [twentieth] century; in fact, we have not liked this teaching. We have said we must tell people to come to Jesus, we must always be positive. We do not like preaching the Law; we do not like the thunderings of the Law; we do not like the Old Testament. The gospel, we say, is a matter of love. And, of course, after a while this omission becomes so common and something we are so accustomed to that we forget all about it. But there is only one thing that keeps us right individually, only one thing ultimately that will make us concerned about others, and that is that we know something about the fear of hell.

There is no question about the necessity for a real conviction of sin. It must always come first, it must always be emphasized because, I repeat, it is this that always keeps us right ourselves. I have heard so many people say, "Oh, I wish I could go back again and get the thrill and the enjoyment of that time when I was converted, when I began to be a Christian." They say that they no longer feel the same enthusiasm, that they have become humdrum Christians living a humdrum kind of Christian life, and they add that they cannot understand it.

And then, of course, in order to try to correct this dullness, they try to work up some sort of excitement. And they organize this or that, something to bring a bit of life back into the church. The church as a whole, as well as the individual, behaves in this way. But do you see the fallacy? It is really like someone who is not feeling very well deciding to drink alcoholic beverages; it is the dangerous argument for taking a stimulant. First find out why you are lacking in spiritual life. Think of a person beginning to feel loss of energy, lack of interest, and so on. The bad doctor is the one who does not try to find out the cause but says, "You need medication" and writes out a prescription. That is very bad medical practice. The doctor should first try to discover why this person who was so full of life and energy is now so low. What is the matter?

And we must do the same in the spiritual realm. The Christian's joy should not only not decrease as time goes on, it should become greater and greater. People do not like to be told this. They say, "No, no; of course, you cannot expect to go on like that through your life. The child is full of exuberance and enthusiasm and gets joy over things. But as children grow up, they become more staid and more settled, and then in middle age they probably become cynical and peter out." But, my dear friends, that is not true of the Christian life. The joy of the Christian life, as I have been trying to show you, is a joy that is based upon knowledge and upon understanding. The joy of the apostle Paul and the other New Testament writers became greater and greater, and the nearer we get to the glory, the greater should be our joy, too.

But if it is not, why not? I suggest that the answer is that we have paid far too much attention to experiences, far too much attention to the initial decision—and, of course, this all belongs to the past and cannot be repeated. You have made your decision or you have had your experience, and now you must go on with the Christian life—it is a matter of duty. Or perhaps when you were young, you belonged to some union or society, and that kept you going, but then you had to go out into the world, and you got married, and the problems of life came. The stimulus that kept you going in those early days has gone, and you lose enthusiasm and say, "I don't seem to have much experience of joy. It was there once—I did have it," and so you just keep going and trudge along.

How wrong that is, how tragically wrong! What is the matter? It is the failure to realize the truth about yourself at all stages and at every point in the Christian life. By nature you are a hell-bound sinner—if you are not as moved and as concerned about that today as you were twenty years ago, there is something radically wrong with you. The Christian should never get over this fact. I do not care how long you have been a Christian, you are nothing but a sinner saved by the grace of God.

As I shared earlier, Daniel Rowland, that great preacher of two hundred years ago, knew what it was to be transported up into the heights in preaching and in private devotion. He had great experiences from God and under God had been the means of leading many thousands to Christ in the amazing Evangelical Awakening in Wales. He was dying at last, and somebody, one of the other preachers, went to him and said, "How are you, Mr. Rowland, what is your experience?" And this is what he said: "I am still nothing but an old sinner saved by the grace of God." That is it! That was his secret. He never forgot that.

And you and I must never forget; we should always be aware of it. Every day when you wake up, you should say to yourself, "I am what I am by the grace of God." Why are you a Christian? Why are you getting on your knees to pray by the side of your bed? Why do you read your Scriptures? Do not just go on mechanically, but ask yourself, "Why am I doing this?" And then say, "It's because God in his infinite grace awakened me, opened my eyes, showed me myself as a guilty sinner bound for hell and eternal destruction, and then showed me what his Son had done for me." Then you will be on your feet rejoicing. You should do that daily. That is how you "rejoice in the Lord always" (Phil. 4:4). You rejoice *in the Lord*—not in your experiences, not in what has happened to you, not in what you are doing, but "in the Lord," and that means that you will be reminded of where you were, the precariousness and the hopelessness of your situation and how you are saved in one way and in one way only.

And if you do that, you will at the same time be reminding yourself immediately, automatically, that all those other poor people are still in that hopeless condition. You have relatives in that condition, you have friends, acquaintances, in that position, people with whom you have worked. The world around you is still in that condition. That is the way to be like the woman of Samaria. "Come, see a man, which told me all things that ever I did."

Men die in darkness at thy side,
Without a hope to cheer the tomb;
Take up the torch and wave it wide,
The torch that lights time's thickest gloom.

Horatius Bonar ("Go, Labor On: Spend, and Be Spent")

This is it. They do not know their state. "Men die in darkness at thy side." They are round and about us, and they do not know it. My dear friends, if you realize this, you cannot be silent, you are bound to tell them. But this is the way to go about it—not by numbers, not because it is the right thing to do, but because you are sorry for them, you are alarmed about them, and you feel that you would be a cad if you did not warn them.

But let me give you one further point. I want to put this positively as I close. This woman's concern for her people has a positive aspect, and it is this: she rushes back out of her desire that the people of her town might also share in the benefits she is enjoying. She does not stop at a negative concern—she is moved by the fact that they are missing what she now has when it is possible for them to enjoy it, too. She is sorry for them, sorry that they should go on eating the husks that are put out for the swine—and in the last analysis that is what civilization is—and she is anxious that they should begin to enjoy the riches, the food, that God has already provided. Was it Samuel Rutherford who said that he had lost his taste for the stale brown bread of this world since he started tasting of the heavenly manna? That is it; she wants everybody else to taste it also.

In other words, when you come to know the joy of the Christian life, you feel you cannot keep it to yourself, you cannot be selfish. There is a great story in 2 Kings 7. The city of Samaria—at that time the capital of Israel—was besieged by the mighty army of the Syrians. Inside the city, all the food had been eaten, and the people were dying of starvation. But then we read of four poor lepers. Because they were lepers, they could not go into the city, and they were outside the city gate. They also had no food and did not know what to do. They said, "If we try to get into the city, we'll die there. We might as well try the Syrians. If they receive us and give us some food, then we'll live; if they put us to death, then we'll die, but we were going to die anyway."

So that evening these lepers took the risk of going to the Syrians' camp. When they got there, they found the camp deserted. The horses, the camels, the food, and everything else were all there, but there were no people. This was because as darkness was falling, God had made the Syrians hear the noise of a vast approaching army, and thinking that this army was coming to the rescue of Samaria, the Syrians had fled in terror. So these lepers suddenly found themselves in the midst of wealth and abundance. They at once began to enjoy the food and drink and to hide the clothes and the silver and gold. It was an instinctive reaction—"I'm alone. I'm on to a good thing. I'll keep it to myself and not let anybody know."

But then the lepers came to themselves and said, "We do not well: this day is a day of good tidings, and we hold our peace" (2 Kings 7:9). All those people in the city were starving. Could these four go on enjoying themselves in selfishness and allow them to die? Could they keep silent when they had discovered riches? No, no; that would be wrong. So they rushed back to the city and told everyone the good news.

That is exactly what the woman of Samaria did. When you have come across such "good tidings," you cannot keep them to yourself. The Christian is not selfish. One of the great changes that takes place is that we cease to be self-centered and to hold it all for ourselves. We want to share it; we want everybody to enjoy it. Why? We are in a common salvation! This is what moved the apostle Paul, as we have seen. This is why he felt he was a "debtor" (Rom. 1:14). This is why he says, "The love of Christ constraineth us" (2 Cor. 5:14).

Look at that great verse, Romans 1:16: "I am not ashamed of the gospel of Christ: for it is the power of God unto salvation to every one that believeth." A man working in Egypt in the early years of this present [twentieth] century found a fragment of papyrus on which were written the words of Romans 1:16, and it gave him most wonderful information. It was written in koine Greek—the common Greek that was spoken in the first century—and he found that instead of the usual Greek word for "power," a word had been used that also meant "prescription." So Romans 1:16 could be translated like this: "I am not ashamed of the gospel of Christ: for it is the prescription of God unto salvation to every one that believeth." Do you see what that tells us? Why was Paul longing to come to Rome? Because he had a prescription.

Can you not see the analogy? Imagine a man who for many years had suffered from some very painful and crippling disease, say, in his joints. He was in agony; he could not move without pain and had almost become a cripple. He had tried his doctor, who had done his best, but the man was no better. So he had tried another doctor, but to no avail. He had tried all the great doctors who had been recommended to him, but not one of them had been able to cure him. At best there had only been a temporary improvement. He was almost at the point of despair.

But at last he heard of a great physician somewhere in another country who seemed to cure people suffering from this ailment. He said, "I must see this doctor," and he traveled to that country. The moment he met this physician, he realized that this man was different; he seemed to understand the suffering man. "Yes," said the physician, "I do understand your condition, and not only that, I can cure you." He sat at his desk and wrote out a prescription. "Take this," he said. "You will lose your pains, your joints will become supple, and you will be perfectly well." So the man went to the chemist with the prescription, got it dispensed, and began taking the medicine. He kept on taking it, and the pain did indeed begin to go away; the joints became free, and he was cured.

Now that man walks up and down the streets of life. One afternoon he sees a man coming up on the other side of the street. He does not know the man, but he knows exactly what that man's trouble is—he can tell by the way the poor man is holding himself and shuffling along. He says, "That man has my old complaint." In his breast pocket is the prescription given by that great physician. What does he do? There is no question; there is no argument; he does not need to be trained or persuaded. He says to himself, "If I don't cross the street and talk to that man, I'm a cad."

So he crosses the street. He does not wait for an introduction; he is not interested in etiquette and formalities. That other man is suffering, and he has the cure. He is bound to speak. He says, "Excuse me, sir, I don't know you, and you don't know me, but I do know what is the matter with you. You have a complaint that I once had. Tell me, have you ever heard of this?" and he produces his prescription. "Take it, and it will cure you as it cured me."

"I am debtor." "The love of Christ constraineth me." The woman of Samaria knows that the one who has cured her of her terrible disease can also cure other people, and all that is necessary is that she should bring them to him, and that is what she does. At the present time, your friends, relatives, associates, and neighbors are dying because of the lack of a cure. Do you have this cure? If you have, and you realize the truth about them, you will feel that you are bound to tell them. You will feel that you are a "debtor" to them and that, indeed, you are a cad if you do not tell them.

55

The Preeminence of Christ—Telling Others

The woman then left her waterpot, and went her way into the city, and saith to the men, Come, see a man, which told me all things that ever I did: is not this the Christ? Then they went out of the city, and came unto him. (John 4:28–30)

It is very important at this present time that we should all know the difference between being religious and being Christian. The failure to understand this difference is certainly the major problem in the church, and therefore, of course, it becomes a major problem in the world. Men and women are outside the church, and they are not interested in it, and I suggest that is largely because they are not interested in a dead, formal religion. I still believe that when they are confronted by the true Christian faith and message as they see it exemplified in Christian lives, they will respond as these people in this city of Samaria did. If you are concerned about the state of the world and of this country, morally and in every other respect, and if you believe that the message of the gospel is the only hope for any individual in the world and for the world itself in general, then this is a very urgent matter for you.

This issue becomes particularly urgent for the individual Christian for this additional reason: we are living in days when it is no longer the custom for people to go to churches and chapels to listen to the preaching of the gospel. The responsibility of the individual Christian therefore becomes correspondingly greater. As at similar times in the past, there is no doubt that it is largely through the personal witness of Christian people that the gospel will be spread in our day and generation.

If everybody in the church acted as this woman did, the situation would be transformed in a very short time. We are therefore analyzing her motives, the things that produce this spontaneous impulse in her, and we have noted some of them. She has something to give. She has found the uniqueness of the person of Jesus. She knows what he has done for her. She is concerned for the people in her town. She longs that they should share what has now come to her.

There is just one other motive that I must mention, and it is, indeed, a kind of climax to everything that I have been saying. This is her desire that all might come to glory in this person, that all might come to praise him. Or, putting it in another way, it is her desire that he might have the glory. As Paul puts it in writing to the Colossians, "that in all things he might have the preeminence" (Col. 1:18).

This, again, is a most delicate and sensitive test, and it can also be illustrated very simply by a human analogy. I have already used the very good analogy of doctor and patient. Our Lord is the great Physician; he is the Healer. Salvation means health, spiritual health, total health. So this is the obvious analogy, and it works very well at this particular point. Whenever people have had experiences of being in trouble with regard to health, they try their physicians or seek specialists' advice, and they keep on trying until at last they find somebody who can help them. And I pointed out last time that when you are better again, your first impulse is to let everybody know about the cure.

But, of course, it does not stop at that. Another element comes in—you are concerned that this particular doctor should have the glory and the praise. You want everybody to feel the same wonder that you feel, and so you are anxious to send everybody to your doctor. Now there is an important double motive here. It is not simply that you are anxious that other suffering people should benefit, though, of course, you are. This desire is instinctive, as we have seen. If you have discovered something good, you want to share it. That is why I have put this first. But over and above that, you are anxious to show your gratitude to the one who has helped you, and the best way of doing that is to send everybody to him or her; you cannot give greater praise. "Oh," you say, "you must go to So-and-So! Don't waste your time anywhere else."

Now this is clearly seen in the woman of Samaria. She is so thrilled by this person and what he has done for her that she wants everybody else to come and admire him and praise him and be astonished at him. And, again, she is no exception. As we read the four Gospels, we find that people were constantly talking about what he had done for them, spreading the news to such an extent that it even became an embarrassment to our Lord, and at times he told them not to do this because his work was being hindered. He could have been kept in any one village, as it were, by everybody coming to him, but he said that he had to go to other places to preach the gospel. So he had to extricate himself from them. But it is emphasized everywhere in the Gospels that this was the inevitable reaction. The Christian is anxious that the Lord should have the praise and the honor and the glory, that everybody should go to him, and that everybody should be filled with the same admiration.

To put it in more theological language, Christians are people who make their boast in the Lord Jesus Christ. And that is why I say this is a very delicate and sensitive test. "He that glorieth," says the apostle Paul, "let him glory in the Lord" (1 Cor. 1:31). This is the test of Christian men and women. They see that this person is the only one who matters. He is the object of their affection and their desire, and they make their boast in him; they glory in him. Watch that word "glory" as you read the epistles, particularly of the apostle Paul. It is said, and I tend to agree, that he uses this word so frequently because it really means "to make your boast." Paul, as a Pharisee, had boasted of his knowledge of the Law, his correctness in a mechanical sense, his morality, and his religion. He shows us that in Philippians 3, in that little bit of autobiography where he is really saying, "I no longer boast in myself or in the fact that I am a Jew of the tribe of Benjamin or in any of these things. I make my boast in Christ." He glories in the Lord, and he wants everybody else to do the same.

We can look at it like this: the Christian is one who talks about the Lord. "Come, see a man, which told me everything that ever I did." You notice that the woman of Samaria does not speak about herself primarily. She does not speak about the benefits that she has received, though she has received them, and we considered them in looking at her motives. But she talks about the Lord Jesus Christ. That does not mean that we never mention our experience of the benefits of the Christian life, but the order here is extremely important. And, again, it is important because we are so anxious to contrast the Christian message, the Christian faith, and the Christian experience with that which belongs to the cults—these counterfeits that the devil introduces to keep people from Christ and from God—and this is one of the ways in which you can see the difference. The adherents of the cults generally talk about themselves and the benefits that they have derived. Of course, they then tell you that you can enjoy the same benefits if you adopt this teaching, but that is their method. But here is something quite different: the Christian talks first and foremost about this blessed person. The benefits are secondary.

Take the exhortation in the New Testament about rejoicing, and notice the way in which it is put: "Rejoice *in the Lord* always: and again I say, Rejoice" (Phil. 4:4). There are times when circumstances are adverse and are inimical to your joy. If you are relying upon nothing but some happy inward sensations, you will not receive the support you need, as feelings are always variable, and you cannot rely on them. The hymnwriter says:

I dare not trust the sweetest frame,
But wholly lean on Jesus' name.
On Christ the solid Rock I stand,
All other ground is sinking sand.

Edward Mote ("My Hope Is Built: The Solid Rock")

And that is perfectly true. If you start with your experiences and with yourself, you will find there will be times when you really have nothing to say. And if you have followed one of the cults and say there is no such thing as disease and then you become ill, you are in a bit of trouble, are you not? But this is not the Christian position at all. Christians start with the Lord. Whatever I may feel, whatever my position may be, he abides ever always the same, and so I can always speak of him.

In every high and stormy gale,
My anchor holds within the veil.

Our anchor is always Christ, everything that is true of him. So we speak of him as the woman does, and we ourselves and our experiences and benefits come afterward.

This is such an important point. Take, for instance, what we are told in the second chapter of the book of Acts. These disciples have been waiting ten days, as our Lord instructed them, for the coming baptism of the Holy Spirit. And then the great day comes, and the Spirit is poured forth upon them. They are all filled with the Spirit, and they begin to speak with other tongues. They have an amazing experience, which obviously has a vital effect upon them, filling them with joy and with ecstasy, with praise and thanksgiving.

And then the crowd comes together and can see at once that something has happened to these people; some of the crowd even suggest that they are filled with new wine. But this is what is interesting: Peter gets up to speak, and what does he do? He does not speak about the experience. He starts off by saying, "This is that which was spoken by the prophet Joel" (Acts 2:16). Yes, but he says that in order to speak about something else. This, he says, is entirely due to this person whom you and your rulers crucified but who rose again. Peter's sermon is about the Lord Jesus Christ. This is what is remarkable. Here the disciples are, filled with the Spirit, with the accompanying phenomena, but they do not talk about that, they talk about him. Of course, our Lord had prophesied that this would be the case. He said that when the Spirit came, he would glorify him (John 16:14), and immediately the Spirit began to do that. The whole emphasis is upon the Lord, his person and work.

There is another equally interesting example in the very next chapter. Peter and John are going up to the Temple at the hour of prayer in order to pray, and they are accosted by a lame man sitting at the Beautiful Gate of the Temple. Then they are given authority and power to help him, and there is great excitement, a phenomenon. Something has happened, a fact. Again the crowd gathers together, and once more Peter begins to preach. Does he say, "You can all be healed, if you like—all of you can get the experience that this man has just had"? No; he says:

> Ye men of Israel, why marvel ye at this? or why look ye so earnestly on us, as though by our own power or holiness we had made this man to walk? The God of Abraham, and of Isaac, and of Jacob, the God of our fathers, hath glorified his Son Jesus; whom ye delivered up, and denied him in the presence of Pilate. (Acts 3:12–13)

It is again a sermon on the Lord Jesus Christ. Go through the book of the Acts of the Apostles, and you will find this same emphasis everywhere. We see it when Peter is preaching in the household of Cornelius. And when we come to the section of Acts that deals with Paul, again and again we find that Paul is not primarily telling the people about what has happened to him and how that can happen to them, but he is recounting the facts about Jesus—he is preaching Christ.

It is equally clear in the epistles—for example, "We preach not ourselves, but Christ Jesus the Lord" (2 Cor. 4:5). The people are always reminded of this great doctrine concerning the Lord. This is what matters; this always comes first. And when we come to the book of Revelation, it is the same. He is there—what he has done, what he is doing, what he is going to do. The entire book of Revelation concentrates on him and finishes by saying, "Even so, come, Lord Jesus."

Now these early Christians were passing through terrible times—persecutions and trials and tribulations—but their message was always a message that glorified Jesus; they gloried in him and wanted others to do the same. As Paul puts it in Colossians 1 (here he is, preaching the gospel to the Gentiles; he is indefatigable, and he explains his teaching, he divides it up and tells us exactly what he is doing): "whom we preach"—that is it, that is his work—"Christ in you, the hope of glory" (v. 27), "warning every man, and teaching every man in all wisdom; that we may present every man perfect in Christ Jesus" (v. 28).

It is always the same, and therefore this is something to which we must pay very great attention. Paul says, "He that glorieth, let him glory in the Lord" (1 Cor. 1:31). And again, "God forbid that I should glory"—he is contrasting himself with false Judaizing teachers who gloried in the flesh, in legalistic details, and in themselves and their converts—"save [except] in the cross of our Lord Jesus Christ" (Gal. 6:14). "From henceforth let no man trouble me," he goes on to say in verse 17. In verses 14–17 he is saying in effect, "Leave me alone. Nothing matters to me except that this person receive all the honor and the glory and praise."

Have you not noticed, as you read, how Paul will suddenly seem to go off on a tangent? The literary pedants, of course, are upset by this. He interrupts his sentences, they say. Sometimes he does not complete them, and he seems to have forgotten what he started saying. But what makes him do this? Oh, it is that he has mentioned the Lord's name, and off he goes to some great apostrophe of praise. What matters to Paul over and above even the doctrine and all that we get by way of experience is the Lord himself. Paul is anxious that Christ should have the preeminence, that he should stand out.

And then when we come to our hymnbooks, we find that the great hymns, especially the great hymns from the great periods of revival, likewise always glorify Christ.

All hail the power of Jesus' Name . . .

This is the note. The desire is this:

Let every kindred, every tribe
On this terrestrial ball,

To him all majesty ascribe,
And crown him Lord of all.
EDWARD PERRONET ("ALL HAIL THE POWER OF JESUS' NAME")

O for a thousand tongues to sing
My great Redeemer's praise.
CHARLES WESLEY ("O FOR A THOUSAND TONGUES TO SING")

That is Edward Perronet's and Charles Wesley's desire. It is the desire of all true Christians. They want the whole world to come to Jesus, to go to him. Once people see him, they will admire him and take glory in him and in him alone. Incidentally, it is interesting to notice where those hymns I have just quoted come in the hymnbook. They do not come under the section headed "Christian Ministry" because they are not only for preachers. The danger is to think, "Well, that is an appropriate hymn for an ordination or just before a sermon." No, no; they are for all Christians. This glorying in the Lord Jesus should be true of every Christian, as it was true of this woman of Samaria. If I am a Christian, surely this is my inevitable reaction. The Christian talks about him, the Christian wants everybody to see him, the Christian wants everybody to know him, the Christian wants everybody to praise him, the Christian wants everybody to follow him. He is the center of the Christian's life.

The reasons, of course, are perfectly clear. Christians alone realize who the Lord is. That is why the apostle Paul writes all about the Lord Jesus Christ in that first chapter of the Epistle to the Colossians. Those foolish people had been listening to some false teachers who were going around the churches. They tended to follow the great apostle wherever he went, and they had a hodgepodge of teachings, a specious mixture of philosophy and Jewish practices. Paul deals with their teaching still more specifically in the second chapter of Colossians—that is his purpose in writing this letter. They talked about experiences and thrills, and the foolish Colossians were listening to all this—it seemed so wonderful. People are always ready to make sacrifices and to become ascetics. They will fast and sweat and pray; if necessary, they will mutilate their bodies. People have done this throughout the centuries. Anything that panders to the flesh gives this idea of "will worship," as the apostle says (2:23).

By contrast, Paul brings in his great message and says, "What are you talking about?" These teachers said there was a whole series of angels, a gradation of angels and intermediaries, between God and man. It all sounded so intellectual, and yet at the same time so thrilling to the emotions. But Paul brushes it all aside. He says in effect, "You would never have looked at that teaching if you had just realized the truth about him. If you had understood this, you would always have given him, and him alone, the preeminence." Why? Because, says Paul, he is who he is, "the firstborn of every creature" (Col. 1:15). He is the one through whom and for whom the world was made. Oh, the glory of the person!

This is what is lacking in us. We are all so subjective; we keep taking our spiritual pulses and are concerned about little aches and pains. We even tend to think of the church as a kind of dispensary where medications are dispensed to make us feel a little bit better and more comfortable. Tell me, what brings you to church? Do you come to praise him, to consider him? Do you come to get more knowledge of him and a better understanding of him so you can go and tell people about him, or do you just come for something you want?

Now do not misunderstand me. I must put it in this extreme form in order to correct the tendency that is in all of us to regard church as being for us, as it were. It is not primarily. The church is "the pillar and ground of the truth" (1 Tim. 3:15), and today's church is as she is because she has forgotten all this. The church is afraid, so she is modifying everything, even her message, in order to attract and interest and hold people. What a travesty! The business of the church is to hold forth Christ. She is "the pillar and ground of the truth," this great pillar that is displayed so that "in all things he might have the preeminence" (Col. 1:18). It is when the church fails to realize this that we go wrong, and the apostle is never tired of showing this.

This is the way, incidentally, to deal with our personal problems. Have you often found that? I have found it many a time, thank God, thank the Lord Jesus Christ. My little problems! When I have met him again, they have gone; I have forgotten all about them. When he comes in, it is like lifting up the blinds and the sun coming in. That is the effect he has. If we only knew him better and realized these truths concerning him, all these other specious false doctrines would be seen for the nonsense that they are and would vanish. All the cleverness of the world—what is the value of it? There is nothing in it. And fancy giving our time and attention to things like that, being misled by them, being troubled by them, when he is here in the midst and we are to look at him, at the glory and the wonder of his very person! At this very moment he is "upholding all things by the word of his power" (Heb. 1:3). That is who he is.

Then the apostle goes on to point out what the Lord has done. How can we talk about anything else? How can we be interested in anything else? Read again Philippians 2:4–11. Think of him "who, being in the form of God, thought it not robbery to be equal with God: but made himself of no reputation." Is there anybody else worth talking about? We glory in people; it is pathetic, is it not? There has never been a man or woman who is worthy of our glory. Everything we have, we have received. We have not created it; we have not produced it. "What hast thou that thou didst not receive?" says Paul to the Corinthians (1 Cor. 4:7). Foolish people, he says, glorying in men. Here is the only worthy one. He has given every man and woman all they have. All abilities, everything, have come from him. Here is one to glory in because he is who and what he is. He is "the brightness of his [God's] glory, and the express image of his person" (Heb. 1:3).

So you see that this woman of Samaria was saying, "Come and see him; come and see this person. Come and see him that you may fall at his feet"—and that is what we are to do. That is our business as Christians. "O 'tis all my business here below," says Charles Wesley, "to cry: 'Behold the Lamb!'" So there it is—the Incarnation, the self-humiliation of the Son of God, born as a man in the likeness of men—yes, "in the likeness of sinful flesh" (Rom. 8:3). That is what he has done.

Of whom do *you* speak? I have given you the human analogy, a doctor, some great statesman, politician, scientist. All right, you admire them because of what they have done. But as you tell the world about what these other people have done, you must speak to them of what Jesus has done. And you must go on to tell them about how he not only took the form of a servant but also humbled himself even to "the death of the cross" (Phil. 2:8), and you tell them about the cross.

> *When I survey the wondrous cross*
> *On which the Prince of glory died,*
> *My richest gain I count but loss,*
> *And pour contempt on all my pride.*
>
> Isaac Watts ("When I Survey the Wondrous Cross")

You do not talk about yourself any longer; you talk about "the Prince of glory," this paradox. As Peter puts it in that sermon recorded in Acts 3, "[You] killed the Prince [author] of life" (v. 15). The Author of life is put to death. You can tell people about that—you are not interested in any other drama because this is *the* drama, and everything else is a pale imitation. So you tell them about what he has done.

In the Epistle to the Philippians, Paul is dealing with a most practical matter—a lack of cooperation among certain people in the church. "Look not every man on his own things," Paul says, "but every man also on the things of others" (2:4). Do not be selfish, he says; share with one another. But Paul cannot even talk about that without going in a different direction at once—the person of Jesus! "Oh," he says in effect, "what am I talking about?" "Let this mind be in you, which was also in Christ Jesus" (v. 5). Here is the solution.

A friend was asking me the other day, "How can I be humble?" He felt there was pride in him, and he wanted to know how to get rid of it. He seemed to think that I had some patent remedy and could tell him, "Do this, that, and the other and you will be humble."

I said, "I have no method or technique. I can't tell you to get down on your knees and believe in prayer because I know you will soon be proud of that. There's only one way to be humble, and that is to look into the face of Jesus Christ; you cannot be anything else when you see him." That is the only way. Humility is not something you can create within yourself; rather, you look at him, you realize who he is and what he has done, and you are humbled.

My richest gain I count but loss,
And pour contempt on all my pride.

The only way to get rid of pride is to regard it with contempt, and he alone will enable you to do this. He humbled himself; his body was broken; his blood was shed. This is actual fact.

Why did he do it? He did it that you and I might be forgiven. He did it that you and I might become the children of God. He did it to redeem us, that we might be "delivered from the power of darkness" to which we all belong by nature and be brought into "the kingdom of his dear Son," the Son of God (Col. 1:13). This is all fact, and once we see it, what else can we talk about?

And then there is his glorious rising, his conquering of death and the grave, the last enemy (1 Cor. 15:26). So Christians begin to look to the future. They make that grand leap that the apostle makes in Philippians 2:

> Wherefore God also hath highly exalted him, and given him a name which is above every name: that at the name of Jesus every knee should bow, of things in heaven, and things in earth, and things under the earth;

> and that every tongue should confess that Jesus Christ is Lord, to the glory of God the Father. (vv. 9–11)

It is all there. And what do Christians want? They want to see the whole world falling at the feet of this blessed person. This is the height of their ambition; this is their greatest desire. They are "looking for and hasting unto the coming of the day of God" (2 Pet. 3:12). They are looking forward to that great day when every tongue shall confess and every knee shall bow. The greatest people the world has ever known and all the potentates and principalities and powers in the heavenly places and on earth and under the earth shall all humble themselves before him and look up in admiration at him and glory in him and "confess that Jesus Christ is Lord, to the glory of God the Father" (Phil. 2:11).

Knowing all these things about him, Christians are inevitably bound to talk about them. They are anxious that everybody else should know this and should bow before him. They realize that people are in ignorance and are rebellious and that their only hope is to get to know him. The Christian's great concern is not simply that other people should get the benefits of knowing him—I have already dealt with that—but that others may see his glory and worship him. It should be intolerable to contemplate that there is anybody who does not acknowledge him—not primarily because they are wrong and are in a state of misery but because they are not bowing the knee to this King immortal, invisible, the Son of God, the Savior of the world. That is the motive, as it clearly is in the case of the woman of Samaria. She longs that these people should come, and she delights in the anticipation of seeing the expression on their faces when they see him and hear what he has to say.

There, then, are the leading motives that urge this woman to leave her waterpot and go and bring the people to see him; and these are the motives that should impel each one of us to do this in our own way and in our own time and generation.

But this leads me to the next question, which is this: how is this work done? I want to be very practical because this is an important and urgent question for every Christian at this hour. I repeat that it is no use bemoaning the times, the increasing immorality and vice, war and the whole horror of the state of the world; there is no point if you do nothing about it. Negative condemnation is utterly useless. The world is ignorant. It needs the gospel message; it needs the truth about this blessed person, and you and I alone can give it. How are we to do it? In the Bible we are given vital instruction.

Now we cannot do precisely what the woman of Samaria does. Our Lord is no longer here as he was in the days of his flesh. What, then, do we do? Thank God, he himself and his disciples, his apostles, the writers of the books of Scripture, have given us the knowledge and instruction of which we stand in need. I will try to summarize it all for you.

Before we come down to the particulars, let us look at this question in general, and again I must remind you hurriedly of the negatives. How is this work to be done? The answer is, first, never mechanically. If it is done mechanically, it will probably do more harm than good. We must never witness to the glory of our Lord merely because we feel it is our duty, that we ought to be doing it, and if we have not, we will feel a bit unhappy when we go to bed at night and pray to God. I hope that all I have been saying gets rid of such notions. Obviously, also, it is not a question of behaving more or less like a parrot and just repeating clichés and formulas. That is inconceivable when you put this into the context with which we have been dealing. Books have been written on this subject, and it is pathetic to notice the tendency to adopt a mechanical approach.

How, then, should you do this work? Well, positively, first, you prepare yourself. This is of the utmost importance. What you are is infinitely more important than what you do, and what you do ultimately depends upon what you are. The danger is that you pick up the manuals and rush off into the details. The Christian always has to prepare himself or herself. I have often illustrated this. This is my experience, my testimony, as a preacher of the gospel. The most important thing for a preacher is to prepare himself. It takes us quite a long time to learn that. The young man prepares his sermon and feels, when he has finished preparing it, that he is right. What a fallacy! I have been very guilty of it—we all have; it takes a man years to learn this lesson. You can have an almost perfect sermon, but if you are not right, it will be no good, it will be "as sounding brass, or a tinkling cymbal"—great knowledge, great learning, polished phrases and sentences. Rubbish! Nonsense! Oh, you will get admiration—"Verily I say unto you, They have their reward" (Matt. 6:2)—but what a reward! No, no; the preparation of the man is the important thing; nothing is so important.

After putting it like that in general, I move on to the next point—the first detail—which is that we bring ourselves to a realization of the seriousness of the task. The seriousness! What do I mean? I am not talking about preaching only. It is true of preaching—preaching is the most serious thing in the world. You see, that is why, if one did not believe in the Holy Spirit and the power that he can give, one would never dare enter a pulpit. "Who is sufficient for these things?" (2 Cor. 2:16). But it is equally true of anybody who talks to an individual about these matters.

First, then, we realize the possibility of our doing great harm and antagonizing people. That is the place to start. Do not rush into this and say it is quite simple—you have this verse and that, and there you are, a pat-answer kind of evangelism. What a terrible thing that is! You must start by realizing the harm you can do. I have had to deal with near tragedies in this respect, harm done to people by injudicious Christian people whose motives were excellent, who wanted to do good and to warn their relatives or friends, but who were speaking mechanically and superficially and had never realized the seriousness of what they were doing.

It sounds as if I am discouraging you, does it not? I am not discouraging you—I am encouraging you to do this work in the right way. Then you will have fruit, and you will have glory with God. So we start by realizing that we are dealing with souls, immortal souls; we are dealing with people not only as regards their life in this world but regarding their eternal destiny. We are not trying to get people to join a club or an institution or to take up a theory in which we are interested. No, no; we are dealing with immortal souls and their everlasting destiny. It is the most serious and responsible work in the world.

Furthermore—and to me this is perhaps the most important point of all—you must always start by realizing that the work you are attempting to do can only be done, finally, by the Holy Spirit. You can never make anybody a Christian—never. You can make them church members, but you never make them Christians. It is impossible. The Holy Spirit alone can do this, and, therefore, we must always be afraid of spurious results, temporary results, something that people have done rather than the Holy Spirit.

To conclude this point, let me put it to you in the words of the great apostle, the man who probably knew more about this work, both in public and in private, than he knew about anything else. This, he tells us, is how he approached it:

> I was with you in weakness, and in fear, and in much trembling. And my speech and my preaching was not with enticing words of man's wisdom, but in demonstration of the Spirit and of power. (1 Cor. 2:3–4)

Why "fear" and "much trembling"? For the reasons I have already given you. Paul knew what he was doing. He knew the danger, the responsibility, the possibility of harm—"in weakness, and in fear, and in much trembling"—this authority, this genius! He knew that he was dealing with the human soul.

Or listen to the apostle saying this again in a very striking way: "Now thanks be unto God, which always causes us to triumph in Christ, and maketh manifest the savour of his knowledge by us in every place." That is what you are doing, for, Paul says, the fact is this: "For we are unto God a sweet savour of Christ, in them that are saved, and in them that perish: to the one we are the savour of death unto death; and to the other the savour of life unto life." And then Paul asks a question: "And who is sufficient for these things?" (2 Cor. 2:14–16).

That is the position of every Christian who speaks to another about the Lord Jesus Christ. You can be "the savour of death unto death" or "of life unto life"—"Who is sufficient for these things?" And once you ask that, you have avoided and evaded most of the terrible dangers, for you are humbled, you realize the seriousness of what you are doing, the tremendous responsibility and the necessity of the presence and power of the Holy Spirit. And that, as I hope to show you, will also be essential for the other practical aspects of the carrying out of this great desire to bring everybody to him, that in all things and by all people he, and he alone, may have the preeminence.

56

More than Conquerors[36]

The woman then left her waterpot, and went her way into the city, and saith to the men, Come, see a man, which told me all things that ever I did: is not this the Christ? Then they went out of the city, and came unto him. (John 4:28–30)

There have been various periods in our history when the masses outside the church have been indifferent to her message. It is at such times that the witness of the individual Christian is greatly enhanced. Today we are living at such a time. But why are people today largely outside the church? Is it because we are failing in our witness as individual Christians? Is it because we are somehow or another different from the woman of Samaria so that those who know us are not attracted, not interested, not concerned about listening to the gospel? This is a very important matter. It is not merely a matter of duty that we should consider this question—it becomes a thorough test of our whole position as Christians. There is something wrong with the Christian who cares simply about himself or herself and has no concern whatsoever about those who are outside.

That is the background to our consideration of verses 28–30, which we are dealing with in a very practical way. Having considered the motives that impelled the woman of Samaria to fetch her fellow townspeople—motives that have always impelled Christian men and women—we are now considering the way in which we bring people to our Lord, and this, again, is all-important. In the case of this woman, all she had to do was invite people to come out of the city to meet our Lord since he was there by the side of the well. We cannot do that, but the principles are perfectly clear, and there are many guidelines in the Scriptures. Once we leave the four Gospels and go on to the book of Acts and the epistles, we find the people in the position that we are in today, and there is abundant teaching with regard to this whole matter.

We have been emphasizing the importance of what we are. We are bound to start here because what we are is altogether more significant than what we do. We are in a century that is activist, and part of its trouble is that, forgetting principles, people rush off into action. So it is essential that we should remind ourselves that though we may do this, that, and the other, if we ourselves are not right, we are wasting our time, and people will not listen to us. "What you are," they say, "speaks louder than what you say." And they are interested in what we are.

So we are considering the kind of impact that we as Christians should be making upon others. As we have seen, the book of Acts records that ordinary Christians, scattered abroad by persecution, spread the gospel. They were in contact with other people, and it was what these others saw in the Christians that aroused the desire to be like them. This is the way that God has always used so strikingly for the extension of his kingdom. What staggered the ancient world was the quality of life of the Christians. Therefore this is a subject that we should consider very carefully.

So what are the characteristics of the Christian? Christian men and women are serious people. They are followers of one who was "a man of sorrows" (Isa. 53:3). They do not take the superficial, giddy view of life that so many have in the midst of tragedy. They are bound to be serious, they cannot help themselves, and they realize the seriousness of what they are doing. They know something of what the apostle Paul experienced when he went to Corinth "in weakness, and in fear, and in much trembling" (1 Cor. 2:3). The days are evil, and it is only Christians who really have an understanding of the times.

But we must hasten to say that Christians also have joy, a joy that no one else has. The seriousness and the joy are not incompatible; they go together. It is a serious joy or a joyful seriousness. It is not solemnity; it is not dullness. The last thing the Christian should ever be is dull. A dull Christian is a contradiction in terms.

But let me suggest some further qualities that, it seems to me, are particularly important at a time such as this. The Christian is one who always conveys a sense of peace. We can use many other words for this—a sense of tranquillity, a heart that is at rest. You see the relevance of this at the present time. The words that really describe the world as it is today are the words of the prophet Isaiah: "But the wicked are like the troubled sea, when it cannot rest, whose waters cast up mire and dirt" (57:20). Is not that the modern world? Oh, the restlessness of this age! The hurry, the tension, the excitement, the lack of stability. It is a time of trouble, a time of confusion, a time of uncertainty. Its waters cast up mire and dirt, and we see that in our newspapers and on our televisions. It is a part of the restlessness.

That is the world in which we live, and that is the description of the wicked. Now we give that word *wicked* much too restricted a meaning. The term means all those who are not Christians. And they are "like the troubled sea," carried about hither and thither, having no center, no central stability, and at the same time, of course, troubled in mind and troubled in spirit.

I need not dwell on this. It has been talked about at great length. This restlessness is the outstanding characteristic of the present age. It is an age that has to live on drugs, tranquilizers, and medications and depends on artificial means to get to sleep. The commonly used words in our vocabulary today are the words *tension* and *stresses* and *strains*. And then, on top of that, there is the mania for pleasure. It is all because of this restlessness, the turmoil of life, and the complete failure to deal with it and to understand it.

Now that being the state and condition of the world, it is obvious that the Christian is to be the exact opposite. The sense of peace that Christians have is one of the most wonderful proofs of the Christian faith, and it is this, when it is seen in us, that attracts others, because, I say again, the world is always more ready to listen when it sees an example than when it hears mere talk. It is familiar with the talk.

The cults, of course, thrive on the condition of the modern world and are always offering easy remedies. But people have tried them, and their philosophies, and are tired of it all. They just find that it does not work. This is what is so significant today. People have only turned to drugs and other forms of escapism because they have lost hope in what the world has to offer them and have lost confidence in human reason and understanding. They have to escape, they say. The world cannot help; there is nothing there. This is a very serious matter. As we said earlier, politically the world tends to turn to dictatorship in a time of restlessness and uncertainty.

All this gives us as Christians an exceptional opportunity. We have the opportunity to show that though we are in the same world and subject to the same pressures, yet we are essentially different, and the big difference is expressed in a line from the hymn by Anna L. Waring: "a heart at leisure from itself." That sense of tranquillity, of peace, of being at rest is the greatest thing of all.

It is my contention that the Christian alone is capable of this. I do not want to weary you with an analysis of all this, but we are aware of the teaching of the Stoics. As in the days when our Lord was here, so now and in every time of strain and stress, this philosophy tends to come. But Stoicism does not teach a heart at rest; it is mere resignation, a mere refusal to face things. That is not true rest; it is a form of repression. If you have the willpower and the health to follow this philosophy, you may give the impression of having a kind of rest in your life, but you do not really have it. Merely to hold things down is not to be at peace. There is no solution there, only grim determination just to go on in spite of everything. I grant you that there may be something quite noble about it, something that at times can even appear to be heroic, but it is always negative, and in any case it is of no value to others because it is entirely dependent upon the willpower and ability of the person concerned.

Some people are born with a phlegmatic kind of temperament. They do not react as others do; they seem to be rendered more insensitive to things that happen. But like the Stoic, the phlegmatic person has nothing to give to anyone else.

But that is not the position of Christians. The reason for their peace, of course, is that they have a solution, an understanding of life. This has not come from anything in themselves; they have received it from the word of the Lord. To quote Matthew Arnold, the Christian is someone who is able to "see life steadily and see it whole," and that is the only thing that gives inward peace and rest. The Christian is no longer frantically looking for some solution or for some understanding. It is the search for understanding that causes the restlessness. The book of Acts describes this perfectly. One of the most sophisticated cities and societies in the ancient world was Athens, the mecca of philosophy, where all the philosophers went. It was the seat of learning and of understanding, and, of course, the great object there was, as the book of Acts tells us, "either to tell, or to hear some new thing" (Acts 17:21).

Why was that the characteristic of the life of Athens? It was because of the perplexities created by the whole problem of life and living. They were trying to understand, and they could not. The philosophers were canceling one another out, and none of them was really satisfactory. And as the secular historians tell us, the rate of suicide among the philosophers was higher proportionately than in any other section of the community. So, you see, the whole society was restless, and it is just the same today.

People are on edge; they are tense and under a tremendous strain. You see it in their faces.

So here is our opportunity, and here is the test for us. Do we have hearts at leisure from themselves? Do we have an inward peace? If we have, it inevitably shows itself. We read of our blessed Lord that "he could not be hid" (Mark 7:24), and this peace, too, simply cannot be hid. This is a great psychological point, of course. What we are inside always shows itself. It shows itself in our faces, in our eyes, in the very atmosphere that we carry with us. There are certain people whom we cannot meet without immediately feeling at rest. We cannot analyze this; we just know it, we are at once conscious of it. Of course, we can all put on appearances, can we not? We can smile and appear to be very content when everything is wrong inside. But here is something different. This peace is not playacting; it is not all on the surface.

People of the world see through all the playacting because that is how they live themselves, but when they come across these Christian people, they know at once that they are different. They see this inward peace; they recognize that Christians have what is called "the quiet heart." This is what the Quakers, in particular, have always been concerned about, and to that extent they are absolutely right. They have tended to turn this into a philosophy and into a cult, and in a very subtle way, because of their departure from the orthodox Christian faith, it becomes for them just a refined form of Stoicism. But the quiet heart itself, the tranquil heart, "a heart at leisure from itself," that they are seeking is always right.

Nothing so opens the door of opportunity as that you and I should have this sense of inward peace and rest. In this way we can influence others and bring them to the Lord Jesus Christ, for our whole testimony is that we are not like this by nature, that some of us were as far removed from this as it is possible for a human being to be. We do not have some sort of bovine stolidity. No; we have been given this peace by the grace of God. Our Lord said, "Peace I leave with you, my peace I give unto you: not as the world giveth, give I unto you. Let not your heart be troubled, neither let it be afraid" (John 14:27). This is the peace of God. And what he has done for us he can do for others.

Then there is something further, which leads logically and directly from that and is an extension of it, but I put it separately because I think one must. People must be able to see that we have inner reserves. I draw the distinction because they must first see that we are at peace. After that they see that we continue to be at peace in spite of what happens to us. This is an important distinction because the great test of life is what we are like when things go wrong.

Very many people give the impression of having inward peace and tranquillity when everything is going well. We can, most of us, put up a very good show when we are well and hale and hearty and young, and everything is prospering, and the sun is shining in the heavens; most of us are fairly good under such conditions. We have wonderful theories and say we will do this, that, and the other. But the test comes when everything goes wrong. Then people find that they have nothing at all, and they break down. That is where the opportunity for the Christian comes in at the present time because never have the outward stresses and strains been greater than they are at this moment.

Our Lord dealt with that once and forever at the end of the Sermon on the Mount in the parable of the two houses. Here is a man who rushes to build his house without a foundation, and he is very amused that the other fellow is so slow. He has his house up before the other man has dug his foundations. "What a fool! This is marvelous! This solves all my problems." Oh, the marvel of shortcuts! But then the rain descends, and the floods come, and the wind blows, and the whole building collapses. That is so typical of the world—its theories and ideas cannot stand up to the test.

And here, again, the Christian is essentially different. This is one of the most profound tests that we can ever apply to ourselves. It is the great test between believism and faith, between taking up religion and being taken up by it, between having it in your head and having it in your heart, in your spirit, at the center of your life. The whole point about Christian men and women is that they are not easily disturbed or shaken by what happens; they are no longer dependent upon circumstances for their happiness and their joy. This is absolutely basic. What has happened to us as Christians is, as it is put so frequently in the New Testament, that we have been delivered from "this present evil world" (Gal. 1:4) and translated "into the kingdom of his [God's] dear Son" (Col. 1:13). Now when Paul says that we have been delivered from "this present evil world," he does not merely mean that we are delivered from its practices, from its habits and customs. These words mean much more. They mean that we have been delivered from the world's way of thinking, from its outlook, from its whole understanding of life and living and the purpose of it all. This is one of the things that is most striking about the Christian. Those who are not Christians, by contrast, are dependent upon what happens to them; they are dependent upon their surroundings and circumstances.

Now there is no need to prove this; it is shouting at us. Why do people spend so much money on drinking and on smoking and on pleasure? It is obvious, is it not? They cannot live without it. They are dependent upon it. They are dependent upon other people; they are dependent upon the state of their health; they are dependent upon success. They are in the hands of circumstances and conditions and the things that are happening around them. The result is that when there is a change, an adverse change, in their circumstances, and everything is collapsing, they have nothing to fall back on. There is no sense of having an inward reserve; there is no satisfaction within. They have been kept going by the things outside. The life of the unbeliever is indeed like a bubble—you keep it going, you go on blowing, and then, if you cannot for some reason, it collapses and is gone.

Here is one of the greatest and most glorious differences between the Christian and the non-Christian. Here is one of the great differences between the child of God and the one who is not a child of God. The psalmist says:

> Unto the upright there ariseth light in the darkness: he is gracious, and full of compassion, and righteous. A good man sheweth favour, and lendeth: he will guide his affairs with discretion. Surely he shall not be moved for ever: the righteous shall be in everlasting remembrance. He shall not be afraid of evil tidings [are you afraid of evil tidings? As for this man, this righteous man]: his heart is fixed, trusting in the LORD. His heart is established, he shall not be afraid. (Ps. 112:4–8)

Now that is the Old Testament. Here is a man writing at least a thousand years before the coming of the Son of God into this world, and yet he is able to say that, and it was true. That is the secret of those great men of the Old Testament—the patriarchs, the psalmists, the prophets, and others. And yet we know that we are in a superior position. They were children of God, yes, but they did not have the knowledge that we have. "He that is least in the kingdom of heaven is greater than he [John the Baptist]"—in position and in understanding (Matt. 11:11); and yet there it is in the Old Testament. And so we ask ourselves this question: are we afraid of evil tidings? The world is as it is because its heart is not fixed, because it is not established in the very center.

Or let me put it another way. The book of Proverbs says, "The name of the LORD is a strong tower: the righteous runneth into it, and is safe" (18:10). In other words, the righteous have a place into which to retreat. When the enemy is attacking powerfully outside, and God's people feel their defenses are being penetrated, and they are tending to lose ground, they are all right, there is no panic. Here is this tower—"a strong tower"—that is impregnable, and "the righteous runneth into it, and is safe." He enters into his fortress, and he knows that no enemy can ever penetrate it.

That is from the Old Testament, but this is obviously so true of Christian men and women. It differentiates them from non-Christians; they have inner resources. And is there anything more glorious and more wonderful about this life than this very fact that there is within us a place that is absolutely impregnable no matter what the world may think or do? And does it not become obvious that the real reason why so many are outside the church is that they do not see people like this inside the church? They say, "Ah, these people, they go to this place on a Sunday, and they affect an interest, but I have watched them when things go wrong and when troubles come, and they are no different from the rest of us. They are just as panicky, and they obviously do not know what to do." Those are the words that are used. They say, "What's the value of all their churchgoing?" And that is a perfectly fair criticism. It is no use talking about the Christian faith if that is how you behave. They say, "What's the value of your faith if it can't help you at the time of trial?"

The New Testament is full of this teaching. Let me give one or two of these glorious examples in order that we may all examine ourselves and, I trust, be filled with a sense of shame and realize that the first thing we must do is put ourselves right and become the sort of people about whom anyone meeting us will say, "I would give the whole world if only I could be like you!"

Let me give you this great example: look at the apostle Paul. Here he is in prison. First-century prisons were dank, damp, horrible in every sense, and Paul is suffering. But one afternoon he is brought out of prison to give a little bit of entertainment to a king and a queen and a Roman governor. They ask him about the Christian faith, and Paul gives them the account of his conversion. Then Paul says, "King Agrippa, believest thou the prophets? I know that thou believest." Agrippa then says to Paul, "Almost thou persuadest me to be a Christian." Do not misunderstand that. Perhaps a better translation is, "Do you think that with just a little talk you can make me a Christian?" But here is the important point. Paul then says, "I would to God, that not only thou, but also all that hear me this day, were both almost, and altogether such as I am, except these bonds" (Acts 26:27–29).

I think that is one of the greatest statements ever made. Here is a man, a prisoner with the chains hanging from his wrists, and he is addressing the king and the queen and the Roman governor. They are at liberty, enjoying life, while he is in a prison. And yet this prisoner is able to say, "I would give anything if only you people could be as I am. Oh, I wish you had the inward peace and the rest that I am enjoying! I wish that you could have the experience that I am having in that prison cell! Oh, that you were as I am!"

Here is a man who is entirely independent of his circumstances—they make no difference to him. He has inner reserves; he has something here that is bigger than the whole universe. It does not matter what man may do to him—he wishes that all others would be as he is. He does not want them to be in bonds, he does not want them to suffer, but what he does want them to have is the rest, the peace, the quiet, the satisfaction that he has. He wants them to discover that the truth is, whatever happens to Christian people, it all ministers to this life they have been given through the Lord Jesus Christ by the Holy Spirit.

Let the apostle himself teach you. He himself gives us the explanation. He tells us why he was able to speak as he did on that occasion to Agrippa and Festus. In a passage in 2 Corinthians 4 he quite honestly and frankly gives us an account of the difficulties that he has been going through. Yet he says this:

> We have this treasure in earthen vessels, that the excellency of the power may be of God, and not of us. We are troubled on every side, yet not distressed; we are perplexed, but not in despair; persecuted, but not forsaken; cast down, but not destroyed; always bearing about in the body the dying of the Lord Jesus, that the life also of Jesus might be made manifest in our body. For we which live are always delivered unto death for Jesus' sake [those were the things that were happening to him, but notice the great contrasts. What is the explanation?]. . . . For which cause we faint not; but though our outward man perish, yet the inward man is renewed day by day.

My dear friends, this is the question: do you know the difference between the outward man and the inward man? Are you living your life entirely on the outward level? So many people are. They live on talk and gossip and excitement and pleasure. It is all outside, and inside there is an emptiness. That is not Christianity. What makes a Christian a Christian is the inward life, new life from God, "the life of God in the soul of man" (Scougal). Christians are "partakers of the divine nature" (2 Pet. 1:4). There is an inward man, and this inward man is entirely independent of the outward man and is being renewed day by day.

And then Paul continues, "For our light affliction"—all that has been happening to him, all that he has been describing, he calls a "light affliction"—"which is but for a moment"—what does he mean by "but for a moment"? Does he know that the persecutions are going to stop? Does he have second sight? Is this sympathetic understanding? Does he know that all his circumstances are suddenly going to change and all is going to be well? Is that what he means? Of course not! That is his view of life in this world. For the Christian, it only lasts "a moment." Of course, for the non-Christian, life in this world is everything. And when physical death comes, that is terrible; it is the end of all things: "Death is coming! I'm getting older. I must do everything to keep young—rejuvenation! I'll go to the end of the earth, get an operation, a new heart!"

What a tragedy! That shows the emptiness of the heart. But what about this "light affliction, which is but for a moment"? What does it do? It "worketh for us a far more exceeding and eternal weight of glory." This word "worketh" is most important. It means "produces," "creates," "stimulates." The "light affliction, which is but for a moment," all these terrible things that are happening, are creating within the apostle, and increasing and enhancing within him, "a far more exceeding and eternal weight of glory." How do they do it? Well, Paul says, the secret is, "while we look not at the things which are seen, but at the things which are not seen."

What another vital distinction this is! What do you spend your time looking at? Are you always looking at something outside? Do you live through the winter by thinking of your summer vacation plans—is that how you get through? Many people are like that. Now let us be reasonable about these things. I am not saying that you should not plan your summer vacation, but what I am saying is that you should not live on that. Some people are always talking about their schemes and plans and proposals as if they cannot enjoy the present moment. They have nothing within them. "We look not at the things which are seen, but at the things which are not seen." The whole secret of Christian men and women is that they see "the things which are not seen," and they can see them wherever they are. Within a prison cell they see them. They are not outside; they are inside.

And so the more adverse and cruel and trying the circumstances, the more they remind Christian people of their imperishable souls and of the Lord Jesus Christ, who had similar experiences when he was in this world. They remind Christians that the Lord has gone on to prepare a place for them and will come again and receive them unto himself. The apostle goes on to put it like this: "For we know that if our earthly house of this tabernacle were dissolved, we have a building of God, an house not made with hands, eternal in the heavens" (2 Cor. 4:7–11, 16; 5:1).

So the more you are afflicted and tried by things that happen to you from the outside and the malice of men, the more it drives you to realize that you do not belong to this world, that you are bigger than it, that you belong to Christ, you belong to heaven, you belong to glory—"a far more exceeding and eternal weight of glory."

The trouble with all of us is that we think so little about that glory; we are looking so much at the outside, at the seen, the visible, that we do not gaze upon the unseen, the eternal, the glorious, which God in Christ is preparing for us. We do not heed the exhortation of Paul to the Colossians: "Set your affection on things above, not on things on the earth" (Col. 3:2). So when afflictions and trials come, they force us to do what we had foolishly not been doing. We cannot enjoy the outside because it is all against us at the moment, and that, therefore, reminds us of the inside, the unseen, the eternal, the spiritual. And the moment we begin to think in that way, we are immune to what happens outside. This builds up, and we see the eternal more and more gloriously, and we know we are going on to it. So even if they kill us, what have they done? They have simply introduced us to that glory at an earlier point than we had expected. "Though our outward man perish, yet the inward man is renewed day by day."

Now, my dear friends, it is the people who give this impression who conquer the world. These are the people who act as magnets, drawing others to the Lord Jesus Christ. The apostle Paul was full of this; clearly it was one of the most important things of all to him. For your encouragement, let me remind you of what he wrote to Timothy. Timothy was so like us. He was nervous, apprehensive, troubled, anxious about the care of the churches, and now he gets a message to say that Paul is not only in prison but is likely to be put to death at any moment. So as well as being worried about himself, Timothy is worried about Paul, and the apostle has to write to him. Look here, says Paul, "For God hath not given us the spirit of fear"—that is what we have by nature, and the world is in the grip of the spirit of fear. What has God given us? ". . . but of power, and of love, and of a sound mind [discipline]."

Then Paul goes on to say:

> Be not therefore ashamed of the testimony of our Lord, nor of me his prisoner: but be thou partaker of the afflictions of the gospel according to the power of God; who hath saved us, and called us with an holy calling, not according to our works, but according to his own purpose and grace, which was given us in Christ Jesus before the world began, but is now made manifest by the appearing of our Saviour Jesus Christ, who hath abolished death, and hath brought life and immortality to light through the gospel: whereunto I am appointed a preacher, and an apostle, and a teacher of the Gentiles. For the which cause I also suffer [I am suffering] these things ["I am in prison, and I have been treated very cruelly and in a most unjust manner." Then comes that blessed word "nevertheless"]: nevertheless I am not ashamed ["I am not troubled, I am not taken unawares, I am not grumbling and complaining, and you must not." Why not?]: for I know whom I have believed, and am persuaded that he is able to keep that which I have committed unto him against that day. (2 Tim. 1:7–12)

Well, there it is, my dear friends. To use again the language of the great apostle, the Christian does not merely manage to get through; that is what the Stoic does. Here is the Christian:

> Who shall separate us from the love of Christ? shall tribulation, or distress, or persecution, or famine, or nakedness, or peril, or sword? As it is written, For thy sake we are killed all the day long; we are accounted as sheep for the slaughter. Nay [this blessed protest, the inner man begins to speak], in all these things we are more than conquerors through him that loved us. For I am persuaded, that neither death, nor life, nor angels, nor principalities, nor powers, nor things present, nor things to come, nor height, nor depth, nor any other creature, shall be able to separate us from the love of God, which is in Christ Jesus our Lord. (Rom. 8:35–39)

Oh, beloved Christians, are you giving everyone the impression that you have inner reserves, that your inner man is growing day by day and is independent of circumstances—of chance, of war, it does not matter what it is—and that all they do is increase this "far more exceeding and eternal weight of glory"? Believe me, when the Christian church, as insignificant as she is today, is filled with people who give that impression, the world will come streaming in, for it is the one thing that it cannot discover because it is only to be found in our blessed Lord and Savior Jesus Christ.

Notes

1. Regarding John 1–2, see D. Martyn Lloyd-Jones, *Joy Unspeakable (Including Prove All Things)* (Eastbourne, UK: Kingsway Publications, 2000).
2. Kenneth E. Kirk, *The Vision of God: The Christian Doctrine of the Summum Bonum* (London: Longmans, Green & Co., 1931; Harrisburg, PA: Morehouse, 1991).
3. The reference here is to the terrible events on October 21, 1966 when 144 people, including 116 children, were killed after tons of coal waste engulfed a school, a cottage, and a farm in the village of Aberfan in Wales.
4. From the old hymn "At Even, Ere the Sun Was Set."
5. This, again, is a reference to the Aberfan disaster (see note 3 above).
6. Held in Britain on the Sunday nearest to November 11.
7. From Wallace E. Henley, "Invictus."
8. This sermon was preached on December 4, 1966.
9. This sermon was preached on December 11, 1966.
10. Joseph Hart, "Come, Holy Spirit, Come."
11. This sermon was preached on December 18, 1966.
12. Christmas Day, 1966.
13. January 1, 1967.
14. Publisher's note: The Brethren of the Common Life started in Holland in the late fourteenth century and spread into southern and western Germany and into Poland.
15. J. H. Alexander, *More Than Notion* (Bedfordshire, UK: Fauconberg Press, 1964).
16. Cecil Frances Alexander, "There Is a Green Hill Far Away."
17. R. R. Marrett, *A Jerseyman at Oxford* (Oxford, UK: Oxford University Press, 1941).
18. March 19, 1967.
19. John Calvin, *Institutes*, III.ii.7.
20. Charles Wesley, "Love Divine, All Loves Excelling."
21. C. P. Snow, *Variety of Men* (New York: Macmillan, 1967).

22. The 1904/1905 revival in Wales.
23. Charles Wesley, "Jesus, Thou Joy of Loving Hearts."
24. Charles Wesley, "Thou Hidden Source of Calm Repose."
25. John G. Whittier, "Immortal Love, Forever Full."
26. Fanny Crosby, "Safe in the Arms of Jesus."
27. See D. Martyn Lloyd-Jones, *Joy Unspeakable (Including Prove All Things)* (Eastbourne, UK: Kingsway Publications, 2000).
28. Kenneth S. Wuest, *Golden Nuggets in the Greek New Testament*. This was reprinted in 1973 by Eerdmans as one of the volumes in a four-volume set, *Word Studies in the Greek New Testament*.
29. Observed in Britain in November. Initially its purpose was to remember those who were killed in World Wars I and II.
30. William Wordsworth, "The World Is Too Much with Us," 1807.
31. This sermon was preached on Christmas Eve, 1967.
32. These sermons have been published in D. Martyn Lloyd-Jones, *Authentic Christianity: Sermons on the Acts of the Apostles*, Vol. 6 (Edinburgh: Banner of Truth Trust, 2006) and in the USA under the title *Compelling Christianity* (Wheaton, IL: Crossway Books, 2007).
33. For Dr. Lloyd-Jones, the coming year would bring serious illness and the end of his ministry at Westminster Chapel. These pages were certainly true of him.
34. Henry Francis Lyte, "Abide with Me."
35. Charles Wesley, "Jesus, Lover of My Soul."
36. This was Dr. Lloyd-Jones's sermon at his last Sunday morning service as the minister of Westminster Chapel.